COMMISSION OF THE EUROPEAN COMMUNITIES

Higher Education in the European Community

Student Handbook

Sixth edition

edited by

Dr Brigitte Mohr

Deutscher Akademischer Austauschdienst (DAAD)
Bonn

Office for Official Publications
of the European Communities

Kogan Page

ORYX PRESS
1990

Every effort has been made to ensure accuracy of the edition at the time of going to press, but inevitably certain parts of the information may have become outdated after publication. No responsibility can be accepted by the editor, the Deutscher Akademischer Austauschdienst or the Commission for any errors or omissions in the text, or for use which might be made of the information.

The rare Arabian Oryx is believed to have inspired the myth of the unicorn. This desert antelope became virtually extinct in the early 1960s. At that time several groups of international conservationists arranged to have 9 animals sent to the Phoenix Zoo to be the nucleus of a captive breeding herd. Today the Oryx population is nearly 800, and over 400 have been returned to reserves in the Middle East.

Published in the United States by
The Oryx Press
2214 North Central at Encanto
Phoenix, AZ 85004-1483

Published in the United Kingdom by
Kogan Page
120 Pentonville Road
London N1 9JN
England

Published simultaneously in Canada

Printed in the United Kingdom

ISBN 0-89774-657-0

Foreword

As 1992 approaches and with it the establishment of the single European market symbolizing the central dynamic of the European Community in the years immediately ahead, the EC has a greater need than ever for young academics who have acquired a sound experience of education and training with a European dimension.

In such a context, the EC action programmes, which are intended to contribute to this European dimension in initial training through increased student mobility, have recently made great progress.

The sixth edition of the *Student Handbook* appears with the Erasmus programme well into its third year of operation. In the course of its first three years, some 40 000 students have received mobility grants helping them to spend a fully recognized part of their studies in another Member State. Meanwhile, around 8 000 professors and lecturers have undertaken study or teaching visits and almost 2 000 cooperation programmes between the institutions of higher education in the Member States have been financially supported by the Commission.

At the same time, following a Council decision, the Comett programme enters its second phase in 1990. The programme strengthens cooperation between institutions of higher education and companies in the field of the new technologies by systematically expanding, for training purposes, the network between higher education and industry and by considerably increasing the number of transnational placements. In the same way, Comett supports joint projects of continuing training and media-supported distance studies.

The ambition of forming a truly European citizenry must lead to an active policy of promoting Community languages. 1989 witnessed the adoption of the Lingua programme which provides for a broad range of promotional measures, and, in particular, the opportunity for future foreign-language teachers to spend a study period of substantial length in the country whose language they will be teaching.

The recognition of higher education degrees is a further important factor contributing towards the freedom of movement of working people.

The implementation of the Council Directive of 21 December 1988, which is planned for 1991, will be a milestone on the path to the recognition of professional and vocational qualifications; for it will be the first time that a general system for the recognition of higher education degrees awarded after a minimum of three years of study has been created. In the meantime the Commission is pursuing its measures intended to facilitate the recognition of vocational and professional training and qualifications at various levels, and to advance the transparency of the labour market.

In the context of the Erasmus programme, 1989 saw the launching of the ECTS scheme (European Community course credit transfer system). The pilot phase of ECTS will last six years. The scheme represents an especially flexible form of academic recognition based on transparency and mutual trust between the individual institutions of higher education.

In publishing this *Student Handbook*, the Commission hopes that it will be useful to all those directly or indirectly involved in the world of higher education, whether as students, parents, teachers, administrators or employers. The information contained in it has been carefully checked so that readers may form an exact idea of the higher education systems of the 12 Member States. The chapter dealing specifically with European initiatives and institutions has been extended and brought up to date.

On behalf of the Commission, I should like to thank the editors at the German Academic Exchange Service (DAAD), the national correspondents and the publishing houses involved for their cooperation in this sixth edition.

VASSO PAPANDREOU
Member of the Commission

Contents

Introduction

When this sixth edition of the EC *Student Handbook* appears, the 'magical date' of 31 December 1992, the completion of the single European market, will have become very close indeed. The awareness of EC citizens is beginning to change. Many have realized that the united Europe towards which we are steering will bring new vocational requirements and demands for the individual as well as, however, new opportunities as regards freedom of movement. Multilingualism will be required, not least of academics. Studies abroad will change from being a luxury for a few to being a necessity for nearly all.

The latest EC programmes are driving this development forward. From implementation of the Erasmus programme in mid-1987 until mid-1990, almost 40 000 students will have been able to spend a recognized period of their studies in another Member State.

Through the Comett programme, which aims at the exchange between institutions of higher education and industry in the field of technology, more than 4 000 students have found places as practical trainees from 1987 to 1989. Lingua, the most recent programme which commences in 1990 is expected to give new impulses to foreign-language teaching at vocational schools, institutions of higher education and at the place of work. For it is often an insufficient knowledge of the language that is the main obstacle to studies and work abroad.

The *Student Handbook* provides information on these programmes. However, the main section is formed by the contributions of the 12 Member States. They are similarly structured. This eases comprehension as well as comparison. The information compiled includes the structure of higher education, the organization and validation of courses, entry requirements, tuition fees (where these apply), scholarships and social aspects such as insurance cover, accommodation and the cost of living. Each national chapter concludes with a detailed appendix. This includes important addresses, a tabular survey of the courses and programmes offered at the higher education institutions in the country, a bibliography and a glossary with specialist terms, which have largely been left in the original language in the text in order to avoid errors of translation. The degree courses in the tables which up until now have remained untranslated for the very same reason, have, due to numerous requests, been supplemented in this edition for the first time by an approximate translation, since it has emerged that this handbook is not only used by students who should have a knowledge of the language of their target country, but also increasingly by politicans, in ministries and other authorities as well as in industry.

These groups, above all, can be expected to be interested in the development of student statistics and structural changes in the higher education sector. Such changes are clearly to be seen: in almost all Member States a greater degree of practical orientation is being called for in the traditional degree courses, vocational-training establishments are being raised to higher education status, short programmes and new diplomas are being introduced because formerly non-academic careers now require higher education level training. The number of students is rising everywhere accordingly.

More and more countries are introducing across-border degree programmes and partially even degrees as well, for example, in economic subjects, European law or environmental science. This tendency will doubtlessly increase. The handbook devotes one short chapter each to the two oldest European study institutions: the European University Insitute in Florence and the College of Europe in Bruges. In 1991, the EC directive on mutual recognition of diplomas in national law will be implemented. It is all the more important that academic recognition between the institutions of higher education also progresses. The European Community course credit transfer system (ECTS) — which has been documented in the appendix — is expected to promote this development. Eighty-two institutions of higher education are cooperating in this pilot project. In the appendix to the handbook, readers will also find a short description of all international information centres for the recognition of certificates, study achievements and diplomas. This network, which is supported by the EC Commission, is called Naric.

The handbook appears in all nine Community languages. The manuscript was completed in May 1989. It should be noted that the national correspondents, who were appointed by their governments and who wrote the individual chapters as well as approving revision through the editors, were compelled to present a condensed description. Indeed, the handbook is not intended to replace the detailed information material of the Member States and their institutions of higher education, but rather refers and points to this information.

The editors wish to thank the national correspondents as well as all those who helped in the compilation of the material for their cooperation.

The handbook may be obtained through book shops, the EC sales offices as well as the publishing houses in the Member States (please see rear inside cover) and also through the Office for Official Publications of the EC in Luxembourg.

List of national correspondents

Belgium	Mlle Ch. Kaufmann	Ministère de l'Education nationale
	de heer N. Vercruysse	Ministerie van Onderwijs
Denmark	Fru L. Thomsen	Undervisningsministeriet
Federal Republic of Germany	Frau Dr Jonen Frau U. Dolezal	Kultusministerkonferenz Bundesministerium für Bildung und Wissenschaft
Greece	Dr M. Eginitou-Panayotidis	Υπουργείο Εθνικής Παιδείας
Spain	Dr F. Haering Pérez	Consejo de Universidades
France	Mme D. Auvergne	Ministère de l'Education nationale
Ireland	Miss R. Dalton	Higher Education Authority
Italy	Dott.ssa A. Cammisa	Ministero della Pubblica Istruzione
Luxembourg	Prof. C. Kieffer	Ministère de l'Education nationale et de la Jeunesse
The Netherlands	de heer M. van Wingerden	Netherlands Universities Foundation for International Cooperation (NUFFIC)
Portugal	Dr M. C. Rosa	CIRAD (Centro de Informação sobre o Reconhecimento Academico de Diplomas)
United Kingdom	Mrs Therese Lloyd	British Council

Belgium

Organization of higher education

Until 1970 the structure of the Belgian State, founded in 1830, was based on the principle of unity between legislation and government for the whole of the State territory. Since then, the Belgian Constitution has been subjected to three fundamental amendments (1970, 1980, 1988), which brought the government system of a unified Belgian State to an end and created an extraordinarily complex type of State, in which the power of the State is divided between the central State, the cultural communities, the regions, the provinces and the local communities.

Education largely belongs to the sectors which fall under the authority of the cultural communities. The central State, however, continues to bear responsibility for the education system, namely in all those sectors which have been assigned to it by the Constitution. This covers:

1. the length of compulsory schooling;
2. the minimal contents of degrees/diplomas;
3. the pension of members of the teaching staff.

In the Belgian Constitution of 1831, the principle of the freedom of teaching is embedded. Within this constitutional framework, two forms of institutions have developed in the higher education sector: on the one hand, the official institutions created and administered by the State, the provinces or the local communities and, on the other, the private institutions, most of which are church-associated.

Students are free to choose the institutions of higher education they wish to attend.

Teaching is done in the language of the region involved: French in the Walloon region, Dutch in the Dutch-speaking region and both languages in the *arrondissement* of Brussels.

All academic degrees issued by institutions of higher education which have been certified and recorded by the supervisory body invested with this authority on the basis of laws and regulations, have the same official value regardless of where the administrative responsibility for the institution of higher education in question lies (State, province, commune or private individual).

Higher education in Belgium was legally structured for the first time on the basis of the Law of 7 July 1970 concerning the general structure of higher education. Thus, for the first time, all training courses following on from secondary school have been legally listed. They are, depending on subject and organization of the studies and the study objective, divided into universities (*enseignement supérieur universitaire/universitair hoger onderwijs*) and non-university higher education (*enseignement supérieur non-universitaire/niet-universitair hoger onderwijs*). The non-university higher education is itself then subdivided into short degree courses (*enseignement de type court/hoger onderwijs van het korte type)* (consisting of a single study stage, lasting between two and three, and sometimes four years) and long degree courses (*enseignement de type long/hoger onderwijs van het lange type)*, which comprise two study stages of two years each (sometimes three years as well) and which correspond to university level.

As is repeatedly emphasized in the preliminary report on the above-mentioned law, the primary task of the universities consists in preserving, disseminating and promoting science and scholarship. Thus the tasks of teaching and research are closely interrelated. The main aim of the other institutions of higher education consists in the dissemination of scientific knowledge and its application in the different professions for which they provide preparation.

The two types of institution of higher education are considered to be on an equal level. Each has its own value and specific aims that determine the structures and teaching methods of the type in question.

Types of higher education institutions

Universities

University education is offered at 17 institutions (for addresses see Appendix 1) with university or equivalent status (*établissement assimilé/gelijkgestelde instelling*). These include six fully-fledged universities: Université de l'État à Liège, Rijksuniversiteit te Gent, Université catholique de Louvain, Katholieke Universiteit te Leuven, Université libre de Bruxelles, Vrije Universiteit Brussel. The other higher education institutions are limited to specific subject areas and, in some cases, to the first stage of studies (two or three years leading to the *diplôme de candidat/diploma van kandidaat*). The Universitaire Instelling Antwerpen offers only the second and third stages.

The complete universities comprise at least the five traditional faculties (philosophy and literature, law, science, medicine, applied science) and may also include a varying number of other faculties or institutes offering specialized courses (art history, archaeology, oriental studies, business and economics, social and political science, criminology, psychology and education, etc.).

Higher education at non-university establishments

The courses of study offered by the remaining institutions of higher education cover a very broad field.

They prepare students for various professions, mainly in industry, commerce, agriculture, paramedical and social work, teaching, interpreting, applied arts and the media.

Thus the non-university higher education sector is divided into the following subject orientations:

(i) technical higher education institutions *(enseignement supérieur technique/technisch hoger onderwijs)*;

(ii) economic higher education institutions *(enseignement supérieur économique/economisch hoger onderwijs)*;

(iii) agricultural higher education institutions *(enseignement su-*

périeur agricole/agrarisch hoger onderwijs);

(iv) higher education institutions for paramedical professions *(enseignement supérieur paramédical/paramedisch hoger onderwijs)*;

(v) higher education institutions for social service professions *(enseignement supérieur social/sociaal hoger onderwijs)*;

(vi) art colleges *(enseignement supérieur artistique/artistiek hoger onderwijs)*;

(vii) higher education colleges of teaching *(enseignement supérieur pédagogique/pedagogisch hoger onderwijs)*;

(viii) higher education institutions for maritime studies *(enseignement supérieur maritime/maritiem hoger onderwijs)*.

The higher education institutions listed under this heading are just as diverse as the courses of study they offer. Some of them, such as the *instituts supérieurs de commerce/handelshogescholen,* have university character. Others, such as the *école normales/normaalscholen,* have retained their own specific character.

In Appendix 2 the student will find a list of all the courses of study offered by this type of higher education institution.

Foreign students wishing information on the range of educational opportunities offered by Belgian institutions of higher education will be interested to know that besides the insitutions classified by the Law of 7 July 1970 and which comprise nearly all of the Belgian higher education institutions, there are still other specialized courses of study offered at the following institutions: music schools, such as the Royal Conservatories and the Institute of Church Music and Music Education. The former prepare their students primarily for their initial prizes and the *diplôme supérieur/hoger diploma* (various instruments), while the latter prepare their students for the *lauréat/laureaat* in music education in organ or harpsichord, piano and singing; art schools such as the Colleges of Decorative Arts and the Royal Academies of Fine Arts which offer various training courses in the broad field of fine arts and decorative arts; the Faculty of Protestant Theology in Brussels and the Faculty of Protestant Theology at Heverle, which grant the degrees of *licencié* and *docteur en théologie/licentiaat* and *doctor in de godgeleerdheid;* the Prince Léopold Institute of Tropical Medicine which leads to special qualifications for doctors, veterinarians and nurses; the Luxembourg University Foundation, which offers a course of study in environmental research at the third stage (instruction only in French); the Schools of Navigation and Radio Navigation, which train the officers of the merchant navy; the School of Civil Aeronautics, which trains airline pilots; the Royal Military Academy, which trains the officers of the land, air and sea forces.

Students interested in any of these courses of study are invited to write for further information to the *Administration de l'enseignement supérieur/Bestuur van het hoger onderwijs* (for addresses see Appendix 1).

B

Student statistics

In 1987—88, 103 522 students were registered at Belgian universities, of which 12 298 (12 %) were foreign students. Of these foreign students, 4 773 (39 %) came from EC Member States.

For the same period, 150 807 students were studying in the non-university sector, of which 10 257 were foreign students (6 %). The number of students coming from EC Member States amounted to 5 903 (57 %).

Organization and validation of courses

Studies in the Belgian system of higher education are organized in stages of studies (*cycles/cycli*) and academic years. The academic year generally begins in September/October and ends in June/July.

Universities

University education is characterized by a strict subdivision into a number of stages. At the end of each stage the student obtains the qualification which he needs to gain admission to the next stage of studies.

In most university courses students obtain the qualification of a *candidat/kandidaat* in two or sometimes three years. This qualification marks the completion of the basic training the student needs for his remaining studies. The second qualification, that of *licencié/licentiaat*, is obtained after a further two or three years of study and involves specialized studies and the submission of a final thesis *(mémoire/verhandeling)*. In some disciplines this second qualification amounts to that of a doctor (human medicine or veterinary medicine), pharmacist or engineer; in such cases, the qualification is granted after three to four years of study. In general, the second-stage qualifications confer upon the student the right to exercise a profession.

An additional qualification is required in order to teach in secondary schools, that of *agrégé de l'enseignement secondaire supérieur/geaggregeerde voor het hoger secundair onderwijs*, which may be awarded directly after the degree of *licencé/licentiaat* has been obtained.

University education in these various stages involves lectures, practical classes and seminars.

The third qualification, that of *docteur/doctor*, can be obtained no less than one or two years after the *licence/licentiaat*. (In practice, however, it often takes much longer.) It presupposes the writing of an original *dissertation/proefschrift* and a *thèse annexe/bijkomende stelling* which must be defended in public. Only such students are accepted for a *doctorat/doctoraat* who seem capable of independent work and scholarly research.

The highest qualification is that of *agrégé de l'enseignement supérieur/geaggregeerde voor het hoger onderwijs*. This qualification cannot be obtained until at least two years after being awarded the title of *docteur/doctor*. It involves the submission and public defence of an original *dissertation/proefschrift* as well as three *thèses annexes/bijkomende stellingen*, the topics of which can be chosen freely by the doctoral candidate, and an oral presentation on a subject proposed by the examining board. The degree of *agrégé de l'enseignement supérieur/geaggregeerde voor het hoger onderwijs* is only awarded to particularly qualifed students.

University degrees are divided into three main categories: national degrees (*grades légaux/wettelijke graden*), scientific degrees (*grades scientifiques/wetenschappelijke graden*) and supplementary or specialized degrees (*grades complémentaire/aanvullende graden*).

The *grades légaux/wettelijke graden,* also termed academic degrees, are awarded upon completion of studies for which admission requirements, curriculum and duration are laid down by law. They prepare students for public service professions such as the bar, the bench, medical professions, etc.

Grades scientifiques/wetenschappelijke graden are awarded upon completion of study for which admission requirements, curriculum and duration are fixed directly by the university, and they include such subjects as economics, sociology, psychology, education, criminology, oriental studies, physical education, geology, political science, etc.

University courses that end with a national or scientific degree generally follow the same pattern (*candidature/kandidatuur, licence/licentiaat, doctorat/doctoraat*) as described above.

Specialist study courses are concluded with the *grades complémentaires/aanvullende graden* or postgraduate degrees which are generally only taken after the second study stage. Requirements for obtaining these degrees are determined by the universities themselves.

Tables indicating the university courses leading to national degrees and tables showing all the available university courses can be found in the appendices.

Higher education at non-university establishments

The different higher education courses outside the university lead to a great variety of qualifications including those of *diplôme/diploma* in architecture, industrial engineering, economic engineering, *licencié/licentiaat* in administrative sciences, *licencié/licentiaat* in business management, *licencié/licentiaat* in interpreting, graduate nursing, primary-school teaching, lower secondary-school teaching, social work/assistant and pre-school education. These study courses are available either as long or short courses.

The tables giving the organization of non-university studies (see Appendix 2) list the training in short study courses as well as in the long study courses and the respective degrees according to subject. A brochure is available upon request from the *Administration de l'enseignement supérieur/Bestuur van het hoger onderwijs* which contains necessary information on every institution (addresses, subjects, degrees, etc.).

B

Admission and registration

Initial information

The sections in this chapter give basic information about the admission and registration of foreign students, who will find an initial source of information by writing to the Belgian Embassy in their own country (Addresses: see appendices).

A student wishing detailed information should definitely contact one of the following institutions:

1. The information service *(service d'information/Dienst voor studie-advies)* at the universities and the course information centre *(centre d'information sur les études/Centrum voor studie-advies).* The addresses can be found in the appendices;
2. For information on study possibilities: the Ministries of Education, *Administration de l'enseignement supérieur/Bestuur van het hoger onderwijs;*
3. For information on entrance requirements, registration and fees: the offices of the registrar *(Service d'inscription/Dienst inschrijvingen)* at the higher education institutions;
4. For information on scholarships: the *Commissariat général aux relations internationales/Commissariaat-generaal voor de internationale culturele samenwerking* and the offices of the registrar at the institutes of higher education;
5. For information on health insurance, employment, and living costs: the social services *(Service social/Sociale dienst)* at the higher education institutions;
6. For information on accommodation: the housing services *(Service de logement/Dienst huisvesting)* at the higher education institutions.

Entry requirements

Universities

In order to qualify for admission to the first level of university studies students must present one of the following Belgian school-leaving certificates or a recognized foreign equivalent. The most important Belgian school-leaving certificates valid for admission to university studies are:

1. the *diplôme d'aptitude à accéder à l'enseignement supérieur/bekwaamheidsdiploma voor het hoger onderwijs,* issued by a secondary school (general, technical or artistic) and officially approved by the *Commission d'homologation/Homologatiecommissie;*
2. the *diplôme d'aptitude à accéder à l'enseignement supérieur/bekwaamheidsdiploma voor het hoger onderwijs (examen de maturité/maturiteitsexamen),* issued by the *Jury d'État de l'enseignement secondaire supérieur/Examencommissie van de Staat voor het hoger secundair onderwijs;*
3. the *diplôme de l'examen d'admission aux études de candidat/diplo-*

ma van het toelatingsexamen voor de opleiding van kandidaat for mathematics, physics, and agricultural engineering, issued by a university or some other institution of higher education entitled to issue these certificates;

4. the *diplôme de l'examen d'admission aux études de candidat/diploma van het toelatingsexamen voor de opleiding van kandidaat* for the study of civil engineering issued by the *Jury d'État de l'enseignement secondaire supérieur / Examencommissie van de Staat voor het hoger secundair onderwijs,* a university or some other institute of higher education entitled to issue this certificate *(établissement assimilé/gelijkgestelde instelling).*
5. the *diplôme d'agrégé de l'enseignement secondaire inférieur/diploma van geaggregeerde voor het lager secundair onderwijs* for general courses;
6. the *diplôme d'ingénieur technicien/diploma van technisch ingenieur* for technical courses;
7. the *diplôme de licencié ou d'ingénieur commercial/diploma van licentiaat of commerciëel ingenieur* for courses in economic engineering; and
8. the *diplôme de l'enseignement supérieur de type court de plein exercice/diploma voor het hoger onderwijs van het korte type (full-time studieprogramma's).*

Students who have a certificate from a secondary school abroad can receive any necessary information from the *Service des équivalences de l'administration de l'enseignement secondaire* (for the French-language institutions)/ *Dienst gelijkwaardigheden van het bestuur van het secundair onderwijs* (for the Dutch-language institutions) (for addresses see Appendix 1).

Students holding the following certificates can be admitted to courses which are validated by a degree specified by the State:

baccalauréat européen issued by a school in Belgium or abroad;

International Baccalaureate, issued by the Office du Baccalauréat International in Geneva;

diplôme de maturité, issued by the SHAPE school, Belgian section;

France: *diplôme de bachelier de l'enseignement du second degré,* all series (enseignement général Bacs A, B, C, D);

Luxembourg: *certificat de fin d'études secondaires;*

Italy: *diploma di maturità scientifica;*

Spain: *Certificado del curso preuniversitario en letras o en ciencias,* certificate of successful completion of the *Curso de Orientación Universitaria;*

The Netherlands: *getuigschrift van een school voor voorbereidend wetenschappelijk onderwijs;*

Federal Republic of Germany: *Allgemeine Hochschulreife (Abitur, Reifezeugnis).*

Foreign students who have already begun university studies in their home countries and want to continue them in Belgium should request information on requirements for studying at a Belgian university by contacting the *Service des équivalences de l'enseignement supérieur/Dienst gelijkwaardigheden van het bestuur van het hoger onderwijs,* when the degree pro-

B

grammes correspond to those for which in Belgium the *grades légaux/wettelijke graden* (State degrees) would be awarded, or apply directly to the university offices for degree programmes for which the *grades scientifiques/wetenschappelijke graden* (scientific degrees) would be conferred.

Higher education at non-university establishments

At the remaining institutions of higher education the entry requirements vary depending on whether or not the institution offers a long or short course.

1. Long course *(enseignement supérieur de type long/hoger onderwijs van het lange type)*: The same entry requirements apply here as for admission to a university.
2. Short course *(enseignement supérieur de type court/hoger onderwijs van het korte type)*: To be admitted to such a course an officially approved *diplôme* or *certificat d'enseignement secondaire du degré supérieur/diploma* or *getuigschrift van secundair onderwijs van de hogere graad* must be presented.

To be admitted to any kind of higher education outside the university, foreign students must first acquire an equivalent to the required Belgian qualification. All necessary information is available from the *Administration de l'enseignement secondaire* (for the French-language institutions)/*Bestuur van het secundair onderwijs* (for the Dutch-language institutions) (for addresses see Appendix I).

This also applies to foreign students who have already begun university studies in their own countries and wish to continue them in Belgium.

Limitations

Access to higher education, in the university sector as well as in higher education outside the universities is, in principle, not subject to any limitations. Higher education is open to all those persons who present the required qualification or a recognized foreign equivalent. Thus foreign students must have applied for admission to the university of their choice before they can register. It must be pointed out, however, that the universities are forced to limit the number of admissions because of restricted capacity, especially in the case of medicine.

If admission is rejected by a State university the student can put in an appeal with the Minister for National Education within 30 days by registered post. The minister can repeal the decision to reject the application within 30 days.

Recognition of foreign certificates and degrees

Belgian law permits recognition of all foreign studies, without regard to level, subject or country in which they were carried out.

Equivalence can be recognized for:

1. periods of study at a foreign institution;
2. examinations taken at foreign institutions;

3. degrees and certificates acquired under foreign regulations.

Decisions on equivalence are general or relevant to individual cases. The recognition of equivalence may be full or partial. In some cases it is granted only after passing additional examinations.

Recognition of equivalence must by no means result in the fact that

1. studies are recognized, the level of which is not comparable with the level of corresponding studies in Belgium;
2. the applicant is admitted to a course of study, to which he would not be admitted in the country in which the degree or certificate was granted (e.g. if access to the studies in question depended on passing an entrance examination).

Entry examinations

There is no entrance examination for foreign students with the required Belgian secondary-school qualification or a recognized foreign equivalent. There is one exception: admission to a civil engineering course is only possible after passing an entrance test. This test is legally prescribed for all Belgian and foreign applicants regardless of the secondary-school qualification they have.

In mathematics, physics and agricultural engineering the universities require entrance examinations for those Belgian or foreign students who can present neither a Belgian *diplôme d'aptitude à accéder à l'enseignement supérieur/bekwaamheidsdiploma voor het hoger onderwijs* nor an equivalent foreign qualification (see section on 'Entry requirements').

Application and registration

Foreign students who wish to begin or continue higher education in Belgium are urgently requested to inquire at least a year prior to their planned departure. They should first contact the *Service culturel/Culturele dienst* of the Belgian Embassy (for addresses see Appendix 1) which can furnish them with general information not contained in this handbook. After that they should contact the higher education institution of their choice. There they will receive precise information regarding the contents of the curriculum and registration particulars.

Foreign students of all nationalities are urgently requested to send their applications for admission together with the required qualifications as early as possible, preferably before 1 May to the office of the registrar *(Service des inscriptions/Inschrijvingsdienst)* of the higher education institution in question (for addresses see Appendix 1).

The universities commence definitive registration at the beginning of September. The students are required to appear in person with an identity card or passport and a passport photograph. They must present the qualifications necessary for admission to the planned course of study, the notification of admission and certification of a recent medical examination. They must pay the tuition fees.

B

For information about possible additional fees the reader should consult the following section on 'Tuition fees'.

Tuition fees

Universities

The amount of fees is determined by the universities. Decisions concerning fees are made before 1 July. For the 1988—89 academic year, the tuition fees amounted to around BFR 15 000 at the Dutch-language higher education institutions and BFR 18 000 at the French-language higher education institutions. This amount covers the costs for matriculation, courses, exams and accident insurance. Foreign students in the following categories pay the same tuition fees as Belgian students:

1. students of foreign nationality whose parents (or legal guardian) have permanent or temporary residence in Belgium and work there (or did so in the past);
2. students who are citizens of an EC Member State;
3. students of foreign nationality, who are resident in Belgium and who have refugee status accorded to them by the Belgian delegation of the United Nations High Commissioner for Refugees;
4. students from a developing country that is recognized as such by Belgium and who have been granted admission to university studies in Belgium by the minister responsible for cooperation with developing countries;
5. students of a country which has concluded a cultural agreement with Belgium and who have received a scholarship within the framework of such an agreement from the ministers responsible for international cultural relations;
6. those foreign students not included in categories 1 to 5 and whose number is limited to 2 % of the number of Belgian students enrolled in the subject in question during the past academic year.

The remaining foreign students can be charged additional fees ranging between BFR 89 000 and BFR 271 000 (1986-87) depending on the subject being studied and the level attained.

In order to determine the exact amount of the fees to be paid, students should contact the office of the registrar as soon as possible *(Service des inscriptions/Inschrijvingsdienst)* at the university where they have applied for admission (for addresses see Appendix 1).

Higher education at non-university establishments

Fees at non-university establishments of higher education amount to:

(i) BFR 7 500 for long study courses,

(ii) BFR 250 for short study courses.

These fees have to be paid by Belgian students and foreign students of the following categories:

1. students who are citizens of an EC Member State;
2. students of foreign nationality, whose father, mother or legal guardian is a Belgian national;

3. students whose parents (or legal guardian) have permanent residence in Belgium;
4. foreign students who are married and whose husbands or wives live in Belgium in the same household and either work or receive a 'substitute income' (government support);
5. students of foreign nationality who are residents in Belgium and have refugee status;
6. foreign students with accommodation in a residence at the expense of OCMW (Belgian social benefit);
7. foreign students who work in Belgium or receive a 'substitute income' (government support);
8. foreign students who come to Belgium to study in the context of an agreement concluded by the *Ministre de l'Éducation/Minister van Onderwijs;*
9. students from a developing country recognized as such by Belgium and who have been granted admission to studies at an institution of higher education other than a university by the minister responsible for cooperation with developing countries;
10. students from a country that has concluded a cultural agreement with Belgium and who have been granted a scholarship within the framework of such an agreement by the ministers responsible for international cooperation.

Foreign students not included in one of these categories must pay additional fees, the amount of which varies according to subject.

Additional information on registration fees in the higher education sector outside the universities is available from the office of the registrar *(Service des inscriptions/Inschrijvingsdienst)* of the higher education institution in question.

B

Knowledge of the language of instruction, language courses and other courses

It should again be pointed out that courses are taught in the language of the region, i.e. French or Dutch.

In order to derive the maximum benefit from their studies, foreign students must possess a good knowledge of the language of instruction. Students whose mother-tongue is not the language of instruction at the higher education institution of their choice or who have not previously completed a course of study in the language in question are generally required to take a language test prior to final admission.

The universities provide intensive language courses for those students who still do not have sufficient language proficiency levels.

A booklet giving details of the various French-language courses which are offered to foreign students in the French-speaking part of Belgium is available at the *Administration de l'enseignement supérieur et de la recherche scientifique* (see Appendix 1 for the address).

Special courses at the universities are intended for all those Belgian and foreign students who, because of their specific study orientation, want to complement their training in the one or another discipline. Information on these courses of study can be obtained from the university offices (for addresses see Appendix 1).

Financial assistance and scholarships

Foreigners who wish to pursue higher education studies in Belgium may be eligible for scholarships under certain conditions. These scholarships come from various sources:

1. scholarships granted by the Belgian Government; some are granted under bilateral cultural agreements, others are reserved for foreign students with temporary residence in Belgium;
2. scholarships granted by foreign governments;
3. scholarships granted by international organizations, foundations, higher education institutions and private individuals;
4. scholarships granted within the framework of the Erasmus programme of the European Communities.

The size of scholarships, the number available and the conditions under which they are granted vary with the type of scholarship and often from one year to the next. For that reason interested students should apply to the *Service culturel/Culturele dienst* at the Belgian Embassy, at the *Commissariat général aux relations internationales/ Commissariaat-generaal voor de internationale culturele samenwerking* or the office of the registrar at the higher education institution in question (for addresses see Appendix 1).

Students must apply for all scholarships before coming to Belgium.

Entry and residence regulations

Students who wish to study in Belgium must register with the authorities of the town where they take up residence within a week of their arrival. They need to take along the following documents:

1. a passport or identity card;
2. a certificate of enrolment at a higher education institution;
3. proof of financial status: certificate of having a scholarship, a certified declaration of the embassy in question to the effect that financial responsibility has been assumed by the family of the student or by a Belgian citizen;
4. three to five passport photographs (depending on the town).

After completing these formalities students will receive a certificate proving that they have been entered in the aliens register. This document alone permits legal residence in Belgium. This certificate is valid for one year and must be renewed regularly during the entire duration of the students' studies.

Social aspects

Social security and health insurance

All students attending higher education institutions in Belgium are required to take out medical insurance with one of the companies in the compulsory insurance scheme.

Students already in a Belgian or foreign compulsory medical insurance scheme are required to present proof of this.

Anyone not in a compulsory medical insurance scheme must join one. He is free to choose the insurance company. He will need to take along a certificate of enrolment from the higher education institution he is attending and a passport or identity card. Membership in a compulsory medical insurance scheme covers doctor, medical and hospital costs.

It should be pointed out that medical expenses for students holding a scholarship from the *Commissariat général aux relations internationales/ Commissariaat-generaal voor de internationale culturele samenwerking* or from the European Communities are paid for by the agency granting the scholarship in question.

Advisory services

Most higher education institutions provide information services and documentary material on curriculum organization and post-graduate job prospects. These advisory services generally include psychological counselling and are there to help students cope with any difficulties that may arise at any time during their studies.

Student employment

Foreign students should be warned against the erroneous idea that they will have no difficulty in obtaining employment, even on a part-time basis. If this should prove necessary it would be best for them to approach the student welfare service (*Service social/Sociale dienst*) of the higher education institution they are attending in order to find out what work is available and to obtain all the necessary information on social legislation, job contracts and work permits. The work offered is rarely as stable and permanent as that covered by a normal contract.

Student organizations

Students, especially at universities, have a long tradition of joining one or other of the numerous student associations that have grown up in response to a large variety of different needs and interests. Some of them reflect cultural or sports interest while others have ideological or political aims.

It is quite natural for foreign students to join together in such associations according to their nationality. These associations represent their members *vis-à-vis* the academic administration and the various university bodies. They have the important function of helping foreign students adjust to Belgian university life and, if need be, provide various kinds of material and moral support.

Cost of living

In 1989 foreign students needed an annual budget (not counting tuition fees) of about BFR 230 000.

Their likely expenditures are as follows: study materials (course aids, books, etc.) BFR 20 000; accommodation (12 × BFR 6 000) BFR 72 000; food (12 × BFR 8 000) BFR 96 000; transport BFR 11 000; cost of membership in a compulsory health insurance scheme BFR 5 000; miscellaneous BFR 26 000.

This estimate is only approximate. Obviously the students' budget will depend on the life-style they adopt.

Accommodation

Foreign students have a choice of various forms of accommodation: university residence halls, rented rooms in town, community houses.

Pertinent information can be had by contacting the housing offices (*Service de logement/Dienst huisvesting*) (for addresses see Appendix I). There, students looking for accommodation will be helped in complying with the formalities necessary to obtain the desired accommodation.

Services for students

The social services (*Services sociaux/Sociale diensten*) generally fulfil the duties of a student service and assume an important role in university life. They have a broad area of responsibility, relating especially to improving living and working conditions for the students. If necessary they can also refer students to specific agencies (for addresses see Appendix 1).

Facilities for disabled students

In general, institutions of higher education take into consideration the special situation in which disabled students find themselves. In each case specific problems are discussed with the student in order to arrive at a satisfactory solution. The social services provide assistance to these students.

B

Appendices

1. Addresses

Belgian embassies in EC countries

Denmark
Øster Allé 7
DK-2100 København
☎ (01) 26 03 88

Federal Republic of Germany
Kaiser-Friedrich-Straße 7
D-5300 Bonn 1
☎ 21 20 01-5

Greece
Sekeri 3
Athina 10 671
☎ 36 178 86/87

Spain
Paseo de la Castellana 18, 6° piso
28046 Madrid
☎ 401 95 58

France
9, rue de Tilsit
F-75840 Paris Cedex 17
☎ 43 80 61 00

Ireland
Shrewsbury House
2 Shrewsbury Road
Ballsbridge
Dublin 4
☎ 69 20 82/69 15 88

Italy
Via dei Monti Parioli, 49
I-00197 Roma
☎ 360 94 41/360 94 45

Luxembourg
4 rue des Girondins
Résidence Champagne
L-1626 Luxembourg
☎ 44 27 46

The Netherlands
Lange Vijverberg 12
2513 's-Gravenhage
☎ 64 49 10

Portugal
Praça Marquês de Pombal 14, 6° piso
Lisboa
☎ 54 92 63

United Kingdom
103 Eaton Square
London SW1 W9 AB
☎ 235 54 22

Ministries

Ministère de l'éducation nationale
- Administration de l'enseignement supérieur et de la recherche scientifique
- Administration de l'enseignement secondaire

Cité administrative de l'État, bloc Arcades D
B-1010 Bruxelles
☎ (02) 210 55 11

- Administration de l'enseignement artistique

Boulevard Pachéco 34
B-1000 Bruxelles
☎ (02) 219 45 80/219 31 30

Commissariat général aux relations internationales de la Communauté française
Rue Stevens 7
B-1000 Bruxelles
☎ (02) 518 14 36

Ministerie van Onderwijs
- Bestuur van het Hoger Onderwijs en het Wetenschappelijk Onderzoek
  Koningsstraat 136
  1000 Brussel
  ☎ (02) 211 42 11
- Bestuur van het Secundair Onderwijs
  Koningstraat 138
  B-1000 Brussel
  ☎ (02) 211 42 11
- Bestuur van het Kunstonderwijs
  Wetstraat 26, 5e verd.
  B-1040 Brussel
  ☎ (02) 230 56 95

Ministerie van de Vlaamse Gemeenschap
- Administratie voor Onderwijs en Permanente Vorming
  Bestuur van Onderwijszaken
  - Dienst voor Studietoelagen
  - Internationale Samenwerking

  Kunstlaan 43
  B-1040 Brussel
  ☎ (02) 513 74 64

Universities

Université de l'État à Liège
- Secrétariat de l'université
- Service des inscriptions
- Service social
- Service de logement
  Place du 20 Août 9
  B-4000 Liège

Rijksuniversiteit te Gent
- Secretariaat
  Sint-Pietersnieuwstraat 25
  B-9000 Gent
- Dienst inschrijvingen
  Rectoraat
  Sint-Pietersnieuwstraat 45
  B-9000 Gent
- Sociale dienst
- Dienst huisvesting
- Buitenlandse studenten
  Sint-Pietersnieuwstraat 45
  B-9000 Gent
- Dienst voor studieadvies
  Sint-Pietersplein 7
  B-9000 Gent

Université catholique de Louvain:
Site de Louvain-la-Neuve (toutes les études universitaires,

sauf celles de médecine, de pharmacie, de science dentaire et de santé publique)
- Secrétariat de l'université (étudiants étrangers)
- Secrétariat des étudiants
  Halles universitaires
  Place de l'Université 1
  B-1348 Louvain-la-Neuve
- Service social
  Grand'rue 16
  B-1348 Louvain-la-Neuve
- Service de logement
  Place Polyvalente 1
  B-1348 Louvain-la-Neuve
- Centre d'information et de documentation sur les études et les professions (CID)
  Rue de la Lanterne Magique 28
  B-1348 Louvain-la-Neuve

Site de Louvain-en-Woluwe (études de médecine, de pharmacie, de science dentaire et de santé publique)
- Secrétariat général et service des inscriptions (étudiants étrangers)
  Avenue Emmanuel Mounier 50
  B-1200 Bruxelles
- Service d'aide aux étudiants
  La Mairie
  Rue Martin V 9
  B-1200 Bruxelles
- Service de logement
  La Mairie
  Rue Martin V 9
  B-1200 Bruxelles

Katholieke Universiteit te Leuven
- Secretariaat
- Dienst inschrijvingen
  Universiteitshal
  Naamsestraat 22
  B-3000 Leuven
- Dienst voor Studieadvies
  Atrecht college
  Naamsestraat 63
  B-3000 Leuven
- Sociale Dienst
- Buitenlandse studenten
- Huisvesting
  Van Dale college
  Naamsestraat 80
  B-3000 Leuven
- Campus Kortrijk
  Faculteitengebouw Letteren en Wijsbegeerte en Rechten
  Universitaire Campus
  B-8500 Kortrijk

Université libre de Bruxelles
- Secrétariat de l'université
- Service d'information et d'accueil des étudiants
- Service des inscriptions
- Service social
  Avenue F. D. Roosevelt 50
  B-1050 Bruxelles
- Service logement
  Cité Universitaire
  Avenue Paul-Héger 22
  B-1050 Bruxelles

Vrije Universiteit Brussel
- Secretariaat
- Dienst inschrijvingen
- Sociale dienst
- Dienst huisvesting
- Buitenlandse studenten
- Dienst studieadvies
  Campus Oefenplein
  Pleinlaan 2
  B-1050 Brussel

Université de l'État à Mons
- Secrétariat de l'université
- Service des inscriptions
  Place du Parc 20
  B-7000 Mons
- Service social
- Service logement
  Rue de la Grande-Triperie 30/34
  B-7000 Mons
- Centre d'information et de counselling (CICO)
  Rue de la Halle, 15
  B-7000 Mons

Rijksuniversitair Centrum Antwerpen
- Rectoraat
  Beukenlaan 12
  B-2020 Antwerpen
- Dienst inschrijvingen
  Groenenborgerlaan 171
  B-2020 Antwerpen
- Sociale dienst
- Buitenlandse studenten
- Dienst studieadvies
- Dienst huisvesting

Middelheimlaan 1
B-2020 Antwerpen

Universitaire Faculteiten Sint-Ignatius te Antwerpen
- Secretariaat
  Venusstraat 35
  B-2000 Antwerpen
- Dienst inschrijvingen
- Sociale dienst
- Dienst huisvesting
  Prinsstraaat 13
  B-2000 Antwerpen

Universitaire Instelling Antwerpen
- Secretariaat
- Dienst inschrijvingen
- Sociale dienst
- Buitenlandse studenten
- Dienst studieadvies
- Dienst huisvesting
  Universiteitsplein 1
  B-2610 Wilrijk

Faculté polytechnique de Mons
- Secrétariat de la faculté
- Service des inscriptions
- Service social
- Service de logement
  Rue de Houdain 9
  B-7000 Mons

Faculté des sciences agronomiques de l'État à Gembloux
- Secrétariat de la faculté
- Service des inscriptions
- Service social
- Service logement
  B-5800 Gembloux

Facultés universitaires Notre-Dame de la Paix à Namur
- Secrétariat des facultés
- Service des inscriptions
- Service social
- Service de logement
  Rue de Bruxelles 61
  B-5000 Namur

Faculté universitaire catholique de Mons
- Secrétariat de la faculté

– Service des inscriptions
– Service social
– Service logement
Chaussée de Binche 151
B-7000 Mons

Facultés universitaires Saint-Louis à Bruxelles
– Secrétariat des facultés
– Service des inscriptions
Boulevard du Jardin Botanique 43
B-1000 Bruxelles
– Service social
– Service logement
Rue du Marais 109
B-1000 Bruxelles

Universitaire Faculteiten Sint-Aloysius te Brussel
– Secretariaat
– Dienst inschrijvingen
– Sociale dienst
– Buitenlandse studenten
– Dienst studieadvies
– Dienst huisvesting
Vrijheidslaan 17
B-1080 Brussel (Koekelberg)

Limburgs Universitair Centrum
– Secretariaat
– Dienst inschrijvingen
– Sociale dienst
– Dienst huisvesting
– Dienst studieadvies
Limburgse Universitaire Campus
Universiteitslaan
B-3610 Diepenbeek

Fondation universitaire luxembourgeoise
Rue des Déportés 140
B-6700 Arlon

Faculté universitaire de théologie protestante/
Universitaire Protestantse Theologische Faculteit
Rue des Bollandistes 40/
Bollandistenstraat 40
B-1040 Bruxelles/Brussel

Evangelische Theologische Faculteit
Sint-Jansbergsesteenweg 97
B-3030 Heverlee

Institut de médecine tropicale Prince Léopold
Nationalestraat 155
B-2000 Antwerpen

Non-university establishments of higher education

The following is a list of addresses of French-language and Dutch-language institutions of higher education in the non-university sector offering long courses.

The list of addresses of institutions offering short courses may be obtained by writing to the *Administration de l'enseignement supérieur/Bestuur van het hoger onderwijs.*

(a) Higher education in the non-university sector (French-language) — long courses

Enseignement supérieur technique

Institut supérieur industriel de Bruxelles
Rue Royale 154-158
B-1000 Bruxelles

Institut supérieur industriel
Avenue Maistriau 8
B-7000 Mons

Institut supérieur industriel
Rue Saint-Victor 3
B-5200 Huy

Institut supérieur industriel
Chemin de Weyler 2
B-6700 Arlon

Institut supérieur industriel de l'HF — IMC
Avenue Émile Gryson 1
B-1070 Bruxelles

Institut supérieur industriel du Hainaut
Boulevard Solvay 31
B-6000 Charleroi

Institut supérieur industriel liégeois
Quai Gloesener 6
B-4020 Liège

Institut supérieur industriel (ECAM + ENRACI)
Rue du Tir 14
B-1060 Bruxelles

Institut supérieur industriel catholique du Hainaut
Avenue de l'Hôpital 27 h
B-7000 Mons

Institut supérieur industriel — Institut Gramme
Quai du Condroz 28
B-4900 Angleur

Institut supérieur industriel Pierrard
B-6760 Virton

Enseignement supérieur économique

Institut supérieur de l'État de traducteurs et interprètes
Rue Hazard 34
B-1180 Bruxelles

Institut Marie Haps
Rue d'Arlon 11
B-1040 Bruxelles

École d'interprètes internationaux
Place Warocqué 17
B-7000 Mons

Institut d'enseignement supérieur Lucien Cooremans
Place Anneessens 11
B-1000 Bruxelles

Institut supérieur de commerce Saint-Louis
Rue du Marais 113
B-1000 Bruxelles

Institut catholique des hautes études commerciales
Boulevard Brand Whitlock 2
B-1150 Bruxelles

École des hautes études commerciales et consulaires
Rue Sohet 21
B-4000 Liège

Enseignement supérieur agricole

Institut supérieur industriel
Rue Saint-Victor 3
B-5200 Huy

Institut supérieur industriel
Boulevard Solvay 31
B-6000 Charleroi

Enseignement supérieur social

Institut des hautes études de communications sociales
Chaussée de Binche 151
B-7000 Mons

Enseignement supérieur artistique

Institut supérieur d'architecture de l'État
Place Flagey 19
B-1050 Bruxelles

Institut supérieur d'architecture Victor Horta
ULB Campus de la Plaine
Boulevard du Triomphe
CP 248
B-1050 Bruxelles

Institut supérieur d'architecture
Rue d'Havré 88
B-7000 Mons

Institut supérieur d'architecture Lambert Lombard
Rue Saint-Gilles 33
B-4000 Liège

Institut supérieur d'architecture Saint Luc
Rue d'Irlande 57
B-1060 Bruxelles

Institut supérieur d'architecture Saint Luc
Chaussée de Tournai 50
B-7721 Ramegnies-Chin

Institut supérieur d'architecture Saint Luc
Rue Sainte-Marie 40
B-4000 Liège

Institut supérieur d'architecture communale
Rue des Halles 11
B-1000 Bruxelles

Institut national supérieur des arts du spectacle et techniques de diffusion
Rue Thérésienne 8
B-1000 Bruxelles

Institut des arts de diffusion
Rue des Blancs Chevaux 38/40
B-1348 Louvain-la-Neuve

Enseignement supérieur maritime

Ecole supérieur de navigation d'Anvers.
Noordkasteel-Est 6
B-2030 Anvers

(b) Higher education in the non-university sector (Dutch-language) — long courses

Technisch hoger onderwijs

Stedelijke Industriële Hogeschool Antwerpen
Paardenmarkt 94
B-2000 Antwerpen

Katholieke Industriële Hogeschool ter Kempen
Technische Schoolstraat 56
B-2440 Geel

Katholieke Industriële Hogeschool Antwerpen
Salesianenlaan 1A
B-2710 Hoboken

Katholieke Industriële Hogeschool De Nayer Mechelen-Geel
J. De Nayerlaan 5
B-2580 St. Katelijne-Waver

Stedelijke Industriële Hogeschool Mechelen
Leopoldstraat 42
B-2800 Mechelen

Industriële Hogeschool van het Rijk
Nijverheidskaai 170
B-1070 Brussel-Anderlecht

Katholieke Industriële Hogeschool Groep T Leuven
Vuurkruisenlaan 4
B-3000 Leuven

Katholieke Industriële Hogeschool voor Limburg
Limburgse Universitaire Campus
Universiteitslaan
B-3600 Diepenbeek

Industriële Hogeschool van het Rijk
Maastrichterstraat 100
B-3500 Hasselt

Industriële Hogeschool van het Rijk BME
Schoonmeersstraat 52
B-9000 Gent

Industriële Hogeschool van het Rijk CTL
Voskenslaan 270
B-9000 Gent

Katholieke Industriële Hogeschool Oost-Vlaanderen
Gebr. de Smetstraat 1
B-9000 Gent

Provinciale Industriële Hogeschool
Karel de Goedelaan
B-8500 Kortrijk

Katholieke Industriële Hogeschool West-Vlaanderen
Zeedijk 101
B-8400 Oostende

Agrarisch hoger onderwijs

Katholieke Industriële Hogeschool ter Kempen
Technische Schoolstraat 56
B-2440 Geel

Industriële Hogeschool van het Rijk BME
Schoonmeersstraat 52
B-9000 Gent

Industriële Hogeschool van het Rijk CTL
Voskenslaan 270
B-9000 Gent

Economisch hoger onderwijs

Handelshogeschool
Korte Nieuwstraat 33
B-2000 Antwerpen

B

Provinciaal Hoger Instituut voor Bestuurswetenschappen
Koningin Elisabethlei 22
B-2018 Antwerpen

Katholieke Vlaamse Hogeschool
— Hoger Technisch Instituut
De Bomstraat 11
B-2018 Antwerpen

Hoger Instituut voor vertalers en tolken
Schildersstraat 41
B-2000 Antwerpen

Economische Hogeschool St-Aloysius
Broekstraat 113
B-1000 Brussel

Administratieve economische Hogeschool
Trierstraat 84 bus 6
B-1040 Brussel

Hoger Rijksinstituut voor vertalers en tolken
Trierstraat 84 — bus 11
B-1040 Brussel

Vlaamse Economische Hogeschool Brussel
Koningsstraat 284
1210 Brussel

Provinciale Hogeschool van Vertalers en Tolken
Brusselspoort 93
B-9000 Gent

Economische Hogeschool Limburg
Limburgse Universitaire Campus
Universiteitslaan
B-3610 Diepenbeek

Provinciaal Instituut voor hoger onderwijs
Henleykaai 83A
B-9000 Gent

Artistiek hoger onderwijs

Hoger Architectuurinstituut van het Rijk
Mutsaertstraat 31
B-2000 Antwerpen

St-Lukas Hoger Architectuurinstituut
Paleizenstraat 70
B-1030 Brussel

Provinciaal Hoger Instituut voor architectuur
Gouv. Verwilghensingel 3
B-3500 Hasselt

Hoger Architectuurinstituut St-Lukas
Zwarte Zusterstraat 34
B-9000 Gent

Hoger Architectuurinstituut van de stad Gent
Prof. Klyskensstraat 6
B-9000 Gent

Pedagogisch hoger onderwijs

Handelshogeschool
Korte Nieuwstraat 33
B-2000 Antwerpen

Economische Hogeschool St-Aloysius
Broekstraat 113
B-1000 Brussel

Administratieve economische Hogeschool
Trierstraat 84 bus 6
B-1040 Brussel

Vlaamse Economische Hogeschool
Koningstraat 284
B-1210 Brussel

Economische Hogeschool Limburg
Limburgse Universitaire Campus
Universiteitslaan
B-3610 Diepenbeek

Technisch hoger onderwijs van de derde graad

Hoger Rijksinstituut voor toneel- en cultuurspreiding
Naamsestraat 54
B-1000 Brussel

Maritiem hoger onderwijs

Hogere Zeevaartschool Antwerpen
Noordkasteel — Oost 6
B-2030 Antwerpen

B

2. Survey of courses of study at higher education institutions

Diagram showing university studies leading to *grades légaux* (French-language institutions)

	Études	Nombre d'années d'études							
		1	2	3	4	5	6	7	
Philosophie et lettres	Philosophie	Candidat en philosophie		Licencié en philosophie		Agrégé de l'enseignement secondaire supérieur	Docteur en philosophie et lettres[1]		AGRÉGÉ DE L'ENSEIGNEMENT SUPÉRIEUR[3]
Philosophie et lettres	Histoire	Kandidaat en histoire		Licencié en histoire					
Philosophie et lettres	Philologie classique	Candidat en philologie classique		Licencié en philologie classique					
Philosophie et lettres	Philologie romane	Candidat en philologie romane		Licencié en philologie romane					
Philosophie et lettres	Philologie germanique	Candidat en philologie germanique		Licencié en philologie germanique					
Droit	Droit et notariat	Candidat en droit		Licencié en droit			Docteur en droit[2] / Lic. en notariat		
Sciences	Mathématiques	Candidat en sciences mathématiques		Licencié en sciences mathématiques		Agrégé de l'enseignement secondaire supérieur	Docteur en sciences[1]		
Sciences	Physique	Candidat en sciences physiques		Licencié en sciences physiques					
Sciences	Chimie	Candidat en sciences chimiques		Licencié en sciences chimiques					
Sciences	Géologie et minéral.	Candidat en sciences géologiques et minéralogiques		Licencié en sciences géologiques et minéralogiques					
Sciences	Biologie	Candidat en sc. biologiques		Licencié en sc. zoologiques / Licencié en sc. botaniques					
Sciences	Géographie	Candidat en sciences géographiques		Licencié en sciences géographiques					
Sciences médicales	Pharmacie	Candidat en sciences pharmaceutiques		Pharmacien					
Sciences médicales	Médecine	Candidat en sciences médicales			Docteur en médecine, chirurgie et accouchements				
Sciences médicales	Science dentaire	Candidat en sciences dentaire		Licencié en science dentaire					
Sciences médicales	Médecine vétérinaire	Candidat en sciences véterinaire			Docteur en médecine vétérinaire				
Sciences appliquées	Mines	Candidat ing. civil		Ingénieur civil des mines					
Sciences appliquées	Constructions	Candidat ing. civil		Ingénieur civil des constr.					
Sciences appliquées	Métallurgie	Candidat ing. civil		Ingénieur civil-métallurgiste					
Sciences appliquées	Chimie	Candidat ing. civil		Ingénieur civil-chimiste					
Sciences appliquées	Électricité	Candidat ing. civil		Ingénieur civil-électricien					
Sciences appliquées	Mécanique	Candidat ing. civil		Ingénieur civil-mécanicien					
Sciences appliquées	Constructions navales	Candidat ing. civil		Ingénieur civil des constructions navales					
Sciences appliquées	Architecture	Candidat ing. civil		Ingénieur civil-architecte					
Sciences appliquées	Industrie textile	Candidat ing. civil		Ingénieur civil de l'industrie textile					
Sciences agronom.	Agronomie et chimie	Candidat ingénieur agronome		Ingénieur agronome / Ingénieur chimiste et des industries agricoles					

Une année d'études au moins après l'obtention du grade de *licencié.*

Deux années d'études au moins après l'obtention du grade de *licencié.*

Deux années au moins après l'obtention du grade *de docteur,* de *licencié en notariat* ou en *science dentaire,* de *pharmacien* ou *d'ingénieur.*

B

Diagram showing university studies leading to a *wettelijke graad* (Dutch-language institutions)

	Studies	Aantal jaren studie						
		1	2	3	4	5	6	7
Letteren en Wijsbegeerte	Wijsbegeerte	Kandidaat in de wijsbegeerte		Licentiaat in de wijsbegeerte		Geaggregeerde voor het hoger secundair onderwijs	Doctor in de letteren en wijsbegeerte[1]	
	Geschiedenis	Kandidaat in de geschiedenis		Licentiaat in de geschiedenis				
	Klassieke filologie	Kandidaat in de klassieke filologie		Licentiaat in de klassieke filologie				
	Romaanse filologie	Kandidaat in de Romaanse filologie		Licentiaat in de Romaanse filologie				
	Germaanse filologie	Kandidaat in de Germaanse filologie		Licentiaat in de Germaanse filologie				
Recht	Rechten en notariaat	Kandidaat in de rechten		Licentiaat in de rechten			Doctor in de rechten[2] / Lic. i.h. notariaat	
Wetenschappen	Wiskunde	Kandidaat in de wiskundige wetenschappen		Licentiaat in de wiskundige wetenschappen		Geaggregeerde voor het hoger secundair onderwijs	Doctor in de wetenschappen[1]	
	Natuurkunde	Kandidaat in de natuurkundige wetenschappen		Licentiaat in de natuurkundige wetenschappen				
	Scheikunde	Kandidaat in de scheikundige wetenschappen		Licentiaat in de scheikundige wetenschappen				
	Aardkunde en delfstofkunde	Kandidaat in de aardkundige en de delfstofkundige wetenschappen		Licentiaat in de aardkundige en de delfstofkundige wetenschappen				
	Biologie	Kandidaat in de biologische wetenschappen		Lic. in de dierkundige wetenschap.				
				Lic. in de plantkundige wetenschap.				
	Aardrijkskunde	Kandidaat in de aardrijkskundige wetenschappen		Licentiaat in de aardrijkskundige wetenschappen				
Medische wetenschappen	Apotheker	Kandidaat farmaceutische wet.		Apotheker				
	Geneeskunde	Kandidaat in de geneeskundige wetenschappen			Doctor in de genees-, heel- en verloskunde			
	Tandheelkunde	Kandidaat in de tandheelkunde		Licentiaat in de tandheelkunde				
	Diergeneeskunde	Kandidaat in de diergeneeskundige wetenschappen			Doctor in de diergeneeskunde			
Toegepaste wetenschappen	Mijnen	Kand. burg. ingenieur		Burgerlijk mijningenieur				
	Bouwkunde	Kand. burg. ingenieur		Burgerlijk bouwkundig ingenieur				
	Metallurgie	Kand. burg. ingenieur		Burgerlijk metallurgisch ingenieur				
	Scheikunde	Kand. burg. ingenieur		Burgerlijk scheikundig ingenieur				
	Electrotechniek	Kand. burg. ingenieur		Burgerlijk electrotechnisch ingenieur				
	Werktuigkunde	Kand. burg. ingenieur		Burgerlijk werktuigkundig ingenieur				
	Scheepsbouwkunde	Kand. burg. ingenieur		Burgerlijk scheepsbouwkundig ingenieur				
	Architectuur	Kand. burg. ingenieur		Burgerlijk ingenieur-architect				
	Textielnijverheid	Kand. burg. ingenieur		Burgerlijk ingenieur der textielnijverheid				
Landbouw-wetensch.	Landbouw en scheikunde	Kandidaat landbouwkundig ingenieur		Landbouwkundig ingenieur				
				Ing. voor de scheikunde en de landbouwindustrieën				

[1] Ten minste één jaar studie na het behalen van het diploma van *licentiaat.*

[2] Ten minste twee jaar studie na het behalen van het diploma van *licentiaat.*

[3] Ten minste twee jaar studie na het behalen van het diploma van *doctor, licentiaat in het notariaat, licentiaat in de tandheelkunde, apotheker* of *ingenie*

B

Survey of courses of study at French-language universities in Belgium

Degree courses concluding with scientific-academic degrees *(grades scientifiques)*

Administration, Commerce, Economics, Political Sciences and Social Sciences

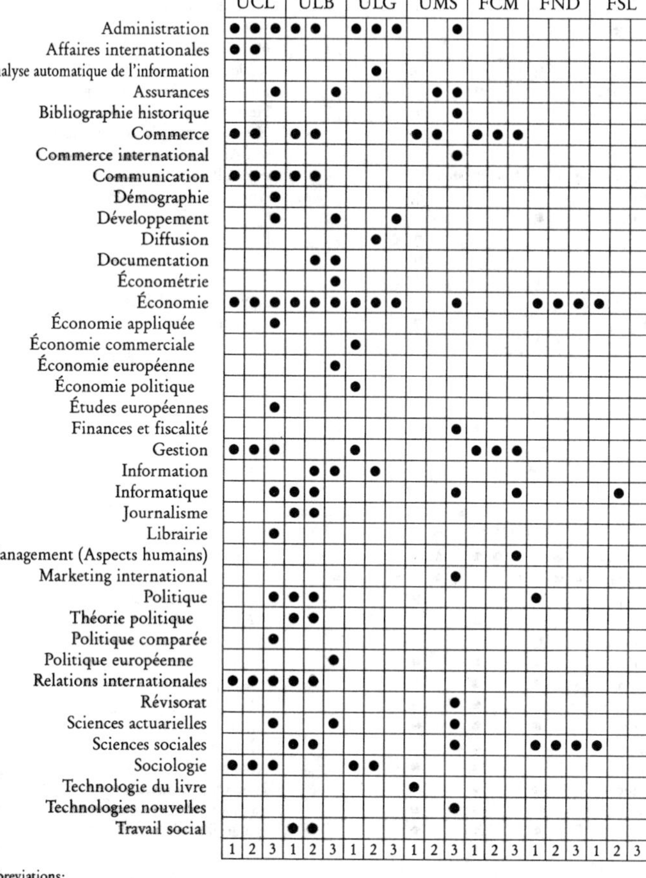

	UCL			ULB			ULG			UMS			FCM			FND			FSL			
	1	2	3	1	2	3	1	2	3	1	2	3	1	2	3	1	2	3	1	2	3	
Administration	●	●	●	●	●		●	●	●			●										Administrative science
Affaires internationales	●	●																				International affairs
Analyse automatique de l'information								●														Data processing
Assurances			●			●					●	●										Insurance
Bibliographie historique												●										Historical bibliography
Commerce	●	●		●	●					●	●		●	●	●							Trade and Commerce
Commerce international												●										International trade
Communication	●	●	●	●	●																	Communications sciences
Démographie			●																			Demography
Développement			●			●			●													Development
Diffusion								●														Public relations
Documentation					●	●																Documentation
Économétrie						●																Economics and Computer science
Économie	●	●	●	●	●	●	●	●	●			●				●	●	●	●			Economics
Économie appliquée			●																			Applied economics
Économie commerciale							●															Trade economics
Économie européenne						●																European economics
Économie politique							●															Political economics
Études européennes			●																			European studies
Finances et fiscalité												●										Financial and fiscal studies
Gestion	●	●	●				●						●	●	●							Business management
Information					●	●		●														Information science
Informatique			●	●	●							●			●					●		Computer science
Journalisme				●	●																	Journalism
Librairie			●																			Librarian studies
Management (Aspects humains)															●							Human resources management
Marketing international												●										International marketing
Politique			●	●	●											●						Political sciences
Théorie politique				●	●																	Political theory
Politique comparée			●																			Comparative political science
Politique européenne						●																European politics
Relations internationales	●	●	●	●	●																	International relations
Révisorat												●										Economic auditing
Sciences actuarielles			●			●						●										Actuarial theory
Sciences sociales				●	●							●				●	●	●	●			Social sciences
Sociologie	●	●	●				●	●														Sociology
Technologie du livre										●												Printing technology
Technologies nouvelles												●										Modern technologies
Travail social				●	●																	Social work
	1	2	3	1	2	3	1	2	3	1	2	3	1	2	3	1	2	3	1	2	3	

bbreviations:

CL Université catholique de Louvain
LB Université libre de Bruxelles
LG Université de l'État à Liège
MS Université de l'État à Mons
G Faculté des sciences agronomiques de l'État à Gembloux
M Faculté universitaire catholique de Mons
ND Facultés universitaires Notre-Dame de la Paix à Namur
M Faculté polytechnique de Mons
L Facultés universitaires Saint-Louis
P Faculté universitaire de théologie protestante de Bruxelles
JL Fondation universitaire luxembourgeoise
T Inter-university programme
First stage of studies.
Second stage of studies.
Third (specialization) stage, postgraduate studies.

Note:

All courses of study listed refer to the qualifications and degrees obtained after the respective course cycles or stages. Doctorates and courses leading to national degrees *(grades légaux/wettelijke graden)* are not contained in these tables.

B

Agriculture and the Environment

	UCL			ULB			FAG			FUL						
Agriculture	●	●		●	●	●	●	●	●							Agricultural science
Agrométéorologie												●				Agricultural meteorology
Agronomie	●	●	●	●	●		●	●	●							Agronomy
Biotechnologie									●							Biotechnology
Brasserie			●													Brewing
Chimie	●	●		●	●	●	●	●								Chemistry
Développement rural			●						●							Rural development
Écologie des eaux: voir Sciences																Water protection, see: Natural sciences
Écologie humaine						●										Human ecology
Économie agraire, Économie rurale			●						●							Agricultural economics
Environnement						●						●				Environmental protection
Génie sanitaire									●							Health-service technology
Hydrologie voir Sciences appliquées																Hydr. engineer./water managem., see: Appl. nat. sc.
Industries agricoles	●	●		●	●	●	●	●								Agricultural industry
Informatique appliquée									●							Applied computer science
Pédologie tropicale			●													Tropical soil science
Phytiatrie, phytogénétique									●							Plant genetics
Phytopharmacie, phytotechnique									●							Plant protection, botany
Régions chaudes			●						●							Tropical regions
Sciences naturelles appliquées			●													Applied natural sciences
Statistique appliquée									●							Applied statistics
	1	2	3	1	2	3	1	2	3	1	2	3				

Law and Criminology

	UCL			ULB			FAG			FUL			FSL			
Criminologie		●			●	●		●	●							Criminology
Droit	●	●		●	●		●	●		●			●			Law
Droit administratif						●			●							Administrative law
Droit aérien						●										Air-traffic law
Droit comparé						●										Comparative law
Droit économique			●			●			●							Economic law
Droit européen			●			●			●							European law
Droit fiscal						●			●							Fiscal law
Droit international			●			●			●							International law
Droit maritime						●										Maritime law
Droit social						●			●							Social law
Économie des assurances			●			●										Insurance business
Fiscalité						●			●							Tax law
Notariat			●			●			●							Notarial studies
	1	2	3	1	2	3	1	2	3	1	2	3	1	2	3	

B

Medicine – Health-Service – Pharmacy

	UCL			ULB			ULG			UMS			FND						
Biologie médicale			●	●	●	●			●										Medical biology
Dentisterie	●	●		●	●		●	●											Dentistry
Éducation physique	●	●	●	●	●		●	●											Physical education
Kinésithérapie	●	●		●	●	●	●	●											Physiotherapy/kinesiotherapy
Logopédie	●	●	●				●	●											Logopaedics
Médecine, chirurgie et accouchements	●	●		●	●		●	●		●			●						Medicine, surgery, obstetrics
Médecine vétérinaire	●						●	●					●						Veterinary medicine
Pharmacie	●	●		●	●		●	●		●			●						Pharmacy
Réadaptation	●	●	●						●										Rehabilitation Therapy
	1	2	3	1	2	3	1	2	3	1	2	3	1	2	3				

Moral code – Religion – Theology

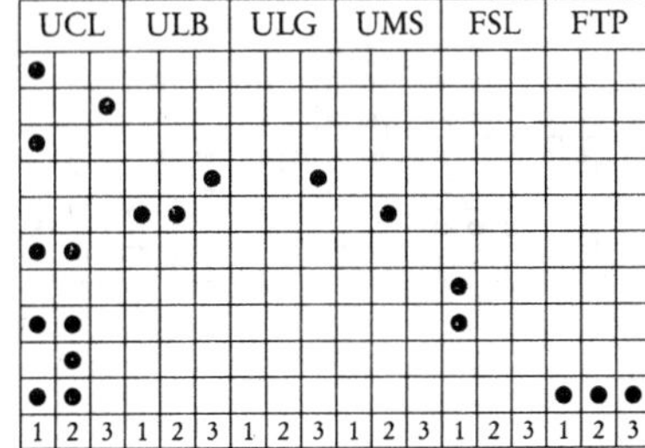

	UCL			ULB			ULG			UMS			FSL			FTP			
Catéchèse	●																		Catechism/religious teaching
Droit canonique			●																Canon law
Évangélisation	●																		Evangelization
Histoire des religions						●			●										Religious history
Morale				●	●						●								Moral code
Philologie biblique	●	●																	Biblical philology
Philosophie													●						Philosophy
Religion	●	●											●						Religion
Sciences ecclésiastiques		●																	Religious sciences
Théologie	●	●														●	●	●	Theology
	1	2	3	1	2	3	1	2	3	1	2	3	1	2	3	1	2	3	

B

Philosophy and the Humanities

	UCL			ULB			ULG			FND			FSL			
	1	2	3	1	2	3	1	2	3	1	2	3	1	2	3	
Africanistique			●			●										African studies
Allemand						●			●							German studies
Anglais - études anglaises et américaines						●			●							English and American studies
Antiquité classique	●	●		●	●		●	●	●	●			●			Classical antiquity
Arabe		●														Arabic
Art - archéologie	●	●		●	●			●	●	●						Archaeology and History of art
Brésil (études brésiliennes)		●														Brazilian studies
Byzantinologie						●										Byzantine studies
Égyptologie					●											Egyptology
Espagnol - études hispaniques		●				●										Hispanic studies
Français (Langue et littérature)				●	●											French (language and literature)
Histoire	●	●	●	●	●		●	●	●	●			●			History
Islamologie		●				●										Islamic sciences
Italien		●				●										Italian
Linguistique		●				●										Linguistics
Littérature	●	●														Literary studies
Moyen-âge			●						●							Medieval studies
Musicologie							●	●								Musicology
Néerlandais						●			●							Dutch
Orientalisme		●		●	●	●	●	●								Oriental studies
Philologie classique	●	●		●	●		●	●		●			●			Classical philology
Philologie germanique	●	●		●	●		●	●		●			●			Germanic philology
Philologie romane	●	●		●	●		●	●		●			●			Romance philology
Philosophie	●	●	●	●	●		●	●	●	●			●			Philosophy
Portugais - études portugaises		●														Portuguese
Slavistique			●	●	●											Slavonic studies

Psychopedagogics – Translation and Interpretation

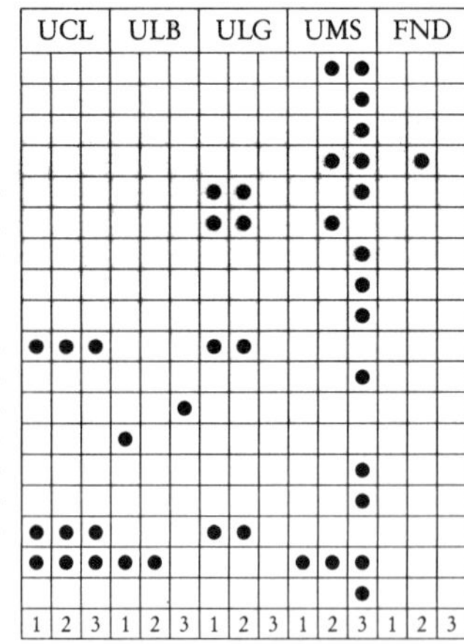

	UCL			ULB			ULG			UMS			FND			
	1	2	3	1	2	3	1	2	3	1	2	3	1	2	3	
Administration scolaire											●	●				School administration sciences
Audio-visuel												●				Audio-visual methodology
Psychologie clinique												●				Clinical psychology
Didactique des langues											●	●		●		Foreign-language didactics
Éducation, éducation permanente							●	●				●				Further training
Formation, formation des adultes							●	●			●					Adult education
Informatique												●				Computer science
Interprétariat et traduction												●				Translation and Interpretation
Linguistique appliquée												●				Applied linguistics
Logopédie	●	●	●				●	●								Logopaedics
Orthopédagogie												●				Orthopedagogics
Pédagogie						●										Pedagogics
Pédagogie appliquée				●												Applied pedagogics
Phonétique												●				Phonetics
Psycholinguistique												●				Psycholinguistics
Psychologie	●	●	●				●	●								Psychology
Psychopédagogie	●	●	●	●	●					●	●	●				Psychopedagogics
Sciences du langage												●				Linguistics

B

Natural sciences

	UCL			ULB			ULG			UMS			FND			INT			
	1	2	3	1	2	3	1	2	3	1	2	3	1	2	3	1	2	3	
Astrophysique									●										Astrophysics
Biochimie		●																	Biochemistry
Biologie	●	●	●	●	●		●	●		●	●		●	●					Biology
Biologie moléculaire						●													Molecular biology
Biophysique									●										Biophysics
Biotechnologie						●													Biotechnology
Botanique	●	●		●	●		●	●											Botany
Cartographie																		●	Cartography
Chimie	●	●	●	●	●		●	●		●	●		●	●					Chemistry
Chimie appliquée						●													Applied chemistry
Développement									●										Development
Écologie des eaux															●				Hydroecology
Géographie, géologie	●	●		●	●		●	●					●					●	Geography, Geology
Géophysique						●													Geophysics
Informatique				●	●	●				●	●	●							Computer science
Mathématique	●	●	●	●	●	●	●	●	●	●	●		●	●					Mathematics
Médecine nucléaire									●										Nuclear medicine
Minéralogie	●	●		●	●		●	●					●						Mineralogy
Mycologie												●							Mycology
Nucléaire									●										Nuclear research
Océanologie									●										Oceanography
Palynologie												●							Palynology
Physique, physique théorique	●	●	●	●	●	●	●	●		●	●		●	●					Physics, theoretical plasmaphysics
Physique des solides, physique médicale									●										Solid-state physics, Medical physics
Radiobiologie						●													Radiobiology
Radiologie, Radioprotection, Rayonnements ionisants			●						●										Radiology, Radiation protection, Ionizing radiation
Statistique			●																Statistics
Télédétection																		●	Aerial reconnaissance
Vétérinaires (sciences -)	●						●	●					●						Veterinary science
Zoologie	●	●		●	●		●	●		●	●		●	●					Zoology
	1	2	3	1	2	3	1	2	3	1	2	3	1	2	3	1	2	3	

B

Applied Sciences

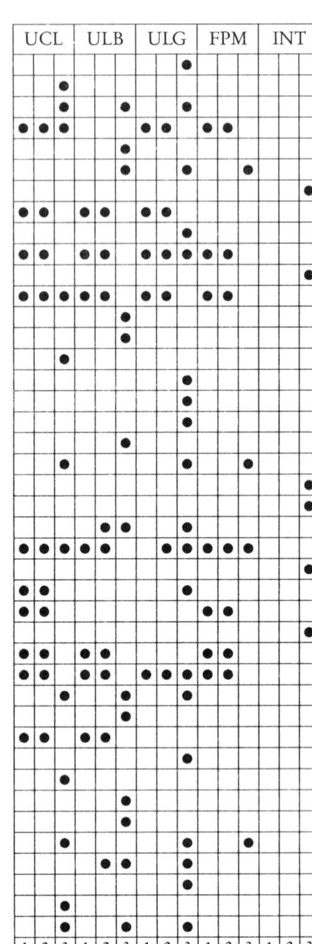

	UCL			ULB			ULG			FPM			INT			
Aéronautique									●							Aviation and space engineering
Algorithmique			●													Algorithmical processes
Aménagement du territoire			●			●			●							Landscape conservation, landscape plannin
Architecture	●	●	●				●	●		●	●					Architecture
Art de bâtir						●										Building design
Automatique						●			●			●				Automation engineering
Catalyse															●	Catalysis
Constructions	●	●		●	●		●	●								Civil engineering
Constructions navales									●							Naval engineering
Chimie	●	●		●	●		●	●	●	●	●					Chemistry
Dynamique des réseaux															●	Network technology
Électricité - électronique	●	●	●	●	●		●	●		●	●					Electricity, electronics
Énergie						●										Energy engineering
Environnement						●										Ecology
Fabrications soudées			●													Welding engineering
Génie civil									●							Civil engineering sciences
Génie médical									●							Health-service technology
Géologie									●							Geology
Géotechnique						●										Geo-engineering
Gestion - gestion industrielle			●						●			●				Industrial management
Haute tension															●	High-voltage engineering
Hydrologie															●	Hydrology
Hygiène du travail					●	●			●							Preventive medicine at the workplace
Informatique	●	●	●	●	●			●	●	●	●	●				Computer science
Ionisation															●	Ionization
Mathématiques appliquées	●	●							●							Applied mathematics
Mécanique	●	●								●	●					Mechanical engineering
Mécanique des roches															●	Stone/rock engineering
Métallurgie	●	●		●	●					●	●					Metallurgy
Mines - minéralogie	●	●		●	●		●	●	●	●	●					Mining, mineralogy
Nucléaire			●			●			●							Nuclear research
Pétrochimie						●										Petrochemistry
Physique	●	●		●	●											Physics
Physique du bâtiment									●							Building physics
Programmation			●													Programming
Rénovation urbaine						●										Urban renewal
Restauration des bâtiments						●										Building renovation
Sciences appliquées			●						●			●				Applied natural science
Sécurité et hygiène du travail					●	●			●							Protection at work
Systèmes et automatique									●							Process and automation engineering
Télécommunications			●													Telecommunications
Urbanisme			●			●			●							Urban planning
	1	2	3	1	2	3	1	2	3	1	2	3	1	2	3	

Survey of courses of study at Dutch-language universities in Belgium

Medicine – Dentistry

	KUL			RUG			VUB			RUCA			UIA			LUC			
Biomedische wetenschappen						●	●	●	●										Biomedical sciences
Diergeneeskunde				●	●	●				●									Veterinary medicine
Farmaceutische Wetenschappen	●	●	●	●	●	●	●	●	●	●				●	●				Pharmacy
Genees-, heel- en verloskunde	●	●	●	●	●	●	●	●	●	●				●	●	●			Medicine and obstetrics
Kinesitherapie en motorische revalidatie	●	●	●	●	●	●	●	●	●										Kinesiotherapy, rehabilitation
Lichamelijke opvoeding	●	●	●	●	●	●	●	●	●										Physical education
Tandheelkunde	●	●	●	●	●	●	●	●	●	●				●	●	●			Dentistry
	1	2	3	1	2	3	1	2	3	1	2	3	1	2	3	1	2	3	

Humanities and Philosophy

	KUL			RUG			VUB			UFSIA			UIA			UFSAL			
Afrikaanse geschiedenis en filologie				●	●	●													African history and philology
Bijbelse filologie	●	●	●																Biblical philology
Germaanse filologie (Nederlands, Engels, Duits)	●	●	●	●	●	●	●	●	●	●				●	●	●			German(ic) philology (Dutch, English, German)
Skandinavische taal					●	●		●	●										Scandinavian languages
Geschiedenis	●	●	●	●	●	●	●	●	●	●						●			History
Klassieke filologie	●	●	●	●	●	●	●	●	●										Classical philology
Kunstgeschiedenis en Oudheidkunde	●	●	●	●	●	●	●	●	●										History of art, archaeology
Literatuurwetenschap			●			●													Literature
Middeleeuwse studies			●																Medieval studies
Moraalwetenschappen				●	●	●	●	●	●										Ethics
Morele begeleiding					●	●			●										Moral code
Neurolinguistiek									●										Neurolinguistics
Oosterse filologie	●	●	●	●	●	●													Oriental studies
Romaanse filologie (Frans, Italiaans, Spaans)	●	●	●	●	●	●	●	●	●	●				●	●	●			Romance philology (French, Italian, Spanish)
Slavische filologie	●	●	●	●	●	●													Slavonic studies
Taalkunde			●			●													Linguistics
Taalpathologie									●										Logopaedics
Wijsbegeerte	●	●	●	●	●	●	●	●	●	●						●			Philosophy
English philosophy	●	●	●																English philosophy
European Studies			●																European studies
Theaterwetenschap			●			●									●				Drama
Amerikaanse studies			●																American studies
	1	2	3	1	2	3	1	2	3	1	2	3	1	2	3	1	2	3	

Abbreviations:

KUL Katholieke Universiteit Leuven
RUG Rijksuniversiteit Gent
VUB Vrije Universiteit Brussel
RUCA Rijksuniversitair Centrum Antwerpen
UIA Universitaire Instelling Antwerpen
UFSIA Universitaire Faculteiten Sint-Ignatius Antwerpen
UFSAL Universitaire Faculteiten Sint-Aloysius Brussel
LUC Limburgs Universitair Centrum
UFPGB Universitaire Faculteit voor Protestantse Godgeleerdheid te Brussel
ETH Evangelische Theologische Faculteit te Heverlee
1 First stage of studies *(kandidatuur)*.
2 Second stage of studies *(licentie;* pharmacists, engineers, physicians, without thesis; upper secondary-school teachers).
3 Third stage of studies, doctoral programme (with thesis; postgraduate and specialization studies).

Note:

All courses of study listed refer to the qualifications and degrees obtained after the respective course cycles or stages. Doctorates and courses leading to national degrees *(grades légaux/wettelijke graden)* are not contained in these tables.

Religion and Theology

	KUL			UFPGB			ETH			
	1	2	3	1	2	3	1	2	3	
Godgeleerdheid	●	●	●							Theology
Godsdienstwetenschappen	●	●	●							Religious sciences
Kerkelijk recht	●	●	●							Canon law
Morele en religieuze wetenschappen	●									Moral and religious history
Protestantse godgeleerdheid					●	●		●	●	Protestant theology
Religious studies (English)	●	●	●							Religious studies (English)
Theology (English)	●	●	●							Theology (English)
Toegepaste Theologie		●	●							Applied theology

Law and Criminology

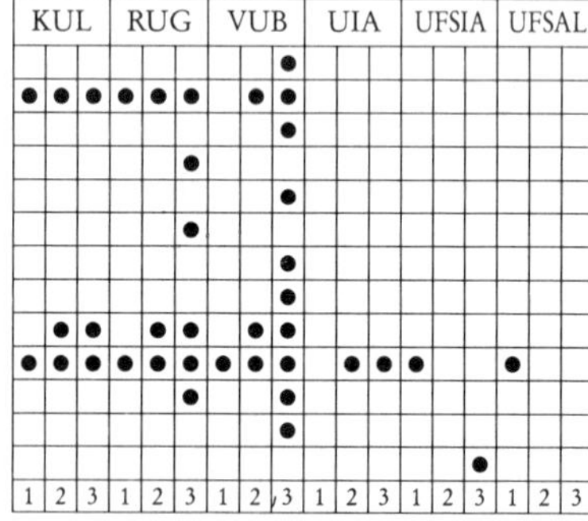

	KUL			RUG			VUB			UIA			UFSIA			UFSAL			
	1	2	3	1	2	3	1	2	3	1	2	3	1	2	3	1	2	3	
Bedrijfsrecht									●										Trade law
Criminologie	●	●	●	●	●	●		●	●										Criminology
Economisch recht									●										Economic law
Europees recht						●													European law
Fiscaal recht									●										Fiscal law
Haven- en maritieme wetenschappen						●													Maritime law
Internationaal en Europees recht									●										International and European law
International Legal cooperation									●										International legal cooperation
Notariaat		●	●		●	●		●	●										Notarial studies
Rechten	●	●	●	●	●	●	●	●	●		●	●	●			●			Law studies (general)
Sociaal recht						●			●										Social law
Staats- en bestuursrecht									●										Administrative law
Zee- en binnenscheepvaartrecht															●				Law of sea and inland water traffic

Economics, Business Administration, Political and Social Sciences

	KUL			RUG			VUB			UFSIA			RUCA			UIA			UFSAL			
	1	2	3	1	2	3	1	2	3	1	2	3	1	2	3	1	2	3	1	2	3	
Accountancy						●																Accountancy
Actuariële wetenschappen		●	●						●													Insurance mathematics
Bedrijfsbeheer						●																Business administration
Bedrijfsinformatica									●													Industrial engineering
Bestuurskunde en overheidsmanagement			●			●																Public administration
Business Administration (English)			●									●										Business administration (English)
Communicatiewetenschappen	●	●	●				●	●	●													Communications sciences
Demografie									●													Demography
Diplomatieke wetenschappen				●	●	●																Diplomacy
Documentatie- en bibliotheekwetenschappen																		●				Documentation and library science
Economische wetenschappen	●	●	●	●	●	●	●	●	●										●			Economics
Financiële wetenschappen						●			●													Financial and fiscal studies
Fiscaliteit en boekhoudkundig onderzoek						●																Taxation and accountancy
Handelswetenschappen - handelsingenieur	●	●	●				●	●	●			●	●	●	●							Commerce (commercial engineering)
Industrial location and development									●													Industrial location and development
Internationale betrekkingen							●	●	●								●	●				International relations
Management						●			●													Management
Marketing						●																Marketing
Maritieme wetenschappen												●										Maritime commerce
Ontwikkelingssamenwerking						●																Studies of developing countries
Openbare administratie							●	●	●													Public administration
Operationeel onderzoek									●													Systems analysis
Pers- en communicatiewetenschappen				●	●	●																Media and communications sciences
Politieke wetenschappen				●	●	●	●	●	●	●							●	●				Political science
olitieke en sociale wetenschappen	●	●	●														●	●				Political and social sciences
Revisoraat									●													Economic auditing
ociale wetenschappen, Sociologie	●	●	●	●	●	●	●	●	●								●	●				Social science, Sociology
aat- en bestuurswetenschappen				●	●	●																Public and administrative studies
Statistiek									●													Statistics
gepaste economische wetenschappen	●	●	●							●	●	●	●	●	●							Business administration, applied
Verzekeringen									●													Insurance studies

Psychology, Pedagogics

	KUL			RUG			VUB			
	1	2	3	1	2	3	1	2	3	
Antropologie			●							Anthropology
Arbeids-, gemeenschaps- en organisatiepsychologie		●	●							Psychology of work, community and organizations
Bedrijfspsychologie					●	●		●	●	Industrial psychology
Beroepsoriëntering en selectie			●							Job orientation and selection
Didactiek			●							Didactics
Forensische gedragswetenschappen									●	Behavioural science
Logopedie			●							Logopaedics
Onderwijskunde		●	●							Psychology of instruction
Ontwikkelings- en/of klinische psychologie		●	●		●	●		●	●	Development and/or clinical psychology
Orthopedagogiek		●	●		●	●		●	●	Special education
Pedagogiek - Pedagogische wetenschappen	●	●	●	●	●	●	●	●	●	Pedagogics, educational sciences
Psycholinguistiek			●							Psycholinguistics
Psychologie - Psychologische wetenschappen	●	●	●	●	●	●	●	●	●	Psychology
Schoolpsychologie		●	●							School psychology
Sociale agogiek					●	●				Social pedagogics
Sociale en culturele antropologie			●							Social and cultural anthropology
Sociale en culturele agogiek							●	●	●	Social and cultural pedagogics
Sociale pedagogiek		●	●							Social pedagogics
Theoretische en/of experimentele psychologie		●	●		●	●	●	●	●	Theoretical and/or experimental psychology

Natural Sciences

	KUL			RUG			VUB			RUCA			UIA			LUC			
	1	2	3	1	2	3	1	2	3	1	2	3	1	2	3	1	2	3	
Aardrijkskunde	●	●	●	●	●	●	●	●	●										Earth sciences
Aard- en delfstofkunde	●	●	●	●	●	●	●	●	●										Geology, Mineralogy
Biochemie														●	●				Biochemistry
Biologie	●			●			●			●									Biology
Biotechnologie			●		●	●								●					Biotechnology
Bodemkunde						●													Soil conservation
Dierkunde, plantkunde		●	●		●	●		●	●					●	●				Zoology, Botany
Informatica	●	●	●	●	●	●	●	●	●	●				●	●	●			Computer science
Moleculaire biologie/ biochemie/biofysica						●			●										Cell biology, Biochemistry, Biophysics
Natuurkunde	●	●	●	●	●	●	●	●	●	●				●	●	●			Physics
Scheikunde	●	●	●	●	●	●	●	●	●	●				●	●	●			Chemistry
Wiskunde	●	●	●	●	●	●	●	●	●	●				●	●	●			Mathematics

B

Agricultural Sciences (Diploma courses)

	KUL			RUG			VUB			
	1	2	3	1	2	3	1	2	3	
Algemene landbouw		●	●		●	●				General agricultural science
Agriculture science (English)			●							Agricultural science (English)
Bio-industriële wetenschappen			●							Bio-industrial sciences
Biotechnologie (toegepaste plantkunde)			●			●			●	Biotechnology (applied botany)
Bodemwetenschappen		●	●		●	●				Soil science
Cel- en gentechnologie		●	●							Cell and genetic technology
Boerderij bouwkunde		●	●							Agricultural building
Fytotechniek		●	●							Phytotechnology
Hydrobiologie (toegepaste dierkunde)					●	●				Hydrobiology (applied zoology)
Irrigation engineering			●							Hydraulic engineering (irrigation)
Landbouweconomie en sociologie		●	●		●	●				Agricultural administration and sociology
Landbouwkunde van tropische en subtropische streken		●	●		●	●				Agriculture, tropical and sub-tropical
Landbouwontwikkeling						●				Agricultural development
Landbouwwetenschappen	●	●	●	●	●	●				Farming science
Milieusanering			●			●				Agricultural ecology
Plantenbescherming		●	●		●	●				Plant protection
Ruimtelijke ordening		●	●		●	●				Regional planning
Scheikunde en landbouwindustrieën	●	●	●	●	●	●	●	●	●	Chemistry and agricultural industry
Tuinbouw		●	●		●	●				Horticulture
Veeteelt		●	●		●	●				Animal husbandry
Water en bossen		●	●		●	●				Forestry and water management

Applied Sciences – Engineering

	KUL			RUG			VUB			
	1	2	3	1	2	3	1	2	3	
Aardkunde			●							Surveying
Architectuur	●	●	●	●	●	●	●	●	●	Architecture
Automatiseringstechnieken						●				Automation
Bedrijfskunde						●				Business administration
Biomedische technieken			●						●	Biomedical technology
Bouwkunde, bouwmechanica	●	●	●	●	●	●	●	●	●	Civil engineering
Computerwetenschappen	●	●	●							Computer sciences
Elektrotechniek	●	●	●	●	●	●	●	●	●	Electrical engineering
Geotechniek						●				Geotechnology
Hydrologie									●	Hydrology
Informatica			●			●			●	Computer science
Industrieel beleid			●							Industrial management
Industriële wiskunde			●							Industrial mathematics
Kernwetenschappen			●			●				Nuclear physics
Lucht- en ruimtevaarttechniek									●	Aero- and aerospace technology
Metaalkunde	●	●	●	●	●	●	●	●	●	Metallurgy
Mijnwezen	●	●	●							Mining
Milieubeheer			●							Conservation of environment
Natuurkunde				●	●	●				Physical engineering
Scheepsbouwkunde				●	●	●				Shipbuilding
Scheikunde	●	●	●	●	●	●	●	●	●	Chemical engineering
Stedebouw en ruimtelijke ordening/ontwikkeling			●			●				Urban and regional planning and development
Textiel				●	●	●				Textiles technology
Toegepaste geologie									●	Applied geology
Toegepaste wetenschappen			●			●			●	Applied natural sciences
Toegepaste wiskunde			●							Applied mathematics
Veiligheidstechnieken			●						●	Safety technology
Werktuigkunde	●	●	●	●	●	●	●	●	●	Machine tools technology
Artificial intelligence			●							Artificial intelligence
Physics of microelectronics and materials sciences			●							Physics of micro electronics and materials sciences
Monumentenzorg			●							Protection and conservation of monuments

B

Organization of studies at non-university establishments (French-language higher education establishments)

	DE TYPE LONG	DE TYPE COURT
Enseignement supérieur technique	Ingénieur industriel en:[1] – Construction – Mécanique ou électromécanique – Électricité – Électronique – Chimie – Énergie nucléaire – Textile – Industrie	Assistant-ingénieur Gradué(e) en régulation et automation Gradué(e) en chimie et biochimie (diverses spécialités) Gradué(e) en construction Gradué(e) en électromécanique Gradué(e) en mécanique Gradué(e) en électronique Gradué(e) en électronique et automation Gradué(e) en photographie-cinéma Gradué(e) en moteur et expertises automobiles Gradué(e) en techniques de l'industrie textile Assistant de laboratoire clinique Gradué(e) en électronique médicale Gradué(e) en informatique industrielle Gradué(e) en techniques d'exploitation des industries de chauffage
Enseignement supérieur économique	Commerce: a) licencié(e) en sciences commerciales et financières b) licencié(e) en sciences commerciales et consulaires c) licencié(e) en sciences commerciales et administratives d) ingénieur commercial e) licencié(e) en sciences commerciales appliquées aux pays en voie de développement Langues: a) licencié(e)-traducteur b) licencié(e)-interprète Administration: licencié(e) en sciences administratives	Gradué(e): Hôtesse d'accueil Assurances Commerce Comptabilité Distribution-marketing Hôtellerie Informatique et programmation Secrétariat: a) de direction b) langues modernes c) médical Tourisme et loisirs Sciences juridiques Gradué(e) en gestion des transports et logistique Gradué(e) en techniques d'accueil Gradué(e) en gestion des collectivités
Enseignement supérieur agricole	Ingénieur industriel en agriculture[1]	Gradué(e) en agronomie a) architecture des jardins et du paysage b) horticulture Gradué(e) agricole a) agriculture des régions tempérées b) agriculture des régions tropicales et subtropicales c) eaux et forêts d) génie rural
Enseignement supérieur paramédical		Infirmier(e) gradué(e) hospitalier(e) Infirmier(e) gradué(e) de pédiatrie Infirmier(e) gradué(e) social(e) Infirmier(e) gradué(e) accoucheur(euse) Infirmier(e) gradué(e) psychiatrie Gradué(e) en kinésithérapie Gradué(e) en ergothérapie Gradué(e) en logopédie Gradué(e) en diététique Gradué(e) en chimie clinique

Organization of studies at non-university establishments (French-language higher education establishments)

	DE TYPE LONG	DE TYPE COURT
Enseignement supérieur social	Du 3e degré:[2] Techniques de diffusion et communications sociales	De type court: Auxiliaire social Conseiller social Assistant(e) en psychologie Bibliothécaire documentaliste Éducateur en éducation physique
Enseignement supérieur artistique	De type long: Architecte Du 3e degré: Arts du spectacle et techniques de diffusion	De type court:[3] Gradué(e): Architecte d'intérieur Arts du tissu Arts graphiques Arts plastiques Dessin d'architecture Esthétique industrielle Stylisme-modélisme Photographie et cinéma Publicité-étalage Arts du spectacle et techniques de diffusion Décoration pour l'industrie de la céramique, du verre et du livre
Enseignement supérieur pédagogique	De type long: Agrégé(e) de l'enseignement secondaire supérieur – commerce	De type court: a) École normale préscolaire: Institutrice préscolaire b) École normale primaire: Instituteur(trice) primaire Éducateur(trice) c) École normale secondaire: Agrégé(e) de l'enseignement secondaire inférieur (régent): – français-histoire – français-morale – néerlandais-anglais – néerlandais-allemand – anglais-allemand – mathématique-physique – mathématique-sciences économiques – mathématique-morale – physique-chimie-biologie – géographie-chimie-biologie – géographie-histoire-sciences sociales et économiques – éducation physique-sports et loisirs d) École normale technique moyenne: Agrégé(e) de l'enseignement secondaire inférieur (régent): – commerce – habillement modéliste – arts plastiques – économie ménagère – économie ménagère agricole – enfance inadaptée – de cours techniques – électromécanique, bois
Enseignement supérieur maritime	Licencié(e) en sciences nautiques	

[1] Nouveau grade créé par la loi du 18 février 1977 concernant l'organisation de l'enseignement supérieur technique et agricole de type long. Il remplace l'ancien grade d'ingénieur technicien.
[2] Classement provisoire.

B

Organization of studies at non-university establishments (Dutch-language higher education establishments)

	LANGE TYPE	KORTE TYPE
Technisch hoger onderwijs	Industrieel ingenieur:[1] – bouwkunde – elektromechanica – elektriciteit – chemie – mechanica – kernenergie – textiel	Gegradueerde: – automechanica – autotechnieken – bedrijfsmechanisatie – biochemie – bouwbedrijf – boekbedrijf – bouwplaatstechnologie – cinematographie – elektromechanica – elektronica – fotografie – gistingsbedrijven – grafische bedrijven – industriële meettechnieken en instrumentatie – industriële onderhoudstechnieken – industriële milieuzorg – industriële chemie, industriële scheikunde – klimatisatie – mechanica – microcompressor- en teletechnieken – onderhoudstechnieken – scheikunde, chemie – textiel – topografie
Economisch hoger onderwijs	Handel: – Lic. handels- en bestuurswetenschappen – Lic. handels- en consulaire wetenschappen – Lic. handels- en financiële wetenschappen – Handelsingenieur Talen: – Licentiaat tolk – Licentiaat vertaler Administratie: – Lic. bestuurswetenschappen	Gegradueerde: – bedrijfsadministratie – boekhouden – boekhouden en administratie – boekhouden en bankwezen – boekhouden en bedrijfsbeheer – boekhouden – fiscaliteit – boekhouden – informatica – boekhouden – organisatie – fiscaliteit – distributie – distributie en marketing – expeditie – handel – informatica informatica-systeemanalyse informatica-programmering – hotelbedrijf – marketing – medisch secretariaat – public relations – public relations – onthaal – secretariaat – secretariaat-distributie

Organization of studies at non-university establishments (Dutch-language higher education establishments)

	LANGE TYPE	KORTE TYPE
		– talen – toerisme – toegepaste communicatiewetenschappen met public relations – vertaler-tolk – verzekering
Agrarisch hoger onderwijs	Industrieel ingenieur:[1] landbouw	Gegradueerde: – landschaps- en tuinarchitectuur
Paramedisch hoger onderwijs		Gegradueerde: – arbeidstherapie – dieetleer – klinische scheikunde – kinesitherapie – logopedie – kinderverpleging – psychiatrische verpleging – sociale verpleging – vroedvrouw – ziekenhuisverpleging – farmaceutische en biologische technieken
Sociaal hoger onderwijs		Gegradueerde: – assistent in de psychologie – lichamelijke opvoeding – maatschappelijk adviseur – maatschappelijk adviseur – maatschappelijke bijstand – orthopedagogie
Hoger kunstonderwijs van de tweede graad	Binnenhuisarchitectuur	
Hoger kunstonderwijs van de derde graad	Industriële vormgeving	
Hoger technisch onderwijs van de tweede graad	Binnenhuisarchitectuur	
Hoger technisch onderwijs van de derde graad	Cultuurspreidingstechnieken – film – toneel – radio – TV – technieken voor sociale communicaties	
Artistiek hoger onderwijs		Architect assistent: gegradueerde: – binnenhuisarchitectuur – cultuurspreidingstechnieken – beeld – geluid – montage – assistentie – animatie – plastische kunsten – sierkunsten

B

Organization of studies at non-university establishments (Dutch-language higher education establishments)

	LANGE TYPE	KORTE TYPE
Pedagogisch hoger onderwijs	Geaggregeerde van het hoger secundair onderwijs	kleuterleid(st)er onderwijzer(es) geaggregeerde van het lager secundair onderwijs: (regentaat) – Frans – geschiedenis – lichamelijke opvoeding – Nederlands – Engels – plastische kunsten – wetenschappen – aardrijkskunde – wiskunde – elektriciteit – handel – hout – huishoudkunde – kleding – land- en tuinbouw – mechanica – nijverheid – plastische kunsten – schoonheidsverzorging
Maritiem hoger onderwijs	Licenciaat	

[1] Nieuwe graad opgericht door de wet van 18 februari 1977 betreffende de organisatie van het onderwijs en inzonderheid van het technisch en agrarisch hoger onderwijs van het lange type.
Deze vervangt de derde graad van ingenieur technicien.

. Student statistics

tudents at universities and non-university establishments absolute figures 1987/88)

	N + F	N	F
Total (Belgian and foreigners)	254 329	142 739	111 590
Total foreigners	22 555	4 004	18 551
Total from non-European countries	11 502	1 695	9 807
Africa	7 664	508	7 156
Central and South America	524	125	399
North America	492	196	296
Asia	2 240	825	1 415
Oceania	8	5	3
USSR	3	/	3
Others	571	36	535
Total Europe	11 053	2 309	8 744
Europe (without EC or unspecified)	77	85	292
EC member states	10 676	2 224	8 452
DK	26	4	22
D	565	235	330
GR	808	81	727
E	1 218	84	1 134
F	1 620	42	1 578
IRL	22	10	12
I	3 144	168	2 976
L	1 076	19	1 057
NL	1 689	1 478	211
P	266	18	248
UK	242	85	157

N+F = Dutch-language and French-language institutions.
N = Dutch-language institutions.
F = French-language institutions.

Students at universities and non-university establishments (relative figures: out of 100 000) 1987/88

	N + F	N	F
Total (Belgian and foreigners)	100 000	100 000	100 000
Total foreigners	8 869	2 805	16 637
Total from non-European countries	4 523	1 187	8 795
Africa	3 013	355	6 417
Central and South Amercia	206	87	357
North America	193	137	265
Asia	880	578	1 269
Oceania	3	3	2
USSR	1	/	2
Others	224	25	479
Total Europe	4 346	1 618	7 842
Europe (without EC or unspecified)	148	59	261
EC Member States	4 198	1 558	7 580
DK	10	2	19
D	222	164	295
GR	317	56	652
E	478	58	1 017
F	637	29	1 415
IRL	8	7	10
I	1 236	117	2 669
L	423	13	947
NL	664	1 035	189
P	104	12	222
UK	95	59	140

N+F = Dutch-language and French-language institutions.
N = Dutch-language institutions.
F = French-language institutions.

Belgian and foreign students at universities, according to subjects, 1987/88

	Belgians & foreigners	Foreigners total	Europe total	EC countries	DK	D	GR	E	F	IRL	I	L	NL	P	UK
Theology & religious studies	1 914	513	146	133	-	8	11	2	15	3	9	4	56	4	21
Philosophy & humanities	13 630	794	535	488	-	53	60	60	40	4	121	36	83	17	14
Law	14 834	733	406	348	-	17	56	33	39	1	89	33	62	9	9
Natural sciences	10 899	1 134	393	367	1	22	37	32	51	1	95	64	42	8	14
Medicine	15 534	2 968	1 130	1 015	2	138	82	146	143	3	136	133	189	23	20
Pharmacy	3 509	395	103	98	-	4	3	9	11	-	23	38	6	3	1
Physical education	3 330	157	110	106	-	6	10	6	12	1	16	35	18	2	-
Veterinary medicine	1 894	197	167	165	-	11	-	5	71	-	7	23	46	1	1
Applied sciences (engineering)	9 948	1 119	311	294	1	8	32	24	35	-	83	57	30	11	13
Agricultural sciences	4 148	511	140	138	-	6	9	9	36	-	20	36	15	1	6
Social, political & economic science	12 590	1 778	687	619	5	38	76	71	65	1	136	110	59	35	22
Business administration, commerce	12 843	1 057	553	524	4	17	32	30	75	2	149	47	142	6	20
Education, psychology	5 976	462	250	241	2	11	24	22	31	2	72	16	44	17	-
Interdisciplinary centres	1 283	480	220	207	1	6	45	76	19	2	17	3	7	23	8
Total N	58 150	2 619	1 198	1 104	3	161	52	31	17	9	48	11	703	11	55
Total F	54 181	9 679	3 951	1 669	13	181	125	145	636	11	925	624	116	141	94
Total N + F	**112 311**	**12 298**	**5 151**	**4 773**	**16**	**345**	**177**	**526**	**653**	**20**	**973**	**635**	**119**	**160**	**119**

N = students at Dutch-language institutions.
F = students at French-language institutions.
N + F = total.

B

4. Bibliography

Brochures and publications in French

Programmes des cours (Course catalogues) published annually by the Belgian universities. Available from the universities in question.

Liste des établissements d'enseignement supérieur. Administration de l'énseignement supérieur, et de la recherche scientifique — Ministère de l'éducation nationale Bruxelles, 1988, 40 pp. Available from the Administration de l'enseignement supérieur, Cité administrative de l'État, bloc Arcades D, B-1010 Bruxelles.

Répertoire des diplômes de l'enseignement supérieur dans la Communauté française de Belgique, Bruxelles, 1988, 94 pp.

Enseignement universitaire — Recueil des lois et des règlements (Collection of laws and regulations), brochure 1 — Administration de l'enseignement supérieur et de la recherche scientifique — Ministère de l'éducation nationale, Bruxelles, 1978, 72 pp., BFR 120. Available from Service des Publications, rue Royale 123, B-1000 Bruxelles.

Rapport annuel 1989 — Bureau des statistiques universitaires. Fondation universitaire, Bruxelles, 1989. Annual report in French and Dutch. Available from the Fondation universitaire, rue d'Egmont 11, Bruxelles.

Les études supérieures — les études universitaires (2 brochures). CEDIEP (Centre de documentation et d'information sur les études et les professions). Bruxelles, 1988. Available from CEDIEP, Bte 8, avenue de Tervuren, B-1150 Bruxelles.

Demain étudiant. Université libre de Bruxelles. Bruxelles, 1988, 154 pp. Available from Université libre de Bruxelles, avenue F.D. Roosevelt 50, B-1050 Bruxelles.

Guide du futur étudiant de l'Université catholique de Louvain. 320 pp. Service d'impression UCL. Available from Centre d'information et de documentation, rue de la Lanterne Magique 28, B-1348 Louvain-la-Neuve.

Brochures and publications in Dutch

Study guides (**Studiegidsen**) and information brochures (**Inlichtingenbrochures**), published by the universities and available from them (1988/89 editions).

Lijst der instellingen voor hoger onderwijs. Bestuur van het hoger onderwijs en het wetenschappelijk onderzoek. Ministerie van Onderwijs, Brussel, 1987. Available from Bestuur voor het hoger onderwijs.

Hoger Onderwijs buiten de Universiteit — Universitair Onderwijs. Officieuze codificatie van onderwijswetgeving en reglementering. Compilation of the legal bases and regulations for non-university and university higher education. Available from: Dienst Informatie en Documentatie, Koningsstraat 150, 1000 Brussel.

University Studies in Flanders (Belgium). Information brochure for foreign students. Published by Vlaamse Universitaire Raad, Egmontstraat 5, B-1050 Bruxelles.

Jaarverslag 1988. Dienst voor universitaire statistiek. Universitaire Stichting, Brussel 1988. Second edition. Available free of charge in French and Dutch from the Universitaire Stichting, Egmontstraat 11, B-1050 Brussel.

Studeren buiten de universiteit. Gegevens bijgewerkt tot juni 1988. Edited by the Centrale voor studie- en beroepsoriëntering en psychomedisch-sociale centra, 320 pp., BFR 290. Available from the CSBO, M. Lemonnierlaan 129, B-1000 Brussel.

Voorlichtingenreeks Mijn Toekomst 25 delen — januari 1988. Series of 25 information brochures 'My future', January 1988. Published by: Economische Hogeschool Limburg, Universitaire Campus, 3610 Diepenbeek, BFR 2 500.

Onderwijsgids Universitair Onderwijs 1988. Study guide for the universities. Published by Vormingscentrum van de R.M.S.-Centra, Brussel. Available from the sales office of the Ministry of Education: Ministerie van Onderwijs, Dienst Verkoop Publikaties, RAC, Arcadengebouw, blok D, B-1010 Brussel.

Study information centres

Further printed information is available from: CEDIEP — Centre de documentation et d'information sur les études et les professions, avenue de Tervueren 222/bte 8, B-1150 Bruxelles.

CID — Centre d'information et de documentation sur les études et les professions, rue de la Lanterne Magique 28, B-1348 Louvain-la-Neuve.

SIEP — Service d'information sur les études et les professions, chaussée de Wavre 205, B-1040 Bruxelles.

5. Glossary

Agrégé de l'enseignement secondaire inférieur/Geaggregeerde voor het lager secundair onderwijs: Higher education degree entitling the holder to teach one or several subjects in lower secondary education.

Agrégé de l'enseignement secondaire supérieur/Geaggregeerde voor het hoger secundair onderwijs: Higher education degree awarded either simultaneously with or after the *licence/licentiaat* and entitling the holder to teach one or several subjects in upper secondary education.

Agrégé de l'enseignement supérieur/Geaggregeerde voor het hoger onderwijs: The highest university degree. It is usually awarded after the *doctorat/doctoraat* and is one of the degrees that entitles the holder to teach at universities.

Candidat/Kandidaat: First university degree or non-university long study course degree obtained after two or three years of study.

Commission d'homologation/Homologatiecommissie: Official commission whose duty it is to see to it that secondary school-leaving qualifications correspond to legal and other regulations, and to compare secondary school leaving qualifications and certificates of qualification which allow students to study at university.

Diplôme /Diploma: An official document confirming the holding of a degree and confirming the rights connected with this degree.

Diplôme d'aptitude à accéder à l'enseignement supérieur/Bekwaamheidsdiploma dat toegang verleent tot het hoger onderwijs: Certificate awarded to holders of the qualification allowing them to study at university by the institution where they have successfully attended the fifth and sixth years of schooling, subdivided in the same way and taking the same form (general education, technical education, creative subjects). This certificate can also be awarded by a national committee for secondary education, after the examinee has successfully gained the *examen de maturité,* the secondary school leaving certificate. Whoever has it is entitled to be admitted to all courses of study in higher education with the exception of civil engineering.

Dissertation/Proefschrift: Original work of high academic quality on an unpublished topic, presented and defended to obtain the degree of *docteur/doctor* or *agrégé de l'enseignement supérieur/geaggregeerde voor het hoger onderwijs.* When presented to obtain the latter degree, it must represent a real contribution to the progress of academic research.

Docteur/Doctor:

1. Second university degree awarded in medicine and veterinary medicine after four and three-year courses, respectively, that follow the *candidature/candidatuur.* Submission of a dissertation is not required.
2. In all other disciplines it is the third university degree. In these cases it is awarded at the end of at least a one or two-year course of study following the *licence/licentiaat.* It requires the presentation and

public defence of a *dissertation/proefschrift.*

École normale/Normaal-school: Teacher training institution *(enseignement supérieur pédagogique/pedagogisch hoger onderwijs)* for pre-school, primary and lower secondary school teachers.

Enseignement supérieur/Hoger onderwijs: General designation for all courses of study following secondary education both of universities *(enseignement universitaire/universitair onderwijs)* and at the other higher education institutions *(enseignement supérieure autre qu'universitaire/hoger onderwijs met uitsluiting van het universitair onderwijs).*

Enseignement supérieur autre qu'universitaire/Hoger onderwijs met uitsluiting van het universitaire onderwijs: This part of the system of higher education includes: *enseignement supérieur technique/technisch hoger onderwijs, enseignement supérieur économique/economisch hoger onderwijs, enseignement supérieur agricole/agrarisch hoger onderwijs, enseignement supérieur paramédical/paramedisch hoger onderwijs, enseignement supérieur social/sociaal hoger onderwijs, enseignement supérieur artistique/artistiek hoger onderwijs, enseignement supérieur pédagogique/pedagogisch hoger onderwijs, enseignement supérieur maritime/maritiem hoger onderwijs.* It prepares mainly for functions on various levels in the different areas of economic life (agriculture, industry, commerce), for the profession of architect or artistic professions, for the professions of translator or interpreter, for professions in the health sector and for teaching professions.

Enseignement universitaire/Universitair onderwijs: Courses of study offered by universities to train top quality experts for research and for the development and the application of scientific knowledge.

Établissement assimilé/Gelijkgestelde instelling: Higher education institutions granted equal status by law with respect to the right to award certain *diplômes lègaux/wettelijke graden.*

Examen de maturité/Maturiteitsexamen: Secondary school final examination with which the *diplôme d'aptitude à accéder à l'enseignement supérieur/bekwaamheidsdiploma voor het hoger onderwijs* is obtained.

Faculté/Faculteit:
1. University department in which the subjects belonging to a main area of academic endeavour are grouped together.
2. Legal designation for institutions of higher education in the university sector that only offer one or several specific courses of study.

Grade/Graad: Degree or qualification marking the division of successive stages in a course of study *(cylce/cyclus)* acquired after passing an examination administered by a competent board.

Grade complémentaire/Aanvullende graad: University degree terminating specialized courses of study completed after obtaining an initial degree *(licencié/licentiaat, docteur/doctor, ingénieur/doctor, ingénieur/ingenieur, etc).*

Grade légal/Wettelijke graad: University degree terminating a course of study, the admission to which and curriculum and duration of which are regulated by law.

Grade scientifique/Wetenschappelijke graad: University degree terminating a course of study, the admission to which and curriculum and duration of which are determined by the university in question.

Gradué/Gegradueerde: Degree in higher education outside the university sector awarded upon completion of studies (courses of 2-3 years) in the various subjects offered by the specific institution.

Instituteur(trice) préscolaire/Kleuterleid(st)er: Degree at the teachers colleges *(enseignement supérieur pédagogique/pedagogisch hoger onderwijs)* for future pre-school teachers (children from 3 to 6 years).

Instituteur(trice) primaire/Onderwijzer(es): Degree at the teachers colleges *(enseignement supérieur pédagogique/pedagogisch hoger onderwijs)* for future primary school teachers (children between 6 and 12 years).

Licencié/Licentiaat: Second university degree (humanities, sciences and law) and in higher education other than at universities (commerce, translator, interpreter). It is awarded at the end of a two or three-year course of study following the *candidature/kandidatuur.*

Mémoire/Eindverhandeling: Final thesis to obtain the degree of *licencié/licentiaat.* It must demonstrate the ability to correctly present the results of personal, objective and methodical research.

Thèse/Stelling: Written thesis which a candidate for the degree of *docteur/doctor* or *agrégé de l'enseignement supérieur/geaggregeerde voor het hoger onderwijs* must defend together with his *dissertation/proefschrift.*

Université/Universiteit: Legal designation for higher education institutions comprising several departments *(faculté/faculteit)* and offering courses of study leading to the acquisition of academic degrees.

B

6. Diagram of the education system

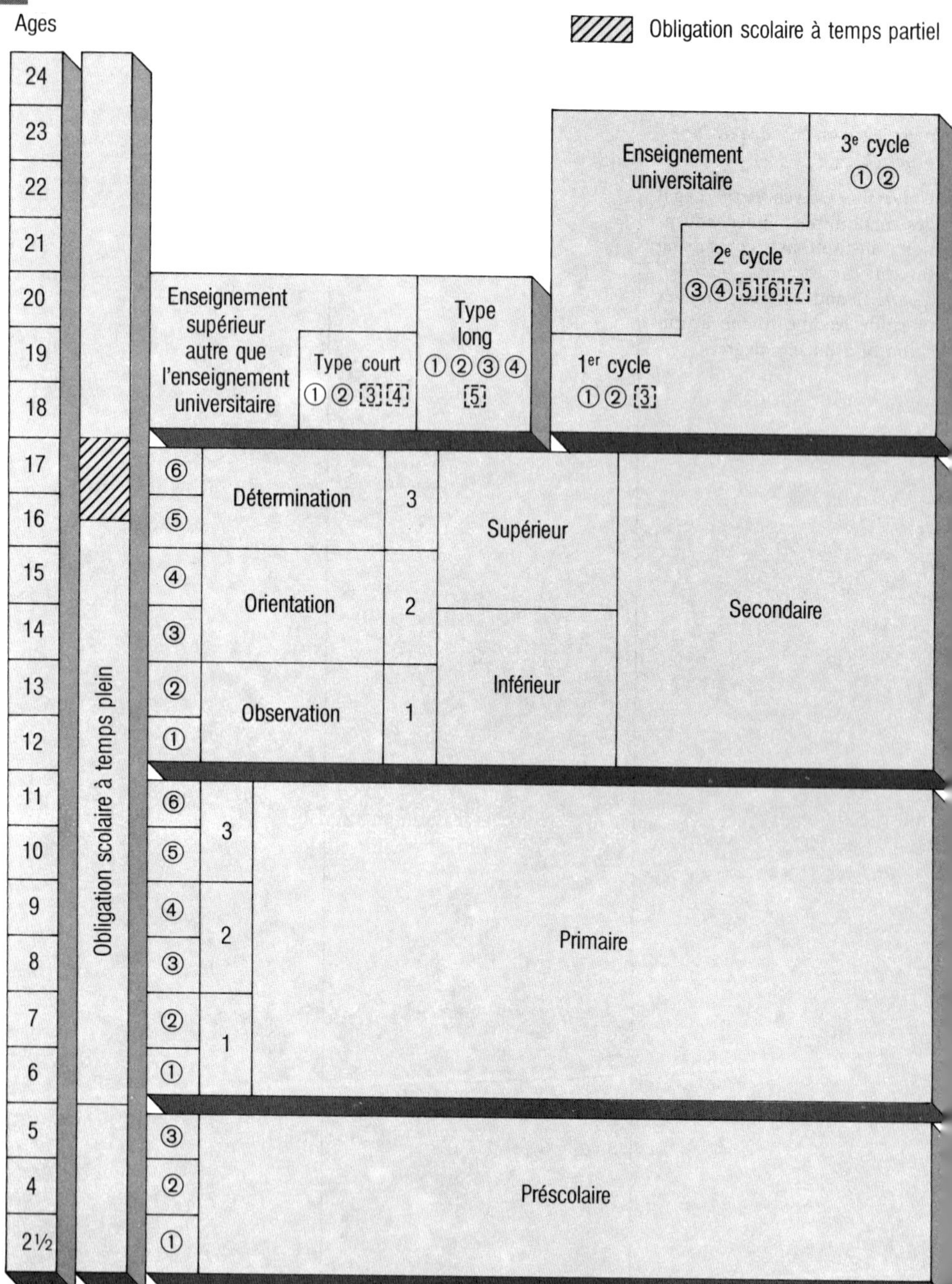
Ages
Obligation scolaire à temps partiel
24
23
22
21
20
19
18
17
16
15
14
13
12
11
10
9
8
7
6
5
4
2½
Obligation scolaire à temps plein
Enseignement universitaire
3e cycle ① ②
2e cycle ③ ④ [5] [6] [7]
1er cycle ① ② [3]
Enseignement supérieur autre que l'enseignement universitaire
Type court ① ② [3] [4]
Type long ① ② ③ ④ [5]
⑥ ⑤ Détermination 3
④ ③ Orientation 2
② ① Observation 1
Supérieur
Inférieur
Secondaire
⑥ ⑤ 3
④ ③ 2
② ① 1
Primaire
③ ② ①
Préscolaire

Explanations and translations of technical terms see facing page.

Legend

Ages — Age.
Inférieur — Secondary schools, lower level.
Obligation scolaire à temps partiel — Compulsory schooling (part-time).
Obligation scolaire à temps plein — Compulsory schooling (full-time).
Préscolaire — Pre-school education.
Primaire — Primary school.
Secondaire — Secondary school.
Supérieur — Secondary schools, upper level.
Supérieur autre que l'enseignement universitaire — Non-university establishments.
Universitaire — Universities.

Denmark

Organization of higher education

In Denmark the concept *videregående uddannelser* (post-secondary education; higher education) includes both higher academic courses of study and a number of other, as a rule shorter, courses of non-academic training.

The government is responsible for higher education: most higher education institutions come under the Ministry of Education, but a few are controlled by the Ministry of Cultural Affairs (schools of architecture, academies of music, the Royal Academy of Fine Arts, schools of librarianship).

All higher education institutions in Denmark are entitled to undertake independent research and teaching, but the ministry responsible determines general curricula, the admission to courses of study, the awarding of degrees, and the appointment of lecturers and other academic staff.

Types of higher education institutions

(a) Higher education institutions are divided into two groups:

1. the universities (*universiteter*) in Copenhagen, Århus and Odense, and the university centres in Roskilde and Aalborg, which engage in research and offer courses of study in traditional university subjects as well as in new fields;
2. The *højere læreanstalter* which offer a number of specialized training courses at university level and which also engage in research work: the *Danmarks Tekniske Højskole* (technical university) and the *Danmarks Ingeniørakademi* (academy of engineers); the *Danmarks Farmaceutiske Højskole* (Royal Danish School of Pharmacy); the *Kgl. Veterinær- og Landbohøjskole* (the Royal Danish Veterinary and Agricultural University); schools of economics, business administration and modern languages; the *Kgl. Danske Kunstakademi* (the Royal Danish Academy of Fine Arts); the schools of architecture; the *Danmarks Lærerhøjskole* (the Royal Danish School of Educational Studies); the academies of music.

The usual requirements for admission to one of these courses of study are the *studentereksamen*, the *højere forberedelseseksamen* or the *højere handelseksamen*.

(b) Other advanced training courses: Besides actual academic training, there are a number of training courses offered at institutions that do not carry out research but at which teaching is based to a certain extent on the results of research at universities and *højere læreanstalter*.

These courses prepare students for the following vocations: librarian (schools of librarianship with two departments); kindergarten and recreation teacher (26 *seminarier*); primary and lower secondary-school teacher (25 *seminarier*);physiotherapist, ergotherapist (eight schools); home economics teacher (two *semi-*

DK

narier); journalist (Danish School of Journalism in Århus); midwife (school of midwifery with two departments); social pedagogue (13 *seminarier*); social worker (four *sociale højskoler* (schools of social work) as well as Aalborg University Centre); *teknikum*-engineer (eight engineering colleges-*teknika*).

Prerequisites for admission to these courses of study vary, since not all of them require the above-mentioned qualifications (*studentereksamen, højere forberedelseseksamen, højere handelseksamen*). In some cases nine to ten years of school plus either work experience or vocational training, an entrance examination or a supplementary examination are enough for admission.

Student statistics

In the 1987/88 academic year approximately 87 000 students were enrolled at Denmark's 19 higher education institutions. Of these, some 2 900 (3 %) were foreigners, of which about 570 (20 %) came from EC Member States. See table in Appendix.

Organization and validation of courses

The basic unit in the Danish system of higher education is the academic year. Lectures are held in two semesters, usually from September to Christmas and from February to June.

Without dealing in detail with the types of courses offered or final degrees awarded by the various higher education institutions (*højere uddannelsesinstitutioner*), an attempt will be made to provide an overall picture of the widely varying degrees. Some degrees or courses of study lead directly to careers in public administration or private industry, while others require vocation-orientated further training. The ministry responsible lays down the general rules for examinations, grades and other examination-related matters by means of ministerial directives. The study and examination regulations are determined by the individual higher education institutions.

At the universities the *kandidateksamen* is the most common final examination in the traditional university subject, i.e. theology, social sciences, medicine, the humanities and the natural sciences. In autumn 1988 a bachelor's degree was introduced. Since then students who have completed the first three years of a *kandidat*-programme and who have passed the appropriately prescribed examinations may gain the title of BA in humanities, theology and social sciences or B.Sc. in the natural sciences and health sciences.

The *magisterkonferens* is a research training programme (six years' duration) which — in contrast to the *kandidat*-programmes — focuses on the methodological disciplines as a whole.

The universities offer a large number of *kandidat*-programmes. Most courses have an officially stipulated duration of five to six years, however, experience has shown that the duration of studies is often longer.

In order to obtain qualifications for the practical pursuit of such professions as secondary-education teaching, medicine, law or the clergy, further training is required in the form of additional courses or practical training outside the universities.

The university centres offer one-year (Aalborg) or two-year (Roskilde), project-orientated basic studies as a basis for the major studies on an intermediate or *kandidat* level.

At some of the *højere læreanstalter* — *Danmarks Tekniske Højskole* (engineering courses), the *Kgl. Veterinær- og Landbohøjskole* (courses in agriculture, veterinary medicine, forestry, horticulture, dairy sciences, food science and technology), *Danmarks Farmaceutiske Højskole* (pharmacy) as well as the *Tandlægehøjskoler* in Copenhagen and Århus (dentistry) — the studies include with the *kandidateksamen* in the corresponding subject. The time stipulated for the studies varies between four and six years.

At the schools of economics, business administration and modern languages there are, in addition to the *kandidatgrader* in economics and business administration and in business/applied languages, a number of degree programmes on an intermediate level which form part of the *kandidateksamen*, but which may, however, be concluded at an earlier stage with the *afgangseksaminer, diplomeksaminer* etc.

The training at the *Danmarks Lærerhøjskole* — which is only open to primary and lower secondary-school teachers — comprises both individual courses for further training as well as studies leading to the *kandidateksamen*.

The *Kunstakademiets Arkitektskole* as well as the *Arkitektskole* in Århus award *afgangsbeviser* upon completion of the architect training. The programme is concluded with a major project. The duration of studies is generally at least six years.

The *Kunstakademi* in Copenhagen offers courses in the fields of the fine arts, art teaching as well as art restoration.

At the *musikkonservatorierne* (academies of music) successful completion of courses at various levels qualifies students for teaching posts (State-registered music teacher) or for employment in orchestras or choirs. Training for soloists is also available but does not involve any specific final certificate. The courses last four to eight years.

Postgraduate degrees

The *licentiatgrad* (Ph.D.) is regarded as the first actual postgraduate degree. For admission to the courses of study leading to this degree, a *kandidateksamen* in the same subject or in a closely-related subject is required. The study project has to be approved by the faculty concerned, and a tutor is appointed for the duration of the studies (two or, at most, three years).

The *doktorgrad* is the highest attainable academic degree. There are no course requirements to obtain this degree. Instead the candidate must present a doctoral thesis (*disputats*) which generally calls for several years of independent and original research at a very high level.

DK

Admission and registration

Initial information

Students who wish to obtain general course information or have queries about their choice of studies or educational opportunities are advised to contact the *Centrale studievejledning, Københavns Universitet* (Central Student Advisory Service at the University of Copenhagen: for address see Appendix 1). This centre has extensive information material at hand or can refer students to further offices.

Students seeking specific information about courses should write to the higher education institutions concerned.

Students who want to receive information on additional courses available should get in touch with the Central Student Advisory Service at the University of Copenhagen.

Entry requirements

There are no uniform requirements for admission to Denmark's higher education institutions. A large number of Danish and foreign examinations and qualifications can lead to acceptance. The qualifications needed for admission are indicated in the admission regulations of the individual higher education institutions. The usual basis for acceptance at higher education institutions is the *studentereksamen* (upper secondary-school leaving examination), the *højere forberedelseseksamen* (higher preparatory examination) or the *højere handelseksamen* (higher commercial examination).

Acceptable foreign university entrance qualifications specifically mentioned in the admission regulations of the higher education institutions include examinations taken in countries with which Denmark has multilateral agreements on the recognition of university entrance qualifications. This applies to all of the EC countries, the Nordic countries and the other Council of Europe countries as well as a number of Unesco countries.

In other words, the academic admission requirements for study at a Danish higher education institution are basically fulfilled when the person concerned has passed an examination in an EC country which qualifies for university studies in that country. Some courses of study are, however subject to specific admission conditions (e.g. proof of 'special ties with Denmark' — see below) or limitations. Moreover, the International Baccalaureate (IB) and the European Baccalaureate (EB) give admission to Danish higher education institutions.

The following arrangement applie to Danish nationals and to the specifi group of EC nationals covered b Article 12 of Regulation (EEC) N 1612/68 concerning the free move ment of labour within the Europea Community: the marks obtained i the examination qualifying the appl cant for university studies (plus an university entrance examination) hav to be converted into the Danish marking system (13-point scale) and the resultant grade is deemed equivalent to that obtained in a corresponding Danish examination.

Course students and occasional students

At some higher education institutions suitably qualified foreigners can be accepted upon application as course students or occasional students. Occasional students (*gæstestuderende*) are not subject to normal admission limitations. Admission depends on whether the institution concerned recognizes the applicant's qualifications and study purpose, and has sufficient capacity to accommodate the applicant's study wishes.

Only qualified foreigners who have studied the subject in question for at least two years at a university or comparable institution in their home country and who wish to include a brief period of study at a Danish university in these studies are admitted as occasional students. They are not permitted to attend introductory courses and are usually admitted for one year and a maximum of two years. In addition to attending lectures, occasional students can take examinations in the subjects they are studying and/or receive certificates on their studies from the higher education institution. However, as occasional students they cannot acquire a full academic degree. Since university instruction is in Danish, a knowlegde of the latter is necessary. (For admissions see 'Admission and registration'.) Requests for information and applications should be sent direct to the institutions in question.

In order to be accepted as course students (*kursusstuderende*), applicants must have sufficient prior knowledge including a knowledge of Danish, despite the fact that studies at the Danish universities are open to everyone who would like to enrol on a university course regardless of previous education and nationality. Course students are entitled to register for an examination after taking a course.

Application: There is no special course prospectus. Information and application forms should be requested from the relevant institution. There is room for only a limited number of students on each course. Only a very small part of higher education instruction is offered in the form of single courses. It should be emphasized that *kursusstuderende* cannot take the *kandidatseksamen*.

Except for foreigners who have a special reason for wanting to complete an entire course of study in Denmark the guest and course studies offered should satisfy the needs of most foreign students wishing to take specialized courses during a brief stay in the country for study purposes.

Limitations

On 1 June 1976 the Folketing passed a law regulating the admission to higher education studies. According to this law, acquisition of a qualification for admission to higher education does not automatically entitle a person to admission to a higher education insti-

DK

tution. This means that such a qualification does not necessarily guarantee that students can enrol in the course of study or at the institution of higher education of their first choice. Instead, students can apply for admission to eight different courses of study at higher education institutions. For foreign students there is a specific quota below 10 %; it generally lies between 2 % and 4 %.

The admission of foreigners to certain courses of study is regulated by the 'special ties with Denmark' requirement. To be admitted to the study of subjects such as medicine, dentristry, pharmacy, agriculture and civil engineering, it is necessary to have special ties with Denmark. It is the responsibility of the higher education institutions to decide for each case on the special ties with Denmark. The following criteria are considered:

1. Equal treatment through agreement

   Students who are members of a specific group of EC country citizens are placed in the same quota as holders of the current Danish entrance examinations. According to Article 12, Section 1 of Regulation (EEC) No 1612/68, the children of EC country citizens who are or were (retired) employed on the territory of another Member State under certain, more closely defined, conditions are admitted to studies at universities and other institutions of higher education in the Member State concerned. The term 'children' includes for this purpose descendants, that is children or grandchildren. At the time of application, these must have their residence on the territory of the Member State.

2. Residence criterion

   (a) At least 24 months' residence prior to 1 September of the year in which the application is submitted;
   (b) upon proof of marriage with a Danish citizen at the time of application, at least 12 months of residence prior to 1 September of the year in which the application is submitted.

3. Family criterion

   The children of Danish citizens: special ties of children of whom neither parent holds Danish citizenship can only be granted when evidence can be produced that the change of citizenship was necessitated by the employment in the service of another State, by professional activity abroad, and similar.

4. Transfer criterion

   The children (under 22 years of age) of foreigners who have been transferred to Denmark or who run a business in Denmark in as far they can prove long-term future residence in the country (normally more than two years).

5. Recognized refugees

   The precondition for admission according to these regulations is the proof of the applicant's academic qualification and sufficient knowledge of Danish in accord ance with the current regulation of the higher education institutions.

Being married to a Danish citizen does not create special rights (except that the residence criterion under item 2 above is deemed to be fulfilled after one year).

For the following courses of study, the criterion of special ties with Denmark applies: architecture, librarianship, ergotherapy and physiotherapy, business economics (full-time studies), midwifery, human medicine, engineering sciences at the Danish engineering academy and the technical university, pharmacy, social worker training, all degree courses at the *Landbohøjskolen* (veterinary science and agriculture), dentistry.

Recognition of foreign certificates and degrees

As stated under 'Entry requirements' above, Denmark recognizes higher education entrance qualifications obtained in other EC countries as well as the international and European baccalaureates. In some cases the qualification is accepted as the basis for admission, while in others applicants must also meet their own country's requirement of a university entrance test.

Foreign academic degrees: Under the European Convention of 14 December 1959 Denmark can recognize the academic degrees of other Member States. Because of the differences in structure and contents of national degrees, direct recognition of foreign degrees is not possible. Requests for recognition are dealt with on an individual basis. For the assessment, the duration of study, subjects studied and examinations taken are compared with the corresponding requirements for a Danish degree.

The recognition of equivalence may thus be based on either the following:

(1) an assessment of the applicant's degree in connection with job applications, acceptance in professional associations, admission to the *pædagogikum* (professional postgraduate teacher-training for upper secondary-school teachers) or issuance of the *jus practicandi* (business permit). (The right of establishment does not include the right to use the Danish title of *kandidat.*);

(2) full or partial recognition: a detailed assessment of examinations passed for admission to higher education studies.

In some cases recognition under (1) depends on certain supplementary requirements. Requests for recognition should be addressed to the institution in question. Applicants should enclose the following in duly authenticated form: certificates, examination requirements, description of studies, major papers, reading lists, etc.

Some institutions (e.g. the University of Copenhagen) have special application forms which should be requested in writing.

A period of two to three months should be allowed for the processing of applications. It is expected that those who apply for recognition of academic degrees will have certain ties with Denmark.

DK

Entry examinations

Students with university entry qualifications from EC member countries fulfil the general requirements. The higher education institutions also require a knowledge of the Danish language. Supplementary tests may have to be taken in subjects required for the studies chosen.

For some courses of study there are entrance examinations (e.g. the academies of music), or work has to be submitted for assessment (Academy of Fine Arts). Information on such requirements is available from the institutions on request.

Application and registration

Since the admission regulations of the institutions of higher education are not uniform, applications for admission are individually processed by the various institutions. Thus, foreign applicants must contact the relevant higher education institution directly or the Central Advisory Service (*studievejledning*) at the University of Copenhagen in good time. When applying to an institution, the following information and duly certified documents must be submitted:

1. higher education entrance qualification;
2. present university studies;
3. knowledge of Danish;
4. subject area to be studied;
5. when studies are to begin;
6. whether the application is for an entire course of study or for a short stay, e.g. as an occasional student;
7. special ties with Denmark.

The applicant is recommended to request information on the following:

1. the possibility of admission in general and/or to the desired course of study;
2. application deadline;
3. beginning and end of the academic year;
4. the requirement of a Danish language test.

Applicants with sufficient information should send the application together with the necessary documents to the indicated address before the application deadline (15 March). Photocopies must be officially certified.

Applicants will receive a preliminary notification by 1 June. If accepted, applicants must follow the instructions for registration at the higher education institution. The registration deadline (*tilmeldingsfristen*) is 1 July.

The higher education institutions send out final notification at the end of July. If the application has been accepted, a student identity card (*årskort*) will be sent out during the month of August.

Subject to certain exceptions, registration can be effected only once a year (until 1 September). It is not possible to change from one course of study to another during the academic year.

Foreign students seeking admission as occasional students (see above) should inquire at the higher education institution concerned as to whether or not relevant facilities exist and about conditions for admission. There is no admission limitation or set application deadline for occasional students, but it is strongly advised to apply well in advance since applications must be given individual consideration by the recipient institutions.

Tuition fees

There are no tuition fees at Danish higher education institutions.

Knowledge of the language of instruction, language courses and other courses

Since lectures and other courses are held in Danish, it stands to reason that a good knowledge of written and spoken Danish is not only important for foreign students, but also a necessity if they are to profit from their studies at one of the higher education institutions in Denmark. In some subjects it may, of course, be possible to manage with less fluency than, say, in the study of languages where an ability to translate accurately both into and from Danish is important. For this, a good command of the language is indispensable. Some institutions have specific language requirements, while others give no details regarding the required knowledge of Danish.

There are no beginners' courses in Danish for foreigners offered at higher education institutions. Foreign students are advised to attend the Danish courses available at the *Studieskole* in Copenhagen, Århus and Odense, and at the municipal evening schools or to take private language instruction. Examinations in Danish held at the *Studieskole* are those recognized and indeed demanded by most higher education institutions as a certificate of proficiency in Danish.

Outside the regular lecture period no classes are held at the universities,

university centres and institutes of higher education. No special courses for foreigners are offered during the normal academic year.

Financial assistance and scholarships

Government educational assistance (*Statens uddannelsesstøtte — SU*) is granted to Danish citizens under specific regulations.

There are also regulations governing the granting of financial assistance to foreigners studying or undergoing training in Denmark. One such regulation applies to children of citizens of EC countries and to foreigners who, with their parents, are permanently resident in Denmark and were under 20 years of age upon entering the country.

Other foreign students or trainees are entitled to *Statens uddannelsesstøtte* if they have been residents of Denmark and employed full time for two consecutive years immediately prior to the application for assistance, or if there are special ties with Denmark. Foreigners who receive educational support from their home countries are not entitled to assistance in Denmark. Foreign students who wish to spend a short period of study in Denmark, e.g. as occasional students will be unable to obtain assistance under the *Statens uddannelsesstøtte* system.

Citizens of EC member countries who consider themselves eligible for assistance should get in touch with the *stipendiekontoret* (scholarship office) at the relevant higher education institution. They will receive an application form for exemption from the requirement of Danish citizenship as well as the application form for financial assistance, both of which they must submit together.

Information on scholarships awarded by private foundations (*legat*) is provided in the *Legathåndbogen* and the *Legater, Studielån, Kollegier-Håndbog*. However, most of these scholarships are reserved for specific categories of recipients.

In addition, there is a limited number of Danish Government scholarships which are especially intended for students who wish to spend a short period of time studying in Denmark. Information on these *udvekslingsstipendier* (exchange scholarships) and, in particular, on the closing date for the submission of applications can be obtained from the relevant authorities (normally the Ministry of Education) in the respective home country.

Entry and residence regulations

Citizens of an EC Member State can reside in Denmark for three months without any special permit. Should they want to extend their stay, e.g. for study purposes, they must apply for a residence permit. The residence permit should normally be requested from the Danish consular service in the students' home country and the students should provide proof that they have been accepted at a higher education institution and have sufficient means to finance their studies.

Citizens of an EC country can also apply for a residence permit from the *Direktoratet for Udlændinge* (Directorate for Foreigners) in Copenhagen or, outside the Copenhagen area, from the local police. In this case too, they must provide evidence of admission to a course of study and of the ability to finance these studies. When applying for a renewal, students must submit a declaration by their professors or the higher education institution they are attending concerning their academic progress.

Students from EC member countries wanting to study in Denmark for more than three months must register within five days of their arrival in Denmark with the residents' registration office (*Folkeregistret*) of the municipality in which they live or

intend to live. After registering they will be issued a personal number certificate (*Centrale Personregister — CPR*).

Social aspects

Social security and health insurance

There are no special arrangements in Denmark for students. Students are insured under the public health insurance system in the same way as other Danish nationals. Students from EC countries who intend to stay in Denmark for more than three months and have obtained a residence permit will automatically receive a health insurance card (*sygesikringsbevis*) entitling them to treatment by doctors and dentists, to hospital treatment, and to prescription allowances on the same basis as Danish nationals. Everyone is entitled to treatment in local hospitals in the event of serious illness or accident.

EC nationals who are covered by a health insurance scheme in their home country should present evidence of this to the residents' registration office of the community in which they reside. Potential claims are automatically transferred to Denmark.

Advisory services

There is no central advisory service for all higher education institutions. Foreign students desiring information on types of courses available, application procedures, deadlines or course content and structure should apply to the individual institution.

The Central Student Advisory Service at the University of Copenhagen (*Centrale Studie- og Erhvervsvejledning*) provides information not only on studies at the University of Copenhagen, but also on educational opportunities in Denmark as a whole and on general university and social questions. The reader is referred to the addresses of the institutions (Appendix 1).

Student counsellors (*studenterrådgivere*) provide advice on personal problems. Social counsellors, psychiatrists and psychologists are also available to students.

Career counselling (*erhvervsvejledning*) is provided by all Danish labour exchanges; everybody is entitled to free counselling services.

Student employment

Danish and foreign students may take up employment during term without special permission from the higher education institution at which they are studying. Income from such work may, however, lead to the reduction of any educational assistance being granted.

Foreign students are required to have a work permit issued by the *Direktoratet for Udlændinge*. Such a permit will not be issued until the applicant has been accepted for a job. Any money earned by working is subject to taxes. The tax-free allowance in Denmark is approximately DKR 25 000 (1989).

In view of widespread unemployment it is difficult for students to find jobs. Consequently, foreign students should not count on being able to finance their stay by means of a regular job or part-time work.

Student organizations

Students in Denmark participate in the running of higher education institutions since they are represented in all the administrative bodies. Students stand for the elections through their political organizations.

There are various political and subject-oriented student associations at the institutions. Membership is voluntary. Information can be obtained from the individual institutions.

Cost of living

Only approximate information can be given concerning the cost of living. For a Danish student living away from home a monthly minimum of about DKR 4 500 should be expected (based on the price index of 1989 prices). Of this sum, DKR 1 000-1 500 will be needed for accommodation and DKR 2 000 for food. In addition to these expenses, the student has to pay for transport, books, laundry, clothes, etc.

Expenses have been calculated for Danish students. They are, without doubt, greater for foreign students. Inflation should be taken into consideration when calculating study costs.

Accommodation

Foreign students registered at Danish higher education institutions are en-

DK

titled to apply for a room in one of the large number of *kollegier* (halls of residence) or other similar student accommodation on an equal footing with Danish students. The rent for a room in a hall of residence amounts to DKR 1 000-1 500 a month.

Foreign students seeking a room in a hall of residence should inquire before travelling to Denmark (preferably three months in advance). They should write to the *indstillingsudvalg* (allocation committee), whose address is given in Appendix 1.

Most rooms in the *kollegier* are allocated by this body. Fewer than 25 % of students live in *kollegier*. Further information is contained in the *Kollegieoversigter* (lists of halls of residence), for instance that published by the *Centrale studievejledning* (Central Student Advisory Service) at the University of Copenhagen.

It is also possible to obtain private accommodation. The advisory services of the higher education institutions supply information on whom to contact.

Services for students

There are student services such as refectories and bookshops at all higher education institutions. Some institutions have crèches and kindergartens. There are sports associations at some higher education institutions which are intended primarily for students.

Student reductions are available for rail, ship or air travel (but not for local public transport). Various admission prices for certain exhibitions, museums and theatre performances are reduced for students. There are no general guidelines.

Facilities for disabled students

Danish applicants with serious physical disabilities stand a good chance of being admitted to tertiary education in Denmark.

Special measures have been taken in almost all areas making it possible to admit the disabled, independent of normal admission procedures, as long as they fulfil formal admission requirements.

The procedures are applied differently, but in general the disabled have better chances of being admitted to the larger institutions, since they are generally regarded as supplementary students. At smaller institutions which do not have the capacity to admit supplementary students, relatively few disabled applicants are accepted.

The question of whether disabled people will be able to use their training professionally is not usually one of the criteria for admission. However, the institution will want to be satisfied that, given the facilities available, the person will be able to cope with the practical problems that occur.

Physically disabled persons are given higher priority than mentally handicapped persons.

There are only a very few instances of special assistance for the disabled (e.g. use of a secretary). The responsibility for this type of help lies with the social authorities. Financial assistance to these students is also considered a

DK

social matter and is rarely a cause for difficulties.

The number of seriously disabled persons enrolled in tertiary education in Denmark is small, since many leave the educational system at an earlier stage.

Appendices

1. Addresses

Danish embassies in EC countries

Belgium
Avenue Louise 221
Boîte 7
B-1050 Bruxelles
☎ 648 25 25

Federal Republic of Germany
Pfälzer Straße 14
D-5300 Bonn 1
☎ (228) 72 99 10

Greece
Philikis Etairias
(Platia Kolonaki)
GR-10673 Athina
☎ (1) 724-9315

Spain
Claudio Coello 91
E-28006 Madrid
☎ (1) 431-8445

France
77 Avenue Marceau
F-75116 Paris
☎ (1) 47 23 54 20/
(1) 47 20 32 66

Ireland
Royal Danish Embassy
121-122 St Stephen's Green
Dublin 2
☎ (1) 75 64 04/(1) 75 64 07/
(1) 75 65 15

Italy
Via dei Monti Parioli 50
I-00197 Roma
☎ (6) 360 04 41/42/43

Luxembourg
11 b, Boulevard Joseph II
L-1840 Luxembourg
☎ 209 64/209 65

The Netherlands
Koninginnegracht 30
Postbus 30838
2500 GV 's-Gravenhage
☎ (070) 65 58 30

Portugal
Rua Castilho 14-3°
1296 Lisboa Codex
☎ (1) 54 50 99/(1) 54 51 24/
(1) 54 52 49

United Kingdom
Royal Danish Embassy
55 Sloane Street
London SW1X 9SR
☎ (1) 235 1255

Ministries and other institutions

Det internationale kontor
Undervisningsministeriet
(International Office at the Ministry of Education)
Frederiksholms Kanal 25 D
DK-1220 København K
☎ (33) 92 50 00

Direktoratet for Udlændinge
(Directorate for Foreigners)
Absalonsgade 9
DK-1658 København V
☎ (31) 21 11 77

Folkeregistret i København
(Resident Registration,
Authority in Copenhagen)
Dahlerupsgade 6
DK-1603 København V
☎ (33) 11 51 00

Styrelsen for Statens
Uddannelsesstøtte (SU)
(State educational assistance)
Danasvej 30
DK-1910 Frederiksberg C
☎ (31) 21 46 66

Danmarks Internationale Studenterkomité (DIS)
(International student committee)
Skindergade 36
DK-1159 København K
☎ (33) 11 11 00

Folkeuniversitetet
i København
(Centre for Adult Education)
Købmagersgade 52
DK-1150 København K
☎ (33) 14 48 27

Universities and student information offices

Københavns Universitet
Det Internationale Kontor
(Information service for students)
Frue Plads, Port A
Postbox 2177
DK-København K
☎ (33) 91 08 28

Studievejledningen og Dispensationskontoret
(Student counselling and matters of exemption)
Fiolstræde 22
DK-1171 København K
☎ (33) 14 15 36

Aarhus Universitet
Nordre Ringgade
DK-8000 Århus C

Odense Unviersitet
Campusvej 55
DK-5230 Odense M

Roskilde Universitetscenter
Postbox 260
DK-4000 Roskilde

Aalborg Universitetscenter
Postbox 159
DK-9100 Aalborg

Arkitektskolen i Århus
Nørreport 20
DK-8000 Århus C

Danmarks farmaceutiske
Højskole
Universitetsparken 2
lK-2100 København Ø

Danmarks Ingeniørakademi
Bygning 101 A
DK-2800 Lyngby

Danmarks Lærerhøjskole
Emdrupvej 101
DK-2400 København NV

Danmarks Tekniske Højskole
Bygning 101 A
DK-2800 Lyngby

Den Kgl. Veterinær- og Landbohøjskole
Bülowsvej 13
DK-1870 Frederiksberg C

Det Jydske Musikkonservatorium
Fuglesangsallé 26
DK-8210 Århus V

Det Kgl. Danske Kunstakademi
Kgs. Nytorv 1
DK-1050 København K

Det Kgl. Danske Musikkonservatorium
Niels Brocks Gade 1
DK-1574 København V

Handelshøjskolen i København
Dalgas Have 15
DK-2000 Frederiksberg

Handelshøjskolen i Århus
Fuglesangsallé 4
DK-8210 Århus V

Kunstakademiets Arkitektskole
Peder Skramsgade 8, st.
DK-1054 København K

Københavens Tandlægehøjskole
Nørre Allé 20
DK-2200 København N

Århus Tandlægehøjskole
Vennelyst Boulevard
DK-8000 Århus C

Other higher education institutions

Information on other higher education institutions and their addresses available from:

Undervisningsministeriets
Internationale Kontor
Frederiksholms Kanal 25 D,
DK-1220 København K

Den centrale studievejledning
Københavns Universitet
Fiolstræde 22
DK-1171 København K
or at higher education institutions

Detailed information will be given by the student advisers of the individual institutions

Danish courses

Studieskolen
Antonigade 6
DK-1106 København K

Folkeuniversitetet i Odense
Niels Bohrs Allé 25
DK-5230 Odense M

Folkeuniversitetet i Århus
Immervad 7
DK-8000 Århus C

Accommodation services

Centralindstillingsudvalget (CIU) (Accommodation board)
Skindergade 36
DK-1159 København K

Kollegiekontoret
(Office for residence halls)
Vester Allé 24
DK-8000 Århus C

Regionale Indstillingsudvalg (RIU) (Regional accommodation board)
Hinderupgård
Niels Bohrs Allé 21
DK-5000 Odense M

Indstillingsudvalget for Aalborgs kollegier (IFAK)
(Selection Committee for residence halls at Aalborg)
Badehusvej 23
DK-9000 Aalborg

Ungdomsinformationen
(Youth information centre)
Magstræde 14
DK-1204 København K

Polyteknisk Kollegiebyggeselskab
(Society for residence hall construction at Polytechnics)
Anker Engelundsvej 1
Bygning 101 F
DK-2800 Lyngby

DK

2. Survey of courses of study at higher education institutions

● Degree-course

Universities

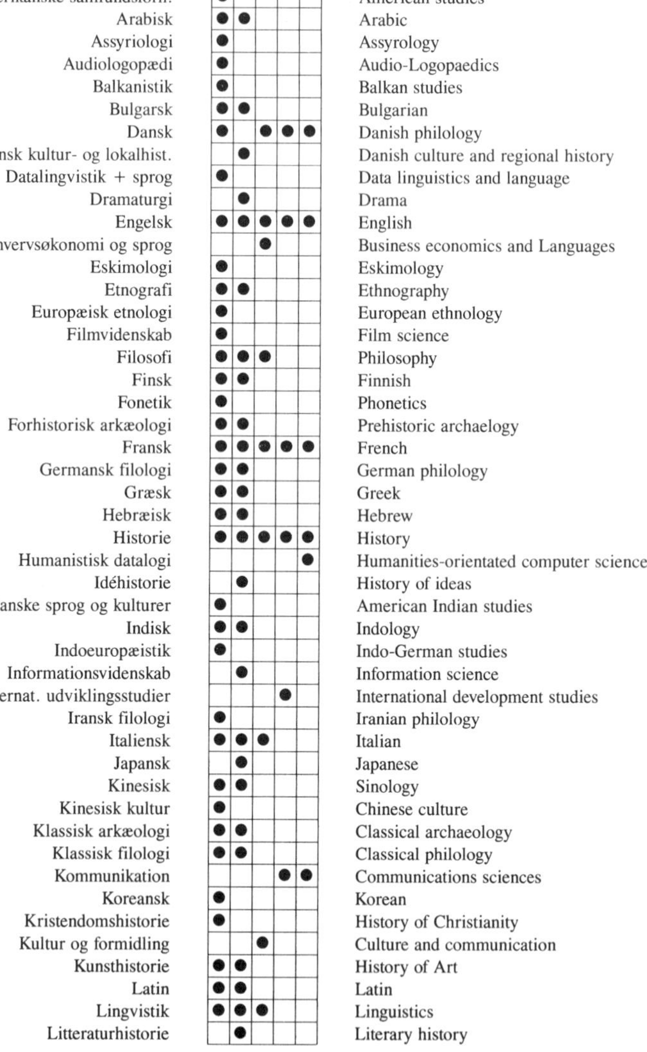

Humaniora:	Københavns Universitet	Århus Universitet	Odense Universitet	Roskilde Universitetscenter	Aalborg Universitetscenter	Humanities:
Afrika, områdestudier	●					African studies
Amerikanske samfundsforh.	●					American studies
Arabisk	●	●				Arabic
Assyriologi	●					Assyrology
Audiologopædi	●					Audio-Logopaedics
Balkanistik	●					Balkan studies
Bulgarsk	●	●				Bulgarian
Dansk	●		●	●	●	Danish philology
Dansk kultur- og lokalhist.		●				Danish culture and regional history
Datalingvistik + sprog	●					Data linguistics and language
Dramaturgi		●				Drama
Engelsk	●	●	●	●	●	English
Erhvervsøkonomi og sprog			●			Business economics and Languages
Eskimologi	●					Eskimology
Etnografi	●	●				Ethnography
Europæisk etnologi	●					European ethnology
Filmvidenskab	●					Film science
Filosofi	●	●	●			Philosophy
Finsk	●	●				Finnish
Fonetik	●					Phonetics
Forhistorisk arkæologi	●	●				Prehistoric archaelogy
Fransk	●	●	●	●	●	French
Germansk filologi	●	●				German philology
Græsk	●	●				Greek
Hebræisk	●	●				Hebrew
Historie	●	●	●	●	●	History
Humanistisk datalogi					●	Humanities-orientated computer science
Idéhistorie		●				History of ideas
Indianske sprog og kulturer	●					American Indian studies
Indisk	●	●				Indology
Indoeuropæistik	●					Indo-German studies
Informationsvidenskab		●				Information science
Internat. udviklingsstudier				●		International development studies
Iransk filologi	●					Iranian philology
Italiensk	●	●	●			Italian
Japansk		●				Japanese
Kinesisk	●	●				Sinology
Kinesisk kultur	●					Chinese culture
Klassisk arkæologi	●	●				Classical archaeology
Klassisk filologi	●	●				Classical philology
Kommunikation				●	●	Communications sciences
Koreansk	●					Korean
Kristendomshistorie	●					History of Christianity
Kultur og formidling			●			Culture and communication
Kunsthistorie	●	●				History of Art
Latin	●	●				Latin
Lingvistik	●	●	●			Linguistics
Litteraturhistorie		●				Literary history

DK

Humaniora:	Københavns Universitet	Århus Universitet	Odense Universitet	Roskilde Universitetscenter	Aalborg Universitetscenter	Humanities (continuation):
Litteraturvidenskab	●		●			Literary studies
Lokalhistorie			●			Local history
Middelalderarkæologi		●				Medieval archaeology
Moderne kultur og -formidl.	●					Modern culture and communication
Musik	●	●			●	Music
Musikterapi					●	Music therapy
Nederlandsk	●	●				Dutch
Nordisk filologi	●	●	●			Nordic philology
Nordisk litteratur	●					Nordic literature
Nordisk folkemindevid.	●					Nordic folklore
Nygræsk	●	●				Modern Greek
Nærorientalsk arkæologi	●					Near Orient archaeology
Oldtidskundskab	●	●				Ancient studies
Polsk	●	●				Polish
Portugisisk	●	●				Portuguese
Psykologi	●	●			●	Psychology
Pædagogik	●					Education science
Religion		●				Religion
Religionshistorie	●	●				History of religions
Religionssociologi	●					Religious sociology
Retorik	●					Rhetoric
Romansk filologi	●	●	●			Romance philology
Rumænsk	●					Romanian
Russisk	●	●	●			Russian
Russisk samfundsvidenskab			●			Russian studies
Samtidshistorie			●			Contemporary history
Semitisk filologi	●	●				Semitic philology
Serbokroatisk	●	●				Serbo-Croat
Slavisk filologi	●	●				Slavonic philology
Slaviske sprog og kulturer	●					Slavonic languages and cultures
Spansk	●	●	●			Spanish
Sprog og internat. forhold					●	Language and international relations
Sprogvidenskab	●					Linguistics (philology)
Teatervidenskab	●					Theatre sciences
Thai	●					Thai
Tibetansk	●					Tibetan
Tjekkisk	●	●				Czech
Tysk	●	●	●	●	●	German
Ungarsk		●				Hungarian
Voksenpædagogik	●					Adult education science
Egyptologi	●					Egyptology
Estetisk kulturarbejde		●				Aesthetics in cultural work
Østasiatiske sprog og kult.	●					East-Asian languages and cultures
Østasiatisk filologi	●					East-Asian philology
Østasiatisk kultur, kunst og sprog	●					East-Asian culture, art and languages
Østasien, områdestudium		●				East-Asian studies
Øststatskundskab	●					Eastern-bloc studies

Naturvidenskab:	Københavns Universitet	Århus Universitet	Odense Universitet	Roskilde Universitetscenter	Aalborg Universitetscenter	Natural sciences:
Akademiingeniør					●	Academy engineering
Astronomi	●	●				Astronomy
Biokemi	●					Biochemistry
Biologi	●	●	●			Biology
Cellebiologi			●			Molecular biology
Civilingeniør					●	Civil engineering
Datalogi	●	●	●	●	●	Computer science
Eksperimentel biologi			●			Experimental biology
Forsikringsvidenskab	●					Insurance science (actuarial studies)
Fysik	●	●	●	●	●	Physics
Geofysik	●					Geophysics
Geodæsi	●					Geodetics
Geografi	●	●		●		Geography
Geologi	●	●				Geology
Kemi	●	●	●	●	●	Chemistry
Landinspektør					●	Development planning and surveying
Legemsøvelser	●		●			Physical education and sports
Matematik	●	●	●	●	●	Mathematics
Matematisk Økonomi		●				Mathematics/economics
Statistik	●	●				Statistics

Samfundsvidenskab:	Københavns Universitet	Århus Universitet	Odense Universitet	Roskilde Universitetscenter	Aalborg Universitetscenter	Social sciences:
Administrativ databehandl.				●		Data-processing in administration
Erhvervsret			●		●	Economic law
Erhvervssprog			●		●	Business/applied languages
Erhvervsøkonomi			●	●	●	Business economics
Forvaltning	●			●		Administration
Forvaltning og datalogi	●					Administration and Computer science
Jura	●	●				Law
Kultursociologi	●					Cultural sociology
Revision			●		●	Auditing
Samfundsfag	●	●	●		●	Political sciences
Samfundsvidenskab					●	Social sciences
Socialrådgiver					●	Social work
Socialvidenskab			●			Social studies
Sociologi	●					Sociology
Statskundskab		●				Political studies and administration
Statsvidenskab	●					Political science
Tekn.-samf. vid. planlægning				●		Technological-sociological planning
Økonomi		●				Economics

	Københavns Universitet	Århus Universitet	Odense Universitet	Roskilde Universitetscenter	Aalborg Universitetscenter	
Medicin	●	●	●			**Medicine**

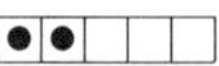

	Københavns Universitet	Århus Universitet	Odense Universitet	Roskilde Universitetscenter	Aalborg Universitetscenter	
Teologi	●	●				**Theology**

DK

Higher education institutions
(højere laereanstalter)

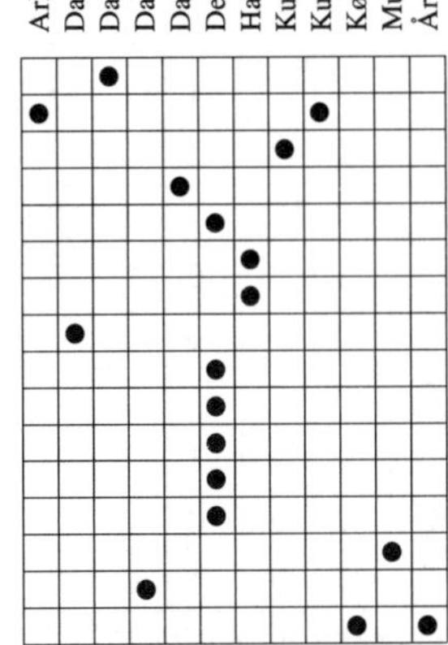

	Arkitektskolen i Århus	Danmarks Farmaceutiske Højskole	Danmarks Ingeniørakademi	Danmarks Lærerhøjskole	Danmarks Tekniske Højskole	Den Kgl. Veterinær- og Landbohøjsk.	Handelshøjskolerne og handelshøjskoleafd.	Kunstakademiet	Kunstakademiets Arkitektskole	Københavns Tandlægehøjskole	Musikkonservatorierne	Århus Tandlægehøjskole	
Akademiingeniør			●										Academy engineering
Arkitektur	●								●				Architecture
Billedkunst								●					Fine arts
Civilingeniør					●								Civil engineering
Dyrlægevidenskab						●							Veterinary science
Erhvervssprog							●						Business/applied languages
Erhvervsøkonomi							●						Business economics
Farmaci		●											Pharmacy
Forstvidenskab						●							Forestry
Havebrugsvidenskab						●							Horticulture
Landbrugsvidenskab						●							Agricultural science
Levnedsmiddelvidenskab						●							Food science
Mejeriingeniørvidenskab						●							Dairy science
Musik											●		Music
Pædagogik				●									Education science
Tandlægevidenskab										●		●	Dentistry

Other institutions

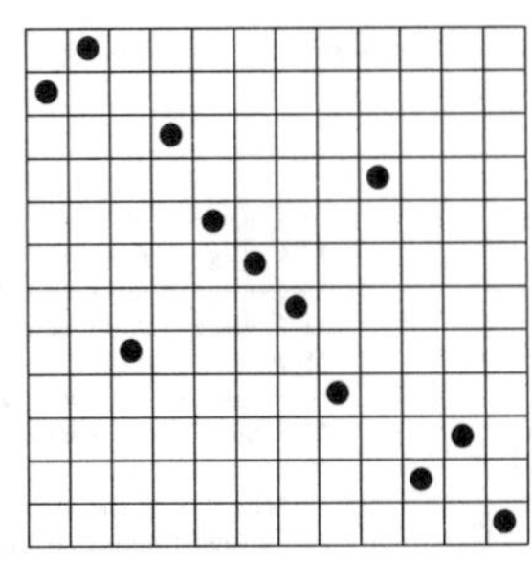

	Børnehaveseminarier	Danmarks Biblioteksskole	Danmarks Jordemoderskole	Ergoterapeutskoler	Fritidspædagogseminarier	Fysioterapeutskoler	Husholdningsseminarier	Journalisthøjskolen	Seminarier	Sociale højskoler	Socialpædagogiske seminarier	Teknika – Ingéniørhøjskoler	
Bibliothekar		●											Librarianship
Børnehavepædagog	●												Kindergarten teacher
Ergoterapeut				●									Ergotherapy
Folkeskolelærer									●				Elementary school teacher
Fritidspædagog					●								Recreation centre teacher
Fysioterapeut						●							Physiotherapy
Husholdningslærer							●						Home economics teacher
Jordemoder			●										Midwifery
Journalist								●					Journalism
Socialpædagog											●		Social educational studies
Socialrådgiver										●			Social work
Teknikumingeniør												●	*Teknikum* engineering

3. Student statistics

Foreign students in Denmark 1987/88

	Total	B	F	D	GR	IRL	I	L	NL	P	E	UK	EC	Nordic countries	Others	Total foreign
1	26 355	4	40	87	2	2	13	0	19	4	7	66	244	251	523	1 018
2	13 178	2	7	80	5	2	5	0	7	2	0	26	136	107	126	369
3	6 120	0	3	18	3	0	1	0	1	1	3	12	42	41	56	139
4	2 994	0	1	10	1	0	0	0	1	0	0	9	22	22	34	78
5	5 693	1	0	9	0	0	0	0	1	1	0	9	21	176	50	247
6	5 037	0	3	17	1	0	1	0	0	0	0	10	32	69	138	239
7	2 232	0	1	4	1	0	2	0	0	0	0	3	11	10	89	110
8	2 746	0	0	7	0	0	0	0	1	0	0	4	12	39	38	89
9	401	0	0	4	0	0	0	0	1	0	0	0	5	1	10	16
10	302	0	0	9	0	0	0	0	0	0	0	0	9	1	3	13
11	867	0	0	5	0	0	0	0	1	0	0	1	7	6	22	35
12	12 525	EC and others unspecified total: 119											*	125	*	244
13	6 068	1	1	4	0	0	0	0	0	0	0	2	8	67	36	111
14	91	0	1	3	0	0	2	0	0	0	0	0	6	38	17	61
15	164	0	0	1	0	0	0	0	0	0	0	0	1	26	1	28
16	30	0	0	0	0	0	0	0	0	0	0	0	0	08	0	8
17	715	0	0	3	0	0	0	0	0	0	0	0	3	13	9	25
18	409	0	0	1	0	0	1	0	0	0	0	2	4	34	3	41
19	210	0	0	3	0	0	0	0	0	0	0	0	3	12	3	18
20	-	-	-	-	-	-	-	-	-	-	-	-	-	-	-	-

* There is no precise information available concerning the *Handelshøjskole* in Copenhagen.

1 University of Copenhagen
2 University of Århus
3 University of Odense
4 University Centre of Roskilde
5 University Centre of Aalborg
6 Technical University of Denmark
7 Engineering Academy of Denmark
8 College of Veterinary Medicine and Agriculture
9 College of Dentistry, Copenhagen
10 College of Dentistry, Århus
11 College of Pharmacy
12 College of Business and Management Sciences, Copenhagen
13 College of Business and Management Sciences, Århus
14 College of Architecture
15 Academy of Fine Arts
16 Academy of Art Restoration
17 School of Architecture, Århus
18 School of Music, Copenhagen
19 School of Music, Århus
20 Teacher training college

4. Bibliography

Education in Denmark. The education system. Published by the Danish Ministry of Education. Also available in French.

Studie- og Erhvervsvalget I og II. 1988/89. Orientering for Gymnasiet og HF. (Guide to studies and occupations I and II. Information for upper secondary schools and the HF). A very valuable reference work on educational and vocational opportunities, educational institutions, duration of studies and admission requirements; published by the *Rådet for Uddannelses- og Erversvejledning* (Council for Educational and Vocational Guidance); may be consulted in libraries and at the student advice centres and similar.

Studieordninger (Study regulations). Information on course organization, regulations and examination requirements is partially contained in the respective study regulations and partially in the descriptions of courses which give a general overview of the study requirements and regulations. Available on request from the student advisory service (*studievejledning*) and the study and information offices (*studiekontor, informationskontor*).

Lektionskataloger or studieprogrammer. Course prospectuses or teaching curricula. These are published each semester for the respective areas of study or individual subjects. Available from the institutions of higher education, for example from the individual departments prior to each semester.

The University of Copenhagen 1987. Published by Københavns Universitet. Available free of charge.

Rules of admission for foreign students. Published by Københavns Universitet. Available free of charge.

Aarhus Universitet. Published by *Aarhus Universitet.* Available free of charge.

The University of Aarhus. Rules of admission for foreign students. Available free of charge.

Odense University. Information about Odense University and rules of admission for foreign students.

Roskilde University Centre. Published by *Roskilde Universitetscenter.*

Roskilde University Centre. Admission for foreign students.

Aalborg University Centre. The University of Aalborg. Published by *Aalborg Universitetscenter.*

The Technical University of Denmark. Published by Danmarks Tekniske Højskole.

Kollegieoversigt. (List of student halls of residence). Published by Studievejledningen (Student advisory service) at Københavns Universitet.

Kollegiehåndbogen. (Guide to student halls of residence). Published by Akademisk Forlag.

Legater, Studielån, Kollegieren Håndbog. (scholarships, student halls of residence — a guide). Published by Akademisk Forlag.

5. Glossary

Afgangsbevis: Certificate obtained upon completion of a course of study.

Afgangseksamen: Final examination on completion of three or four years of study at all schools of economics, business administration and modern languages and Roskilde *Universitetscenter.*

Bachelor: Degree which is awarded after the first three years of a *kandidat* programme (*kandidatuddannelse*) in humanities, social sciences, theology, natural sciences and health science subjects.

Bifag: The humanities or science subsidiary (minor) which, combined with the *hovedfag* (major), makes up the humanities *kandidateksamen.* The study of the minor subjects takes two to three years. For humanities subjects, this was replaced in 1985 by the basic studies, the *Grunduddannelsen.*

Diplomeksamen: Examination for a degree in business economics (HD) and business/applied languages (ED) after three or four years of part-time study.

Doktorgraden: The highest academic degree. Awarded only for a doctoral thesis (*disputats*) based on many years of independent and highly qualified research.

Grunduddannelse: The first part of the *kandidateksamen* in the humanities and social sciences. The basic studies last two years and form the prerequisite for admission to the main studies (*overbygningsuddannelsen*).

Hovedfag: The major subject is the one — more important — humanities or natural science subject. The officially stipulated time of study of the major subject which leads to the degree of 'cand. phil.' is four years. The *speciale* (thesis) is an important part of the studies in the major subject.

Højere forberedelseseksamen (HF): This examination presupposes a two-year course of study and is one of the higher education admission qualifications. It comprises a number of compulsory subjects and two or three optional subjects.

Højere handelseksamen (HH): Qualification obtained at business-orientated academic-stream upper secondary schools (*handelsgymnasium*), providing access to universities and other higher education institutions.

Højere læreanstalter: This term which appears for instance in the expression *Polyteknisk læreanstalt,* includes those higher education institutions that offer courses of study leading to the *kandidat* degree in the technical sciences, business economics, business/applied languages, veterinary medicine, food science, horticulture, dairy science, agricultural science, forestry science, dentistry, pharmacy, the fine arts and architecture, music as well as in the context of further training for primary-school teachers. The instruction offered is at university level.

Højere uddannelser: Courses of training at institutions at which research is conducted and which grant the *kandidat, licentiat* and doctoral degrees (universities and other higher education institutions).

Højskole: The term *højskole* (higher education institution) is used in compounds as a designation for part of the higher education institutions (e.g. *handelshøjskolen, farmaceutisk højskole. Danmarks tekniske højskole*). Instruction offered is at university level. There are also *Ingeniørhøjskolerteknika,* which offer engineering courses.

Kandidateksamen: The most common examination for a degree at the higher education institutions of the country requiring four to six years of study. The *kandidatgrad* is used in the Latin form (*candidatus, -a*) followed by the Latin term for the subject (e.g. *candidatus theologiae*, abbreviated cand. theol.) or subject area (e.g. *candidatus polytechnices*, cand. polyt.).

Kortere videregående uddannelser: These include a number of non-academic courses of training with a maximum duration of three years. They comprise both theoretical and practical instruction with emphasis being placed on practical instruction.

Licentiatgrad: *(Ph. D. degree).* A postgraduate degree which presupposes a *kandidateksamen,* a *magistergrad* or a corresponding academic degree. Application for admission to *licentiat* studies must be directed to the vice-chancellor or principal of the institution in question and be approved by the faculty or departmental body responsible. The duration of studies is fixed at two and at the most three years and is concluded with a written academic-scientific thesis.

Længere videregående uddannelser: These courses of study take from three to eight years and include academic studies at the *universiteter, højere læreanstalter* and training at various *seminarier,* colleges and higher education institutions. These courses of study are either entirely (as with academic courses) or predominantly theoretical.

Magistergrad: This degree can be awarded in the humanities and certain areas of the social sciences. It differs from the *kandidatgrad* in the duration of studies (six years) and in the independent, scholarly nature of studies.

Overbygningsuddannelse: Two-year main studies which follow the basic studies and are taken in the same or related subjects. They lead to the title of 'cand.phil.'. Two-year main studies in the same subjects together with a supplementary or combination course (*modul*) or three-year main studies in the same subjects lead to the title of 'cand.mag.'. Four-year main studies (i.e. cand. phil. plus two years) in the same subjects or within the same discipline (magister) lead to the title of 'mag. art.'.

Pædagogikum: Five-month postgraduate teacher training for candidates in humanities and science education and some social science subjects leading to teaching qualifications for the upper secondary level.

Seminarier: Training for primary and lower secondary school teachers, home economics teachers, kindergarten teachers and recreation centre teachers, etc. is offered at

seminarier. The course of training takes three to four years.

Statens uddannelsesstøtte (SU): Educational assistance provided for by law. The scheme offers assistance as loans or scholarships for students at higher education institutions.

Studentereksamen: The most common higher education admission qualification. It is acquired on completion of three years of upper secondary education (*gymnasium*) or after a two-year course, i.e. 12 years of schooling. Since the 1988 reform, the upper secondary classes have been divided into two streams: a language (modern) and a mathematical stream. There are compulsory and optional subjects. The *studentereksamen* consists of 10 oral and written tests and, in addition, a major paper. Basically, the *studentereksamen* gives admission to all sorts of courses and training in higher education; however, there may be specific requirements for certain courses of study with regard to the optional subjects at upper secondary school.

Teknikum: *Teknikum* is the designation for the engineering colleges that lead to a *teknikum* engineering degree. The course of study takes four years, including a period of on-the-job training, and primarily involves training in practical engineering skills.

Udvekslingsstipendier: Exchange scholarships. Denmark has exchange scholarship agreements with the following EC countries: Belgium, the Federal Republic of Germany, France, Greece, Ireland, Italy, the Netherlands, Portugal, Spain and the United Kingdom.

Universitetscenter: Defines the two higher education institutions in Roskilde (RUC) and Aalborg (AUC) where interdisciplinary project-oriented basic studies are the foundation for further study leading to an examination at medium or *kandidat* level in the social sciences, humanities, natural sciences and technical sciences.

Årskort: Identity card for enrolled students, necessary when registering for an examination, etc. The student card must be renewed annually.

DK

6. Diagram of the education system

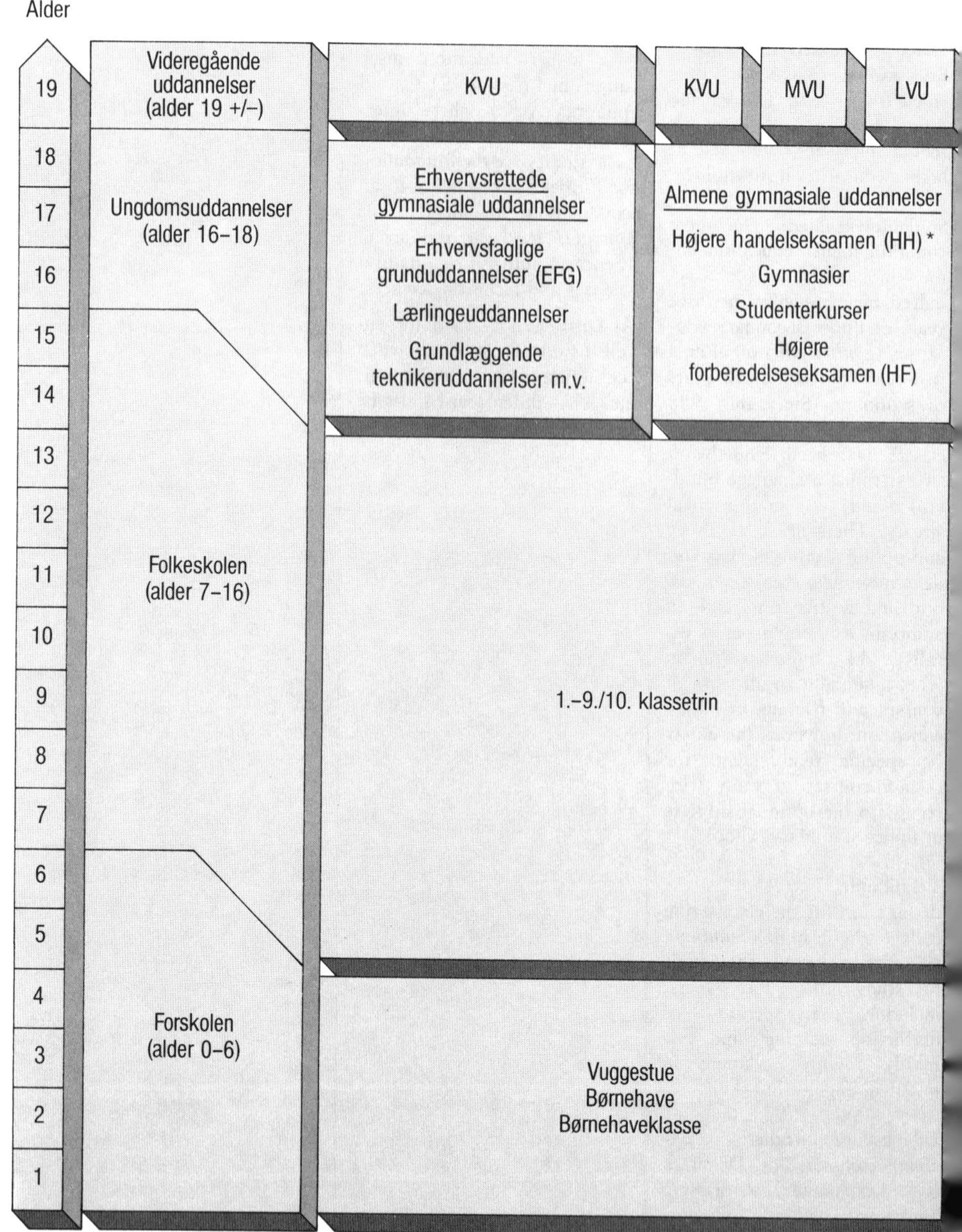
Alder
19
18
17
16
15
14
13
12
11
10
9
8
7
6
5
4
3
2
1
Videregående uddannelser (alder 19 +/–)
Ungdomsuddannelser (alder 16–18)
Folkeskolen (alder 7–16)
Forskolen (alder 0–6)
KVU
KVU
MVU
LVU
Erhvervsrettede gymnasiale uddannelser
Erhvervsfaglige grunduddannelser (EFG)
Lærlingeuddannelser
Grundlæggende teknikeruddannelser m.v.
Almene gymnasiale uddannelser
Højere handelseksamen (HH) *
Gymnasier
Studenterkurser
Højere forberedelseseksamen (HF)
1.–9./10. klassetrin
Vuggestue
Børnehave
Børnehaveklasse

Explanations and translations of technical terms see facing page.

Legend

Almene gymnasiale uddannelser — General upper secondary level; Higher commercial examination (HH)*, upper secondary schools; adult upper secondary level courses; higher preparatory examination (HF).
Erhvervsrettede gymnasiale uddannelser — Vocational upper secondary level; basic vocational education courses (EFG), apprenticeship training; basic technical courses (technicans and others).
Folkeskolen — Primary and lower secondary school.
Forskolen — Pre-school establishments.
1.-9./10. klassetrin — 1st-9th/10th class.
KVU = Korte videregående uddannelser — Short-cycle courses.
LVU = Lange videregående uddannelser — Long-cycle courses.
MVU = Mellemlange videregående uddannelser — Medium-cycle courses.
Ungdomsuddannelser — Youth education.
Videregående uddannelser — Post-secondary education.
Vuggestue, Børnehave, Børnehaveklasse — Crèche; kindergarten; pre-schooling.

* Højere handelseksamen kan tages enten som en 2-årig overbygning efter en erhvervsrettet gymnasial uddannelse eller som en 1-årig overbygning efter en almen gymnasial uddannelse.

* The higher commerical examination is either taken after a two-year supplementary course following the vocational upper secondary level or after a one-year supplementary course following the general upper secondary level.

Federal Republic of Germany

Organization of higher education

The Federal Republic of Germany consists of the States of Baden-Württemberg, Bavaria, Bremen, Hamburg, Hesse, Lower Saxony, North Rhine-Westphalia, Rhineland-Palatinate, Saarland and Schleswig-Holstein. Berlin has special four-power status.

The responsibility for educational policy and planning in the Federal Republic of Germany is determined by its federative governmental structure. According to the constitution of the Federal Republic of Germany, the individual States are responsible for most of the education system whereas only individual specified areas of responsibility are assigned to the Federal Government. Its responsibilities comprise the decree containing guidelines for the general principles of higher education (*see Hochschulrahmengesetz* (HRG) in glossary), the promotion of research, financial assistance for students, vocational training outside schools and vocational guidance.

The building of institutions of higher education, educational planning, and the support/promotion of supra-regional research institutions are considered to be the joint responsibility of Federation and *Länder*.

As a rule, higher education establishments are public institutions of the individual States; they have a right to self-government within the framework of the law. Their statutes require approval from the responsible state ministry. There are also church higher education establishments and a few private institutions.

The functions of higher education institutions, in keeping with the purposes assigned to them, include the cultivation and development of science and arts through research, teaching and studies. They are intended to prepare students for professional occupations requiring the application of scientific knowledge and methods or ability in the creative arts. Their functions also include the encouragement of young talent in the sciences and arts as well as scientific-academic further training which will gain ever more importance over the coming years.

Types of higher education institutions

There are at present in the Federal Republic of Germany 243 State and State-recognized higher education institutions. They can be divided as follows:

1. universities and equivalent higher education institutions such as technical universities, *Gesamthochschulen*, special subject colleges, e.g. colleges of medicine, sports academies, academies for postgraduate, administrative studies, colleges of philosophy and theology (Catholic) and colleges of theology (Protestant) as well as teacher training colleges;
2. colleges of art and music;
3. *Fachhochschulen*.

The courses of study offered by the universities and the *Technische Hoch-*

D

schulen/Universitäten and *Gesamthochschulen* include, as a rule, the subject areas of philology and cultural studies, law, economics and social sciences, mathematics, natural sciences, medicine, agricultural, forest and food sciences, engineering, fine arts and sports.

The courses of study offered by the *Universitäten- Gesamthochschulen,* which exist in two of the states, include university and *Fachhochschule* courses, and occasionally courses in art. They offer courses of varying length and with different final examinations.

Pädagogische Hochschulen/Erziehungswissenschaftliche Hochschulen, which exist in only three of the States, provide training for primary and lower secondary school teachers and for special education. Otherwise, teacher training takes place at universities, *Technische Universitäten/Hochschulen, Gesamthochschulen* as well as *Kunsthochschulen* and *Musikhochschulen* (art and music colleges).

Kunst- und Musikhochschulen and the corresponding subject areas in the universities and *Gesamthochschulen* provide training in the fine and the performing arts, and also in music subjects.

Fachhochschulen have the task of preparing students for later professions which require the application of academic knowledge and methods, or ability in the creative arts by means of practice-oriented teaching on an academic or artistic basis. They offer shorter courses above all for engineers, and in the areas of economics, social services, agriculture and the creative arts.

Besides the above-named public higher education institutions, there are special forms of higher education (e.g. the Federal Armed Forces and *Fachhochschulen* within the administration service), which are not considered in the following.

Distance learning

At all of the previously mentioned institutions of higher education, the studies are undertaken as full-time studies with compulsory attendance. In some subjects, however, it is also possible to undertake further and continued training through distance learning. By comparison with some of the neighbouring States, distance learning is at present quantitatively only poorly developed in the Federal Republic of Germany. Such courses are offered by public and private sector institutions of higher education and by some commercial distance-teaching institutes.

The possibility of gaining a higher education degree ist currently only offered by the Distance University of Hagen *(Fernuniversität/Gesamthochschule Hagen)* (with 38 000 students) and the Higher Education Institution for the Employed in Rendsburg (*Hochschule für Berufstätige, Rendsburg*), a State-recognized Polytechnical College concluding with the degree of *Diplom-Betriebswirt* and *Diplom-Wirtschaftsingenieur*. For applicants with a certificate of aptitude for higher education or polytechnical studies (*Hochschul- or Fachhochschulreife*) *Diplom* degrees are currently being offered by the *Fernuniversität-Gesamthochschule Hagen* in mathematics, economics, computer sciences and electrical engineering as well as newly-developed degree programmes with temporally-staged degrees (for full-time studies generally after six or eight semesters).

Moreover, there is the opportunity at the Distance University in Hagen to achieve a *Magister* degree (MA) in some subject combinations. The requirements for admission to this course of study are a general or subject-related certificate of aptitude for higher education study.

The range of study courses at the Distance University may also be taken advantage of by Germans living abroad or by foreigners. For students with sight deficiencies, a considerable portion of the range of courses is available in braille. For a course of studies at the Distance University and the study materials, full-time students must reckon with fees of about DM 300 on average per semester. For part-time students the fees are correspondingly lower.

A catalogue of distance teaching and distance studies published by the Federal Institute for Vocational Training (*Bundesinstitut für Berufsbildung*) on behalf of the Federal Minister for Education and Science will inform interested persons on the range of distance studies/distance teaching in the Federal Republic of Germany.

Student statistics

During the winter semester of 1988/89, 1 470 500 students were enrolled at higher education institutions in the Federal Republic of Germany, 343 732 (23.4%) of which were at *Fachhochschulen*. The percentage of foreign students amounted to 5.9% or 86 700 students, of which 16 000 were at *Fachhochschulen*. A total of 19 500 or 24% of all foreign students in 1987/88 came from Member States of the European Community.

The student statistics in Appendix 3 are broken down according to country of origin, type of higher education institution and subject area.

Organization and validation of courses

The academic year is divided into a winter semester and a summer semester at all higher education institutions. Particularly in technical and science subjects, students can only begin their studies in the winter semester at many higher education establishments.

For every course, the examination regulations stipulate a period of time within which students should complete their studies. This states how long it takes for students to pass the exam they are aiming at in a particular course. For university courses, this is usually eight or nine semesters; for the study of medicine, it is six years and three months. After completion of the study of medicine, a practical training period of 18 months' duration must be served. The general period of study is often one or two years longer than the recommended period. At *Fachhochschulen* the stipulated duration of studies — six semesters (without practicals) and eight semesters for degree programmes with integrated practical

D

semesters — is as a rule only insignificantly overstepped.

Studies at higher education institutions are generally divided into two different stages. Stage I (*Grundstudium*) usually consisting of four semesters and of two to four semesters at *Fachhochschulen* ends with an intermediate examination *(Zwischenprüfung)*. Stage II *(Hauptstudium)* ends with the final examination.

Depending on the course, studies terminate either with a State examination or some other higher education examination. In addition, church examinations can also be taken after a course of theological studies at a university. In a way, they correspond to the State examination in other subjects.

In some subjects, studies end with a *Staatsprüfung* (State examination), i.e. an examination for which the State lays down the required standards, e.g. doctors, veterinarians, dentists, teachers, lawyers, pharmacists and food chemists. State examinations are administered by a State examining board, part of which is comprised of higher education teaching staff.

Higher education institutions are authorized by law to administer examinations leading to higher education degrees. The most important are the *Diplom, Magister* and *Doktor*. Generally *Diplom* degrees are granted in engineering, economics, social sciences and natural sciences. In *Diplom* courses, emphasis is placed on one subject.

Particularly in modern languages and cultural studies, sometimes also in social sciences and economics, courses are offered which lead to the *Magister* examination. *Magister* courses enable students to combine several separate subjects, as a rule two major subjects or one major subject with two subsidiaries.

At universities and equivalent institutions of higher education with the right to confer doctorates (technical colleges/universities, colleges of education, and *Gesamthochschulen)* studies can be continued after the *Staatsexamen,* the *Diplomprüfung,* or the *Magisterprüfung* with postgraduate studies which lead to the *Promotion* (doctoral degree). The *Promotion* requires students to have obtained a particularly good qualification in their first degree examinations. Apart from students studying medicine and chemistry only a relatively small number of students in the Federal Republic of Germany go on to study for a doctorate after acquiring the degree necessary for their future occupation. The doctorate ist obtained on the basis of an independently written doctoral thesis, for which, as a rule, two to four years of study after the first degree and an oral examination are needed. As a rule, a doctoral candidate must have studied at least two semesters at the institution in question. The department of the university in question (i.e. *Fakultät*) decides whether an academic degree taken abroad is sufficient for acceptance as a doctoral candidate. Questions concerning taking a doctorate are dealt with by the *Promotionsordnung* of the relevant *Fakultät* or *Fachbereich* (department).

The subjects offered at *Fachhochschulen* correspond in part to those at universities and other higher education institutions. Studies there, however, differ from university studies in that they are more strongly practice-oriented, the duration of studies is shorter, and in some States there are additional practical training semesters incorporated into the course of study. Studies end with a final or degree examination. The *Diplom* with the adjunct 'FH' *(Fachhochschule)* is awarded after this examination has been passed.

Postgraduate studies

Numerous institutions of higher education offer postgraduate, supplementary and complementary programmes (graduate studies) in individual subjects. These graduate studies serve professional qualification, the specialization or in-depth study of the basic study stage subject. The form of certification for successful participation ranges from certificates of supplementary examinations in the field of teacher training to academic degrees *(Diplom, Magister, Lizentiat)*. A higher education degree may only be gained in a part (40 %) of the further training range of study courses. Thus, for example, at the University of the Saarland German and foreign law graduates may gain a European Certificate in a one-year course on European Integration, and with a further six months may gain a *Magister* in European Law. At present the number of universities that offer postgraduate courses for foreign law graduates has grown to 16. Further examples of graduate programmes with an international orientation are the courses in International Economic Relations at the University of Mannheim and the University of Konstanz, International Marketing at the *Fachhochschule* Reutlingen and European Environmental Science at Kaiserslautern, Trier and Saarbrücken. An overview of the subjects on offer can be found in *Studien- und Berufswahl 1988/89*, (see bibliography). More detailed information about courses which may be of interest to Third World students is given in a publication of the *Deutsche Stiftung für Internationale Entwicklung* (see bibliography).

Moreover, graduate courses are to be increasingly established at special graduate colleges *(Graduiertenkollegs)* and graduate courses over the next few years. The graduate colleges are institutes belonging to institutions of higher education aimed to promote research and young scientific-academic graduates (doctorate candidates) in thematically defined research groups. By contrast, graduate courses are short courses (ranging from a weekend to two to three weeks) also serving an intensive scientific-academic exchange of ideas between doctorate candidates and higher education lecturers and professors on a thematically limited research field.

D

Admission and registration

Initial information

Students wishing to take up a course of study in the Federal Republic of Germany should, before leaving their home countries, acquire all necessary information. By doing this, students can avoid difficulties later in their studies.

Information on studying in the Federal Republic of Germany can be obtained from the German diplomatic missions abroad, the branch offices of the DAAD or the DAAD central office in Bonn, the Goethe Institutes abroad and the *Akademisches Auslandsamt* or the administrative office of the higher education institution at which the student wishes to study (for addresses see Appendix 1).

Entry requirements

The prerequisite for admission to higher education studies in the Federal Republic of Germany is basically achieved through a secondary school-leaving certificate which establishes aptitude for higher education. For the admission of German applicants, a differentiation is made between the following types of higher education admission prerequisites:

(i) the general certificate of aptitude for higher education *(Allgemeine Hochschulreife)*, which confers the right to study at all higher education institutions without limitations in certain subjects or subject areas;

(ii) the subject-related certificate of aptitude for higher education *(Fachgebundene Hochschulreife)*, which confers the right to study the subjects listed in the certificate at universities and equivalent higher education institutions as well as at the polytechnics *(Fachhochschulen)*;

(iii) The *Fachoberschul*-certificate of aptitude for higher education *(Fachhochschulreife)* entitles the holder to study at *Fachhochschulen* and at the university-level *Universitäts-Gesamthochschulen* in North-Rhine Westphalia as well as at the *Gesamthochschule* in Kassel for the newly established diploma degree programmes with temporally staged degrees.

The general or subject-related certificate of aptitude for higher education is awarded after 13 school years of progress at the end of the upper secondary stage of a *Gymnsasium* or of a vocationally-related training course at an upper secondary level, also leading to the general certificate of aptitude for higher education. Upper secondary evening institutes *(Abendgymnasien)* for the employed and institutes preparing students for higher education *(Kollegs)* as well as examinations to determine the aptitude for higher education of particularly-gifted employed persons represent additional possibilities for gaining the general certificate of aptitude for higher education. The certificate of aptitude for *Fachhochschul*-studies is usually awarded after

12 years of concurrent, progressive schooling and is generally gained at the *Fachoberschulen*. The certificate of aptitude for study at a *Fachhochschule* may also be gained by taking a supplementary programme at specialized vocational schools *(Berufsfachschulen)* as well as at the technical colleges *(Fachschulen)* (see diagram and glossary in Appendices). In principle, the general and, in most cases, the subject-related certificates of aptitude for higher education entitle the holder to study at a *Fachhochschule*. Furthermore, some *Fachhochschulen* additionally require proof of a preliminary practical related to the desired training area. Depending on subject orientation, its duration may range from six weeks to 12 months.

At the colleges of art and music *(Kunst- und Musikhochschulen)* proof of artistic ability is required in addition to the certificate of aptitude for higher education. In exclusively artistic degree courses, that means not those leading to a teaching qualification, studies are possible without the certificate of aptitude for higher education in most of the *Länder* if exceptional artistic ability can be proven. A further exception is formed by the sports-practical aptitude tests for the study of sport, which is, however, not required by all institutions of higher education for courses leading to qualification as a sports teacher or sports scientist.

The requirements for the admission of *foreign* applicants to universities, technical universities/institutions of higher education, teacher training colleges/colleges of education *(Universitäten, Technische Universitäten/Hochschulen, Pädagogischen/Erziehungswissenschaftlichen Hochschulen/Gesamthochschulen)* is a foreign certificate of higher education aptitude which has been recognized as equivalent to the German certificate of general aptitude for higher education.

Proof of previous education in EC Member States which represents the higher education aptitude certificate in those countries is as a rule recognized as being equivalent to the general certificate of higher education aptitude. However, the required language proficiency must be additionally proven. Secondary school-leaving certificates from EC Member States which only entitle holders to university studies in certain subjects are as a rule recognized as equivalent to the German subject-related certificate of aptitude for higher education. With regard to the precise degree of subject related limitation, foreign applicants are advised to turn to the higher education institution at which they wish to take up their studies.

For foreign students applying to the *Fachhochschule* the following is in force: as a rule those are entitled to admission to a *Fachhochschule* whose certificate would also entitle the holder to admission to a course of study at a German university, technical university/institution of higher education and *Gesamthochschule*. Frequently a subject-related preliminary practical is also required as a requirement for a course of study at the *Fachhochschulen*, as mentioned above.

Due to the different arrangements in each country, students are urgently advised to inquire in good time at the

Fachhochschule of their choice. Prior to admission to degree courses in the arts or sport, foreigners, as well as Germans, must under certain circumstances take an aptitude examination.

Students from EC countries must meet three requirements if they wish to study in the Federal Republic of Germany:

1. They must have a document proving that their prior education entitles them to study at a university in their home country or that they have actually been granted admission.
2. They must have a good knowledge of German, to be proven by examinations.
3. There must be a secure financial basis for their studies.

In certain courses of study, a *Praktikum* (period of practical training) must be completed before beginning with studies or by the third semester on a regular basis in the periods between terms.

Limitations

In some courses of study, which make up only a relatively small part of the overall number of courses offered, there are admission restrictions *(numerus clausus)* for German first-year students at all higher education institutions in the Federal Republic of Germany. In these degree courses (currently architecture, business administration, biology, forestry, home economics and nutritional sciences, computer science, food chemistry, medicine, pharmacy, psychology, veterinary science and political economy between 6 and 8 % of the study places available have been reserved for foreign first-time students.

Foreign students apply as a rule to the higher education institution of their choice.

If the number of foreign applicants is greater than the number of places available, a selection procedure has to be employed for the applicants. The main criterion in this selection procedure is the applicant's qualification (the grades on the secondary school leaving certificate). Special circumstances in favour of an applicant's being admitted can also be considered in the course of the selection procedure.

Foreign applicants with a German certificate of aptitude for higher education are subject to special regulations. Further information on this procedure may be found in the ZVS-Info sheet, published by the Central Office for the Allocation of Places in Higher Education *(Zentralstelle für die Vergabe von Studienplätzen (ZVS))* (see bibliography).

In addition to these nationwide admission restrictions, there are local restrictions in a few other courses of study at individual higher education institutions. Information on this can be obtained from the higher education institutions themselves.

In those subjects in which there is no *numerus clausus*, there is no admission quota for foreign students. There are no quotas for foreigners from specific countries, so that the higher education institutions are free to decide on the admission of foreigners within the limitations of available places.

Some subjects or courses of study at *Fachhochschulen* are also subject to admission restrictions. This is often the case for the technical and economic subject orientations.

Recognition of foreign certificates and degrees

Agreements on reciprocal recognition or accreditation of periods of study, courses and examinations, exist between the Federal Republic of Germany and France (10 July 1980 and 27 October 1986) and with the Netherlands (23 March 1980), as well as with the Republic of Austria (19 January 1983). An agreement with the Republic of Italy has been drafted. Agreements with other countries, which are not members of the EC, are being prepared.

Responsibility for the recognition and accreditation of foreign certificates of education lies with:

1. Certificates from general education and vocational schools (except in the case of admission to higher education) should be presented to the responsible ministries of education and cultural affairs (see addresses in Appendix 1).
2. Application for admission to higher education studies (first semester) should be addressed to the university or *Fachhochschule* chosen *(Akademisches Auslandsamt* or *Studentensekretariat).*
3. Applications for accreditation of courses already taken towards a degree course at a German institution are decided on by the *Fakultät (Fachbereich)* in question. In the case of courses of study involving medical, pharmaceutical, or education degrees, responsibility lies with the *Landesprüfungsamt* (local *Länder* examination board) for medicine, the *Landesprüfungsamt* for pharmacy or the respective *Prüfungsamt* at the institution in question and in the case of law courses with the *Justizprüfungsamt* (examination board for law).

The higher education establishment in question has to decide whether foreign qualifications allow students to take up their studies in Germany. In case of doubt, recognition must be obtained from special offices in the state ministries for education and science or in offices indicated by them. Anyone wishing recognition in the Federal Republic of Germany of an academic degree or certificate acquired abroad should apply to the State authority responsible for the subject area in question.

Entry examinations

Applicants from EC countries having a secondary school leaving certificate which entitles them to admission to higher education studies in their home country or who have already been admitted to a course of study at a university in their home country are, as a rule, not subject to an entry examination *(Feststellungsprüfung).*

However, all higher education institutions make admission to studies or registration dependent upon passing a German language test (see 'Knowledge of the language of instruction').

D

Foreign applicants whose secondary school leaving certificates have not been recognized as equivalent to the German certificate of aptitude for higher education are required to take the so-called *Feststellungsprüfung*, an entry examination. Students may attend a *Studienkolleg*, an institute at which applicants are prepared for higher education.

Application and registration

1. Application

Foreign students wishing to apply for admission should send an *Antrag auf Zulassung zum Studium und auf Immatrikulation* (in German) to the higher education institution in question. The application must be made by all students wishing to enrol regardless of whether they are first-year students or are continuing their studies in the Federal Republic of Germany.

Foreign students will receive application forms and information concerning admission upon request from the *Akademische Auslandsämter* or secretariats of the institutions of higher education. They can also acquire them from diplomatic or consular missions of the Federal Republic of Germany abroad or from the branch offices of the *Deutscher Akademischer Austauschdienst (DAAD)*.

Foreign and stateless applicants will find all necessary information in the leaflet called 'Zulassungsinformation für ausländische und staatenlose Studienbewerber' (see bibliography).

An application for admission should always be made as early as possible. Only if it arrives before the closing date for applications can the institution point out deficiencies in the application for admission or the documents to the applicant. The closing date for the receipt of applications and all the necessary documents is:

1. 15 July for the following winter semester (beginning 1 October);
2. 15 January for the following summer semester (beginning 1 April).

The date stamped on the application upon receipt by the higher education institution is decisive. These dates also represent the final deadlines for submitting documents possibly still missing. For this reason it is very important, that the time it takes for mail to arrive be considered, especially if the application and documents are sent from abroad.

Information on application dates and on the beginning of term can be obtained from the *Akademische Auslandsämter*.

The higher education institutions coordinate their admission decisions concerning courses with a limited number of places, i.e. medicine, dentistry, veterinary medicine, pharmacy and psychology, before notifying applicants. Applicants requesting admission to more than one higher education institution will receive only one reply. Applicants with important reasons for wanting to study at a particular higher education institution should mention these in their applications. Otherwise, applicants have no influence on the decision as to which of the universities they have applied to will admit them.

A longer time-span can lie between the closing date for applications and notification of the student in the form of a letter of acceptance or rejection; letters of acceptance are usually not sent out until only a few weeks before the semester begins, so that the period of time between the date of arrival of a notification of acceptance and the necessary date of departure may possibly be very short. The notification of acceptance includes information about the matriculation date and necessary documents.

Classes begin in the winter semester in early October/November and end in mid/late February; summer semester courses begin in early April/May, ending in mid/late July. Numerous *Fachhochschulen* and some universities have their curricula organized in such a way that it is only possible to begin with studies in the winter semester. Precise information can be obtained from the higher education institutions themselves. Students interested in enrolling in the winter semester should apply in the period from May to June (at some *Fachhochschulen* the application deadline is in May!); those interested in enrolling in the summer semester should apply in the period from November to January.

Foreign students wishing to continue their studies in the Federal Republic of Germany must observe the following: academic and examination results from abroad entitle the student to begin his studies in an advanced semester in the Federal Republic of Germany only if these results are given recognition by the German higher education institution concerned.

Applicants should apply early for this recognition to the higher education institution in question, or, as the case may be, to some other responsible authority.

If the application is rejected, the applicant will not be able to enrol in a course of study until the next term (see 'Recognition of foreign certificates and degrees') and then only in the first semester of a course.

2. Registration

The closing dates for registration at the respective institutions of higher education must be observed for all degree programmes. The applicants can only be registered at a higher education institution in the Federal Republic of Germany if they possess a letter of admission. All students must appear in person for *Immatrikulation* (registration).

Foreign students must present the following documents:

1. the letter of acceptance from the higher education institution in question or in exceptional cases from the *Zentralstelle für die Vergabe von Studienplätzen* (see under 'limitations');
2. the originals of school and university certificates sent to the higher education institution as certified copies;
3. the originals of certified translations sent to the higher education institution as part of the application for admission;
4. a certificate of exmatriculation or proof of leave from study if the applicant was previously enrolled at a different higher education institution either in the Federal Republic of Germany or abroad;

5. the results of the university entrance examination *(Feststellungsprüfung)* if one was taken,
6. proof of sufficient financial means (a bank guarantee or the letter of a private individual who is willing to guarantee the financing of the applicant's studies);
7. travel document or identity card with valid residence permit;
8. a certificate of registration from the local resident registration office;
9. a health certificate issued by the local public health authority;
10. certificate of sufficient coverage from a German medical health insurance scheme (e.g. AOK); students from EC Member States must submit evidence of sufficient insurance coverage in their country of origin;
11. receipt proving the student has paid the semester contribution for the *Studentenwerk* (student welfare organization);
12. if required, certificate proving completion of the required period of practical experience for the specific course of study;
13. four passport-size photos.

The foreign applicant becomes a student at a higher education institution in the Federal Republic of Germany, and can obtain a student identity card, only upon completing *Immatrikulation* (registration).

Tuition fees

The paying of registration, tuition and examination fees is not required of German and foreign students at higher education institutions in the Federal Republic of Germany. (Some private institutions are an exception to this rule.)

However, all registered students are required to pay a *Sozialbeitrag* or an *Studentenwerksbeitrag.* This varies from place to place and amounts to between DM 30 and DM 50 per semester.

If there is an *Allgemeiner Studentenausschuß (AStA)* (a student committee) at the higher education institution in question, a student union fee must be paid which is either included in the social fee or is charged separately. This fee at present amounts to about DM 10 (see 'Student organizations').

Knowledge of the language of instruction, language courses and other courses

Lectures, classes and seminars are held in German. A good knowledge of German is thus indispensable for studies in the Federal Republic of Germany.

All higher education institutions make admission or registration dependent upon passing a German language test which, as a rule, is administered by the higher education institutions themselves and must be taken before commencing studies. Its degree of difficulty corresponds, at least, to the level of the *Zentrale Mittelstufenprüfung* of the Goethe Institute or comparable courses.

Graduates of German-French secondary schools have the same status as German applicants and are thus generally exempted from the language test. At some German schools abroad, the German language diploma (language diploma II) of the KMK (*Kultusministerkonferenz*) can be taken, which also gives exemption from the language test. In the same way, the Minor German Language Diploma (*Kleines Deutsches Sprachdiplom*) awarded by the Goethe Institute represents the level of exemption from the language test.

German language courses are held at numerous foreign universities, at the Goethe Institutes and German cultural institutes abroad. Information can be obtained from the diplomatic and consular missions of the Federal Republic of Germany abroad as well as the Goethe Institutes or the German cultural institutes abroad (for addresses see Appendix 1).

If it is not possible for applicants to attend a German language course in their home country, they may enrol on a course at one of the teaching centres of the Goethe Institute (fees) in the Federal Republic of Germany (for addresses see Appendix 1), or on a course at the higher education establishment they have chosen, in order to learn German. Information can be obtained from the *Akademisches Auslandsamt* (Foreign students' office) of the chosen university. However, attending a language course at a German higher education establishment does not automatically give the student the right of admission to studies.

At the higher education institutions in the Federal Republic of Germany language courses are offered for foreign students in the form of summer holiday courses, pre-study courses, and courses accompanying regular studies. Details on this are contained in the brochure published by the *Deutscher Akademischer Austauschdienst* (German Academic Exchange Service — DAAD) called 'Dokumentation Deutsch als Fremdsprache', and the DAAD brochure ('Hochschulferienkurse und Feriensprachkurse — Bundesrepublik Deutschland', see bibliography).

D

Financial assistance and scholarships

(a) The financing of studies under the *Bundesausbildungsförderungsgesetz*: German citizens and, under certain circumstances, also foreigners who do not have sufficient financial means to cover living and study costs from other sources (in particular their parents' income) are entitled to financial assistance for their studies under the *Bundesausbildungsförderungsgesetz* (Federal Financial Assistance to Education Act) or BAföG, as it is generally referred to. Students have a legal right to this form of assistance. About one fifth of German students receive payments in accordance with the BAföG. This support covers all of the time regarded as normal for studies in this subject (*Regelstudienzeit*).

The amount of assistance per month depends on the financial circumstances of the student and the relatives who are liable for financial support. Financial assistance is also given during holidays to cover the students' needs. Students who do not live with their parents can receive up to DM 845 per month (DM 725 for their living expenses, DM 45 for national health insurance and up to DM 75 rent subsidy). The financial assistance is granted as an interest-free loan. How the loan is repaid is dependent on social and financial factors. Information about the procedure for applying for grants, and the conditions students must fulfil in order to get them can be obtained from the *Amt für Ausbildungsförderung* (student administration offices for financial assistance) within the *Studentenwerk*.

Studies abroad can be financed if at least partly they can be recognized as part of the stipulated period of study, or if studies in the Federal Republic of Germany cannot be undertaken because of admission restrictions. These possibilities also apply to EC foreigners with the exception of studies in the country of origin.

As a rule, grants for studies abroad cover one year; with subjects that have admissions restrictions, grants beyond the one-year limit are only given when the studying period is carried out in Europe. A practical period of study which is laid down within the framework of the studies can also be financed if there is a guarantee that this will be recognized by a higher education establishment in the Federal Republic of Germany. The supplementary grants given under the German requirements clause, as well as fees and travel costs necessary for attending foreign education establishments, are given as a subsidy and do not have to be paid back later.

According to the BAföG, foreigners can also be given grants for studying in the Federal Republic of Germany for the whole of their studies, if they have the same legal status as German citizens. This is the case, if the foreigner in question:

1. is stateless;
2. has his usual residence in the Federal Republic of Germany and as a result of the *Asylverfahrensgesetz* (law concerning political asylum) has been recognized as entitled to political asylum or as a refugee under Section 1 of the law concerning measures for refugees received within the framework of humanitarian relief action;
3. has permanent residence in the Federal Republic of Germany or Berlin (West) and one parent is German;
4. is the child of parents of EC Member State citizenship who are or have been employed in the Federal Republic of Germany including Berlin (West) and is thus granted freedom of movement or residence under the *Aufenthaltsgesetz*/EWG (law concerning the residence of EC member country nationals).

BAföG assistance will only be granted to other foreigners:

1. if they have lived for five years in the Federal Republic of Germany or Berlin (West) prior to beginning their studies and have been legally employed during that period;
2. if at least one parent has been resident in the Federal Republic of Germany or Berlin (West) for a total of three years in the six years previous to the beginning of higher education and has been legally working there; otherwise a grant can be awarded from the point during the course of the students' education when these conditions are, in fact, fulfilled.

This regulation is currently undergoing modification for migrant workers from EC Member States on the basis of a verdict of the European Court. A change in the law is to be expected in the course of 1990. Information may be obtained from the *Akademische Auslandsämter* or secretariats of the institutions of higher education as well as the Offices for Educational Promotion (*Ämter für Ausbildungsförderung*).

(b) Scholarships for particularly gifted students from the *Begabtenförderungswerke* (foundation for the furtherance of particularly talented students): Particularly gifted students, also if they are in the same group defined under section (a) above can, as a rule, receive a scholarship (supplement) from the *Begabtenförderungswerke*. The *Begabtenförderungswerke* themselves decide which students they will award grants to. The level of support is income-related. Of the eight *Begabtenförderungswerke*, four are connected to the main political parties, two are connected to the two churches (Protestant and Catholic churches), one is a trade union institution, and the largest, the *Studienstiftung des deutschen Volkes*, is politically and ideologically neutral. All of

D

the *Begabtenförderungswerke* also give grants for doctorate candidates. Students are recommended to contact one of the tutor representatives in the higher education establishment where they want to study, before making an application.

As a rule names and addresses of these tutors can be found in the *Vorlesungsverzeichnis* (course catalogue) of the higher education establishment concerned.

(c) Grants from the Deutsche Akademische Austauschdienst (DAAD), the German Academic Exchange Service:

The DAAD offers students and younger academics scholarships for periods of basic or advanced study at German universities and other higher education institutions. DAAD scholarships are, as a rule, granted for a period of one year. They are available to applicants who have successfully completed at least two years of study in their home country. Applications should be submitted to the responsible educational authority of the country in question. Moreover, the DAAD is the national agency in the Federal Republic of Germany in the context of the EC Erasmus programme and grants Erasmus scholarships to German students. Information can be obtained from German diplomatic or consular missions in the applicant's home country as well as the branch office of the DAAD in Paris and London.

A list of further institutions in the Federal Republic of Germany which offer financial assistance to students is contained in the brochure called 'Der ausländische Student in der Bundesrepublik Deutschland' (see bibliography).

In certain cases, the higher education institutions in the Federal Republic of Germany are able to offer scholarships to students at higher education institutions abroad within the framework of partnership agreements. Information on such partnerships can be obtained from institutions of higher education in the applicant's home country or from German higher education establishments.

Entry and residence regulations

Specific regulations apply for entering the Federal Republic of Germany, depending on the person's country of origin.

There are no special entry formalities for nationals of other Member States of the EC. For study purposes, however, they need a residence permit, which is obtainable from the local aliens authority in Germany. To apply for a residence permit, students need a letter of admission from a German higher education institution and proof of sufficient financial means.

Nationals of other countries[1] require a residence permit in the form of a visa prior to entering the Federal Republic of Germany. Visas are available at the German diplomatic missions in the country of origin. It is recommended that applicants inquire with the German diplomatic mission in question early on, regarding regulations on entering the Federal Republic for educational purposes. A tourist visa cannot be converted to a residence permit of this kind once the applicant is in Germany.

As soon as foreign students have arrived in the Federal Republic of Germany, they must report their presence to the aliens authority responsible for their place of residence. They must also register with the aliens authority if they already have a residence permit from a diplomatic mission in their home country.

Students need to register their place of residence at the relevant *Einwohnermeldeamt*. If they should change addresses, they must report their new place of residence to the *Einwohnermeldeamt* within a week after moving. This also applies to changes of address within the same town.

Important: An extension of the residence permit must be applied for before it expires.

[1] Exept the Dominican Republic, Honduras, Liechtenstein, Monaco, Austria, Switzerland and the United States of America.

D

Social aspects

Social security and health insurance

Up until now, any student wishing to register was required to provide evidence of having taken out the legally prescribed medical insurance. Amendments to the law, however, envisage that from 1 April 1989 onwards students without proof of sufficient medical insurance may have themselves exempted from membership in an insurance scheme without the need to give any special reasons for this, and that the compulsory insurance cover with one of the statutory health insurance schemes for students is as a rule limited to 14 study semesters and at most up to the age of 30. Students who leave the statutory insurance scheme on account of this regulation may, however, continue to have health insurance, albeit at a higher cost, in the same health insurance scheme.

The monthly contribution for the statutory health insurance scheme at present amounts to about DM 64. Private health insurance companies also offer favourable student rates. Since the Federal Republic of Germany has concluded social insurance agreements with all EC Member States, students are advised to check first whether there is not already sufficient insurance cover.

More detailed information on questions concerning social security and medical insurance can be obtained from the social office of the student representation, the *Studentenwerk*, or the *Akademische Auslandsämter*.

Advisory services

At the universities, technical colleges/universities and *Gesamthochschulen* foreign students can go to the *Akademische Auslandsämter*, for advice. Foreign students also have access to student advisory services (*Zentrale Studienberatungsstelle, Studienbegleitende Fachberatung*). It is recommended that foreign students write to the *Akademisches Auslandsamt* of the higher education institution of their choice in order to clarify questions concerning study opportunities, courses of study, admission, recognition of foreign qualifications, etc., in writing if possible a year befor beginning their studies (for addresses, see Appendix 1). Students applying to other higher education institutions should direct their inquiries to the administrative offices of these institutions.

At the beginning of a course of study at a German higher education institution, a general advisory service to students is important. This includes orientation sessions held by the *Akademisches Auslandsamt* or administrative office at the higher education institution in question. At many institutions these offices provide information on how to fill in registration forms. General information and tips on how to organize one's studies can be obtained at introductory sessions for foreign first-year students. Here, students can also find out what formalities need to be observed during re-registration (*Rückmeldung*) or exmatriculation, which extra-curricular programmes are available at the institution, etc. German institutions of higher education do not give any careers advice or have job-placement services. The Labour Offices (*Arbeitsämter*) are responsible for this.

Student employment

Students from EC Member States are not required to have a work permit for employment in the Federal Republic of Germany. Students should be warned not to harbour illusions that their studies can be financed on the basis of part-time jobs. On the one hand, studies are tightly organized and, on the other, the present job-market situation narrowly restricts the possibilities of finding work.

Student organizations

In most States, apart from those of Baden-Württemberg and Bavaria, students automatically become members of a community referred to as the *Studentenschaft* (student body) upon registration. The way in which students are organized to look after their own interests in the individual higher education establishments is laid down differently by the various States. In most States, the student body is represented by the *Studentenparlament* (in Bremen the *Studentenrat*), or by the *Allgemeine Studentenausschuß* (AStA), the executive body of student self-administration. One of the AStA's functions is providing practical assistance to foreign students.

Membership in one of the various political groups at the higher education institutions and participation in their political work is open to all students.

The German Committee of the World University Service, which is represented at a number of higher education establishments, looks after the interests of foreign students.

The Catholic and Protestant Churches have established student community centres which are directed by student chaplains. Considerable attention is often devoted to meetings between German and foreign students.

Cost of living

The cost of living varies from location to location and in accordance with individual needs. On average, foreign students will have to reckon with spending about DM 850 per month, including rent and study materials.

Accommodation

German higher education institutions do not have the campus system in which all students are assured of accommodation upon registration. Student halls of residence do exist, but the majority of German and foreign students have to find their own accommodation themselves on the

D

open market. Thus foreign students should come to Germany to arrange accommodation as soon as possible after receiving their letter of acceptance, before the beginning of the semester. On account of the very high student numbers, it is at present, however, extremely difficult at many higher education institution locations. Like German students, foreign students must reckon with having to take a room in the suburbs and nearby surroundings.

It would be wise to stay in a youth hostel, a boarding house or some other cheap accommodation (list available from the *Akademisches Auslandsamt*) for a limited period of time until more adequate accommodation can be found. The *Auslandsämter, Studentenwerke* (see section 'Services for students') and other university services provide assistance.

The *Studentenwerke*, as well as religious and private organizations, have built *Studentenwohnheime* (student halls of residence) at almost all university locations so that about 10 % of all German and foreign students find a place in a hall of residence. Foreign students should thus inquire at the *Auslandsamt* or administrative office of the higher education institution they wish to attend about the possibility of finding accommodation in a student hall of residence. The selection of applicants takes place six months prior to the beginning of the semester. It is absolutely necessary to make inquiries and apply well in advance.

Rent in student residences depends on the size of the room and the conveniences it offers. Prices vary considerably at the various university locations, but the present range is generally between DM 180 and DM 200 a month.

In any case, the rent is considerably lower than on the private accommodation market where rent is dependent on the desired form of accommodation as well as on the higher education institution's location and ranges from DM 250 to DM 400 and in the large university cities rising rents are to be expected.

Information can be obtained from the *Akademische Auslandsämter*, the *Studentenwerke* or the student housing offices at the higher education institutions in question.

Services for students

At the institutions of higher education there are the so-called *Studentenwerke* (student welfare offices) which are regarded as legally independent establishments.

These are responsible for organizing social welfare services at higher education institutions. Thus they provide students with economic, social and medical assistance. In several of the States these *Studentenwerke* also represent the cultural interests of the students. Traditionally, *Studentenwerke* have three main areas of activity: financial assistance, meals and accommodation.

Students eat for the most part in the *Mensen* (student canteens) belonging to the institute of higher education where inexpensive meals (from DM 2) can be bought. The *Studentenwerke* also run cafeterias and refreshment rooms.

Substantial government subsidies are granted to the *Studentenwerke* to assist them in carrying out the services they provide.

German and foreign students receive a *Studentenausweis* upon registration at a German higher education institution and can, as a rule, use public transport (bus, tram) at reduced prices.

All students, regardless of whether or not they are sports students, can freely use the sports facilities of their higher education institution.

For further details reference should be made to the DAAD brochure 'Der ausländische Student in der Bundesrepublik Deutschland' (see bibliography), which is available in several languages.

Facilities for disabled students

As far as possible the same study conditions are to be created for disabled students as exist for non-disabled students.

Higher education institutions in the Federal Republic are only in part equipped to deal with the needs of handicapped students, particularly those with severe physical disabilities. In recent years, however, the situation has improved in many places.

In Bochum, Hannover, Heidelberg, Marburg and Regensburg there are residences with appropriate facilities for physically handicapped students. In addition, there are student residences equipped for wheelchair users at numerous locations. With regard to study achievements and examinations, disabled students are granted an appropriate disadvantage compensation. Information may be obtained from the Examination Offices (*Prüfungsämter*) or Examination Committees (*Prüfungsausschüsse*).

The central student welfare organization (*Deutsches Studentenwerk eV*) has established a counselling office for disabled applicants and students (D-5300 Bonn 1, Weberstr. 55, Telephone: (0228) 29 90 60). A brochure published by *Deutsches Studentenwerk,* entitled 'Behinderte studieren', provides practical information, including the names and telephone numbers of the counsellors for the disabled at the various higher education institutions (see bibliography).

D

Appendices

1. Addresses

German embassies in EC countries

Belgium
Botschaft der Bundesrepublik Deutschland
Avenue de Tervueren 190
B-1150 Bruxelles

Denmark
Botschaft der Bundesrepublik Deutschland
Stockholmsgade 57
DK-2100 København Ø

Greece
Botschaft der Bundesrepublik Deutschland
Vassilissis Sofias 10
POB 610
GR-15124 Amaroussio

Spain
Botschaft der Bundesrepublik Deutschland
Calle de Fortuny 8
E-28010 Madrid

France
Botschaft der Bundesrepublik Deutschland
13/15 avenue Franklin
D. Roosevelt
F-75008 Paris

Ireland
Botschaft der Bundesrepublik Deutschland
31 Trimleston Avenue
Booterstown
Blackrock, Co. Dublin

Italy
Botschaft der Bundesrepublik Deutschland
Via Po 25c
I-00198 Roma

Luxembourg
Botschaft der Bundesrepublik Deutschland
20-22 av. Émile Reuter
L-2420 Luxembourg

The Netherlands
Botschaft der Bundesrepublik Deutschland
Groot Hertoginnelaan 18-20
2517 EG 's-Gravenhage

Portugal
Botschaft der Bundesrepublik Deutschland
Campo dos Mártires
da Pátria 38
P-1100 Lisboa

United Kingdom
Botschaft der Bundesrepublik Deutschland
23 Belgrave Square
London SW1X 8PZ

DAAD central office and branch offices in EC countries

Deutscher Akademischer Austauschdienst (DAAD)
Kennedyallee 50
D-5300 Bonn 2
☎ (02) 28 88 21

Büro Berlin
Deutscher Akademischer Austauschdienst (DAAD)
Steinplatz 2
D-1000 Berlin 12
☎ (0 30) 31 04 61

Büro London
German Academic Exchange Service
17 Bloomsbury Square
London WC1A 2LP
☎ (01) 404 4065

Büro Paris
Office Allemand d'Échanges Universitaires
15, rue de Verneuil
F-75007 Paris
☎ 2 61 58 57

Maison Heinrich Heine
27C, bd Jourdan
F-75014 Paris
☎ 5 89 32 26

The DAAD branch offices also serve as contact offices for the Westdeutsche Rektorenkonferenz

Goethe-Institut: German-language teaching centres in the Federal Republic and German cultural institutes in EC countries

Goethe-Institut
Lenbachplatz 3
Postfach 20 1009
D-8000 München 2
☎ (0 89) 5 99 90

German-language training centres (Unterrichtsstätten)

(Unterrichtsstätten)
Knesebeckstr. 38-48
D-1000 Berlin 15

Helene-Pagès-Str. 9
D-5407 Boppard/Rhein

Kennedyallee 91-103
D-5300 Bonn 2

Fedelhören 78
D-2800 Bremen

Willi-Becker-Allee 10
D-4000 Düsseldorf

Barckhausstr. 1-3
D-6000 Frankfurt/Main

Schnewlinstr. 1
D-7800 Freiburg

Merkelstr. 4
D-3400 Göttingen

Stennerstraße 4
D-5860 Iserlohn/Westf.

Projektgruppe Kiel
Kleiner Kuhberg 2-4
D-2300 Kiel 1

Goethe-Institut
Ifflandstr. 2-6
D-6800 Mannheim 1

Goethe-Institut
Sonnenstr. 25
D-8000 München 2

Wasserburger Straße 54
D-8018 Grafing

Seidlstr. 17
D-8110 Murnau/Obb.

Goethestraße 1
D-8210 Prien/Chiemsee

Herrngasse 17
D-8803 Rothenburg o.d.T.

Am Spitalbach 8
D-7170 Schwäbisch Hall/Württ.

Rempart 7
D-7813 Staufen/Breisgau

Belgium
Goethe-Institut
Deutsche Bibliothek
rue Belliard 58
B-1040 Brussel
☎ 2 30 39 70

Denmark
Deutsches Kulturinstitut
Nørre Voldgade 106
DK-1358 København K.
☎ 01 13 34 54

Greece
Goethe-Institut
Omirou Str. 14-16
POB 30383
100 33 Athen
☎ 360 81 11/15

Goethe-Institut
Digeni Akrita 3
73100 Chania/Kreta
☎ 2 37 78

Goethe-Institut
Agiou Nikolaou 99
26225 Patras
☎ 27 34 46

Goethe-Institut
Leoforos Nikis 15/POB: 10268
54110 Thessaloniki
☎ 27 26 44/22 61 89, 23 91 69

Spain
Deutsches Kulturinstitut
Instituto Alemán de Cultura
Gran Via de les Corts Catalanes 591, 3º
08007 Barcelona
☎ 3 17 38 86/90
3 18 80 36/40

Deutsches Kulturinstitut
Instituto Alemán
Calle Zurbarán 21
28010 Madrid
☎ 4 19 32 35

France
Goethe-Institut
Centre Culturel Allemand
16ter, rue Boudet
F-33000 Bordeaux
☎ 44 67 06

Goethe-Institut
Centre Culturel Allemand
98, rue des Stations
F-59800 Lille
☎ 57 02 44/57 27 21

Goethe-Institut
Centre Culturel Allemand
16-18, rue François Dauphin
F-69002 Lyon
☎ 8 42 88 27

Goethe-Institut
Centre Culturel Allemand
171, rue de Rome
F-13006 Marseille
☎ 47 63 81

Goethe-Institut
Centre Culturel Allemand
39, rue de la Ravinelle
F-54052 Nancy
☎ 3 35 44 36

Goethe-Institut
Centre Culturel Allemand
17, avenue d'Iéna
F-75116 Paris
☎ 7 23 61 21

Goethe-Institut
6bis, rue Clémence Isaure
F-31000 Toulouse
☎ 23 08 34

Ireland
Goethe-Institut
37 Merrion Square
Dublin 2
☎ 61 11 55/61 11 56

Sprachabteilung
62 Fitzwilliam Square
Dublin 2
☎ 76 22 13

Italy
Goethe-Institut
Centro culturale tedesco
Salita Santa Caterina, 4
I-16123 Genova
☎ 58 10 11/54 27 88

Goethe-Institut
Centro culturale tedesco
Via San Paolo
I-20121 Milano
☎ 79 92 40/78 47 91, 78 34 74/79 58 13

Goethe-Institut
Palazzo Spalletti
Riviera di Chiaia 202
I-80121 Napoli
☎ 41 19 23/41 39 43

Goethe-Institut
Centro culturale tedesco
Via Vaccarini, 1
I-90143 Palermo
☎ 30 27 99/30 27 52

Goethe-Institut
Centro Culturale Tedesco
I-Via Savoia 15
I-00198 Roma
☎ 884 17 25

Goethe-Institut
Centro culturale tedesco
Via del Coroneo, 15
I-34133 Trieste
☎ 73 20 57/73 20 58

Goethe-Institut
Centro culturale tedesco
Piazza San Carlo 206
I-10121 Torino
☎ 5 57 52 26/54 38 30

D

Luxembourg
Thomas-Mann-Bibliothek
42 Boulevard Joseph II
L-1840 Luxembourg
☎ 45 31 04/45 31 05

The Netherlands
Goethe-Institut
Herengracht 470
1017 CA Amsterdam
☎ 23 04 21

Goethe-Institut
's-Gravendijkwal 50-52
3014 ED Rotterdam
☎ 436 54 11

Portugal
Goethe-Institut
Instituto Alemão
Campo dos Mártires
da Pátria 37
1198 Lisboa Codex
☎ 52 01 49/53 03 05/
54 90 73

Goethe-Institut
Instituto Alemão
Rua Alexandre Herculano
21 B
3000 Coimbra
☎ 2 69 25

Goethe-Institut
Instituto Alemão
Rua do Campo Alegre,
298-1°
P-4100 Porto
☎ 69 14 08

United Kingdom
Goethe Institute
3 Park Circus
74 Victoria Crescent Road
Glasgow G3 6AX
☎ 332 25 55

Goethe-Insitut London
50 Princes Gate
Exhibition Rd
London SW7 2PH
☎ 5 81 33 44/5 81 33 47

Goethe-Institut
Ridgefield House
14 John Dalton Street
Manchester M2 6JR
☎ 8 34 46 35

Goethe-Institut
The King's Manor
Exhibition Square
York Y01 2EP
☎ 61 11 22

State ministries responsible for academic affairs

Baden-Württemberg
Ministerium für Wissenschaft
und Kunst
Postfach 401
Königstraße 46
D-7000 Stuttgart 1
☎ (07 11) 2 00 31

Bayern
Bayerisches Staatsministerium
für Wissenschaft und Kunst
Salvatorplatz 2
D-8000 München
☎ (0 89) 2 18 61

Berlin
Der Senator für Wissenschaft
und Forschung
Bredtschneiderstraße 5-8
D-1000 Berlin 19
☎ (0 30) 3 03 21

Bremen
Der Senator für Bildung, Wissenschaft und Kunst
Rembertiring 8-12
D-2800 Bremen
☎ (04 21) 36 11

Hamburg
Freie und Hansestadt
Hamburg
Behörde für Wissenschaft und
Forschung
Postfach 5668
Hamburger Straße 37
D-2000 Hamburg 76
☎ (0 40) 29 18 81

Hessen
Hessisches Ministerium für
Wissenschaft und Kunst
Luisenplatz 10
D-6200 Wiesbaden
☎ (0 61 21) 36 80

Niedersachsen
Niedersächsisches Ministerium
für Wissenschaft und Kunst
Prinzenstraße 14
D-3000 Hannover
☎ (05 11) 12 01

Nordrhein-Westfalen
Der Minister für Wissenschaft
und Forschung des Landes
NRW
Völklinger Straße 49
D-4000 Düsseldorf
☎ (02 11) 3 03 21

Rheinland-Pfalz
Kultusministerium Rheinland-Pfalz
Postfach 3220
Mittlere Bleiche 61
D-6500 Mainz
☎ (0 61 31) 1 61

Saarland
Minister für Kultus, Bildung
und Wissenschaft
Postfach 1010
Hohenzollernstraße 60
D-6600 Saarbrücken
☎ (06 81) 50 31

Schleswig-Holstein
Kultusministerium Schleswig-Holstein
Düsternbrooker Weg 64-68
Landeshaus, Nebengebäude A
D-2300 Kiel
☎ (04 31) 59 61

Federal ministry

Bundesministerium für Bildung
und Wissenschaft
Heinemannstr. 2
D-5300 Bonn 2
☎ (02 28) 5 71

Kultusministerkonferenz

Sekretariat der Ständigen Konferenz der Kultusminister der
Länder in der Bundesrepublik
Deutschland
Postfach 2240
Nassestr. 8
D-5300 Bonn 1
☎ (02 28) 50 10

Westdeutsche Rektorenkonferenz (WRK)

Westdeutsche Rektorenkonferenz
Sekretariat
Ahrstr. 39
D-5300 Bonn 2
☎ (02 28) 37 69 11

Abbreviations and addresses of institutions of higher education

Abbreviations

ABK	Akademie der Bildenden Künste
DSH	Deutsche Sporthochschule
EuropWH	Europäische Wirtschaftshochschule
FernU	Fernuniversität
FH	Fachhochschule
FU	Freie Universität
GH	Gesamthochschule
HbK	Hochschule für bildende Kunst
HdK	Hochschule der Künste
HfB	Hochschule für Berufstätige
HfK	Hochschule für Künste
HFF	Hochschule für Fernsehen und Film
HfM	Hochschule für Musik
HfP	Hochschule für Politik
HfV	Hochschule für Verwaltungswissenschaften
HJS	Hochschule für Jüdische Studien
HS	Hochschule
HWP	Hochschule für Wirtschaft und Politik
H	Kirchliche Hochschule (evang.)
MeHo	Medizinische Hochschule
MeU	Medizinische Universität
PTH	Philosophische-Theologische Hochschule (kath.)
PTL	Physikalisch-Technische Lehranstalt
TH	Technische Hochschule
TiHo	Tierärtzliche Hochschule
TU	Technische Universität
U	Universität
U-GH	Universität-Gesamthochschule
WHU	Wissenschaftliche Hochschule für Unternehmensführung

Addresses

Universities, technical universities (Technische Hochschulen and Gesamthochschulen)

Aachen TH
Bergdriesch 37
D-5100 Aachen

Augsburg U
Universitätsstraße 2
D-8900 Augsburg

Bamberg U
Kapuzinerstr. 16
D-8600 Bamberg

Bayreuth U
Postfach 10 12 51
D-8580 Bayreuth

Berlin FU
Boltzmannstr. 3
D-1000 Berlin 33

Berlin TU
Straße des 17. Juni 135
D-1000 Berlin 12

Bielefeld U
Universitätsstr. 25
D-4800 Bielefeld

Bochum U
Postfach 10 21 48
D-4630 Bochum

Bonn U
Postfach 2220
D-5300 Bonn

Braunschweig TU
Konstantin-Uhde-Str. 16
D-3300 Braunschweig

Bremen U
Postfach 33 04 40
D-2800 Bremen 33

Clausthal TU
Postfach 1253
D-3392 Clausthal-Zellerfeld

Darmstadt TH
Karolinenplatz 5
D-6100 Darmstadt

Dortmund U
Postfach 50 05 00
D-4600 Dortmund 50

Düsseldorf U
Universitätsstr. 1
D-400 Düsseldorf

Duisburg U-GH
Lotharstr. 65
D-4100 Duisburg

Eichstätt U kath.
Ostenstr. 26
D-8078 Eichstätt

Erlangen-Nürnberg U
Postfach 3520
D-8520 Erlangen

Essen U-GH
Universitätsstr. 2
D-4300 Essen

Frankfurt U
Postfach 11 19 32
D-6000 Frankfurt 11

Freiburg U
Heinrich-v.-Stephan-Str. 25
D-7800 Freiburg

Gießen U
Ludwigstr. 23
D-6300 Gießen

Göttingen U
Burgstraße 51
D-3400 Göttingen

Hagen FernU-GH
Konkordiastr. 5
D-5800 Hagen

Hamburg U
Edmund-Siemers-Allee 1
D-2000 Hamburg 13

Hamburg-Harburg TU
Postfach 901403
D-2100 Hamburg 90

Hannover U
Welfengarten 1
D-3000 Hannover

Hannover MeHo
Konstanty-Gutschow-Str. 8
Hannover 61

Hannover TiHo
Bischofsholer Damm 15
D-3000 Hannover

Heidelberg U
Seminarstr. 2
D-6900 Heidelberg

Hildesheim HS
Marienburger-Platz 22
D-3200 Hildesheim

Hohenheim U
Postfach 70 05 62
D-7000 Stuttgart 70

Kaiserslautern U
Erwin-Schrödinger-Str.
D-6750 Kaiserlautern

Karlsruhe U
Postfach 83 80
D-7500 Karlsruhe

Kassel U-GH
Postfach
D-3500 Kassel

Kiel U
Olshausenstr. 40
D-2300 Kiel

Koblenz WHU
Wissenschaftliche Hochschule
für Unternehmensführung
Heerstraße 52 (Haus d'Ester)
5414 Vallendar

Köln U
Albertus-Magnus-Platz
D-5000 Köln

Konstanz U
Postfach 55 60
D-7750 Konstanz

Lübeck MeU
Ratzeburger Allee 160
D-2400 Lübeck

Lüneburg HS
Wilschenbrucher Weg 84
D-2120 Lüneburg

Mainz U
Postfach 39 80
D-6500 Mainz

Mannheim U
L 9, 7
D-6800 Mannheim

Marburg U
Biegenstr. 10
D-3550 Marburg

München U
Geschwister-Scholl-Platz 1
D-8000 München

München TU
Arcisstr. 21
D-8000 München

Münster U
Schloßplatz 2
D-4400 Münster

Oldenburg U
Postfach 25 03
D-2900 Oldenburg

Osnabrück U
Postfach 44 69
D-4500 Osnabrück

Paderborn U-GH
Postfach 16 21
D-4790 Paderborn

Passau U
Innstr. 29
D-8390 Passau

Regensburg U
Postfach 397
D-8400 Regensburg

Saarbrücken U
Im Stadtwald
D-6600 Saarbrücken

Siegen U-GH
Herrengarten 3
D-5900 Siegen

Stuttgart U
Postfach 10 60 37
D-7000 Stuttgart

Trier U
Postfach 3825
D-5500 Trier

Tübingen U
Wilhelmstr. 11
D-7400 Tübingen

Ulm U
Oberer Eselsberg
D-7900 Ulm

Witten-Herdecke U
Postfach 24 80
D-5810 Witten-Herdecke

Würzburg U
Sanderring 2
D-8700 Würzburg

Wuppertal U-GH
Gaußstr. 20
D-5600 Wuppertal

Church-related colleges

Berlin KH
Teltower Damm 120-122
D-1000 Berlin 37

Bethel KH
Remterweg 45
D-4800 Bielefeld 13

Neuendettelsau GH
Postfach 20
D-8806 Neuendettelsau

Oberursel KH
Altkönigstr. 150
D-6370 Oberursel

Wuppertal KH
Missionsstraße 9 b
D-5600 Wuppertal

Colleges of philosophy and theology

Benediktbeuren PTH
Don-Bosco-Str. 1
D-8174 Benediktbeuren

Frankfurt PTH
Offenbacher Landstr. 224
D-6000 Frankfurt 70

Fulda PTH
Domplatz 2
D-6400 Fulda

Hennef PTH
Waldstr. 9
D-5202 Hennef/Sieg

München PTH
Kaulbachstr. 33
D-8000 München

Münster PTH
Hörster Platz 5
D-4400 Münster

Paderborn PTH
Kamp 6
D-4790 Paderborn

Sankt Augustin PTH
Arnold-Janssen-Str. 30
D-5205 Sankt Augustin

Trier PTH
Jesuitenstr. 13
D-5500 Trier

Vallendar PTH
Pallottistr. 3
D-5414 Vallendar

Art colleges, academies

Berlin HdK
Postfach 12 67 20
D-1000 Berlin 12

Braunschweig HbK
Johannes-Selenka-Platz 1
Postfach 28 28
D-3300 Braunschweig

Bremen HfK
Am Wandrahm 23
D-2800 Bremen

Düsseldorf HbK Kunstakademie
Eiskellerstr. 1
D-4000 Düsseldorf

Frankfurt HbK
Dürerstr. 10
D-6000 Frankfurt

Hamburg HbK
Lerchenfeld 2
D-2000 Hamburg 76

Karlsruhe ABK
Reinhold-Frank-Str. 81-83
D-7500 Karlsruhe

München ABK
Akademiestr. 2
D-8000 München

Nürnberg ABK
Bingstr. 60
D-8500 Nürnberg

Offenbach HbK
Schloßstr. 31
D-6050 Offenbach

Stuttgart ABK
Am Weißenhof 1
D-7000 Stuttgart

Music colleges

Berlin HdK
Postfach 12 67 20
D-1000 Berlin 12

Bremen HfK
Am Wandrahm 23
D-2800 Bremen

Detmold HfM
Allee 22
D-4930 Detmold

Dortmund HfM[1]
Emil-Figge-Str. 44
D-4600 Dortmund

Münster HfM[1]
Ludgeriplatz 1
D-4400 Münster

Robert-Schumann-Hochschule HfM
Fischerstraße 110
D-4000 Düsseldorf

Essen HfM
Abtei
D-4300 Essen 16

Duisburg HfM[1]
Düsseldorfer Str. 19
D-4100 Duisburg

[1] The indented institutions are associated with the before-named university.

Frankfurt HfM
Eschersheimer Landstr. 29-39
D-6000 Frankfurt

Freiburg HfM
Schwarzwaldstr. 141
D-7800 Freiburg

Hamburg HfM
Harvestehuder Weg 12
D-2000 Hamburg 13

Hannover HfM
Emmichplatz 1
D-3000 Hannover

Heidelberg-Mannheim HfM
L 15, 16
D-6800 Mannheim

Karlsruhe HfM
Weberstr. 8
D-7500 Karlsruhe

Köln HfM
Dagobertstr. 38
D-5000 Köln

Aachen HfM[1]
Postfach 12 65
D-5100 Aachen

Wuppertal HfM[1]
Friedrich-Ebert-Str. 141
D-5600 Wuppertal-Elberfeld

Lübeck HfM
Gr. Petersgrube 17-29
D-2400 Lübeck

München HfM
Arcisstr. 12
D-8000 München 2

Saarbrücken HfM
Bismarckstr. 1
D-6600 Saarbrücken 3

Stuttgart HfM
Urbanplatz 2
D-7000 Stuttgart

Trossingen HfM
Schultheiß-Koch-Platz 5
D-7218 Trossingen

Würzburg HfM
Hofstallstr. 6-8
D-8700 Würzburg

D

Other institutions of higher education

Berlin EuropWH
Breitscheidplatz
Europa-Center
1000 Berlin 3

Hamburg HWP
Von-Melle-Park 9
D-2000 Hamburg 13

Heidelberg HJS
Friedrichstr. 9
D-6900 Heidelberg

Köln DSH
Postfach 45 03 27
D-5000 Köln 41

München HFF
Frankenthaler Straße 23
D-8000 München 90

München HfP
Ludwigstr. 8
D-8000 München 22

Speyer HfV
Postfach 14 09
D-6720 Speyer

Teacher training colleges

Baden-Württemberg

Freiburg PH
Kunzenweg 21
D-7800 Freiburg

Heidelberg PH
Keplerstr. 87
D-6900 Heidelberg

Karlsruhe PH
Bismarckstr. 10
Postfach 4960
D-7500 Karlsruhe

Ludwigsburg PH
Reuteallee 46
D-7140 Ludwigsburg

Schwäbisch Gmünd PH
Oberbrettringer Str. 200
D-7070 Schwäbisch Gmünd

Weingarten PH
Kirchplatz 2
D-7987 Weingarten

Rheinland-Pfalz

Koblenz
Abteilung der EWH Rheinland-Pfalz
Rheinau 3-4
D-5400 Koblenz

Landau
Abteilung der EWH Rheinland-Pfalz
Im Fort 7
D-6740 Landau

Schleswig-Holstein

Flensburg PH
Mürwiker Str. 77
D-2390 Flensburg

Kiel PH
Olshausenstr. 75
D-2300 Kiel

Addresses of Fachhochschulen *and other higher education institutions with* Fachhochschule *courses of study*

Baden-Württemberg

Aalen FH
Beethovenstr. 1
D-7080 Aalen

Biberach FH
Karlstr. 9-11
D-7950 Biberach

Eßlingen FH
für Sozialwesen
Flandernstr. 101
D-7300 Eßlingen

Eßlingen FH
für Technik
Kanalstr. 33
D-7300 Eßlingen

Freiburg FH
f. Sozialwesen, Religionspädagogik und Gemeindediakonie
Bugginger Str. 38
D-7800 Freibrug i. Br.

Kath. FH f. Sozialwesen und Religionspädagogik
Karlstr. 34
D-7800 Freibrug i. Br.

Furtwangen FH
Postfach 28
D-7743 Furtwangen 1

Heidelberg FH
der Stiftung Rehabilitation
Postfach 101 409
D-6900 Heidelberg 1

Heilbronn FH
Max-Planck-Str. 39
D-7100 Heilbronn

Isny
Naturwiss.-Technische Akademie
Seidenstr. 16
D-7922 Isny

Karlsruhe FH
Moltkestr. 4
D-7500 Karlsruhe

Konstanz FH
Brauneggerstr. 55
D-7750 Konstanz

Mannheim FH
f. Technik
Speyerer Str. 4
D-6800 Mannheim 1

Mannheim FH
f. Sozialwesen
Pettenkoferstr. 24-30
D-6800 Mannheim 1

Mannheim FH
f. Gestaltung, E3, 16
D-6800 Mannheim 1

Nürtingen FH
Neckarsteige 10
D-7440 Nütringen

Offenburg FH
Badstr. 24
D-7600 Offenburg

Pforzheim FH
f. Wirtschaft
Tiefenbronnerstr. 65
D-7530 Pforzheim

Pforzheim FH
f. Gestaltung
Holzgartenstr. 36
D-7530 Pforzheim

Ravensburg-Weingarten FH
Postfach 1261
D-7987 Weingarten

Reutlingen FH
f. Technik u. Wirstschaft
Pestalozzistr. 73
D-7410 Reutlingen

Reutlingen FH
f. Sozialwesen
Ringelbachstr. 221
D-7410 Reutlingen

Schwäbisch Gmünd FH
f. Gestaltung
Postf. 1308
D-7070 Schwäbisch Gmünd

Sigmaringen FH
Anton-Günther-Str. 51
D-7480 Sigmaringen

Stuttgart FH
f. Technik
Postfach 10 14 52
D-7000 Stuttgart 1

Stuttgart FH
f. Druck
Nobelstr. 10
D-7000 Stuttgart 80

Stuttgart FH
f. Bibliothekswesen
Feuerbacher Heide 38-42
D-7000 Stuttgart 10

Ulm FH
Postf. 3860
D-7900 Ulm

Bayern

Augsburg FH
Baumgartnerstr. 16
D-8900 Augsburg

Bamberg U
Kapuzinerstr. 16
D-8600 Bamberg

Coburg FH
Friedrich-Streib-Str. 2
D-8630 Coburg (mit Abteilung in Münchberg)

Eichstätt Kath. U
Ostenstr. 26
D-8078 Eichstätt

Kempten FH
Balinhofstraße 61
D-8960 Kempten/Allgäu

Landshut FH
Am Lurzenhof 4
D-8300 Landshut

München FH
Lothstr. 34
D-8000 München 2

Kath. Stiftungsfachhochschule Mü.
Preysingstr. 83
D-8000 München 80 (m. Abt. in Benediktbeuern)

Nürnberg FH
Keßlerplatz 12
D-8500 Nürnberg 21

Nürnberg FH
Ev. Stiftungsfachhochschule N
Burgschmietstr. 10
D-8500 Nürnberg 90

Regensburg FH
Prüfeningerstr. 58
D-8400 Regensburg

Rosenheim FH
Marienberger Str. 26
D-8200 Rosenheim

Weihenstephan FH
D-8050 Freising 12 (mit Abt. in Schönbrunn und Triesdorf)

Würzburg-Schweinfurt FH
Münzstr. 12
D-8700 Würzburg

Berlin

Technische FH Berlin
Luxemburgerstr. 10
D-1000 Berlin 65

FH f. Wirtschaft
Badensche Str. 50-51
D-1000 Berlin 62

FH f. Sozialarbeit und Sozialpädagogik
Karl-Schrader-Str. 6
D-1000 Berlin 30

Ev. FH f. Sozialarbeit u. Sozialpädagogik
Reinerzstr. 40
D-1000 Berlin 33

Bremen

Bremen FH
Hochschule Bremen
Neustadtwall 30
D-2800 Bremen

Bremen FH
Hochschule HfK
Am Wandrahm 23
D-2800 Bremen

Bremerhaven
Hochschule Bremerhaven
An der Karlstadt 8
D-2850 Bremerhaven

Hamburg

Hamburg FH
Winterhuder Weg 29
D-2000 Hamburg 76

Ev. FH f. Sozialpädagogik
Horner Weg 170
D-2000 Hamburg 74

Hessen

Darmstadt FH
Schöfferstr. 1
D-6100 Darmstadt

Ev. FH Darmstadt
Zweifalltorweg 12
D-6100 Darmstadt

Frankfurt FH
Kleiststr. 31
f. WiSo: Limescorso 5
D-6000 Frankfurt/M.

FH. Bibliotheksschule in Ff. a. M.
Wiesenau 1
D-6000 Frankfurt

Fulda FH
Marquardstr. 35
D-6400 Fulda

Gießen-Friedberg FH
Ludwigstr. 7
D-6300 Gießen
(m. Abt. in Friedberg)

Kassel U-GH
Mönchebergstr. 11
D-3500 Kassel

Oestrich-Winkel
European Business School
Schloß Reichartshausen
D-6227 Oestrich-Winkel

Wiesbaden FH
Kurt-Schumacher-Ring 18
D-6200 Wiesbaden
(mit Abteilungen in Geisenheim, Idstein, Rüsselsheim)

Wiesbaden FH Fresenius
Dambachtal 20
D-6200 Wiesbaden

Niedersachsen

Braunschweig-Wolfenbüttel FH
Ludwig-Winter-Str. 2
D-3300 Braunschweig
(mit Abt. in Wolfenbüttel)

Emden FH Ostfriesland
Constantiaplatz 4
D-2970 Emden
(mit Abteilung in Leer)

Hannover FH
Ricklinger Stadtweg 118
D-3000 Hannover 91
(mit Abteilung in Nienburg)

Ev. FH in Hannover
Postf. 690309
D-3000 Hannover 61

Hildesheim-Holzminden FH
Hohnsen 1
D-3200 Hildesheim
(mit Abteilungen in Göttingen u. Holzminden)

Lüneburg FH Nordostniedersachsen
Münstermannskamp 1
D-2120 Lüneburg
(m. Abteilungen in Buxtehude u. Suderburg)

Oldenburg FH
Ofener Str. 16
D-2900 Oldenburg
(mit Abt. in Elsfleht)

Osnabrück FH
Neuer Graben (Schloß)
D-4500 Osnabrück

Kath. FH Norddeutschland
Detmarstr. 2
D-4500 Osnabrück
(mit Abteilung in Vechta)

Ottersberg FH
Freie Kunst-Studienstätte
Am Wiestebruch 66/68
D-2802 Ottersberg

Wilhelmshaven FH
Friedrich-Paffrath-Str. 101
D-2940 Wilhelmshaven

Nordrhein-Westfalen

Aachen FH
D-5100 Aachen
(m. Abt. in Jülich)

Bielefeld FH
Kurt-Schumacher-Str. 6
D-4800 Bielefeld 1
(m. Abt. in Minden)

Bochum FH
Postf. 100741
D-4630 Bochum
(m. Abt. in Gelsenkirchen)

FH Bergbau
Herner Str. 45
D-4630 Bochum

Ev. FH Rheinland, Westfalen-Lippe. Abt. Bochum
Immanuel-Kant-Str. 20
D-4630 Bochum

Bonn FH
Fachhochschule für das öffentliche Bibliothekswesen
Wittelsbacherring 9
D-5300 Bonn

Dortmund FH
Sonnenstr. 96
D-4600 Dortmund 1

Düsseldorf FH
Universitätsstraße
(Geb. 23.31/32)
D-4000 Düsseldorf 1

Duisburg U-GH
Lotharstr. 65
D-4100 Duisburg

Essen Univ.-Gesamthochschule Essen
Universitätsstr. 2
D-4300 Essen 1

Iserlohn, Märkische FH
Frauenstuhlweg 31
5860 Iserlohn

Köln FH
Claudiusstr. 1
D-5000 Köln 21
(mit Abt. in Gummersbach)

Rheinische FH Köln
Hohenstaufenring 16-18
D-5000 Köln 1

Kath. FH Nordrhein-Westfalen,
Wörthstr. 10
D-5000 Köln 1

FH f. Bibliotheks- und Dokumentationswesen
Claudiusstraße 1
D-5000 Köln 41

Krefeld FH Niederrhein
Postf. 2850
D-4150 Krefeld 1
(m. Abt. in Mönchengladbach)

Lemgo FH Lippe
Liebigstr. 87
D-4920 Lemgo 1
(m. Abt. in Detmold)

Münster FH
Corrensstr. 25
D-4400 Münster
(m. Abt. in Steinfurt)

Paderborn U-GH
Postf. 1621
D-4790 Paderborn
(mit Abt. in Höxter, Meschede u. Soest)

Siegen U-GH
Herrengarten 3
D-5900 Siegen

Wuppertal U-GH
Gaußstr. 20
D-5600 Wuppertal 1

Rheinland-Pfalz

Bingen FH
d. Landes Rheinland-Pfalz
Rochusallee 4
D-6530 Bingen 1
(mit Abt. in Aachen, Köln, Münster u. Paderborn)

Kaiserslautern FH
d. L. Rheinland-Pfalz
Morlautererstr. 31
D-6750 Kaiserslautern

Koblenz FH
d. L. Rheinland-Pfalz
Am Finkenherd 4
D-5400 Koblenz-Karthause
(m. Abt. in Höhr-Grenzhausen)

Ludwigshafen FH
d. L. Rheinland-Pfalz
Ernst-Böhe-Str. 4
D-6700 Ludwigshafen
(m. Abt. in Worms)

Ludwigshafen FH
Ev. FH für Sozialwesen
Maxstraße 29
D-6700 Ludwigshafen

Mainz FH
d. L. Rheinland-Pfalz
Holzstr. 36
D-6500 Mainz

Mainz FH
d. L. Rheinland-Pfalz
Abteilung Mainz II
An der Bruchspitze 50
D-6500 Mainz

Mainz FH
Kath. FH
für Sozialarbeit, Sozialpädagogik und praktische Theologie
Saarstraße 2
D-6500 Mainz

Trier FH
d. L. Rheinland-Pfalz
Schneidershof
D-5500 Trier

Saarland

Saarbrücken FH des Saarlandes
Goebenstraße 40
D-6600 Saarbrücken 1

Saarbrücken FH
Kath. Fachhochschule für Sozialwesen
Rastpfuhl 12 a
D-6600 Saarbrücken

Schleswig-Holstein

Flensburg FH
Kanzleistr. 91-93
D-2390 Flensburg

Kiel FH
Breiter Weg 10
D-2300 Kiel
(m. Abt. in Eckernförde u. Rendsburg)

Lübeck FH
Stephensonstr. 3
D-2400 Lübeck 1

Rendsburg HfB
Neuer Wall 37
D-2000 Hamburg 36

Wedel FH, PTL Wedel
Feldstr. 143
D-2000 Wedel

D

2. Survey of courses of study at higher education institutions

Universities, technical universities/ Technische Hochschulen, Gesamthochschulen

Source:
'Studien- und Berufswahl 1989/90'
Verlag K. H. Bock,
Bad Honnef

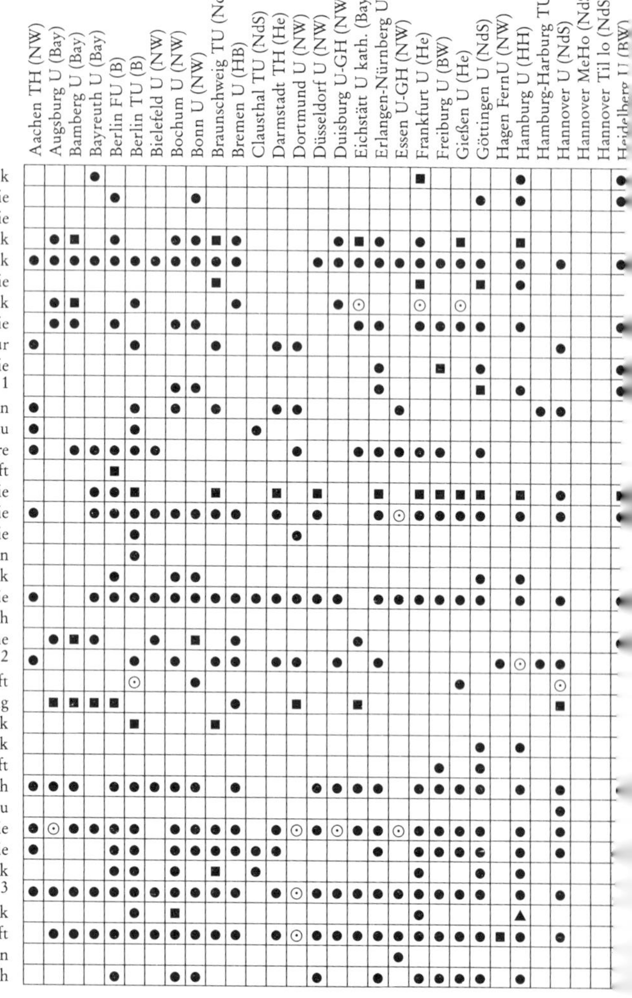

	Aachen TH (NW)	Augsburg U (Bay)	Bamberg U (Bay)	Bayreuth U (Bay)	Berlin FU (B)	Berlin TU (B)	Bielefeld U (NW)	Bochum U (NW)	Bonn U (NW)	Braunschweig TU (NdS)	Bremen U (HB)	Clausthal TU (NdS)	Darmstadt TH (He)	Dortmund U (NW)	Düsseldorf U (NW)	Duisburg U-GH (NW)	Eichstätt U kath. (Bay)	Erlangen-Nürnberg U (Bay)	Essen U-GH (NW)	Frankfurt U (He)	Freiburg U (BW)	Gießen U (He)	Göttingen U (NdS)	Hagen FernU (NW)	Hamburg U (HH)	Hamburg-Harburg TU (HH)	Hannover U (NdS)	Hannover MeHo (NdS)	Hannover Til lo (NdS)	Heidelberg U (BW)
Afrikanistik				●																■					●					●
Ägyptologie					●				●														●		●					●
Agrarökonomie																														
Amerikanistik		●	■		●			●	●	■	●					●	■	●		●		■			■					
Anglistik	●	●	●	●	●	●	●	●	●	●	●				●	●	●	●	●	●	●	●	●		●		●			●
Anthropologie										■										■			■		●					
Arbeitslehre/Technik		●	■			●					●					●	⊙			⊙		⊙								
Archäologie		●	●		●			●	●								●	●		●	●	●	●		●					●
Architektur	●					●				●			●	●													●			
Assyriologie																		●			■		●							●
Astronomie, Astrophysik [1]								●	●									●					■		●					●
Bauingenieurwesen	●					●		●		●			●	●					●							●	●			
Bergbau	●					●						●																		
Betriebswirtschaftslehre	●		●	●	●	●	●							●			●	●	●	●	●		●							
Bibliothekswissenschaft					■																									
Biochemie				●	●	■				■			■		■			■		■	■	■	■		■		●			■
Biologie	●			●	●	●	●	●	●	●	●		●		●			●	⊙	●	●	●	●		●		●			●
Biotechnologie						●								●																
Brauwesen						●																								
Byzantinistik					●			●	●														●		●					
Chemie	●			●	●	●	●	●	●	●	●	●	●	●	●	●		●	●	●	●	●	●		●		●			●
Dänisch																														
Deutsch als Fremdsprache		●	■	●			●		■		●						●													●
Elektrotechnik [2]	●					●		●		●	●		●	●		●		●						●	⊙	●	●			
Ernährungswissenschaft						⊙			●													●					⊙			
Erwachsenenbildung		■	■	■	■						●			■			■										■			
Feinwerktechnik						■				■																				
Finno-Ugristik																							●		●					
Forstwissenschaft																					●		●							
Französisch	●	●	●		●	●	●	●	●		●				●	●	●	●		●	●	●	●		●		●			●
Gartenbau																											●			
Geographie	●	⊙	●	●	●	●		●	●	●	●		●	⊙	●	⊙	●	●	⊙	●	●	●	●		●		●			
Geologie	●				●	●		●	●	●	●	●	●					●		●	●	●	●		●		●			
Geophysik					●	●		●		■		●								●			●		●					
Germanistik [3]	●	●	●	●	●	●	●	●	●	●	●		●	⊙	●	●	●	●	●	●	●	●	●		●		●			
Geschichte d. Naturw./Technik						●		■												●					▲					
Geschichtswissenschaft		●	●	●	●	●	●	●	●	●	●		●	⊙	●	●	●	●	●	●	●	●	●	■	●		●			
Gestaltung, Design																			●											
Griechisch, klassisch					●			●	●						●			●		●	●	●	●		●					

For abbreviations of the higher education institutions, see p. 115.

Abbreviations of the Länder

BW Baden-Württemberg
Bay Bayern
B Berlin
HB Hansestadt Bremen
HH Hansestadt Hamburg
He Hessen
NdS Niedersachsen
NW Nordrhein-Westfalen
RPf Rheinland-Pfalz
Saar Saarland
SH Schleswig-Holstein

● Complete course of study
■ Advanced segment of course or minor subject only
⊙ Exclusively teacher training
▲ 'Hauptstudium' only (up from fifth semester)

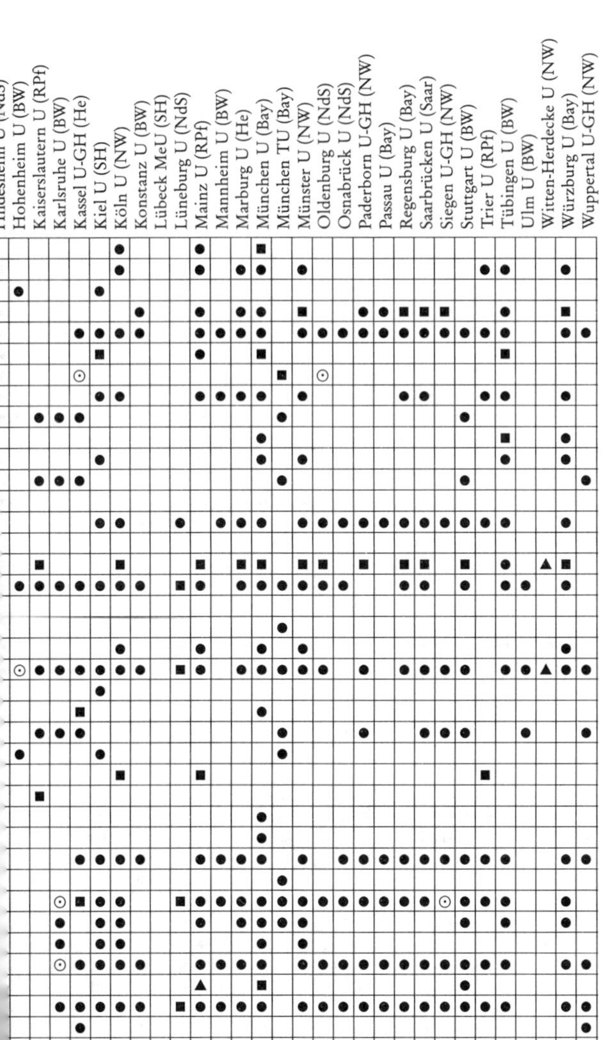

Hildesheim U (NdS)	Hohenheim U (BW)	Kaiserslautern U (RPf)	Karlsruhe U (BW)	Kassel U-GH (He)	Kiel U (SH)	Köln U (NW)	Konstanz U (BW)	Lübeck MeU (SH)	Lüneburg U (NdS)	Mainz U (RPf)	Mannheim U (BW)	Marburg U (He)	München U (Bay)	München TU (Bay)	Münster U (NW)	Oldenburg U (NdS)	Osnabrück U (NdS)	Paderborn U-GH (NW)	Passau U (Bay)	Regensburg U (Bay)	Saarbrücken U (Saar)	Siegen U-GH (NW)	Stuttgart U (BW)	Trier U (RPf)	Tübingen U (BW)	Ulm U (BW)	Witten-Herdecke U (NW)	Würzburg U (Bay)	Wuppertal U-GH (NW)	
						●				●			■																	African studies
						●				●		●	●		●									●	●			●		Egyptology
	●				●																									Agricultural economics
							●			●		●	●		■			●	●	■	■	■			●			■		American studies
				●	●	●	●			●	●	●	●		●	●	●	●	●	●	●	●	●	●	●			●	●	English studies
					■					●			■												■					Anthropology
				⊙										■		⊙														Job orientation/Technical instruction
					●	●				●	●	●	●		●					●	●			●	●			●		Archeology
		●	●	●										●									●							Architecture
													●												■			●		Assyrian studies
					●								●		●										●			●		Astronomy, Astro-physics[1]
		●	●	●										●									●						●	Civil engineering
																														Mining
					●	●			●		●	●	●		●	●	●	●	●	●	●	●	●	●	●			●		Business administration
																														Library science
		■				■				■		■	■		■	■		■		■	■		■		●		▲	■		Biochemistry
	●	●	●	●	●	●	●		■	●		●	●	●	●	●	●			●	●		●		●	●		●		Biology
																														Biotechnology
														●																Brewing technology
						●				●			●		●													●		Byzantine studies
	⊙	●	●	●	●	●	●		■	●		●	●	●	●	●		●		●	●	●	●		●	●	▲	●	●	Chemistry
					●																									Danish studies
				■									●																	German as a foreign language
		●	●	●										●				●			●	●	●			●			●	Electrical engineering[2]
	●				●									●																Home economics and nutrition
						■				■														■						Adult education
		■																												Precision instruments engineering
													●																	Finno-ugristics
													●																	Forestry
				●	●	●	●			●	●	●	●		●		●	●	●	●	●	●	●	●	●			●	●	French studies
														●																Horticulture
			⊙	■	●	●			■	●	●	●	●	●	●	●	●	●	●	●	●	⊙	●	●	●			●		Geography
			●		●	●				●		●	●	●	●								●		●			●		Geology
			●		●	●							●		●															Geophysics
			⊙	●	●	●	●			●	●	●	●		●	●	●	●	●	●	●	●	●	●	●			●	●	German(ic) philology[3]
										▲			■										●							History
			●	●	●	●	●		■	●	●	●	●		●	●	●	●	●	●	●	●	●	●	●			●	●	History of science and technology
				●																									●	Design
					●	●	●			●	●	●	●		●					●	●			●	●			●		Classical Greek

Mostly combined with physics; leading to a doctoral degree.
TU Berlin: up from the fifth semester also combined with media technology.
U Kiel: also Frisian philology.

D

Study possibilities at universities, technical universities/ Technische Hochschulen, Gesamthochschulen

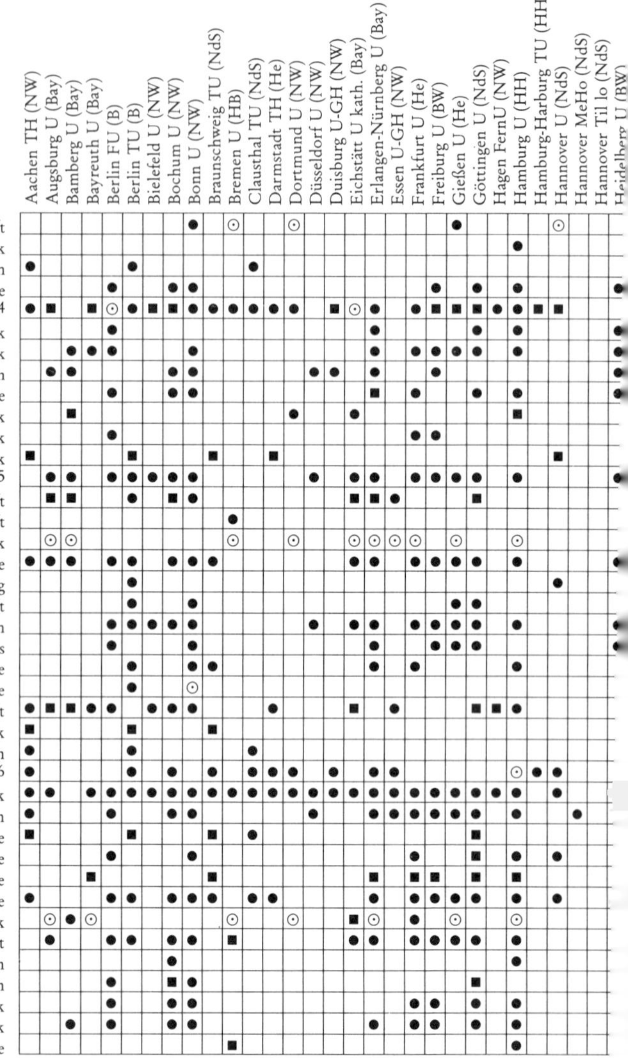

	Aachen TH (NW)	Augsburg U (Bay)	Bamberg U (Bay)	Bayreuth U (Bay)	Berlin FU (B)	Berlin TU (B)	Bielefeld U (NW)	Bochum U (NW)	Bonn U (NW)	Braunschweig TU (NdS)	Bremen U (HB)	Clausthal TU (NdS)	Darmstadt TH (He)	Dortmund U (NW)	Düsseldorf U (NW)	Duisburg U-GH (NW)	Eichstätt U kath. (Bay)	Erlangen-Nürnberg U (Bay)	Essen U-GH (NW)	Frankfurt U (He)	Freiburg U (BW)	Gießen U (He)	Göttingen U (NdS)	Hagen FernU (NW)	Hamburg U (HH)	Hamburg-Harburg TU (HH)	Hannover U (NdS)	Hannover MeHo (NdS)	Hannover TiHo (NdS)	Heidelberg U (BW)
Haushaltswissenschaft									●		⊙			⊙								●					⊙			
Holzwirtschaft, Holztechnik																									●					
Hüttenwesen	●					●						●																		
Indologie					●			●	●												●		●		●					●
Informatik [4]	●	■		■	⊙	●	■	■	●	●	●	●	●	●		■	⊙	●		●	■	■	■	●	●	■	■			
Iranistik/Indoiranistik					●													●					●		●					●
Islamwissenschaft, Semitistik			●	●	●				●									●		●	●	●	●		●					●
Italienisch		●	●					●	●						●	●		●			●									●
Japanologie					●			●	●									■		●			●		●					●
Journalistik			■											●			●								■					
Judaistik					●															●	●									
Kerntechnik, Reaktortechnik	■					■				■			■														■			
Klassische Philologie [5]		●	●		●	●	●	●	●						●		●	●		●	●	●	●		●					●
Kommunikationswissenschaft		■	■			●		■	●								■	■	●				■							
Kulturwissenschaft											●																			
Kunst/Kunstpädagogik		⊙	⊙								⊙			⊙			⊙	⊙	⊙	⊙		⊙			⊙					
Kunstgeschichte	●	●	●		●	●		●	●	●							●	●		●	●	●	●		●					●
Landespflege/Landschaftsplanung						●																					●			
Landwirtschaft/Agrarwissenschaft						●			●													●	●							
Latein					●	●	●	●	●						●		●	●		●	●	●	●		●					●
Latein. Philologie des Mittelalters					●				●									●			●	●	●							●
Lebensmittelchemie						●			●	●								●		●					●					
Lebensmitteltechnologie						●			⊙																					
Literaturwissenschaft	●	■	■	●	●		●	●	●				●				■		●				■	■	●					
Luft- und Raumfahrttechnik	■					■				■																				
Markscheidewesen	●					●						●																		
Maschinenbau [6]	●					●		●		●		●	●	●		●		●	●						⊙	●	●			
Mathematik	●	●		●	●	●	●	●	●	●	●	●	●	●	●	●	●	●	●	●	●	●	●	●	●		●			
Medizin	●				●			●	●						●			●	●	●	●	●	●		●			●		
Metallkunde	■					■				■		●											■							
Meteorologie					●				●											●			■		●		●			
Mikrobiologie				■						■								■		■	■		■		■					
Mineralogie	●				●	●		●	●	●		●	●					●		●	●	●	●		●		●			
Musik/Musikpädagogik		⊙	●	⊙							⊙			⊙			■	⊙		●		⊙			⊙					
Musikwissenschaft		●			●	●		●	●		■						●	●		●	●	●	●		●					
Neugriechisch								●																	●					
Niederländisch					●			■	●														■							
Nordistik/Skandinavistik					●			●	●											●	●		●		●					
Orientalistik			●		●			●	●									●		●	●		●		●					
Ozeanographie											■														●					

[4] Also as complete course of study at the EWH Koblenz.

[5] U Augsburg , TU Berlin, U Bielefeld , cath. U Eichstätt, U Osnabrück: Latin only

D

- ● Complete course of study
- ■ Advanced segment of course or minor subject only
- ⊙ Exclusively teacher training
- ▲ 'Hauptstudium' only (up from fifth semester)

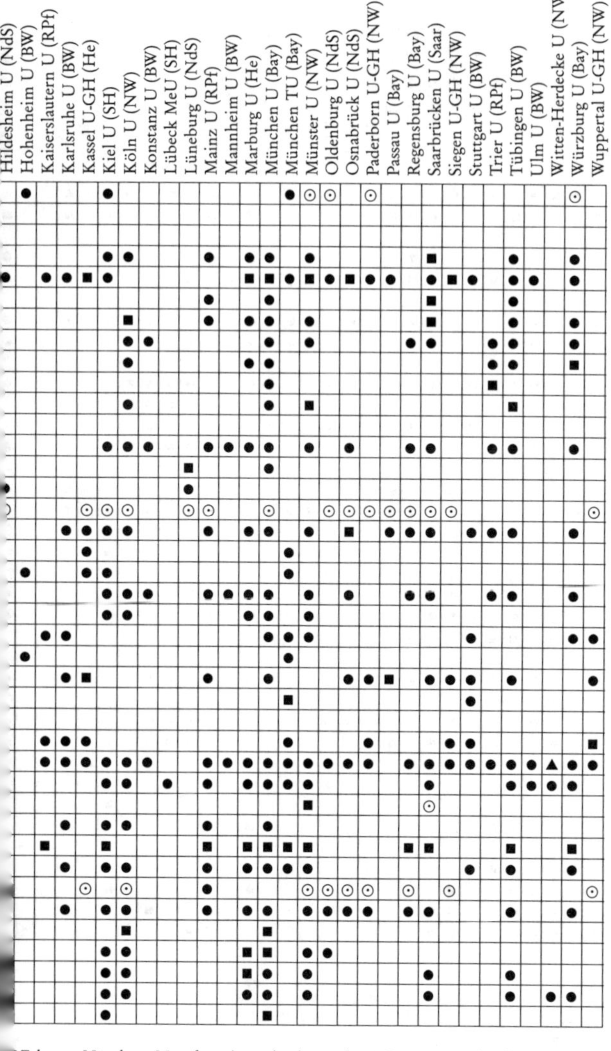

Subject	Hildesheim U (NdS)	Hohenheim U (BW)	Kaiserslautern U (RPf)	Karlsruhe U (BW)	Kassel U-GH (He)	Kiel U (SH)	Köln U (NW)	Konstanz U (BW)	Lübeck MeU (SH)	Lüneburg U (NdS)	Mainz U (RPf)	Mannheim U (BW)	Marburg U (He)	München U (Bay)	München TU (Bay)	Münster U (NW)	Oldenburg U (NdS)	Osnabrück U (NdS)	Paderborn U-GH (NW)	Passau U (Bay)	Regensburg U (Bay)	Saarbrücken U (Saar)	Siegen U-GH (NW)	Stuttgart U (BW)	Trier U (RPf)	Tübingen U (BW)	Ulm U (BW)	Witten-Herdecke U (NW)	Würzburg U (Bay)	Wuppertal U-GH (NW)
Home economics		●				●									●	⊙	⊙		⊙										⊙	
Woods economics and technology																														
Metallurgical engineering																														
Indian studies						●	●				●		●	●		●						■				●			●	
Computer sciences[4]	●		●	●	■	●							■	■	●	■	●	■	●	●		●	■	●		●	●		●	
Iranian, Indo-Iranian studies											●			●								■				●				
Islamic studies, Semitic studies							■				●		●	●		●						■				●			●	
Italien studies							●	●						●		●					●	●			●	●			●	
Japanese studies							●						●	●											●	●			■	
Journalism														●											■					
Judaic studies							●							●		■										■				
Nuclear and reactor physics																														
Classical philology[5]						●	●	●			●	●	●	●		●		●			●	●			●	●			●	
Communication sciences										■				●																
Humanities	●									●																				
Art, art education	⊙				⊙	⊙	⊙			⊙	⊙			⊙			⊙	⊙	⊙	⊙	⊙	⊙	⊙							⊙
History of art				●	●	●	●				●		●	●		●		■		●	●	●		●	●	●			●	
Land conservation, land planning					●										●															
Agricultural sciences		●			●	●									●															
Latin						●	●	●			●	●	●	●		●		●			●	●			●	●			●	
Latin, philology of the Middle Ages						●	●						●	●		●														
Food chemistry			●	●										●	●	●								●					●	●
Food technology		●													●															
Literature				●	■						●			●				●	●	■		●	●	●		●				●
Aeronautical and aerospace engineering															■									●						
Mine surveyeing																														
Mechanical engineering[6]			●	●	●										●				●				●	●						■
Mathematics			●	●	●	●	●	●			●	●	●	●	●	●	●	●	●		●	●	●	●	●	●	●	▲	●	●
Medicine						●	●		●		●		●	●	●	●						●				●	●	●	●	
Metallurgy																■						⊙								
Meteorology				●		●	●				●			●																
Microbiology			■			■					■		■	■	■	■					■	■				■			■	
Mineralogy				●		●	●				●		●	●	●	●								●		●			●	
Music, Music education					⊙		⊙				●					⊙	⊙	⊙	⊙		⊙		⊙							⊙
Musicology				●		●	●				●		●	●		●	●	●	●		●	●				●			●	
Modern Greek							■							■																
Dutch studies						●	●						■	■		●	●													
Scandinavian studies						●	●						■	●		●						●				●				
Oriental studies						●	●						●	●		●						●				●		●	●	
Oceanography						●								■																

[6] Erlangen-Nürnberg: Manufacturing technology only; U-GH Wuppertal: Safety technology only.

D

Universities technical universities/ Technische Hochschulen, Gesamthochschulen

	Aachen TH (NW)	Augsburg U (Bay)	Bamberg U (Bay)	Bayreuth U (Bay)	Berlin FU (B)	Berlin TU (B)	Bielefeld U (NW)	Bochum U (NW)	Bonn U (NW)	Braunschweig TU (NdS)	Bremen U (HB)	Clausthal TU (NdS)	Darmstadt TH (He)	Dortmund U (NW)	Düsseldorf U (NW)	Duisburg U-GH (NW)	Eichstätt U kath. (Bay)	Erlangen-Nürnberg U (Bay)	Essen U-GH (NW)	Frankfurt U (He)	Freiburg U (BW)	Gießen U (He)	Göttingen U (NdS)	Hagen FernU (NW)	Hamburg U (HH)	Hamburg-Harburg TU (HH)	Hannover U (NdS)	Hannover MeHo (NdS)	Hannover Til lo (NdS)	Heidelberg U (BW)
Pädagogik/Erziehungswissenschaft		●	●	●	●	●	●	●		●	●		●	●	●	●	●	●	●	●	●	●	●	●	●		●			●
Paläontologie	■				■				●	■	■	■						■		■	■	■	●		●		■			■
Papieringenieurwesen													■																	
Pharmazie					●				●	●					●			●		●	●				●					●
Philosophie	●	●	●	●	●	●	●	●	●	●	●		●		●	●	●	●	●	●	●	●	●		●		●			●
Phonetik																				●					●					
Physik	●			●	●	●	●	●	●	●	●	●	●	●	●	●		●	●	●	●	●	●		●		●			●
Politikwissenschaft	●	●	●	■	●	●	⊙	■	●	●	●		●			■	●	●	⊙	●	●	●	■		●		●			●
Produktionstechnik						■				■	●	■		■																
Psychologie [7]	▲	■	●	■	●	●	●	●	●	●	●		●	■	●	⊙	●	●		●	●	●	●	■	●					●
Publizistik			■		●	■		●														■	■							
Raumplanung						●	■			■				●			■						■							
Rechtswissenschaft		●		●	●		●	●	●		●							●		●	●	●	●	■	●		●			●
Religionspädagogik											●						●													
Religionswissenschaft				●	●				●		●												●				■			
Romanistik	●	●	●	●	●	●	●	●	●	●	●				●	●	●	●		●	●	●	●		●		●			●
Russisch			⊙	⊙	⊙			⊙	⊙									⊙		⊙		⊙	⊙		⊙					⊙
Schiffstechnik	■					■										●									●					
Sicherheitstechnik																														
Sinologie					●			●	●									●		●	●		●		●					●
Slawistik			●		●		●	●	●									●		●	●	●	●		●					●
Sozialpädagogik			■		■	■				■	●			⊙		■	■													
Sozialwesen			●														●													
Sozialwissenschaften/Soziologie	●	●	●	●	●	●	●	●	⊙	●	●		●	■	●	●	●	●		●	●	●	●		●		●			●
Spanisch	⊙	⊙	⊙		⊙			⊙	⊙						⊙	⊙		⊙			⊙		⊙		⊙					⊙
Sport/Leibeserziehung [8]		●		●	⊙		⊙	●			⊙		●	⊙	⊙			⊙	⊙	●	●	●	●		●		⊙			●
Sprachwissenschaft, Linguistik		●	■		●	●	●	●	●		●				●		■	●	●		●	●	●		●					●
Städtebau	■					●				■				●												▲	■			
Statistik														●																
Südostasienwissenschaft																				■					■					
Techn. Gesundheitswesen						■												■												
Technische Kybernetik																														
Technomathematik						●						●				■														
Theaterwissenschaft [9]				●	●			●										●				●			■					
Theologie, evang.	⊙	●	●	●	●		⊙	●	●					⊙		⊙		●	⊙	●		●	●		●		⊙			
Theologie, kath.	⊙	●	●	●	●		⊙	●	●					⊙		⊙	●		⊙	●	●	●					⊙			

[7] TH Aachen: Psychology of work, enterprises and organization only; Bavaria: Specialization. school psychology; also offered as degree course at the EWH Landau.

[8] Cologne: Sports studies are carried out at the Deutsche Sporthochschule (DSH).

D

● Complete course of study
■ Advanced segment of course or minor subject only
⊙ Exclusively teacher training
▲ 'Hauptstudium' only (up from fifth semester)

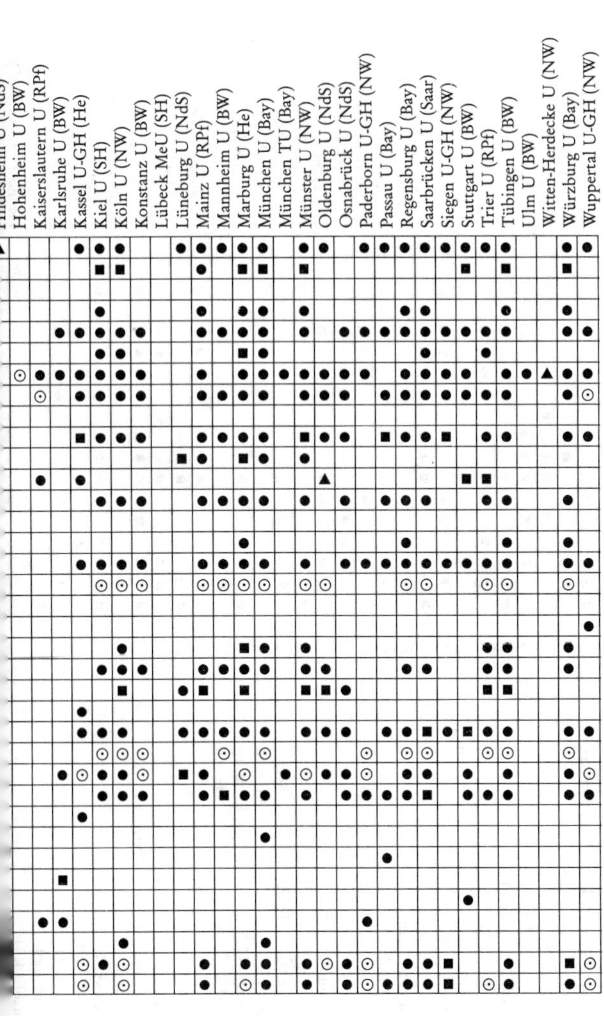

Subject	Hildesheim U (NdS)	Hohenheim U (BW)	Kaiserslautern U (RPf)	Karlsruhe U (BW)	Kassel U-GH (He)	Kiel U (SH)	Köln U (NW)	Konstanz U (BW)	Lübeck MeU (SH)	Lüneburg U (NdS)	Mainz U (RPf)	Mannheim U (BW)	Marburg U (He)	München U (Bay)	München TU (Bay)
Pedagogy/eductional science	▲				●	●	●			●	●	●	●	●	
Paleontology						■	■				●		■	■	
Paper engineering															
Pharmacy						●					●		●	●	
Philosophy				●	●	●	●	●			●	●	●	●	
Phonetics						●	●						■	●	
Physics		⊙	●	●	●	●	●	●			●		●	●	●
Political science			⊙		●	●	●	●			●	●	●	●	
Production engineering															
Psychology[7]					■	●	●	●			●	●	●	●	
Publicism										■	●		■	●	
Regional planning			●		●										
Law						●	●	●			●	●	●	●	
Religious studies/teaching															
Divinity													●		
Romance studies					●	●	●	●			●	●	●	●	
Russian studies						⊙	⊙	⊙			⊙	⊙	⊙	⊙	
Naval technology															
Safety technology															
Sinology							●						■	●	
Slavonic studies						●	●	●			●	●	●	●	
Social pedagogy							■			●	■		■		
Social affairs					●										
Social science, Sociology					●	●	●			●	●	●	●	●	
Hispanic studies						⊙	⊙	⊙				⊙		⊙	
Sports, Physical education[8]				●	⊙	●	●	⊙		■	●		⊙		●
Linguistics, Philology						●	●	●			●	■	●	●	
Urban planning					●										
Statistics														●	
South-East-Asian studies															
Public health technology				■											
Technical cybernetics															
Technical mathematics			●	●											
Drama[9]							●							●	
Theology, Protestant					⊙	●	⊙				●		●	●	
Theology, Catholic					⊙		⊙				●		⊙	●	

Subject	Münster U (NW)	Oldenburg U (NdS)	Osnabrück U (NdS)	Paderborn U-GH (NW)	Passau U (Bay)	Regensburg U (Bay)	Saarbrücken U (Saar)	Siegen U-GH (NW)	Stuttgart U (BW)	Trier U (RPf)	Tübingen U (BW)	Ulm U (BW)	Witten-Herdecke U (NW)	Würzburg U (Bay)	Wuppertal U-GH (NW)
Pedagogy/eductional science	●	●		●	●	●	●	●	●	●	●			●	●
Paleontology	■								■		■			■	
Paper engineering															
Pharmacy	●					●	●				●			●	
Philosophy	●		●	●	●	●	●	●	●	●	●			●	●
Phonetics							●			●					
Physics	●	●	●	●		●	●	●	●		●	●	▲	●	●
Political science	●	●	●		●	●	●	●	●	●	●			●	⊙
Production engineering															
Psychology[7]	■	●	●		■	●	●	■		●	●			●	●
Publicism	●														
Regional planning		▲							■	■					
Law	●		●		●	●	●			●	●			●	
Religious studies/teaching															
Divinity						●					●			●	
Romance studies	●		●	●	●	●	●	●	●	●	●			●	●
Russian studies	⊙	⊙				⊙	⊙			⊙	⊙			⊙	
Naval technology															
Safety technology															●
Sinology	●									●	●			●	
Slavonic studies	●	●				●	●			●	●			●	
Social pedagogy	■	■	●							■	■				
Social affairs															
Social science, Sociology	●	●	●		●	●	■	●	■	●	●			●	●
Hispanic studies				⊙		⊙	⊙			⊙	⊙			⊙	
Sports, Physical education[8]	⊙	●	●	⊙		●	●		●		●			●	⊙
Linguistics, Philology	●		●	●	●	●	■		●	●	●			●	●
Urban planning															
Statistics															
South-East-Asian studies					●										
Public health technology															
Technical cybernetics									●						
Technical mathematics				●											
Drama[9]															
Theology, Protestant	●	⊙	●	⊙		●	●	■			●			■	⊙
Theology, Catholic	●		●	⊙	●	●	●	■		⊙	●			●	⊙

Hamburg: Integrated course of study of HfM and university.

Universities technical universities/ Technische Hochschulen, Gesamthochschulen

	Aachen TH (NW)	Augsburg U (Bay)	Bamberg U (Bay)	Bayreuth U (Bay)	Berlin FU (B)	Berlin TU (B)	Bielefeld U (NW)	Bochum U (NW)	Bonn U (NW)	Braunschweig TU (NdS)	Bremen U (HB)	Clausthal TU (NdS)	Darmstadt TH (He)	Dortmund U (NW)	Düsseldorf U (NW)	Duisburg U-GH (NW)	Eichstätt U kath. (Bay)	Erlangen-Nürnberg U (Bay)	Essen U-GH (NW)	Frankfurt U (He)	Freiburg U (BW)	Gießen U (He)	Göttingen U (NdS)	Hagen FernU (NW)	Hamburg U (HH)	Hamburg-Harburg TU (HH)	Hannover U (NdS)	Hannover MeHo (NdS)	Hannover Til lo (NdS)
Theologie, altkatholisch									●																				
Tiermedizin					●																	●							●
Turkologie			●																	■		●	●		●				
Übersetzungswesen [10]									●						●														
Umweltschutz				■		●		■		■		■		■								■	■			■	■		
Ur- und Frühgeschichte					●			●	●									●		●	●	●	●		●				
Verfahrenstechn./Chemieingenieurw.	■					●				■		●	■	●				●	⊙							●	■		
Vermessungswesen						●			●				●														●		
Verwaltungswissenschaften			■																										
Völkerkunde/Ethnologie				●	●				●											●	●		●		●				
Volkskunde/Europ. Ethnologie		●	●	■					●								●			●	●		●		●				
Volkswirtschaftslehre			●	●	●	●	●		●					●				●		●	●	●	●		●				
Werkstoffwissenschaften	■					●		■		■		●		■				●								●	■		
Wirtschaftsinformatik			●	■				■					●			■							■						
Wirtschaftsingenieurwesen						●							●												●	●			
Wirtschaftsmathematik		●		●		●	●							●		■						■	■		●				
Wirtschaftspädagogik, -wissenschaft [11]	⊙	●			⊙			●			●			⊙		●		⊙	●	⊙		●	⊙	●	⊙		●		
Zahnmedizin	●				●				●						●			●		●	●	●	●		●			●	

[10] U Bonn : exclusively languages of the Near, Middle and Far East.

Teacher training at Pädagogischen/ Erziehungswissen-schaftlichen Hochschulen and universities/ Gesamthochschulen

Source:
'Studien- und Berufswahl 1989/90'
Verlag K.H. Bock, Bad Honnef

<table>
<tr><th></th><th colspan="6">Baden-Württemberg</th><th colspan="9">Bayern</th><th>Berlin</th><th>Bremen</th><th>Hamburg</th><th colspan="4">Hessen</th><th colspan="7">Niedersachsen</th></tr>
<tr><th></th><th>Freiburg PH</th><th>Heidelberg PH</th><th>Karlsruhe PH</th><th>Ludwigsburg PH</th><th>Schwäbisch Gmünd PH</th><th>Weingarten PH</th><th>Augsburg U</th><th>Bamberg U</th><th>Bayreuth U</th><th>Eichstätt U kath.</th><th>München U</th><th>Nürnberg (U Erlangen-Nürnberg)</th><th>Passau U</th><th>Regensburg U</th><th>Würzburg U</th><th>Berlin FU, TU, HdK</th><th>Bremen U</th><th>Hamburg U</th><th>Frankfurt U</th><th>Gießen U</th><th>Kassel U-GH</th><th>Marburg U</th><th>Braunschweig TU</th><th>Göttingen U</th><th>Hannover U</th><th>Hildesheim U</th><th>Lüneburg U</th><th>Oldenburg U</th><th>Osnabrück U</th></tr>
<tr><td>Lehramt an Grundschulen</td><td rowspan="2">●</td><td rowspan="2">●</td><td rowspan="2">●</td><td rowspan="2">●</td><td rowspan="2">●</td><td rowspan="2">●</td><td>●</td><td>●</td><td>●</td><td>●</td><td>●</td><td>●</td><td>●</td><td>●</td><td>●</td><td>●</td><td></td><td></td><td>●</td><td>●</td><td></td><td></td><td rowspan="2">●</td><td rowspan="2"></td><td rowspan="2">●</td><td rowspan="2">●</td><td rowspan="2">●</td><td rowspan="2">●</td><td rowspan="2">●</td></tr>
<tr><td>Lehramt an Hauptschulen</td><td>●</td><td>●</td><td>●</td><td>●</td><td>●</td><td>●</td><td>●</td><td>●</td><td>●</td><td>●</td><td></td><td></td><td rowspan="2">●</td><td rowspan="2">●</td><td></td><td></td></tr>
<tr><td>Lehramt an Realschulen</td><td>●</td><td>●</td><td></td><td>●</td><td></td><td>●</td><td>●</td><td>●</td><td>●</td><td>●</td><td>●</td><td>●</td><td>●</td><td>●</td><td>●</td><td>●</td><td></td><td></td><td></td><td></td><td>●</td><td></td><td>●</td><td></td><td></td><td>●</td><td>●</td></tr>
<tr><td>Lehramt an Sonderschulen [1]</td><td></td><td>●</td><td></td><td>●</td><td></td><td></td><td></td><td></td><td></td><td></td><td>●</td><td></td><td></td><td></td><td>●</td><td>●</td><td>●</td><td>●</td><td>●</td><td>●</td><td></td><td>△</td><td></td><td></td><td>●</td><td></td><td></td><td>●</td><td></td></tr>
<tr><td>Lehramt für Primarstufe/Grundstufe</td><td></td><td></td><td></td><td></td><td></td><td></td><td></td><td></td><td></td><td></td><td></td><td></td><td></td><td></td><td></td><td></td><td>●</td><td>●</td><td></td><td></td><td>●</td><td></td><td></td><td></td><td></td><td></td><td></td><td></td><td></td></tr>
<tr><td>Lehramt für Sekundarstufe/Mittelstufe</td><td></td><td></td><td></td><td></td><td></td><td></td><td></td><td></td><td></td><td></td><td></td><td></td><td></td><td></td><td></td><td></td><td>●</td><td>●</td><td></td><td></td><td>●</td><td></td><td></td><td></td><td></td><td></td><td></td><td></td><td></td></tr>
<tr><td>Pädagogik</td><td>●</td><td>●</td><td>●</td><td>●</td><td>●</td><td></td><td>●</td><td>●</td><td>●</td><td>●</td><td>●</td><td>●</td><td>●</td><td>●</td><td>●</td><td>●</td><td>●</td><td>●</td><td>●</td><td>●</td><td>●</td><td>●</td><td>●</td><td>●</td><td>●</td><td>●</td><td>●</td><td>●</td><td>●</td></tr>
<tr><td>Deutsch für Ausländer [2]</td><td></td><td>●</td><td>●</td><td></td><td>●</td><td></td><td>●</td><td>■</td><td></td><td>●</td><td>●</td><td>●</td><td></td><td></td><td></td><td></td><td>●</td><td></td><td></td><td></td><td></td><td></td><td></td><td></td><td></td><td></td><td></td><td></td><td></td></tr>
</table>

[1] PH Ludwigsburg: Studies take place at Reutlingen.
[2] In Baden-Württemberg and Bavaria only as a supplementary subject.

● Complete course of study
■ Advanced segment of course or minor subject only
⊙ Exclusively teacher training
▲ 'Hauptstudium' only (up from fifth semester)

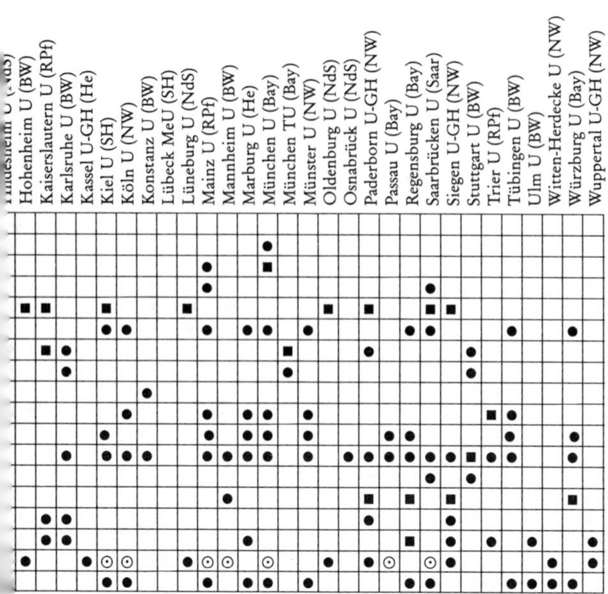

	Hohenheim U (BW)	Kaiserslautern U (RPf)	Karlsruhe U (BW)	Kassel U-GH (He)	Kiel U (SH)	Köln U (NW)	Konstanz U (BW)	Lübeck MeU (SH)	Lüneburg U (NdS)	Mainz U (RPf)	Mannheim U (BW)	Marburg U (He)	München U (Bay)	München TU (Bay)	Münster U (NW)	Oldenburg U (NdS)	Osnabrück U (NdS)	Paderborn U-GH (NW)	Passau U (Bay)	Regensburg U (Bay)	Saarbrücken U (Saar)	Siegen U-GH (NW)	Stuttgart U (BW)	Trier U (RPf)	Tübingen U (BW)	Ulm U (BW)	Witten-Herdecke U (NW)	Würzburg U (Bay)	Wuppertal U-GH (NW)
Theology, old Catholic																													
Veterinary medicine													●																
Turkish studies										●			■																
Translating 10										●											●								
Environmental science	■	■			■				■							■		■			■	■							
Pre-history, Early history					●	●				●		●	●		●					●	●				●			●	
Process engineering, Chemical engineering		■	●											■				●					●						
Surveying			●											●									●						
Public administration							●																						
Ethnology						●				●		●	●		●									■	●				
Folklore/European ethnology					●					●		●	●		●				●	●					●			●	
Political economy			●		●	●	●			●	●	●	●		●		●	●	●	●	●	●	■	●	●			●	
Materials science																					●		●						
Business computing											●							■		■		■						■	
Industrial engineering		●	●															●				●							
Industrial mathematics		●	●									●								■		●		●		●			●
Economic studies (also for teaching) 11	●			●	⊙	⊙			●	⊙	⊙		⊙			●		●	⊙		⊙	●					●		●
Dentistry					●	●				●		●	●		●					●	●				●	●	●	●	

U Bochum: also economics of film and television.

● Complete course of study
■ Area focus of course or minor subject only
△ Postgraduate studies (after first degree)

<table>
<tr><th></th><th>Dortmund U</th><th>Duisburg U-GH</th><th>Essen U-GH</th><th>Köln U</th><th>Münster U</th><th>Paderborn U-GH</th><th>Siegen U-GH</th><th>Wuppertal U-GH</th><th colspan="2">Rheinland-Pfalz</th><th>Saarland</th><th colspan="2">Schleswig-Holstein</th></tr>
<tr><th></th><th></th><th></th><th></th><th></th><th></th><th></th><th></th><th></th><th>Koblenz EWH</th><th>Landau EWH</th><th>Saarbrücken U</th><th>Flensburg PH</th><th>Kiel PH</th></tr>
<tr><td>Teaching at primary schools</td><td></td><td></td><td></td><td></td><td></td><td></td><td></td><td></td><td rowspan="2">●</td><td rowspan="2">●</td><td rowspan="2">●</td><td rowspan="2">●</td><td rowspan="2">●</td></tr>
<tr><td>Teaching at lower secondary schools (Hauptschulen)</td><td></td><td></td><td></td><td></td><td></td><td></td><td></td><td></td></tr>
<tr><td>Teaching at intermediate schools (Realschulen)</td><td></td><td></td><td></td><td></td><td></td><td></td><td></td><td></td><td>●</td><td>●</td><td>●</td><td>●</td><td>●</td></tr>
<tr><td>Teaching at special schools (Sonderschulen) 1</td><td>●</td><td></td><td></td><td>●</td><td></td><td></td><td></td><td></td><td></td><td></td><td></td><td></td><td>●</td></tr>
<tr><td>Teaching at primary level</td><td>●</td><td></td><td>●</td><td>●</td><td>●</td><td>●</td><td>●</td><td>●</td><td></td><td></td><td></td><td></td><td></td></tr>
<tr><td>Teaching at lower secondary level</td><td>●</td><td>●</td><td></td><td>●</td><td>●</td><td>●</td><td>●</td><td>●</td><td></td><td></td><td></td><td></td><td></td></tr>
<tr><td>Pedagogy</td><td>●</td><td>●</td><td>●</td><td>●</td><td>●</td><td>●</td><td></td><td>●</td><td>●</td><td>●</td><td>●</td><td>●</td><td>●</td></tr>
<tr><td>German for foreigners 2</td><td></td><td></td><td>●</td><td></td><td></td><td></td><td></td><td></td><td></td><td>●</td><td></td><td></td><td></td></tr>
</table>

Teacher training of *Grund-* and *Hauptschulen* (primary and lower secondary level), special schools, *Realschulen* (lower secondary level) was transferred to the universities in most of the *Länder*, just like the training of grammar school and vocational school teachers. Only three *Länder* have separate teacher training institutions and colleges of education. These institutions offer beside teaching degrees, also other degrees *(Magister, Diplom)* in a number of subjects and eventually lead to the *Promotion* (doctorate).

D

Courses of study at other institutions of higher education

Source:
'Studien- und Berufswahl 1989/90',
Verlag K. H. Bock,
Bad Honnef

	Kirchliche Hochschulen					**Philosophisch-Theologische Hochschulen**										**Hochschulen/Akademien für bildende Künste**												
	Berlin KH	Bethel KH (Bielefeld)	Neuendettelsau KH	Oberursel KH	Wuppertal KH	Benediktbeuern PTH	Frankfurt PTH	Fulda Theol. Fak.	Hennef PTH	München PTH	Münster PTH	Paderborn Theol. Fak.	Sankt Augustin PTH	Trier Theol. Fak.	Vallendar Theol. H.	Berlin HdK	Braunschweig HbK	Bremen HfK	Düsseldorf HbK	Frankfurt HbK	Hamburg HbK	Karlsruhe ABK	München ABK	Münster HbK	Nürnberg ABK	Offenbach HS Gestaltung	Saarbrücken HbK	Stuttgart ABK
Architektur																●					●							
Betriebswirtschaftslehre																												
Dokumentarfilm, Fersehpublizistik																					■							
Druckereitechnik																●					■							
Film und Fernsehspiel																	■		■	●	■							
Fotografie																■	■	●	■		■							
Gestaltung, Design																●	●	●			●				●	●	●	●
Innenarchitektur																							●		●			●
Jüdische Studien																												
Kunst																●	●	●	●	●	●	●	●	●	●		●	●
Musik																												
Musikwissenschaft																												
Philosophie [1]						■	■	●	■	●	●		■		■													
Politologie *(Diplom)*																												
Soziologie																												
Sport *(Diplom)*																												
Städtebau																					■							
Theologie, evangelisch	●	●	●	●	●																							
Theologie, katholisch						●	●	●	●		●	●	●	●	●													
Toningenieur/Tonmeister																												
Verwaltungswissenschaft																												
Volkswirtschaftslehre																												
Wirtschaftswissenschaften																												

[1] Only in the context of the diploma course in Catholic Theology.

The indented institutions are associated with the before-named college.

D

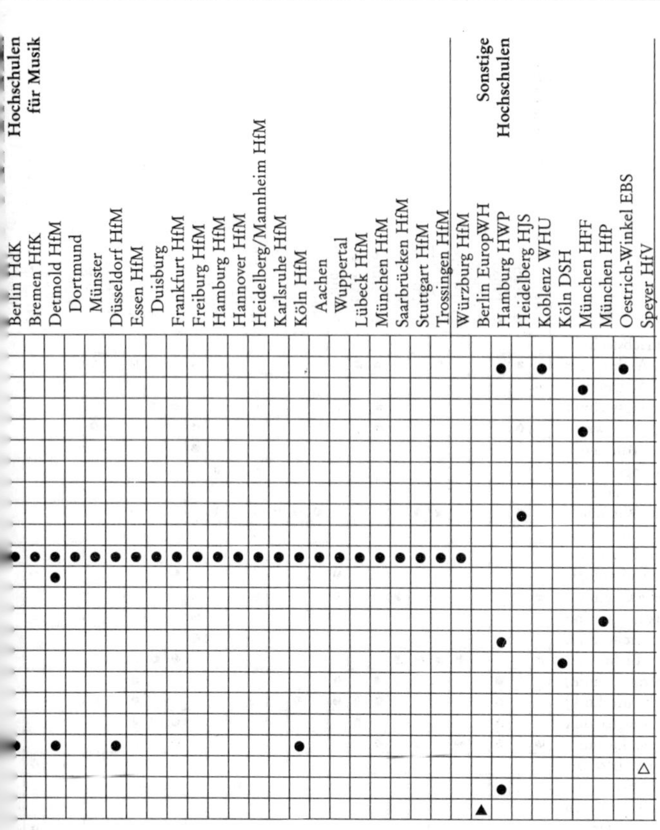

	Berlin HdK	Bremen HfK	Detmold HfM	Dortmund	Münster	Düsseldorf HfM	Essen HfM	Duisburg	Frankfurt HfM	Freiburg HfM	Hamburg HfM	Hannover HfM	Heidelberg/Mannheim HfM	Karlsruhe HfM	Köln HfM	Aachen	Wuppertal	Lübeck HfM	München HfM	Saarbrücken HfM	Stuttgart HfM	Trossingen HfM	Würzburg HfM	Berlin EuropWH	Hamburg HWP	Heidelberg HJS	Koblenz WHU	Köln DSH	München HFF	München HfP	Oestrich-Winkel EBS	Speyer HfV
	Hochschulen für Musik																							Sonstige Hochschulen								
Architecture																																
Business administration																									●		●				●	
Documentary film, TV journalism																													●			
Printing technology																																
Film- and TV-production																													●			
Photography																																
Design																																
Interior design																																
Jewish studies																										●						
Art																																
Music	●	●	●	●	●	●	●	●	●	●	●	●	●	●	●	●	●	●	●	●	●	●	●									
Musicology			●																													
Philosophy [1]																																
Political science (diploma)																														●		
Sociology																									●							
Sports (diploma)																												●				
Urban planning																																
Theology, Protestant																																
Theology, Catholic																																
Sound engineering	●		●			●									●																	
Administrative science																																△
Political economy																									●							
Economics																								▲								

● Complete course of study
■ Advanced segment of course or minor subject only
▲ 'Hauptstudium' only (up from fifth semester)
△ Postgraduate studies (after first degree)

D

Courses of study at Fachhochschulen and corresponding courses at Gesamthochschulen/ Universitäten

Source:
'Studien- und Berufswahl 1989/90'
Verlag K. H. Bock,
Bad Honnef

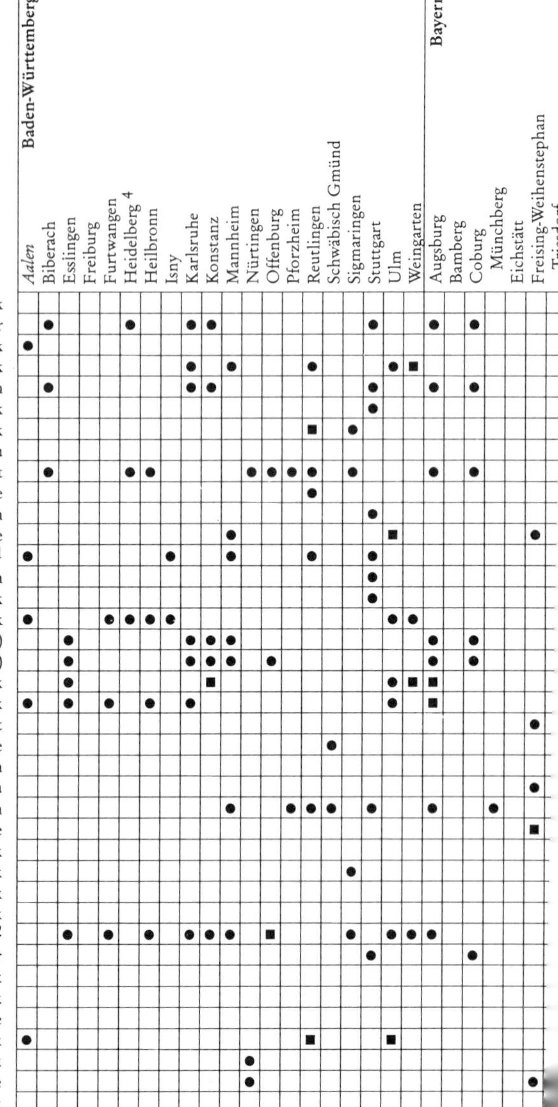

	Baden-Württemberg																				Bayern						
	Aalen	Biberach	Esslingen	Freiburg	Furtwangen	Heidelberg [4]	Heilbronn	Isny	Karlsruhe	Konstanz	Mannheim	Nürtingen	Offenburg	Pforzheim	Reutlingen	Schwäbisch Gmünd	Sigmaringen	Stuttgart	Ulm	Weingarten	Augsburg	Bamberg	Coburg	Münchberg	Eichstätt	Freising-Weihenstephan	Triesdorf
Anlagenbetriebstechnik																											
Architektur		●				●			●	●								●			●		●				
Augenoptik	●																										
Automatisierungstechnik									●		●				●				●	■							
Bauingenieurwesen		●							●	●								●			●		●				
Bauphysik																		●									
Bekleidungstechnik															■		●										
Bergbau																											
Betriebswirtschaft/Wirtschaft		●				●	●					●	●	●	●		●				●		●				
Betriebswirtschaft, europäische															●												
Bibliothekswesen																		●									
Biotechnologie											●								■							●	
Chemie, Technische Chemie [1]	●							●			●				●			●									
Dokumentation																		●									
Druckereitechnik																		●									
Elektronik	●				●	●	●	●											●	●							
Elektrotechnik (Energietechnik)			●						●	●	●										●		●				
Elektrotechnik (Nachrichtentechnik)			●						●	●	●		●								●		●				
Fahrzeugtechnik			●							■									●	■	■						
Feinwerktechnik	●		●		●		●		●										●		■						
Forstwirtschaft																										●	
Fotografie																●											
Fotoingenieurwesen																											
Gartenbau																										●	
Gestaltung/Design											●			●	●	●		●			●			●			
Getränketechnologie																										■	
Glastechnik																											
Haushalts- und Ernährungstechnik																	●										
Holzwirtschaft, Holztechnik																											
Hüttentechnik/Gießereitechnik																											
Informatik [2]			●		●		●		●	●	●		■				●		●	●	●						
Innenarchitektur																		●					●				
Keramik																											
Kerntechnik, Reaktortechnik																											
Kunst, bildende																											
Kunststofftechnik	●														■				■								
Kunsttherapie/-pädagogik												●															
Landespflege												●														●	
Landmaschinenbau/-technik																											

[1] FH Druck (Printing), Stuttgart: Department Colour.

[2] FH Heilbronn: only medical computer science, together with the Univer sity of Heidelberg; access to these studies only with Abitur *(allgemeine Hochschulreife)*.

[3] HfB Rendsburg; distance studies.

[4] Heidelberg: FH for rehabilitation.

Indented institutions: departments of the before-named *Fachhochschule.*

D

● Complete course of study
■ Advanced segment of course

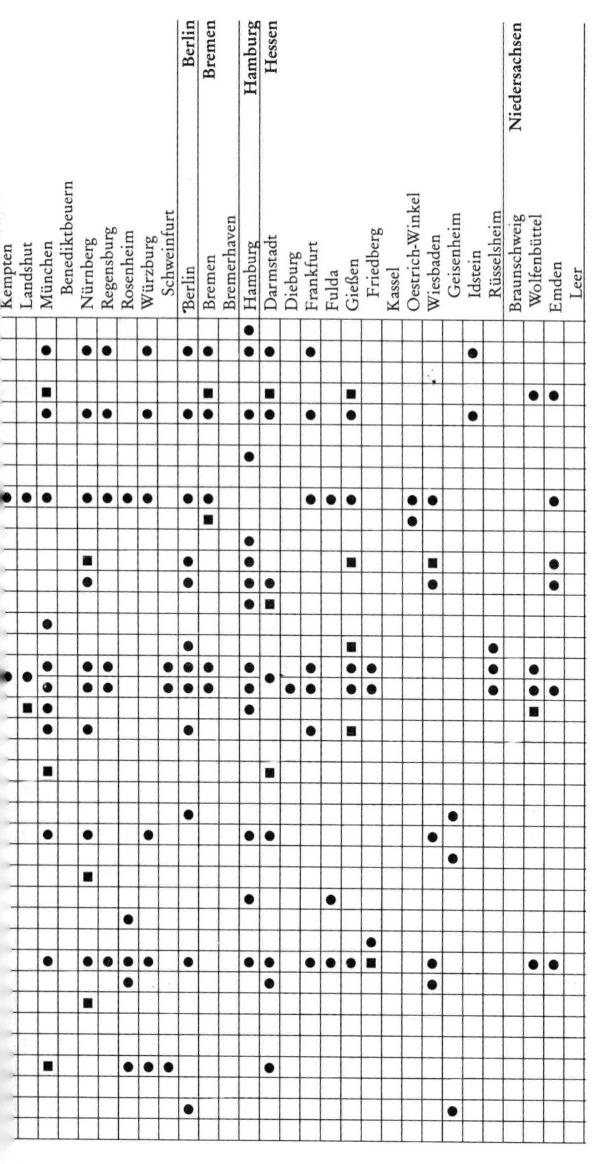

	Kempten	Landshut	München	Benediktbeuern	Nürnberg	Regensburg	Rosenheim	Würzburg	Schweinfurt	Berlin	Bremen	Bremerhaven	Hamburg	Darmstadt	Dieburg	Frankfurt	Fulda	Gießen	Friedberg	Kassel	Oestrich-Winkel	Wiesbaden	Geisenheim	Idstein	Rüsselsheim	Braunschweig	Wolfenbüttel	Emden	Leer
										Berlin	Bremen		Hamburg	Hessen												Niedersachsen			
Plant operations and systems													●																
Architecture			●		●	●		●		●	●		●	●		●								●					
Applied optics																													
Automation			■								■			■				■									●	●	
Civil engineering			●		●	●		●		●	●		●	●		●		●						●					
Structural physics																													
Clothing technology													●																
Mining																													
Business administration/Economics	●	●	●		●	●	●	●		●	●					●	●	●			●	●						●	
European business administration											■										●								
Library science													●																
Biotechnology					■					●			●					■				■						●	
Chemistry, chemical technology[1]					●					●			●	●								●						●	
Documentation													●	■															
Printing technology			●																										
Electronics										●								■							●				
Electrical engineering, power engineering	●	●	●		●	●			●	●	●		●	●		●		●	●						●		●		
Electrical (communications) engineering			●		●	●			●	●	●		●		●	●		●	●						●		●	●	
Vehicle engineering		■	●										●														■		
Precision engineering			●		●					●						●		■											
Forestry																													
Photography			■											■															
Photographic technology																													
Horticulture										●													●						
Design			●		●			●					●	●								●							
Technology of beverages																							●						
Glass technology					■																								
Household and nutrition technology													●				●												
Wood technology and economics							●																						
Metallurgical and foundry engineering																			●										
Computer science[2]			●		●	●	●	●		●			●	●		●	●	●	■			●					●	●	
Interior design							●							●								●							
Ceramics					■																								
Nuclear and reactor technology																													
Fine arts																													
Plastic technology			■				●	●	●					●															
Art therapy, Art education																													
Landscape mangament										●													●						
Agricultural machines/technology																													

D

Courses of study at Fachhochschulen and corresponding courses at Gesamthochschulen/ Universitäten

															Nordrhein-Westfalen														
	Hannover	Nienburg	Hildesheim	Göttingen	Holzminden	Lüneburg	Buxtehude	Suderburg	Oldenburg	Elsfleth	Osnabrück	Vechta	Ottersberg	Wilhelmshaven	Aachen	Jülich	Bielefeld	Minden	Bochum	Gelsenkirchen	Bonn	Dortmund	Düsseldorf	Duisburg	Essen	Iserlohn	Hagen	Köln	Gummersbach
Anlagenbetriebstechnik																													
Architektur	●	●	●		●		●		●						●			●	●			●	●					●	
Augenoptik																													
Automatisierungstechnik	●										●			■		●			●				●					●	●
Bauingenieurwesen	●	●	●		●		●	●	●						●			●	●									●	
Bauphysik																													
Bekleidungstechnik																													
Bergbau																			●										
Betriebswirtschaft/Wirtschaft [3]						●					●			●	●		●		●			●	●					●	
Betriebswirtschaft, europäische											●											●							
Bibliothekswesen	●																				●							●	
Biotechnologie																■										■			
Chemie, Technische Chemie															●	●													
Dokumentation	●																											●	
Druckereitechnik																													
Elektronik																													
Elektrotechnik (Energietechnik)	●										●			●	●	●	●		■	●		●	●				●	●	●
Elektrotechnik (Nachrichtentechnik)	●										●			●	●		●		●	●		●	●					●	
Fahrzeugtechnik																												●	
Feinwerktechnik														●															
Forstwirtschaft				●																									
Fotografie																	●					●						●	
Fotoingenieurwesen																												●	
Gartenbau											●																		
Gestaltung/Design	●		●												●		●					●	●		●			●	
Getränketechnologie																													
Glastechnik																								●					
Haushalts- und Ernährungstechnik											●																		
Holzwirtschaft, Holztechnik			●																										
Hüttentechnik/Gießereitechnik																								●					
Informatik	●										●											●							
Innenarchitektur	●		●																				●						
Keramik																								●					
Kerntechnik, Reaktortechnik																●													
Kunst, bildende	●		●										●															●	
Kunststofftechnik															■		■									■			
Kunsttherapie/-pädagogik													●																
Landespflege											●														●				
Landmaschinenbau/-technik																												●	

Footnotes, , see p. 132.

D

● Complete course of study
■ Advanced segment of course

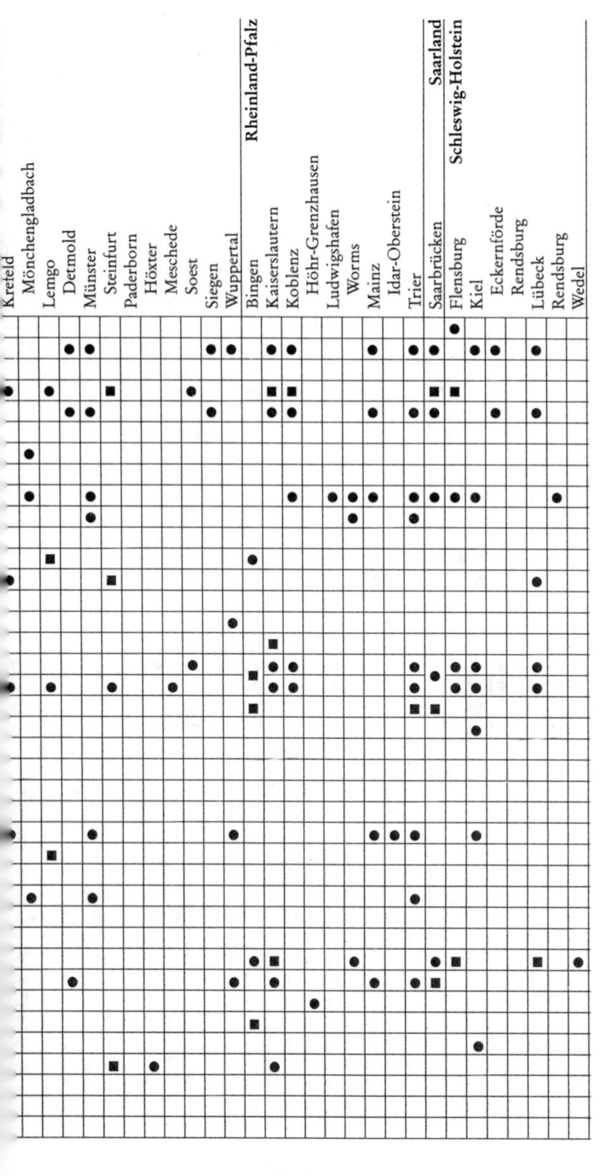

Course													Rheinland-Pfalz									Saarland	Schleswig-Holstein						
	Krefeld	Mönchengladbach	Lemgo	Detmold	Münster	Steinfurt	Paderborn	Höxter	Meschede	Soest	Siegen	Wuppertal	Bingen	Kaiserslautern	Koblenz	Höhr-Grenzhausen	Ludwigshafen	Worms	Mainz	Idar-Oberstein	Trier	Saarbrücken	Flensburg	Kiel	Eckernförde	Rendsburg	Lübeck	Rendsburg	Wedel
Plant operations and systems																							●						
Architecture				●	●						●	●		●	●				●		●	●		●	●		●		
Applied optics																													
Automation	●		●			■				●				■	■							■	■						
Civil engineering				●	●						●			●	●				●		●	●			●		●		
Structural physics																													
Clothing technology		●																											
Mining																													
Business administration/Economics [3]		●			●										●		●	●	●		●	●	●	●				●	
European business administration					●													●			●								
Library science																													
Biotechnology			■										●																
Chemistry, chemical technology	●					■																					●		
Documentation																													
Printing technology												●																	
Electronics														■															
Electrical engineering, power engineering										●			■	●	●						●	●	●	●			●		
Electrical (communications) engineering	●		●			●			●				■	●	●						●	●	●	●			●		
Vehicle enigneering													■								■	■							
Precision engineering																								●					
Forestry																													
Photography																													
Photographic technology																													
Horticulture																													
Design	●				●							●							●	●	●			●					
Technology of beverages			■																										
Glass technology																													
Household and nutrition technology		●			●																●								
Wood technology and economics																													
Metallurgical and foundry engineering																													
Computer science													●	■				●				●	■				■		●
Interior design				●								●		●					●		●	■							
Ceramics																●													
Nuclear and reactor technology													■																
Fine arts																								●					
Plastics technology						■		●						●															
Art therapy, Art education																													
Landscape management																													
Agricultual machines/technology																													

D

Courses of study at Fachhochschulen and corresponding courses at Gesamthochschulen/ Universitäten

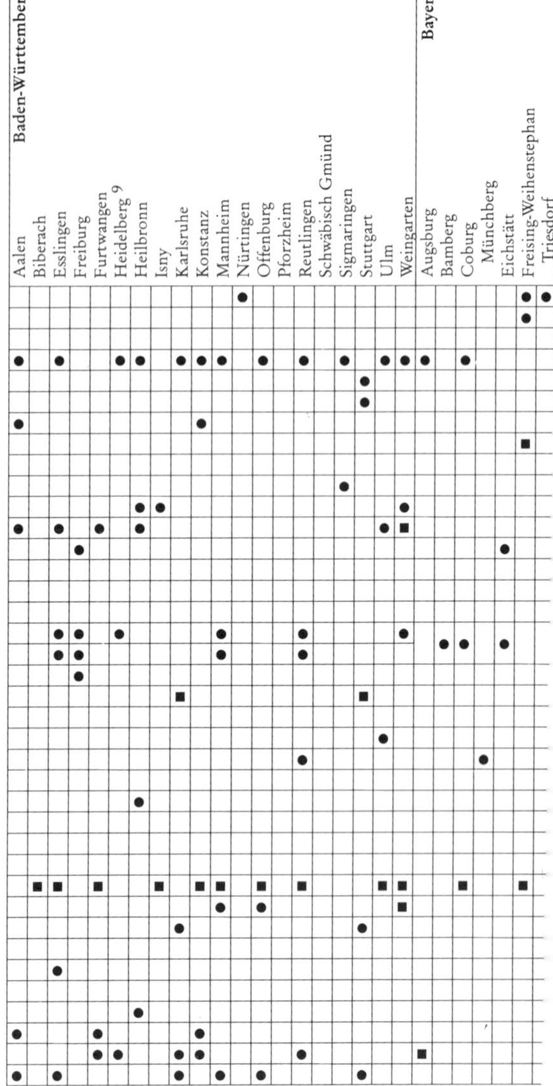

	Baden-Württemberg																				Bayern						
	Aalen	Biberach	Esslingen	Freiburg	Furtwangen	Heidelberg [9]	Heilbronn	Isny	Karlsruhe	Konstanz	Mannheim	Nürtingen	Offenburg	Pforzheim	Reutlingen	Schwäbisch Gmünd	Sigmaringen	Stuttgart	Ulm	Weingarten	Augsburg	Bamberg	Coburg	Münchberg	Eichstätt	Freising-Weihenstephan	Triesdorf
Landwirtschaft/Agrarwirtschaft												●														●	●
Lebensmitteltechnologie [5]																										●	
Luft- und Raumfahrttechnik																											
Maschinenbau	●		●			●	●		●	●	●		●		●		●		●	●	●		●				
Mathematik																		●									
Medientechnik																		●									
Metallkunde	●									●																	
Milch- und Molkereiwirtschaft																										■	
Papiertechnik																											
Pharmatechnik																	●										
Physikalische Technik/Physik							●	●												●							
Produktionstechnik	●		●		●		●												●	■							
Religionspädagogik [6]				●																					●		
Schiffbau																											
Schiffsbetriebstechnik																											
Seefahrt/Nautik																											
Sozialwesen (Sozialarbeit) [7]			●	●		●					●				●					●		●	●		●		
Sozialwesen (Sozialpädagogik) [7]			●	●							●				●												
Sozialwesen (Heilpädagogik)				●																							
Städtebau									■									■									
Systemanalyse																											
Technisches Gesundheitswesen [8]																			●								
Textiltechnik															●									●			
Ton- und Bildtechnik																											
Touristik							●																				
Transportwesen																											
Triebwerkbau																											
Übersetzungswesen																											
Umweltschutz/Umwelttechnik		■	■		■			■		■	■		■		■				■	■			■			■	
Verfahrenstechnik											●		●							■							
Vermessungs- und Kartenwesen									●									●									
Versicherungswesen																											
Versorgungstechnik (Energie/Wärme)			●																								
Wasserbau/Wasserwirtschaft																											
Weinbau/Weinwirtschaft							●																				
Werkstofftechnik	●				●					●																	
Wirtschaftsinformatik					●	●			●	●					●						■						
Wirtschaftsingenieurwesen	●		●						●		●		●					●									

[5] This course of study is held at the TU Munich.
[6] Munich: FH course of study of the KH Neuendettelsau; Paderborn: Department of the Catholic FH of North-Rhine-Westphalia, Cologne.
[7] Bavaria: Combined course of study for social work/therapeutic pedagogy.
[8] FH Ulm. Medical technology.
[9] Heidelberg: FH for Rehabilitation.

D

● Complete course of study
■ Advanced segment of course

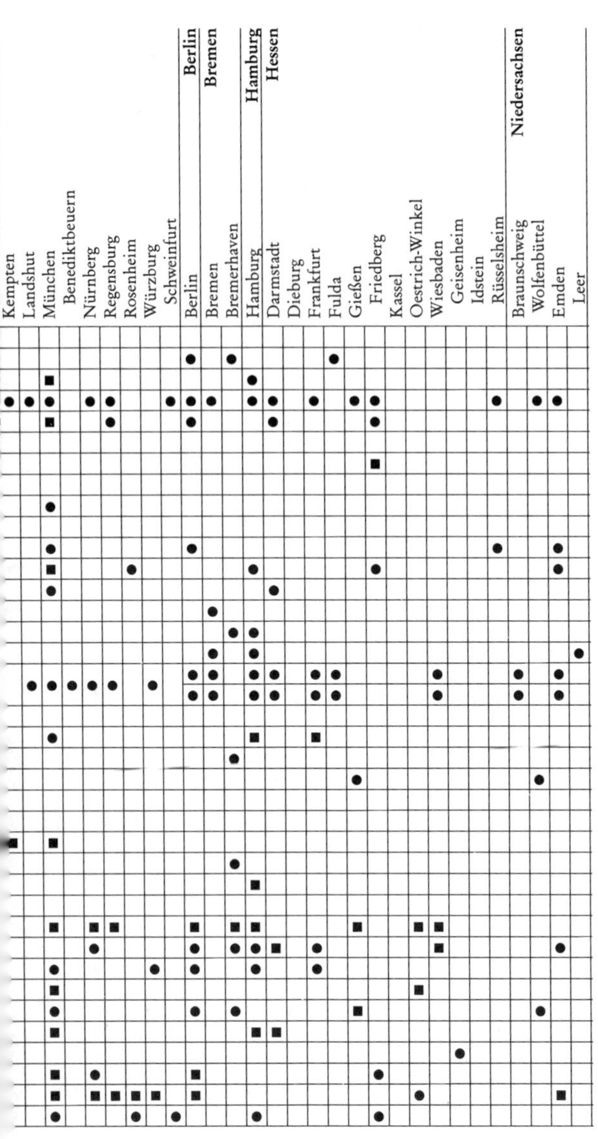

Subject	Kempten	Landshut	München	Benediktbeuern	Nürnberg	Regensburg	Rosenheim	Würzburg	Schweinfurt	Berlin	Bremen	Bremerhaven	Hamburg	Darmstadt	Dieburg	Frankfurt	Fulda	Gießen	Friedberg	Kassel	Oestrich-Winkel	Wiesbaden	Geisenheim	Idstein	Rüsselsheim	Braunschweig	Wolfenbüttel	Emden	Leer
										Berlin	Bremen		Hamburg	Hessen												Niedersachsen			
Agriculture, agronomy																													
Food technology[5]										●		●					●												
Aeronautical and aerospace engineering			■										●																
Mechanical engineering	●	●	●		●	●			●	●	●		●	●		●		●	●						●		●	●	
Mathematics			■			●				●				●					●										
Media engineering																													
Metallurgy																			■										
Milk production and dairy management																													
Paper technology			●																										
Pharmatechnology																													
Physical engineering/Physics			●							●															●			●	
Production engineering			■				●						●						●									●	
Religious education[6]			●											●															
Naval architecture											●																		
Ship operation												●	●																
Navigation/Nautics											●		●																●
Social work[7]		●	●	●	●	●		●		●	●		●	●		●	●					●				●		●	
Social pedagogy[7]										●	●		●	●		●	●					●				●		●	
Social work (therapeutic pedagogy)																													
Urban planning			●										■			■													
Systems analysis												●																	
Public health technology[8]																		●									●		
Textiles technology																													
Sound and picture technology																													
Tourism	■		■																										
Transports administration												●																	
Engine technology													■																
Translating																													
Environmental protection and technology			■		■	■				■		■	■					■			■	■							
Process engineering					●					●		●	●	■		●						■						●	
Surveying and cartography			●					●		●			●			●													
Insurance studies			■																		■								
Services engineering (energy)			●							●		●						■									●		
Hydraulic engineering, water management			■										■	■															
Viticulture, wine business																							●						
Materials technology			■		●					■									●										
Business computing			■		■	■	■	■		■											●							■	
Industrial engineering			●				●		●				●						●										

D

Courses of study at Fachhochschulen and corresponding courses at Gesamthochschulen/ Universitäten

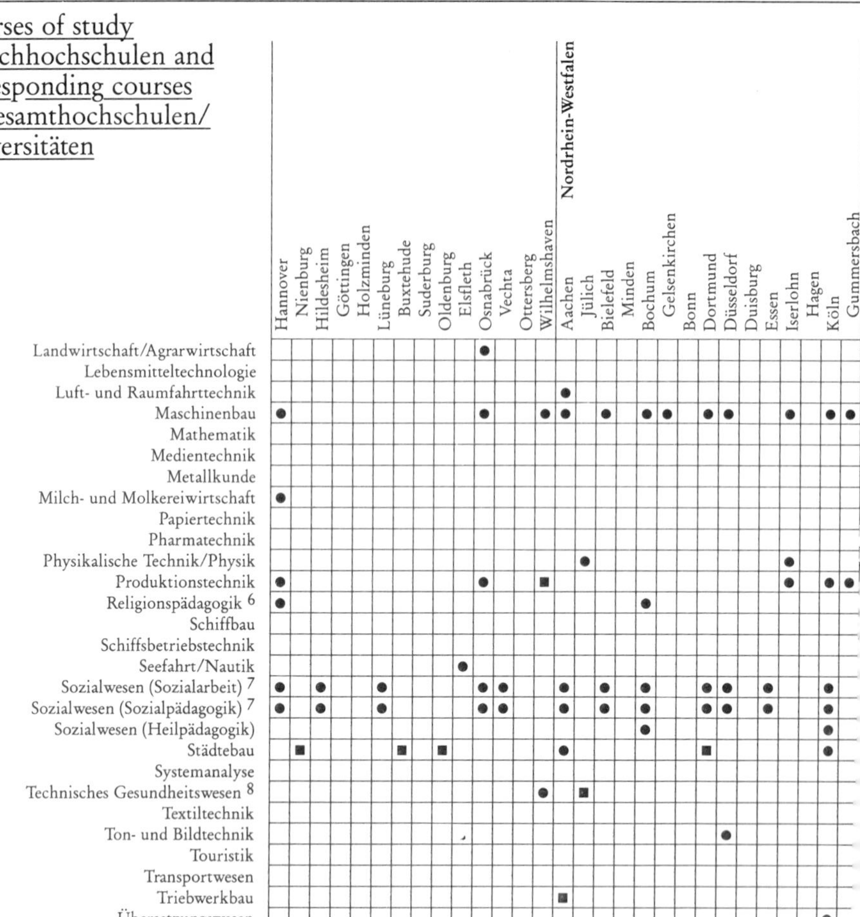

	Hannover	Nienburg	Hildesheim	Göttingen	Holzminden	Lüneburg	Buxtehude	Suderburg	Oldenburg	Elsfleth	Osnabrück	Vechta	Ottersberg	Wilhelmshaven	Nordrhein-Westfalen Aachen	Jülich	Bielefeld	Minden	Bochum	Gelsenkirchen	Bonn	Dortmund	Düsseldorf	Duisburg	Essen	Iserlohn	Hagen	Köln	Gummersbach
Landwirtschaft/Agrarwirtschaft											●																		
Lebensmitteltechnologie																													
Luft- und Raumfahrttechnik															●														
Maschinenbau	●										●			●	●		●		●	●		●	●			●		●	●
Mathematik																													
Medientechnik																													
Metallkunde																													
Milch- und Molkereiwirtschaft	●																												
Papiertechnik																													
Pharmatechnik																													
Physikalische Technik/Physik																●										●			
Produktionstechnik	●										●			■												●		●	●
Religionspädagogik [6]	●																		●										
Schiffbau																													
Schiffsbetriebstechnik																													
Seefahrt/Nautik										●																			
Sozialwesen (Sozialarbeit) [7]	●		●			●					●	●			●		●		●			●	●		●			●	
Sozialwesen (Sozialpädagogik) [7]	●		●			●					●	●			●		●		●			●	●		●			●	
Sozialwesen (Heilpädagogik)																			●									●	
Städtebau		■					■		■						●							■						●	
Systemanalyse																													
Technisches Gesundheitswesen [8]														●		■													
Textiltechnik																													
Ton- und Bildtechnik																							●						
Touristik																													
Transportwesen																													
Triebwerkbau															■														
Übersetzungswesen																												●	
Umweltschutz/Umwelttechnik				■										■		●												■	
Verfahrenstechnik															■				●				●					●	
Vermessungs- und Kartenwesen									●										●						●				
Versicherungswesen																												●	
Versorgungstechnik (Energie/Wärme)																				●								●	
Wasserbau/Wasserwirtschaft					●			●							●			■	●									●	
Weinbau/Weinwirtschaft																													
Werkstofftechnik											●											●		●					
Wirtschaftsinformatik						●					●											●							●
Wirtschaftsingenieurwesen														●			●												

Footnotes, see p. 136.

● Complete course of study
■ Advanced segment of course

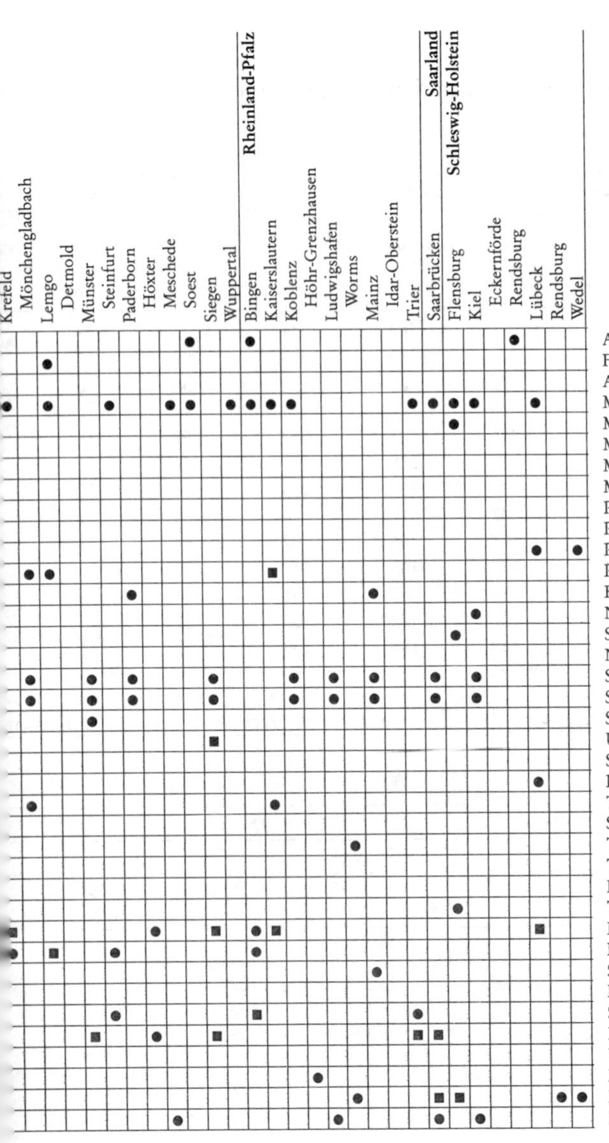

													Rheinland-Pfalz									Saarland	Schleswig-Holstein						
	Krefeld	Mönchengladbach	Lemgo	Detmold	Münster	Steinfurt	Paderborn	Höxter	Meschede	Soest	Siegen	Wuppertal	Bingen	Kaiserslautern	Koblenz	Höhr-Grenzhausen	Ludwigshafen	Worms	Mainz	Idar-Oberstein	Trier	Saarbrücken	Flensburg	Kiel	Eckernförde	Rendsburg	Lübeck	Rendsburg	Wedel
Ariculture, agronomy										●			●													●			
Food technology			●																										
Aeronautical and aerospace engineering																													
Mechanical engineering	●		●			●			●	●		●	●	●	●						●	●	●	●			●		
Mathematics																							●						
Media engineering																													
Metallurgy																													
Milk production and dairy management																													
Paper technology																													
Pharmatechnology																													
Physical engineering/Physics																											●		●
Production engineering		●	●											■															
Religious education[6]							●												●										
Naval architecture																								●					
Ship operation																							●						
Navigation/Nautics																													
Social work[7]		●			●		●				●				●		●		●			●		●					
Social pedagogy[7]		●			●		●				●				●		●		●			●		●					
Social work (therapeutic pedagogy)					●																								
Urban planning											■																		
Systems analysis																													
Public health technology[8]																											●		
Textiles technology		●												●															
Sound and picture technology																													
Tourism																		●											
Transports administration																													
Engine technology																													
Translating																							●						
Environmental protection and technology	■							●			■		●	■													■		
Process engineering	●		■			●							●																
Surveying and cartography																			●										
Insurance studies																													
Services engineering (energy)						●							■								●								
Hydraulic engineering, water management					■			●			■										■	■							
Viticulture, wine business																													
Materials technology																●													
Business computing																		●				■	■					●	●
Industrial engineering									●								●					●		●					

D

3. Student statistics

Students from EC Member States broken down according to subject areas, winter semester 1987/88

Country of origin	Foreign students in subject group					
	Humanities including languages and sports	Law, economics and social science	Mathematics, natural sciences engineering	Engineering	Medicine, dentistry veterinary medicine	Agricultural and nutritional sciences
Europe	13954	10056	5362	9741	3037	527
EC Member States	7889	4373	2553	3333	1099	211
Belgium	215	97	67	99	39	6
Denmark	109	59	29	41	17	7
Greece	1775	1 456	1125	1257	559	36
Spain	774	384	208	314	99	25
France	1 528	620	165	254	56	27
Ireland	151	37	17	4	4	1
Italy	1 104	478	256	362	89	18
Luxembourg	306	172	165	347	52	25
The Nederlands	648	454	283	411	107	46
Portugal	161	127	52	105	22	5
United Kingdom	1118	489	186	139	55	15

Students from EC Member States broken down according to types of higher education institutions

Country of origin	Foreign students				
	Total		There of		
			Universities	Art academies	Fachhoch-schulen
	Total number	%	Number		
Europe	42677	52,6	33273	1107	8297
EC Member States	19458	24,0	16114	490	2854
Belgium	523	0,6	394	16	113
Denmark	262	0,3	215	8	39
Greece	6 208	7,7	5598	51	559
Spain	1 804	2,2	1468	41	295
France	2 650	3,3	2 086	89	475
Ireland	214	0,3	196	10	8
Italy	2 307	2,8	1 795	87	425
Luxembourg	1 067	1,3	950	25	92
The Nederlands	1 949	2,4	1 486	70	393
Portugal	472	0,6	349	10	113
United Kingdom	2 002	2,5	1 577	83	342

Source: Grund- und Strukturdaten 1988/89,
published by Bundesministerium für Bildung und Wissenschaft.

4. Bibliography

The educational system in the Federal Republic of Germany. Governance, structures, courses. Published by: Foreign Office of the Federal Republic of Germany. (Bonn, 1982, resp. 1984), Ed. Ständige Konferenz der Kultusminister; also available in French and Spanish.

Die Bedeutung der Fachhochschulausbildung und ihrer Abschlüsse in der Bundesrepublik Deutschland und im internationalen Rahmen. (German, English, French, Spanish). Ed.: Ständige Konferenz der Kultusminister (KMK), Bonn, 1986, 54 pp. (2nd ed.). Available free of charge from the KMK, Nassestr. 8, 5300 Bonn 1.

Fachhochschulführer. Ständige Konferenz der Rektoren und Präsidenten der Staatlichen Fachhochschulen in der Bundesrepublik Deutschland. Frankfurt, Verlag Campus, 1989, 367 pp. Price: DM 36 (English, French and Spanish editions in preparation). A detailed reference book on the 69 *Fachhochschulen* in the Federal Republic which provides information on more than 750 degree courses in more than 40 subjects and which, among other things, contains information on foreign partner higher education institutions, language courses and other details.

Informationsschrift zur Förderung partnerschaftlicher Beziehungen zu Hochschulen in Entwicklungsländern. Contains a survey of existing relations (as of November 1987), Bonn, 1987, 32 pp. and about 140 pp. of enclosures. Ed.: Ständige Konferenz der Kultusminister der Länder (KMK), Nassestr. 8, 5300 Bonn 1.

Aus Tradition in die Zukunft — Die Hochschulen in der Bundesrepublik Deutschland. Series: Bildung und Wissenschaft (BW 1/2 1987). 36 pp. Published by and available free of charge from Inter Nationes e. V., Kennedyallee 91-103, D-5300 Bonn 2. (Also available in English, French and Spanish.)

Vademecum deutscher Stätten der Lehre. Part 1: Universities, 9th ed. Published by Editorial Board of the Deutschen Universitätszeitung, Publishing house: Raabe, 1989, 1 400 pp. Price: DM 360.

Studien- und Berufswahl 1988/89. Entscheidungshilfen für Abiturienten und Absolventen der Fachoberschulen. Published by: Bund-Länder-Kommission für Bildungsplanung und Bundesantalt für Arbeit. Bad Honnef: Bock, 400 pp. This book appears annually and is distributed free of charge to pupils in their final school year.

Vorlesungsverzeichnisse (course catalogues) of the higher education institutions, newly published every summer and winter semester. Available from bookshops in student towns.

ZVS-Kurzinfo. Appears new every semester. Available free of charge from the Central Office for the Allocation of Places in Higher Education (ZVS), 4600 Dortmund 1, Sonnenstr. 171, Postfach 8000.

Deutscher Akademischer Austauschdienst (DAAD). (German Academic Exchange Service), Kennedyallee 50, 5300 Bonn 2, informs students on studies in the Federal Republic with the following brochures that are available free of charge and which may also be consulted in the *Auslandsämter* at the institutions of higher education.

Das Studium in der Bundesrepublik Deutschland, Wissenschaftliche Hochschulen. Sixteen-page instruction pamphlet for foreign students (German, English, French, Spanish, Portuguese, Turkish, Indonesian, Arabic, Japanese).

Das Studium in der Bundesrepublik Deutschland. Fachhochschulen. (German, English, French, Spanish, Portuguese, Arabic, Indonesian). Access to studies via *Studienkollegs* for foreign students (German, English, French, Spanish, Portuguese, Arabic, Indonesian). Students from EC Member States are not required to attend a *Studienkolleg*.

Zulassungsinformationen. Information on admission for foreign and stateless applicants to higher education at a university in the Federal Republic of Germany, including Berlin (West). Fourpage leaflet (German, English, French, Spanish).

Antrag auf Zulassung zum Studium/Immatrikulation. Form for admission to/registration at an institute of higher education. Four-page form available from the institutions of higher education themselves.

Degree courses at Institutions of Higher Education in the Federal Republic of Germany.

Cursus d'études dans les établissements d'enseignement supérieur en République fédérale d'Allemagne.

D

Carreras de enseñanza superior en la Répública Federal Alemania.
These three brochures are a translated extract of the abovementioned 'Studien- und Berufswahl' published by Bock. Aufbaustudiengänge in der Bundesrepublik Deutschland. Postgraduate courses in the Federal Republic of Germany (German, foreign language editions in preparation)
For some study areas, the DAAD has published special *Fachstudienführer* (subject area study guides). Namely,
Biosciences (German, English, French, Spanish),
German language and literature,
History (German, English, Spanish, French versions in preparation),
Engineering sciences (German, foreign language editions in preparation),
Colleges of Music,
Courses in German as a foreign language and, as a supplementary volume, a detailed description of the range of language teaching,
German as a foreign language at the institutions of higher education and *Studienkollegs* in the Federal Republic of Germany, including Berlin (West).

Sommerkurse in der Bundesrepublik Deutschland: Sprache, Literatur, Musik, Landeskunde. Summer courses in the Federal Republic of Germany covering language, literature, music and general studies. This brochure is updated at the end of each year.

Scholarships for postgraduate courses, with special relevance to developing countries at universities and Fachhochschulen in the Federal Republic of Germany, 1989/90. This brochure, which is also available in Spanish, describes the postgraduate courses which are of particular interest to students from developing countries.

Förderungsmöglichkeiten für deutsche und ausländische Hochschulangehörige — ein Leitfaden. Short, general guide to scholarships and other educational study assistance.

Studienland EG — Geförderte Kooperationsprogramme deutscher Hochschulen 1988/89. Provides a detailed survey of all group exchange programmes at German universities and *Fachhochschulen* with institutions of higher education in other EC Member States which have been promoted within the framework of the Erasmus programme of the EC, by financial means from the DAAD programme 'Integrated studies abroad' or by the German-French Higher Education *Kolleg*.

Publications of the Westdeutsche Rektorenkonferenz (WRK). The following publications are available free of charge from the office of the WRK, Ahrstraße 39, 5300 Bonn 2:

Übersicht über Studienmöglichkeiten und Zulassungsbeschränkungen für deutsche Studienanfänger an den Hochschulen der Bundesrepublik Deutschland. Twelve-page brochure newly published every semester. Available free of charge from: WRK, Ahrstraße 39, 5300 Bonn 2.

Übersicht über Bewerbungs- und Anmeldungsfristen, Einschreibung, Beginn und Ende der Vorlesungen der wissenschaftlichen Hochschulen der Bundesrepublik Deutschland. Brochure, newly published every semester, available free of charge from WRK.

Kooperationsvereinbarungen (Partnerschaften) zwischen deutschen und ausländischen Hochschulen. sixth edition as of September 1987. Extracts available free of charge upon request.

Publications from the Federal Ministry of Education and Science, Heinemannstr. 2, 5300 Bonn 2:

Äquivalenzen im Hochschulbereich 2/88 from the series: 'Bildung-Wissenschaft-Aktuell' of the Ministry of Education and Science, Postfach 20 01 08, 5300 Bonn 2.

BAFöG 1988/89; Gesetze und Beispiele. Published by: Federal Ministry of Education and Science 91 pp. Valid as of spring 1989. Available free of charge from the Ministry.

Die Begabtenförderungswerke in der Bundesrepublik Deutschland. Published by: Bundesministerium für Bildung und Wissenschaft. Bonn: 1987, 95 pp. Also free of charge.

Mobilität von Studenten und Wissenschaftlern. Series: Bildung Wissenschaft aktuell, issue 1/87. Published by: Bundesministerium für Bildung und Wissenschaft.

Other publications:

Kleiner Wegweiser zu entwicklungsländerbezogenen Postgraduierten-Studiengängen und Weiterbildungsangeboten an Hochschulen in der Bundesrepublik Deutschland einschließlich Berlin (West). 2nd extended ed., Bonn 1986, 55 pp. Published by: Deutsche Stiftung für internationale Entwicklung, Hans-Böckler-Straße 5, D-5300 Bonn 3.

Förderungsmöglichkeiten für Studierende: Published by: Deutsches Studentenwerk, 8th ed. Publishing house: Bock, Bad Honnef, 338 pp. Price: DM 22,80.

Behinderte studieren. Praktische Tips und Informationen der Beratungsstelle für behinderte Studienbewerber und Studenten des Deutschen Studentenwerks e.V. 3rd edition. Published by: Deutsches Studentenwerk, Bonn e.V. 1989, 186 pp. Free of charge.

Presse- und Informationsamt der Bundesregierung: Tatsachen über Deutschland (German, English, French, Spanish, Portuguese, Italian, Brazilian-Portuguese, Arabic), Bonn. Available free of charge from: Presse- und Informationsamt der Bundesregierung, Welckerstraße 11, D-5300 Bonn 1.

5. Glossary

Akademisches Auslandsamt: A body at a higher education establishment which provides assistance to foreign students and manages the university's international academic relations.

Allgemeine Hochschulreife: Qualification obtained as a rule by taking a final examination *(Abiturprüfung)* after 13 years of schooling, including upper secondary education, as a rule at a *Gymnasium*. The holder has in general the right to study at all institutions of higher education without restrictions with regard to subject areas.

Allgemeiner Studentenausschuß (AStA): Student self-administration body (in most states) which occupies itself with the academic and social interests of the students.

Bundesausbildungsförderungsgesetz (BAföG): Regulates the payment of loans and subsidies to finance the studies of German and (in special cases) foreign students.

Deutscher Akademischer Austauschdienst (DAAD) (German Academic Exchange Service): Organization of the higher education establishments for the promotion of relations between higher education establishments and abroad. It is almost exclusively financed by the Federal Government. Gives information about possibilities of studying in the Federal Republic of Germany and abroad, and awards grants to foreign and German students and young academics within the framework of specific programmes.

Diplomgrad: Academic degree which is awarded as a higher education qualification after an examination, particularly in natural and engineering sciences, economics and social sciences.

Doktorgrad: Academic degree awarded after completion of a doctoral thesis *(Dissertation)* and an oral examination *(Rigorosum)*. In principle, only those students are permitted to work for a doctorate who have already completed a *Diplom* or other examination.

Exmatrikulation: Removal of a student from the list of students of a higher education institution.

Fachbereich (Fakultät): Basic organizational unit of the higher education institution representing one or more related subjects.

Fachhochschule: Institution of higher education offering academic training with a practical bias, particularly in engineering, economics, social affairs, agriculture and design.

Fachhochschulreife: Qualification obtained, as a rule, by taking a final examination after 12 years of schooling, the last two years at a *Fachoberschule*. It provides access to studies at *Fachhochschulen* and the corresponding courses of study at *Gesamthochschulen*.

Fakultät see *Fachbereich*.

Feststellungsprüfung: Foreign applicants for higher education whose secondary school-leaving certificate has not been recognized as equivalent to a German certificate of aptitude for higher education must take this examination. Students attend the *Studienkolleg* to prepare for this exam.

Fernuniversität: A *Gesamthochschule* in existence since 1975, which offers part-time and continuing studies in particular. Written and audio-visual media are complemented by classes which students have to attend. 39 regional centres look after the needs of the students.

Gesamthochschule: Institution of higher education existing in two *Länder* combining functions of the universities, *Fachhochschulen* and, in some cases, colleges of art and music. They offer courses of studies of various duration and leading to different degrees.

Grundstudium: The degree courses at institutions of higher education are generally divided into an initial stage *(Grundstudium)* or Part 1 and second stage *(Hauptstudium),* Part 2. Part 1 is concluded with an intermediate or preliminary examination and lasts four semesters at universities and between two and four semesters at *Fachhochschulen.*

Habilitation: The *Habilitation* is, depending on the requirements of the post, one of the preconditions for employment for professors. Through the *Habilitation* the applicant's capacity to independently represent a scientific-academic subject in teaching and research is formally proven. To be admitted to the *Habilitation* the candidate must have a doctorate and must have continued scientific-academic work after the doctorate.

Hauptstudium: After passing an intermediate or preliminary examination, the second study stage commences. This is concluded with a higher education, a State or a church examination.

Hochschulrahmengesetz (HRG): A Federal law in effect since 1976 which regulates the general principles of higher education.

Immatrikulation: Admission to a higher education establishment by entering one's name in the students' register.

Magister Artium (MA): Higher edcuation qualification (academic degree) which is awarded as a result of a higher education examination, particularly in arts and humanities subjects.

Numerus clausus: Name for the admission restrictions which only apply when there are not sufficient places available on a particular course for the number of applicants. This applies to German and foreign students. Admission procedure in these cases is settled by the individual States in a *Staatsvertrag* (State document), on the basis of the *Hochschulrahmengesetz.* These restricted places are allocated by the 'Zentralstelle für die Vergabe von Studienplätzen' in Dortmund.

Praxis semester: Practical periods outside of the institution of higher education are integrated into the studies. The duration of these practical periods, one or two practical semesters, differs from one *Land* to the next.

Promotion: *See Doktorgrad.*

Regelstudienzeit: The duration of studies in which the examination that is being prepared for can be achieved is laid down in the study regulations for each course of study.

Rückmeldung: Required re-registration at the beginning of every semester within determined time-limits which are listed in the *Vorlesungsverzeichnis* of the higher education institutions in question.

Sekretariat: Administrative office at the higher education institutions at which registration (matriculation) takes place.

Sozialbeitrag (-gebühren)/Studentenwerksbeitrag: Compulsory fee to be paid upon matriculation which contributes to financing various student service institutions. At some higher education institutions a contribution to financing student self-administration is also contained in the fee.

Staatsexamen (-prüfung): State examination terminating a course of study at higher education institutions for which the State determines requirements. This examination is a prerequisite for entering a profession in only part of the courses of study (all medical professions, teachers, lawyers, pharmacists, food chemists).

Studentenausweis: Proof of registration (matriculation) at a higher education institution; provides various benefits for foreign and German students in different areas of everyday life.

Studentenschaft: There is a so-called *verfaßte Studentenschaft* in most States at every higher education establishment. It is a student organization with obligatory membership and fees. The tasks of the *Studentenschaft* are connected with the higher education establishment (looking after the academic, social and cultural interests of the students).

Studentenverbände: Membership of one of the various associations active in higher education politics and participation in their political or cultural work is open to all students.

Studentenwerk: Institution which provides social assistance for the students at every higher education establishment, runs the *Mensa* (refectory) and student halls of residence, and which also usually takes over the payment of *BAföG* to the students.

Studienkolleg: In order to prepare for the *Feststellungsprüfung,* foreign applicants for higher education may attend a *Studienkolleg*. The training at this institution generally lasts for two half-year periods. In order that foreign students may prepare for their intended studies purposefully, the *Studienkolleg* courses are focused on larger study fields.

Vorlesungsverzeichnis: Catalogue of the courses taught at a higher education institution containing at the same time a list of the teaching staff, relevant dates and other important information on studying at the institution in question. Available in the bookshops at the higher education insitution location. In some EC Member States, they can be consulted in the branch offices of the DAAD or one of the Goethe Institutes.

Vorprüfung: See *Zwischenprüfung*.

Westdeutsche Rektorenkonferenz (WRK): Conference for the university presidents and rectors of the higher education establishments in the Federal Republic of Germany, which sits in Bonn.

Zwischenprüfung: For degree courses with a normal study duration of at least four years and concluding with a higher education examination, an intermediate examination is held which may be taken concurrently with the studies.

D

6. Diagram of the education system

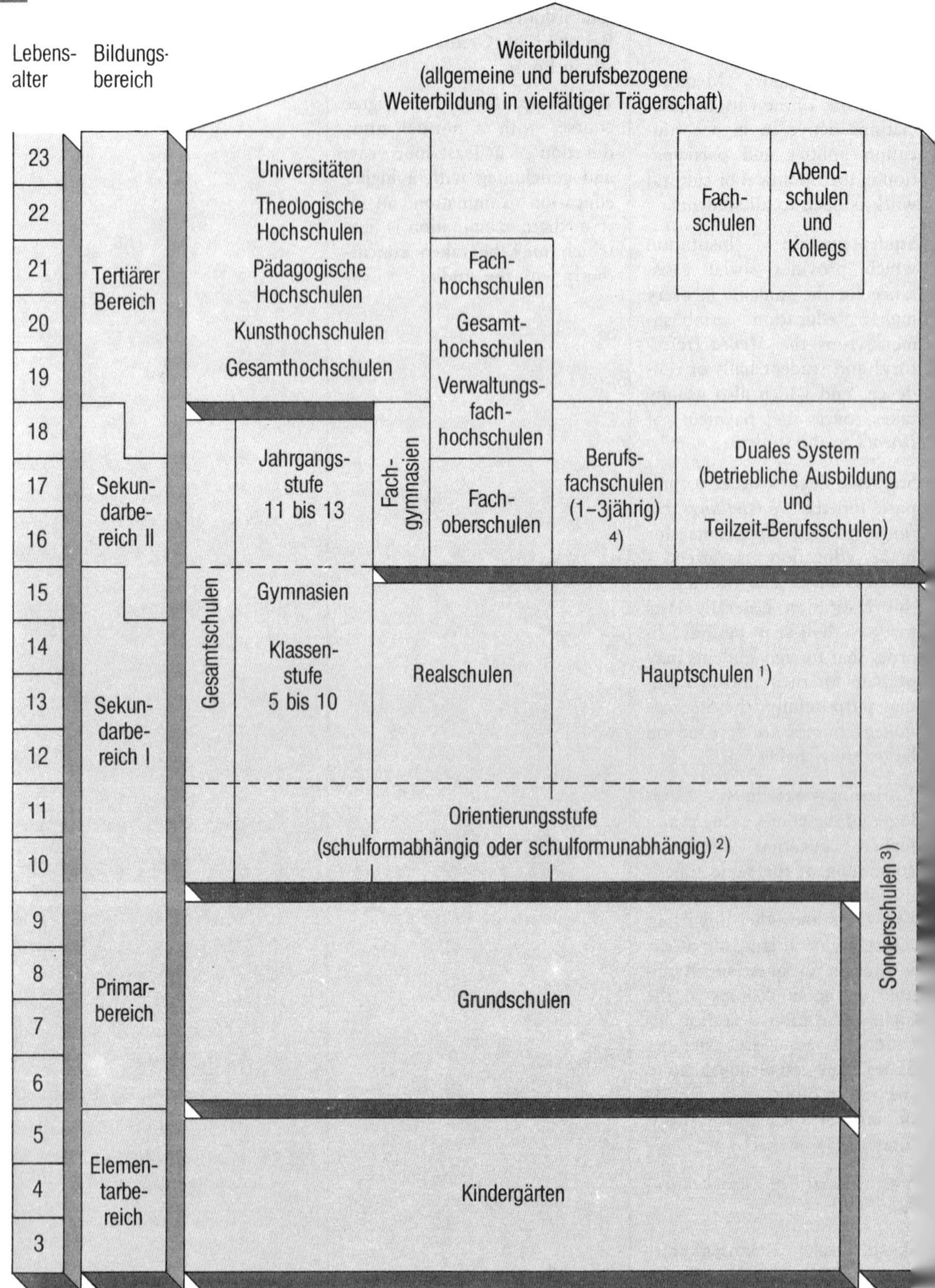

Lebens-alter
Bildungs-bereich
Weiterbildung
(allgemeine und berufsbezogene
Weiterbildung in vielfältiger Trägerschaft)
23
22
21
20
19
18
17
16
15
14
13
12
11
10
9
8
7
6
5
4
3
Tertiärer Bereich
Sekundarbereich II
Sekundarbereich I
Primarbereich
Elementarbereich
Universitäten
Theologische Hochschulen
Pädagogische Hochschulen
Kunsthochschulen
Gesamthochschulen
Fachhochschulen
Gesamthochschulen
Verwaltungsfachhochschulen
Fachschulen
Abendschulen und Kollegs
Jahrgangsstufe 11 bis 13
Fachgymnasien
Fachoberschulen
Berufsfachschulen (1–3jährig) 4)
Duales System (betriebliche Ausbildung und Teilzeit-Berufsschulen)
Gesamtschulen
Gymnasien
Klassenstufe 5 bis 10
Realschulen
Hauptschulen 1)
Orientierungsstufe
(schulformabhängig oder schulformunabhängig) 2)
Sonderschulen 3)
Grundschulen
Kindergärten

Explanations and translations of technical terms see facing page.

Footnotes, see p. 148.

Legend

Abendschulen und Kollegs — Evening schools for employed adults and full-time institutions offering instruction to adults who want to qualify for higher education.
Berufliche Schulen — Vocational schools.
Bildungsbereich — Level of education.
Duales System — Dual system (training in enterprises and vocational schools).
Elementarbereich — Pre-school level.
Fachgymnasium — Grammar school, upper level, 11th to 13th forms leading to a general university entrance qualification, but providing also vocational education in special, career-orientated areas (e.g. economics, technology social work).
Fachhochschulen — Institution of higher education offering academic training with a practical bias, particularly in engineering, economics, social affairs.
Fachoberschulen — Technical secondary school (11th and 12th forms) providing general education along with specialized instruction in various subject areas (e.g. economics, technology, social work). The leaving certificate qualifies students to enter *Fachhochschulen.*
Fachschule — Technical school providing advanced vocational training, e.g. for technicians who want to become 'State-examined engineer' or craftsmen who want to be 'Meister' in their trade. Usually two-year programmes of study.
Gesamthochschule — The type of higher education institutions exists only in two of the 11 *Länder*. It combines functions of the universities, the *Fachhochschulen* and, in some cases, of colleges of art and music. Courses of study of varying duration are offered, and they lead to different degrees.
Gesamtschule — Comprehensive school.
Grundschule — Primary school.
Gymnasium — Grammar school/secondary school, 5th to 13th forms providing general education and, after successful completion, giving access to university studies.
Hauptschule — Secondary school, lower level (5th to 9th forms or, in some cases, 10th). Upon graduation, most pupils enter employment, but some continue at grammar schools.
Jahrgangsstufe — Classes 11-13.
Kindergarten — Kindergarten (voluntary).
Klassenstufe — Classes 5-10.
Kunsthochschule — College/Academy of art and music.
Lebensalter — Age.
Orientierungsstufe — 5th and 6th forms may be organized as an orientation stage during which the decision on a particular school type is left open.
Pädagogische Hochschule — Teacher training college.
Primarbereich — Primary school level.

D

Realschulen — General secondary school, lower level, normally 5th to 10th forms, giving access to upper secondary education and to middle-level careers.
Sekundarbereich I — Lower secondary level.
Sekundarbereich II — Upper secondary level.
Sonderschulen — Special schools for handicapped children.
Tertiärer Bereich — Tertiary level.
Theologische Hochschule — College of theology and philosophy.
Universitäten — Universities.
Verwaltungsfachhochschulen — Administrative colleges (for civil servants).
Weiterbildung — Further or continuing education of varying duration, e.g. for graduates who want to specialize in a certain subject or with a view to obtain a doctorate. There are numerous higher education institutions as well as other organizations offering further studies or training of a general education or vocational type.

1 About 30% of all pupils attend the *Hauptschulen* for 10 years.
2 The orientation stage is attended by around 73% of pupils in the 5th and 6th years of schooling.
3 Appropriate institutions are also to be found on the level of *Realschulen* and grammar schools as well as in the vocational schools.
4 Differentiated system of up to three-year schools which lead to a certificate of vocational qualification.

Schematic representation of the typical structure of the education system in the Federal Republic of Germany. There are differences in the individual *Länder*.

The allocation of age to the educational institutions is valid for the earliest possible, typical entr and for uninterrupted progress through the educational system.

The size of the rectangles is not proportionate to the numbers attending.

Greece

Note

The Colleges (Ανώτατες Σχολές) which have been renamed as Universities (Πανεπιστήμια) are referred to in this Handbook by their original names, since the manuscript had already been sent to press when the relevant law was passed.

The new names will be adopted in the 7th edition of the Student Handbook.

Organization of tertiary education

Tertiary education in Greece falls under the responsibility of the Ministry of Education and Religion; it comprises higher education with its universities (AEI) and the technical tertiary education level with its technical training facilities (TEI).

Furthermore, the following educational institutions which are part of the non-university tertiary sector fall under the auspices of the Ministry of Education:

1. Charohopios — School of Home Economics;
2. Department of Technician Training (Asetem) of the training institution for vocational and technical training (Selete);
3. Training seminary for priests in Athens;
   (Admission: candidates must submit an admissions application form and are then selected in special examinations).

Moreover, there are institutions of the tertiary education sector which fall under the responsibility of other ministries:

(a) Ministry of National Defence
(Officer training schools of the army, the navy and the air force: the Ikaros school, the military academy for female medical officers. All of these institutions have been placed on a equal footing with the AEI institutions of higher education through Law 1351/1983).

(b) Ministry of Agriculture
(the Mediterranean Institute for Agriculture in Chania, the International Higher Education Centre for Studies on the Agriculture of the Mediterranean Region);

(c) Ministry of Public Order
(Officer training schools of the Greek police, officer training schools of the fire service);

(d) Ministry of Merchant Shipping
(State training centres of the merchant navy for captains, engineers and radio engineers).

In the whole of tertiary education in Greece only a limited number of applicants can be accepted (entry limitations). The prospective students for study places in tertiary education in Greece sit general examinations after they have gained a secondary school-leaving certificate; these examinations are held annually in the second half of June. These examinations cover a certain number of subjects which lead to the corresponding study subjects in higher education. Students are instructed in these subjects during the last class of upper secondary schooling. For this reason, they must indicate at the beginning of the school year which direction they wish to take. School-leavers from previous years may take these subjects at post-schooling preparation centres (MPK), which are maintained in all districts of the country.

Admission to the institutions of tertiary education depends upon the mark, the number of available study places and the level of the respective subject area in which the applicant is to be accepted. The total number of points that each candidate can achieve is calculated from the sum of points in four subjects, which are equally weighted. One of these subjects is regarded as the major subject for one subject area each: the candidate must achieve at least the required minimum number of points in this subject, at least 10 (of 20 possible) points. If this is not the case, then the student cannot be admitted.

Furthermore, a fixed number of foreigners and Greeks with residence abroad as well as scholarship holders are admitted.

EDUCATION IN THE UNIVERSITY SECTOR (ΑΝΩΤΑΤΗ ΕΚΠΑΙΔΕΥΣΗ)

Article 16 of the 1975 Greek Constitution stipulates that art, science, research and teaching are free and that it is the duty of the State to develop and support them.

The same article in the Greek Constitution states that higher education is to be provided by autonomous public institutions. These institutions are under the supervision of the State, which is responsible for their funding. Their function and organization is regulated by higher education laws. Private higher education institutions are forbidden.

Generally, higher education begins after 12 years of schooling: six years of primary education and six years of secondary education.

Law 1268/82 'on the structure and function of the universities (AEI)' was tabled and adopted in the Greek Parliament with the objective of promoting structural changes for the democratization and modernization of institutions of higher education; it has been in force since 16 July 1982.

The primary objectives of the comprehensive reform which Law 1268/82 introduced are the safeguarding of the quality of higher education which is imperative from both national and social points of view and the creation of a free and democratic system of higher education. The fundamental organizational changes introduced by this law were:

1. the abolition of the institution of professorial chairs, the establishment of departments (τμήματα), and the division of these departments into subject areas (τομείς). Each of these subject areas will coordinate the teaching of a part of the field covered by its department. The faculty is responsible for the guidelines on training and research of the respective science whilst the departments are expected to implement the general objectives of the faculty.
2. the establishment of advisory and decision-making bodies. These are the National Academy of Education and Science (EAGE) and

the Council on Higher Education (SAP), each with its own clearly-defined responsibilities. The National Academy for Education and Science (EAGE), which has not yet been founded, will be expected to advise the government on questions relating to higher education training; it will plan and supervise research at the universities in the context of decisions made by the SAP.

The (Advisory) Council on Higher Education (SAP) is an institution of public supervision on which representatives from higher education, from the ministry as well as from the parties sit. It reports to the government on topics relating to higher education training. The Council for Higher Education (SAP) has already been founded and has been operating since April 1986;

3. the division of the university sector into departments, subject areas, faculties (Σχολή), and higher education institutions — AEIs (Ανώτατα Εκπαιδευτικά Ιδρύματα). The departmental full assembly is the authoritative body which on the one hand sets down the guidelines for training and research and on the other hand in its function as a democratic control body is responsible for the overall working of the department. The universities (AEIs) are organized in faculties. The bodies of the universities (AEIs) are the senate, the conference of rectors and the rector;
4. the guaranteed autonomy of university staff (DEP) in the execution of their teaching and research activities. The university staff is divided into four levels: professors, associate professors, assistant professors and lecturers;
5. the consolidation and guaranteed existence of autonomous, immune and free universities, as well as of the free exchange of ideas and of pluralism at universities.

Types of higher education institutions (AEIs)

Higher education institutions are categorized as follows:

Universities

These are the Universities of Athens (founded 1837), Thessalonica (1925), Patras (1964), Ioannina (1970), Thrace (1973), Crete (1973), the Aegaeon (which commenced teaching in the 1985/86 academic year), the Ionian University with its seat in Kerkyra (Corfu), which also commenced teaching in the 1985/86 academic year and the University of Thessaly with its seat in Volos, where teaching commenced in the 1988/89 academic year.

Polytechnic colleges (Πολυτεχνεία)

These are the polytechnic institutions of higher education in Athens (National Polytechnic Institutions of Higher Education, Metsovio, founded 1836, with the status of a university since 1914) and Crete (1977).

Independent institutions of higher education (Σχολές αυτοτελείς)

These are: the College of Trade and Industry (Athens, 1920); the College of Agriculture (Athens, 1920); the College of Art (1930, with university

status since 1935); the Panteios College of Political Sciences (Athens, 1930); the College of Industrial Studies (Piraeus, 1938, with university status since 1958); the College of Industrial Studies (Thessaloniki, 1948, with university status since 1958).

Students at AEIs

In the 1986/87 academic year a total of 115 908 students were registered at Greek universities, 35 884 of which were studying in Athens. The numbers of foreign students coming from EC Member States and registered in Greece can be seen in the table in the appendix.

Organization and validation of courses

Organization of courses

Undergraduate studies

Teaching in individual subject areas is organized along the lines of a study programme. This programme is drawn up by each department's general meeting. It is reviewed every April and includes a list of compulsory subjects and a list from which a choice of subjects must be made. This programme also includes a definition of course content for each course and a weekly schedule.

The study programme is based on the lowest possible number of semesters (two per year) which are needed to attain a degree (πτυχίο). The required number of semesters for each degree is defined by a presidential directive, which is issued after consultation with the SAP and the faculties: a minimum of eight semesters is required.

Each semester consists of a number of credit hours. One credit hour corresponds to either:

— a weekly one-hour course comprising only one lecture; or

— a one- to three-hour per week lecture or practical class for other courses, depending on the decisions of the departmental general meeting.

The study programme also defines the minimum number of credit hours required to earn a degree.

The academic year is divided into two semesters. Each semester consists of 13 full teaching weeks and two examination weeks. The first semester begins in the second half of September, the second semester ends in the first half of June. The senate sets the exact dates.

Students are marked in each subject by the professor teaching the course, who is also responsible for setting and holding written and oral examinations as necessary. Students who fail compulsory subjects are required to repeat that subject in the following semester. Students who fail courses they selected from the given list can either repeat that course in the following semester or opt for another course on the list.

Postgraduate studies

Law 1566/85 provided a new framework for the organization of postgraduate studies. This Law states that:

(a) with the permission of the Minister for National Education and Religion, each department may establish and run a postgraduate studies programme in the field for which it is responsible. Permission is granted upon application by the department and after reports by the senate and by the Council for Higher Education (SAP). Each postgraduate studies programme aims to award a postgraduate degree for a specialized field;

(b) each specialized field is defined by the subject area, or respectively, the subject areas jointly responsible for it. It is possible to establish an inter-departmental or inter-university programme. For this an application by the departments must be made and reports must be submitted by the senate and the SAP. Alternatively, the senate may submit the application followed by an assessment report by the SAP;

(c) a committee for postgraduate studies and for research will be established at every higher education institution (AEI);

(d) postgraduate students can take advantage of the same rights and reductions as undergraduate students.

Validation of courses

Students are awarded a degree (πτυχίο) after successful participation in a final examination. Degree holders can attain a doctorate, provided they produce a doctoral thesis in Greek (or Latin if the thesis is being submitted to the philosophy faculty) and successfully pass a public viva voce. In general (with the exception of the College of Art), a doctorate is required of anyone wishing to join the teaching and research staff of a higher education institution.

Postgraduate students who successfully complete their courses are awarded a corresponding title, which is important for the salary grade of graduates who are already in the civil service, and which must always be taken into consideration as a substantial qualification for grade assessments during any civil service career. There is the possibility for occasional students to take part in some classes. An application must be filed at the faculty and the permission of the respective lecturer sought.

EDUCATION IN THE TERTIARY TECHNICAL SECTOR (ΤΡΙΤΟΒΑΘΜΙΑ ΤΕΧΝΟΛΟΓΙΚΗ ΕΚΠΑΙΔΕΥΣΗ)

Tertiary technical education in Greece is covered by the TEIs which were established on the basis of Law 1404/83. Within the framework of this law and of their own statutes these TEIs are autonomous public institutions. The TEIs are supervised by the State, which funds them.

The TEIs are expected to offer theoretical and practical training suited to enabling the student to apply academic, technical, artistic and other knowledge and skills to a later career.

The legislation which laid down the foundation of the TEIs also envisaged the establishment of the following:

(a) new advisory and decision-making bodies — namely, the Council for Technological Education (STE) and the Institute for Technological Education (ITE), each with its

GR

own clearly defined responsibilities;
(b) administrative bodies on four levels: sub-department, department, faculty and TEI. At the same time the TEIs were given the legal status of guaranteed autonomous, immune and free places of learning.

Teaching is primarily the responsibility of the teaching staff (EP), which is divided into the following levels: professor, assistant professor, and lecturer.

Types of TEIs (τεχνολογικά Εκπαιδευτικά ιδρύματα)

In addition to the 11 TEIs which have been established in Greece and which are situated in Athens, Thessaloniki, Piraeus, Patras, Larissa, Heraklion, Kavala, Kosani, Chalkida, Serres and Messolongi, some of the TEIs have also opened up affiliated colleges. A TEI affiliated college is a teaching institution which is situated more than 30 kilometres from the parent TEI and which has only one faculty or at most three independent departments. The following TEIs maintain affiliated colleges:

Patras	in Kalamata;
Larissa	in Lamia and Karditsa;
Heraklion	in Chania;
Kavala	in Drama;
Kosani	in Florina;
Messolongi	in Ioannina, Arta and Karpenissi.

Students at TEIs

In the 1986/87 academic year, a total of 64 000 students were registered at Greek TEIs of which 16 288 were studying at the TEI of Athens.

Organization and validation of courses

Study courses at TEIs are based on specialized classes and lectures. Subjects are categorized as general subjects, compulsory subjects, subjects chosen from a given list and purely optional subjects.

Each department's study programme is drawn up at the departmental general meeting. The study programme is reviewed at least once every two years and students are informed about changes in good time.

The departmental study programme is drawn up in line with the general directive on study programmes, and is defined and put into effect on the basis of the respective curriculum by the Minister for National Education and Religion after consultation with the ITE.

At the beginning of each semester, students are expected to announce their desired individual semester schedule, although two requirements must be met:

1. they may not participate in a course for which another course is required, unless the required course has been successfully completed; and
2. the weekly schedule must consist of between 20 and 45 hours.

The form of teaching and the assessment criteria for each subject are

defined by collective decisions made by the relevant departmental bodies. In effect, student assessment is based on three criteria:
(a) on the student's active participation in the course;
(b) on the student's performance in various course activities throughout the semester; and
(c) on the student's performance in the final examinations.

In order to receive a degree, a student must also:
(a) successfully complete all the compulsory subjects as defined by the department;
(b) successfully complete a certain number of subjects which the student must choose from a given list;
(c) successfully complete a number of purely optional subjects which may also be chosen from other departments; and
(d) complete six months of practical vocational training.

Compulsory attendance is in force for all TEI lectures and classes. Students who fail a course must repeat it. The minimum length of studies at a TEI is six semesters. Each academic year is split into two independent teaching sessions. Each teaching semester comprises 15 full teaching weeks and two examination periods, each lasting two weeks. TEI degree holders are entitled to practize a profession as defined and regulated by the presidential directive drawn up after consultation with the education minister, and in some cases with the minister responsible for certain professional groups, and with the STE.

Admission and registration

Initial information

The authorities which offer information on undergraduate and postgraduate studies in Greece are:
(a) local Greek diplomatic and consular representations;
(b) the Ministry of Education, the Department of AEI Studies and Student Care; further, the Department of Research, Statistics and Organization in AEIs, and the Administrative Office for TEIs;
(c) the Public Relations Office of the Athens University Club; and
(d) the respective universities' administrative offices.

Entry requirements

Undergraduate studies

The basic requirement for admission to an institution of higher education is a school-leaving certificate from a Greek *lycée* (λύκειο) or proof of six to seven years of successful secondary schooling at a gymnasium (γυμνάσιο). Equivalent certificates from other Greek schools, or a school-leaving certificate from a foreign school, both in Greece and abroad, which entitles the holder to immatriculation at a university in the country of origin are regarded as equal to this basic requirement. The same requirement is needed for admission to a TEI. The College of Art is an exception to this rule, since up to 15 % of all its successful applicants may be admitted with a school-leaving certificate showing only three years of secondary schooling, if these applicants can show themselves to have extraordinary artistic talent.

Postgraduate studies

The requirements for admission to a postgraduate course of study are a first degree from a Greek or an equivalent foreign institution of higher education. There are no formal postgraduate studies at the TEIs. However, within the framework of their mandate, these do organize specialized programmes in order to enable TEI degree holders or equivalent degree holders to carry out work on a more specific section of their field of study. These so-called 'specialization programmes' last up to 10 months and include simultaneous practical training periods in relevant vocational and professional fields. At the end of these specialization programmes, participants receive appropriate certificates.

Limitations

Undergraduate studies

There is restricted entry to the institutions of higher education, since the number of available places is limited. The total number of places for each institution of higher education, or respectively each department, is laid down annually for each academic year by the Minister for Education, after consultation with the respective higher education institution, the senate and the Council for Higher Education, the SAP. A ministerial directive may admit applicants from the following categories over and above the total number of available places and up to a 20% share of the total number of successful applicants for higher education places.

For the 1988/89 academic year, the share of higher education places for these special categories was laid down as follows:

(a) foreign students — 1% — (this category includes foreigners not of Greek origin whose parents are not Greek citizens, neither by birth nor by naturalization);

(b) students of Greek origin who have lived abroad for more than five years — 5% — (this category includes Greeks or the children of Greeks [at least one parent must be Greek by birth or naturalization] who have themselves or who have had one parent living in Greece for at least five of the last 10 years). These applicants must have spent at least three years at a foreign school. This schooling must be equivalent to the same number of school years at a Greek secondary school. Or the applicants are expected to have completed the last two years at a Greek *lycée;*

(c) foreigners or applicants of Greek origin who have been awarded a Greek government scholarship — 1%.

5% of the available places at technical colleges, at schools of medicine and dentistry, and at veterinary colleges are reserved for Cypriots. In other academic branches, the share of reserved places for Cypriots is 10%. Admission is decided by entry examinations held by the Cypriot Ministry of Education.

The above-listed entry requirements are also valid for the TEIs.

Postgraduate studies

The number of postgraduate study places differs from subject to subject. For information concerning the entry requirements for foreigners to postgraduate study courses and for other details, foreign applicants should address themselves to the administrative office of the respective faculty or institution of higher education.

Recognition of foreign certificates and degrees

I. The Inter-university Institute for the Recognition of Foreign Certificates and Degrees (Dikatsa), which began its work in 1979, is an independent public body. Its mandate is to examine and then decide on the equivalence of degrees from foreign institutions of higher education with corresponding Greek degrees. Further, this office assesses the level of foreign higher education institutions in comparison with Greek institutions. In order to determine the equivalence of a certificate or degree, each case is individually examined. For this, the individual course of study of each applicant will be taken into consideration.

In making its decision, the Dikatsa must answer three questions.

1. Whether the institution of higher education is equal in status to its Greek counterpart.
2. Whether the teaching and research at the institution of higher education is equivalent to that at a similar Greek institution.
3. Whether the degree is equivalent. The curriculum of the course in question forms the basis for this decision.

If the course of study cannot be adjudged to be fully equivalent, then the following alternatives exist:

(a) enrolment into a specific year (at the equivalent level);
(b) an additional examination in certain subjects which cannot be regarded as equivalent.

In those cases where no equivalent course of study is offered by Greek institutions of higher education, the applicant is issued with a special certificate of degree equivalence, without any Greek degree being defined as its equivalent.

II. The Institute for Technological Education (ITE), which was founded in 1983, is an authority which comes under the jurisdiction of the Ministry of National Education. The ITE's function, among others, is to determine the equivalence of certificates and degrees conferred abroad with those conferred by Greek TEIs.

The ITE takes the following criteria into consideration in making its decision on the application of an interested student:

(a) the equivalence of higher education institutions or departments in the tertiary, non-university sector of the foreign country's educa-

GR

tion system with Greek TEIs, and the equivalence of degrees which these institutions confer for their study courses, if possible, with degrees conferred by Greek TEIs;

(b) the level (semester or year) into which an applicant is to be enrolled, or the additional examinations for certain subjects at a TEI department which the applicant must take, if the equivalent foreign degree does not correspond as far as course content is concerned with that of Greek TEIs, or if it is not possible to recognize the equivalence of the degree with that awarded by Greek TEIs. In such cases, foreign degree holders are awarded a degree by the TEI department responsible after they have fulfilled the stipulated requirements;

(c) the recognition of the equivalence of degrees which Greek technical colleges under the jurisdiction of other ministries have awarded with degrees conferred by the TEIs (after a mutual resolution has been passed by the Minister for Education and Religion and the other respective minister);

(d) the equivalence or superior level of credits earned at institutions in foreign tertiary education in comparison with specialized qualifications earned at Greek TEIs.

(e) the level and value of certificates and degrees and the equivalence of degrees from foreign higher education institutions or departments on an equal level to the Asetem degree of the Selete.

(f) the assignment to the appropriate semester at a TEI department or at the Asetem of the Selete of technical college students, of students with diplomas or degrees from Greek tertiary education institutions, of students from the Asetem of the Selete, or of students from abroad in accordance with the guidelines of Law 1286/82.

Entry examinations

Undergraduate studies

As a rule there are no entry examinations for foreign students wishing to enter a Greek institution of higher education. The selection of foreign students is based solely on the marks of their school-leaving certificates. The entry examination must be taken by applicants of Greek origin who, as the children of Greek public servants on duty abroad in the past and at present, have been raised abroad. The examination is held in September.

Postgraduate studies

The selection of applicants for postgraduate study differs from one higher education institution to the next. In those cases where foreign language skills are required, it is necessary that these skills be examined.

Application and registration

Application

Undergraduate studies

Foreign and Greek applicants who are selected must submit the following documents: an application form (with two passport photographs); this application form must also show the certified final mark received on completion of secondary education; applicants should also state their order of preference for the higher education institutions. The order of preference given by applicants is binding. The order in which the institutions are listed will be regarded as the order of preference. It is not possible to admit applicants to higher education institutions not named on this list. This is also true in cases where the applicant has not been admitted to any of the chosen institutions because the average secondary schooling mark, or respectively, the entry examination mark is lower than that of all the successful applicants. In cases where the applicants have been successful in their applications to two or more higher education institutions, only the institution highest in the order of preference will count.

Foreign applicants must submit the following documents:

(a) a document issued by the relevant authority in the student's country of origin in which the citizenship of the applicant and of both parents is shown;
(b) confirmation of the applicant's final average mark achieved on completion of secondary schooling, transferred to a scale of 1—20 (20 equals excellent), if it is not shown on the certificate itself, and a school-leaving certificate which shows that the applicant has qualified for admission to an institution of higher education;

Greek applicants who are or have been living abroad for more than five years must submit the following documents:

a) confirmation by the Greek diplomatic or consular representation responsible for the foreign country of the applicant's or applicant's parents' period abroad;
(b) confirmation of the number of completed years of secondary schooling in Greece and abroad;
(c) confirmation that the applicant is qualified for admission to an institution of higher education and a school-leaving certificate from a *lycée*.

Applicants in the category of foreign scholarship holders and Greek scholarship holders with residence abroad must submit the following documents:

(a) an application form;
(b) a school-leaving certificate from the *lycée*;
(c) a statement of confirmation that the applicant has been granted a scholarship to study a specialized subject or area and that the applicant's proficiency in Greek is acceptable;
(d) (for Greek applicants) a certificate stating the duration of the applicant's stay abroad.

Application forms and all other documents must be submitted either in person, or by an authorized representative, to the Ministry of Education (the Department of AEI Studies and Student Care). In special cases scholarship holders can apply directly to the higher education institution.

The deadlines for submitting applications are:

(a) applicants of Greek origin — 1 to 10 July;
(b) for foreign and Greek scholarship holders — 1 to 10 October;
(c) for foreign applicants — 1 to 10 August.

Postgraduate studies
The higher education institution involved decides itself which documents are necessary for the application procedure.

Registration

Undergraduate studies
Registration follows the publication of a list of successful applicants by the Ministry of Education. Registration takes place at the higher education institutions themselves and must be completed by the registration deadline, which is announced in the daily press.

Before a foreign student is allowed to register, it is required that a sufficient knowledge of Greek be proved. This is the case if the student has a school-leaving certificate from a Greek *lycée* or from a Greek six-year secondary school, or if the student has acquired a statement of confirmation from the Athens University Club or from the Greek Language Institute at the University of Thessaloniki.

If proof of a sufficient knowledge of Greek cannot be submitted by the registration deadline, then the student's right to acceptance by a Greek university expires. In special cases, a prolongation of the deadline is permitted to enable the student to submit the above-mentioned proof of language proficiency: the new deadline is then next year's registration deadline for students entering university for the first time.

The above-mentioned regulations regarding entry examinations, admissions, application procedures and registration at the AEIs are also valid for the TEIs.

Tuition fees

Higher education in Greece is free. Exceptions to this rule are foreign students attending undergraduate or postgraduate courses, be it as full-time students or as occasional students. They are required to pay tuition and registration fees.

Scholarship holders are exempted from the payment of fees. Students from countries where Greek students do not have to pay tuition fees are also exempted, if a statement of confirmation to this effect issued by the Ministry of Education in their country of origin can be presented. Students with Greek citizenship are completely exempted from the payment of any such fees.

The tuition fees for the 1988/89 academic year amounted to DR 54 000. The tuition fees for schools of medicine and dentistry and for veterinary colleges as well as for all the colleges of technology differ from this sum: at such establishments the annual tuition fee amounts to DR 72 000. The fees for instruction in Greek at the special departments of the Universities of Athens and Thessaloniki amount to DR 27 000.

These amounts may be paid in two instalments. Foreign students in financial difficulties who have shown extraordinary suitability and performance in their studies may be granted a scholarship which will cover all or part of the tuition and registration fees. This scholarship is awarded on the basis of a ministerial decision by the Minister for Education, after consultation with the higher education institution involved.

The following groups are exempted from the payment of tuition and registration fees for undergraduate and postgraduate studies:

(a) foreign students with a scholarship from the Holy Synod of the Greek Church;
(b) foreign students who have confirmation from an international organization that they are the victims of persecution in their countries of origin;
(c) foreign students from countries where, under like conditions, Greeks are fully exempted from tuition fees;
(d) foreign students who have received a scholarship from the Greek Government and who have a certificate to this effect;
(e) students of Greek origin;
(f) foreigners married to Greek citizens.
(g) children of diplomats;
(h) Palestinians in possession of a certificate issued by the PLO.

In contrast to attendance at the AEIs, attendance at the TEIs is free, both for Greek and for foreign students.

Knowledge of the language of instruction, language courses and other courses

A sufficient knowledge of the Greek language is an indispensable prerequisite for anyone wishing to study at a Greek tertiary education institution, AEI or TEI.

Instruction in Greek can be obtained from the Foreign Language Institute of the Athens University Club and from the Institute for Modern Greek at the University of Thessaloniki. The following documents are required for registration at these institutes:

1. a secondary school-leaving certificate, translated and authenticated by the Greek consulate in the country of origin;
2. a certificate from the foreign student's embassy in Greece confirming that the school-leaving certificate entitles the student to attend an institution of higher education in the country of origin;
3. three passport photographs and two DR 20 fee stamps;
4. the translated and authenticated birth certificate;

The University of Thessaloniki additionally requires a short curriculum vitae and proof of the average school-leaving mark transferred into the Greek marking system (1 — 20, where 20 equals excellent).

Registration takes place from 1 to

20 October. Attendance in person is required.

The winter semester in Athens begins on 21 October and lasts until 30 June. At the University of Thessaloniki, the winter term begins in mid-September and ends on 15 June. At the Institute for Modern Greek in Thessaloniki, a summer semester has been established which runs from 16 August to 15 September; the tuition fees for this summer course amount to DR 15 000. In Athens, there are three hours of teaching a day, in Thessaloniki, four hours a day. The tuition fees amount to DR 27 000. The tuition fees are to be paid in two equal instalments.

The documents required for registration at the Institute for Modern Greek in Thessaloniki (summer semester) must be submitted by 30 April, (winter semester) by 10 September.

The same students as are listed in the section on 'Tuition fees' are exempted from payment of the registration fees as well as the fees for language courses.

Financial assistance and scholarships

The Greek State has been granting undergraduate and postgraduate students at Greek higher education institutions (AEIs) and at TEIs interest free loans as financial assistance for the students' studies since the 1983/84 academic year. The granting of such loans depends on:

(a) the student's academic record — (independent of marks, the student is expected to complete a certain number of courses);
(b) the financial circumstances of the student and of the family.

The National Scholarship Board (IKY) will award scholarships to:

(a) students in tertiary education with an outstanding academic record and aptitude;
(b) Greek Cypriots, to enable these to undertake undergraduate studies in Greece;
(c) Greeks who are degree holders from a tertiary level institution in order to allow them to participate in postgraduate studies abroad or in Greece — first they must take part in a special (IKY) selection competition;
(d) Greeks who are holders of a foreign higher education degree in order to allow them to prepare a doctoral thesis in Greece;
(e) foreign holders of degrees who originate from Member States of the

Council of Europe or from Asian, African and Latin American countries in order to enable them to prepare a doctoral thesis in Greece.

Applicants from groups (d) and (e) must be holders of an M.Sc. or DEA or of an equivalent foreign degree which has been recognized as such by Dikatsa. The initial duration of the scholarship is one year and it can be prolonged if the performance of the scholarship holder has been assessed as satisfactory in all respects by the administrative council of the IKY.

Scholarship holders of Greek origin and foreign scholarship holders who wish to continue their education in Greece are granted:

(a) a monthly allowance towards the cost of living amounting to DR 40 000;
(b) a one-off payment of DR 50 000 for travelling costs and initial accommodation costs; and
(c) a payment of up to DR 60 000 for the printing costs of a doctoral thesis.

The amount of the scholarships for Greek students is determined by the Administrative Council of the National Scholarship Board.

The University of Athens has an Educational Assistance Office (ταμείο αρωγής φοιτητών) which provides moral and material support for students at this university. This support can take the form of advice, materials and of money. This support is not limited to Greek students.

From the 1988/89 academic year onwards, the IKY was appointed as the national authority for the allocation of scholarships for students within the framework of the EC Erasmus programme. Moreover, from the 1986/87 academic year onwards, scholarships will be awarded to Greek research fellows who wish to undertake postgraduate studies at the European University Institute in Florence. This occurs in accordance with the regulations and conditions which are prescribed by the paragraphs of Law 1628/1986 and additionally by the IKY statutes.

GR

Entry and residence regulations

(Editor's note: The Greek Ministry of Education was not in a position to contribute a text to this section.)

Social aspects

Social security and health insurance

Undergraduate and postgraduate students at AEIs as well as at TEIs, Greek citizens, students of Greek origin, and foreigners are entitled to free medical care, including visits to doctors, medication and hospital stays. Each course of study has been ascribed a minimum number of semesters. The time limit is in force for both undergraduate and postgraduate students. Medical care is free for one and a half times the number of semesters ascribed to the student's course. Free medical care includes: medical examination and treatment; hospital examination and treatment; medication; laboratory analyses; house calls; maternity care; physiotherapy; dentistry; and orthopaedic aids, contact lenses and spectacles. Moreover, there is the possibility of treatment abroad if the illness cannot be diagnosed or treated in Greece.

In order to make use of the above-listed medical care, the students should show the doctor their student medical care book. This book is issued to students on registration at any Greek higher education institution (AEI or TEI).

Advisory services

Foreign students can obtain information and advice on planning and organizing their studies from the employees of the relevant university club: at Athens University this is the Publicity Office of the Athens University Club.

Student employment

(*Editor's note:* The Greek Ministry of Education was not in a position to contribute a text to this section.)

Student organizations

There are no restrictions on foreign students wishing to join student organizations.

There are student organizations affiliated to the various higher education institutions and there are also student organizations with political and religious aims which are affiliated to bodies outside the higher education institutions. Organizations for foreign students also exist.

Cost of living

No precise information about the cost of living can be given. However, students should reckon with a minimum of DR 50 000 per month for basic needs.

Accommodation

The National Youth Foundation Board (φοιτητικές εστίες) decides upon applications for accommodation in student halls of residence. Successful applications are decided upon on grounds of the applicant's family's financial circumstances. Eight per cent of the available places in the halls of residence are reserved for foreign students. Foreign students should either submit their application to the director of the hall of residence or submit it directly to the National Youth Foundation's Catering and Accommodation Office. The National Youth Foundation Board is responsible for distributing the places to foreigners. Those foreigners are favoured in whose countries national liberation movements exist, as well as those who are Greek government scholarship holders. More information can be obtained from the housing offices at the university clubs, which will also assist students in finding accommodation.

At the University of Athens, this information is available from the Secretariat for Public Relations of the University Club.

Services for students

On registration at a tertiary education institution, students are issued with a student pass. Holders of valid student passes are granted certain reductions, for example, in theatres, museums, etc. The administrative offices or, where applicable, the students' unions will issue certificates with which students can obtain 50% reductions on inner city public transport. Students are also granted a 50% reduction on ship and rail journeys. Moreover, there is a reduction of 25% on the price of tickets for cross-country buses within Greece and of 50% for the journey from home to university town.

The handbooks on which the courses and examinations are based are issued to students free of charge.

Facilities for disabled students

Disabled students receive preferential treatment in the admissions procedure to higher education institutions. These students, whether Greeks or foreigners, are not subject to admissions restrictions to appropriate higher education institutions in the home towns of their parents.

Medical care and hospital stays are free. The administration offices of Greek higher education institutions are obliged to ease the burden of studying in various ways for these students (for example, in the organization of timetables and examinations). Facilities for disabled students such as ramps for wheelchairs as well as special lifts are being installed.

Appendices

1. Addresses

Greek embassies in EC countries

Belgium
430, avenue Louise
B-1050 Bruxelles
☎ 648 17 30

Denmark
Borgergade 16
DK-1300 København K
☎ 01 11 45 33

Federal Republic of Germany
Rheinallee 76
D-5300 Bonn 2
☎ 35 50 36/7
35 57 01

Spain
Serrano 140
E-28006 Madrid
☎ 4 11 33 45/4 11 32 96

France
17, rue Auguste Vacquerie
F-75116 Paris
☎ 7237228/29/30/31

Ireland
1 Upper Pembroke Street
Dublin 2
☎ 767254/5

Italy
Viale Gioacchino Rossini 4
I-Roma
☎ 85 96 30

Luxembourg
23, avenue Monterey
L-2163 Luxembourg
☎ 47 43 41

The Netherlands
Koninginnegracht 37
NL-'s-Gravenhage
☎ 63 87 00/60 28 80

Portugal
Rua Visconde de Santárem
71-5°
P-Lisboa
☎ 55 89 52/3

United Kingdom
1a Holland Park
London W11 3TP
☎ 727 80 40

Addresses of general interest

Υπουργείο Εθνικής Παιδείας και Θρησκευμάτων
☎ κέντρο 3 23 04 61-5
α) Διεύθυνση Σπουδών και Φοιτητικής Μέριμνας
β) Ειδική Γραμματεία Τ Ε Ι
γ) Συμβούλιο Ανωτάτης Εκπαίδευσης
Μητροπόλεως 15
GR-10185 Αθήνα
(Ministry of National Education and Religion
(a) Department of Studies and Student Care
(b) Special Department of TEI Administration
(c) Council of Higher Education)

Πανεπιστημιακή Λέσχη Πανεπιστημίου Αθηνών
Γραφείο Δημοσίων Σχέσεων (προϊστάμενος κ. Μ. Γεράρδου
☎ 3609295)
Ιπποκράτους 15
GR-10679 Αθήνα
(Athens University Club – Public Relations Office)

Ίδρυμα Κρατικών Υποτροφιών
Λυσικράτους 14
GR-10558 Αθήνα
☎ 3 25 43 85
(National Scholarship Foundation)

Παιδαγωγικό Ινστιτούτο
Μεσογείων 396
Αγία Παρασκευή
GR-15341 Αττική
☎ 6 56 73 64
(Pedagogical Institute)

Διαπανεπιστημιακό Κέντρο Αναγνωρίσεως Τίτλων Σπουδών Αλλοδαπής (ΔΙΚΑΤΣΑ)
Συγγρού 112
GR-11741 Αθήνα
☎ 9 22 25 26
(Central office for the recognition of foreign degrees and certificates)

Ινστιτούτο Τεχνολογικής Εκπαίδευσης
(ITE)
Συγγρού 56
GR-11745 Αθήνα
☎ 9 21 45 02
(Institute of Technical Education)

Institutions of higher education (AEIs)

Πανεπιστήμιο Αθηνών
Ελ. Βενιζέλου 30
GR-10679 Αθήνα
(University of Athens)

Εθνικό Μετσόβειο Πολυτεχνείο
28ης Οκτωβρίου 42
GR-10682 Αθήνα
(National Polytechnic College Metsovio)

Πανεπιστήμιο Θεσσαλονίκης
Πανεπιστημιούπολη
GR-54006 Θεσσαλονίκη
(University of Thessaloniki)

Ανωτάτη Σχολή Οικονομικών και Εμπορικών Επιστημών
28ης Οκτωβρίου 76
GR-10434 Αθήνα
(College of Trade and Industry, Athens)

Ανωτάτη Γεωπονική Σχολή Αθηνών
Ιερά Οδός 75
GR-11855 Αθήνα
(College of Agriculture, Athens)

Πάντειος Ανωτάτη Σχολή Πολιτικών Επιστημών
Λεωφ. Συγγρού 136
GR-17671 Καλλιθέα-Αθήνα
(Panteios College of Political Science, Athens)

Ανωτάτη Βιομηχανική Σχολή Πειραιώς
Κουντουριώτου 98-100
GR-18532 Πειραιάς
(College of Industrial Studies, Piraeus)

Ανωτάτη Βιομηχανική Σχολή Θεσσαλονίκης
Τσιμισκή 45
GR-54110 Θεσσαλονίκη
(College of Industrial Studies, Thessaloniki)

Πανεπιστήμιο Πατρών
Πανεπιστημιούπολη
GR-26001 Πάτρα
(University of Patras)

Πανεπιστήμιο Ιωαννίνων
Δαβόλη 30
GR-45110 Ιωάννινα
(University of Ioannina)

Πανεπιστήμιο Θράκης
Δημοκρίτου 17
69100 Κομοτηνή
(University of Thrace)

Ανωτάτη Σχολή καλών Τεχνών
28ης Οκτωβρίου 42
GR-10682 Αθήνα
(College of Art, Athens)

Πανεττιστήμιο Κρήτης
Δημητρακάκη 17
GR-74100 Ρέθυμνο
(University of Crete, Rethymnon)

Πολυτεχνείο Κρήτης
Ελ. Βενιζέλου 34
GR-73132 Χανία
(Crete Polytechnic Institute, Chania)

Πανεπιστήμιο Αιγαίου
Κανάρη 9 (ΔΕ)*
Διοικούσα Επιτροπή
GR-10671 Αθήνα
(University of the Aegaeon: Administrative Committee)
Μυτιλήνη
α) Τμήμα Περιβάλλοντος
β) Τμήμα Κοινωνικής Ανθρωπολογίας
Καραντώνη 17
GR-81100 Μυτιλήνη
(Lesvos
(a) Department of environmental technology
b) Department of social anthropology)
Χίος
Τμήμα Διοίκησης Επιχειρήσεων
Μιχάλων 8
GR-82100 Χιος
Chios: Department of administration of enterprises)
Ρόδος
α) Παιδαγωγικό Τμήμα δημοτικής Εκπαίδευσης
β) Παιδαγωγικό Τμήμα Νηπιαγωγών
οδός Δημοκρατίας
GR-85100 Ροδος
(Rhodos
(a) Department of pedagogy (primary-school teacher training)
(b) Department of pedagogy (pre-school teacher training)
Σάμος
Τμήμα μαθυματικών
Καρλόβασι
GR-83200 Σαμος
(Samos: Department of mathematics)

Ιόνιο Πανεπιστήμιο
Δεληγιώργη 55-59
Κέρκυρα
(Ionian University, Kerkyra/Corfu)

Πανεπιστήμιο Θεσσαλίας
α) Μητροπόλεως 60
GR-10563 Αθήνα
β) Τ. Οικονομάκη 47 και Γκαμβέτα
GR-38221 Βολος
(University of Thessaly)
Διοικούσα Επιτροπή

Institutions of technical tertiary education (TEIs)

Αθήνας
Αγ. Σπυρίδωνα και Δημητσάνας
GR-12243 Αιγαλεω
(TEI, Athens)
Πειραιά

Π. Ράλλη και Θηβών 250
GR-12244 Αιγαλεω
(TEI, Piraeus)

Θεσσαλονίκης
Τ.Θ. 14561
GR-54110 Θεσσαλόνικη
(TEI, Thessaloniki)

Πάτρας
Κουκούλι
GR-26334 Πάτρα
(TEI, Patras)

Λάρισας
Τ.Ε.Ι. Λάρισας
GR-41110 Λαρίσα
(TEI, Larissa)

Ηρακλείου
Θέση εσταυρωμένος
GR-71500 Ηρακλειο
(TEI, Herakleion)

Καβάλας

Εθνικής Αντίστασης 80
GR-65403 Καβάλα
(TEI, Kavala)

Κοζάνης

Κοίλα
GR-50161 Κοζάνη
(TEI, Kosani)

Χαλκίδας
Ψαχνά
GR-34400 Χαλκίδα
(TEI, Chalkida)

Σερρών
Υψηλάντου 1
GR-62123 Σερρες (Διδακτήρια)
(TEI, Serres)

Μεσολογγίου
Νέα Κτίρια
GR-30200 Μεσολογγί
(TEI, Messolongi)

Other institutions of tertiary education

Χαροκόπειος Ανωτάτη Σχολή
Οικιακής οικονομίας
Ελ. Βενιζέλου 70
GR-17676 Καλλιθεα
(Charokopios School of Home Economics)
Ανώτερη Σχολή Εκπαίδευσης Τεχνολόγων Μηχανικών (Α.Σ.Ε.Τ.Ε.Μ.)
Κτήμα Μακρυκώστα
GR-15125 Μαρουσι
(Department for Technician Training)
Ανώτερη Εκκλησιαστική Σχολή Αθηνών

Θεμιστοκλέους και Χρυσαλίδος
GR-14561 Κηφισία
(Training seminary for priests)

Other ministries responsible for institutions of tertiary education

Ministry of Defence
Γενικό Επιτελείο Εθνικής Άμυνας
Δ/νοη Ανθρωπίνου Δυναμικού
Σ.Τ.Γ. 1020 Χολλργος

Ministry of Agriculture
Δ/νοη Γεωργικής Πολιτικής και Τεκμηρίωσης
Αχαρνών 5
GR-10176 Αθήνα

Ministry of Public Order

1. Ελληνική Αστυνομία, Δ/νοη Εκπαίδευσης
   Κατεχάκη 1
   GR-10177 Αθήνα
2. Αρχηγείο Πυροσβεστικού Σώματος
   Δ/νοη IV Μελετών-Οργάνωσης Εκπαίδευσης
   Μουρούζη 4
   GR-10172 Αθήνα

Ministry of Merchant Shipping
Διεύθυνση Ναυτικών
GR-18518 Πειραίας

GR

2. Survey of courses of study at higher education institutions

Degree courses

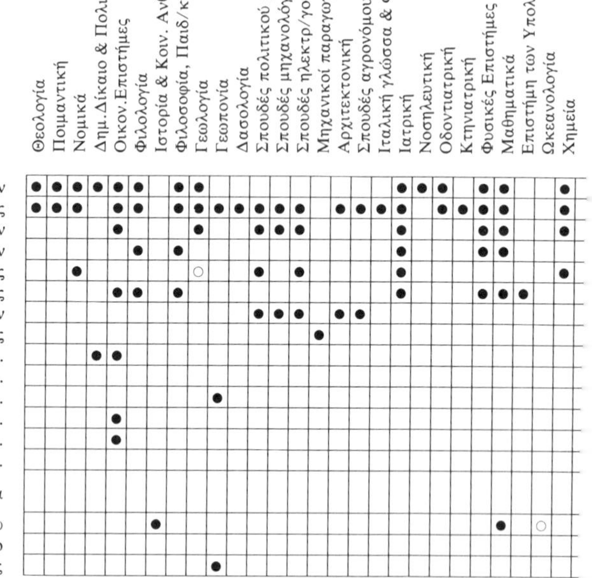

	Θεολογία / Theology	Ποιμαντική / Religious teaching	Νομικά / Law	Δημ.Δίκαιο & Πολιτ.Επιστήμες / Public law and politics	Οικον.Επιστήμες / Economics	Φιλολογία / Literature, Philology	Ιστορία & Κοιν. Ανθρωπολογία / History and Sociology	Φιλοσοφία, Παιδ/κή & Ψυχολογία / Philosophy, Pedagogy, Psychology	Γεωλογία / Geology	Γεωπονία / Agriculture	Δασολογία / Forestry	Σπουδές πολιτικού μηχανικού / Civil engineering	Σπουδές μηχανολόγου-μηχανικού / Mechanical engineering	Σπουδές ηλεκτρ/γου-μηχανικού / Electrical engineering	Μηχανικοί παραγωγής & διοίκησης. / Production engineering and administration	Αρχιτεκτονική / Architecture	Σπουδές αγρονόμου-τοπογράφου μηχανικού / Rural engineering and topography	Ιταλική γλώσσα & Φιλολογία / Italian language and literature	Ιατρική / Medicine	Νοσηλευτική / Paramedical training	Οδοντιατρική / Dentistry	Κτηνιατρική / Veterinary medicine	Φυσικές Επιστήμες / Natural sciences	Μαθηματικά / Mathematics	Επιστήμη των Υπολογιστών / Computer sciene	Ωκεανολογία / Oceanography	Χημεία / Chemistry
Πανεπιστήμιο Αθηνών	●	●	●	●	●	●		●	●										●	●	●		●	●			●
Παν/μιο Θεσ/νίκης	●	●	●		●	●		●	●	●	●	●	●	●		●	●	●	●		●	●	●	●			●
Παν/μιο Πατρών					●				●			●	●	●					●				●	●			●
Παν/μιο Ιωαννίνων						●		●											●				●	●			
Παν/μιο Θράκης			●						○			●		●					●								●
Παν/μιο Κρήτης					●	●		●											●				●	●	●		
Πολυτεχνείο Αθηνών												●	●	●		●	●										
Πολυτεχνείο Κρήτης															●												
Α.Σ.Ο.Ε.Ε.				●	●																						
Π.Α.Σ.Π.Ε.																											
Α.Γ.Σ.Α.										●																	
Α.Β.Σ.Π.					●																						
Α.Β.Σ.Θ.					●																						
Α.Σ.Κ.Τ.																											
Νέα Πανεπιστήμια																											
Παν/μιο Αιγαίου							●																	●		○	
Ιόνιο Παν/μιο																											
Παν/μιο Θεσσαλίας										●																	

● Degree course
○ Course of study planned

	Φαρμακευτική / Pharmacology	Βιολογία / Biology	Ιστορικές σπουδές, αρχαιολογία / History, Archaeology	Ψυχολογία / Psychology	Παιδ.τμήματα δημοτ. εκπ/σης / Pedagogy (teacher training)	Παιδ. τμήμα Νηπιαγωγών / Pedagogy (pre-school teachers)	Αγγλική γλώσσα & Φιλολογία / English language and literature	Γαλλική γλώσσα & Φιλολογία / French language and literature	Γερμανική γλώσσα & Φιλολογία / German language and literature	Σπουδές χημικού μηχανικού / Chemical engineering	Σπουδές ναυπηγού μηχανολόγου μηχανικού / Naval architecture	Σπουδές μηχανικού μεταλλείων μεταλλουργών / Metal construction, Metallurgy	Σπουδές μηχανικών ηλεκτρονικών υπολογιστών & Πληροφ/κής / Computer sciences	Οργάνωση & διοίκηση επιχ/σεων / Organiz. and administration of enterprises	Στατιστική & ασφαλιστική επιστήμη / Statistics and insurances	Πολιτική επιστήμη / Political science	Δημόσια Διοίκηση / Public administration	Κοινωνιολογία / Sociology	Ζωγραφική / Painting	Γλυπτική / Sculpture	Χαρακτική / Engraving	Φυσική αγωγή & αθλητισμός / Physical education, Sports	Μουσικές σπουδές / Music	Ξένες γλώσσες, μετάφραση και διερμηνεία / Foreign languages, translating and interpreting	Αρχειονομία & Βιβλιοθηκονομία / Documentation, Library science	Χωροταξία & Περιφερειακή ανάπτυξη / Soil conservation	Στατιστική & Πληροφορική / Statistics and Computing	Μηχανική Ορυκτών Πόρων / Mining
University of Athens	●	●	●		●	●	●	●	●							●						●						
University of Thessaloniki	●	●	●		●	●	●	●	●	●									●	●	●	●	●					
University of Patras	●	●			●	●				●			●															
University of Ioannina			●		●	●																						
University of Thrace					●	●																●						
University of Crete		●	●	●	●	●												●										
Polytechnic College of Athens										●	●	●																
Polytechnic College of Crete			●																									●
ASOEE College of Trade and Industry, Athens														●													●	
PASPE Panteios College of Political Sciences																●	●	●										
AGSA College of Agriculture, Athens																												
ABSP College of Industrial Studies, Piraeus														●	●													
ABSTH College of Industrial Studies, Thessaloniki														●														
ASKT College of Art, Athens																			●	●	●							
New institutions:																												
Ionian University of the Aegaeon					●	●								●														
Ionian University, Kerkyra			●																				○	●	○			
University of Thessaly, Volos					●	●																○				●		

GR

2a. Post-graduate studies

ΠΙΝΑΚΑΣ ΜΕΤΑΠΤΥΧΙΑΚΩΝ ΣΠΟΥΔΩΝ

	Ωκεανογραφία / Oceanography	Ηλεκτρονική & Ραδιοηλεκτρολογία / Electronic and Radio-electricity	Ηλεκτρονικός αυτοματισμός / Automation	Μετεωρολογία / Meteorology	Πληροφορική & Επιχειρησιακή έρευνα / Computer science and market research	Ιδιωτικό δίκαιο / Civil law	Δημόσιο δίκαιο & Πολιτικές επιστήμες / Public law, Politics	Ποινική επιστήμη / Penal law	Οικονομική επιστήμη / Economics	Γενετική βελτίωση φυτών και γεωργίας / Genetic improvement of plants in agriculture	Ζωοτεχνία και διατροφή αγροτικών ζώων / Cattlebreeding and economics	Έγγειες βελτιώσεις / Irrigation	Υγιεινή τροφίμων Ιοικής προέλευσης / Sanitary control of food of animal origin	Μικροβιολογία και λοιμώδη νοσήματα / Microbiology and contagious diseases	Ερμηνευτική Θεολογία / Hermeneutic theology	Ιστορική Θεολογία / Historical theology	Συστηματική Θεολογία / Systematic theology	Πρακτική Θεολογία / Practical theology	Γαλακτοκομία / Milk and dairy industry	Ψυχολογία / Psychology	Παιδαγωγικές σπουδές / Pedagogics	Περιφερειακή ανάπτυξη / Regional development	Χαρτογράφηση υδατική / Hydrocartography	Οικονομία εδαφών / Soil conservation	Διοίκηση επιχειρήσεων / Business administration	
Πανεπιστήμιο Αθηνών	●	●	●	●	●																					University of Athens
Πανεπιστήμιο Θεσσαλονίκης		●				●	●	●	●	●	●	●	●	●	●	●	●	●		●	●			●		University of Thessaloni
Ανωτάτη Γεωπονική Σχολή Αθηνών																			●						●	AGSA College of Agriculture, Athens
Ανωτάτη Σχολή Οικονομικών και Εμπορικών Επιστημών									●														●			ASOEE College of Trade and Industry, Athens
Πάντειος Ανωτάτη Σχολή Πολιτικών Επιστημών																						●				PASPE Panteios College of Political Sciences

2b. Survey of courses of study at TEIs and Asetems Seletes

Faculties and Departments	1	2	3	4	4a	5	5a	5b	6	6a	7	7a	8	8a
				Patras		Larissa			Heraklion		Kavala		Kozani	
	Athen	Thessaloniki	Piraeus	Κεντρικό Πάτρα	Παρ/μα Καλαμάτα	Κεντρικό Λάρισα	1° Παρ/μα Λαμία	2° Παρ/μα Καρδίτσα	Κεντρικό Ηράκλειο	Παρ/μα Χανιά	Κεντρικό Καβάλα	Παρ/μα Δράμα	Κεντρικό Κοζάνη	Παρ/μα Φλώρινα
1. Σχολή γραφικών τεχνών και καλλιτεχνικών σπουδών														
Γραφιστικής	⊕													
Διακοσμητικής	⊕													
Γραφικών Τεχνών	⊕													
Φωτογραφίας	⊕													
Συντήρησης αρχαιοτήτων και έργων τέχνης	⊕													
2. Σχολή διοίκησης και οικονομίας														
Εμπορίας και διαφήμισης	⊕	⊕												
Διοίκησης επιχειρήσεων	⊕		⊕	⊕		⊕					⊕		⊕	
Λογιστικής		⊕	⊕	⊕		⊕			⊕		⊕		⊕	
Τουριστικών επιχειρήσεων	⊕	⊕		⊕		⊕			⊕					
Βιβλιοθηκονομίας	⊕	⊕												
Στελεχών συνεταιριστικών οργανώσεων και εκμεταλλεύσεων									⊕					
Διοίκησης μονάδων υγείας και πρόνοιας	⊕													
3. Σχολή επαγγελμάτων υγείας και πρόνοιας														
Νοσηλευτικής	⊕	⊕		⊕		⊕	⊕		⊕					
Μαιευτικής	⊕	⊕												
Φυσικοθεραπείας	⊕	⊕												
Εργοθεραπείας	⊕													
Ραδιολογίας-Ακτινολογίας	⊕													
Ιατρικών εργαστηρίων	⊕	⊕				⊕								
Οδοντοτεχνικής	⊕													
Δημόσιας υγιεινής	⊕													
Οπτικής	⊕													
Αισθητικής	⊕	⊕												
Κοινωνικής εργασίας	⊕			⊕					⊕					
Βρεφονηπιοκομίας	⊕	⊕												
Επισκεπτών και επισκεπτριών υγείας	⊕													

9	10	11	11a	11b	11c			
		Messolongi				Asetem/Seletem	Duration of study, semesters	
Chalkis	Serres	Κετρικό Μεσολσγγι	1° Παρ/μυ ΚαρπενΗαι	2° Παρ/μυ Ιωάννινα	3° Παρ/μα Αρτα			
								Fine arts, Graphic arts
							7 ct.	Graphic arts
							7 ct.	Decorative arts
							7 ct.	Technology and graphic art
							7 ct.	Photography
							7 ct.	Restoration of cultural heritage and works of art
								Economics, business administration
							6 ct.	Commerce and Public Relations (Marketing)
⊕	⊕						6 ct.	Business administration
⊕	⊕	⊕					6 ct.	Accountancy, auditing
							6 ct.	Business administration/tourism
							6 ct.	Business administration/libraries
		⊕					6 ct.	Rural development and cooperatives
							6 ct.	Hospital administration and health care
								Professions of the health and social sector
				⊕			6 ct.	Paramedical professions
							6 ct.	Obstetrics (training of midwives)
							6 ct.	Physiotherapy
							6 ct.	Ergotherapy
							6 ct.	Radiology and actinology
							6 ct.	Medical laboratories
							6 ct.	Dental protheses
							6 ct.	Public hygiene
							6 ct.	Optics
							6 ct.	Cosmetics
							6 ct.	Social assistance
				⊕			6 ct.	Infant nursing
							6 ct.	Health counselling

Faculties and Departments

	1	2	3	4	4a	5	5a	5b	6	6a	7	7a	8	8a
				Patras		Larissa			Heraklion		Kavala		Kozani	
	Athen	Thessaloniki	Piraeus	Κεντρικό Πάτρα	Παρ/μα Καλαμάτα	Κεντρικό Λάρισα	1° Παρ/μα Λαμία	2° Παρ/μα Καρδίτσα	Κεντρικό Ηράκλειο	Παρ/μα Χανιά	Κεντρικό Καβάλα	Παρ/μα Δράμα	Κεντρικό Κοζάνη	Παρ/μα Φλώρινα
4. Σχολή τεχνολογικών εφαρμογών														
Δομικών έργων			⊕						⊕					
Έργων υποδομής	⊕	⊕		⊕		⊕								
Πολιτικών														
Τοπογραφίας	⊕													
Μηχανολογίας			⊕	⊕		⊕			⊕		⊕		⊕	
Τεχνολογίας ιατρικών οργάνων	⊕													
Ηλεκτρολογίας			⊕	⊕	⊕	⊕	⊕		⊕		⊕		⊕	
Ηλεκτρονικής	⊕	⊕	⊕				⊕			⊕				
Πληροφορικής	⊕	⊕												
Ηλεκτρονικών υπολογιστικών συστημάτων			⊕											
Ναυπηγικής	⊕													
Κλωστοϋφαντουργίας			⊕											
Τεχνολογίας πετρελαίου											⊕			
Οχημάτων		⊕												
Αυτοματισμού			⊕											
Ενεργειακής τεχνικής	⊕													
Τεχνολογίας ορυχείων													⊕	
5. Σχολή τεχνολογίας τροφίμων														
Τεχνολογίας τροφίμων	⊕	⊕												
Οινολογίας και τεχνολογίας ποτών	⊕													
Διατροφής		⊕												
6. Σχολή τεχνολογίας γεωπονίας														
Φυτικής παραγωγής		⊕				⊕			⊕					⊕
Ζωικής παραγωγής		⊕				⊕								⊕
Ιχθυοκομίας-αλιείας														
Γεωργικών μηχανημάτων αρδεύσεων						⊕								
Δασοπονίας								⊕				⊕		
Ανθοκομίας και θερμοκηπίων									⊕					
Διοίκησης γεωργικών εκμεταλλεύσεων		⊕												

9	10	11	11a	11b	11c			
		Messolongi						
Chalkis	Serres	Κετρικό Μεσολσγγι	1ο Παρ/μυ ΚαρπενΉαι	2ο Παρ/μυ Ιωάννινα	3ο Παρ/μα Αρτα	Asetem/Seletem	Duration of study, semesters	
								Technology applied
⊕							6 ct.	Infrastructural building
							6 ct.	Public works of infrastructure
						⊕		Civil engineering
							6 ct.	Topography
⊕	⊕					⊕	6 ct.	Mechanical engineering
							7 ct.	Technology of medical instruments
⊕						⊕	6 ct.	Electrical engineering
						⊕	6 ct.	Electronic engineering
							6 ct.	Computer science, applied
							6 ct.	Computer systems
							6 ct.	Naval construction
							6 ct.	Textile industry
							6 ct.	Petrol technology
							6 ct.	Vehicle technology
							7 ct.	Automation
							6 ct.	Energy techniques
							6 ct.	Mining technology
								Food technology
							7 ct.	Nutrition
							7 ct.	Viniculture and technology of liquid food
							7 ct.	Food technology
								Agricultural technology
					⊕		6 ct.	Plant production
							6 ct.	Animal production
		⊕					6 ct.	Fishery and pisciculture
							6 ct.	Agricultural machines and irrigation systems
			⊕				6 ct.	Forestry
							6 ct.	Green-house systems, Floriculture
							6 ct.	Agricultural exploitation and planning

GR

3. Student statistics

Foreign students at Greek universities
(broken down according to country of origin)

	Πανεπιστήμιο Αθηνών University of Athens	Ε.Μ.Π. National Polytechnic Institute Metsoviou	Α.Π.Θ. Aristotle University of Thessalonica	Α.Σ.Ο.Ε.Ε. College of Trade and Industry	Α.Γ.Σ.Α. College of Agriculture	Α.Σ.Κ.Τ. College of Art	Π.Α.Σ.Π.Ε. Pandios College of Political Sciences	Α.Β.Σ.Π. College of Industrial Studies, Patras	Α.Β.Σ.Θ. College of Industrial Studies, Thessalonica	Παν/μιο Πατρών University of Patras	Παν/μιο Ιωαννίνων University of Ioannina	Δημ/τειο Παν/μιο Θράκης University of Thrace	Παν/μιο Κρήτης University Crete	Πολυτεχνείο Κρήτης Polytechnic Institute of Higher Education, Crete	Παν/μιο Αιγαίου University of the Aegeaon	Ιόνιο Παν/μιο Ionian University	Παν/μιο Θεσσαλίας University of Thessaly
Belgium	2		1														
Federal Republic of Germany	26	2	31				1			11	3		1			1	
Denmark	1		1														
Spain			1														
France	2	1	10			1	1										
Ireland			1														
Italy	1	1	12				3			1						1	
Luxembourg																	
The Netherlands			3														
Portugal																	
United Kingdom	3		1								1						

GR

4. Bibliography

The Ministry of Education and Religion publishes a brochure entitled **Faculties and subjects at the TEI** in Greek and in English.
A brochure entitled **Guide to admission into tertiary education for foreigners and others born abroad** is also produced in Greek and English by the Ministry of Education and Religion.
Also available: **Study guide after upper secondary schooling**, School Book Publishing House, Athens 1988.

Yearbooks: Each year Greece's institutions of higher education (AEIs) jointly publish a students' handbook which contains information on the teaching staff at each institution, on courses of study offered for each academic year, on entry requirements, on the number of students admitted per subject, on examinations, etc. This handbook also provides information on financial assistance, on scholarships and on medical care and facilities.

AEI guides: Each year, every higher education institution (AEI) also publishes its own guide, including a course schedule for the academic year.

Information leaflets and booklets: The Institute of Modern Greek at the Aristotle University in Thessaloniki publishes several information leaflets and booklets in Greek and English on summer and winter courses in modern Greek. The titles of these leaflets and booklets are: **Summer/winter courses in modern Greek language,** Aristotle University in Thessaloniki, School of Modern Greek Language; and
Courses on Greek language, history and culture, Institute for Balkan Studies, International Summer School.

General information: The Greek Ministry of National Education and Religion and the European Commission (Administration Office for Education in the European Community: European Information Centre Eurydice) has produced a brochure which provides detailed information on all the levels of the State-run Greek education system. This brochure called **The Greek education system** (Brussels 1988), is available in Greek, English and French.

5. Glossary

Γυμνάσιο: three-year secondary school which follows six years of primary schooling (approximately equivalent to Secondary level I). The six and seven-year secondary schools mentioned in the text above are school types which no longer exist, following a review of secondary education in Greece.

Λύκειο: *lycée* — three-year secondary school which follows Secondary level I and which is approximately equivalent to Secondary level II.

Ίδρυμα Κρατικών Υποτροφιών (IKY): the National Scholarship Board — the authority responsible for scholarship matters.

Law 105: this law requires that applicants make a sworn statement in which they confirm the correctness of the personal data given on the application forms. Applicants who provide false data may be prosecuted.

Πτυχίο: first university degree.

AEI: abbreviation for Ανώτατα Εκπαιδευτικά Ιδρύματα, university level higher education institutions.

TEI: abbreviation for Τεχνολογικά Εκπαιδευτικά Ιδρύματα, non-university level (technical) education institutions.

STE: abbreviation for Συμβούλιο Τεχνολογικής Εκπαίδευσης, Council for Technological Education.

ITE: abbreviation for Ινστιτούτο Τεχνολογικής Εκπαίδευσης, Institute of Technological Education.

Dikatsa: abbreviation for Διαπανεπιστημιακό Κέντρο Αναγνωρίσεως Τίτλων Σπουδών Αλλοδαπής, Inter-university Institute for the recognition of foreign certificates and degrees.

EAGE: abbreviation for Εθνική Ακαδημία Γραμμάτων και Επιστημών, The National Academy of Education and Sciences.

Greece has bilateral agreements (programmes) on cultural exchange and scholarships for foreign students with the following countries: Belgium, Denmark, the Federal Republic of Germany, France, Italy, the Netherlands, the United Kingdom and Ireland.

SAP: Συμβούλιο Ανώτατης Παιδείας (Council of Higher Education)

UPEPTH: Υπουργείο Εθνικής Παιδείας και Θρησκευμάτων (Ministry of Education and Religion)

OESB: Οργανισμός Εκδόσεως Σχολικών Βιβλίων (Publishing house for school textbooks).

6. Diagram of the education system

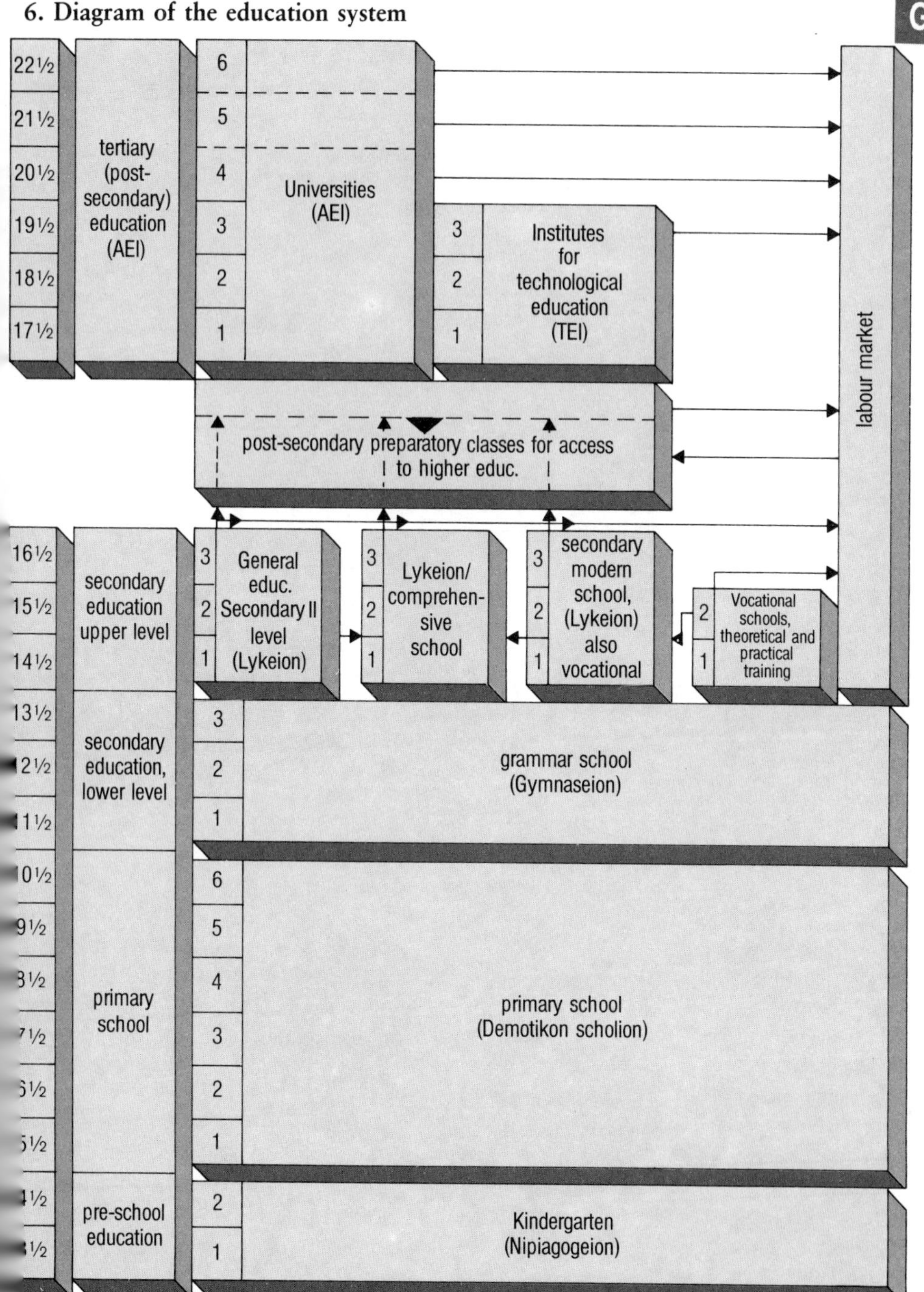
22½
21½
20½
19½
18½
17½
tertiary (post-secondary) education (AEI)
6
5
4
3
2
1
Universities (AEI)
3
2
1
Institutes for technological education (TEI)
labour market
post-secondary preparatory classes for access to higher educ.
16½
15½
14½
secondary education upper level
3
2
1
General educ. Secondary II level (Lykeion)
3
2
1
Lykeion/ comprehen-sive school
3
2
1
secondary modern school, (Lykeion) also vocational
2
1
Vocational schools, theoretical and practical training
13½
12½
11½
secondary education, lower level
3
2
1
grammar school (Gymnaseion)
10½
9½
8½
7½
6½
5½
primary school
6
5
4
3
2
1
primary school (Demotikon scholion)
4½
3½
pre-school education
2
1
Kindergarten (Nipiagogeion)

Spain

E

Organization of higher education

The Spanish Constitution of 1978 established a new model of regional division which replaced the old, centralized model and which was greatly decentralized. Within this framework Autonomous Communities, new regional bodies placed on a level between State and local administration and having, according to Article 2 of the Constitution, the right to self-determination, are able to assume responsibility in the field of higher education.

The 1983 Law on the Reformation of Higher Education is the legal foundation for the Spanish higher education system today. This law specifies the basic principle of self-administration for institutions of higher education contained in Article 27, Paragraph 10 of the Constitution and also defines the areas of responsibility with regard to the higher education policy of the State, the Autonomous Communities and of the universities themselves. This law also created the University Council as a coordinating, organizing, planning and advisory body (Article 23 of the Higher Education Reform Law).

Nevertheless, only seven (out of a total of 17) Autonomous Communities at present exercise their responsibility for the education system, including higher education. Autonomy of the institutions of higher education within the legal framework mentioned above extends to essentially four different aspects:

1. freedom of decision over internal administration;
2. freedom of choice over teaching staff and other personnel;
3. freedom of administration over the budget;
4. approval of degree curricula and right to award higher education diplomas and degrees.

Since 1983, various developments have taken place in the individual points. In some, the planned programmes are approaching completion (for example, the drawing up of statutes for the regulation of the international administration of the relevant institution). In others, (such as in the reform of the degree programmes and curricula), the process of defining the overall structure is still at an intermediate stage.

Types of higher education institutions

Since 1970 there have been only a few highly specialized subject areas at tertiary level outside the university system in Spain. So the universities comprise practically the whole higher education system.

There are 36 [1] universities, 32 State-run and four under the responsi-

1 The State-run University of Navarre was recently established and is expected to open in the 1989/90 academic year.

bility of the Roman Catholic Church, which among other things are subject to the 1962 Concordat and the 1979 Agreement with the Holy See. Of the 32 universities, 30 are general (four of these being polytechnics) and two are universities with specialist characteristics: the National Correspondence University, which has some legal peculiarities because of the nature of the courses of study available, and the International University (Universidad International Menéndez y Pelayo), offering seminars on topical issues (Universidad de Extensión cultural).

Courses at Spanish universities vary according to the types of higher education institutions at which they are offered:

1. *Facultades*,
2. *Escuelas Técnicas Superiores de Ingeniería y Arquitectura*,
3. *Escuelas Universitarias*,
4. *Colegios Universitarios*.

In the non-university sector a differentiation is made between two types of degree programme. First, degree programmes which are equivalent to those at universities with regard to structure, entry requirements and academic level: Merchant shipping (at present being introduced at universities), Sport and Tourism. Secondly, degree programmes in the arts field with their own structure and entry requirements: Drama and dance, singing and music (higher education level).

Student statistics

The total number of students registered at Spanish higher education institutions in the 1986/87 academic year amounted to 903 166; of these 872 621 were studying at State-run universities and 30 545 at private ones.

Figures for foreign students and above all students from the other European Community Member States are classified according to nationality in a table in the appendix.

The number of students in the non-university sector in the 1984/85 academic year totalled 36 684. (More recent figures are currently not available.)

Organization and validation of courses

Various degrees and certificates are awarded for the successful completion of courses at Spanish higher education:

Long-term courses of study

1. *Licenciado*: this degree is awarded after five or six years of study at a *Facultad*.
2. *Ingeniero Superior y Arquitecto*: these degrees are conferred after a course of study lasting five or six years at an *Escuela Técnica Superior*.

   The first three years may be completed at the *Colegios Universitarios* finishing with the licentiate degree. Originally, these were founded in towns and cities in which there was no institution of higher education, however, in the last few years they have spread everywhere. They are in all cases – albeit in differing forms – affiliated to a university.

E

Short-term courses of study

1. *Diplomado*: this degree is awarded after three years of study at an *Escuela Universitaria*.
2. *Ingeniero Técnico y Arquitecto Técnico*: this degree is awarded after three years' study of engineering and architecture at an *Escuela Técnica de Ingenería y Arquitectura*.

In addition to these, there is the academic title of Doctor, which corresponds to the third cycle of studies and which was recently regulated by Royal Decree 185/85 of 23 January. Candidates for this degree are required to participate in a special course (Ph.D. programme) and subsequently to present an individual academic thesis on independent research work. In general, only a small proportion of graduates continue to this level.

Finally, on account of their autonomy the institutions are in a position to offer various other degree programmes over and above those already mentioned. These are then completed with degrees which are conferred by the relevant institution of higher education. These degrees are not valid in all parts of the country, unless they are at some later date recognized through an appropriate process.

With a view to this eventuality, the range of postgraduate courses at individual universities has been increased considerably in the past few years.

Admission and registration

Initial information

Although current reforms aim at the abolition of the higher education regions and admission zones, those students are presently being given preference in admission to higher education institutions who have completed their secondary education in the zone concerned, unless they wish to embark on courses of study which do not exist there. In this case, students who have to leave their region are regarded in exactly the same way as students from the region concerned. In Madrid and Barcelona (where there are several universities) there are universal distribution systems which take the preferences of students and their marks into consideration.

Applicants from outside Spain are not subject to these restrictions; thus they can address their applications to any institution or university of their choice. It is, however, strongly recommended that applicants carry out all relevant formalities within the prescribed periods, and that they gather information about the university and course in question as early as possible.

Entry requirements

The entry requirement for Spaniards to a course of study is the certificate awarded upon successful completion of secondary education (*Bachillerato Unificado y Polivalente* — BUP) and the completion of a one-year introductory course (*Curso de Orientación Universitaria* — COU). Although admission to higher education is also possible by other means (secondary stage vocational training for certain *Escuelas Universitarias*, special examinations for people over 25 years of age), the vast majority of students choose this way. In general, lectures take place from October to June (which represents the academic year).

The situation with regard to admission to higher education institutions is very varied: at times the difference between various subject areas at one and the same institution of higher education is even more extreme because of the differing demand for certain courses of study. For some courses (medicine, dentistry, veterinary medicine and certain engineering branches), fierce competition may exist.

According to the regulations in force, a 5 % quota is reserved for foreign students at institutions of higher education where admissions are limited. It must, however, be noted that Royal Decree 943/86 of 9 May 1986 established the principle of equal treatment for students from other EC Member States and Spanish students as far as admission to higher education institutions is concerned.

Limitations

The only limitation provided for by the Law for the Reformation of the Higher Education System is the one as regards the capacity of each institution. To this end, the determination of some general regulations is envisaged which should be used by higher education institutions in determining the number of vacancies. When this is not the case, the University Council determines the number of students to be admitted to a first course of study, setting the number in accordance with the justified proposals made by the universities which require this.

In the last few years nearly all universities have established admission quotas for a number of subject areas using the above-mentioned process as a basis. If no quotas exist, only the general regulations for admission to higher education are applied.

Recognition of foreign certificates and degrees

In general, and with regard to the other countries, the following regulations are in force:

1. admission to the first course: certificate required for admission to higher education in the country of origin;
2. admission to further courses and postgraduate courses: the recognition of individual study achievements is the responsibility of the relevant institution of higher education;
3. completed courses and degrees awarded: the decision as to recognition is the responsibility of the Ministry of Education and Science.

E

All this is valid without prejudice to European Community regulations concerning the right of EC citizens to settle and to carry out certain professions anywhere within the Community.

Entry examinations

According to regulations in force, all Spanish and foreign applicants must take a general examination (*prueba de acceso a la Universidad*), which takes place in July and September. This examination is imperative for admission to *Facultades* and *Escuelas Técnicas Superiores*. The examination is carried out by the higher education institutions themselves. The National Open University holds these examinations in the Spanish embassies in some countries. This is generally the case where a large number of applicants is involved.

Application and registration

All applicants must submit an application to the institution at which they wish to study. For their first course, they must name various alternatives, as it is difficult, on account of the number of applicants and the existing limitations, to guarantee the consideration of the preferences of applicants in all cases.

As soon as the university has given the student permission to register for a certain subject area, he must formally enrol upon presentation of the required documents.

Tuition fees

Fees are determined annually by the University Council and the governments of the Autonomous Communities with responsibility for higher education (Catalonia, the Basque Country, Galicia, Andalusia, Valencia, the Canary Island and Navarre). The Ministry of Education and Science determines the fees for the remaining institutions of higher education.

Generally, fees for the academic year 1987/88 amounted to between PTA 37 065 and 52 500 (with minor variations). Higher education institutions under the auspices of the Church determine their own fees.

The above refers to courses of study which lead to officially recognized degrees for the whole of the sovereign territory of Spain. For other degree programmes and degrees which are offered by an institution of higher education within the scope of its autonomy, the tuition fees are determined by the relevant institution.

Knowledge of the language of instruction, language courses and other courses

For a course of study at a Spanish institution of higher education, a good knowledge of Spanish is imperative, as courses and lectures are generally conducted in Spanish. It should be noted that the Autonomous Communities where there is a second official language (Catalonian in Catalonia and on the Balearic Islands, Basque in the Basque Country and in Navarre, Galician in Galicia and Valencian in Valencia), some lectures may be held in those languages.

The universities and other educational establishments themselves offer a variety of courses in Spanish for foreign students. The language and literature courses offered by the Menéndes y Pelayo International University in summer are a special facility. Here, a wide range of courses on various subjects is offered.

Financial assistance and scholarships

The scholarship system administered by the Ministry of Education and Science applies only to students with Spanish citizenship or those with legal residence in Spain. Furthermore, there are other forms of financial assistance for foreign students. It is granted by different national institutions based on bilateral agreements between Spain and other countries or programmes for specific academic and research purposes.

For these, it is highly recommended that applicants collect general information and, in particular, consult the following: the Ministry of Foreign Affairs, and especially the Spanish embassy in the country concerned. Students from Latin America should address their inquiries to the *Instituto de Cooperación Iberoamericana*. Other State and private institutions grant financial assistance to a limited extent. In any case, it is imperative that students submit their applications for a grant or financial assistance at the earliest opportunity and always before arrival in Spain.

E

Entry and residence regulations

For nationals of EC Countries and of some other countries (it is imperative to inquire beforehand) a visa is not required for entry and for residence of up to three months. For longer residence a permit must be obtained in all cases from the authorities concerned (Ministry of the Interior and Police Commissioner's Department). For this, reasons for residence must be given and proof of sufficient financial means produced.

Since the relevant regulations will only apply in full from 1992 onwards, Royal Decree 1099/86 of 26 May generally regulates the situation of nationals from other European Community Member States positively.

Social aspects

Social security and health insurance

All Spanish students under the age of 28 and registered at Spanish institutions of higher education are included in a students' insurance fund. This fund will gradually be transferred into the social security system, however, as a special entity.

The students' insurance fund also caters for a considerable number of students from other countries as a result of reciprocal agreements. Students from EC States are among those equally covered by this programme. Students over the age of 28 are strongly advised to take out additional private insurance, primarily to cover medical care and other services.

Advisory services

General information can primarily be obtained from Spanish embassies and from Spanish cultural institutions if they exist in the foreign country concerned.

The Ministry of Education and Science operates several departments which give relevant information to foreign students: *Servicio de Información* for matters of recognition of periods of study (see Appendix). Finally there are similar bodies in various forms at every institution of higher education: student secretariats (*vicerrectorados de alumnos*) and information offices for foreign students (*unidades de información*). Exact details about course structure can be obtained there.

Student employment

Without the relevant work permit from the employment exchange employment is not permitted. Temporary employment is possible in principle, but in view of the present labour market situation in Spain, opportunities are limited.

At some institutions of higher education, there are information centres which help students find jobs, and which may also be of use to foreign students. Foreign students, however, need the work permit mentioned above.

After the period of transition in Spain's Treaty of Accession to the EC has expired, students from other EC Member States will, to all intents and purposes, have the same rights as Spanish students.

Up to this time, the above-mentioned regulations (Royal Decree 1099/86 of 26 May) will be in force which envisage a relatively flexible special treatment for this group.

Student organizations

For various reasons, student organizations are still underdeveloped. However, at the individual higher education institutions all types of student-run organizations are emerging which have different aims and goals. At the national level, the first steps have also been taken towards forming large organizations.

At present, the foreign student would be advised to request information from student bodies at the individual institutions.

Cost of living

It is difficult to determine exactly the average cost of living for each individual with regard to all items. In addition to registration fees and equipment costs, an amount of at least PTA 45 000 per month can be assumed.

Although vast differences do not exist between the various zones and regions of Spain, it can be assumed that the amounts in Madrid and Barcelona are somewhat higher.

Experience shows that foreign students must allow for somewhat higher average costs than Spanish students.

Accommodation

There are a number of student halls of residence (*Colegios Mayores*) at the institutions of higher education and in comparison with the demand, places available are in short supply. More detailed information regarding this should be requested from the institution concerned.

The availability of private accommodation is varied and depends on the situation in the town concerned. In some cases, accommodation scarcity has led to relatively steep price increases.

Within and outside the higher education institutions there are some bodies which assist students in finding accommodation. They receive offers and advertise places in the student media.

Services for students

In general, there is a wide range of services (cafeterias, refectories, transportation, etc.), cultural and sports facilities. In practically all cases, they are limited to the local, or at most, the regional area, so it is difficult to compile a general register.

In all cases, student status allows access to those services which are open to all students without exception.

Facilities for disabled students

All relevant information should be requested from the university or faculty itself.

Whether facilities exist for disabled students depends largely on the structure of the building. With few exceptions, only relatively modern buildings are fitted with appropriate equipment. Admittedly great efforts are being made in this respect to incorporate this group of students into university life.

E

Appendices

1. Addresses

Spanish embassies in EC countries

Belgium
19 rue de la Science
B-1040 Bruxelles
☎ 2 30 03 40
Telex: 22 092

Denmark
Upsalagade 26
DK-2100 København
☎ (01) 42 47 00/(01) 42 22 66
Telex: 27 145 ESCO DK

Federal Republic of Germany
Schloßstr. 4
D-5300 Bonn 1
☎ 21 70 94/95, 21 75 27
Telex: 886 792 ESPEM D

Greece
Vassilissis Sofias 29
GR-10674 Athina
☎ 721 48 85/721 53 52/722 42 42
Telex: 215 860 PRIS GR.

France
13, Av. George V
F-75381 Paris
☎ 47 23 61 83/47 23 46 35/47 23 32 27/47 23 40 85/47 23 83 77
Telex: 280 689 AMBESPA PARIS

Ireland
17A Merlyn Park
Dublin 4
☎ 69 16 49/69 25 97
Telex: 25 549 EMES EI

Italy
Palazzo Borghese, Largo Fontanella di Borghese, 19
I-00186 Roma
☎ 679 85 06/07
Telex: 626 126 EMSPAN I.

Luxembourg
4 Blvd Emmanuel Servais
BP 290
L-2535 Luxembourg
☎ 46 02 55
Telex: 1 545 EMELUX LU.

The Netherlands
Lange Voorhout 50
's-Gravenhage 2514 EG
☎ 64 38 14/15/16/17, 45 15 23
Telex: 32 373 EMBES-NL

Portugal
Rua do Salitre, 1
P-1296 Lisboa
☎ 37 23 81/82/83/84
Telex: EMEPOR 12505

United Kingdom
24 Belgrave Square
London SW 1X8QA
☎ (01) 235 55 55
Telex: 21 110 and 261 333 SPANISHEMB LDN

Ministry of Education and Science

Ministerio de Educación y Ciencia (Ministry of Education and Science)

- Sede central (Central office)
  Alcalá 34
  E-28014 Madrid
  ☎ 532 13 00
- Secretaría General Técnica (General administration)
  Alcalá 34
  E-28014 Madrid
  ☎ 532 13 00

  Subdirección General de Cooperación Internacional (Subdepartment for international cooperation)
  Paseo del Prado 28
  E-28014 Madrid
  ☎ 467 11 54

  Subdirección General de Homologación de Títulos (Subdepartment for the recognition of degrees)
  Paseo del Prado 28
  E-28014 Madrid
  ☎ 467 11 54

  Servicio de Información, Iniciativas y Reclamaciones (Office for information, initiatives and complaints)
  Alcalá 34
  E-28014 Madrid
  ☎ 532 13 00

  Dirección General de Promoción Educativa (Department of educational promotion)
  Los Madrazo 15-17
  E-28014 Madrid
  ☎ 222 11 00

Other authorities

- Consejo de Universidades (University Council)
  Secretaría General —
  Ciudad Universitaria s/n
  E-28040 Madrid
  ☎ 449 66 65/75/78, 449 74 37
- Ministerio de Trabajo y Seguridad Social (Ministry of Labour and Social Security)
  Agustín Bethencourt 4
  E-28071 Madrid
  ☎ 253 60 00
- Ministerio del Interior (Ministry of the Interior)
  Amador de los Ríos 7
  E-28071 Madrid
  ☎ 419 39 00
- Ministerio de Asuntos Exteriores (Ministry of Foreign Affairs)
  Plaza de la Provincia 1
  E-28071 Madrid
  ☎ 266 48 00/266 50 00

E

– Consejerías de Educación de los Gobiernos de las Comunidades Autónomas (Education Offices of the Autonomous Communities)

Junta de Andalucía
Consejería de Educación y Ciencia
República Argentina 21
E-41071 Sevilla
☎ 45 92 11

Generalitat de Catalunya
Departamento de Enseñanza
Avda. Diagonal 682
E-08071 Barcelona
☎ 205 10 00

Gobierno de Canarias
Consejería de Educación
J. R. Hamilton
E-Santa Cruz de Tenerife
(Islas Canarias)
☎ 27 54 50

Junta de Galicia
Consejería de Educación
Edif. Admvo. San Cayetano
E-Santiago de Compostela
☎ 56 41 00

País Vasco
Departamento de Educación, Universidades e Investigación
Duque de Wellington s/n
E-01071 Vitoria
☎ 24 99 00

Generalitat Valenciana
Consejería de Cultura, Educación y Ciencia
Avda. Campanar 32
E-46071 Valencia
☎ 349 02 44

Comunidad F ral de Navarra
Consejería de Educación y Cultura
Avda. de San Ignacio 5
E-31002 Pamplona
☎ 984 22 72 00

Universities

Alcalá de Henares
Carretera de Barcelona km 33
E-28014 Madrid

Alicante
San Vicente del Raspeig
E-03071 Alicante

Barcelona
Gran Via de les Corts Catalanes 585
E-08071 Barcelona

Barcelona Autónoma
Campus de Bellaterra
E-08071 Barcelona

Cádiz
Plaza de Fragela s/n
E-11071 Cádiz

Politécnica de Canarias
Plaza de la Constitución 72
E-35071 Las Palmas

Cantabria
Avda. de los Castros s/n
E-39071 Santander

Castilla-La Mancha
La Paloma 9
E-13071 Ciudad Real

Politécnica de Cataluña
Avda. Gregorio Marañón s/n
E-08071 Barcelona

Córdoba
Alfonso XIII 17
E-14071 Córdoba

Extremadura
Avda. de Elvas s/n
E-06071 Badajoz

Granada
Cuesta del Hospicio s/n
(Hospital Real)
E-18071 Granada

Islas Baleares
Miguel de los Santos Oliver 2
E-07071 Palma de Mallorca

La Laguna
Molinos de Agua s/n
E-Tenerife

León
Campus de Vegazana
E-24071 León

Madrid Autónoma
Carretera de Colmenar Viejo km 15
Cantoblanco
E-28071 Madrid

Madrid Complutense
Ciudad Universitaria
Pabellón de Gobierno
E-28071 Madrid

Madrid Politécnica
Ramiro de Maeztu s/n
E-28071 Madrid

Málaga
Plaza de El Ejido s/n
E-29071 Málaga

Murcia
Santo Cristo 1
E-30071 Murcia

Universidad Pública de Navarra
Avda. del Ejército 2, 6a
E-Pamplona

Oviedo
San Francisco 3
E-33071 Oviedo

País Vasco
Ciudad Universitaria
Campus de Lejona
E-48071 Vizcaya

Salamanca
Patio de Escuelas 1
E-37071 Salamanca

Santiago
Plaza del Obradoiro
Palacio San Jerónimo
E-Santiago de Compostela
(La Coruña)

Sevilla
San Fernando 4
E-41071 Sevilla

UNED
Ciudad Universitaria s/n
E-28071 Madrid

Valencia
Nave 2
E-46071 Valencia

Valencia Politécnica
Camino de Vera s/n
E-46071 Valencia

Valladolid
Cárcel 6
E-47071 Valladolid

Zaragoza
Plaza de San Francisco s/n
E-50071 Zaragoza

Menéndez y Pelayo
Amador de los Ríos 1
E-28071 Madrid

Private universities

Pontificia de Comillas
Canto Blanco
E-28049 Madrid

Deusto
E-48071 Bilbao

Navarra
E-31071 Navarra

Pontificia de Salamanca
E-37071 Salamanca

Non-university sector

Institutos nacionales de Educación Física

Barcelona
San Mateo, s/n
Carretera de Esplugas

Granada
Carretera de Alfácar, s/n
C.P: 18011

La Coruña
Carretera de Bastiagueiro, s/n
C.P: 15179 Oleiros
(La Coruña)

Las Palmas
Pérez del Toro, I
C.P: 35004

León
Facultad de Biología
Universidad de León
Campus de Vegazana
C.P: 24071

Lérida
Partida de La Caparrella, s/n
C.P: 25000

Valencia
Carretera de Valencia a Cheste, s/n
C.P: 46380 Cheste (Valencia)

Vitoria
Carretera de Lasarte, s/n
C.P: 01007

Madrid
Avda. Martín Fierro
Ciudad Universitaria

Escuelas Superiores de Marina Civil

La Coruña
Paseo de Ronda, s/n

Gijón
Avda. Eduardo Castro, s/n

Santander
Avda. Carrero Blanco, s/n

Bilbao
María Díaz Haro
Portugalete (Vizcaya)

Barcelona
Plaza de Palacio, 18

Cádiz
Duque de Nájera, s/n

Sta. Cruz de Tenerife
Avda. de Anaga, s/n

Escuelas de Turismo

Centro Estatal:

Madrid
Plaza de Roma, 16
(For addresses of the 51 private schools, see bibliography *Estudios en España*).

Escuelas de Arte Dramático y Danza

Alicante
San Fernando, 30

Córdoba
Blanco Belmonte, 16

Madrid
Plaza Isabel II, s/n

Málaga
El Egido, s/n

Murcia
Angel Guirao, s/n

Sevilla
Jesús del Gran Poder, 49

Valencia
Plaza de San Esteban, 3

Barcelano
Instituto del Teatro
Plaza del Conde de Güell

Escuela Superior de Canto

Madrid
San Bernardo, 44

Conservatorio de Música – Grado superior

Alicante
San Fernando, 30

Córdoba
Angel Saavedra, 1

Madrid
Plaza de Isabel II, s/n

Málaga
El Égido, s/n

Murcia
Angel Guirao, s/n

Sevilla
Jesús del Gran Poder, 49

Valencia
Plaza de San Esteban, 3

Badajoz
Ramón Albarrán, 13

Barcelona Municipal
Bruc, 100

Barcelona Liceo
Ramblas, 63

San Sebastián
Easo, 39

Santa Cruz de Tenerife
Teobaldo Pover, 3

E

2. Survey of courses of study at higher education institutions

2.1. University sector

Facultades

	Alcalá de Henares	Alicante	Barcelona	Autónoma de Barcelona	Politécnica de Cataluña	Cádiz	Cantabria	Castilla-La Mancha	Córdoba	Extremadura	Granada	Islas Baleares	La Laguna	León	Autónoma de Madrid	Complutense de Madrid	Politécnica de Madrid	
Geografía e Historia																		**Geography and History**
Geografía	●	●	●	●			●	●	●	●	●	●	●	●	●	●		Geography
Historia	●	●	●	●		●	●	●	●	●	●	●	●	●	●	●		History
Historia de América			●													●		American history
Historia del Arte			●						●	●		●			●	●		History of art
Arte				●									●	●				Art sciences
Prehistoria															●			Prehistory
Historia Antigua															●			Ancient history
Historia Medieval															●			Medieval history
Historia Moderna															●			Modern history
Historia Contemporánea															●			Contemporary history
Derecho	●	●	●[1]	●		●	●	●	●	●	●	●	●	●	●	●		Law
Bellas Artes			●					●			●		●			●		Art
Informática				●	●												●	Applied information science
Ciencias de la Información				●									●			●		Information science
Medicina	●	●	●[4]	●		●	●		●	●	●		●		●	●		Medicine
Farmacia	●		●								●		●			●		Pharmacy
Odontología			●								●					●		Dentistry
Veterinaria				●					●	●			●	●		●		Veterinary medicine
Matemáticas		●	●	●			●			●	●		●		●	●		Mathematics
Física		●	●	●			●			●	●	●	●		●	●		Physics
Geología		●	●	●							●					●		Geology
Biología	●	●	●	●					●	●	●	●	●	●	●	●		Biology
Química	●	●	●[5]	●		●		●	●	●	●	●	●		●	●		Chemistry
Ciencias del Mar																		Oceanography
Psicología			●	●							●		●		●	●		Psychology
Fil. y C. Educación																		**Philology and Education science**
Filosofía			●	●				●			●	●	●		●	●		Philosophy
C. Educación			●	●								●	●			●		Education science

● State sector
■ Private sector

[1] There are two law faculties at the University of Barcelona: Barcelona and Lérida.
[2] There are two law faculties at the University of Santiago: Santiago and La Coruña.
[3] There are two law faculties at the University of Valladolid: Valladolid and Burgos.
[4] There are three faculties of medicine at the University of Barcelona: Barcelona, Lérida and Reus.
[5] There are two faculties of chemistry at the University of Barcelona: Barcelona and Tarragona.
[6] There are two faculties of chemistry at the University of Basque country: Bilbao and San Sebastian.
[7] There are two faculties of chemistry at the University of Sevilla: Sevilla and Huelva.

E

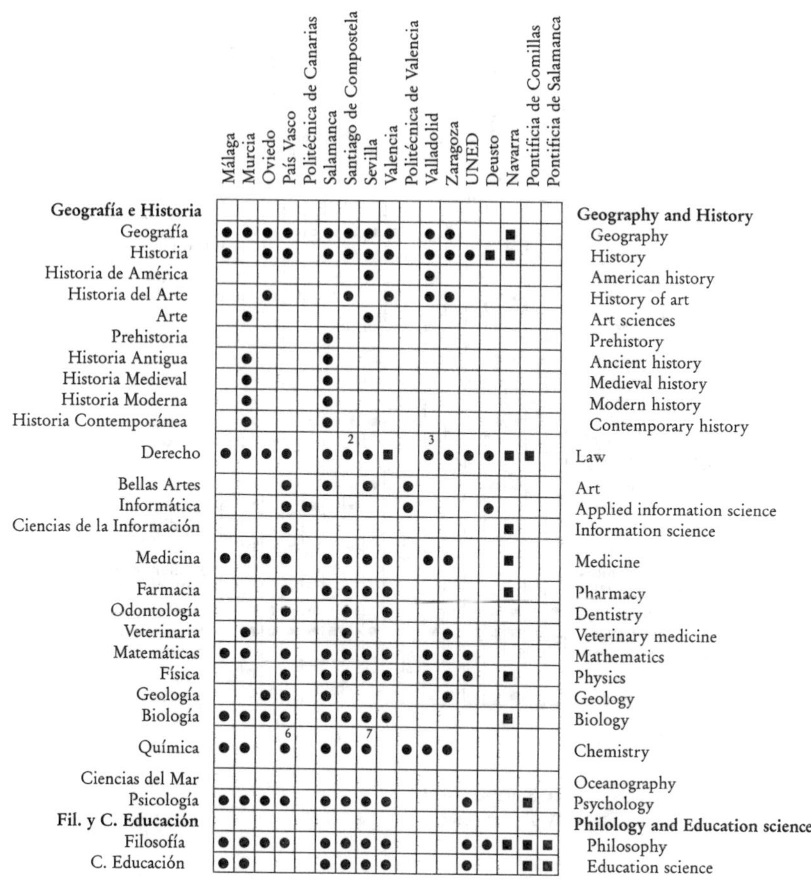

	Málaga	Murcia	Oviedo	País Vasco	Politécnica de Canarias	Salamanca	Santiago de Compostela	Sevilla	Valencia	Politécnica de Valencia	Valladolid	Zaragoza	UNED	Deusto	Navarra	Pontificia de Comillas	Pontificia de Salamanca	
Geografía e Historia																		**Geography and History**
Geografía	●	●	●	●		●	●	●	●		●	●			■			Geography
Historia	●		●	●		●	●	●	●		●	●	●	■	■			History
Historia de América								●			●							American history
Historia del Arte			●				●		●		●	●						History of art
Arte		●						●										Art sciences
Prehistoria						●												Prehistory
Historia Antigua		●				●												Ancient history
Historia Medieval		●				●												Medieval history
Historia Moderna		●				●												Modern history
Historia Contemporánea		●				●												Contemporary history
Derecho	●	●	●	●		●	2 ●	●	■		3 ●	●	●	●	■	■		Law
Bellas Artes				●		●		●		●								Art
Informática				●	●					●				●				Applied information science
Ciencias de la Información				●											■			Information science
Medicina	●	●	●	●		●	●	●	●		●	●			■			Medicine
Farmacia				●		●	●	●	●						■			Pharmacy
Odontología				●			●		●									Dentistry
Veterinaria		●					●					●						Veterinary medicine
Matemáticas	●	●		●		●	●	●	●		●	●	●					Mathematics
Física				●		●	●	●	●		●	●	●		■			Physics
Geología			●	●		●						●						Geology
Biología	●	●	●	●		●	●	●	●						■			Biology
Química	●	●		6 ●		●	●	7 ●		●	●	●						Chemistry
Ciencias del Mar																		Oceanography
Psicología	●	●	●	●		●	●	●	●				●			■		Psychology
Fil. y C. Educación																		**Philology and Education science**
Filosofía	●	●	●	●		●	●	●	●				●	●	■	■	■	Philosophy
C. Educación	●	●				●	●	●	●				●			■	■	Education science

E

2.1. University sector

Facultades

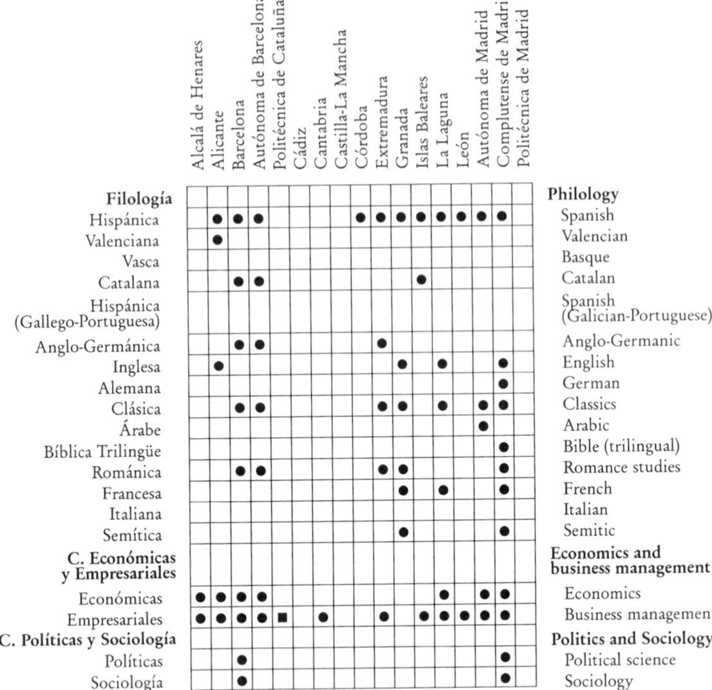

	Alcalá de Henares	Alicante	Barcelona	Autónoma de Barcelona	Politécnica de Cataluña	Cádiz	Cantabria	Castilla-La Mancha	Córdoba	Extremadura	Granada	Islas Baleares	La Laguna	León	Autónoma de Madrid	Complutense de Madrid	Politécnica de Madrid	
Filología																		**Philology**
Hispánica		●	●	●					●	●	●	●	●	●	●	●		Spanish
Valenciana		●																Valencian
Vasca																		Basque
Catalana			●	●								●						Catalan
Hispánica (Gallego-Portuguesa)																		Spanish (Galician-Portuguese)
Anglo-Germánica			●	●						●								Anglo-Germanic
Inglesa		●									●		●			●		English
Alemana																●		German
Clásica			●	●						●	●		●		●	●		Classics
Árabe															●			Arabic
Bíblica Trilingüe																●		Bible (trilingual)
Románica			●	●						●	●					●		Romance studies
Francesa											●		●			●		French
Italiana																		Italian
Semítica											●					●		Semitic
C. Económicas y Empresariales																		**Economics and business management**
Económicas	●	●	●	●									●		●	●		Economics
Empresariales	●	●	●	●	■		●			●		●	●	●	●	●		Business management
C. Políticas y Sociología																		**Politics and Sociology**
Políticas			●													●		Political science
Sociología			●													●		Sociology

● State sector
■ Private sector

1 There are two faculties of economics and business management: Vigo and Santiago.
2 There are two faculties of economics and business management: Deusto and San Sebastian.

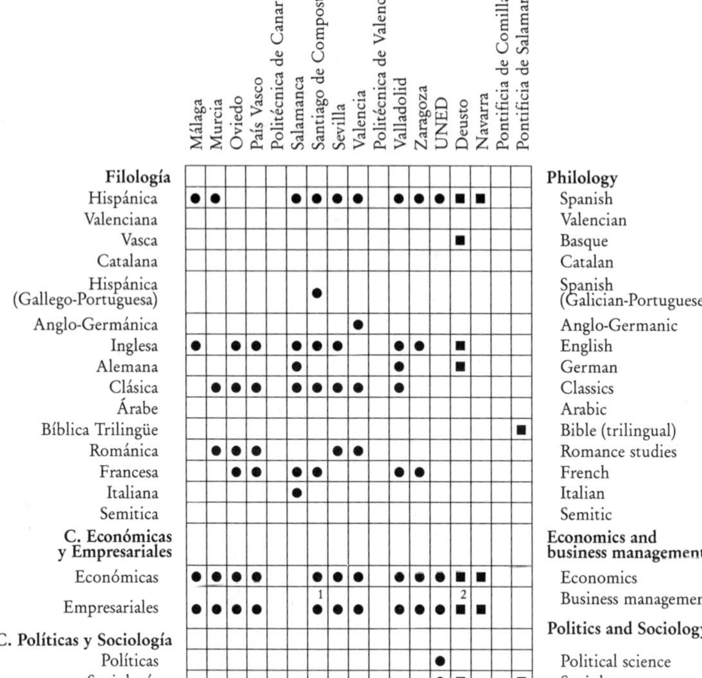

	Málaga	Murcia	Oviedo	País Vasco	Politécnica de Canarias	Salamanca	Santiago de Compostela	Sevilla	Valencia	Politécnica de Valencia	Valladolid	Zaragoza	UNED	Deusto	Navarra	Pontificia de Comillas	Pontificia de Salamanca	
Filología																		**Philology**
Hispánica	●	●				●	●	●	●		●	●	●	■	■			Spanish
Valenciana																		Valencian
Vasca														■				Basque
Catalana																		Catalan
Hispánica (Gallego-Portuguesa)							●											Spanish (Galician-Portuguese)
Anglo-Germánica									●									Anglo-Germanic
Inglesa	●		●	●		●	●	●			●	●		■				English
Alemana						●					●			■				German
Clásica		●	●	●		●	●	●	●		●							Classics
Árabe																		Arabic
Bíblica Trilingüe																	■	Bible (trilingual)
Románica		●	●	●				●	●									Romance studies
Francesa			●	●		●	●				●	●						French
Italiana						●												Italian
Semitica																		Semitic
C. Económicas y Empresariales																		**Economics and business management**
Económicas	●	●	●	●			●	●	●		●	●	●	■	■			Economics
Empresariales	●	●	●	●			1 ●	●	●		●	●	●	2 ■	■			Business management
C. Políticas y Sociología																		**Politics and Sociology**
Políticas													●					Political science
Sociología													●	■			■	Sociology

E

2.1. University sector

Escuelas Técnicas Superiores

	Alcalá de Henares	Alicante	Barcelona	Autónoma de Barcelona	Politécnica de Cataluña	Cádiz	Cantabria	Castilla-La Mancha	Córdoba	Extremadura	Granada	Islas Baleares	La Laguna	León	Autónoma de Madrid	Complutense de Madrid	Politécnica de Madrid	
Arquitectura																		Architecture
Edificación					●[1]												●	Structural engineering
Urbanismo					●												●	Town planning
Ingenieros Agrónomos																		Agricultural sciences
Economía Agraria									●								●	Agricultural economics
Industrias Agrarias					●				●								●	Agricultural engineering
Ingeniería Rural									●								●	Rural engineering
Fitotecnia					●				●								●	Plant breeding
Zootecnia									●								●	Animal husbandry
Ingenieros Aeronaúticos																		Aeronautical engineering
Aeronaves																	●	Aircraft
Aeropuertos																	●	Airports
Ingenieros de Caminos, Canales y Puertos					●		●										●	Engineering for roads, canals, and bridges
Ingenieros Electromecánicos																		Electrical engineering
Ingenieros de Minas																		Mining engineering
Combustibles y Energía																	●	Fuels and energy
Geología y Geofísica																	●	Geology and Geophysics
Minería y Explosivos																	●	Mining and explosives
Metalugia y Mineralurgia																	●	Metallurgy and Mineralogy
Ingeniero de Montes																		Forestry engineering
Industrias Forestales																	●	Forestry economics
Silvicultura y Piscicultura																	●	Forest cultivation and fish breeding
Ingenieros Navales																		Naval engineering
Arquitectura Naval																	●	Naval architecture
Máquinas Marinas																	●	Marine engineering
Ingenieros de Telecomunicación																		Telecommunications engineering
Comunicaciones					●												●	Communications
Electrónica					●												●	Electronics

● State sector
■ Private sector

1 There are two *Escuelas Técnicas Superiores* for architecture at the *Universidad Politécnica de Cataluña:* Barcelona and Tarra
2 There is one *Escuela Técnica Superior* for agricultural science at Lugo.

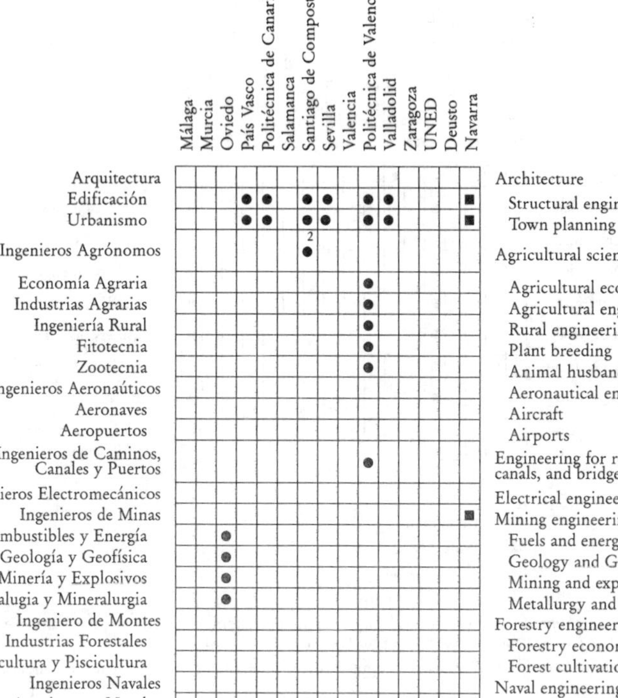

	Málaga	Murcia	Oviedo	País Vasco	Politécnica de Canarias	Salamanca	Santiago de Compostela	Sevilla	Valencia	Politécnica de Valencia	Valladolid	Zaragoza	UNED	Deusto	Navarra	
Arquitectura																Architecture
Edificación				●	●		●	●		●	●				■	Structural engineering
Urbanismo				●	●		●	●		●	●				■	Town planning
Ingenieros Agrónomos							2 ●									Agricultural sciences
Economía Agraria										●						Agricultural economics
Industrias Agrarias										●						Agricultural engineering
Ingeniería Rural										●						Rural engineering
Fitotecnia										●						Plant breeding
Zootecnia										●						Animal husbandry
Ingenieros Aeronaúticos																Aeronautical engineering
Aeronaves																Aircraft
Aeropuertos																Airports
Ingenieros de Caminos, Canales y Puertos										●						Engineering for roads, canals, and bridges
Ingenieros Electromecánicos																Electrical engineering
Ingenieros de Minas															■	Mining engineering
Combustibles y Energía			●													Fuels and energy
Geología y Geofísica			●													Geology and Geophysics
Minería y Explosivos			●													Mining and explosives
Metalugia y Mineralurgia			●													Metallurgy and Mineralogy
Ingeniero de Montes																Forestry engineering
Industrias Forestales																Forestry economics
Silvicultura y Piscicultura																Forest cultivation and fish breeding
Ingenieros Navales																Naval engineering
Arquitectura Naval																Naval architecture
Máquinas Marinas																Marine engineering
Ingenieros de Telecomunicación				●	●				●							Telecommunications engineering
Comunicaciones																Communications
Electrónica																Electronics

E

2.1. University sector

Escuelas Técnicas Superiores

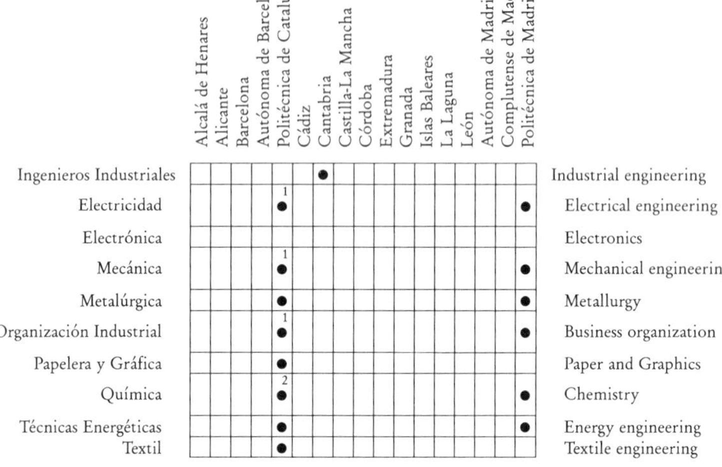

	Alcalá de Henares	Alicante	Barcelona	Autónoma de Barcelona	Politécnica de Cataluña	Cádiz	Cantabria	Castilla-La Mancha	Córdoba	Extremadura	Granada	Islas Baleares	La Laguna	León	Autónoma de Madrid	Complutense de Madrid	Politécnica de Madrid	
Ingenieros Industriales							●											Industrial engineering
Electricidad					● [1]												●	Electrical engineering
Electrónica																		Electronics
Mecánica					● [1]												●	Mechanical engineering
Metalúrgica					●												●	Metallurgy
Organización Industrial					● [1]												●	Business organization
Papelera y Gráfica					●													Paper and Graphics
Química					● [2]												●	Chemistry
Técnicas Energéticas					●												●	Energy engineering
Textil					●													Textile engineering

● State sector
■ Private sector

[1] There are two *Escuelas Técnicas Superiores* for mechanical engineering, specializing in electricity, mechanical engineering an business organization at the *Universidad Politécnica de Cataluña:* Barcelona und Tarrasa.

[2] There are two *Escuelas Técnicas Superiores* for industrial engineering, specializing in chemistry at the *Universidad Politécnic de Cataluña*.

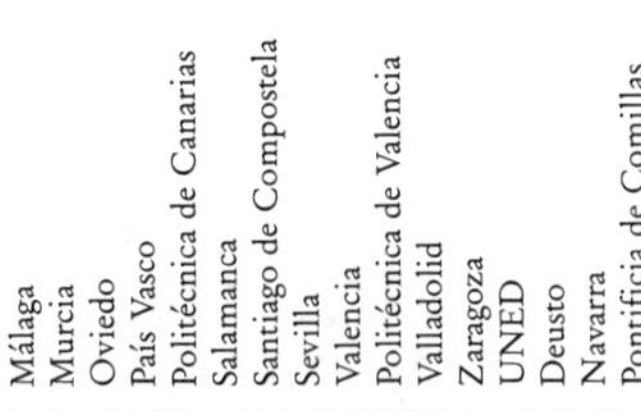

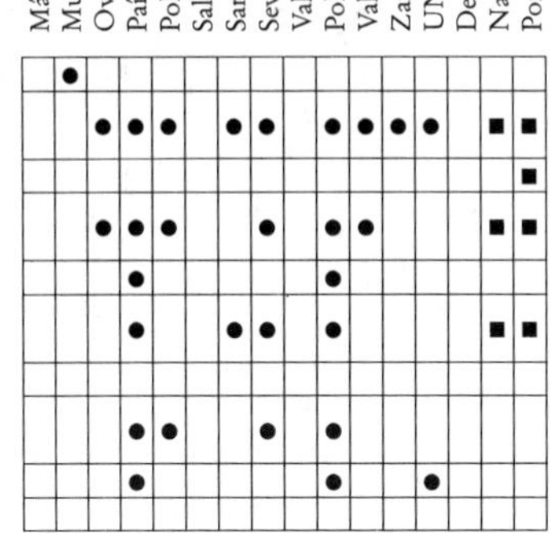

	Málaga	Murcia	Oviedo	País Vasco	Politécnica de Canarias	Salamanca	Santiago de Compostela	Sevilla	Valencia	Politécnica de Valencia	Valladolid	Zaragoza	UNED	Deusto	Navarra	Pontificia de Comillas	
Ingenieros Industriales		●															Industrial engineering
Electricidad			●	●	●		●	●		●	●	●	●		■	■	Electrical engineering
Electrónica																■	Electronics
Mecánica			●	●	●			●		●	●				■	■	Mechanical engineering
Metalúrgica				●						●							Metallurgy
Organización Industrial				●			●	●		●					■	■	Business organization
Papelera y Gráfica																	Paper and graphics
Química				●	●			●		●							Chemistry
Técnicas Energéticas				●						●			●				Energy engineering
Textil																	Textile engineering

E

2.1. University sector

Escuelas Universitarias

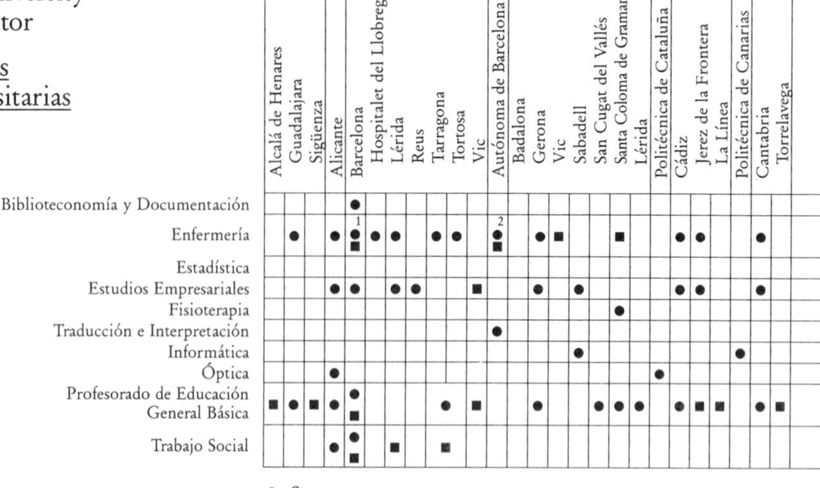

	Alcalá de Henares	Guadalajara	Sigüenza	Alicante	Barcelona	Hospitalet del Llobregat	Lérida	Reus	Tarragona	Tortosa	Vic	Autónoma de Barcelona	Badalona	Gerona	Vic	Sabadell	San Cugat del Vallés	Santa Coloma de Gramanet	Lérida	Politécnica de Cataluña	Cádiz	Jerez de la Frontera	La Línea	Politécnica de Canarias	Cantabria	Torrelavega
Biblioteconomía y Documentación					●																					
Enfermería		●		●	[1] ● ■	●	●		●	●		[2] ● ■		●	■			■			●	●			●	
Estadística																										
Estudios Empresariales				●	●		●	●			■			●		●					●	●			●	
Fisioterapia																		●								
Traducción e Interpretación												●														
Informática																●								●		
Óptica				●																●						
Profesorado de Educación General Básica	■	●	■	●	● ■				●		■			●			●	●	●		●	■	■		●	■
Trabajo Social				●	● ■		■		■																	

● State sector
■ Private sector

1 There are four *Escuelas Universitarias de Enfermería* in Barcelona, two State-run and two private.
2 There are three *Escuelas Universitarias de Enfermería* in Barcelona Autónoma, two State-run and one private.
3 There are two *Escuelas Universitarias de Enfermería* in Badajoz.
4 There are two *Escuelas Universitarias de Enfermería* in Granada.

	La Laguna	Santa Cruz de Tenerife	Las Palmas	León	Ponferrada	Autónoma de Madrid	Segovia	Complutense de Madrid	Politécnica de Madrid	Málaga	Ronda	Antequera	Murcia	Cartagena	Oviedo	Gijón	País Vasco	Derio	San Sebastián	Vitoria	Bilbao	Oñate	Escoridza	Salamanca	Zamora	Ávila
Biblioteconomía y Documentación													■											■		
Enfermería		●	●	●		[1] ● ■		●		[2] ●	■		[3] ●		●	●	●		●	●				●	●	●
Estadística								●																		
Estudios Empresariales		●	●	●				●		●			●	●	●	[6] ●			●		●	■		●		
Fisioterapia	●					■		●																●		
Traducción e Interpretación																								●		
Informática									●	●			●		●	●										
Óptica								●																		
Profesorado de Educación General Básica	●	■	●	●	■	● ■	●	[7] ● ■		●		■	●		● ■			■	● ■	●	●		■	●	●	●
Trabajo Social		■	■	■				■	■						●	■			■	■				●		

● State sector
■ Private sector

1 There are three *Escuelas Universitarias* at the Autonomous University of Madrid, two State-run and one privat
2 There are two *Escuelas Universitarias* in Málaga.
3 There are two *Escuelas Universitarias* in Murcia.
4 There are two *Escuelas Universitarias* in Sevilla.
5 There are four *Escuelas Universitarias* in Valencia, three State-run and one private.
6 There are two *Escuelas Universitarias* for business administration in Gijón.
7 There are five *Escuelas Universitarias* for teaching (primary school), two State-run and three private.

	Castilla-La Mancha	Albacete	Cuenca	Ciudad Real	Toledo	Córdoba	Extremadura	Badajoz	Cáceres	Mérida	Plasencia	Almendralejo	Granada	Almería	Ceuta	Jaén	Melilla	Guádix	Linares	Úbeda	Pontificia de Comillas	Madrid	Islas Baleares	Palma de Mallorca
Librarianship and documentation													●											
Hospital administration		●	●	●		●		[3] ●		●	●		[4] ● ■	●	■	●	■				●			●
Statistics																								
Business administration						■		●	●				●	●		●	●						●	
Physiotherapy																								
Languages													●											
Applied information science		●				●			●	●			●										●	
Optics																								
Teaching qualification, primary school		●	●	●	●	● ■		●	●			■	● ■	●	●	●	●	■	●	●			● ■	
Social work													■								■		■	

	Santiago de Compostela	El Ferrol	La Coruña	Lugo	Pontevedra	Vigo	Orense	Sevilla	Huelva	Valencia	Castellón de la Plana	Cheste	Politécnica de Valencia	Alicante	Valladolid	Burgos	Palencia	Soria	Zaragoza	Huesca	Logroño	Pamplona	Teruel	Navarra	Pontificia de Salamanca
Librarianship and documentation																									
Hospital administration	●		●	●	●	●		[4] ●	●	[5] ● ■	●				●	●	●	●	●	●	●	●	●	■	■
Statistics																									
Business administration			●	●		●	●	●		●					●	●			●		●	●			
Physiotherapy										●									●						
Languages																									
Applied informations science			●					●					●	●	●										
Optics																									
Teaching qualification, primary school	●		●	●	●	■	●	● ■	●	● ■					● ■	●	●	●	● ■	●	●	●	●		■
Social work	■							■	●	■					■				● ■		■	●		■	

E

2.1. University sector

Escuelas Universitarias

	Alcalá de Henares	Politécnica de Cataluña	— Gerona	— Igualada	— Lérida	— Manresa	— Mataró	— Tarrasa	— Tarragona	— Villanueva y la Geltrú	— Canet de Mar	Cádiz	— Algeciras	Cantabria	— Torrelavega	Castilla-La Mancha	— Almadén	— Toledo	— Albacete	
Arquitectos Técnicos		●	●																	Technical architecture
Ingenieros Técnicos Aeronáuticos																				Technical engineering for aviation
Ingenieros Técnicos Agrícolas																			●	Technical engineering for agriculture
Explotaciones Agropecuarias		●	●		●											●			■	for agricultural enterprises
Hortofruticultura y Jardinería		●																		for fruit, vegetable and market gardening
Industrias Agrícolas		●																		for agricultural industry
Mecanización Agraria y Construcciones Rurales																				for agricultural mechanization and farming
Ingenieros Técnicos Forestales					●															Technical engineering for forestry
Explotaciones Forestales																			●	Forestry
Industrias de los Productos Forestales																			●	Forestry industry
Ingenieros Técnicos Industriales				●			●		●								●	●	●	Technical engineering for industry
Mecánica		●	●	●	●	●		●		●		●		●						Mechanical engineering
Electrónica Industrial										●										Industrial electronics
Eléctrica Industrial		●	●			●		●		●			●	●						Industrial electrics
Química																				Chemistry
Textil		●						●												Textile engineering
Organización Industrial																				Business organization
Ingenieros Técnicos de Minas																	●			Technical engineering for mining
Explotación de Minas						●									●					Mine management
Instalaciones de Combustibles y Explosivos																				Fuel and explosives plants
Instalaciones Electromecánicas Mineras																				Electromechanical mining plants
Metalurgia						●									●					Metallurgy
Sondeos y Prospecciones Mineras																				Mining drilling and research
Ingenieros Técnicos Navales														●						Technical engineering for nautics
Ingenieros Técnicos Obras Públicas		●																		Technical engineering for public buildings
Construcciones Civiles																				Civil buildings
Hidrología																				Hydrology
Transportes y Servicios																				Transportation and services
Ingenieros Técnicos Textiles											■									Technical engineering for textiles
Topógrafos		●																		Topography
Ingenieros Técnicos de Telecomunicación	●									●				●						Technical engineering for telecommunications
Equipos Electrónicos		■																		Electronic apparatus
Radiocomunicación		■																		Radio
Sonido e Imagen		■																		Sound and pictures
Telefonía y Transmisión de datos																				Telephone and data transfer

● State sector ■ Private sector

E

	Córdoba	— Bélmez	Extremadura	— Almendralejo	— Cáceres	— Mérida	Granada	— Almería	— Jaén	— Linares	León	Politécnica de Madrid	— Villalva	Málaga	Murcia	— Cartagena	Oviedo	— Mieres	— Gijón	
Arquitectos Técnicos					●		●					●								Technical architecture
Ingenieros Técnicos Aeronáuticos												●								Technical engineering for aviation
Ingenieros Técnicos Agrícolas				■				●					●			●				Technical engineering for agriculture
Explotaciones Agropecuarias			●								●	●								for agricultural enterprises
Hortofruticultura y Jardinería												■								for fruit, vegetable and market gardening
Industrias Agrícolas												■								for agricultural industry
Mecanización Agraria y Construcciones Rurales												● ■								for agricultural mechanization and farming
Ingenieros Técnicos Forestales																				Technical engineering for forestry
Explotaciones Forestales												●								Forestry
Industrias de los Productos Forestales												●								Forestry industry
Ingenieros Técnicos Industriales	●		●								●			●						Technical engineering for industry
Mecánica									■	●		●				●			●	Mechanical engineering
Electrónica Industrial																				Industrial electronics
Eléctrica Industrial										●		●							●	Industrial electrics
Química																				Chemistry
Textil																				Textile engineering
Organización Industrial																				Business organization
Ingenieros Técnicos de Minas																●				Technical engineering for mining
Explotación de Minas		●								●	●							●		Mine management
Instalaciones de Combustibles y Explosivos																				Fuel and explosives plants
Instalaciones Electromecánicas Mineras		●																●		Electromechanical mining plants
Metalurgia										●								●		Metallurgy
Sondeos y Prospecciones Mineras		●									●							●		Mining drilling and research
Ingenieros Técnicos Navales																●				Technical engineering for nautics
Ingenieros Técnicos Obras Públicas				●	●															Technical engineering for public buildings
Construcciones Civiles												●								Civil buildings
Hidrología												●								Hydrology
Transportes y Servicios												●								Transportation and services
Ingenieros Técnicos Textiles																				Technical engineering for textiles
Topógrafos						●						●								Topography
Ingenieros Técnicos de Telecomunicación																				Technical engineering for telecommunications
Equipos Electrónicos												●								Electronic apparatus
Radiocomunicación												●								Radio
Sonido e Imagen												●								Sound and pictures
Telefonía y Transmisión de datos												●								Telephone and data transfer

E

2.1. University sector

Escuelas Universitarias

	País Vasco	— Baracaldo	— Eibar	— Mondragón	— San Sebastián	— Vitoria	Politécnica de Canarias	— La Laguna	Salamanca	— Béjar	— Zamora	Santiago de Compostela	— La Coruña	— Lugo	— Vigo	— El Ferrol	
Arquitectos Técnicos								●					●				Technical architecture
Ingenieros Técnicos Aeronáuticos																	Technical engineering for aviation
Ingenieros Técnicos Agrícolas																	Technical engineering for agriculture
Explotaciones Agropecuarias								●						●			for agricultural enterprises
Hortofruticultura y Jardinería																	for fruit, vegetable and market gardening
Industrias Agrícolas																	for agricultural industry
Mecanización Agraria y Construcciones Rurales																	for agricultural mechanization and farming
Ingenieros Técnicos Forestales																	Technical engineering for forestry
Explotaciones Forestales																	Forestry
Industrias de los Productos Forestales																	Forestry industry
Ingenieros Técnicos Industriales			●														Technical engineering for industry
Mecánica	●			●	●	●	●			●	●				●		Mechanical engineering
Electrónica Industrial					●												Industrial electronics
Eléctrica Industrial	●				●	●	●								●		Industrial electrics
Química																	Chemistry
Textil										●							Textile engineering
Organización Industrial					●												Business organization
Ingenieros Técnicos de Minas																	Technical engineering for mining
Explotación de Minas		●															Mining management
Instalaciones de Combustibles y Explosivos		●															Fuel and explosives plants
Instalaciones Electromecánicas Mineras																	Electromechanical mining plants
Metalurgia		●															Metallurgy
Sondeos y Prospecciones Mineras																	Mining drilling and research
Ingenieros Técnicos Navales							●									●	Technical engineering for nautics
Ingenieros Técnicos Obras Públicas																	Technical engineering for public buildings
Construcciones Civiles							●										Civil buildings
Hidrología							●										Hydrology
Transportes y Servicios																	Transportation and services
Ingenieros Técnicos Textiles																	Technical engineering for textiles
Topógrafos							●										Topography
Ingenieros Técnicos de Telecomunicación							●										Technical engineering for telecommunications
Equipos Electrónicos																	Electronic apparatus
Radiocomunicación																	Radio
Sonido e Imagen																	Sound and pictures
Telefonía y Transmisión de datos																	Telephone and data transfer

● State sector ■ Private sector

	Sevilla	– Palos de la Frontera	Valencia	Politécnica de Valencia	– Orihuela	– Alcoy	– Alicante	Valladolid	– Burgos	– Palencia	– Zaragoza	– La Almunia	– Logroño	– Huesca	Pontificia de Comillas	Navarra	
Arquitectos Técnicos	●			●			●		●								Technical architecture
Ingenieros Técnicos Aeronáuticos																	Technical engineering for aviation
Ingenieros Técnicos Agrícolas	●	●			●			■						●			Technical engineering for agriculture
Explotaciones Agropecuarias				●						●							for agricultural enterprises
Hortofruticultura y Jardinería				■								■					for fruit, vegetable and market gardening
Industrias Agrícolas											■						for agricultural industry
Mecanización Agraria y Construcciones Rurales																	for agricultural mechanization and farming
Ingenieros Técnicos Forestales										●							Technical engineering for forestry
Explotaciones Forestales		●															Forestry
Industrias de los Productos Forestales																	Forestry industry
Ingenieros Técnicos Industriales									●			■					Technical engineering for industry
Mecánica	●	●		●		●		●			●		●		■	■	Mechanical engineering
Electrónica Industrial						●											Industrial electronics
Eléctrica Industrial	●	●	●			●		●			●			●	■		Industrial electrics
Química																	Chemistry
Textil				●		●											Textile engineering
Organización Industrial																	Business organization
Ingenieros Técnicos de Minas																	Technical engineering for mining
Explotación de Minas		●															Mining management
Instalaciones de Combustibles y Explosivos		●															Fuel and explosives plants
Instalaciones Electromecánicas Mineras		●															Electromechanical mining plants
Metalurgia		●															Metallurgy
Sondeos y Prospecciones Mineras		●															Mining drilling and research
Ingenieros Técnicos Navales																	Technical engineering for nautics
Ingenieros Técnicos Obras Públicas																	Technical engineering for public buildings
Construcciones Civiles							●		●								Civil buildings
Hidrología							●										Hydrology
Transportes y Servicios							●										Transportation and services
Ingenieros Técnicos Textiles																	Technical engineering for textiles
Topógrafos																	Topography
Ingenieros Técnicos de Telecomunicación								●									Technical engineering for telecommunications
Equipos Electrónicos																	Electronic apparatus
Radiocomunicación																	Radio
Sonido e Imagen																	Sound and pictures
Telefonía y Transmisión de datos																	Telephone and data transfer

● State sector ■ Private sector

2.1. University sector

Colegios Universitarios

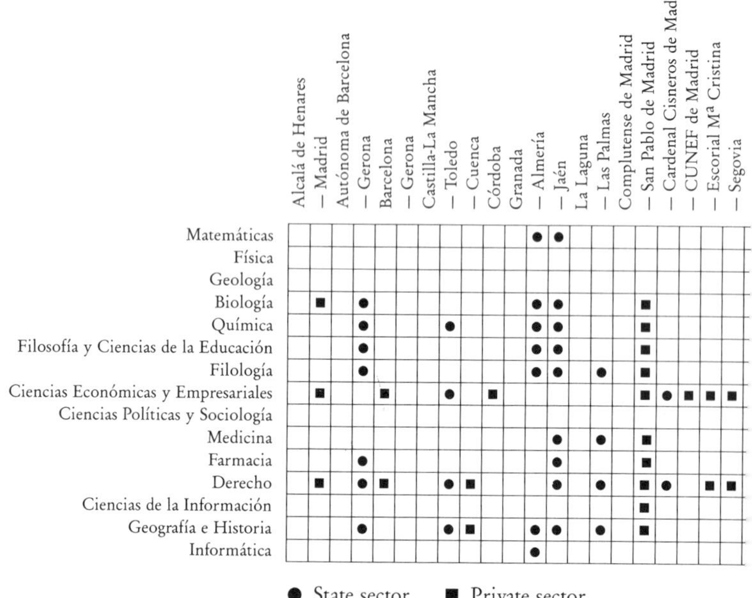

	Alcalá de Henares	— Madrid	Autónoma de Barcelona	— Gerona	Barcelona	— Gerona	Castilla-La Mancha	— Toledo	— Cuenca	Córdoba	Granada	— Almería	— Jaén	La Laguna	— Las Palmas	Complutense de Madrid	— San Pablo de Madrid	— Cardenal Cisneros de Madrid	— CUNEF de Madrid	— Escorial Mª Cristina	— Segovia
Matemáticas												●	●								
Física																					
Geología																					
Biología		■		●								●	●				■				
Química				●				●				●	●				■				
Filosofía y Ciencias de la Educación				●								●	●				■				
Filología				●								●	●		●		■				
Ciencias Económicas y Empresariales		■			■			●		■							■	●	■	■	■
Ciencias Políticas y Sociología																					
Medicina													●		●		■				
Farmacia				●									●				■				
Derecho		■		●	■			●	■				●		●		■	●		■	■
Ciencias de la Información																	■				
Geografía e Historia				●				●	■			●	●		●		■				
Informática												●									

● State sector ■ Private sector

2.2. Non-university sector

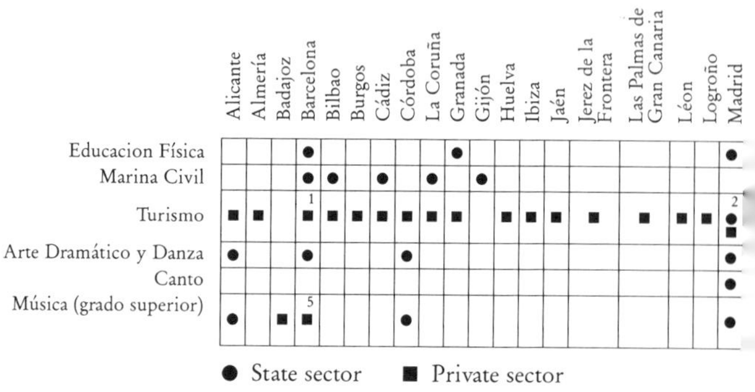

	Alicante	Almería	Badajoz	Barcelona	Bilbao	Burgos	Cádiz	Córdoba	La Coruña	Granada	Gijón	Huelva	Ibiza	Jaén	Jerez de la Frontera	Las Palmas de Gran Canaria	Léon	Logroño	Madrid
Educacion Física				●						●									●
Marina Civil				●	●		●		●		●								
Turismo	■	■		■ [1]	■	■	■	■	■	■		■	■	■	■	■	■	■	● ■ [2]
Arte Dramático y Danza	●			●				●											●
Canto																			●
Música (grado superior)	●		■	■ [5]				●											●

● State sector ■ Private sector

1 There are eight private schools for tourism in Barcelona.
2 There are eight private schools for tourism in Madrid.
3 There are two private schools for tourism in Palma de Mallorca.
4 There are two private schools for tourism in Valencia.
5 There are two private schools for music (higher education) in Barcelona.

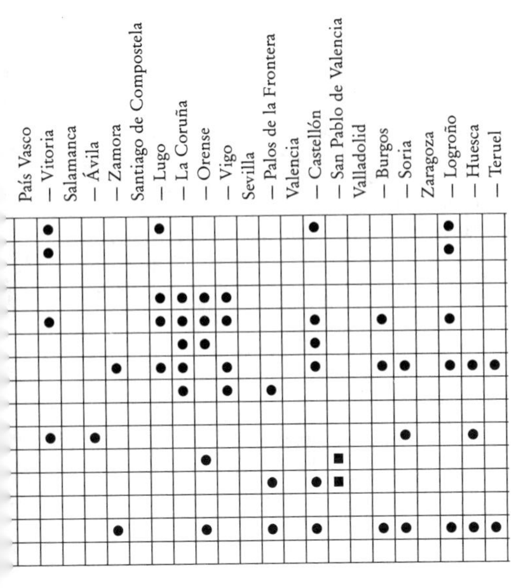

País Vasco	– Vitoria	Salamanca	– Ávila	– Zamora	Santiago de Compostela	– Lugo	– La Coruña	– Orense	– Vigo	Sevilla	– Palos de la Frontera	Valencia	– Castellón	– San Pablo de Valencia	Valladolid	– Burgos	– Soria	Zaragoza	– Logroño	– Huesca	– Teruel	
	●					●							●						●			Mathematics
	●																		●			Physics
																						Geology
						●	●	●	●													Biology
	●					●	●	●	●				●			●			●			Chemistry
							●	●					●									Philosophy and Education sciences
				●		●	●		●				●			●	●		●	●	●	Philology
							●		●		●											Economics and Business management
																						Political science and Sociology
	●		●														●			●		Medicine
								●						■								Pharmacy
											●		●	■								Law
																						Information sciences
				●				●			●		●			●	●		●	●	●	Geography and History
																						Applied information science

Mahón	Málaga	Mérida	Murcia	Oviedo	Palma de Mallorca	Pamplona	Salamanca	Santander	San Sebastián	Santa Cruz de Tenerife	Segovia	Sevilla	Valencia	Valladolid	Vigo	Zaragoza	
																	Physical education
								●		●							Merchant shipping
■	■	■	■	■	■[3]	■	■	■	■	■	■	■	■[4]	■	■	■	Tourism
	●		●									●	●				Drama and dance
																	Singing
	●		●						■	■		●	●				Music (higher education)

E

3. Student statistics

Foreign students at Spanish institutions of higher education

Figures for the academic year 1986/87

Total number of students:	903 166
Foreign students (total) (2.6 %):	24 883

Breakdown according to EC Member States:

Belgium	479
Denmark	28
FR of Germany	2 315
Greece	69
France	3 498
Ireland	24
Italy	217
Luxembourg	11
The Netherlands	193
Portugal	368
United Kingdom	763
Total	7 965

4. Bibliography

Anuario y guía de cada una de las universidades. Yearbook and guide of individual higher education institutions.

Estudios en España. II Nivel universitario. Cuadernos de Información. Ministerio de Educación y Ciencia. 1986. Ministry of Education and Science, information brochure on second cycle of university studies.

Becas y ayudas al estudio. Nivel universitario. Cuadernos de Información. Ministerio de Educación y Ciencia. 1985. Ministry of Education and Science, information brochure on grants and scholarships in higher education.

Cursos de español para extranjeros. Ministerio de Educación y Ciencia. 1985. Spanish courses for foreigners. Ministry of Education and Science. 1985.

Guía de la Universidad. Secretaría General. Consejo de Universidades. Centro de Publicaciones. Minsterio de Educacíon y Ciencia. Madrid 1988. (University guidelines of the University Council)

Información Universitaria. Centro de Publicaciones. Ministerio de Educación y Ciencia. Madrid 1987. General information on university studies. Ministry of Education and Science. Madrid 1987.

5. Glossary

Bachillerato Unificado y Polivalente (BUP): (uniform and polyvalent A-levels) Term for certificate of completion of secondary education.

Curso de Orientación Universitaria (COU): (Orientation course for institutions of higher education) Course following the BUP at the *Institutos de Bachillerato* after completion of secondary education and before entry into higher education.

Facultad: Type of institute of higher education where long-term courses are offered in almost all academic disciplines (except technical courses).

Escuela Técnica Superior: Type of institute of higher education where long-term technical courses are offered.

Escuela Universitaria: Type of institute of higher education where short-term courses are offered in a variety of subjects.

Escuela Universitaria de Ingeniería Técnica: Type of institute of higher education where short-term technical courses are offered.

Colegio Universitario: Institute where the first three years of study leading to *licenciado* can be completed.

Licenciado: Degree awarded upon completion of a course at a *facultad.*

Ingeniero: Degree awarded upon completion of a course of study at an *Escuela Técnica Superior.*

Arquitecto: Degree awarded upon completion of a course of study at an *Escuela Técnica Superior*.

Diplomado: Degree awarded upon completion of a course of study at an *Escuela Universitaria*.

Ingeniero Técnico: Degree awarded upon completion of a course of study at an *Escuela Técnica Universitaria*.

Arquitecto Técnico: Degree awarded upon completion of a course of study at an *Escuela Técnica Universitaria*.

Doctor: Title after a third level, awarded after completion of a doctor's programme and successful defence of an individual academic thesis.

Ciclo: Period during which courses of study are completed on a certain level.

Matrícula: Registration at an institution of higher education to take up a course of study.

Tasas: Fee to be paid by the student upon matriculation.

Prueba de Acceso a la Universidad (PAU): (university entrance examination) This is a requirement for a place at the *Facultades* and *Escuelas Técnicas Superiores*.

E

6. Diagram of the education system

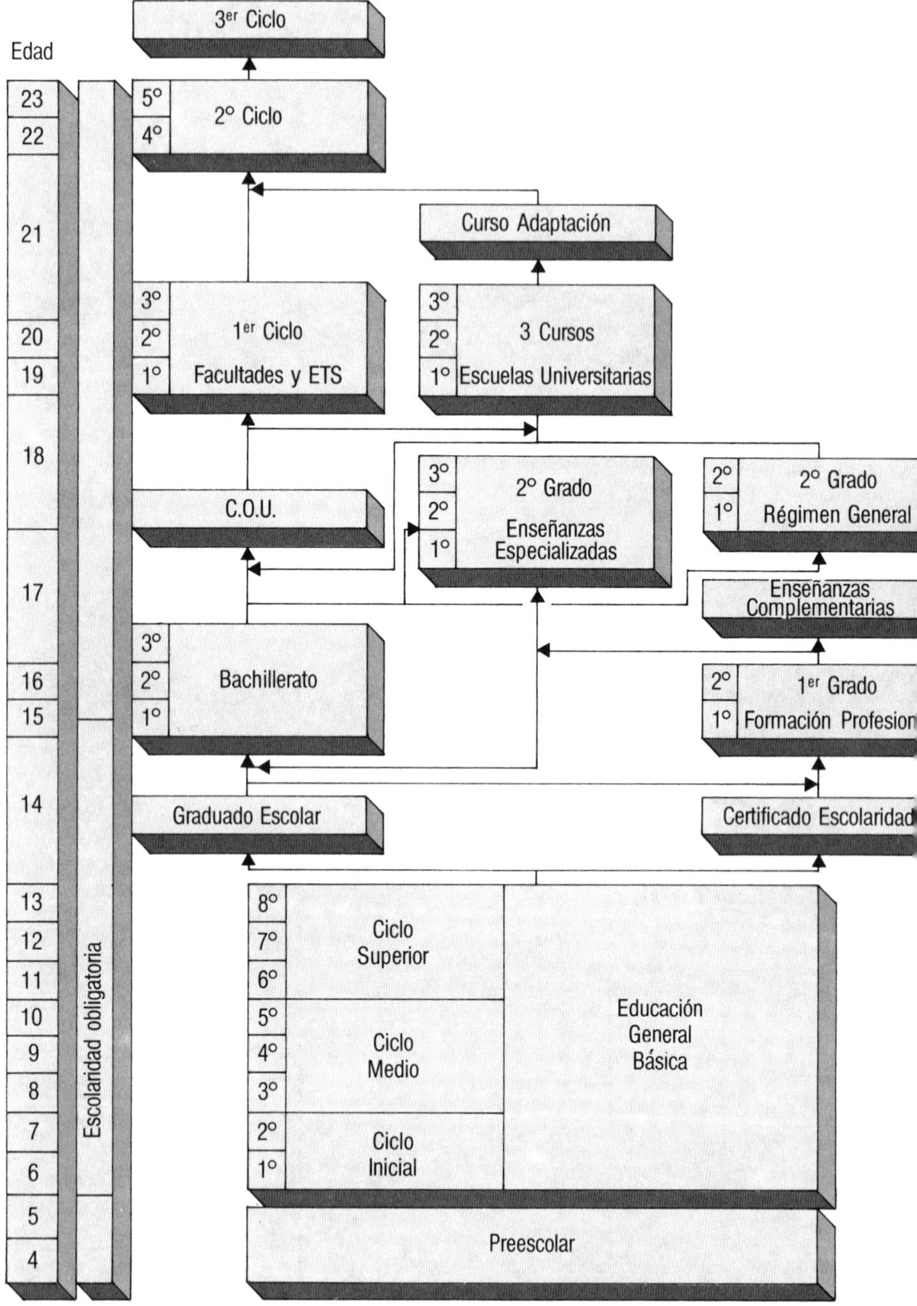

3er Ciclo
Edad
23
22
21
20
19
18
17
16
15
14
13
12
11
10
9
8
7
6
5
4
Escolaridad obligatoria
5°
4°
2° Ciclo
Curso Adaptación
3°
2°
1°
1er Ciclo
Facultades y ETS
3°
2°
1°
3 Cursos
Escuelas Universitarias
3°
2°
1°
2° Grado
Enseñanzas
Especializadas
2°
1°
2° Grado
Régimen General
C.O.U.
Enseñanzas
Complementarias
3°
2°
1°
Bachillerato
2°
1°
1er Grado
Formación Profesion
Graduado Escolar
Certificado Escolaridad
8°
7°
6°
Ciclo
Superior
5°
4°
3°
Ciclo
Medio
2°
1°
Ciclo
Inicial
Educación
General
Básica
Preescolar

Explanations and translations of technical terms see facing page.

Legend

Bachillerato – Secondary-school leaving certificate after three years of secondary school, upper level (Bachillerato Unificado Polivalente), giving access to university studies after a preparatory course (COU).
Certificado escolaridad – School-leaving certificate.
1er ciclo; 2[o] ciclo; 3er ciclo – 1st, 2nd and 3rd cycle of studies.
C.O.U.: Curso de Orientación universitaria – Preparatory course for university studies, duration: one year.
Curso adaptación – Adaption course.
Edad – Age.
Educación General Básica – General basic education (lower, medium, upper level).
Enseñanzas complementarias – Supplementary instruction.
Enseñanzas especializadas – Specialized education, 1st to 3rd grade.
Escuelas universitarias – University schools, three years of study.
Escolaridad obligatoria – Compulsory education.
Facultades y ETS – University faculties and higher education institutions for technical studies.
Formación profesional – Vocational education, first and second grade.
Graduado escolar – School-leaving certificate, qualifying for a Bachillerato course.
Preescolar – Pre-school education.
Régimen general – General system.

France

Organization of higher education

Higher education in France is characterized by a large variety of educational establishments, whose organization and entrance requirements depend on the nature of each establishment and its educational aims. Most of them come under the Ministry of Education, or are at least supervised by it. This variety is reinforced by the fact that not only the Ministry of Education, but also other Ministries (Defence, Agriculture, Public Health, etc.) have some responsibility in the field of higher education, whether in the administration of State-run higher education establishments or in the supervision of private bodies.

On the one hand there are the *Universities*, all of them State-run, which take in large numbers of students, and whose courses are equally divided between foundation courses and practical courses backed up by research and its application with regard to regional development. On the other hand, there are the *Grandes écoles*, which have a selective admissions procedure and therefore, in practice, restricted student numbers. These offer a high standard of education and have definite professional goals: the education of teachers and engineers, and higher education in the fields of business and economics.

The entrance requirement of both the universities and the *grandes écoles* is the *baccalauréat* (French school-leaving certificate), gained at the end of *études secondaires* (secondary school studies). Pupils who have gained their *baccalauréat* have a choice between a selection system as practised in the *écoles* and shorter technological courses, and an orientation system which is in force in the universities, where a wide range of subjects of increasing degrees of difficulty is offered, and progressive selection is carried out during successive courses of study.

Types of higher education institutions

A — *Enseignement supérieur court* (short study courses)

These include the areas of technology and business administration. This type of course takes two to three years and attracts around 30% of all pupils holding the *baccalauréat.*

1. *The* Instituts universitaires de technologie (IUT)

These 68 colleges offer two-year courses which end with the *diplôme universitaire de technologie* (DUT). The courses are taught through methods suitable for equipping DUT students to take on managerial responsibility in all areas of industry and commerce.

Admission to the IUT is subject to rigorous selection, carried out by a selection committee and based on an appraisal of school reports. There are 19 different departments in the IUT.

F

In 1988 there were a total of 63 780 students.

2. *The* Technicien supérieur *departments in* lycées

These courses are similar to those of the IUT, with the difference that they are more highly specialized and related to definite areas of work, which can mean that changes in career direction can prove difficult later on. The two-year course leads to the *brevet de technicien supérieur* (BTS). There are 87 areas of specialization in the BTS. In 1988, 135 000 pupils were enrolled in State or private *sections de technicien supérieur (STS),* which fall under the supervision of the Ministry of the National Education of Youth and Sport.

3. *Short courses in subjects relating to the paramedical and social sector*

Courses in speech therapy, sight therapy and audioprosthetics are offered at universities. Midwifery courses, offered at colleges which come under the Ministry of Public Health, are closely connected with the medical faculties, whose examining boards are also responsible for examining midwifery candidates. Colleges for social workers and certain medicine-related professions offer a specific professional training in two to three years.

The highly selective admissions procedures — competitive examinations and others, tests or interviews — are carried out after the *baccalauréat.*

B — *Etudes longues* (long-study courses)

These are offered by the universities and the *Grandes écoles,* and take three or more years. The *Grandes écoles* select their students by means of a competitive examination, for which they must complete two preparatory years in the *classes préparatoires* at a *lycée.* 58% of French students are currently following long study courses, 9.9% of them in *classes préparatoires.*

1. *The universities*

The 72 universities are multidisciplinary and largely autonomous, particularly as far as choice of subjects and aims, validation and organization of courses are concerned.

Each university is headed by a president elected by a university council. The universities consist of a varying number of colleges, institutions and *unités de formation et de recherche* (UFR) — education and research departments — which are themselves administered by an elected council. The universities offer an extremely wide variety of courses and confer national degrees including doctorates and university degrees like the *magistère,* engineering degrees, specialized national diplomas (midwifery, etc.) and certificates.

In 1988, 989 461 students were matriculated at the universities.

2. *The* Grandes écoles

The *Grandes écoles* and *écoles supérieures* number around 300 and have about 70 000 students. They offer long study courses which are very much in demand, and prepare their students for managerial positions in industry, commerce and administration. Some of them, notably the teacher training and engineering colleges, can confer doctorates. Many of them come under the Ministry of Education. Most of them are State-run, a few are private institutions. Although they vary greatly in the subjects that they offer, they have their highly selective entrance procedure in common.

The *baccalauréat* is not enough to secure a place. There is also a competitive examination, for which the candidates must complete two years in the *classes préparatoires* at a *lycée*, at university or at the *écoles* themselves. The reputation of each *école* is based on the difficulty of its entrance exam, the high standard of research carried out there and the length of the courses, which take between two and five years.

There are:

(a) The *Grandes écoles scientifiques* (Colleges of natural science). These are all State-run, and are by far the most numerous. In 1988, 47 500 students were matriculated there. They train engineers and executives for both civil and military walks of life.

(b) The *Grandes écoles de formation des professeurs du second degré,* which train *lycée* and university teachers and researchers, and the *Grandes écoles littéraires* for arts subjects. All of them are State-run. The four *Ecoles normales supérieures* (ENS) are made up of departments of the arts, science and technology.

(c) The *Écoles nationales supérieures agronomiques et vétérinaires* for agriculture and veterinary science. All of them are State-run.

(d) The *Grandes écoles de commerce et de gestion,* colleges of commerce and business administration. All are private and most of them come under the Chambers of Commerce. They confer a nationally recognized degree. They charge annual fees of between FF 12 000 and FF 22 000.

3. *The* Instituts catholiques

These institutions in Paris, Lille, Lyons, Angers and Toulouse are private establishments recognized by the Ministry of Education. They provide university education. The students — 16 473 of them in 1988 — take their exams before university examination boards.

4. *The* Instituts d'études politiques

Political science is taught at the *Institut d'études politiques* (IEP) in Paris ('Sciences po') and at the *Instituts d'études politiques* which are affiliated to the universities of Aix-Marseille, Bordeaux, Grenoble, Lyon, Strasbourg and Toulouse. These institutes prepare students for a wide range of managerial careers in administration, in professions relating to finance and industry, particularly banking, and in politics. The courses last three years, including a preparatory year. After the first year, a large number of students is eliminated following an examination. Entry requirements for the second year vary. Students with a *licence* or a foreign degree of a similar standard may be admitted.

C — Further education for people in employment

One type of education offered in the universities or the *écoles* allows people in employment to take part in evening courses by taking advantage of specially planned timetables, and to gain university qualifications. The *Conservatoire national des arts et métiers* (CNAM) and its regional centres admit people who already have jobs, without requiring any special qualifications, and this can eventually lead to an engineering degree.

D — Correspondence courses

University correspondence courses are available to students who wish to study for a national degree, but cannot attend university courses because of their circumstances (health, distance, job and family commitments). These courses are also aimed at a wider public which consists of interested adults rather than actual students. More than 30 000 students take part in university correspondence courses. These are taught through:

(i) 21 universities equipped with distance learning centres (same content and degrees as the students who actually attend the lectures);

(ii) the *Centre national d'enseignement à distance,* which prepares students for competitive exams (administration, CAPES, *agrégation*) or gives specific training (accountancy, modern languages, etc.)

Student statistics

In the 1987/88 academic year 12.5% of the 989 461 students registered at French universities were foreigners, a number which corresponds to 123 978 formally registered students. Of these, 33.8% were in the first stage of their studies, 28.7% in the second, and 35.8% in the third. These students were predominantly registered for arts and humanities subjects (34.5%); otherwise they were fairly equally distributed among the natural sciences subjects (22.8%), economics and law (21.4%) and medicine-related subjects (15.8%).

Of these students, 18 133 — that corresponds to 14.6% — came from EC Member States and were distributed as follows among the following countries of origin:

Federal Republic of Germany	20.1%	3 660
Greece	15.3%	2 768
Spain	14.7%	2 663
Portugal	14.5%	2 634
United Kingdom	11.5%	2 086
Italy	8.2%	1 482
Luxembourg	5.3%	964
Belgium	4.9%	890
The Netherlands	2.9%	560

About 1% came from Denmark (219) and Ireland (197). The total number of foreign students is estimated at 123 978 for the academic year 1987/88.

Organization and validation of courses

A — Universities

In general, long study courses (*études longues*) are divided into three successive stages *(cycles),* each lasting two years, which end with the conferment of a national diploma.

1. The first stage is a general course which serves as a period of

orientation for the students and is open to those who hold the *baccalauréat.*

The first stage courses, which last two years, lead to the *diplôme d'études universitaires générales* (DEUG), which specifies pass mark and subject studied. They comprise a more or less multidisciplinary education, including an orientation period, and offer a great variety of courses.

The DEUG was essentially devised to prepare students with the *baccalauréat* for the *études longues*. However, it also allows some students to finish their studies with the *diplôme d'études universitaires scientifiques et techniques* (DEUST), in subject areas which correspond to national and regional requirements.

2. The second stage, including more detailed studies, general academic education and high level specialized training, prepares the students for taking on professional responsibility. It takes two or three years of study after the DEUG and leads to one of the following types of training:

(i) basic, professional and/or specialized training, aiming at *licence* and *maîtrise* degrees (DEUG + 1 year = *licence; licence* + 1 year = *maîtrise);*

(ii) professional training devised as an indivisible block of two years, leading to the degrees of *Maîtrise des sciences et techniques* (MST), *Maîtrise de sciences de gestion* (MSG), *Maîtrise de méthodes informatiques appliquées à la gestion* (MIAGE);

(iii) courses leading to engineering degrees devised as a block of three years;

(iv) university courses devised as an indivisible block of three years, leading to the *Magistère* (DEUG or DUT + 3 years = *Magistère*).

The new degree of *magistère,* introduced in 1985/86, combines the acquisition of basic knowledge, an introduction to research, and its practical application within a professional framework. The admissions procedure is based on previous achievements and is very selective. The *magistère* is a university degree and must be approved by the Ministry. In 1988, 67 *magistère* courses were introduced: 11 in law, 14 in economics and business administration, 10 in human and social sciences, 2 in regional planning, 1 in chemistry, 5 in mathematics, 4 in computing, 3 in geosciences, 6 in life sciences, 4 in physics, 3 in physical chemistry, 1 in industrial science, 3 in communication science.

3. The third stage, which is highly specialized and trains students in research, consists of one or more preparatory years. Entry to the third stage is subject to selection of holders of the *maîtrise* or an engineering degree or equivalent. Two ways are offered:

(i) that of a *diplôme d'études supérieures spécialisées* (DESS), a professional training in one year, including an obligatory period of practical work within a company (*maîtrise* + 1 year = DESS);

(ii) that of the *doctorat*, whose first year ends with the *diplôme d'études approfondies* (DEA) (DEA + 2 to 4 years = *doctorat*; Ing. + DEA + 2 to 4 years = *doctorat*).

4. Long study courses in medical subjects

The study of medicine, dentistry, pharmacy and human biology, while still following the division into three stages, is also divided into years. The length of the courses varies according to the discipline: 8 to 10 years for the national degree of Doctor of Medicine, 5 years for that of Doctor of Dentistry, and 6 years for that of Doctor of Pharmacy.

At the end of the first year there is a selective exam. The number of candidates allowed to enter the second year is laid down by ministerial decree. At the end of the second stage, a competitive exam decides who will be allowed admission to the *internat en médicine* (clinical stage).

Foreign students who wish to obtain the French degree of Doctor of Medicine are obliged to sit a competitive exam at the end of the first year, even if they have already completed part of their medical studies in their own country.

This exam is part of a very rigorous selection procedure which eliminates 80% of all candidates, who are only permitted to sit the exam twice. In the medicine-related courses, students who wish to observe lectures only (*auditeurs libres*) are not allowed.

B — The *Grandes écoles*

Entry to the *Grandes écoles* (GE) requires two years spent in the *classes préparatoires* (CPGE) of the *lycées*, or, exceptionally, in the GE themselves. The *baccalauréat* is necessary but not sufficient. A file containing copies of reports from *baccalauréat* classes and teachers' remarks must be submitted. Thus pupils are preselected for entry to the 'Prépa'. Foreign students are subject to the same rules as French ones for admission to the first preparatory year. After two years of preparation in the CPGE or at university, success in the competitive exam is necessary for entry to the first year at the *école*. However, candidates with a *maîtrise* or an equivalent foreign degree can be admitted directly into the second year of the engineering course. Student exchanges are offered by those GE which have twinning arrangements with certain universities or colleges abroad. The same is true of university studies. In addition, foreign nationals in the administrative service of their country can take part in a course lasting 14 months at the *École nationale d'administration* (ENA).

The following degrees are conferred by the *écoles:*

(i) the *diplôme d'ingénieur,* which is recognized by the Commission of Engineers, after 5 years of study (2 preparatory years + 3 years of engineering training);

(ii) the *diplôme de haut enseignement commercial,* whose value depends on the reputation of the school, particularly if it has official recognition (1 preparatory year + 3 years at the *école)*;

(iii) as far as the *Écoles normales supérieures* are concerned, they prepare students for the national university diplomas such as *Licence, Maîtrise, Doctorat* as well as for the competitive placement exams for teachers (CAPES, Agrégation);

(iv) the *Mastère* is a title conferred by

the conference of *Grandes écoles*. It signals the completion of a one-year course of special training of which four months are spent in practical training.

C — The *Instituts d'études politiques* (IEP)

Each IEP has its own degree to be conferred for the study of politics. Students gaining this degree can sit the competitive entrance examination for the *Ecole Nationale d'Administration* (ENA). Some of them continue their studies at university until DESS, DEA or *doctorat* level.

The IEP in Paris offers a one-year course for foreign students, where they can gain the *certificat d'études politiques* (not to be confused with the IEP degree). As regards the IEP which are affiliated to the Universities of Aix-Marseille III, Bordeaux I, Grenoble II, Lyon II, Strasbourg III and Toulouse I, these IEP themselves will supply information direct.

Admission and registration

Initial information

The cultural services of the French embassies abroad have access to the registers of the *Office national d'information sur les enseignements et les professions* (ONISEP) as well as brochures issued by the *Bureau d'information et d'orientation* at the Ministry of Education (DESUP 9). The latter will be able to provide any information concerning public State-run higher education establishments in France. Students may also write for information to the *Centre national des œuvres universitaires et scolaires* (CNOUS). In France students can ask for information at the *services commun universitaire d'information et d'orientation des étudiants* (SCUIO), of which there is one in every university.

Entry requirements

A — Universities

The enrolment of foreign students at French universities is based on three essential principles:

1. equality of rights for foreign and French students;
2. equality among foreign candidates;
3. respect for the autonomy of the universities in deciding on admissions.

F

Admission to the universities can only be achieved through proof of successful completion of education leading to a certificate of aptitude for higher education study *(baccalauréat)* or of an equivalent qualification.

Admission:
In stage III studies *(troisième cycle)* the rules are the same as for French students. Application for admission involves an exchange of letters between the applicant and the professor in charge of the course of study. In this correspondence, the applicant must be informed that the Academic Council is prepared to admit the applicant on condition that the other prerequisites have been fulfilled.

In stage II studies *(deuxième cycle)* admission is the same as for French students. However, although a student with the requisite school leaving certificate and proof of completing two years of university studies may consider himself to be on an academic level sufficient for admission to the first year of stage II studies, the university in question may refuse admission to the second cycle and invite the applicant to enrol in stage I studies. Thus, to ensure being admitted, it is recommended that students follow the procedure for admission to stage I studies.

In stage I studies *(premier cycle)* foreign students must submit an application for admission in the case of initial enrolment.

Exceptions to this procedure are indicated in the section 'Application and registration'.

B — *Écoles* and *Grandes écoles*

The same conditions apply for deciding on the admission of foreign students as is the case for French students, i.e. success in a competitive entrance examination or admission on the basis of case-by-case examination of students' previous school and academic records, in accordance with the rules effective at each institution.

Most of these institutions recruit their students by means of competitive examinations, making it necessary for applicants to undergo appropriate preparatory training in special classes *(classes préparatoires aux grandes écoles)*.

Holders of the *baccalauréat* or an equivalent will be admitted to preparatory classes on the basis of their school records. These must be submitted to the principal of the *Grande école* before 1 May. A selection committee decides on admission to the preparatory classes. These classes are held in the *lycées*. The duration of these studies is generally two years (one year for commercial studies).

Limitations

A — Universities

The only numerical limitation on admissions for foreign students is in the first year of stage I *(premier cycle)* medical and dental studies (PCEM) at universities in and around Paris. The number of foreign students admitted cannot exceed 5 % of the number of French students enrolled.

B — *Écoles* and *grandes écoles*

Foreign students are admitted in accordance with a variable quota depending on the institution in question and defined each year by the Ministry of Education.

Recognition of foreign certificates and degrees

In France there is no list of foreign certificates or degrees and their equivalents to French certificates and degrees, with one exception: those that originate from the agreement of 10 July 1980, between the French and German Governments concerning school-leaving certificates, examinations and degrees in the sciences, humanities and social sciences.

The president or director of the institute concerned is responsible for deciding on the recognition of the previous education of candidates. This is done on the basis of a proposal made by the responsible commission after examining the student's transcripts.

The enrolment of foreign students in the first year of university studies depends on their having a qualification that provides access to higher education studies in their own country and which qualifies them to enrol in the degree they have indicated.

For other course years admission is decided on the basis of the applicant's academic record. No matter what certificates or degrees the applicant has obtained previously, admission is not automatic. It depends from case to case on the decision by the university which is quite independent in its decision on the evaluation of the contents of diplomas which constitute one and the same subject: therefore, an applicant may be admitted at one university and not at another.

Students should have a very good command of French. Universities insist on a test to determine French proficiency, no matter what the admission procedure is.

Entry examinations

No entry examination is required for admission to universities. However, applicants must prove they are in possession of a level of French proficiency adequate for the type of course they wish to enrol in (see 'Knowledge of the language of instruction').

At non-university schools or institutes of higher education, *Écoles normales supérieures*, and *Écoles d'ingénieurs* entrance examinations are organized in accordance with rules particular to each individual institution.

Application and registration

No matter what the registration procedure is at a given university (preliminary admission application to the university or registration for stage II or stage III studies), like French students, the foreign student must register definitively with the *service de scolarité* at the university in question. Registration is yearly. Unless special arrangements have been made, students may not register for a term *(trimestre)* or a semester.

F

Registration deadlines are 31 July for initial registration and 15 October for all other registrations. However, students are advised to inquire at the university of their choice, since the closing date for registrations is earlier at some universities.

Preliminary admission application

Students must fill in a form for initial registration in stage I studies *(dossier de demande de première admission en premier cycle)* between 1 December and 15 January of the following year and hand it in by 1 February at the latest. The latter date is final. (Exceptions to this procedure are indicated below). This form is available from the cultural sections of French embassies and, in France, from the university closest to the applicant's place of residence. Applicants must present a residence permit valid for at least a year, or that of their parents if the latter are in possession of a three-year residence permit.

Applicants must name three universities of their choice, at least two of which must be in the provinces.

Exempted from the application procedure for preliminary admission are:

1. holders of the French *baccalauréat,* the French *baccalauréat* with an international option, a Franco-German *baccalauréat,* a European *baccalauréat* and the holders of a French certificate issued exempting the holder from the need to present a *baccalauréat* on the basis of a national regulation;
2. students who have come to France within the framework of a programme based on an intergovernmental agreement or within the framework of an inter-university arrangement;
3. holders of scholarships provided by the French Government, international organizations or foreign governments when these scholarships are administered by a French body (CNOUS or CIES);
4. stateless persons, refugees or persons awaiting response to a request for asylum.

These students must nevertheless inquire about conditions for registration at the university of their choice.

Definitive registration

(a) Administrative registration

Students must present:

1. proof of past studies (original certificates obtained and translations authorized by a consulate),
2. certificate of French proficiency (students are required to take a French test),
3. proof of family status.

The university in question may require the presentation of other documents as well.

(b) Course registration *(inscription pédagogique)*

It takes place at the beginning of the academic year. It involves choosing optional subjects, as well as registration for seminars and practical working groups.

Tuition fees

Administrative registration involves the payment of tuition fees. Various other costs need to be added to these fees which amounted to FF 450 in the 1988/89 academic year: these are obligatory ones (such as provisions for health insurance and social security) or voluntary ones (such as additional insurance or membership fees for student sport clubs, etc.). Students should reckon with a total of FF 1 100 to 1 500 for registration, depending on the options chosen.

After payment of registration fees, students are issued a student identity card *(carte d'étudiant)* which entitles them to course registration *(inscription pédagogique),* the services of the student administration (refectory, halls of residence) and access to the libraries.

Knowledge of the language of instruction, language courses and other courses

To be admitted to stage I studies *(premier cycle)* students are required to take a French proficiency test to determine whether or not proficiency levels are adequate for the subject to be studied.

Exempted from these tests are the holders of secondary school leaving certificates *(baccalauréat)* for which the majority of tests taken were administered in French.

The proficiency level required is that of the DALF *(diplôme approfondi de langue française).*

For admission to stage II and stage III studies *(deuxième et troisième cycles)* tests are administered by the various universities in accordance with their own regulations.

French cultural services abroad will indicate to applicants all of the possibilities available for learning or improving French in the area in question. In addition, they will be able to provide two brochures published annually by the French Foreign Office which lists all of the French courses available to foreign students in France during the academic year and during the summer.

Some universities organize special courses for foreign students aimed at improving their linguistic and academic skills and improving their inte-

F

gration in the French university system. The applicant may get information on this from the university's Information and Student Advice Service (Service commun d'information et d'orientation).

Financial assistance and scholarships

Except in specific cases (e.g. scholarship from an international organization or a private foundation) all scholarships granted by the French Government to foreign students are conferred in the applicant's country of origin by the cultural service of the French embassy. No scholarships are conferred in France. Students are advised to request information from the cultural service of the French embassy at least 18 months prior to applying for a scholarship.

Holders of scholarships provided by the French Government are exempted from paying tuition fees. It is absolutely necessary for scholarship holders to adhere fully to instructions given by the embassy.

Foreign students whose parents (and brothers or sisters) have resided in France for two years can apply for a higher education scholarship from the Ministry of Education. In addition, the French Government awards grants for periods of practical training to foreign students. Information can be obtained from the cultural department of the French Embassy.

Higher education scholarships awarded for reasons of need can only be granted for one academic year; they must be reapplied for every year. These scholarships are granted according to certain criteria.

The applicant must:

(i) come from a family which does not have sufficient means at its disposal, in accordance with upper income limits which are annually determined nationwide;

(ii) be registered at a State or private institution of higher education or participate in a degree programme which is authorized for scholarship holders or be registered at certain institutions of higher education in one of the Member States of the European Community which have the same study level as in France;

(iii) be under 26 years of age on first application, except when the studies have been interrupted for more than three years. This age-limit is extended by the time of military service if this has been served and by one year per child raised.

The application for a higher education scholarship may be obtained from:

(a) the scholarships section of the school attended;

(b) the Department of Higher Education Scholarships at the Rector's Office belonging to the academy at the student's place of residence;

(c) the French consulate in the home-country.

The annual amounts which higher education scholarship holders received in the 1988/89 academic year were between FF 4 212 and FF 14 580 depending on the scholarship approved.

Entry and residence regulations

European Community nationals may enter France and reside there for three months simply on the basis of an identity card. After this period of time, foreign students will have to apply for a temporary residence card (*carte de séjour temporaire*) from the services of the Ministry of the Interior (*préfecture de police* in Paris, *préfecture* or *commissariat de police* in the *départements*).

Furthermore, they must also be in a position to prove that they have financial resources at their disposal which are at least equal to the amount of the scholarship provided by the French Government (basic amount: FF 2 800 per month at the beginning of 1987).

F

Social aspects

Social security and health insurance

Students who are European Community nationals are automatically eligible for social security if they are registered at a recognized institution (virtually all institutions of university level) and if they are under 26 years of age.

Students older than 26 are required to take out voluntary insurance in their country of origin or, on arriving in France, voluntary insurance under the French social security system. Premiums are determined on the basis of income.

Students have social security and health insurance coverage on completing administrative registration *(inscription administrative).* This coverage entitles them to reimbursement of approximately 70% of expenses for medical consultations, medicines and hospital costs. The obligatory premium for non-scholarship holders for the academic year 1988/89 was FF 640.

Coverage under this insurance scheme permits supplementary reimbursement of expenses and also provides third-party coverage as well as coverage in cases of invalidity and death.

Entry into a national or regional mutual scheme *(Mutuelle)* which is registered as a health insurance scheme for students is recommended for all students. The health insurance scheme carries additional reimbursement of costs as well as offering personal liability, invalidity and life insurance. The holders of scholarships from the French Government are reimbursed the costs for premiums to the *Mutuelle.*

The procedures involved in acquiring supplementary insurance coverage *(Mutuelle)* are indicated along with those for social security.

Advisory services

French cultural services abroad are able to provide the principal information necessary to students who wish to study in France. Students are advised first of all to request information from them (see Appendix 1 for the addresses of French embassies in the European Community countries).

Each university has a *Service commun universitaire d'information et d'orientation* (SCUIO) which provides information on the organization of studies and future employment prospects (see Appendix 1 for university addresses) as well as a *Service universitaire pour étudiants étrangers* (SUEE).

At the Ministry of Education there is a *Bureau d'information et d'orientation* in charge of higher education (Bureau DESUP 9, 61-65, rue Dutot, F-75015 Paris, Tel. (1) 40 60 65 40 extensions 6270 and 6747).

Student employment

In principle, European Community students have the same right as French students to seek temporary employment, provided they are in possession of a valid residence permit. However, given the present economic situation, this type of work is very difficult to find (see 'Initial information').

Student organizations

There is a very large number of student organizations. The associations at universities are different from those at other higher education institutions. Before joining any of these organizations foreign students should familiarize themselves with these organizations and their political tendencies.

Cost of living

It is difficult to define a minimum budget for students. In January, 1987, the *Centre national des œuvres universitaires* (CNOUS) estimated that a student needs between FF 3 000 and FF 4 600 per month in Paris, having taken advantage of all student reductions, and a little less in the provinces.

Experience has shown that even though foreign students enjoy the same facilities as their French counterparts, the amount of money per month they need is somewhat above the average.

Accommodation

Foreign students must make their own arrangements for accommodation. In Paris a room costs between FF 1 500 and 2 000. The membership card of the *Œuvres universitaires* (student service) makes students eligible for a room in a hall of residence. However, places are limited and demand is large. In 1987, a room in a student hall of residence in Paris cost FF 700 per month per person sharing a double room and FF 900 to FF 1 200 for a single room.

Services for students

In all material and social problems, students should turn to the *Centres régionaux des œuvres universitaires et scolaires* (CROUS). They offer advice and practical assistance in all questions relating to life at university and outside: employment opportunities, accommodation, budget, leisure-time activities and social legislation. In Paris students may apply directly to the *Centre national des œuvres universitaires* (CNOUS).

Facilities for disabled students

In general, three measures have been prescribed to assist the integration of disabled students into higher education. These are:

(a) personal reception and full accessibility for disabled students to all premises;
(b) special financial support;

F

(c) organization of appropriate teaching.

(a) The personal reception is undertaken by a person appointed by the university who will take particular care of the disabled students. This person is situated either in the *Service commun universitaire d'information et d'orientation* or in the *Service de la scolarité.*

Full accessibility to all premises means that as from 1 March 1979 teaching establishments must, from the outset, be equipped with sloping surfaces, lifts that are suitable for the disabled, etc. Other establishments have had to be modified in accordance with an adaptability programme. Over and above this, students are assisted in finding accommodation: 380 rooms have been especially equipped in the CROUS halls of residence.

(b) Special financial assistance is granted:

(i) reimbursement of travelling expenses from place of residence to the teaching establishment by the *Conseil Régional* in the provinces and by the Rector's offices in Paris, Créteil, Versailles, and in the Ile de France;

(ii) additional points for the calculation criteria for the determination of scholarships for those in need;

(iii) the opportunity to raise the age-limit for student health insurance by four years

(iv) these students can take advantage of the higher education institute's solidarity fund which is always administered by the CROUS, as well as the assistance of social services, the office for preventive medicine, which is to be found at every university.

(c) Furthermore, adapted teaching allows the period of study leading to the diplomas of the first study stage to be extended. A large number of universities is now equipped with the appropriate teaching materials: cassettes, magnetic tapes, teaching using data telecommunications.

The regulations also envisage a special organization of the examinations in order to give the students additional time, materials and, if necessary, personal assistance.

The 21 universities that prepare students through correspondence courses for taking the national diploma in about 40 subjects should also be mentioned (see pp. 256-257).

Appendices

1. Addresses

French embassies in EC countries

Belgium
Rue Ducale 65
B-1000 Bruxelles

Denmark
Kongens Nytorv 4
DK-1050 København

Federal Republic of Germany
Kapellenweg 1A
D-5300 Bonn 2

Greece
7, avenue de la Reine Sophie
GR-Athina

Spain
Héroes del 10 de Agosto 9
E-28001 Madrid

Ireland
36 Ailesbury Road
Dublin 4

Italy
Piazza Farnese 67
I-00186 Roma

Luxembourg
2, rue Bertholet
L-1233 Luxembourg

The Netherlands
Smidsplein 1 — BP 683
'sGravenhage

Portugal
Calvada Marquês de Abrantes 123
P-Lisboa

United Kingdom
Knightsbridge 58
London SWI

Organizations

Ministère de l'Education nationale — Direction des enseignements supérieurs
Sous-direction de la vie étudiante et de la formation permanente — Bureau de l'information de l'accueil, de l'orientation et de l'insertion professionnelle
(Bureau DESUP 9)
61-65, rue Dutot
F-75732 Paris Cedex 15
☎ 40 60 65 40
(provides information which describes the whole higher education system: higher education establishments, courses of study, and the information advice offices — SCUIO — which exist at all universities).

Centre national des œuvres universitaires et scolaires (CNOUS)
69, quai d'Orsay
F-75007 Paris
☎ 4705 3110

Accueil des étudiants étrangers
6-8, rue Jean-Calvin
F-75005 Paris
☎ 4707 6170
(provides general information and the list of Centres régionaux des œuvres universitaires on request)

Office national d'information sur les enseignements et les professions (ONISEP)
168, boulevard du Montparnasse
F-75014 Paris
☎ 4335 1598

Sold on the basis of written requests:

ONISEP Diffusion
F-75225 Paris Cedex 05

Centre d'information et de documentation jeunesse (CIDJ)
101, quai Branly
F-75015 Paris
☎ 4566 4020

Centre de documentation et d'information rurale (CDIR)
(for summer employment)
92, rue du Dessous-des-Berges
F-75013 Paris
☎ 4583 0492

Les Services communs universitaires d'information et d'orientation des universités (SCUIO) (see the list of universities)

Centre national d'enseignement à distance (CNED)
Tour Paris-Lyon 209-211, Rue de Bercy
F-75585 Paris Cedex 12
- 39-41, boulevard Gambetta
  F-38000 Grenoble
- 34, rue Jean Bart
  F-59046 Lille Cedex
- 100 bis, rue Hénon
  F-69316 Lyon Cedex 1
- 2, rue du Docteur Fleury
  F-76130 Rouen
  Mont-Saint-Aignan
- 109, rue Vauquelin
  F-31300 Toulouse

Universities

Académie d'Aix-Marseille
Université de Provence
(Aix-Marseille I)
UNIVAIXMA 1
1, place Victor Hugo
F-13331 Marseille Cedex 3

Université d'Aix-Marseille
(Aix-Marseille II)
UNIVAIXMA 2
Jardin Emile Duclaux
58, boulevard Charles Livon
F-13007 Marseille

Université de Droit, d'Économie et des Sciences
(Aix-Marseille III)
UNIVAIXMA 3
3, avenue Robert Schuman
F-13621 Aix-en-Provence

Université d'Avignon
UNIVAVIGNO
35, rue Joseph Vernet
F-84000 Avignon

F

Académie d'Amiens
Université de Picardie
(Amiens) UNIVAMIENS
Rue Salomon Malhangu
F-80025 Amiens Cedex

Académie des Antilles-Guyane
Université des Antilles-Guyane
UNIVANTILL
Boulevard Légitimus
Boîte postale 771
F-97173 Pointe-à-Pitre Cedex
(Guadeloupe)

Académie de Besançon
Université de Franche-Comté
(Besançon) UNIVBESANC
30, avenue de l'Observatoire
F-25030 Besançon Cedex

Académie de Bordeaux
Université de Bordeaux I
UNIVBORDE 1
351, cours de la Libération
F-33405 Talence Cedex

Université de Bordeaux II
UNIVBORDE 2
146, rue Léo Saignat
F-33076 Bordeaux Cedex

Université de Bordeaux III
UNIVBORDE 3
Domaine universitaire —
Esplanade Michel de Montaigne
F-33405 Talence Cedex

Université de Pau et pays de l'Adour UNIVPAU
Villa Lawrence
68, rue Montpensier
Boîte postale 576
F-64010 Pau Cedex

Académie de Caen
UNIVCAEN
Esplanade de la Paix
F-14032 Caen Cedex

Académie de Clermont-Ferrand
Université Clermont-Ferrand I
UNIVCLERM 1
49, boulevard Gergovia
Boîte postale 32
F-63001 Clermont-Ferrand

Université de Clermont-Ferrand II
34, avenue Carnot
Boîte postale 185
F-63006 Clermont-Ferrand Cedex

Académie de Corse (Corte)
UNIVCORSE
7, avenue Jean Nicoli,
Boîte postale 24
F-20250 Corte

Académie de Dijon
Université de Bourgogne
(Dijon) UNIVDIJON
Campus universitaire de Montmuzard,
Boîte postale 138
F-21004 Dijon Cedex

Académie de Grenoble
Université scientifique, technologique et médicale
(Grenoble I) UNIVGRENO 1
Boîte postale 68
F-38042 Saint-Martin-d'Hères Cedex

Université des sciences sociales
(Grenoble II) UNIVGRENO 2
Domaine universitaire
Saint-Martin-d'Hères,
Boîte postale 47 X
F-38040 Grenoble Cedex

Université des langues et lettres
(Grenoble III)
UNIVGRENO 3
Domaine universitaire
Saint-Martin-d'Hères,
Boîte postale 25 X
F-38040 Grenoble Cedex

Université de Savoie
(Chambéry) UNIVCHAMBE
Domaine universitaire de Jacob
Bellecombette
Boîte postale 1104
F-73011 Chambéry Cedex

Académie de Lille
Université des sciences et techniques (Lille I) UNIVLILLE 1
Domaine universitaire scientifique
F-59655 Villeneuve d'Ascq
Cedex

Université du droit et de la santé (Lille II) UNIVLILLE
42, rue Paul Duez
F-59800 Lille

Université des sciences humaines, des lettres et des arts
(Lille III) UNIVLILLE
Domaine universitaire littéraire et juridique de Villeneuve-d'Ascq — Pont-de-Bois
Boîte postale 149
F-59653 Villeneuve-d'Ascq
Cedex

Université de Valenciennes et du Hainaut-Cambrésis
UNIVVALENC
Le Mont Houy
F-59326 Valenciennes Cedex

Académie de Limoges
Université de Limoges
UNIVLIMOGE
13, rue de Genève
F-87065 Limoges Cedex

Académie de Lyon
Université Claude Bernard
(Lyon I) UNIVLYON 1
86, rue Pasteur
F-69365 Lyon Cedex 07

Université Lyon II
UNIVLYON 2
86, rue Pasteur
F-69365 Lyon Cedex 2

Université Jean Moulin
(Lyon III) UNIVLYON 3
1, rue de l'Université
Lyon 7e
Boîte postale 0638
F-69339 Lyon Cedex 02

Université de Sainte-Etienne
34, rue Francis Baulier
UNIVSTETIE
F-42013 Saint-Etienne Cedex

Académie de Montpellier
Université Montpellier I
UNIVMONTP 1
5, boulevard Henri IV

Boîte postale 1017
F-34006 Montpellier Cedex

Université des sciences et techniques du Languedoc (Montpellier II)
UNIVMONTP 2
Place Eugène Bataillon
F-34060 Montpellier Cedex

Université Paul Valéry (Montpellier III) UNIVMONTP 3
Route de Mende
Boîte postale 5043
F-34032 Montpellier Cedex

Université de Perpignan
UNIVPERPIG
Avenue de Villeneuve
F-66025 Perpignan Cedex

Université Nancy I
UNIVNANCY I
24-30, rue Lionnois
Boîte postale 3137
F-54013 Nancy Cedex

Université Nancy II
UNIVNANCY 2*
25, rue Baron Louis
Boîte postale 454
F-54001 Nancy Cedex

Université de Metz
UNIMETZ
Ile du Saulcy
Boîte postale 794
F-57012 Metz Cedex

Académie de Nantes
Université d'Angers
UNIVANGERS
30, rue des Arènes
Boîte postale 3532
F-49035 Angers Cedex

Université du Maine
(Le Mans) UNIVLEMANS
Route de Laval
Boîte postale 535
F-72017 Le Mans Cedex

* The *Centre européen universitaire* at the University of Nancy II offers a one-year training course for Europe specialists which is open to French and foreign students who have a *maîtrise* or appropriate diploma. The students may be supported with grants.

Université de Nantes
UNIVNANTES
1, quai de Tourville
Boîte postale 1026
F-44035 Nantes Cedex

Académie de Nice
Université de Nice
UNIVNICE
Parc Valrose
F-06034 Nice Cedex

Université de Toulon et du Var
UNIVTOULON
Avenue de l'Université
F-83130 La Garde

Académie d'Orleans-Tours
Université d'Orléans
UNIVORLEAN
Château de la Source
Boîte postale 6479
F-45046 Orléans Cedex 2

Université François Rabelais
(Tours) UNIVTOURS
3, rue des Tanneurs
F-37041 Tours Cedex

Académie de Paris
Université Panthéon-Sorbonne
(Paris I) UNIVPARIS I
12, place du Panthéon
F-75231 Paris Cedex 05

Université de droit, d'économie et de sciences sociales
(Paris II) UNIVPARIS 2
12, place du Panthéon
F-75231 Paris Cedex 05

Université de la Sorbonne-Nouvelle (Paris III)
UNIVPARIS 3
17, place de la Sorbonne
F-75230 Paris Cedex 05

Université de Paris-Sorbonne
(Paris IV) UNIVPARIS 4
1, rue Victor Cousin
F-75230 Paris Cedex 05

Université René Descartes
(Paris V) UNIVPARIS 5
12, rue de l'École de médecine
F-75270 Paris Cedex 06

Université Pierre et Marie Curie (Paris VI)
UNIVPARIS 6
4, place Jussieu
F-75230 Paris Cedex 05

Université Paris VII
UNIVPARIS 7
2, place Jussieu
F-75251 Paris Cedex 05

Université Paris-Dauphine
(Paris IX)
UNIVPARIS 9
Place du Maréchal de Lattre de Tassigny
F-75775 Paris Cedex 16

Académie de Créteil
Université Paris-Vincennes-Saint-Denis (Paris VIII)
UNIVPARIS 8
2, rue de la Liberté
F-93526 Saint-Denis Cedex

Université Paris-Val-de-Marne
(Paris XII) UNIVPARIS 12
Avenue du Général de Gaulle
F-94010 Créteil Cedex

Université Paris-Nord
(Paris XIII) UNIVPARIS 13
Avenue Jean-Baptiste Clément
F-93430 Villetaneuse

Académie de Versailles
Université Paris-Nanterre
(Paris X) UNIVPARIS 10
200, avenue de la République
F-92001 Nanterre Cedex

Université Paris-Sud (Paris XI)
UNIVPARIS 11
15, rue Georges Clémenceau
F-91405 Orsay Cedex

Académie de Poiters
Université de Poitiers
UNIVPOITIE
15, rue de Blessac
F-86034 Poitiers Cedex

Académie de Reims
Université de Reims
UNIVREIMS
23, rue Boulard
F-51100 Reims

Académie de Rennes
Université de Bretagne occidentale
(Brest) UNIVBREST
Rue des Archives
Boîte postale 137
F-29269 Brest Cedex

Université Rennes I
UNIVRENNE 1
2, rue du Thabor
F-35000 Rennes

Université de Haute-Bretagne (Rennes II) UNIVRENNE 2
6, avenue Gaston Berger
F-35043 Rennes Cedex

Académie de la Réunion
Université de La Réunion
UNIVRÉUN
15, avenue René Gassin
F-97489 Saint-Denis Cedex

Académie de Rouen
Université du Havre
UNIVLEHAVR
25, rue Philippe Lebon
Boîte postale 1123
F-76063 Le Havre Cedex

Université de Rouen
UNIVROUEN
Haute-Normandie
Rue Thomas Beckett
F-76130 Mont-Saint-Aignan

Académie de Strasbourg
Université Louis Pasteur (Strasbourg I) UNIVSTRAS 1
4, rue Blaise Pascal
F-67070 Strasbourg Cedex

Université des sciences humaines (Strasbourg II)
UNIVSTRAS 2
22, rue Descartes
F-67084 Strasbourg Cedex

Université des sciences juridiques, politiques, sociales et de technologie (Strasbourg III)
UNIVSTRAS 3
Place d'Athènes
F-67084 Strasbourg Cedex

Université de Haute-Alsace
(Mulhouse) UNIVMULHOU
Maison de l'Université
2, rue des Frères Lumière
F-68093 Mulhouse Cedex

Académie de Toulouse
Université des sciences sociales
(Toulouse I) UNIVTOULO 1
Place Anatole-France
F-31042 Toulouse Cedex

Université de Toulouse
Le Mirail (Toulouse II)
UNIVTOULO 2
5, allée Antonio Machado
F-31058 Toulouse Cedex

Université Paul Sabatier
(Toulouse III)
UNIVTOULO 3
118, route de Narbonne
F-31062 Toulouse Cedex

Territoires d'outre-mer
Université du Pacifique
UNIVPACIFI
Boîte postale 4635
Papeete
Tahiti – Polynésie Française

Other institutions

Engineering training colleges recognized by the Commission du titre

Écoles relevant de l'Éducation nationale

Écoles publiques

Écoles centrales
ECP Paris — École centrale des arts et manufactures
Grande-Voie-des-Vignes
F-92290 Châtenay-Malabry

ECL Lyon — École centrale de Lyon
36, avenue Guy-Collongue
Boîte postale 163
F-69131 Écully Cedex

ENSAM: École nationale supérieure des arts et métiers et écoles nationales assimilées
ENSAM Paris —
151, boulevard de l'Hôpital
F-75640 Paris Cedex 13

6 Centres régionaux de l'ENSAM
- 2, cours des Arts et Métiers, F-13617 Aix-en-Provence
- 2, boulevard du Ronceray
  Boîte postale 35-25
  F-49035 Angers
- Esplanade de l'université
  F-33405 Talence
- 3, rue de La Rochefoucauld
  Boîte postale 508
  F-51006 Châlons-sur-Marne
- F-71250 Cluny
- 8, boulevard Louis-XIV
  F-59046 Lille Cedex

ENSAIS Strasbourg (arts et industries)
24, boulevard de la Victoire
F-67084 Strasbourg Cedex

ENSCI Limoges (céramique industrielle)
47, rue Albert Thomas
F-87065 Limoges Cedex

ENSEA Cergy (l'électronique et de ses applications)
Allée des Chênes-Pourpres
F-95000 Cergy

ENSAIT Roubaix (arts et industries textiles)
2, place des Martyrs-de-la-Résistance
F-59070 Roubaix Cedex 01

INSA: Instituts nationaux des sciences appliquées
INSA Lyon
20, avenue Albert-Einstein
F-69621 Villeurbanne Cedex

INSA Rennes
20, avenue des Buttes-de-Coësmes
F-35043 Rennes Cedex

INSA Rouen
Place Émile Blondel
Boîte postale 8
F-76130 Mont-Saint-Aignan

INSA Toulouse
Avenue de Rangueil
F-31077 Toulouse Cedex

UTC Compiègne — Université de technologie de Compiègne
Rue Roger Couttolenc
Boîte postale 233
F-60206 Compiègne Cedex

ENI: Écoles nationales d'ingénieurs

ENIB Belfort
8, boulevard Anatole-France
Boîte postale 525
F-90016 Belfort Cedex
(4 ans)

ENIB Brest
Avenue Le Gorgeu
F-29287 Brest Cedex
(5 ans)

ENIM Metz
Ile du Saulcy
F-57045 Metz Cedex
(5 ans)

ENISE Saint-Étienne
58, rue Jean-Parot
F-42023 Saint-Étienne
Cédex 2
(5 ans)

ENIT Tarbes
Chemin d'Azereix
Boîte postale 311
F-65013 Tarbes Cedex
(5 ans)

Écoles diverses

IDN Lille — Institut Industriel du Nord de la France, domaine universitaire scientifique de Lille
Boîte postale 48
F-59651 Villeneuve-d'Ascq

CESTI Saint-Ouen — Centre d'études supérieures des techniques industrielles
3, rue Fernand-Hainaut
F-93407 Saint-Ouen

ISMCM Saint-Ouen — Institut supérieur des matériaux et de la construction mécanique
3, rue Fernand-Hainaut
F-93407 Saint-Ouen
(École de spécialisation)

ENSI: Écoles nationales supérieures d'ingénieurs au sein des universités et INP

ENSMM Besançon — ENSI de mécanique et des microtechniques route de Gray
La Bouloie
F-25030 Besançon

ENSCPB Bordeaux — ENSI de chimie et de physique
351, cours de la Libération
F-33405 Talence

ENSERB Bordeaux — ENSI d'électronique et de radioélectricité
351, cours de la Libération
F-33405 Talence

ISMRA Caen — Institut des sciences de la matière et du rayonnement
5, avenue d'Edimbourg
F-14032 Caen Cedex

ENSCCF Clermont-Ferrand — ENSI de chimie, Ensemble scientifique des Cézeaux
24, avenue des Landais
Boîte postale 71
F-63170 Aubière

ENSBANA Dijon — ENSI de biologie appliquée à la nutrition et à l'alimentation
Campus universitaire Montmuzard
F-21100 Dijon

ENSEEG Grenoble — ENSI d'électrochimie et d'électrométallurgie, domaine universitaire
Boîte postale 75
F-38402 Saint-Martin-d'Hères
(INP de Grenoble)

ENSERG Grenoble — ENSI d'électronique et de radio-électricité
23, rue des Martyrs
F-38031 Grenoble
(INP de Grenoble)

ENSIEG Grenoble — ENSI d'ingénieurs électriciens, domaine universitaire
Boîte postale 46
F-38402 Saint-Martin-d'Hères
(INP de Grenoble)

ENSHMG Grenoble — ENSI d'hydraulique et de mécanique, domaine universitaire
Boîte postale 95
F-3840 Saint-Martin-d'Hères
Centre de tri
F-38041 Grenoble Cedex
(INP de Grenoble)

ENSIMAG Grenoble — ENSI d'informatique et de mathématiques appliquées, domaine universitaire
Boîte postale 68
F-38402 Saint-Martin-d'Hères
Cedex
(INP de Grenoble)

ENSPG Grenoble — ENSI de physique, domaine universitaire
Boîte postale 46
F-38402 Saint-Martin-d'Hères
Cedex
(INP de Grenoble)

ENSCL Lille — ENSI de chimie domaine universitaire scientifique
Boîte postale 108
F-59652 Villeneuve-d'Ascq

ENSPMA Marseille — ENSI de physique domaine universitaire Saint-Jérôme
avenue de l'escadrille Normandie-Niemen
F-13397 Marseille Cedex 13

ENSCM Montpellier — ENSI de chimie
8, rue de l'École Normale
F-34075 Montpellier Cedex

ENSCMU Mulhouse — ENSI de chimie
3, rue Alfred-Werner
F-68093 Mulhouse Cedex

ENSITM Mulhouse — ENSI des industries textiles
11, rue Alfred-Werner
F-68093 Mulhouse Cedex

ENSAIA Nancy — ENSI d'agronomie et des industries alimentaires
2, avenue de la Forêt-de-Haye
F-54500 Vandœuvre-lès-Nancy
(INP de Lorraine)

ENSEM Nancy — ENSI d'électricité et de mécanique
2, rue de la Citadelle
Boîte postale 850
F-54011 Nancy Cedex
(INP de Lorraine)

ENSG Nancy — ENSI de géologie appliquée et de prospection minière
94, avenue de-Lattre-de-Tassigny
Boîte postale 452
F-54001 Nancy Cedex
(INP de Lorraine)

ENSIC Nancy — ENSI des industries chimiques
1, rue Grandville
F-54042 Nancy Cedex
(INP de Lorraine)

ENSM Nancy — ENSI des mines
Parc de Saurupt
F-54042 Nancy Cedex
(INP de Lorraine)

ENSM Nantes — ENSI de mécanique
1, rue de la Noé
F-44072 Nantes Cedex

ENSCP Paris — ENSI de chimie
11, rue Pierre et Marie-Curie
F-75231 Paris Cedex 05
poste 3840

ENSMA Poitiers — ENSI de mécanique et d'aérotechnique
Rue Guillaume-VII,
F-86034 Poitiers Cedex

ENSCR Rennes — ENSI de chimie
Avenue du Général-Leclerc
F-35700 Beaulieu-Rennes

EHICS Strasbourg — École européenne des hautes études des industries chimiques
1, rue Blaise-Pascal
Boîte postale 296 R8
F-67008 Strasbourg Cedex

ENSPS Strasbourg — ENSI de physique
7, rue de l'Université
F-67000 Strasbourg

ENSAT Toulouse — ENSI agronomique
145, avenue de Muret
F-31076 Toulouse
(INP de Toulouse)

ENSCT Toulouse — ENSI de chimie
118, route de Narbonne
F-31077 Toulouse Cedex
(INP de Toulouse)

ENSEEIHT Toulouse — ENSI d'électrotechnique, d'électronique, d'informatique et d'hydraulique
2, rue Charles-Camichel
F-31071 Toulouse Cedex
(INP de Toulouse)

ENSIGC Toulouse — ENSI des ingénieurs de génie chimique
Chemin de la Loge
F-31078 Toulouse Cedex
(INP de Toulouse)

ENSIMEV Valenciennes — ENSI d'ingénieurs de mécanique et d'énergétique
Le Mont-Houy
F-59326 Valenciennes

Écoles de spécialisation

ESIPSOI Marseille — École supérieure d'ingénierie de pétroléochimie et de synthèse organique industrielle d'Aix-Marseille III,
domaine universitaire Saint-Jérôme
avenue de l'Escadrille Normandie-Niemen
F-13397 Marseille Cedex 4

EAHP Strasbourg — École d'application des hauts polymères de Strasbourg I
4, rue Boussingault
F-67000 Strasbourg

IPGS Strasbourg — Institut de physique du globe de Strasbourg I
5, rue René-Descartes
F-67084 Strasbourg

INSTN Gif-sur-Yvette — Institut national des sciences et techniques nucléaires
F-91191 Gif-sur-Yvette Cedex
(également sous tutelle du ministère de l'Industrie)

Écoles universitaires d'ingénieurs

IUSTI Aix-Marseille I — Institut universitaire des systèmes thermiques industriels de l'université d'Aix-en-Provence
Centre de Saint-Jérôme
rue Henri-Poincaré
F-13397 Marseille Cedex 13

IUSPIM Aix-Marseille III — Institut des sciences pour l'ingénieur
rue Henri-Poincaré
F-13397 Marseille Cedex 13

ISTAB Bordeaux I — Institut des sciences et techniques des aliments
Avenue des Facultés
F-33405 Talence

CUST Clermont-Ferrand II — Centre universitaire de sciences et techniques
rue des Meuniers
Boîte postale 48
F-63170 Aubière

ISTG Grenoble I — Institut des sciences et techniques de

l'université, domaine universitaire
Boîte postale 68
F-38402 Saint-Martin-d'Hères Cedex

EUDIL Lille I — École universitaire d'ingénieurs
Boîte postale 36
F-59655 Villeneuve-d'Ascq Cedex

IAAL Lille I — Institut agricole et alimentaire de l'université
Cité scientifique
F-59655 Villeneuve-d'Ascq Cedex

ISIM Montpellier II — Institut des sciences de l'ingénieur
Place Eugène-Bataillon
F-34060 Montpellier Cedex

ESSTIB Nancy I — École supérieure des sciences et technologies des industries du bois de l'université
Allée des Hêtres
F-88000 Épinal

ESSTIN Nancy I — École supérieure des sciences et technologies de l'ingénieur de l'université
Parc Robert-Ventz
F-54000 Vandœuvre

IRESTE Nantes — Institut de recherche et d'enseignement supérieur aux techniques de l'électronique de l'université
3, rue du Maréchal-Joffre
F-44041 Nantes Cedex

ISITEM Nantes — Institut des sciences de l'ingénieur en thermique énergétique et matériaux de l'université
2, rue de la Houssinière
F-44072 Nantes

ESSI Nice — École supérieure en sciences informatiques de l'université
Parc Valrose
F-06034 Nice Cedex

ESEM Orléans — École supérieure de l'énergie et des matériaux de l'université
F-45046 Orléans Cedex

ISTP Poitiers — Institut des sciences et techniques de l'université
40, avenue du Recteur-Pineau
F-86022 Poitiers

IST Paris VI — Institut des sciences et technologies de l'université
4, place Jussieu
F-75230 Parix Cedex 05

FIUPSO Parix XI — Formation ingénieur universitaire Paris-Sud de l'université
15, rue Georges-Clémenceau
F-91405 Orsay

CSP Paris XIII — Centre scientifique polytechnique de l'université
Avenue Jean-Baptiste-Clément
F-93340 Villetaneuse
Poste 4138

IMAC — Institut image et communication de l'université
Place du 8-Mai 1945
F-93206 Saint-Denis Cedex

ING Reims — Unité des sciences de l'université
Boîte postale 347
F-51062 Reims Cedex

ENSSAT Rennes I — École nationale supérieure de sciences appliquées et de technologies de l'université
Boîte postale 150
F-22302 Lannion Cedex

ESBS Strasbourg I — École supérieure de biotechnologie de l'université
11, rue Humann
F-67085 Strasbourg

Écoles privées rattachées aux universités
ESE/SUPELEC Gif-sur-Yvette — École supérieure d'électricité
Plateau du Moulon
F-91190 Gif-sur-Yvette

EFP Grenoble — École française de papeterie,
domaine universitaire de Saint-Martin-d'Hères
Boîte postale 65
F-38402 Saint-Martin-d'Hères

ESCIL Lyon — École supérieure de chimie industrielle
43, boulevard du 11-novembre 1918
Boîte postale 2077
F-69616 Villeurbanne Cedex

ESCM Marseille — École supérieure de chimie de la Chambre de commerce et d'industrie
Centre Saint-Jerôme
Avenue de l'Escadrille Normandie-Niemen
F-13397 Marseille Cedex 13

ESO Orsay — École supérieure d'optique
Bâtiment 503
Centre universitaire d'Orsay
Institut d'optique
Boîte postale 43
F-91406 Orsay Cedex

Conservatoire National des Arts et Métiers
CNAMING Paris
292, rue Saint-Martin
F-75141 Paris Cedex 03

IFFI Paris — Institut français du froid industriel (CNAM)
292, rue Saint-Martin
F-75141 Paris Cedex 03

ESGT Évry — École supérieure des géomètres et topographes (CNAM),
18, allée Jean-Rostand
F-91000 Évry

IIE Évry — Institut d'informatique d'entreprise (CNAM)
18, allée Jean-Rostand
Boîte postale 77
F-91002 Évry Cedex
Poste 162 B

Écoles privées

ESEO Angers — École supérieure d'électronique de l'Ouest
4, rue Merlet-de-la-Boulaye
F-49000 Angers

ITF Boulogne-Billancourt — Institut textile de France de Boulogne
35, rue des Abondances
Boîte postale 79
F-92105 Boulogne-Billancourt

ESITE Épinal — École supérieure des industries textiles
85, rue d'Alsace
F-88000 Épinal

ESTACA Levallois-Perret — École supérieure des techniques aéronautiques et de construction automobile
3, rue Pablo-Neruda
F-92300 Levallois-Perret

HEI Lille — École des hautes études industrielles
13, rue de Toul
F-59046 Cedex

ICAM Lille — Institut catholique d'arts et métiers
6, rue Auber
F-59046 Lille Cedex

ISEN Lille — Institut supérieur d'électronique du Nord
41, boulevard Vauban
F-59046 Lille Cedex

ECAM Lyon — École catholique d'arts et métiers
40, montée Saint-Barthélèmy
F-69321 Lyon Cedex 05

ESCEPEA Lyon — École supérieure du cuir et des peintures, encres et adhésifs
181-203, avenue Jean-Jaurès
F-69007 Lyon Cedex

ICPI Lyon — Institut de chimie et de physique industrielles
31, place Bellecour
F-69288 Lyon Cedex

ESIM Marseille — École supérieure d'ingénieurs
28, rue des Électriciens
Boîte postale 64
F-13375 Marseille Cedex 12

ISBA Marseille — Institut supérieur du béton armé
28, rue des Électriciens
F-13012 Marseille

ESTA Orsay — École supérieure des techniques aérospatiales
bâtiment 502 bis, campus universitaire
F-91405 Orsay

CESI Paris — Centre d'études supérieures industrielles siège
297, rue de Vaugirard
F-75015 Paris
(trois centres Paris et région parisienne: Paris 13e, Évry, Gentilly et en province: Aix-en-Provence, Arrâs, Balma, Blanquefort, Bordeaux, Écully, Évry, Le Mans, Lyon, Nantes, Orléans, Rennes, Rouen, Strasbourg, Toulouse, Vandœuvre)

EFREI Paris — École française d'électronique et d'informatique
10, rue Amyot et 12, rue Laromiguière
F-75005 Paris

ESCOM Paris — École supérieure de chimie organique et minérale
12, rue Cassette
F-75006 Paris

ESB Paris — École supérieure du Bois
6, avenue de Saint-Mandé
F-75012 Paris
(également sous tutelle ministère de l'Agriculture)

ESME Paris — École spéciale de mécanique et d'électricité, Sudria
4, rue Blaise-Desgoffe
F-75006 Paris

ETP Paris — École spéciale des travaux publics, du bâtiment et de l'industrie
57, boulevard Saint-Germain
F-75240 Cedex 05

ISEP Paris — Institut supérieur d'électronique
21, rue d'Assas
F-75270 Parix Cedex 06

ESIEA Paris — École supérieure d'informatique, électronique, automatique
9, rue Vésale
F-75005 Paris

ESIEE Paris — École supérieure d'ingénieurs en électrotechnique et électronique de la Chambre de commerce et d'industrie de Paris
Cité Descartes
2, boulevard Blaise-Pascal
Boîte postale 99
F-93162 Noisy-le-Grand

ESSA Paris — École supérieure du soudage et de ses applications
32, boulevard de la Chapelle
F-75018 Paris

ESACG Pessac
— École supérieure d'application des corps gras,
Rue Monge
Parc industriel de Pessac
F-33600 Pessac

ESIG/ELEC Rouen — École supérieure d'ingénieurs en génie électrique
58, rue Méridienne
Boîte postale 1012
F-76100 Rouen

EPF Sceaux — École polytechnique féminine
3 bis, rue Lakanal
F-92330 Sceaux

ESF Sèvres — École supérieure de fonderie
44, avenue de la Division-Leclerc
F-92310 Sèvres

EIT Tours — École d'ingénieurat de Tours
L'Auberdière
F-37200 Tours

ESTIT Villeneuve-d'Ascq — École supérieure des techniques industrielles et des textiles
allée Lakanal
F-59650 Villeneuve-d'Ascq

ESICA Vitry-sur-Seine — École supérieure des industries du caoutchouc
60, rue Auber
F-94408 Vitry-sur-Seine

Écoles relevant de l'agriculture

Écoles publiques

ENSA: Écoles nationales supérieures agronomiques

INA Paris — Institut national agronomique Paris-Grignon
16, rue Claude-Bernard
F-75005 Paris

ENSAMMONTPE
9, place Viala
F-34060 Montpellier Cedex

ENSAR Rennes
65, rue de St-Brieuc
F-35042 Rennes Cedex

ENITA: Écoles nationales des ingénieurs des travaux agricoles

ENITAH Angers — École nationale d'ingénieurs des travaux de l'horticulture et du paysage
2, rue Le-Nôtre
F-49045 Angers

ENITABORDE
1, cours du Général-de-Gaulle
F-33170 Gradignan-Bordeaux

ENITACLERM Marmilhat — École nationale d'ingénieurs des travaux agricoles
F-63370 Lempdes-Clermont-Ferrand

ENITADIJON
21, boulevard Olivier-de-Serres
Boîte postale 42
F-21802 Dijon-Quétigny

ENITIAA Nantes — École nationale d'ingénieurs des techniques et industries agricoles et alimentaires
Chemin de la Geraudière
F-44072 Nantes Cedex

ENITEF Nogent-sur-Vernisson — École nationale d'ingénieurs des travaux des eaux et forêts
domaine des Barres
F-45290 Nogent-sur-Vernisson

ENITRTS Strasbourg — École nationale des ingénieurs des travaux ruraux et des techniques sanitaires
1, quai Koch
Boîte postale 1039 F
F-67070 Strasbourg Cedex

Écoles d'application

INPSA Dijon — Institut national de promotion supérieure agricole
Rue des Champs-Prévois
F-21000 Dijon

ENSSAA Dijon — École nationale supérieure des sciences agronomiques appliquées
26, boulevard du Docteur-Petitjean
F-21100 Dijon

ENSIA Massy — École nationale supérieure des industries agricoles et alimentaires
1, avenue des Olympiades
F-91305 Massy

CNEARC Montpellier — Centre national d'études agronomiques des régions chaudes,
domaine de Lavalette
Boîte postale 5098
F-34033 Montpellier Cedex

ESAT Montpellier — École supérieure d'agronomie tropicale
Avenue du Val-de-Montjenaud
Boîte postale 5098
F-34033 Montpellier Cedex

ENGREF Paris — École nationale du génie rural, des eaux et des forêts
19, avenue du Maine
F-75732 Paris Cedex 15

IESIEL Paris — Institut d'études supérieures d'industrie et d'économie laitières
16, rue Claude-Bernard
F-75231 Paris Cedex 05

ENSFA Rennes — École nationale supérieure féminine agronomique
65, rue de Saint-Brieuc
F-35042 Rennes Cedex

ENSH Versailles — ENS d'horticulture
4, rue Hardy
F-78000 Versailles

Écoles privées

ESA Angers — École supérieure d'agriculture
24, rue Auguste-Fonteneau
F-49044 Angers Cedex

ISAB Beauvais — Institut supérieur agricole
rue Pierre-Waguet
Boîte postale 313
F-60026 Beauvais Cedex

ISALILLE — Institut supérieur d'agriculture
13, rue de Toul
F-59046 Lille Cedex

ISARA Lyon — Institut supérieur d'agriculture Rhône-Alpes
31, place Bellecour
F-69288 Lyon

ESAP Purpan-Toulouse — École supérieure d'agriculture
271, avenue de Grande-Bretagne
F-31076 Purpan-Toulouse Cedex

ESITPA Val de Reuil — École supérieure d'ingénieurs et de techniciens pour l'agriculture
Boîte postale 201
Rue Grande
F-27100 Val de Reuil

F

Écoles relevant de la défense
Écoles publiques

ENSIETA Arcueil — École nationale supérieure d'ingénieurs des études et techniques d'armement, centre d'Arcueil
24, avenue Prieur-de-la-Côte-d'Or
F-94114 Arcueil

ENSIETA Brest — Centre de Brest Naval
Pontanezen
F-29200 Brest

EN Lanveoc-Poulmic — École Navale
F-29240 Brest naval

EP/X Palaiseau — École Polytechnique
route de Saclay
F-91128 Palaiseau Cedex

COSAR Paris — Cours supérieur d'armement, école militaire
1, place Joffre
F- 75007 Paris

COSEM Paris — Cours supérieur des systèmes d'armes terrestres, école militaire
1, place Joffre
F-75007 Paris

ENSTA Paris — École nationale supérieure de techniques avancées
32, boulevard Victor
F-75015 Paris

ESEAT Rennes — École supérieure de l'électronique de l'armée de terre
Quartier Leschi
F-35998 Rennes

ESMSTCYR — École spéciale militaire Saint-Cyr
F-66210 Coëtquidan

EA Salon-de-Provence — École de l'Air
F-13661 Salon-de-Provence Cedex

ENSAE Toulouse — École nationale supérieure de l'aéronautique et de l'espace
10, avenue Édouard-Belin
Boîte postale 4032
F-31055 Toulouse Cedex

ENSICA Toulouse — École nationale supérieure d'ingénieurs de constructions aéronautiques
49, avenue Léon-Blum
F-31056 Toulouse Cedex

ETSTM Vaulx-en-Velin — École technique supérieure des travaux maritimes, rue Maurice-Audin
F-69120 Vaulx-en-Velin

ESGM Versailles — École supérieure du génie militaire
3, rue de l'Indépendance Américaine
F-78013 Versailles

Écoles relevant de l'environnement
Écoles publiques

ENPC Paris — École nationale des ponts et chaussées
28, rue des Saints-Pères
F-75007 Paris

ENPC Puyricard, établissement décentralisé, clos Guiot
Boulevard des Camus
F-13540 Puyricard
(annexe de la rue des Saints-Pères)

ENSGSTMAN — École nationale des sciences géographiques (rattachée à l'Institut géographique national de Saint-Mandé)
2, avenue Pasteur
F-94160 Saint-Mandé

ENTPE Vaulx-en-Velin — École nationale des travaux publics de l'État
Rue Maurice-Audin
Boîte postale 4
F-69120 Vaulx-en-Velin

Écoles relevant de l'industrie
Écoles publiques

ENSTIMA Alès — École nationale supérieure des techniques industrielles et des mines
6, avenue de Clavières
F-30107 Alès Cedex

ENSTIMD Douai — École nationale supérieure des techniques industrielles et des mines
941, rue Charles-Bourseul
Boîte postale 838
F-59508 Douai Cedex

ESM Douai — École supérieure de métrologie
941, rue Charles-Bourseul
Boîte postale 838
F-59508 Douai Cedex

ENSMP Paris — ENS des mines
60, boulevard Saint-Michel
F-75006 Paris

ENSPM Rueil-Malmaison — École nationale supérieure des pétroles et des moteurs
4, avenue de Bois-Préau
Boîte postale 311
F-92506 Rueil-Malmaison

ENSMSE Saint-Étienne — ENS des mines
158, cours Fauriel
F-42023 Saint-Étienne

Écoles relevant des PTT
Écoles publiques

ENST/BR Brest — École nationale supérieure des télécommunications de Bretagne
Boîte postale 832
F-29285 Brest Cedex

ENST Paris — École nationale supérieure des télécommunications
46, rue Barrault
F-75634 Paris

INT Évry — Institut national des télécommunications
Îlot des Épinettes
F-91011 Évry

F

Écoles relevant de l'équipement, de l'aménagement du territoire et des transports

Écoles publiques

ENAC, Toulouse — École nationale de l'aviation civile
7, avenue Edouard-Belin
Boîte postale 4005
F-31055 Toulouse Cedex

ENM Toulouse — École nationale de la météorologie
42, avenue Gustave-Coriolis
F-31057 Toulouse Cedex

École relevant des affaires sociales et de l'emploi

École publique

ENSP Rennes — École nationale de la santé publique
Avenue du professeur Léon-Bernard
F-35043 Rennes

Écoles relevant de la Ville de Paris

Écoles publiques

ESPCI/PC Paris — École supérieure de physique et de chimie industrielles de la ville de Paris
10, rue Vauquelin
F-75231 Paris Cedex 05

IVP Paris — École des ingénieurs de la ville de Paris
57, boulevard Saint-Germain
F-75006 Paris

Écoles normales supérieures et grandes écoles

École normale supérieure d'Ulm
45, rue d'Ulm
F-75005 Paris

École normale supérieure de Saint-Cloud
2, avenue du Palais
F-92211 Saint-Cloud (transférée à Lyon)

École normale supérieure de jeunes filles de Jourdan
48, boulevard Jourdan
F-75014 Paris

École normale supérieure de Fontenay-aux-Roses
5, rue Boucicaut
F-92260 Fontenay-aux-Roses

École normale supérieure de l'enseignement technique (ENSET)
61, avenue du Président-Wilson
F-94000 Cachan

Grands établissements

Collège de France
11, place Marcelin-Berthelot
F-75005 Paris

Muséum national d'histoire naturelle
57, rue Cuvier
F-75231 Paris Cedex 05

École pratique des hautes études
46, rue Saint-Jacques
F-75005 Paris

École nationale des chartes
19, rue de la Sorbonne
F-75005 Paris

École nationale supérieure des bibliothécaires
17-21, boulevard du 11-Novembre-1918
F-69100 Villeurbanne

Conservatoire national des arts et métiers
292, rue Saint-Martin
F-75003 Paris

École des hautes études en sciences sociales
54, boulevard Raspail
F-75006 Paris

Observatoire de Paris
61, avenue de l'Observatoire
F-75014 Paris

Palais de la Découverte
Avenue Franklin-Roosevelt
F-75008 Paris

Institut d'études politiques
27, rue Saint-Guillaume
F-75007 Paris

Institut national des langues et civilisations orientales
2, rue Lille
F-75007 Paris

Grands établissements à l'étranger

École française de Rome
67, Piazza Farnese
I-00186 Rome

École française d'Athènes
6, rue Didot
Athènes

École française d'Extrême-Orient
22, avenue du Président-Wilson
F-75116 Paris

Casa de Velasquez
Cité universitaire
Madrid (3)

Institut français d'archéologie du Caire
37, rue El-Cheikh-Aly-Youssef
Le Caire, Égypte

Instituts d'enseignement supérieur privés: Institut catholiques

Institut catholique de Paris
21, rue d'Assas
F-75006 Paris

Institut catholique de Lille
60, boulevard Vauban
F-59000 Lille

Institut catholique de Lyon
25, rue du Plat
F-59000 Lyon

Institut catholique d'Angers
Boîte postale 858
Place André-Leroy
F-49000 Angers

Institut catholique de Toulouse
31, rue de la Fonderie
F-31000 Toulouse

Formation en sciences vétérinaires

Écoles vétérinaires sous tutelle du ministère de l'Agriculture

École nationale vétérinaire d'Alfort
7, avenue du Général-de-Gaulle
F-94704 Maisons-Alfort Cedex

École nationale vétérinaire de Lyon
Marcy l'Étoile
F-69200 Charbonnières

École nationale vétérinaire de Toulouse
23, chemin des Capelles
F-31076 Toulouse Cedex

École nationale vétérinaire de Nantes
« La Chartrerie »
Route de Gachet
F-44300 Nantes

Formation en matière d'architecture
Établissement privé sous tutelle du ministère de l'Éducation nationale
École spéciale d'architecture de Paris
254, boulevard Raspail
F-75014 Paris

Écoles d'architecture sous tutelle du ministère de l'Urbanisme, du Logement et des Transports

a) Région parisienne

Paris-Villemin
11, quai Malaquais
F-75006 Paris

Paris-Nanterre
58, avenue Salvador-Allende
F-92023 Nanterre Cedex

Petites Écuries du Roy
2, avenue de Paris
F-78000 Versailles

Paris-Conflans
11, rue du Séminaire de Conflans
F-94220 Charenton-le-Pont

58, avenue Salvador-Allende
F-92400 Nanterre

Paris-la-Villette
144, rue de Flandre
F-75019 Paris

Paris-Tolbriac
5, rue Javelot
F-75645 Paris Cedex 13

78, rue de Revéral
F-75019 Paris

Paris-la Seine
14, rue Bonaparte
F-75272 Paris Cedex 06

b) Province

Bordeaux
Domaine de Raba
Cours de la Libération
F-33405 Talence

Clermont-Ferrand
2, rue d'Enfert
F-63000 Clermont-Ferrand

Grenoble
25, rue Lesdiquières
F-38000 Grenoble

Lille
Rue Verte
Quartier de l'Hôtel-de-Ville
F-59650 Villeneuve-d'Ascq

Lyon
27, rue de Villeneuve
F-69130 Écully

Marseille
Route Léon-Lachamp
F-13009 Marseille-Luminy

Montpellier
179, rue de l'Espéron
F-34100 Montpellier

Nancy
Parc de Rémicourt
F-54600 Villiers-les-Nancy

Nantes
« La Mulotière »
Rue Massenet
F-44300 Nantes

Rennes
34, rue Hoche
F-35000 Rennes

Rouen
Aire Saint-Maclou
186, rue Martainville
F-76000 Rouen

Saint-Étienne
1, rue Buisson
F-42000 Saint-Étienne

Strasbourg
Palais du Rhin
3, place de la République
F-67000 Strasbourg

Toulouse
Chemin du Mirail
F-31300 Toulouse-en-Mirail

Établissements d'enseignement supérieur commercial
1. Établissements habilités à délivrer un diplôme revêtu du visa officiel

École des hautes études commerciales (IIEC)
Rue de la Libération
F-78350 Jouy-en-Josas

École supérieure des sciences économiques et commerciales (ESSEC)
Boîte postale 105
F-95001 Cergy

École supérieure de commerce de Paris
79, avenue de la République
F-75001 Paris

École supérieure de commerce de Lyon
Boîte postale 174
23, avenue Guy-de-Collongue
F-69130 Écully

Écoles supérieures de commerce et d'administration des entreprises (ESCAE)

18 ESCAE, à savoir:

Amiens
18, place St-Michel
F-80038 Amiens

Bordeaux
Domaine de Raba
680, cours de la Libération
F-33405 Talence Cedex

Brest
Avenue de Provence
Boîte postale 24
F-29272 Clermont-Ferrand Cedex

Dijon
29, rue Sabin
F-21000 Dijon

Le Havre
Rue Émile-Zola
F-76090 Le Havre Cedex

Lille
Avenue Gaston-Berger
F-59045 Lille Cedex

Marseille
Marseille-Luminy, case 911
F-13288 Marseille Cedex 9

Montpellier
2300, avenue des Moulins
Boîte postale 6969
F-34030 Montpellier Cedex

Nantes
8, route de la Jonelière
Boîte postale 72
F-44003 Nantes Cedex

Nice
CERAM Sophia Antipolis
Boîte postale 20
F-06561 Valbonne Cedex

Pau
74, allée de Morlaas
F-64000 Pau

Poitiers
62, rue Jean-Jaurès
Boîte postale 5
F-86001 Poitiers

Reims
59, rue Pierre-Taittinger
Boîte postale 302
F-51000 Reims Cedex

Rouen
Boulevard André-Siegfried
Boîte postale 34
F-76130 Mont-Saint-Aignan

Tours
2, rue Jules-Favre
F-37000 Tours
(autorisée à délivrer un diplôme revêtu du visa officiel à partir de 1985)

Toulouse
Hôtel Saint-Jean
2, rue de la Dalbade
F-31068 Toulouse Cedex

Grenoble
6, boulevard Gambetta
F-39028 Grenoble Cedex

Clermont-Ferrand
4, boulevard Trudaine
F-63037 Clermont-Ferrand Cedex

Académie commerciale internationale
43, rue de Tocqueville
F-75017 Paris

École supérieure libre des sciences commerciales appliquées
1, rue de Bougainville
F-75007 Paris

École des hautes études commerciales du Nord
58, rue du Port
F-59046 Lille Cedex

Institut supérieur du commerce
(à compter de 1983)
22, boulevard du Fort de Vaux
F-75017 Paris

Institut supérieur de gestion commerciale
21, rue d'Arcole
F-42000 Saint-Étienne

Institut supérieur des affaires
1, rue de la Libération
F-78350 Jouy-en-Josas

Centre de perfectionnement dans l'administration des affaires de Paris
108, boulevard Malesherbes
F-75017 Paris

Centre de perfectionnement dans l'administration des affaires de Lyon
Boîte postale 174
23, avenue Guy-de-Collongue
F-69130 Écully

Institut de commerce international
5, avenue Pierre-1er-de-Serbie
F-75016 Paris

Institut d'économie d'entreprise et de formation sociale pour ingénieurs
41, rue du Port
F-59046 Lille Cedex

Centre d'études supérieures européennes de management de Reims
Boîte postale 302
59, rue Pierre-Taittinger
F-51061 Reims Cedex

École supérieure des sciences commerciales
1, rue Lakanal
F-49045 Angers

2. Établissements non habilités à délivrer un diplôme revêtu du visa officiel

École des cadres et des affaires économiques
92, avenue de Neuilly
F-92000 Neuilly

Institut commercial supérieur
(École Bégué)
15, place de la République
F-75003 Paris

Institut de préparation à l'administration et à la gestion des entreprises
184, boulevard Saint-Germain
F-75005 Paris

Collège des sciences sociales et économiques
184, boulevard Saint-Germain
F-75005 Paris

Institut supérieur privé des sciences techniques et économie de Paris (ISTEC)
24, rue Hamelin
F-75116 Paris

École de commerce de la Chambre de commerce et d'industrie de la Savoie
Route de St-Cassin Jacob Bellecombette
F-73000 Chambéry

École de commerce et de gestion d'entreprises
Place Jules-Ferry
F-88100 Saint-Dié

École européenne des affaires
108, boulevard Malesherbes
F-75017 Paris

École franco-allemande de commerce et d'industrie (EFACI)
105, boulevard Malesherbes
F-75017 Paris

Institut de formation d'animateurs-conseillers d'entreprise de Paris (IFACE)
108, boulevard Malesherbes
F-75017 Paris

Centre d'études supérieures de la distribution de Paris
79, avenue de la République
F-75011 Paris

F

2. Survey of courses of study at higher education institutions

Universities by academic geographic region

	Santé: Médecine / Medicine	Santé: Odontologie / Dentistry	Santé: Pharmacie / Pharmacy	Santé: Éducation physique et sportive / Physical education and Sport	Droit / Law	I.E.P. / Political science	Sciences économiques / Economics	Administration économique et sociale / Economic and social administration	Lettres et arts / Humanities	Langues / Modern languages	Sciences humaines / Human sciences	Histoire/géographie / History/Geography	Sciences / Natural sciences	Formations d'ingénieurs / Engineering	Mathématiques appliquées aux sciences sociales / Applied mathematics in social sciences	Technologie IUT Secteur industrie / Technology (industry sector)	Technologie IUT Secteur tertiaire / Technology (administration, trade and commerce sectors)
Académie d'Aix Marseille																	
Université Aix-Marseille I								○	●	●	●	●	●	●	●		
Université Aix-Marseille II	●	●	●	●			●	○ □			□ ∧	●	●		●	●	●
Université Aix-Marseille III					●	▲	●	○ □		∧	∧	□ ∧	●	●	○ □	●	●
Université Avignon							○	○	○ □	○ □	□	●	○				
Académie d'Amiens																	
Université Amiens	●		●		●		●		●	●	●	●	●			●	●
Académie d'Antilles Guyane																	
Université Antilles-Guyane					●		○ □		○ □	●	∧	○ □	○ □				
Académie de Besançon																	
Université Besançon	●		●	●	○ □		●	○	●	●	●	●	●	●	○	●	●
Académie de Bordeaux																	
Université Bordeaux I					●	▲	●	○ □			∧	∧	●	●		●	●
Université Bordeaux II	●	●	●	●			○				●		○		○		
Université Bordeaux III									●	●	●	●				●	●
Université Pau et pays de l'Adour					●		●	○	○ □	●		●	●		○ □	●	●
Académie de Caen																	
Université Caen	●		●	●	●		●	○ □	●	●	●	●	●	●		●	●
Académie de Clermont-Ferrand																	
Université Clermont-Ferrand I	●	●	●		●		●									●	●
Université Clermont-Ferrand II				●			□		●	●	●	●	●	●		●	●
Académie de Corse																	
Université Corse					●		○ □		□	○ □			○ □				●
Académie de Dijon																	
Université Dijon	●		●	●	●		●	○ □	●	●	●	●	●	●		●	●

Santé = Health-services

Full course of study (First, second and third cycles)
First cycle
Second cycle
Third cycle
IEP: Institut d'études politiques

F

Universities by academic geographic region

	Santé: Médecine (Medicine)	Santé: Odontologie (Dentistry)	Santé: Pharmacie (Pharmacy)	Santé: Éducation physique et sportive (Physical education and Sport)	Droit (Law)	I.E.P. (Political science)	Sciences économiques (Economics)	Administration économique et sociale (Economic and social administration)	Lettres et arts (Humanities)	Langues (Modern languages)	Sciences humaines (Human sciences)	Histoire/géographie (History/Geography)	Sciences (Natural sciences)	Formations d'ingénieurs (Engineering)	Mathématiques appliquées aux sciences sociales (Applied mathematics in social sciences)	Technologie IUT Secteur industrie (Technology (industry sector))	Technologie IUT Secteur tertiaire (Technology (administration,
Académie de Grenoble																	
Université Grenoble I	●		●	●			○				∧	●	●	●		●	●
Université Grenoble II					●	▲	●	○ □	●	□	●		∧		○ ∧	●	●
Université Grenoble III							□		●	●	□ ∧	●					
Université Chambéry					○ □			○	●	○ □	○ □	●	●			●	●
Académie de Lille																	
Université Lille I							●				●	●	●	●		●	●
Université Lille II	●	●	●	●	●		□ ∧	○ □									●
Université Lille III								○ □	●	●	●	●	○		●	●	●
Université Valenciennes					○ □		□		○ □	○ □	∧		∧	●		●	●
Académie de Limoges																	
Université Limoges	●		●		●		●	○ □	●	●	□	●	●			●	●
Académie de Lyon																	
Université Lyon I	●	●	●	●			□ ∧				∧		●		●	●	●
Université Lyon II					●	▲	●	○ □	●	●	●	●	∧		○ □		
Université Lyon III					●		●	○ □	●	●	●	●			○		
Université Saint-Etienne	●				●		○ □	○	●	●	□	●	●			●	●
Académie de Montpellier																	
Université Montpellier I	●	●	●	●	●		●	○ □			∧						
Université Montpellier II							□ ∧						●	●		●	●
Université Montpellier III							□	●	●	●	●	●	○		●		
Université Perpignan					○ □		□ ∧	○ □	○ □	●		○	●			●	●

Health-services

- ● Full course of study (First, second and third cycles)
- ○ First cycle
- □ Second cycle
- ∧ Third cycle
- ▲ IEP: Institut d'études politiques

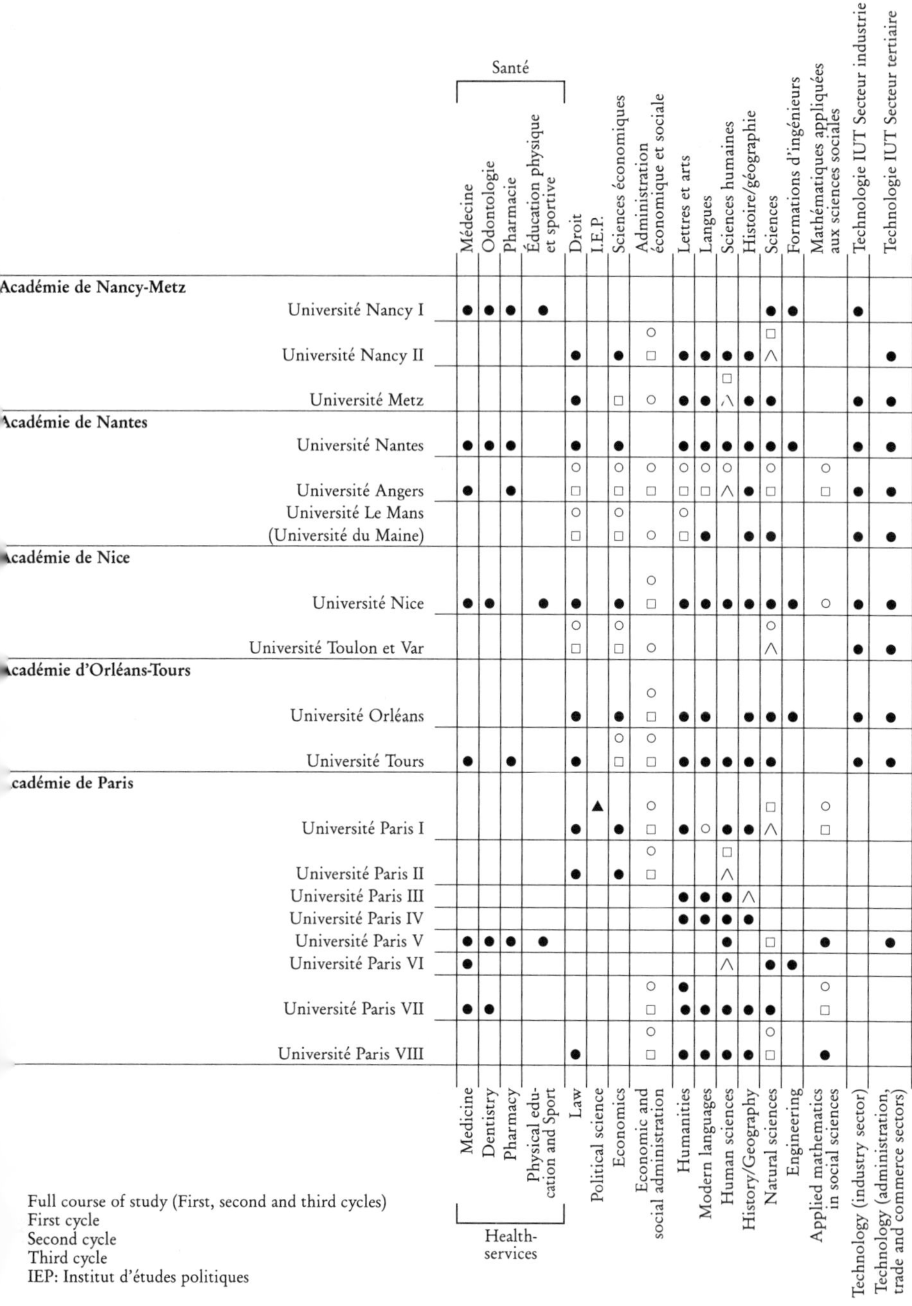

	Santé																
	Médecine	Odontologie	Pharmacie	Éducation physique et sportive	Droit	I.E.P.	Sciences économiques	Administration économique et sociale	Lettres et arts	Langues	Sciences humaines	Histoire/géographie	Sciences	Formations d'ingénieurs	Mathématiques appliquées aux sciences sociales	Technologie IUT Secteur industrie	Technologie IUT Secteur tertiaire
Académie de Nancy-Metz																	
Université Nancy I	●	●	●	●									●	●		●	
Université Nancy II					●		●	○ □	●	●	●	●	□ ∧				●
Université Metz					●		□	○	●	●	□ ∧	●	●			●	●
Académie de Nantes																	
Université Nantes	●	●	●		●		●		●	●	●	●	●	●		●	●
Université Angers	●		●		○ □		○ □	○ □	○ □	○ □	○ ∧	●	○ □		○ □	●	●
Université Le Mans (Université du Maine)					○ □		○ □	○	○ □	●		●	●			●	●
Académie de Nice																	
Université Nice	●	●		●	●		●	○ □	●	●	●	●	●	●	○	●	●
Université Toulon et Var					○ □		○ □	○					○ ∧			●	●
Académie d'Orléans-Tours																	
Université Orléans					●		●	○ □	●	●		●	●	●		●	●
Université Tours	●		●		●		○ □	○ □	●	●	●	●	●			●	●
Académie de Paris																	
Université Paris I					●	▲	●	○ □	●	○	●	●	□ ∧		○ □		
Université Paris II					●		●	○ □			□ ∧						
Université Paris III									●	●	●	∧					
Université Paris IV									●	●	●	●					
Université Paris V	●	●	●	●							●		□		●		●
Université Paris VI	●										∧		●	●			
Université Paris VII	●	●						○ □	● ●	●	●	●	●		○ □		
Université Paris VIII					●			○ □	●	●	●	●	○ □		●		
	Medicine	Dentistry	Pharmacy	Physical education and Sport	Law	Political science	Economics	Economic and social administration	Humanities	Modern languages	Human sciences	History/Geography	Natural sciences	Engineering	Applied mathematics in social sciences	Technology (industry sector)	Technology (administration, trade and commerce sectors)
	Health-services																

Full course of study (First, second and third cycles)
First cycle
Second cycle
Third cycle
IEP: Institut d'études politiques

F

Universities by academic geographic region

	Santé: Médecine (Health-services: Medicine)	Santé: Odontologie (Dentistry)	Santé: Pharmacie (Pharmacy)	Santé: Éducation physique et sportive (Physical education and Sport)	Droit (Law)	I.E.P. (Political science)	Sciences économiques (Economics)	Administration économique et sociale (Economic and social administration)	Lettres et arts (Humanities)	Langues (Modern languages)	Sciences humaines (Human sciences)	Histoire/géographie (History/Geography)	Sciences (Natural sciences)	Formations d'ingénieurs (Engineering)	Mathématiques appliquées aux sciences sociales (Applied mathematics in social sciences)	Technologie IUT Secteur industrie (Technology (industry sector))	Technologie IUT Secteur tertiaire (Technology (administration,
Académie de Paris (continued)																	
Université Paris IX					●		●				∧		□ ∧		●		
Académie de Versailles																	
Université Paris X				●	●		●	○ □	●	●	●	●			○ □	●	
Université Paris XI	●		●	●	●						∧		●	●		●	●
Académie de Créteil																	
Université Paris XII	●				●		●	○ □	●	●	○ □	●	●			●	●
Université Paris XIII					●			○ □	●	●	∧	○ □	●	●		●	●
Académie de Poitiers																	
Université Poitiers	●		●	●	●		●	○ □	●	●	●	●	●	●		●	●
Académie de Reims																	
Université Reims	●	●	●		●		○ □	○	●	●	●	●	●			●	●
Académie de Rennes																	
Université Rennes I	●	●	●		●		●	○ □			●	□	●	●		●	●
Université Rennes II				●				○ □	●	●	●	●			●		●
Université Brest	●	●			●		○ □	○ □	●	●	○	○ □	●			●	●
Académie de la Réunion																	
Université de la Réunion					○ □		○ □		○ □	●	○ □	○ □	○ □				
Académie de Rouen																	
Université Rouen	●		●		●		●		●	●	●	●	●			●	●
Université Le Havre							□	○					○			●	●

● Full course of study (First, second and third cycles)
○ First cycle
□ Second cycle
∧ Third cycle
▲ IEP: Institut d'études politiques

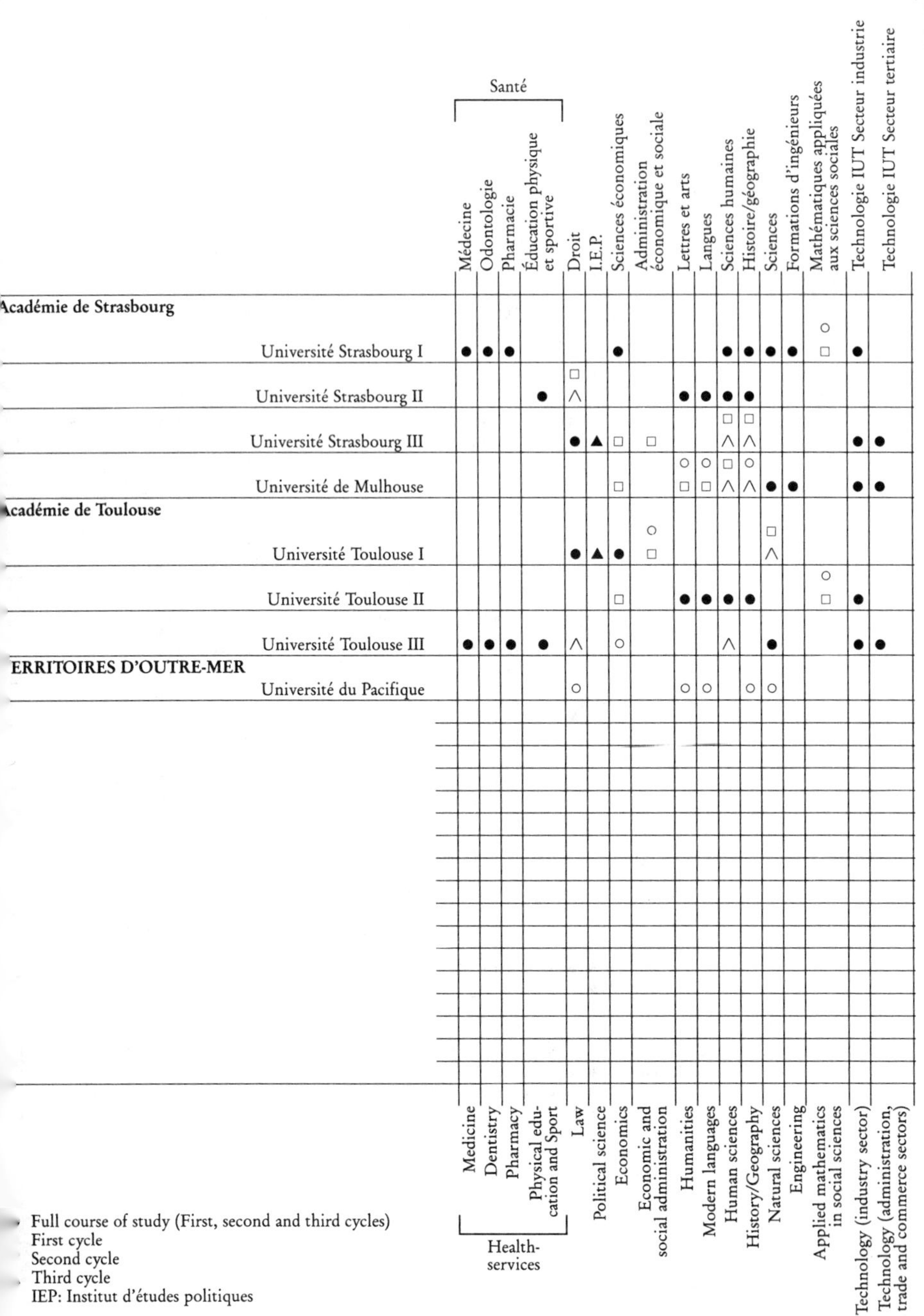

	Médecine (Medicine)	Odontologie (Dentistry)	Pharmacie (Pharmacy)	Éducation physique et sportive (Physical education and Sport)	Droit (Law)	I.E.P. (Political science)	Sciences économiques (Economics)	Administration économique et sociale (Economic and social administration)	Lettres et arts (Humanities)	Langues (Modern languages)	Sciences humaines (Human sciences)	Histoire/géographie (History/Geography)	Sciences (Natural sciences)	Formations d'ingénieurs (Engineering)	Mathématiques appliquées aux sciences sociales (Applied mathematics in social sciences)	Technologie IUT Secteur industrie (Technology (industry sector))	Technologie IUT Secteur tertiaire (Technology (administration, trade and commerce sectors))
Académie de Strasbourg																	
Université Strasbourg I	●	●	●				●				●	●	●	●	○ □	●	
Université Strasbourg II				●	□ ∧				●	●	●	●					
Université Strasbourg III					●	▲	□	□			□ ∧	□ ∧				●	●
Université de Mulhouse							□		○ □	○ □	□ ∧	○ ∧	●	●		●	●
Académie de Toulouse																	
Université Toulouse I					●	▲	●	○ □					□ ∧				
Université Toulouse II							□		●	●	●	●			○ □	●	
Université Toulouse III	●	●	●	●	∧		○				∧		●			●	●
TERRITOIRES D'OUTRE-MER																	
Université du Pacifique					○				○	○		○	○				

Santé / Health-services: Médecine, Odontologie, Pharmacie, Éducation physique et sportive

● Full course of study (First, second and third cycles)
○ First cycle
□ Second cycle
∧ Third cycle
▲ IEP: Institut d'études politiques

F

3. Correspondence courses at French universities (1988/89)

Disciplines			Aix-Marseille I	Besançon	Bordeaux III	Caen	Clermont-Fd II	Dijon	Grenoble II	Lille III	Montpellier III	Antilles-Guayane	Nantes	Nancy II
Lettres			■ ● (m)		■ ● (c, m)	■ ● (m)		■ ● ○ (m) △		■ ● (m)	■ ● ○ (m)			
Linguistique														
Langues étrangères	filières lettres et civilisations étrangères	Allemand	■				□			■ ●	■			
		Anglais	■ ●		■ ●	■ ●	■ ●			■ ●	■ ● ○			■ ● ○ △
		Espagnol			■ ●		□			■ ●	■ ●	5		
		Italien	■ ●							■				
		Polonais								■				
		Russe								■				
		Arabe			■ ●					■				
		Hébreu								■				
		Portugais									●			
		Néerlandais								■				
		Breton												
	filières langues étrangères appliquées[3]	Allemand								■ ●←	■ ● ○←			
		Anglais			■←					■ ●←	■ ● ○←			
		Espagnol			■←									
		Portugais									■ ● ○←			
		Italien	●							■				
		Néerlandais								■				
		Russe								■				
		Grec									■ ●←			
		Tchèque									■ ● ○←			
Français langue étrangère														
Musique														
Histoire des arts										■				
Philosophie			■							■				
Psychologie							■							
Sociologie														
Sciences de l'éducation														
Histoire			■ ●	■ ●	■ ●	■				■ ●	■	5		
Géographie			■ 4		■					■ 4				
Droit									■ ● ○					
Sciences économiques									■ ● ○ △					
Adm. écon. et sociale				■										
Sciences physiques			■ ●	■								5	■	■ 4
Mathématiques			■ ●	■ ●									■	■ 4
Sciences de la Nature			■											

First cycle
- □ First year
- ■ First an second year

(Studies leading to the DEUG)

Second cycle
- ● studies leading to the *licence*
- ○ studies leading to the *maîtrise*

Third cycle
- △ studies leading to the DEA
- ▲ studies leading to the DESS

(c) Classical philology (m) Romance studies: French

Note: In order to simplify this table,
- we occasionally used the same symbols for the whole range of programmes as well as for individual subject areas, leading to the DEUG diplomas, *licence* and *maîtrise;*
- the subjects mentioned do not correspond in all cases with the official definitions of the various DEUG sections; rather these subjects are classified in accordance with the diplomas of the second stage *(licence maîtrise)* into which students may be admitted via the various DEUG sections.

Further information may be obtained from the corresponding university.

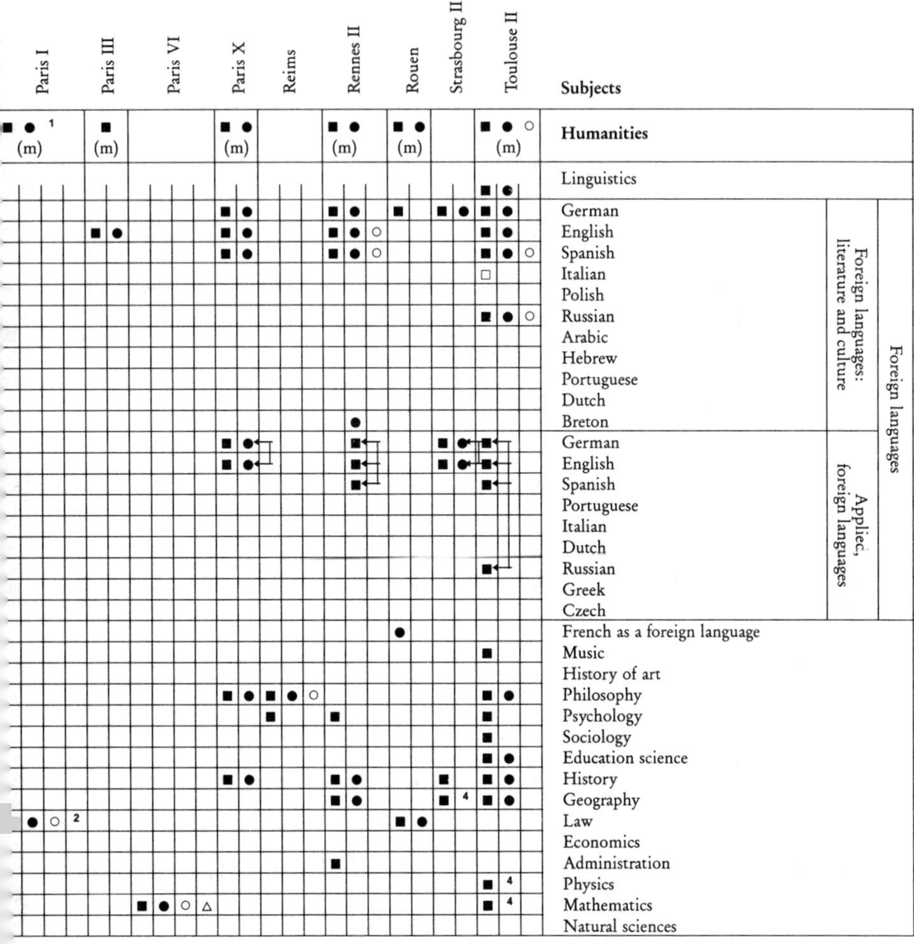

Paris I	Paris III	Paris VI	Paris X	Reims	Rennes II	Rouen	Strasbourg II	Toulouse II	Subjects		
■ ● [1] (m)	■ (m)		■ ● (m)		■ ● (m)	■ ● (m)		■ ● ○ (m)	**Humanities**		
								■ ●	Linguistics		
			■ ●		■ ●	■	■ ●	■ ●	German	Foreign languages: literature and culture	Foreign languages
	■ ●		■ ●		■ ● ○			■ ●	English		
			■ ●		■ ● ○			■ ● ○	Spanish		
								□	Italian		
									Polish		
								■ ● ○	Russian		
									Arabic		
									Hebrew		
									Portuguese		
									Dutch		
					●				Breton		
			■ ●		■		■ ●	■	German	Applied foreign languages	
			■ ●		■		■ ●	■	English		
					■			■	Spanish		
									Portuguese		
									Italian		
									Dutch		
								■	Russian		
									Greek		
									Czech		
						●			French as a foreign language		
								■	Music		
									History of art		
			■ ●	■ ● ○				■ ●	Philosophy		
				■	■			■	Psychology		
								■	Sociology		
								■ ●	Education science		
			■ ●		■ ●		■	■ ●	History		
					■ ●		■ [4]	■ ●	Geography		
● ○ [2]						■ ●			Law		
									Economics		
					■				Administration		
								■ [4]	Physics		
		■ ● ○ △						■ [4]	Mathematics		
									Natural sciences		

Lectures broadcast from the lecture hall by Radio Sorbonne.
The audio-visual centre at the University of Paris I serves correspondence students in law from the Universities of Paris I, II, V, X, XII and XIII.
The applied foreign languages programme comprises two modern foreign languages; arrows indicate the possible subject combinations.
The university leads to the corresponding DEUG degree, cooperating with another university; Aix-Marseille with ... etc.
Distance courses are transmitted via radio station on Guadaloupe and Martinique.

F

4. Student statistics

Foreign students from EC Member States
at French universities 1987/88
according to home country and subject groups

Home country / Subject-groups	Law and economic sciences		Humanities and social sciences	Natural-sciences	Health sciences			Others	IUT	Total
					Medicine	Pharmacy	Dentistry			
Belgium	124	80	298	149	164	19	13	21	22	890
Denmark	18	11	149	18	8	1	0	10	4	219
FR of Germany	298	222	2 352	316	275	14	12	140	31	3 660
Greece	353	172	1 554	372	128	17	10	49	8	2 663
Spain	163	133	1 238	355	704	15	11	90	59	2 768
Ireland	10	17	135	24	1	0	0	6	4	197
Italy	145	98	714	181	201	5	48	55	45	1 492
Luxembourg	197	177	276	142	135	8	14	14	1	964
The Netherlands	50	33	347	55	30	6	4	24	11	560
Portugal	303	258	1 243	311	154	23	6	140	196	2 634
United Kingdom	220	170	1 397	114	32	4	2	82	65	2 086
Total of all EC Member States	1 881	1 371	9 703	2 037	1 832	112	120	631	446	18 133
	17,9 %		53,5%	11,4%	11,4%			3,5%	2,5%	100 %

Classification of students from EC Member States at French universities 1987/88 according to study levels

	1st cycle	2nd cycle	3rd cycle	Total
Belgium	288	274	328	890
Denmark	150	44	25	219
FR of Germany	1537	1666	457	3660
Greece	645	675	1343	2663
Spain	979	820	969	2768
Ireland	74	87	36	197
Italy	583	411	498	1492
Luxembourg	325	459	180	964
The Netherlands	324	139	97	560
Portugal	1630	688	316	2634
United Kingdom	1301	605	180	2086
Total	7836	5868	4429	18133
	43,2%	32,4%	24,4%	100%
(For comparison: total students in France	50,3%	30,0%	17,9%	100%

Source: DEP.

F

5. Bibliography

Publications of the Bureau d'information et d'orientation (DESUP 9) at the Ministry of Education (Directorate of Higher Education). Available from the Cultural Sections of French embassies:

Les établissements d'enseignement supérieur et leurs formations. Includes information leaflets with courses of study and maps (1988/89).

Les diplômes de premier cycle dans les universités (1988/89). Accompanied by an update on degrees created by the reform.

Formations de deuxième cycle dispensées dans les universités françaises (1988/89). Includes courses of study oriented towards professional training.

La recherche à l'université Diplômes de 3ème cycle 1988/89).

Les diplômes d'études supérieures spécialisées: année 1988/89.

Instituts universitaires de technologie (1988/89).
Liste des écoles d'ingénieurs établie par la Commission des titres d'ingénieurs (1988/89).

15 subject-oriented leaflets of the collection SUP: academic year 1988/89:

Leaflet on the organization of the higher education system 'Enseignement supérieur'.
Two leaflets: 'Etudiants étrangers': Registration formalities; Higher education studies in France.
10 leaflets with information on the various courses of study and subjects at French institutions of higher education:

- law and political science
- economics and business management
- classical philology, French and art *(lettres et arts)*
- modern languages
- human sciences: psychology, sociology, philosphy, communication sciences
- education paths in human sciences: history/geography
- mathematics, information science, physics, chemistry
- biosciences, geology
- science and technology: electronics, electrical engineering, automation, mechanics
- health-system-orientated degree programmes (medicine, dentistry, pharmacy, and paramedical studies).

Two special leaflets: Engineering training in France; Correspondence courses offered by universities.

La formation des ingénieurs en France: Télé-enseignement universitaire.
Brochure on the *Pôles FIRTECH* (Formation des ingénieurs par la rechereche technologique). These are associations for the promotion of scientific and technical research in which the universities, *Grands écoles,* national research establishments and industry are involved.

ONISEP publications. Available from French embassies and sold by ONISEP (see addresses of organizations):

Bac ou pas bac (sientifiques et littéraires), que faire après? (1988).

Études de débouchés professionnels après
- un DEUG lettres et arts;
- un DEUG sciences humaines;
- un DEUG droit, sciences économiques, administration économique et sociale (1985), FF 31;
- les DEUG scientifiques (1983), FF 27.

ONISEP also publishes a series of *Cahiers* and a magazine entitled *Avenirs.* Each issue presents different professional careers and includes a section on corresponding courses of study.

Je vais en France. CNOUS, Paris, 1988, pp. 192, FF 45. General information on access to higher education and practical life in France. This brochure is addressed to foreign students and is available at French embassies. Sold by CNOUS, 8, rue Jean Calvin, F-75007 Paris.

Cours de français pour étudiants étrangers (1988/89; summer 1988). Available from French embassies and various student information bodies. Published by: Association pour la diffusion de la pensée française, 9, rue Anatole de la Forge, F-75017 Paris.

F

6. Glossary

Académie: From a geographical point of view, the *académie* generally encompasses several *départements*. At its head there is a *recteur* who is responsible for primary, secondary and higher education. He is the chancellor (*chancelier*) of the universities and as such represents the minister responsible for higher education.

Baccalauréat: Secondary school leaving certificate qualifying for admission to universities and considered the first higher education degree.

Bureau d'information et d'orientation (bureau DESUP 9): Office of Information and Orientation at the Ministry of Education. It distributes information on the entire higher education system (legal regulations, higher education facilities, degree programmes, student life). Ministry tele-information service: 36 14 code ENSUP via Minitel (a type of teletext service).

Centre d'Information Documentation Jeunesse (CIDJ): Centre for Information and Documentation on Youth Affairs.

Centre national des œuvres universitaires et scolaires (CNOUS): State authority for student welfare services.

Centre régional des œuvres universitaires et scolaires (CROUS): Student welfare services, provide various facilitations.

Concours: Examinations organized by a State board or institution on the basis of which applicants are selected for admission to courses with limited capacities (engineering, medicine, etc.).

Cycle: Period of study corresponding to a specific course level.

Diplôme approfondi de langue française (DALF): Follows the *diplôme élémentaire de langue française (DELF)*. The DALF certifies a level of French proficiency sufficient for higher education studies in France.

Diplôme d'études approfondies (DEA): Stage III degree awarded at the end of the first year of doctoral studies.

Diplôme d'études supérieures spécialisées (DESS): Career-oriented stage III degree awarded on completion of a highly specialized course of applied training and after a year of research.

Diplôme d'études universitaires générales (DEUG): Degree awarded on completion of stage I studies.

Diplôme d'études universitaires scientifiques et techniques (DEUST): Degree awarded on completion of studies that end with stage I. These courses of study are intended to provide pre-vocational training.

Diplôme national de l'enseignement supérieur: Final degree for which the same regulations apply at all higher education institutions and which grant all holders the same rights.

Diplôme universitaire de technologie (DUT): Degree awarded on completion of a course of study at university institutes of technology.

Doctorat: The doctoral degree is conferred when the candidate has successfully defended a thesis or completed a series of scholarly or scientific studies. The university that awarded the degree is mentioned after the doctoral title. The doctorate is an academic degree that attests to the holder's ability to conduct scholarly or scientific research. The *habilitation* certifies the holder's ability to direct research.

Inscription: All of the formalities that have to be complied with for admission to higher education.

Inscription administrative: Formalities to be completed at the *Service de la scolarité* of the university in question.

Inscription pédagogique: Registration for courses, seminars and practical working groups. Takes place in the secretariats of the *Unités de formation et de recherche, 'unités des universités'.*

Institut universitaire de technologie (IUT): Institute that is part of a university and provides short courses of higher education oriented primarily towards specific careers.

Licence: Degree awarded on completion of the first year of stage II studies *(deuxième cycle)* at universities.

Magistère: University degree recently established and conferred under the auspices of the Ministry of Education. It may be awarded for numerous subjects. The degree confirms the successful completion of three years of specialist study after completion of a DEUG of DUT.

Maîtrise: Degree awarded on completion of the second year of stage II studies *(deuxième cycle)* at universities.

Mastère: Degree conferred by the Conference of *Grandes écoles* and awarded after 12 months of specialist study.

F

Œuvres universitaires: Membership in the *Œuvres universitaires* makes students eligible for certain facilitations, e.g. cheap meals, accommodation in residence halls, cultural activities, etc.

Services communs universitaires d'information et d'orientation (SCUIO): Service organization providing information and orientation at universities.

F

7. Diagram of the education system

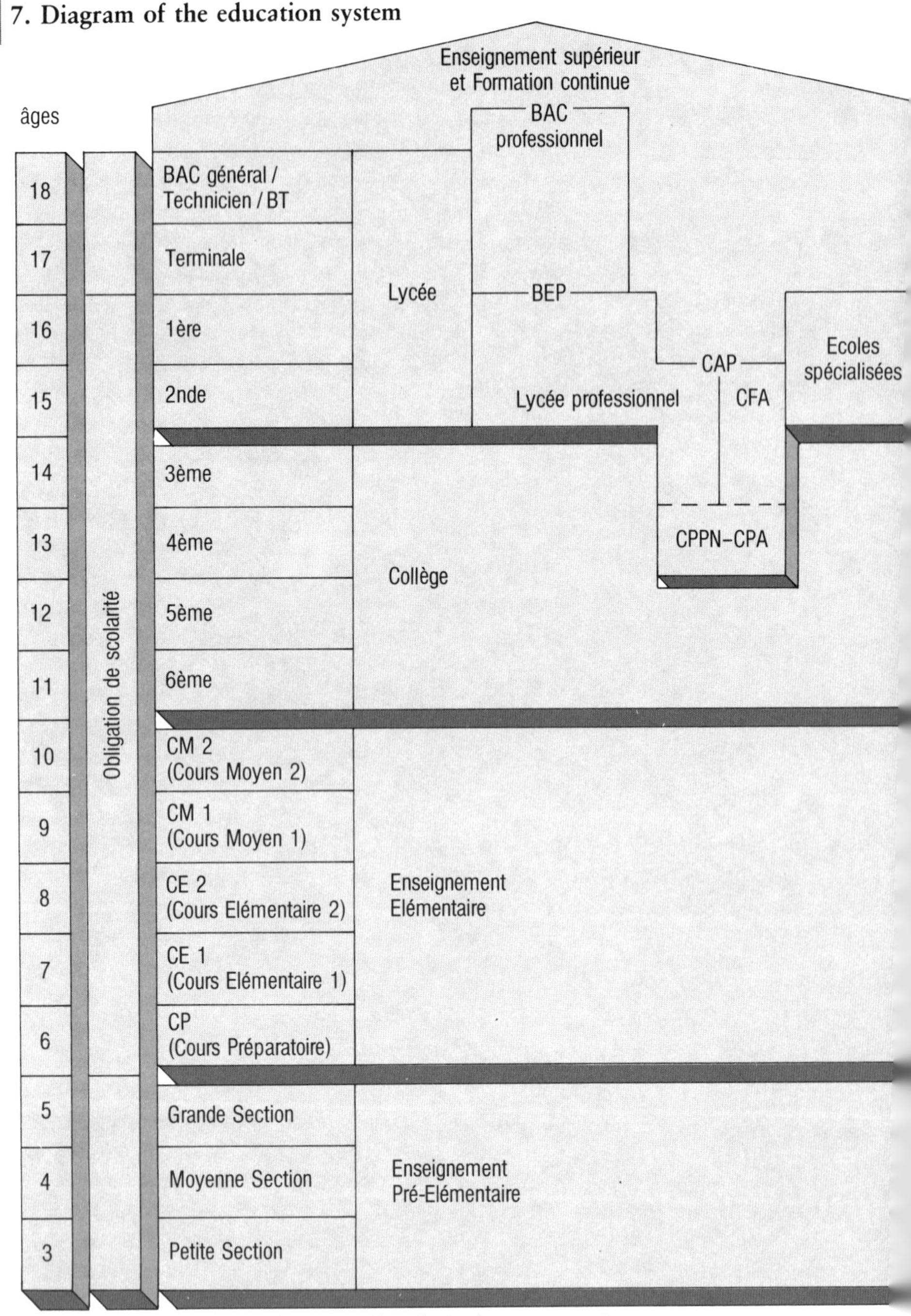
Enseignement supérieur
et Formation continue
âges
BAC
professionnel
18
BAC général /
Technicien / BT
17
Terminale
Lycée
BEP
16
1ère
CAP
Ecoles
spécialisées
15
2nde
Lycée professionnel
CFA
14
3ème
13
4ème
CPPN–CPA
Collège
12
5ème
Obligation de scolarité
11
6ème
10
CM 2
(Cours Moyen 2)
9
CM 1
(Cours Moyen 1)
8
CE 2
(Cours Elémentaire 2)
Enseignement
Elémentaire
7
CE 1
(Cours Elémentaire 1)
6
CP
(Cours Préparatoire)
5
Grande Section
4
Moyenne Section
Enseignement
Pré-Elémentaire
3
Petite Section

Explanations and translations of technical terms see facing page.

Legend

BAC: Baccalauréat — Certificate of aptitude for higher education awarded after completion of upper secondary education.
BEP: Brevet d'études professionnelles — Vocational qualification.
BT: Brevet de technicien — Technical qualification.
CAP: Certificat d'aptitude professionnelle — Vocational certificate of aptitude.
CFA: Centre de formation des apprentis — Apprentice centre.
CPA: Classe préparatoire à l'apprentissage — Preparatory classes for apprenticeship.
CPPN: Classe pré-professionnelle de niveau — Preparatory classes for the CAP
BAC général/Technicien — General/technical upper-secondary school-leaving certificate.
BAC professionnel — Vocational upper-secondary school-leaving certificate.
Collège — Secondary school.
Enseignement élémentaire — Primary school levels (preparatory, elementary [1 and 2], intermediate [1 and 2])).
Enseignement pré-élémentaire — Pre-school education(lower, middle and upper group).
Enseignement supérieur et formation continue — Higher and further education.
Lycée — Secondary school, academic branch.
Lycée professionnel — Vocational secondary school.

Degrees and diplomas at French universities

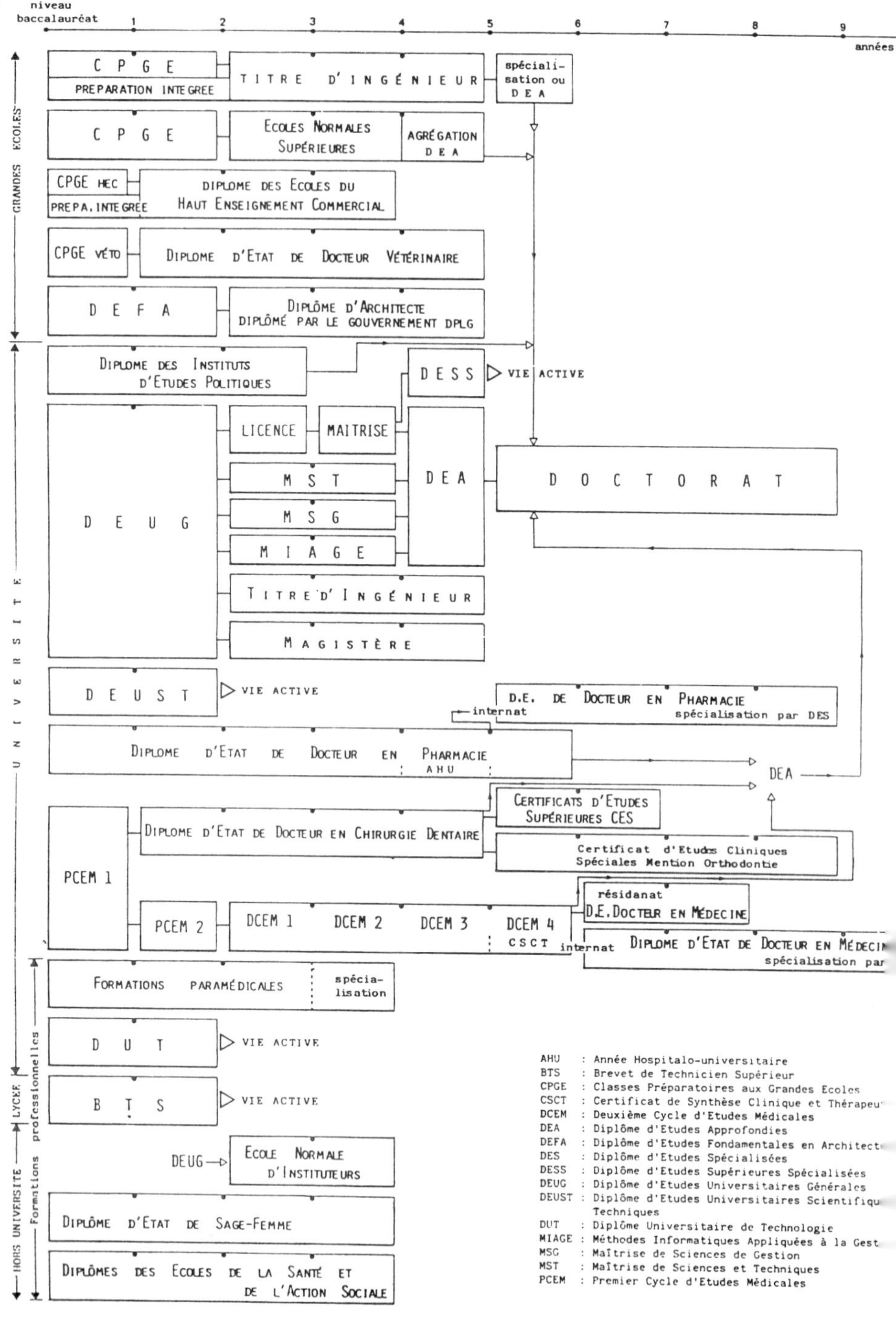

niveau baccalauréat
1
2
3
4
5
6
7
8
9
années
GRANDES ECOLES
CPGE
PREPARATION INTEGREE
TITRE D'INGÉNIEUR
spécialisation ou DEA
CPGE
ECOLES NORMALES SUPÉRIEURES
AGRÉGATION DEA
CPGE HEC
PREPA. INTEGREE
DIPLOME DES ECOLES DU HAUT ENSEIGNEMENT COMMERCIAL
CPGE VÉTO
DIPLOME D'ETAT DE DOCTEUR VÉTÉRINAIRE
DEFA
DIPLÔME D'ARCHITECTE DIPLÔMÉ PAR LE GOUVERNEMENT DPLG
UNIVERSITE
DIPLOME DES INSTITUTS D'ETUDES POLITIQUES
DESS
VIE ACTIVE
DEUG
LICENCE
MAITRISE
MST
MSG
MIAGE
DEA
DOCTORAT
TITRE D'INGÉNIEUR
MAGISTÈRE
DEUST
VIE ACTIVE
D.E. DE DOCTEUR EN PHARMACIE
spécialisation par DES
internat
DIPLOME D'ETAT DE DOCTEUR EN PHARMACIE
AHU
DEA
CERTIFICATS D'ETUDES SUPÉRIEURES CES
DIPLOME D'ETAT DE DOCTEUR EN CHIRURGIE DENTAIRE
Certificat d'Etudes Cliniques Spéciales Mention Orthodontie
PCEM 1
résidanat
D.E. DOCTEUR EN MÉDECINE
PCEM 2
DCEM 1
DCEM 2
DCEM 3
DCEM 4
CSCT
internat
DIPLOME D'ETAT DE DOCTEUR EN MÉDECIN
spécialisation par
HORS UNIVERSITE
LYCEE
Formations professionnelles
FORMATIONS PARAMÉDICALES
spécialisation
DUT
VIE ACTIVE
BTS
VIE ACTIVE
DEUG
ECOLE NORMALE D'INSTITUTEURS
DIPLÔME D'ETAT DE SAGE-FEMME
DIPLÔMES DES ECOLES DE LA SANTÉ ET DE L'ACTION SOCIALE
AHU : Année Hospitalo-universitaire
BTS : Brevet de Technicien Supérieur
CPGE : Classes Préparatoires aux Grandes Ecoles
CSCT : Certificat de Synthèse Clinique et Thérapeu
DCEM : Deuxième Cycle d'Etudes Médicales
DEA : Diplôme d'Etudes Approfondies
DEFA : Diplôme d'Etudes Fondamentales en Architect
DES : Diplôme d'Etudes Spécialisées
DESS : Diplôme d'Etudes Supérieures Spécialisées
DEUG : Diplôme d'Etudes Universitaires Générales
DEUST : Diplôme d'Etudes Universitaires Scientifiqu Techniques
DUT : Diplôme Universitaire de Technologie
MIAGE : Méthodes Informatiques Appliquées à la Gest
MSG : Maîtrise de Sciences de Gestion
MST : Maîtrise de Sciences et Techniques
PCEM : Premier Cycle d'Etudes Médicales

Ireland

Organization of higher education

Higher education in Ireland is provided mainly by universities, technological colleges and colleges of education but also by a number of other institutions providing specialized training in such fields an art and design, medicine, theology, music and law. By far the greater proportion of education is provided in institutions supported very substantially by the State (e.g. universities and technological colleges receive over 68% of their income from this source) although State subvention as a percentage of college income has been decreasing over the past few years.

Types of higher education institutions

The major types of higher education institutions are dealt with below.

Universities

There are three universities in Ireland — the National University of Ireland, Dublin University and the Pontifical University, which is outside the system of State-funded higher education.

The National University of Ireland (NUI) has three constituent colleges (University College, Dublin, University College, Cork and University College, Galway).

The National University also has five 'recognized' colleges, St Patrick's College, Maynooth, The Royal College of Surgeons in Ireland and three other colleges, two of which specialize in the education of primary school teachers and one in the training of teachers of home economics. Courses and teachers at these colleges are 'recognized' by the University and degrees are awarded by the University to students successfully completing recognized courses.

Trinity College, Dublin (TCD), is the only college of Dublin University. Three colleges of education which specialize in the education of primary school teachers and the college which specializes in the education of teachers of home economics are associated with Trinity College.

The University of Dublin is also the awarding body for a number of degree-level courses offered in the colleges of the Dublin Institute of Technology (see below).

The Pontifical University is located on the campus of St Patrick's College, Maynooth. It confers degrees in Canon Law, Philosophy and Theology, and also runs courses in Mission Studies and Religious Studies.

In addition to the universities, higher education is provided by the National Institute for Higher Education, Limerick; the National Institute for Higher Education, Dublin; colleges of technology and other colleges run by various local Vocational Education Committees; Regional Technical Colleges; teacher training colleges and a small number of institutions providing specialized courses of study.

National Institutes for Higher Education

The National Institutes for Higher Education (NIHEs) at Dublin and Limerick, which provide education oriented towards science and business studies, engineering and design, computer studies, communications studies and other fields, and incorporate a strong element of work/outside experience were granted university status in early 1989.

They are now known as Dublin City University and the University of Limerick. Dublin City University is also the national centre for distance education. The first diploma course available through distance education, in Information Technology, commenced in 1986/87.

Higher education at non-university institutions

Regional Technical Colleges (RTCs) at Athlone, Carlow, Cork, Dundalk, Galway, Letterkenny, Sligo, Tralee and Waterford provide third-level technological and commercial courses. The courses range from one-year certificate programmes to courses of more than three years' duration leading to a degree-level or professional award. The main awarding body is the NCEA.

In the cities of Dublin, Cork and Limerick, colleges are operated by Vocational Education Committees which provide third-level courses in applied science, architecture, engineering, quantity surveying, hotel and catering management and commercial studies of various kinds. Many of the courses lead to qualifications of professional institutes, (see 'Professional training' in the Glossary) and some of the courses in the Dublin Institute of Technology (DIT) lead to a degree award from the University of Dublin (Trinity College). Degree awards for other colleges are made by the NCEA. In these colleges, as in the RTCs, there is also a wide range of certificate and diploma programmes.

The Royal College of Surgeons in Ireland is a medical school which provides both undergraduate and postgraduate training for doctors, postgraduate training for dentists and courses for nurses. Its qualifications have acceptance in many countries and the majority of its students are from outside Ireland.

The Honourable Society of King's Inns and the Incorporated Law Society are responsible for professional training in law. The courses run by the Honourable Society of King's Inns lead to the professional qualification of barrister-at-law, while the courses run by the Incorporated Law Society lead to qualifications enabling the holder to practise as a solicitor.

The National College of Art and Design provides courses at degree and diploma level. The National College of Industrial Relations is an independent institution which specializes in the field of business and industrial relations. A four-year diploma in hotel management is offered at the Shannon International Hotel School. Other specialist colleges are listed in the addresses in Appendix 1.

Teacher education

There are five colleges in the State which train teachers for primary schools. Two are 'recognized colleges' of the National University of Ireland and three are associated with Trinity College, Dublin. The courses lead to degrees and to qualifications as a national or primary teacher. Secondary teachers mostly qualify by taking a one-year diploma course in education following the primary degree.

The Thomond College of Education, Limerick, provides courses for teachers of specialist subjects at secondary level. These include physical education, wood and building technology, metal and engineering sciences, business studies and general and rural science.

Courses for teachers of home economics, art and music are provided at other specialist colleges in Ireland.

Student statistics

In 1986/87, there were just under 57 000 full-time students in higher education in Ireland. The participation ratio of the relevant age-group in full-time education is 25%.

As in most other European countries the growth in higher education was low until after the Second World War. The number of students in higher education attending non-university institutions has almost quadrupled since their foundation and is now over 29 600.

Of the 56 911 full-time students in 1986/87, 27 270 were in the university institutions, 2 748 were in teacher training colleges and 26 893 were in other institutions. Of the 27 270 university students 1 603 (6%) were from outside the Republic: 484 were from Northern Ireland, 125 from the rest of the United Kingdom and 162 from other EC countries – thus 48% of all foreign students were from EC Member States.

Of the remaining 832, 3% were from other European countries, 36% from Asia, 38 % from North America, 21% from Africa, with the remaining 1% from South America and Oceania.

Exact figures for the other colleges are not available for 1986/87, but in general the percentage of students from outside the Republic is very small, except in the Royal College of Surgeons in Ireland where of the 863 students, 604 (70%) were from outside the State, 59 (10%) of these being from other EC countries.

Organization and validation of courses

The academic year in Irish colleges normally begins in October, in some cases in September.

It is generally organized into three terms, with annual examinations being held in June or, in some cases, in September.

The range of faculties, departments and subjects varies from college to college (see Appendices).

At the colleges of the National University of Ireland, the duration of study for the first degree, the Bachelor's degree, in Arts and Humanities, the Social Sciences, Law and Commerce/Business Studies, is (with some exceptions) three years. Cognate degrees would generally be of four years' duration at Trinity College.

First-degree courses in Engineering, Agriculture and Science generally take four years; five years in the case of Architecture and Veterinary Medicine, five or six years for Dentistry. Six years are required for Medicine.

The first postgraduate degree, the Master's degree, requires another one to three years of study and can be taken either by thesis or by examination and minor thesis. A further two years at least are normally required for the degree of Doctor of Philosophy (Ph.D.) and four years for a higher Doctorate, such as Doctor of Science (D.Sc.) or Doctor of Literature (D. Litt.).

About a third of primary degree graduates proceed to further study, which includes postgraduate degrees, teacher training and other professional training.

The programmes of study offered in the institutions other than universities may include a period of work outside the universities as part of the course of study. The majority of courses outside the universities are at undergraduate level; certificate courses generally last for two years and diploma courses take four years, except in some Colleges of Education for primary school teachers where they last three years.

The NCEA provides formal recognition and validation on a national basis for a large proportion of courses outside the universities and confers degrees, diplomas and certificates on students who have successfully completed such courses.

For students wishing to study in the Republic of Ireland, the Irish embassies may be an initial source of information.

Admission and registration

Initial information

It is advisable to have begun the process of collecting information one year before the date on which the student proposes to begin a course of study. This is particularly important in the case of those colleges listed in the next paragraph, applications for admission to which must be made through the Central Applications Office (CAO).

Students seeking information on how to make application for entry to undergraduate degree or diploma courses at University College, Dublin, University College, Cork, University College, Galway, Trinity College, Dublin, St Patrick's College, Maynooth, the National Institute for Higher Education, Dublin, and the National Institute for Higher Education, Limerick, the degree courses in the colleges of the Dublin Institute of Technology, or the degree courses in Art and Design Education at the National College of Art and Design, should write to the CAO. Application to various colleges is made on a single form, with colleges listed in order of preference — this eliminates duplication of applications.

The CAO will supply general information on courses available. More specific or detailed information can be obtained from the calendar or prospectus of the appropriate college. Information regarding matriculation should be sought directly from the colleges (see 'Entry requirements' below).

Applications for admission to courses other than degree programmes in the Dublin Institute of Technology should be made to the DIT Admissions Office.

In the case of all other colleges and courses intending students should write directly to the appropriate college requesting general information on the subject area(s) in which they are interested.

Foreign students may apply for admission to Trinity College, Dublin for one year or one term. Inquiries should be made to the Admissions Office of the College. Information about short-term studies at the other institutions can be obtained directly from the institution concerned.

Entry requirements

The main entry requirement for higher education is the Leaving Certificate, which is taken after 13 years of schooling, eight in primary (junior or first-level) school, then three in the junior cycle of secondary school and two or three in the senior cycle. Most pupils are aged four on entering, 17 or 18 on leaving school. Because of competition for places, a student leaving school in Ireland and possessing the academic qualifications for university entry is not automatically entitled to a place at university. EC and other overseas students will be accepted on the basis of the secondary school-leaving examination entitling them to access to higher education in their own country. Specific subjects will be required for certain faculties. It is difficult to make a general statement on the necessary level of performance, as individual applications will be assessed by colleges.

The academic requirements for entry to colleges other than university colleges vary. Many have entry standards which are almost identical with those of the university colleges. In each case it is advisable to seek detailed information on entry requirements from the Admissions Officer at the appropriate college. As with the universities, students will be exempted from entrance examinations on the basis of satisfactory performance at equivalent examinations.

In general, prospective undergraduate students at the university colleges are accepted on the basis of examination performance and are not interviewed by the college in question. However, many of the other colleges do interview students before accepting them. It is advisable, when asking for information, to inquire whether an interview will be required before acceptance.

The closing date for the acceptance of applications from students from EC countries for entrance to the colleges which are members of the CAO is 1 February of the year of admission. The procedures to be followed will be specified in the literature which the CAO supplies to prospective students.

To obtain entry to a postgraduate programme, students must be recommended by the professor in the area of study proposed in the institution where they have studied, and be accepted by the relevant faculty. For most courses, they must have a first-class or second-class (grade I) honours degree though students with a lower grade of honours in their degree may also be accepted (see Glossary under 'Honours degree'). In this case, the student may be required to take a qualifying examination. Students are advised to apply to the registrar of the college in question before the end of the year prior to the year of admission.

When seeking admission to postgraduate courses, students should write directly to the registrar of the college concerned. In the case of Trinity College, application should be made to the Dean of Graduate Studies.

Closing dates for application vary, but will in any case be specified in the college calendar or prospectus. The literature supplied with the application form(s) will also specify what the college requires in terms of evidence of previous qualifications, courses of study, etc.

Recognition of foreign certificates and degrees

The National Academic Recognition Information Centre (NARIC) was established in June 1984 and is now located in the Higher Education Authority. The Centre acts as an information point supplying general information to foreign students. Decisions on the recognition of foreign qualifications are not taken by the Centre — they are dealt with on an individual basis by the college authorities after consultation with the faculty within the college concerned.

Precise information should be given by the applicant on the qualifications held, the content and length of course followed in achieving the qualification, and the marks obtained. Particulars should also be given of the institution or body which awarded the qualification. The course which the applicant wishes to follow in the Irish institution should be clearly indicated.

There are no bilateral or multilateral agreements between Ireland and the other EC countries on the recognition of foreign qualifications.

There are also no agreements as regards the admission of young people who have been at school in a host country and who return to study at third level in Ireland: this is a matter for the receiving institution.

Limitations

The institutions reserve the right to restrict the number of students entering first-year undergraduate courses. There tend to be more applicants than places for most courses. Where it is found necessary to limit the number of entrants to a course, places are allocated in order of merit on the basis of qualifications in the final secondary school-leaving examination.

There is no uniform policy on the admission of overseas applicants to colleges of higher education, either at the universities or elsewhere. In general a student from outside the Republic is more likely to be accepted for a degree course in arts (excluding social science), science, agricultural science and commerce/business studies.

Certain courses at colleges other than the universities also have limited entry. This is particularly true in the colleges of education, which also have a requirement for proficiency in the Irish language.

Entry examinations

Colleges differ in whether they require entrance examinations, tests or interviews from prospective students from outside the Republic. The university colleges do not have entrance examinations or tests and will generally accept foreign students on the appropriate evidence supplied from the student's country of origin. Many of the other colleges do have entrance examinations or interviews and students are advised to clarify this question with the college to which they intend to apply.

Competence in English, written and oral, is part of the entry requirement for most colleges, and a college may decide to test a prospective student's competence in English.

Application and registration

Applications to institutions of higher education must all be made on the official application form. These should be obtained well in advance from the CAO or the office to which application must be made.

Students are advised to inquire, when applying, as to how soon they will be informed of acceptance or rejection of their application.

Registration normally takes place within two weeks of the opening of the academic year. The calendar or handbook of the college will inform students of what documents they should have when registering: generally, these include birth certificate or passport, letter of admission to the college/course and receipt for fees paid. Some colleges make provision for late registration, but in the university colleges students generally cannot be registered, or attend any course, until they have paid the prescribed fees or any other fees required to be paid when registering.

In a number of colleges a student is required to pay only half the annual fees before registration while the remaining instalment is paid in the second term soon after Christmas. The method of payment of fees will normally be specified in the literature or information which a college supplies to students when they have been accepted. Students are advised to clarify, at the time of registration or before, what extra fees (e.g. examination fees) may have to be paid during the course of the year.

Tuition fees

All Irish institutions of higher education charge fees to students. Since the commencement of the academic year 1980/81, these fees are the same for students from all Member States of the European Community as for home students.

The items for which fees are charged include tuition, registration costs, capitation (i.e. membership of students' union and certain clubs and societies), examinations and conferring of degrees and diplomas. As mentioned in the section above on application and registration, colleges differ in the method in which fees are collected.

Fees vary according to the course of study, ranging between approximately IRL 1 000 for arts or business studies and IRL 1 500 for courses in science/medicine at the university colleges. In the case of some professional courses (mainly medical courses), fees for later years were slightly higher. In recent years fee levels have been revised annually and fees for subsequent years will be higher than those quoted above, which apply to 1988/89.

Fees for the first year of postgraduate degree courses in the academic year 1988/89 were, at minimum, IRL 500 to 600 in arts or commerce/business studies, and from IRL 700 in science. In general, for postgraduate courses, fees in the second or subsequent years are lower.

In the colleges of technology and regional technical colleges, fees tended to be considerably lower in the academic year 1988/89. Fees at the new universities at Dublin and Limerick ranged between approximately IRL 1 000 and IRL 1 500 for degree courses. Fees at the National College of Art and Design were IRL 868 per annum for first-year courses. The tuition fees at the Royal College of Surgeons in Ireland in 1988/89 were IRL 11 000. As with the university colleges, fees are adjusted annually and details are normally specified in the literature which colleges will send to interested applicants.

Knowledge of the language of instruction, language courses and other courses

English is required for all courses of study in colleges of higher education in Ireland. Competence in English, oral and written, is part of the entry requirement for most colleges.

In general, colleges do not make special arrangements for the attainment of competence in English by overseas students. In Dublin and some of the larger towns where colleges of higher education are situated, courses in English are organized, generally by specialized language schools, recognized by the Department of Education, and a list of these schools is available from Dublin Tourism.

At University College, Galway, a number of degree courses can be taken through the medium of Irish, and full-time courses taught in Irish are also offered in some other colleges.

Each year, normally in the month of July, the university colleges organize summer schools for visiting students and interested adults of all nationalities. The summer school programmes aim to introduce student visitors to the Irish people and to Ireland. Lectures, tutorial classes and discussions are given by university teaching staff and guest lecturers and deal with Irish art, folklore, economics, history, literature and politics. In addition to lectures and discussions, there are excursions and visits to places of historical and artistic interest and various entertainments are organized.

A limited number of scholarships are awarded by the committees organizing these summer schools. Details of the summer schools should be obtained directly from the college concerned.

Financial assistance and scholarships

The higher education grants scheme in the Republic is confined to students whose parents are ordinarily resident in the Republic of Ireland. Eligibility for this scheme is based on performance in the national school-leaving certificate examination and also on parents' means. A scholarship scheme is operated on a similar basis by the Vocational Education Committees for students pursuing courses in technological institutions of higher education.

Most Irish colleges offer some scholarships and prizes both on entry into the college and for students already in the college. The majority of these are confined to Irish citizens, but non-nationals are eligible to compete for some scholarships offered to students who are already studying in the college concerned. Details of these scholarships are normally provided in the literature sent to applicants.

The Irish Government has a number of arrangements for scholarships of interest exclusively to students from other EC countries. Details of these scholarships can be obtained from the responsible authorities in the countries concerned or in Ireland from the Department of Education (for address see Appendix 1).

Entry and residence regulations

Entry and residence regulations in Ireland vary according to the person's country of origin.

Students who are nationals of another EC Member State and who enter the Republic from any place (other than the United Kingdom) must present themselves to the Immigration Officer at the port or airport of entry. The following documents should be presented to the Immigration Officer:

1. valid passport;
2. evidence of acceptance as a student at a college of higher education;
3. evidence of the ability to maintain themselves for the period of study. (Sufficient evidence, for example, would be a bank statement or a letter from a parent or guardian.)

Students from an EC country who enter the Republic of Ireland from the United Kingdom do not have to report to the immigration authorities at the port or airport of entry.

A student born in the United Kingdom is not required either to register as an alien or to apply to the immigration authorities to enter or remain in the State.

Within one month, students from other EC countries must report to the Registration Officer in the District in which they are residing. In Dublin this is the Aliens Registrations Officer, Harcourt Square, Dublin 2. In other areas students have to report within three months to the local Superintendent of the Garde Síochána.

The documents which are required for registration are the same as those which must be presented to the Immigration Officer. Four passport-sized photographs will also be required.

Students are advised to seek the assistance of the students' union at the appropriate college in registering as an alien.

IRL

Social aspects

Social security and health insurance

Health services in the Republic are administered by eight regional health boards. A person who is unable, without undue hardship, to provide general practitioner services for himself and his dependants has full eligibility for health services. Full eligibility entitles holders of a medical card to the services of a doctor of their choice (provided the doctor is in the scheme and agrees to accept the patient), free hospital treatment in public wards, specialist services at outpatient departments, prescribed medicines, dental treatment and various other services. A student from an EC country coming to Ireland who is covered by social insurance in his home country may have full eligibility under the Irish General Medical Services. Students are advised to make arrangements with the health administration in their home country to ensure that appropriate benefits can be carried over and appropriate documentation provided. Students from countries other than EC countries are assessed for eligibility on the same basis as Irish students and their family circumstances are taken into account.

The relevant application forms will normally be made available to the student on registration at a college. Students wishing to register in the health scheme have to apply to the appropriate regional health board from which they will obtain their medical cards. The offices of the students' union in a college will advise students encountering difficulties in registering under the scheme, and students are recommended to obtain the advice of the union on their entitlements.

Advisory services

Formal arrangements for counselling vary between colleges and depend to some extent on the size of a college. Some of the university colleges have a health service for students and provide medical and psychiatric assistance. The facilities provided by colleges are not intended in any way to supersede those of a student's own physician or the services to which a student may be entitled under the State medical scheme.

In some colleges students are assigned to one or more tutors in the subjects which they are studying and tutors will advise on academic and curricular matters. Informally, many tutors also act as counsellors on personal matters. In Trinity College the tutor is specifically not a supervisor of studies but represents the students before the college authorities and gives confidential advice on matters affecting the student.

In most colleges there are also a number of chaplains of different denominations who provide a counselling service. In the larger colleges the students' union has a full-time Welfare Officer, one of whose functions is to supply information to students wishing to avail themselves of counselling agencies or services.

The universities and some other colleges have Careers and Appointments Offices or equivalent, which inform and advise students about career opportunities and, where possible, help them obtain employment when they leave the college. In other colleges this function is sometimes performed informally by tutors.

Student employment

There is no organization catering for student employment in any formal way. In certain colleges student organizations run bureaux which provide information on possible opportunities. Some colleges assist students in obtaining vacation employment relevant to a professional course of studies. The National Institutes for Higher Education run cooperative education programmes whereby students taking diploma and degree courses are placed in paid employment outside the Institute as part of their course of study. Similar industrial internship programmes are in operation in some of the Regional Technical Colleges.

Student organizations

Most colleges have a wide range of student organizations and societies which receive financial assistance from college resources. These societies cater for academic, cultural, political and other general social activities. Sporting activities are generally well catered for, especially in the larger colleges.

All colleges of higher education have a students' union. The main function of the students' union at a college is to represent student interests in matters relating to academic, cultural and social activities at the college, to provide services in terms of travel and other facilities, to coordinate information on residential accommodation and to represent student interest and opinion at national level. The range of activities and services provided for students varies with the size of colleges. Both the college authorities and the students' union in the larger colleges produce a handbook at the beginning of the academic year which is a guide to many of the facilities available to students. This can normally be obtained at the time of registration. In larger colleges it is also common around the date of registration for an exhibition to be held indicating the various societies and organizations which students may wish to join or whose services they may wish to use.

The Irish Council for Overseas Students provides a full-time advisory service for students from outside the Republic.

It also makes specific arrangements with colleges and other training bodies for the provision of services including:

(i) reception and orientation courses;
(ii) accommodation and welfare services;
(iii) social and cultural programmes.

Cost of living

It was estimated by the Union of Students in Ireland that the cost of living for an Irish student for a period of nine months in 1987 amounted to IRL 300 per month.

This figure does not include student fees, and may be higher in urban areas.

Accommodation

Most students do not reside on campus in Irish colleges, although accommodation is available to a limited extent in some institutions. Rooms on campus tend to be more expensive than those off campus: the average for a room in college would be about IRL 35 per week, for a flat or room outside, from IRL 20 upwards. In some colleges, those who are not living at home are required to live in accommodation recognized by the college as suitable for students. Most colleges assist students in obtaining accommodation and keep lists of recognized hostels, flats or lodgings. In larger colleges this is under the charge of the Officer or Dean of Residence. A student wishing to enquire about residential accommodation should write to the Officer or Dean of Residence at the college in which the student is to be registered. In colleges where there is no Dean or Officer of Residence, the chaplains normally provide this service.

The students' union in the larger colleges provides information on flats and apartments and will also provide details on tenant rights and the legal aspects of renting accommodation.

Services for students

International students' identity cards are available in most colleges from the office of the students' union. Students with this card can obtain discounts in many stores and in a number of restaurants. Lists are compiled of the stores and restaurants where discounts can be obtained and these are normally obtainable at the students' union office. The cost of the card is IRL 5.

The international student identity card also confers eligibility for student flights operated by USIT, the student travel company, and other member organizations of the International Student Travel Conference.

If the international student identity card is endorsed by Córas Iompair Éireann (CIE), the national transport company, a student is entitled to a 50% reduction on the single adult fare on buses and trains travelling between towns and cities. A monthly commuter ticket, price IRL 27, is available to students in the Dublin area. The card can be endorsed at the head office of USIT or its branches in college centres throughout Ireland for a fee of IRL 6.

Facilities for disabled students

All university colleges and some of the other colleges in Ireland offer special facilities for handicapped students. Further information can be obtained from the college in which the respective student intends to study.

Appendices

1. Addresses

Irish embassies in EC countries

Belgium
Rue du Luxembourg 19
B-1040 Brussel

Denmark
Østbanegade 21
DK-2100 København

Federal Republic of Germany
Godesberger Allee 119
D-5300 Bonn

Greece
7 Leoforos Vasileos
Konstantinou
GR-10674 Athina

Spain
Claudio Coello 73
E-28001 Madrid 1

France
12, avenue Foch
F-75116 Paris

Italy
Largo del Nazareno 3
I-00187 Roma

Luxembourg
28, route d'Arlon
L-1140 Luxembourg

The Netherlands
9 Dr Kuyperstraat
2514 BA 's-Gravenhage

Portugal
Rua da Imprensa
(a Estrela) 1–4
P-1200 Lisboa

United Kingdom
17 Grosvenor Place
London SW1X 7HR

Departments and organizations

Department of Education
Marlborough Street
Dublin 1
☎ (01) 73 47 00

Higher Education Authority
21 Fitzwilliam Square
Dublin 2
☎ (01) 61 27 48

Central Applications Office
Tower House
Eglinton Street
Galway
☎ (091) 633 18

Dublin Institute of Technology
Admissions Office
14 Upper Mount Street
Dublin 2
☎ (01) 76 65 84

Irish Council for Overseas Students
41 Morehampton Rd
Dublin 4
☎ (01) 60 52 33

National Council for Educational Awards
26 Mountjoy Square
Dublin 1
☎ (01) 74 15 26

Union of Students in Ireland
16 North Great George's St
Dublin 1
☎ (01) 78 63 66

Union of Students in Ireland Travel (USIT)
19 Aston Quay
Dublin 2
☎ (01) 77 81 17

Dublin Tourism
14 Upper O'Connell Street
Dublin 1
☎ (01) 74 77 33

National Academic Recognition Information Centre
Higher Education Authority
21 Fitzwilliam Square
Dublin 2
☎ (01) 61 27 48

National Grant Awarding Agency (Erasmus)
Higher Education Authority
21 Fitzwilliam Square
Dublin 2
☎ (01) 61 27 48

Institutions of higher education

Universities and University colleges

University of Dublin
Trinity College
Dublin 2

National University of Ireland
49 Merrion Square
Dublin 2

University College
Belfield
Dublin 4

University College
Cork

University College
Galway

St Patrick's College
Maynooth
Co. Kildare

National Institutes for Higher Education

Dublin City University (DCU)
Glasnevin
Dublin 9

University of Limerick
Plassey Technological Park
Limerick

Regional Technical Colleges and other technological institutions

Regional Technical College
Dublin Road
Athlone
Co.Westmeath

Regional Technical College
Kilkenny Road
Carlow

IRL

Regional Technical College
Rossa Avenue
Bishopstown
Cork

Regional Technical College
Dundalk
Co. Louth

Regional Technical College
Dublin Road
Galway

Donogh O'Malley Regional Technical College
Port Road
Letterkenny
Co. Donegal

Regional Technical College
Ballinode
Sligo

Regional Technical College
Clash
Tralee
Co. Kerry

Regional Technical College
Cork Road
Waterford

Limerick College of Art, Commerce and Technology
Moylish Park
Limerick

Dublin Institute of Technology

College of Technology
Bolton Street
Dublin 1

College of Technology
Kevin Street
Dublin 8

College of Commerce
Rathmines
Dublin 6

College of Marketing and Design
40-45 Mountjoy Square
Dublin 1

College of Music
Chatham Row
Dublin 2

Dublin College of Catering
Cathal Brugha Street
Dublin 1

Colleges of education

Thomond College of Education
Castletroy
Limerick

St Patrick's College of Education
Drumcondra
Dublin 9

Mary Immaculate College of Education
South Circular Road
Limerick

Church of Ireland College of Education
96 Upper Rathmines Road
Dublin 6

St Mary's Training College of Education
Marino
Dublin 9

St Catherine's College of Home Economics
Sion Hill
Blackrock
Co. Dublin

Froebel College
Sion Hill
Blackrock
Co. Dublin

St Angela's College of Education for Home Economics
Lough Gill
Sligo

Mater Dei Institute of Education
Clonliffe Road
Dublin 3

Institute of Religious Education
Mount Oliver
Dundalk
Co. Louth

Colleges of commerce and industrial relations

College of Commerce
Rathmines
Dublin 6

College of Marketing and Design
40–45 Mountjoy Square
Dublin 1

College of Industrial Relations
Sandford Road
Dublin 6

Medical and paramedical schools

Royal College of Surgeons in Ireland
123 St Stephen's Green
Dublin 2

School of Pharmacy
Trinity College
18 Shrewsbury Road
Dublin 4

Royal College of Physicians of Ireland
6 Kildare Street
Dublin 2

Each of the university colleges, with the exception of St Patrick's College, Maynooth, has a medical school

Professional law schools

The Honourable Society of King's Inns
Henrietta Street
Dublin 1

The Incorporated Law Society of Ireland
Blackhall Place
Dublin 7

Art schools

National College of Art and Design
100 Thomas Street
Dublin 8

Dun Laoghaire School of Art
Carriglea Park, Kill Avenue
Dun Laoghaire
Co. Dublin

Crawford College of Art and Design
Sharman Crawford Street
Cork

Most of the Regional Technical Colleges provide courses in Art (See also Limerick College of Art, Commerce and Technology)

Music schools

Royal Irish Academy of Music
86 Westland Row
Dublin 2

Limerick School of Music
Mulgrave Street
Limerick

School of Music
Chatham Row
Dublin 2

Army School of Music
Cathal Brugha Barracks
Dublin 6

Municipal School of Music
Union Quay
Cork

Hotel schools

Dublin College of Catering
Cathal Brugha Street
Dublin 1

Shannon International Hotel School
Shannon Free Airport
Co. Clare

Hotel Training School
Killybegs
Co. Donegal

Colleges of theology and divinity

Pontifical University
St Patrick's College
Maynooth
Co. Kildare

Milltown Institute of Theology and Philosophy
Milltown Park
Dublin 6

Holy Cross College
Clonliffe Road
Dublin 3

St Patrick's College
Carlow

St Patrick's College
Thurles
Co. Tipperary

St Kieran's College
Kilkenny

St Peter's College
Wexford

St John's College
Waterford

All Hallows College
Drumcondra
Dublin 9

St Columban's College
Dalgan Park
Navan
Co. Meath

St Patrick's College
Kiltegan
Co. Wicklow

Holy Ghost Missionary College
Kimmage Manor
Dublin 12

St Mary's College
Tallaght
Dublin 24

Church of Ireland Theological College
Braemor Park
Dublin 14

Irish School of Ecumenics
Milltown Park
Dublin 6

Agricultural and related colleges

Agricultural College
Ballyhaise
Co. Cavan

Agricultural College
Clonakilty
Co. Cork

Mellows Agricultural College
Athenry
Co. Galway

Kildalton Agricultural & Horticultural College
Piltown
Co. Kilkenny

IRL

2. Survey of courses of study at higher education institutions

Subjects in which undergraduate degrees and diplomas are awarded

Art and Design/Fine Arts

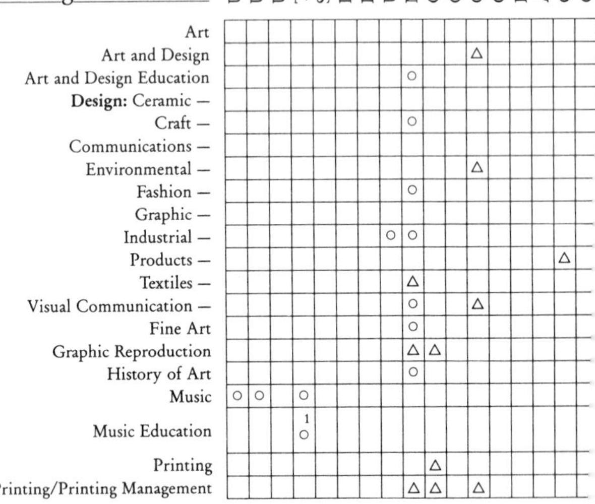

	University College, Dublin	University College, Cork	University College, Galway	Trinity College Dublin	St Patrick's College, Maynooth	Pontifical University	Dublin City University (DCU)	University of Limerick	National College of Art and Design	College of Technology, Bolton Street	College of Technology, Kevin Street	College of Marketing and Design	College of Commerce	Dublin College of Catering	Athlone Regional Technical College	Carlow Regional Technical College	Cork Regional Technical College
Art																	
Art and Design												△					
Art and Design Education									○								
Design: Ceramic –																	
Craft –									○								
Communications –																	
Environmental –												△					
Fashion –									○								
Graphic –																	
Industrial –								○	○								
Products –																△	
Textiles –									△								
Visual Communication –									○			△					
Fine Art									○								
Graphic Reproduction									△	△							
History of Art									○								
Music	○	○		○													
Music Education				[1] ○													
Printing										△							
Printing/Printing Management									△	△		△					

Arts/Humanities/Theology

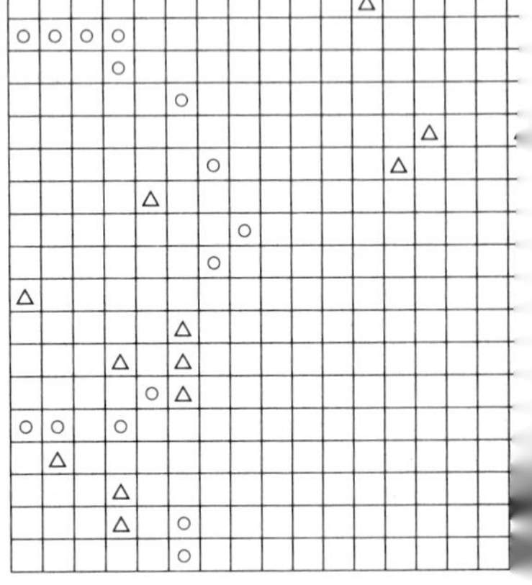

	University College, Dublin	University College, Cork	University College, Galway	Trinity College Dublin	St Patrick's College, Maynooth	Pontifical University	Dublin City University (DCU)	University of Limerick	National College of Art and Design	College of Technology, Bolton Street	College of Technology, Kevin Street	College of Marketing and Design	College of Commerce	Dublin College of Catering	Athlone Regional Technical College	Carlow Regional Technical College	Cork Regional Technical College
Applied Social Studies												△					
Arts [2]	○	○	○	○													
Biblical and Theological Studies				○													
Canon Law						○											
Child Care														△			
Communications Studies							○						△				
Community Service					△												
European Studies								○									
Languages - Applied							○										
Library & Information Studies	△																
Mission Studies						△											
Philosophy				△		△											
Philosophy and Arts					○	△											
Social Science	○	○		○													
Social Work		△															
Theatre Studies				△													
Theology				△		○											
Theology and Arts						○											

[1] Music education in Trinity College Dublin: Joint course with the College of Music and the Royal Irish Academy of Music.

IRL

Donogh O'Malley Regional Technical College	Dundalk Regional Technical College	Galway Regional Technical College	Sligo Regional Technical College	Tralee Regional Technical College	Waterford Regional Technical College	Limerick College of Art, Commerce and Technology	Dun Laoghaire School of Art and Design
		△	△		△	△	△
						△	
					△	△	△
						△	
						△	
						△	
		△					
		△		△			
					○		

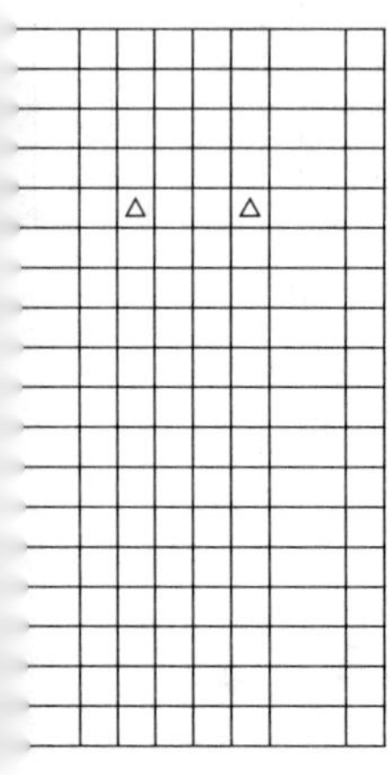

Donogh O'Malley Regional Technical College	Dundalk Regional Technical College	Galway Regional Technical College	Sligo Regional Technical College	Tralee Regional Technical College	Waterford Regional Technical College	Limerick College of Art, Commerce and Technology	Dun Laoghaire School of Art and Design
		△			△		

A detailed list of subjects available can be obtained from the individual colleges or from the Higher Education Authority.

Note:

1. This list includes only full-time undergraduate courses at degree and diploma level. Courses of a strictly professional nature are omitted.
2. A list of postgraduate courses and qualifications in Ireland can be obtained from the Higher Education Autority.
3. Colleges of Education are omitted from this table. A complete list appears in Appendix 1.
4. The universities and institutions of higher education listed in this Appendix generally have facilities for disabled students.
5. Further details of courses listed and others available can be obtained from the individual institutions.

Symbols:

○ Course available to degree level

△ Course available at diploma level only

Subjects in which undergraduate degrees and diplomas are awarded (continued)

Business Studies and Commerce	University College, Dublin	University College, Cork	University College, Galway	Trinity College Dublin	St Patrick's College, Maynooth	Pontifical University	Dublin City University (DCU)	University of Limerick	National College of Art and Design	College of Technology, Bolton Street	College of Technology, Kevin Street	College of Marketing and Design	College of Commerce	Dublin College of Catering	Athlone Regional Technical College	Carlow Regional Technical College	Cork Regional Technical College
Accounting																△	
Accounting and Finance							○										
Auctioneering, Valuation and Estate Agency										△							
Bakery Production and Management											△						
Banking								△									
Business Management												△					
Business Studies							○	○					○		△	△	△
Catering Management														△			
Commerce: General —	○	○	○														
Accounting —	○																
Banking & Finance —	○																
Economics —	○																
International —	○																
Management —	○																
Computer Systems (Business)								○									
Export Law																	
Hotel & Catering Management													○	△			
Hotel & Catering Supervision													△				
International Marketing and Languages							○										
Management Finance															△		
Marketing												○				△	
Marketing Administration												△					
Marketing Institute																	
Marketing & Sales Management																△	
Marketing & Small Business Development																	
Personnel Management								△									
Public Administration								△									
Recreation & Leisure																	
Training Management																	
Work Study																	

Donogh O'Malley Regional Technical College	Dundalk Regional Technical College	Galway Regional Technical College	Sligo Regional Technical College	Tralee Regional Technical College	Waterford Regional Technical College	Limerick College of Art, Commerce and Technology	Dun Laoghaire School of Art and Design
Δ	Δ	Δ	Δ		Δ	Δ	
		Δ				Δ	
	Δ	Δ	Δ	Δ			
				Δ	Δ		
	○						
			Δ		Δ		
	Δ	Δ					
Δ							
						Δ	
						Δ	

IRL

Subjects in which undergraduate degrees and diplomas are awarded
(continued)

Engineering and Architecture

Engineering and Architecture	University College, Dublin	University College, Cork	University College, Galway	Trinity College Dublin	St. Patrick's College, Maynooth	Pontifical University	Dublin City University (DCU)	University of Limerick	National College of Art and Design	College of Technology, Bolton Street	College of Technology, Kevin Street	College of Marketing and Design	College of Commerce	Dublin College of Catering	Athlone Regional Technical College	Carlow Regional Technical College	Cork Regional Technical College
Architectural Technician										△							
Architectural Technology																	△
Architecture	○									○							△
Automobile Engineering																	△
Building Management																	
Building Surveying																	
Chartered Surveying																	
Construction Economics										○							△
Construction Management																	
Construction Studies																	△
Construction Technician										△							
Electrical Engineering Technician											△						
Electronic and Radio Communications																	
Electronic Engineering Technician											△						△
Electronics																△	○
Engineering: Agricultural and Food —	○																
Building Services —										○							
Chemical —	○																○
Civil —	○	○	○	○						△							△
Computer —								○									
Electrical —	○	○	○	○													
Electrical/Electronic —				○							○						
Electronic —	○		○	○			○	○								△	○
Electronic Production —								○									
Highway and Traffic —															△		
Industrial —			○					○									
Marine & Plant —																	[illegible]

Donogh O'Malley Regional Technical College	Dundalk Regional Technical College	Galway Regional Technical College	Sligo Regional Technical College	Tralee Regional Technical College	Waterford Regional Technical College	Limerick College of Art, Commerce and Technology	Dun Laoghaire School of Art and Design
						△	
						△	
		△					
	△						
						△	
					△		
					○		
	△		△	△		△	
						△	
	△	△					
△							
△	△	△				△	

Subjects in which undergraduate degrees and diplomas are awarded

(continued)

Engineering and Architecture (contd)	University College, Dublin	University College, Cork	University College, Galway	Trinity College Dublin	St. Patrick's College, Maynooth	Pontifical University	Dublin City University (DCU)	University of Limerick	National College of Art and Design	College of Technology, Bolton Street	College of Technology, Kevin Street	College of Marketing and Design	College of Commerce	Dublin College of Catering	Athlone Regional Technical College	Carlow Regional Technical College	Cork Regional Technical College
Engineering: Materials —								○									
Mineral —															△		
Mechanical —	○		○	○				○			○				△	△	○
Manufacturing —																	
Software —																○	
Plastics —															△		
Production —								△		○	○						
Structural —										○							
Tool Design —																	
Water —																	
Geo-Surveying										△							
Management Science and Industrial Systems Studies				○													
Manufacturing Technology								○									
Production Management								○								○	
Property Economics/Valuation Surveying										○							
Technician Engineering:																	
Telecommunications & Electronics											△						
Technology: Construction Management —																	
Quality Control —																	
Transport Engineering/Motor																	
Industry Management										△							
Law/Legal studies																	
Law or Legal Studies	○	○		○									△				
Medical and health-related sciences																	
Addiction Studies				△													
Dental Science/Dentistry		○		○													
Environmental Health														○			
Healthcare Technology														△			
Human Nutrition and Dietetics											○						
Medicine	○	○	○	○													
Nursing	○																
Occupational Therapy				○													
Pharmacy				○													
Physiotherapy	○			○													
Public Health Nursing	△																
Radiography	○																
Remedial Linguistics				○													
Veterinary Medicine	○																

Donogh O'Malley Regional Technical College	Dundalk Regional Technical College	Galway Regional Technical College	Sligo Regional Technical College	Tralee Regional Technical College	Waterford Regional Technical College	Limerick College of Art, Commerce and Technology	Dun Laoghaire School of Art and Design
		○					
						△	
		○					
	△	△		△			
			△				
			△				
					△		
						△	
					○		
			△				

Subjects in which undergraduate degrees and diplomas are awarded
(continued)

Science

Science	University College, Dublin	University College, Cork	University College, Galway	Trinity College Dublin	St. Patrick's College, Maynooth	Pontifical University	Dublin City University (DCU)	University of Limerick	National College of Art and Design	College of Technology, Bolton Street	College of Technology, Kevin Street	College of Marketing and Design	College of Commerce	Dublin College of Catering	Athlone Regional Technical College	Carlow Regional Technical College	Cork Regional Technical College
Agricultural Science	○																
Analytical Methods															△		
Analytical Science							○										
Applied Science Technician											△						
Applied Sciences							○				○						
Aquaculture																	
Aquatic Sciences																	
Biotechnology							○										
Chemical Instrumentation																	
Chemical Technology																	△
Chemistry: Analytical —																	
Applied —																	
Computer Applications							○										
Computer Science				○							△						
Computer Studies															○		○
Computer Systems								○									
Computing - Applied								○							△	△	○
Environmental Management														△			
Environmental Science																	
Fine Chemicals and Pharmaceuticals																	
Food Processing & Technology														△			
Food Science & Food Technology		○															△
Industrial Biology																△	
Industrial Chemistry								○									
Industrial Instrumentation								○									
Instrument Physics																	△
Mathematical Sciences				○				○									
Mathematical Sciences - Applied							○	○									
Mathematics - Applied								○									
Meat Science		△															
Medical Laboratory Sciences											△						△
Nautical Science																	△
Ophthalmic Optics											△						
Pharmaceutical Technicians				△													
Physics - Applied							○										
Science - General [1]	○	○	○	○													
Technology: Polymer —															○		
Toxicology —															△		

Donogh O'Malley Regional Technical College	Dundalk Regional Technical College	Galway Regional Technical College	Sligo Regional Technical College	Tralee Regional Technical College	Waterford Regional Technical College	Limerick College of Art, Commerce and Technology	Dun Laoghaire School of Art and Design
		○					
		△					
					△		
						△	
			△				
					△		
		△					
	△	△	△	△	△	○	
			○				
		△					
	△						
		△					

A detailed list of subjects available can be obtained from the individual colleges or from the Higher Education Authority.

3. Bibliography

Central Applications Office, Handbook. Available free of charge from the CAO. This handbook gives information on how to apply for admission to full-time undergraduate courses in the institutions for which applications are dealt with by the CAO.

CAO College Guide 1988. Careers and Educational Publishers, Claremorris, Co. Mayo. This contains information on all aspects of the CAO applicants scheme in addition to other helpful information for students.

The NCEA directory of approved courses in higher education, 1988 (fifth edition), IRL 3.50. This is a detailed guide to degree, diploma and certificate courses approved by the NCEA.

The National University of Ireland, **Matriculation regulations and courses for 1988,** Dublin. IRL 0.80 plus postage, available from the National University of Ireland. This pamphlet contains information on methods of matriculation, subjects and the syllabus for the examination.

Getting into college, Mary O'Donnell, The Desmond Press 1987. IRL 2.95. This is a guide to getting a place at college and outlines the relevant application procedures.

Regional Technical Colleges 1988/89. Bureau for Educational Services and Training, Old Timoleague Road, Clonakilty, Co. Cork. This contains information on courses offered in the Regional Technical Colleges and Limerick College of Art, Commerce and Technology.

Each college **produces a handbook** or brochure providing general information for students. These are usually provided free of charge. In some of the colleges there are in addition more detailed booklets on specific matters (e.g. courses of study, scholarships, etc.).

4. Glossary

Capitation: The capitation fee, which all students must pay, is a fixed sum which entitles students to membership of the students' union in their college and also of a large number of societies and clubs.

Central Applications Office (CAO): The CAO is the central processing agency for applications to the university colleges, the National Institutes for Higher Education at Limerick and Dublin, Thomond College of Education and degree courses in the colleges of the Dublin Institute of Technology.

Certificate courses: One- or more commonly two-year courses provided at undergraduate level in a wide range of third-level institutions in Ireland, but most commonly outside the universities. It may be possible to proceed to diploma level on successful completion of a certificate course.

College of education: Institutions of higher education providing courses of a minimum duration of three years leading to qualifications as teachers in primary education or as teachers of specialist subjects in secondary education.

Constituent college: In the National University of Ireland a term used for the colleges which form the teaching and research organs of the University. These colleges are represented on the Senate of the University which decides on academic standards and on senior academic appointments in the constituent colleges. For most other purposes the colleges are autonomous.

Dean of Residence: In some colleges there is an officer with the title 'Dean of Residence'. Such officers, who are often chaplains, are responsible for ensuring that students living away from home reside in approved lodgings.

Diploma courses: This term is generally applied to courses of three years' duration at undergraduate level. Postgraduate diplomas, generally lasting one or two years, are also available.

Doctoral degree: A postgraduate degree of an advanced level, usually involving at least three years' study. There are two levels of Doctorates: Doctor of Philosophy (Ph.D.) and Higher Doctorates (D.Sc., D.Litt., etc.).

First degree: The first, Bachelor's, or primary degree is the basic qualification obtained from the university colleges after a minimum of three years' study. Bachelor's degree courses are also followed at colleges of education and, to a lesser extent, in other non-university colleges.

Higher Education Grants Scheme: The Higher Education Grants Scheme was established in 1968 to assist students from lower-income groups to participate in higher education. Eligibility for a grant under this scheme is assessed on the basis of Leaving Certificate performance and of a means-test, and the scheme is confined to students whose parents are ordinarily resident in the Republic of Ireland. The grant is composed of a tuition fee and a maintenance element; a sliding scale is in operation with respect to the maintenance element.

Honourable Society of King's Inns: The Society provides a course of professional education and training which enables its students to be admitted to the degree of barrister-at-law and to be called to the Bar of Ireland by the Chief Justice and admitted to practice in the courts of Ireland.

Honours degree: Undergraduate degrees and some Master's degrees are graded on the basis of the student's attainment at the final examination. Awards are divided between pass and honours. In turn, honours degrees are divided between first class, second class (sometimes subdivided between upper and lower division) and also third-class honours. For some undergraduate degree courses, called general degree courses, only pass or general degrees are awarded.

Incorporated Law Society: The Society is the representative body of the solicitor's profession. It exercises a statutory function in connection with legal education and other matters relating to the profession. In its Law School education and training in the professional aspects of the law are provided.

Master's degree: The first postgraduate degree, which may be taken on completion of the primary degree. Master's degrees can be obtained by course work/examination, or by research and thesis.

Matriculation: Matriculation is the term applied to meeting the minimum requirements laid down by the universities for entry to their courses. Applicants must matriculate in a group of six subjects from a matriculation programme. In certain cases exemptions may be made, if evidence of having passed an equivalent examination can be produced by the applicant, or on the grounds of mature years. A separate matriculation examination is available and is of particular relevance to students who wish to enter the colleges of the NUI.

National Council for Educational Awards (NCEA): A body established by the government to validate courses in non-university higher education institutions and to grant and confer awards on those who successfully take approved courses. The awards are at certificate, diploma and degree level.

Postgraduate degree: A postgraduate degree is a higher qualification taken after the first degree has been obtained (provided a minimum standard has been reached in the first degree examination). Specified periods of study are required after the primary degree is obtained before the student can obtain a postgraduate degree. (See Master's degree, Doctoral degree).

Professional training: To a great extent, this is provided outside the institutions of higher education in Ireland. For instance, graduates in Commerce or Business Studies will need to pass more examinations set by professional bodies in order to qualify in accountancy. The primary degree will, however, provide basic training in specific areas.

Recognized college: A term used for a number of institutions of higher education which are associated with the Nation-

IRL

al University of Ireland. Their courses must be approved by the Senate of the University for the award of degrees and other qualifications of the University. Qualifications of the academic staff of such colleges must also be approved by the University Senate.

Royal College of Surgeons in Ireland: A medical school established in 1784 which provides training in medicine at both the undergraduate and postgraduate levels. It has also faculties of anaesthetics, radiology and nursing, each of which conduct training courses and examinations.

Students' union: The students' union is the representative body of all students in a college. As well as their representative function, students' unions provide a variety of services to students (particularly in relation to travel concessions) and coordinate the work of clubs and societies. In many cases they also provide a welfare service which, where it cannot solve a problem directly, can refer to expert professional opinion.

Tutor: A member of a college's academic staff who teaches students in small groups (tutorials). Many tutors also act informally as counsellors on personal matters.

IRL

5. Diagram of the education system

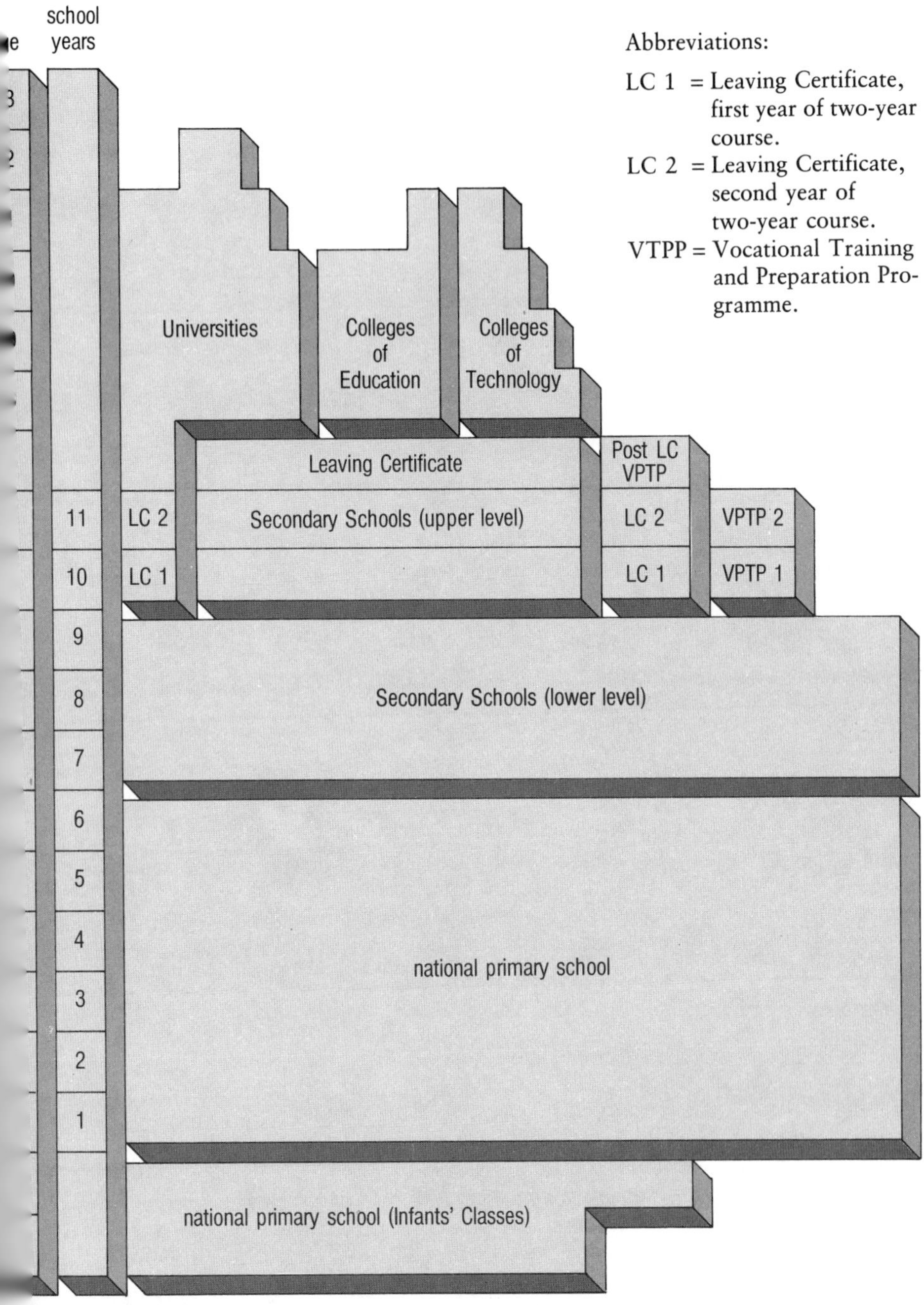

school years
11
10
9
8
7
6
5
4
3
2
1
Universities
Colleges of Education
Colleges of Technology
Leaving Certificate
Post LC VPTP
LC 2
LC 1
Secondary Schools (upper level)
LC 2
LC 1
VPTP 2
VPTP 1
Secondary Schools (lower level)
national primary school
national primary school (Infants' Classes)

Abbreviations:

LC 1 = Leaving Certificate, first year of two-year course.

LC 2 = Leaving Certificate, second year of two-year course.

VTPP = Vocational Training and Preparation Programme.

Italy

I

Organization of higher education

In Italy training in tertiary education is offered at the higher education institutions. The latter are public law bodies. There are two types of higher education institutions, State universities and State-recognized universities. The State institutions are dependent on public funding and administration. The legally recognized, or independent, institutions were founded by various bodies or organizations but have been recognized by the State which approves their statutes and accords the same status to their degrees as those awarded by the State universities.

Types of higher education institutions

Higher education institutions may have various designations: universities, polytechnics (which only have faculties of engineering and architecture), *istituti universitari* (generally with only one faculty), *magistero* (courses of study primarily for teachers).

There are 55 universities in Italy, of which 46 are State-run and nine private. In addition to these, there are two *istituti universitari con ordinamento speciale* (university establishments with special responsibility; see Glossary) and 11 *istituti superiori statali di educazione fisica*, higher education institutions offering physical education; one of these is State-run and 10 are State-recognized institutions.

Furthermore, there are the art colleges *(accademie di belle arti)* and conservatories *(conservatori di musica)* which are not included in the university sector. The art colleges offer artistic training on a post-secondary level. The conservatories offer music lessons for beginners and advanced students.

Student statistics

The total number of students enrolled during the academic year 1986/87 amounted to 1 086 501. Of these 23 264 or 2.2% were foreign students. (For statistics regarding students from other EC Member States, see Appendix).

Organization and validation of courses

The academic year begins on 1 November and ends on 31 October. Lectures and exercise classes normally commence in the first 10 days of November and continue until the end of May. At some institutions of higher education, degree programmes have been organized in semesters following the DPR 382/80 didactic reform directive. As a consequence, lectures commence on 1 October at these institutions of higher education.

The duration of a course of study at a higher education institution is four or five years depending on the faculty (six years for medicine and surgery). A faculty can be divided into different *corsi di laurea* (degree courses). Thus, for instance, the *facoltà di scienze matematiche, fisiche e naturali* is divided into the following *corsi di laurea:* mathematics, physics, biology, geology, and natural sciences.

Ministerial directive DPR 382/80 permits universities to establish departments which are to comprise homogeneous research sectors. These may involve more than one faculty or may include several *laurea* courses. The departmental structure implicitly refers to research only; the structure of teaching is not affected.

For each academic year, examinations are to be taken for those subjects which are in the curriculum.

The curriculum can be either one established by the faculty or one proposed by the student at the beginning of his studies and approved by the Faculty Council *(Consiglio di facoltà)*. There are two regular examination periods, in summer and in the autumn, and one special period in February. The individual examinations can only be taken once in a given examination period and not more than twice in the same academic year. If the student withdraws from an examination he is regarded as having failed.

In Italy there are three academic degrees, i.e. the *diploma,* the *laurea* and the *dottorato di ricerca,* a research doctorate. Both the *laurea* and the *dottorato di ricerca* degrees entitle the holder to use the title of Dr *(dottore)*.

Prior to the recent change in regulations for the higher education sector, the only subjects in which a diploma could be obtained at universities were statistics *(Diploma di statistica)* and diplomas for principals in primary schools *(Diploma di abilitazione alla vigilanza nelle scuole elementari)*. The DPR of 10 march 1982, No 162, reorganized those courses of study at the *scuole dirette a fini speciali* which are affiliated to the universities. After a course duration of two to three years they are concluded by means of a State examination and a diploma *(Diploma postsecondario)* which entitles the holder to employment not requiring the *laurea*, but for which cultural and specific training at tertiary level is required.

In order to be admitted to these training courses, applicants must pass a written examination, if the number of candidates is higher than the number of places available.

The *laurea* is awarded to students who have passed all the annual examnations in the prescribed number of years in the major and minor subjects included in the curriculum of the *corso di laurea* in question. In addition, the student must submit and defend a *tesi scritta* (written thesis) on a topic previously agreed upon with the professor of the subject in question.

The research doctorate *(dottorato di ricerca)*, a *post lauream* degree which is only of significance within the sphere of scientific-academic research, was created by the 1980 university reform act (Law No 28 of 21 February 1980, and Directive DPR No 382 of 11 July 1980).

Through an entry examination for doctoral candidates which consists of a written paper and a viva voce, the aptitude of the candidate for scientific-academic research is established.

After admission, Italian research students may be awarded a research grant of LIT 10 million if their personal annual income does not exceed LIT 8 million. Should they be studying or researching abroad, then the amount may be increased to 15 million. Foreign citizens may be admitted to half of the research doctorate places available. The invitation to the entry examination for the research doctorate is annually published in an official publication, the *Gazzetta ufficiale dei concorsi* and is available from the Italian Foreign Ministry and from diplomatic missions abroad. The number of places available for research doctorate candidates changes from year to year and may be increased on the basis of agreements with public research institutions. In the 1988/89 academic year, the Ministry of Education was able to offer for competition 2 916 places spread over all institutions of higher education. In addition to these, there were 700 places on offer through external agreements. The doctorate programmes are carried through at the previously determined institutions of higher education, where either strongly-specialized subjects or interdisciplinary research activities are developed. The doctorate is finally awarded through a decree of the Ministry of Education to those who have achieved research results of high scientific-academic value. This must be proven through an independent research work paper which must be defended in front of an examination committee.

After the *laurea, corsi di perfezionamento* are taken. These are in-depth, intensification courses. Admission is also restricted. These advanced training courses are intended either to treat the 'cultural requirements of consolidation in certain areas of knowledge', or are to make post-qualification within the context of 'life-long learning' possible. The *scuole di specializzazione* pursue similar objectives; diplomas conferred by these within the framework of the chosen career field are intended to enable holders to advance within their careers as specialists. It is not permitted to be enrolled simultaneously for *corsi perfezionamento, corsi di specializzazione* and for a research doctorate.

The *scuole di specializzazione* may be established upon formal request of the universities and through a corresponding decree of the Ministry of Education. The total number of students that may be admitted depends on the internal structure, the technical equipment as well as the teaching and other staff of the institution of higher education. Around 60 000 students were enrolled for such advanced training courses in *scuole di specializzazione* and *scuole di perfezionamento* at the last count. The duration of the programmes at the *scuole di specializzazione* varies from between two and five years. The *corsi di perfezionamento*, in-depth courses, by contrast, are established through a directive of the Chancellor of the university; their duration should not exceed one year.

Admission and registration

Initial information

Students may obtain general information from the following sources:

1. Italian embassies and consulates;
2. Italian cultural institutes;
3. the Ministry of Education: Ministero della Pubblica Istruzione, Direzione Generale dell'Istruzione, Universitaria, Viale Trastevere 76, 00153 Roma;
4. the Ministry of Foreign Affairs; Ministero degli Affari Esteri, DGRC Ufficio VI, Piazzale Farnesina 00162 Roma;
5. CIMEA (Centro d'Informazione sulla Mobilità e le Equivalenze accademiche), Via XXI Aprile 36, 00162 Roma.

For specific enquiries, please refer to the students' secretariats *(Segretariato degli studenti stranieri)* of the institutions concerned.

Entry requirements: *Corsi di laurea*

The basic requirement for admission to a higher education institution for all applicants is the possession of an upper-secondary school-leaving certificate equivalent to the *diploma di maturità*.

The following rules apply to all foreign applications for admission:

1. Foreigners with school-leaving certificates obtained abroad are admitted on the basis of their certificates under the same conditions as those in force in the country in which the school-leaving certificate was awarded.
2. Applicants from countries in which there is either no university or the desired discipline is not offered can only be admitted to a higher education institution if they can provide proof of at least 12 years of school attendance (beginning with the first year of primary school).

Limitations

In principle, there are no entry limitations to university courses. Such an entry limitation *(numerus clausus)* only exists for *laurea degree* programmes in dentistry and orthodontics. An allocation of student places, the *numero programmato,* brought about by bottlenecks in teaching capacity has only been introduced at some universities (for example, the Universities of Calabria and Rome II), and only for certain degree programmes (medicine and surgery, veterinary medicine, international studies and environmental sciences). Entry examinations are only envisaged for acceptance to a research doctorate programme, to the *scuole di specializzazione,* the *scuole di perfezionamento,* the *scuole dirette a fini speciali* and the institutes of physical education. In general, 10% of the places available in the *laurea* degree programmes subject to the *numero programmato* are reserved for foreigners.

I

According to Law 590 of 14 August 1982, new universities should not have more than 40 000 students, as a rule. The purpose of this is to achieve a more balanced development in institutions of higher education throughout the country.

Recognition of foreign certificates and degrees

Foreign citizens who have an academic degree which was earned at universities or university institutions abroad may apply for the recognition of these in Italy. The academic bodies responsible at the university decide upon the application after examination of each case, involving the evaluation of the degree and of the previous intermediate examinations. The academic bodies may establish that the foreign degree is fully equivalent to the corresponding degree conferred by Italian universities, but may also admit the applicant to the *laurea* or diploma examination, completely or partially exempting the student from the intermediate examinations which are prescribed in the statutes of the university for this degree programme.

If an international agreement exists, then the recognition will be undertaken according to the conditions stipulated in this.

The recognition of the degree, however, is only of academic value. It does not permit from the outset any entry into a professional register *(albo professionale)*, with which the right to exercise a profession in connected.

The application is forwarded together with the prescribed documentation to the Rector of the chosen university by the Italian diplomatic mission in the applicant's home country. Applicants should also turn to the diplomatic mission for information on closing dates and details regarding application. Academic degrees which correspond to degrees conferred by the Italian *scuole di specializzazione* cannot be recognized in as far as this is not regulated by any special bilateral agreements or by directives of the European Community.

Entry examinations

Before being admitted, all foreign students are required to pass a test intended to determine whether or not their knowledge of Italian is sufficient to profitably pursue their chosen course of study.

According to the legal regulations currently in force, this examination is carried out by specialized competent lecturers. The applicant is informed in advance by the Italian Ministry of Foreign Affairs at which university this examination takes place. This is held either in September or October prior to the beginning of next academic year. (The examination for the 1988/89 academic year was held on 26 September. The examination date for the 1989/90 academic year was 31 October.) Students who do not take the test or who do not pass cannot be admitted and will not be permitted to repeat the test until the following academic year. Those students who have passed this language examination are admitted to courses at Italian institutions of higher education according to quotas of vacant places laid down by each institution for each course. The relevant decisions are taken in respect of admission capacity and the situation regarding premises and equipment.

Places available are awarded with preference to:

(a) citizens of EC Member States;
(b) citizens of developing countries;
(c) students from countries which have no tertiary education institutions or in which no course of the desired type is offered.

The following groups of applicants must pass the language examination, but are exempted from admission limitations according to quotas:

(a) political refugees who must apply to the International Social Service in Rome — *Servizio Sociale Internazionale,* Via Veneto 96, Roma;
(b) embassy staff accredited to the State of Italy;
(c) citizens of another EC Member State residing in Italy, including their dependants (spouse, children, brothers, sisters and parents);
(d) foreign grant holders receiving their grant from the Italian Government, from their own government or from international sources are exempted from the admissions limitation quota as well as from the Italian language test, although they must sit any subject-related examinations that may be required.

The following are exempted from both the entry examination and admission limitations according to quotas:

(a) students who have completed education at a State secondary school in the border area where the language of instruction is Italian;
(b) students who have received their school-leaving certificate from the German schools in Italy, from the French *Lycée Chateaubriand* in Rome or from the Spanish *Cervantes* grammar school, which has been recognized for admission to Italian universities in accordance with the bilateral government agreements, since students already take an examination in Italian language and literature as part of the upper-secondary school-leaving examination;
(c) students in possession of school-leaving certificates from the European schools in Luxembourg, Brussels, Varese, Mol, Karlsruhe or Bergen (see Law 108 of 3 January 1960);
(d) students who have taken an international school-leaving certificate *(diploma di baccalaureato internazionale)* as recognized by the Italian State (Law 738 of 30 October 1986);
(e) foreigners who have completed five years of secondary education leading to an Italian school certificate.

Application and registration

Laurea courses

Foreign students wishing to be admitted to Italian universities must direct their application for preliminary registration *(domanda di pre-iscrizione)*

I

and all necessary documents by 31 July to the Italian diplomatic mission responsible.

Four universities must be selected and listed in order of preference from a list of higher education institutions enclosed with the application form.

In addition, applicants must comply with the following requirements:

1. if their place of residence is abroad, they must sign a declaration that they will return home after expiry of their student visa. (This visa will only be renewed if the entry examination has been successfully completed);
2. students must commit themselves to pass at least three examinations in the first two academic years and in the following years at least three annually;
3. they must register for examinations at the institution concerned with a preliminary residence permit issued for study purposes.

Moreover, applicants from non-EC countries must in addition guarantee not to pursue remunerative employment. They must be in possession of an insurance policy valid in Italy and also attach to their application for admission a photocopy and a certified translation of a bank credit note. This note of credit must be valid in Italy and guarantee monthly payment of LIT 800 000 for the cost of living and study.

From 10 October onwards, applicants may consult lists of institutions of higher education at the Italian mission responsible or at the information bureau of the Ministero della Pubblica Istruzione in order to determine at which university they may sit the entry examination.

Of course, registration is not possible if the applicant has not passed the examination. Furthermore, it is also not possible to sit the entry examination at an institution of higher education other than that which has been assigned or for a degree programme other than that which had been named in the application. During the first academic year it is not possible to apply for transfer to another university or to another faculty.

Students wishing to apply to a free, non-State run institution of higher education may only name one location of their choice (see Appendix for the addresses of private institutions of higher education). The admissions application forms for the 1989/90 academic year which are also forwarded by the Italian diplomatic missions abroad must be submitted by 31 July 1989.

Admission: short-term courses

Scuole dirette a fini speciali

The same admissions conditions apply to these short-study courses as for admission to a *laurea* course. If the number of applicants is greater than the number of places available, a multiple choice test is carried out possibly together with an interview and evaluation of the applicant's school reports. Applicants are admitted according to their examination results until the vacant places of the quota are filled. Applications from foreigners are forwarded by the Italian missions to the university to which the *scuola diretta* is affiliated.

Admission: *dottorato di ricerca*

Admission to a research doctoral programme *(dottorati di ricerca)* is subject to *numerus clausus*. Prior to admission appropriate examinations have to be passed. Furthermore, foreigners may be admitted to up to half of the places available. Applications must be addressed via the respective Italian diplomatic missions which are annually informed with regard to the number of available research vacancies as well as the closing dates for application.

Admission: *scuole di specializzazione*

Admission to these courses is subject to an entry examination. If there is a difference between the number of places available and the number of applicants, the remaining places may be given to foreigners. The number of foreigners may not exceed 20% of the total number of Italian citizens.

Admissions limitations or special admissions conditions for foreigners are listed in the statutes of each university and in the announcement of vacant places *(bando di concorso)*. Applications from foreigners are forwarded via the Italian mission.

Admission: other courses

For admission to the institutes for physical education and to the in-depth courses at the *scuole di perfezionamento,* it is also necessary to submit applications for preliminary registration annually on the dates determined to the Italian diplomatic missions and to have the applications forwarded by the mission. Similarly, the embassies or consulates process the student applications for admission to the individual courses *(corsi singoli)* with temporary student status as well as to practicals, and to the academies of fine arts and the music conservatories.

Tuition fees

Fees and other contributions are paid upon admission and can be paid in instalments or in one sum. Payment is effected on special postal account forms obtained from the office of the registrar of the faculty. No other form of payment is accepted. The total amount may vary from university to university and from faculty to faculty. As a rough guideline it can be said to be between LIT 300 000 minimum and LIT 400 000 maximum per academic year.

The free universities may determine their tuition fees autonomously. In some cases they may be graded according to the student's family income. In general they are well above those of the State universities.

Exemption from fees: In some cases complete or partial exemption from fees is provided for. Application for exemption from fees should be addressed to the rector and included with the application for matriculation (or registration). It must contain full details concerning the applicant, the place of residence of his family, the faculty and *corso di laurea* in which the applicant is enrolling.

Foreign students who are scholarship holders of the Italian Government

I

or an international institution must submit, in addition to the application:

1. a certificate of foreign citizenship if this is not apparent from the other documents;
2. a certificate or other attestation providing proof that a scholarship has been awarded;
3. a document proving that their family is resident abroad.

Italian students having permanent residence abroad should submit:

1. a certificate of Italian citizenship;
2. a document proving that they belong to a family which has emigrated and has its permanent residence abroad. (This document is issued by a consular authority.)

Students who are citizens of an EC Member State and whose parents are or were employed in Italy and reside there are entitled to the same rights as Italian students regarding course fees.

Knowledge of the language of instruction, language courses and other courses

The foreign student must have a level of proficiency in Italian sufficient to enable him to follow courses without difficulty, given the fact that instruction is given exclusively in Italian.

Foreign students who wish to attend Italian language courses in their home countries may apply to the Italian cultural institutes (for addresses see Appendix 1) or other institutions such as the Società Dante Alighieri.

In Italy there are language courses for foreigners at several universities, such as in Bologna, Macerata and Urbino. All year round the Foreigners' University in Perugia *(Università per stranieri)* and the School of Italian Language and Culture *(Scuola di lingua e cultura italiana per stranieri)* in Siena offer courses on different levels. The addresses of the universities, other institutes and private organizations can be found in the brochure *Corsi di lingua e cultura per stranieri in Italia,* published by the Direzione Generale delle Relazioni culturali (DGRC) of the Ministry of Foreign Affairs (for address see Appendix).

Financial assistance and scholarships

The most important State scholarships, called the *assegno di studio* or *presalario*, are awarded through public competition. The regional offices for the 'Right to study' *(diritto allo studio)* annually publish the conditions for this competition, in which parental income and school achievements play a role, as well as the procedures, closing dates and other criteria for the awarding of scholarships. The following may take advantage of this financial assistance: Italian students as well as students who are the sons or daughters of citizens from other EC Member States who are pursuing or have pursued paid employment in Italy for public or private employers.

Recipients of this financial assistance, which amounts to an average of LIT 1 million per year or which may be paid in lieu through service (refectory, place in hall of residence, etc.), are automatically exempted from the payment of tuition fees and other contributions for the respective academic year. The individual 'Right to study' offices can also supply information on further reductions, grants, etc.

Foreign students may be granted scholarships through public or private institutions in Italy or abroad. Information on the scholarships announced annually may be obtained from the Italian Ministry of Foreign Affairs *(Ministero degli Affari Esteri, Direzione Generale delle Relazioni Culturali, Ufficio IX)* or abroad from the Italian diplomatic missions.

I

Entry and residence regulations

Foreign students must present themselves for the entry examination at the university allocated to them with a residence permit for study purposes valid until 31 December. This residence permit must be applied for within three days of arrival on Italian territory from the police station responsible *(Pubblica Sicurezza),* which will issue this upon presentation of the passport together with the necessary consular certificate (for citizens from EC Member States) or a visa for study purposes (for citizens of non-EC States). As soon as admission to the university has been granted, they should report to the *questura (Autorità Provinciale di Pubblica Sicurezza).* Here they will receive a residence permit for study purposes for the whole academic year. As has been previously mentioned, unless they pass at least three examinations in the first two academic years and in the following years at least three per year, this residence permit will be revoked and they will have to return to their country of origin.

Social aspects

Social security and health insurance

There is no social security scheme exclusively for the use of Italian and foreign students. Italian students by law are covered by a compulsory health insurance scheme administered by the regional health services. Foreign students from EC countries who are in a national health insurance scheme in their own country are entitled to use the health insurance scheme in Italy and can do so by presenting a form from the given national insurance scheme to the offices of the *Unità sanitaria locale.* Similar benefits are foreseen for the citizens of all countries with which Italy has concluded relevant agreements.

The authorities for the right to higher education *(diritto allo studio)* which, at the regional level, are responsible for financial assistance to students, administer health services and provide medical preventive services.

Foreign students with scholarships from the Italian Government are given life, accident and health insurance coverage for the duration of their stay in Italy.

All duly registered students are, in addition, insured against accidents which could happen at university in the course of experiments or practical exercises contained in the planned curriculum and carried out under the supervision of professors or assistants.

For disabled students, particular services are provided in many provinces *(regioni)*, e.g. means of transportation.

Advisory services

At all universities there is a Foreign Student Office *(segreteria studenti stranieri)* which can provide all information necessary for planning a course of study as well as information on which professors have been charged with advising the students.

Over and above this, most of the 'Right to study' centres *(diritto allo studio)* also offer students information on the routine of university life as well as on social services.

Student employment

Students wishing to complete their studies successfully must invest so much time and energy that they would be ill-advised to pursue any remunerative activity. In this respect attention is drawn to the fact that applicants from countries outside the EC must commit themselves upon admission not to engage in gainful employment.

Student organizations

The student associations at each university provide advisory services to students and assist in their social integration.

Cost of living

No exact information can be given as to the cost of living due to the constant rise of prices and the fact that they vary greatly from place to place. It can be assumed that the average expenditure for food and accommodation for a year (12 months) will be about LIT 10 million. This sum will be lower if the student eats in the *messa universitaria* where a meal on the average costs less than LIT 3 000.

Accommodation

Foreign students only rarely find accommodation in residence halls *(casa dello studente)*. There are residence halls at every university location. They provide rooms with one, two or three beds at modest prices. Upon arriving in Italy, the foreign student can turn to the regional 'Right to study' centres or to the tourist offices in the province, *ente provinciale per il turismo* (EPT) for information or assistance.

Accommodation in residence halls is granted on the basis of a public competition *(concorso)*. Those students who receive a State subsidy are given preference.

In case of acceptance the monthly residence hall fee is deducted from the subsidy.

The rent for a private room is about LIT 300 000 monthly.

Services for students

Both Italian and foreign students are entitled to weekly or monthly rail cards.

In order to be issued a subscription ticket they must present a certificate of registration from the university and a document from the residence authority at the responsible office of the local railway station.

In all Italian towns and cities, monthly tickets are available for students.

There are also reductions on entry to almost all cultural events, such as concerts, theatre, etc.

The regional institutes for *diritto allo studio* also concern themselves with the organization of athletic and recreational activities for students, including cultural and tourist events.

Facilities for disabled students

Special forms of assistance for disabled students are planned in a number of Italian regions (e.g. transport facilities).

In order to facilitate the participation of disabled students in the courses and in the cultural life at the universities, an advisory service has been established at some of the regional 'Right to study' centres. These centres may grant annual subsidies for the purchasing of special technical aids or for the costs of an escort, assistants or translators.

Appendices

1. Addresses

Italian embassies in EC countries

Belgium
28, rue Émile Claus
B-1050 Bruxelles
☎ 649 97 00

Denmark
Gammel Vartov Vej, 7
DK-2900 Hellerup
☎ 62 68 77

Federal Republic of Germany
Karl Finkelnburgstraße 49-51
D-5300 Bonn 2
☎ 82 00 60

Greece
Sekeri 2
GR-Athina 10674
☎ 361 17 22

Spain
Calle Lagasca 98
E-Madrid
☎ 402 54 36/37

France
47, rue de Varenne
F-75007 Paris VII
☎ 45 44 38 90

Ireland
63-65 Northumberland Road
Dublin 4
☎ 60 17 44

Luxembourg
5, rue Marie-Adelaïde
L-2128 Luxembourg
☎ 44 36 44

The Netherlands
Alexanderstraat 8
2514 JL's-Gravenhage
☎ 46 92 49

Portugal
Largo Conde de Pombeiro 6
P-Lisboa
☎ 54 61 44

United Kingdom
14 Three Kings Yard
London W1
☎ 629 82 00

Italian cultural institutes

Belgium
38, rue de Livourne
B-Bruxelles
☎ 537 90 56

Denmark
Gjørlingsvej 11
DK-2900 Hellerup
☎ 62 06 96

Federal Republic of Germany
Hansastraße 6
D-2000 Hamburg
☎ 44 04 41

Karl Finkelnburgstraße 51
D-5300 Bonn 2
☎ 36 27 92

Universitätsstraße 81
D-5000 Köln
☎ 4 00 87

Hermann-Schmid-Straße 8
D-8000 München
☎ 76 45 63

Kolbstraße 6
D-7000 Stuttgart
☎ 60 59 80

Porscherstraße 74-d
3180 Wolfsburg
☎ 229 33

Greece
Oktovriou Parission 47
GR-Athina Odos 28
☎ 522 92 94

France
50, rue de Varenne
F-75008 Paris VII
☎ 42 22 12 78

7 rue de Lesidiguières
F-Grenoble
☎ 76 54 18 54

6, rue Fernand Pauriol
F-Marseille
☎ 48 51 94

7, rue Schweighaeuser
F-Strasbourg
☎ 619 86

2, rue d'Isly
F-Lille
☎ 20 93 32 95

5, rue Commandant, Fauraux
F-Lione
☎ 93 00 17

17, rue du Conseiller
Collignon
F-Nantes
☎ 45 20 78 22

Ireland
11 Fitzwilliam Square
Dublin 2
☎ 76 66 62

Luxembourg
5-7 rue Marie Adelaïde
☎ 44 36 44

The Netherlands
Keizersgracht 564
NL-Amsterdam
☎ 26 53 14

Portugal
Rua do Salitre, 146
Lisboa
☎ 68 41 72

Rua de Restauração, 409
Oporto
☎ 262 43

United Kingdom
39, Belgrave Square
London SW1
☎ 235 14 61

2, Melville Crescent
Edinburgh EH3 THW
☎ 226 36 31

Ministries

Ministero degli affari esteri
Direzione Generale delle relazioni culturali
Piazzale della Farnesina, 1
I-00194 Roma
☎ (06) 369 11

I

Ministero della pubblica istruzione
Direzione generale istruzione universitaria
Via Trastevere, 76
I-00153 Roma
☎ (06) 584 91

Institutions for foreigners

Università italiana per stranieri
Palazzo Gallenga
Piazza Fortebraccio, 4
I-06100 Perugia
☎ (075) 643 44

Scuola di lingua e cultura italiana per stranieri
Piazetta Grassi, 2
I-53100 Siena
☎ (0577) 492 60

Youth associations and organizations

IAESTE
(International association for the exchange of students for technical experience) — Sede italiana presso il politecnico di Torino
Corso Duca degli Abruzzi, 24
Torino
☎ (011) 55 34 23/556 63 94

AIESEC
(Association internationale des étudiants en sciences economiques et commerciales) — Sede italiana presso l'Università Bocconi
Via Sarfatti, 25
I-20136 Milano
☎ (02) 832 17 56

SISM
(Segretariado italiano studenti medicina)
Sede italiana dell 'international federation of medical students association'
Policlinico s. Orsola
Via Massarenti, 9
I-40138 Bologna
☎ (051) 39 95 07

UCSEI
Ufficio centrale studenti esteri in Italia
Piazza Mariotti, 1
I-06100 Perugia

Fondazione Rui
Via XXI Aprile, 36
I-00162 Roma
☎ (06) 832 12 81

Information centre

CIMEA
(Centro di informazione sulla mobilità e le equivalenze accademiche)
Via XXI Aprile, 36
I-00162 Roma
☎ (06) 832 12 81

Universities
Università statali

Università degli studi di Ancona
Piazza Roma, 22-23
I-60100 Ancona
☎ (071) 589 31

Università degli studi di Bari
Pal. Ateneo
Piazza Umberto I, 2
I-70121 Bari
☎ (080) 31 11 11

Università degli studi della Basilicata
Via Sauro, 85
I-85100 Potenza
☎ (0971) 33 41 11

Università degli studi di Bologna
Via Zamboni, 33
I-40126 Bologna
☎ (051) 27 29 33

Università degli studi di Brescia
Piazza del Mercato, 15
I-25100 Brescia
☎ (030) 298 81

Università degli studi della Calabria
Rende-Fraz. Commenda
I-87036 Cosenza
☎ (0984) 83 95 11/86 19 61

Università degli studi di Cagliari
Via Università, 40
I-09124 Cagliari
☎ (070) 66 85 04

Università degli studi di Camerino
Via del Bastione, 3
I-62032 Camerino
☎ (0737) 40 11

Università degli studi di Cassino
Via Marconi
(Bivio Monte Cassino)
I-03043 Cassino (Frosinone)
☎ (0776) 29 91

Università degli studi di Catania
Piazza dell'Università, 2
I-95129 Catania
☎ (095) 32 53 33

Università degli studi 'G. D'Annunzio'
Via dei Vestini
I-66013 Chieti
☎ (0871) 58 01

Università degli studi di Ferrara
Via Savonarola, 9
I-44100 Ferrara
☎ (0532) 391 81

Università degli studi di Firenze
Piazza San Marco, 4
I-50121 Firenze
☎ (055) 275 71

Università degli studi di Genova
Via Balbi, 5
I-16126 Genova
☎ (010) 20 99

Università degli studi de L'Aquila
Piazza dell Annunziata
I-67100 L'Aquila
☎ (0862) 64 61

Università degli studi di Lecce
Viale Taranto
I-73100 Lecce
☎ (0832) 40 61

Università degli studi di Macerata
Piazza dell'Università, 2
I-62100 Macerata
☎ (0733) 41 81

Università degli studi di Messina
Via T. Cannizzaro
I-98100 Messina
☎ (090) 71 10 21

Università degli studi di Milano
Via Festa del Perdono, 7
I-20122 Milano
☎ (02) 884 61

Università degli studi di Modena
Via Università, 4
I-41100 Modena
☎ (059) 32 91 11

Università degli studi del Molise
Via Garibaldi, 127
I-86100 Campobasso
☎ (0874) 31 42 33

Università degli studi di Napoli
Corso Umberto I, 2
I-80138 Napoli
☎ (081) 781 91 11

Università degli studi di Padova
Via VIII Febbraio 2
I-35100 Padova
☎ (049) 65 14 00

Università degli studi di Palermo
Via L. Maqueda, 175
I-90134 Palermo
☎ (091) 58 31 77

Università degli studi di Parma
Via Cavestre, 7
I-43100 Parma
☎ (051) 49 16 41

Università degli studi di Pavia
Corso Strada Nuova, 65
I-27100 Pavia
☎ (0382) 38 71

Università degli studi di Perugia
Piazza dell'Università
I-06100 Perugia
☎ (075) 46 91

Università degli studi di Pisa
Lungarno Pacinotti, 43
I-56100 Pisa
☎ (050) 59 00 00

Università degli studi di Reggio Calabria
Via A. Cimino, 2
I-89125 Reggio Calabria
☎ (0965) 951 24

Università degli studi di Roma I
'La Sapienza'
Piazzale Aldo Moro, 5
I-00185 Roma
☎ (06) 49 91

Università degli studi di Roma II
'Tor Vergata'
Via Orazie Raimondi
Località Romanina
I-00173 Roma
☎ (06) 797 91

Università degli studi di Salerno
Strada Prov. le Ponte Don Melillo
I-84100 Salerno
☎ (089) 96 11 11

Università degli studi di Sassari
Piazza Università, 21
I-07100 Sassari
☎ (079) 21 91 11

Università degli studi di Siena
Via Banchi di Sotto, 55
I-53100 Siena
☎ (0577) 29 80 00

Università degli studi di Torino
Via G. Verdi, 8
I-10124 Torino
☎ (011) 880 21

Università degli studi di Trento
Via Belenzani, 12
I-38100 Trento
☎ (0461) 98 11 36

Università degli studi di Trieste
Piazzale Europa, 1
I-34100 Trieste
☎ (040) 560 38

Università degli studi di Udine
Via Antonini, 8
I-33100 Udine
☎ (0432) 50 30 85

Università degli studi di Venezia
Dorsoduro 3246
I-30123 Venezia
☎ (041) 528 54 20

Università degli studi di Verona
Via dell'Artigliere, 8
I-37129 Verona
☎ (045) 809 81 11

Università degli studi della Tuscia Viterbo
Via S. Giovanni Decollato, 1
I-01100 Viterbo
☎ (0761) 25 71

Politecnico di Milano
Piazza Leonardo da Vinci, 32
I-20123 Milano
☎ (02) 239 91

Politecnico di Torino
Corso Duca degli Abruzzi, 24
I-10129 Torino
☎ (011) 556 61

Istituto universitario di architettura Venezia
Santa Croce, Campazzo dei Tolentini, 191
I-30125 Venezia
☎ (041) 529 77 11

Istituto universitario orientale di Napoli
Piazza S. Giovanni Maggiore, 30
I-80133 Napoli
☎ (081) 553 41 59

I

Istituto universitario navale di Napoli
Via Ammiraglio Acton, 38
I-80133 Napoli
☎ (081) 551 22 49

State-run institutes with special responsibilities

Scuola normale superiore di Pisa
Piazza dei Cavalieri, 7
I-56100 Pisa
☎ (050) 59 71 11

Scuola superiore di studi universitari e di perfezionamento di Pisa
Via Carducci, 40
I-56100 Pisa
☎ (050) 453 77

Free universities (Università libere)

Università cattolica del sacro cuore di Milano
Largo A. Gemelli, 1
I-20123 Milano
☎ (02) 88 56

Università degli studi 'L. Bocconi' di Milano
Via R. Sarfatti, 25
I-20136 Milano
☎ (02) 838 41

Libera università internazionale studi sociali 'LUISS' di Roma
Viale Pola, 12
I-00198 Roma
☎ (06) 884 10 51

Università degli studi di Urbino
Via Saffi, 2
I-61029 Urbino
☎ (0722) 45 11/29 17

Istituto universitario di lingue moderne di Milano
Piazza dei Volontari, 3
I-20145 Milano
☎ (02) 31 39 22

Istituto universitario di lingue letterature straniere di Bergamo
Via Salvecchio, 19
I-24100 Bergamo
☎ (035) 21 71 95

Magistero pareggiato 'Suor Orsola Benincasa' di Napoli
Corso Vittorio Emanuele, 290
I-80135 Napoli
☎ (081) 40 00 70

Istituto universitario di magistero di Catania
Via Ofelia
I-95124 Catania
☎ (095) 32 90 25

Magistero pareggiato 'Maria SS. Assunta' di Roma
Via della Transpontina, 21
I-00193 Roma
☎ (06) 686 44 43

Higher education institutions for physical education (Istituti superiori di educazione fisica)

Istituto superiore di educazione fisica di Bologna
Via San Vitale, 15
I-40125 Bologna
☎ (051) 23 94 93

Istituto superiore di educazione fisica di Firenze
Via Nicolodi, 2
I-50137 Firenze
☎ (055) 57 19 97

Istituto superiore di educazione fisica di Palermo
Via Imperatore Federico, 61
I-90143 Palermo
☎ (091) 54 61 03

Istituto superiore di educazione fisica di Napoli
P. le Tecchio c/o Mostra d'Oltremare
I-80100 Napoli
☎ (081) 61 52 41

Istituto superiore di educazione fisica di Torino
Piazza Bernini, 12
I-10143 Torino
☎ (011) 74 57 74

Istituto superiore di educazione fisica di Urbino
Via dell'Annunziata, 4
I-61029 Urbino
☎ (0722) 32 91 52

Istituto superiore di educazione fisica Lombardia Milano
Piazza S. Alessandro, 1
I-20123 Milano
☎ (02) 869 34 31

Istituto superiore di educazione fisica L'Aquila
Via Francesco Crispi, 7
I-67100 L'Aquila
☎ (0862) 41 02 04

Istituto superiore di educazione fisica di Perugia
Via Campo di Marte, 10/A
I-06100 Perugia
☎ (075) 75 42 06

Istituto superiore di educazione fisica di Milano
Largo Frà A. Gemelli, 1
I-20123 Milano
☎ (02) 885 63 42

Istituto superiore di educazione fisica di Roma
Foro Italico
Piazza de Bosis, 15
I-00194 Roma
☎ (06) 39 06 16

Academies of Art

Accademia di belle arti
Via De Vitofrancesco, 2/1-13
I-70124 Bari
☎ (3980) 22 11 41

Accademia di belle arti
Via Belle Arti, 54
I-40100 Bologna
☎ (3951) 23 79 61

Accademia di belle arti
Via Roma, 1
I-54033 Carrara
☎ (39 585) 716 58

Accademia di belle arti
Via A. Di Sangiuliano, 257
I-95100 Catania
☎ (39 95) 31 73 60

Accademia di belle arti
Via De Filippis
I-88100 Catanzaro
☎ (39 961) 510 49

Accademia di belle arti
Via Ricasoli, 66
I-50100 Firenze
☎ (39 55) 21 54 49

Accademia di belle arti
Corso Garibaldi, 35
I-71100 Foggia
☎ (39 881) 263 01

Accademia di belle arti
Via S.S. Monti Lepini
I-03100 Frosinone
☎ (39 775) 803 25

Accademia di belle arti
Corso Vittorio Emanuele
I-67100 L'Aquila
☎ (39 862) 280 03

Accademia di belle arti
Via Ibertini, 3
I-73100 Lecce
☎ (39 832) 248 15

Accademia di belle arti
Via Don Minzoni, 1
I-62100 Macerata
☎ (39 733) 480 11

Accademia di belle arti
Via Brera, 28
I-20121 Milano
☎ (39 2) 80 69 69

Accademia di belle arti
Via Costantinopoli, 107 A
I-80100 Napoli
☎ (39 81) 34 10 32

Accademia di belle arti
Via Papireto, 18
I-90100 Palermo
☎ (39 91) 58 08 76

Accademia di belle arti
Via XXV Luglio, 10
I-89100 Reggio Calabria
☎ (39 965) 968 52

Accademia di belle arti
Via Ripetta, 222
I-00100 Roma
☎ (39 6) 679 88 61

Accademia nazionale d'arte drammatica
Lungotevere Mellini, 10
I-00100 Roma
☎ (39 6) 678 45 52

Accademia nazionale di danza
Largo Arrigo VII, 5
I-00100 Roma
☎ (39 6) 57 32 84

Accademia di belle arti
'Accademia Albertina'
Via Academia Albertina, 6
I-10100 Torino
☎ (39 11) 839 70 08

Accademia di belle arti
Via dei Maceri, 2
I-61029 Urbino
☎ (39 772) 41 96

Accademia di belle arti
Campo della Carità, 1050
I-30100 Venezia
☎ (39 41) 253 96

2. Survey of courses of study at higher education institutions

Corsi di studio: laurea (*Laurea* subjects of study)

	University locations / State-run universities	Ancona	Bari	Basilicata (Potenza)	Bologna	Brescia	Cagliari	Calabria (Cosenza)	Camerino	Cassino	Catania	Chieti (Pescara e Teramo)	Ferrara	Firenze	Genova
Agricoltura tropicale e subtropicale														●	
Architettura												●		●	●
Astronomia					●										
Chimica			●	●	●		●	●	●		●		●	●	●
Chimica e tecnologia farmaceutiche			●		●		●		●		●		●	●	●
Chimica industriale					●		●				●				●
Commercio internazionale e dei mercati valutari															
Conservazione dei beni culturali															
Discipline delle arti, musica e spettacolo					●			●							
Discipline economiche e sociali															
Economia aziendale															
Economia e commercio		●	●		●	●	●			●	●	●		●	●
Economia marittima e dei trasporti															
Economia politica															
Farmacia			●		●		●		●		●		●	●	●
Filologia e storia dell 'Europa orientale															
Filosofia			●		●		●	●			●	●		●	●
Fisica			●		●		●	●	●		●		●	●	●
Geografia [1]															●
Giurisprudenza			●		●		●		●		●	●	●	●	●
Ingegneria (biennio)													●		
Ingegneria aeronautica															
Ingegneria aerospaziale [2]															
Ingegneria chimica					●		●							●	●
Ingegneria civile: edile, idraulica, trasporti [3]		●	●	●	●	●	●				●			●	●
Ingegneria civile: di fesa del suolo e pianificazione territoriale		●		●				●							
Ingegneria elettronica		●	●		●						●			●	●
Ingegneria elettrotecnica			●		●		●			●	●				●
Ingegneria forestale															
Ingegneria idraulica				●											
Ingegneria dei materiali															
Ingegneria meccanica		●	●		●	●	●			●	●			●	
Ingegneria mineraria					●		●								
Ingegneria navale e meccanica															●
Ingegneria nucleare					●										
Ingegneria tecnica, industriale, economica, organizzativa															

1 Admission from the third year of studying onwards in humanities, natural sciences, biology, geology, political science, statistics, economics.

2 Admission with the *laurea* in engineering.

3 The *laurea* programme for civil engineers (excluding buildings) comprises the three departments of building engineering, hydraulic engineering and transport studies. In Ancona, Basilicata, l'Aquila, Rome II and Trieste only the transport studies programme is offered, at the University of Pavia, hydraulic engineering and transport studies.

● Full-time study

L'Aquila	Lecce	Macerata	Messina	Milano	Milano Politecnico	Modena	Molise (Campobasso)	Napoli	Napoli, Ist. Univ. Navale	Napoli, Ist. Univ. Orientale	Padova	Palermo	Parma	Durata anni (Duration (years))	
														4	Tropical and sub-tropical agriculture
					●			●				●		5	Architecture
											●			4	Astronomy
			●	●		●		●			●	●	●	5	Chemistry
			●	●		●		●			●		●	5	Chemistry and pharmaceutical technology
			●	●				●			●		●	5	Industrial chemistry
									●					4	International trade and business
														4	Studies on cultural heritage
														4	Music, drama, art
														5	Business and social studies
														4	Business studies
			●			●		●				●	●	4	Economics
									●					4	Maritime and transport studies
														4	Political economy
			●	●		●		●			●	●		4	Pharmacy
										●				4	Eastern European studies
	●	●	●	●				●		●	●	●		4	Philosophy
●	●		●	●		●		●			●	●	●	4	Physics
														4	Geography[1]
		●	●	●		●		●			●	●	●	4	Law
			●			●								2	Engineering
					●			●				●		5	Aeronautical engineering
														2	Aerospace engineering[2]
					●			●			●	●		5	Chemical engineering
					●			●			●	●		5	Civil engineering[3]
					●									5	Environmental engineering
					●			●			●	●	●	5	Electronic engineering
					●	●		●			●	●		5	Electrotechnical engineering
														5	Agricultural engineering
													●	5	Hydraulic engineering
														5	Materials technology
					●			●			●	●	●	5	Mechanical engineering
														5	Mining engineering
								●						5	Naval and marine engineering
					●							●		5	Nuclear engineering
					●									5	Industrial engineering

Corsi di studio: laurea (*Laurea* subjects of study)

	University locations State-run universities	Pavia	Perugia	Pisa	Reggio Calabria	Roma I La Sapienza	Roma II Tor Vergata	Salerno	Sassari	Siena	Torino	Torino Politecnico	Trento	Trieste	Tuscia (Viterbo)
Agricoltura tropicale e subtropicale															
Architettura					●	●						●			
Astronomia															
Chimica		●	●	●		●		●	●		●			●	
Chimica e tecnologia farmaceutiche		●	●	●		●			●	●	●			●	
Chimica industriale				●		●					●				
Commercio internazionale e dei mercati valutari															
Conservazione dei beni culturali															●
Discipline delle arti, musica e spettacolo															
Discipline economiche e sociali															
Economia aziendale				●											
Economia e commercio		●	●	●		●	●	●			●		●	●	
Economia marittima e dei trasporti															
Economia politica													●		
Farmacia		●	●	●		●			●	●	●			●	
Filologia e storia dell 'Europa orientale															
Filosofia		●	●	●		●	●	●		●	●			●	
Fisica		●	●	●		●	●	●			●		●	●	
Geografia [1]						●									
Giurisprudenza		●	●	●	●	●	●	●	●	●	●		●	●	
Ingegneria (biennio)			●							●	●				
Ingegneria aeronautica				●		●						●			
Ingegneria aerospaziale [2]						●						●			
Ingegneria chimica		●		●		●						●		●	
Ingegneria civile: edile, idraulica, trasporti [3]		●		●	●	●	●					●	●	●	
Ingegneria civile: di fesa del suolo e pianificazione territoriale		●						●							
Ingegneria elettronica		●		●		●	●					●		●	
Ingegneria elettrotecnica		●		●		●						●		●	
Ingegneria forestale													●		
Ingegneria idraulica															
Ingegneria dei materiali													●		
Ingegneria meccanica		●	●	●		●	●					●		●	
Ingegneria mineraria							●					●		●	
Ingegneria navale e meccanica														●	
Ingegneria nucleare				●		●						●			
Ingegneria tecnica, industriale, economica, organizzativa															

1 Admission from the third year of studying onwards in humanities, natural sciences, biology, geology, political science, statistics, economics.

2 Admission with the *laurea* in engineering.

3 The *laurea* programme for civil engineers (excluding buildings) comprises the three departments of building engineering, hydraulic engineering and transport studies. In Ancona, Basilicata, l'Aquila, Rome II and Trieste only the transport studies programme is offered, at the University of Pavia, hydraulic engineering and transport studies.

4 The Catholic University of Sacro Cuore offers the following degree courses in Milan: humanities, political science, economics, and law; furthermore courses leading to a teaching qualification and mathematics, physics, natural sciences in Brescia, agricultural science in Piacenza, medicine and surger Rome.

● Full-time study

Udine	Venezia	Venezia, Ist. Univ. di Architettura	Verona	Free universities	Bergamo	Catania, Ist. Univ. di Magistero	Milano Bocconi	Milano S. Cuore (Cattolica) 4	Milano, Ist. Univ. di Lingue moderne	Napoli, Magistero pareggiato	Roma (LUISS)	Roma, Magistero pareggiato	Urbino	Durata anni (Duration (years))	
														4	Tropical and sub-tropical agriculture
		●												5	Architecture
														4	Astronomy
													●	5	Chemistry
														5	Chemistry and pharmaceutical technology
	●													5	Industrial chemistry
														4	International trade and business
●														4	Studies on cultural heritage
														4	Music, drama, art
							●							5	Business and social studies
	●						●							4	Business studies
	●		●		●			●	●		●		●	4	Economics
														4	Maritime and transport studies
							●							4	Political economy
													●	4	Pharmacy
														4	Eastern European studies
	●							●					●	4	Philosophy
													●	4	Physics
														4	Geography[1]
								●			●		●	4	Law
								●						2	Engineering
														5	Aeronautical engineering
														2	Aerospace engineering[2]
														5	Chemical engineering
														5	Civil engineering[3]
														5	Environmental engineering
														5	Electronic engineering
														5	Electrotechnical engineering
														5	Agricultural engineering
														5	Hydraulic engineering
														5	Materials technology
														5	Mechanical engineering
														5	Mining engineering
														5	Naval and marine engineering
														5	Nuclear engineering
														5	Industrial engineering

Corsi di studio: laurea (*Laurea* subjects of study)

	University locations State-run universities	Ancona	Bari	Basilicata (Potenza)	Bologna	Brescia	Cagliari	Calabria (Cosenza)	Camerino	Cassino	Catania	Chieti (Pescara e Teramo)	Ferrara	Firenze	Genova
Tecnologie industriali								●							
Interpreti e traduttori															
Lettere			●		●		●	●			●	●		●	●
Lingue e letterature orientali															
Lingue e letterature straniere			●		●		●	●				●		●	●
Lingue e letterature straniere moderne				●	●			●			●			●	●
Lingue e civiltà orientali															
Matematica			●	●	●		●	●	●		●		●	●	●
Materie letterarie			●		●		●			●			●	●	●
Medicina e chirurgia		●	●		●	●	●				●	●	●	●	●
Medicina veterinaria			●		●										
Musicologia															
Odontoiatria e protesi dentaria		●	●		●	●	●				●	●	●	●	●
Pedagogia			●		●		●			●			●	●	●
Pianificazione territoriale e urbanistica															
Psicologia															
Scienze agrarie		●	●	●	●						●				
Scienze ambientali															
Scienze dell'amministrazione															
Scienze bancarie e assicurative															
Scienze biologiche			●		●		●	●	●		●		●	●	●
Scienze dell'informazione			●		●										●
Scienze economiche															
Scienze economiche e bancarie															
Scienze economiche e sociali								●							
Scienze forestali			●	●										●	
Scienze geologiche			●		●		●	●	●	●	●		●	●	
Scienze naturali			●		●		●	●	●		●		●	●	
Scienze politiche			●		●		●		●		●	●		●	
Scienze delle preparazioni alimentari				●											
Scienze della produzione animale					●										
Scienze statistiche e attuariali															
Scienze statistiche e demografiche					●										
Scienze statistiche e economiche			●		●										
Sociologia															
Storia					●			●						●	
Storia e conservazione beni architettonici e ambientali															
Studi islamici [1]															
Scienze internazionali e diplomatiche															

[1] Admission granted to students with *Laurea* in law, political science, languages, literature and philosophy and who, after two years of study, have passe[d] an examination of proficiency in Arabic.

● Full-time study

L'Aquila	Lecce	Macerata	Messina	Milano	Milano Politecnico	Modena	Molise (Campobasso)	Napoli	Napoli, Ist. Univ. Navale	Napoli, Ist. Univ. Orientale	Padova	Palermo	Parma	Durata anni (Duration (years))	
												●		5	Industrial engineering
														4	Interpretation and translation
	●	●	●	●				●		●	●	●		4	Humanities
														4	Eastern languages and literature
●	●		●									●	●	4	Foreign languages and literature
		●	●	●				●		●	●	●		4	Modern foreign languages and literature
										●				4	Eastern languages and civilizations
●	●		●	●		●		●			●	●	●	4	Mathematics
●	●		●								●	●	●	4	Humanities
●			●	●		●		●			●	●	●	6	Medicine and surgery
			●	●				●					●	5	Veterinary studies
														4	Music
●			●	●		●		●			●	●	●	5	Dentistry
●	●										●	●	●	4	Education
			●											5	Urban and environmental studies
											●	●		5	Psychology
				●			●	●			●	●		5	Agricultural sciences
														5	Environmental sciences
														4	Administrative sciences
			●											4	Financial management
●	●		●	●		●		●			●	●	●	5	Biology
●				●										4	Computer science
														4	Economics
	●													4	Economics and financial studies
							●							4	Economic and social sciences
											●			5	Forestry
				●		●		●			●	●	●	4	Geology
			●	●		●		●			●	●	●	4	General sciences
		●	●	●				●		●	●	●		4	Political science
				●			●	●						5	Food and dietetics
				●										5	Animal sciences
														4	Statistics and financial mathematics
			●								●			4	Demographic statistics
											●	●		4	Economic statistics
								●						4	Sociology
			●											4	History
														5	Environmental and architectural studies
										●				2	Islamic studies[1]
														4	International relations

Corsi di studio: laurea (*Laurea* subjects of study)

	University locations State-run universities	Pavia	Perugia	Pisa	Reggio Calabria	Roma I La Sapienza	Roma II Tor Vergata	Salerno	Sassari	Siena	Torino	Torino Politecnico	Trento	Trieste	Tusçia (Viterbo)
Tecnologie industriali								●							
Interpreti e traduttori														●	
Lettere		●	●	●		●	●	●		●	●		●	●	
Lingue e letterature orientali															
Lingue e letterature straniere				●		●		●	●	●	●			●	
Lingue e letterature straniere moderne		●	●	●		●		●			●		●	●	●
Lingue e civiltà orientali															
Matematica		●	●	●		●	●	●		●	●		●	●	
Materie letterarie			●			●		●	●	●	●			●	
Medicina e chirurgia		●	●	●	●	●	●		●	●	●			●	
Medicina veterinaria			●	●					●		●				
Musicologia		●													
Odontoiatría e protesi dentaria		●	●	●	●	●	●		●	●	●			●	
Pedagogia			●			●		●	●	●	●			●	
Pianificazione territoriale e urbanistica					●										
Psicologia						●									
Scienze agrarie			●	●	●				●		●				●
Scienze ambientali															
Scienze dell'amministrazione					●										
Scienze bancarie e assicurative															
Scienze biologiche		●	●	●		●	●		●	●	●		●	●	●
Scienze dell'informazione				●		●		●			●				
Scienze economiche										●					
Scienze economiche e bancarie										●					
Scienze economiche e sociali															
Scienze forestali					●						●				●
Scienze geologiche		●	●	●		●				●	●			●	
Scienze naturali		●	●	●		●			●	●	●			●	
Scienze politiche		●	●	●		●		●	●	●	●			●	
Scienze delle preparazioni alimentari															
Scienze della produzione animale				●											
Scienze statistiche e attuariali						●								●	
Scienze statistiche e demografiche						●									
Scienze statistiche e economiche						●		●		●					
Sociologia						●									
Storia				●						●				●	
Storia e conservazione beni architettonicie ambientali					●										
Studi islamici [1]															
Scienze internazionali e diplomatiche														●	

[1] Admission granted to students with *Laurea* in law, political science, languages, literature and philosophy and who, after two years of study, have passe an examination of proficiency in Arabic.

● Full-time study

Udine	Venezia	Venezia, Ist. Univ. di Architettura	Verona	Free universities	Bergamo	Catania, Ist. Univ. di Magistero	Milano Bocconi	Milano S. Cuore (Cattolica) 3	Milano, Ist. Univ. di Lingue moderne	Napoli, Magistero pareggiato	Roma (LUISS)	Roma, Magistero pareggiato	Urbino	Durata anni (Duration (years))	
														5	Industrial engineering
								●						4	Interpretation and translation
	●							●					●	4	Humanities
	●													4	Eastern languages and literature
●	●		●		●	●		●	●	●		●	●	4	Foreign languages and literature
								●					●	4	Modern foreign languages and literature
														4	Eastern languages and civilizations
●								●						4	Mathematics
			●			●		●		●		●	●	4	Humanities
			●					●						6	Medicine and surgery
														5	Veterinary studies
														4	Music
			●					●						5	Dentistry
			●			●		●		●		●	●	4	Education
		●												5	Urban and environmental studies
														5	Psychology
●							●							5	Agricultural sciences
	●													5	Environmental sciences
														4	Administrative sciences
														4	Financial management
													●	5	Biology
														4	Computer science
														4	Economics
								●						4	Economics and financial studies
														4	Economic and social sciences
														5	Forestry
													●	4	Geology
														4	General science
								●			●		●	4	Political science
														5	Food and dietetics
														5	Animal sciences
														4	Statistics and financial mathematics
														4	Demographic statistics
														4	Economic statistics
													●	4	Sociology
	●													4	History
														5	Environmental and architectural studies
														2	Islamic studies [1]
														4	International relations

Corsi di studio post-laurea (*Post-Laurea* subjects of study)

University locations (State-run universities)	Agraria / Agriculture	Architettura / Architecture	Chimica industriale / Industrial chemistry	Economia e commercio: scienze statistiche / Economics and Statistics	Farmacia / Pharmacy	Giurisprudenza / Law	Ingegneria / Engineering	Lettere e filosofia: magistero, lingue e letterature straniere / Humanities and Philosophy, Foreign languages and literature	Medicina e chirurgia / Medicine and surgery	Medicina veterinaria / Veterinary medicine	Scienze economiche e bancarie / Economics and financial studies	Scienze matematiche, fisiche e naturali / Mathematics, physics, natural sciences
Ancona									•			
Bari	•			•	•	•	•	•	•			•
Basilicata (Potenza)												
Bologna	•		•	•	•	•	•	•	•	•		•
Brescia									•			
Cagliari					•		•	•	•			
Calabria (Cosenza)				•			•					
Camerino					•	•						•
Cassino								•				
Catania				•		•		•	•			•
Chieti e Pescara e Teramo						•			•			
Ferrara					•	•			•			•
Firenze	•	•		•	•		•	•	•			•
Genova		•					•	•	•			•
L'Aquila									•			
Lecce								•				
Macerata						•		•				
Messina				•	•			•	•			•
Milano	•				•	•		•	•	•		•
Milano Politecnico							•					
Modena						•			•			•
Molise (Campobasso)												
Napoli	•	•			•	•	•	•	•	•		•
Napoli, Ist. Univ. Navale												
Napoli, Ist. Univ. Orientale								•				
Padova	•			•	•	•	•	•	•			•
Palermo	•			•	•	•	•		•			
Parma					•	•		•	•	•		•
Pavia				•	•	•		•	•			•

(Facoltà / Faculty)

• Specializing schools

Facoltà / Faculty	Agraria / Agriculture	Architettura / Architecture	Chimica industriale / Industrial chemistry	Economia e commercio: scienze statistiche / Economics and Statistics	Farmacia / Pharmacy	Giurisprudenza / Law	Ingegneria / Engineering	Lettere e filosofia magistero, lingue e letterature straniere / Humanities and Philosophy, Foreign languages and literature	Medicina e chirurgia / Medicine and surgery	Medicina veterinaria / Veterinary medicine	Scienze economiche e bancarie / Economics and financial studies	Scienze matematiche, fisiche e naturali / Mathematics, physics, natural sciences	Scienze politiche / Political science
University locations (State-run universities)													
Perugia	●				●				●	●			
Pisa	●				●		●		●	●		●	
Reggio Calabria									●				
Roma I La Sapienza		●		●	●	●	●	●	●			●	●
Roma II Tor Vergata							●		●				
Salerno												●	
Sassari	●					●			●	●			
Siena					●			●	●		●	●	
Torino	●			●	●			●	●	●		●	
Torino Politecnico							●						
Trento													
Trieste						●		●	●			●	
Tuscia (Viterbo)													
Udine													
Venezia								●					
Venezia, Ist. Univ. di Architettura													
Verona									●				
Università libere (Free universities)													
Bergamo													
Catania, Ist. Univ. di Magistero													
Milano Bocconi				●									
Milano, Ist. Univ. di Lingue moderne								●					
Milano S. Cuore (Cattolica)	●			●		●		●	●				●
Napoli, magistero pareggiato													
Roma (LUISS)				●								●	
Roma, magistero pareggiato								●					
Urbino								●					

3. Student statistics

Students from EC Member States according to subject groups

Country of origin	Mathematics, physics, natural scien.	Pharmacy	Medicine and surgery	Engineering	Architecture	Agriculture	Veterinary medicine	Economics	Political science	Law	Humanities and philosophy	Pedagogics	Other faculties	Total
Belgium	6	1	13	3	5	2	3	18	10	6	16	5	5	93
Denmark	1	1	—	1	2	—	2	5	1	—	7	1	—	21
FR of Germany	70	15	1064	31	80	10	200	67	24	34	167	51	29	1842
Greece	835	1132	2806	789	767	142	92	274	114	306	832	404	117	8610
Spain	6	4	16	4	6	—	1	5	4	16	31	6	4	103
France	25	12	54	15	16	3	17	35	15	13	68	36	32	341
Ireland	—	—	—	—	—	—	—	—	—	2	5	3	1	11
Italy														
Luxembourg	1	—	—	—	2	—	—	1	1	1	4	2	2	14
The Netherlands	7	—	4	7	—	3	4	13	5	1	10	3	7	64
Portugal	2	1	5	2	1	—	—	3	1	2	4	3	—	24
United Kingdom	10	2	27	19	13	1	2	20	10	8	51	30	12	205
Total	963	1168	3989	871	892	161	321	441	185	389	1195	544	209	11328

Italian and foreign students at institutions of higher education in Italy

University locations State-run universities	Fully registered students: Italians and Foreigners	Foreigners
Ancona	6 731	459
Bari	56 245	648
Basilicata	1 532	–
Bologna	58 724	1 791
Brescia	5 074	145
Cagliari	18 961	199
Calabria (Cosenza)	6 169	24
Camerino	3 275	405
Cassino	3 389	2
Catania	28 415	443
Chieti e Pescara e Teramo	19 553	–
Ferrara	4 632	293
Firenze	41 383	1 075
Genova	30 347	477
L'Aquila	4 723	187
Lecce	7 252	199
Macerata	4 922	161
Messina	28 603	421
Milano	67 535	1 037
Milano Politecnico	29 651	815
Modena	7 445	169
Molise (Campobasso)	601	–
Napoli	73 176	1 155
Napoli, Ist. Univ. Navale	2 171	40
Napoli, Ist. Univ. Orientale	8 246	54
Padova	42 562	1 425
Palermo	36 998	510
Parma	14 020	273
Pavia	18 627	928
Perugia	16 968	1 022
Pisa	30 662	387
Reggio Calabria	10 732	178
Roma I, La Sapienza	158 670	4 299
Roma II, Tor Vergata	4 123	20
Salerno	21 350	29
Sassari	8 378	78
Siena	11 540	387
Torino	46 911	596
Torino Politecnico	10 459	344
Trento	4 862	27
Trieste	13 974	953
Tuscia (Viterbo)	1 394	22
Udine	4 448	66
Venezia	14 606	122
Venezia, Istit. Univ. di Architettura	8 288	547
Verona	9 175	240
Freie Universitäten		
Bergamo	3 859	13
Catania	2 859	10
Milano Bocconi	9 797	86
Milano, Ist. Univ. di Lingue moderne	2 622	57
Milano S. Cuore (Cattolica)	22 340	186
Napoli, Magistero pareggiato	3 867	16
Roma (LUISS)	2 755	25
Roma, Magistero pareggiato	708	27
Urbino	12 431	152
Total	1 068 690	23 206

ISEF = Istituto superiore di educazione fisica (Institutes of physical education)

Institute	Italians and Foreigners	Foreigners
ISEF Bologna	1 755	2
ISEF Firenze	1 479	6
ISEF Genova	689	–
ISEF L'Aquila	1 611	19
ISEF Lombardia	946	3
ISEF Milano	797	1
ISEF Napoli	2 970	–
ISEF Palermo	1 889	5
ISEF Perugia	773	–
ISEF Roma	2 185	5
ISEF Torino	1 224	4
ISEF Urbino	1 493	13
Total	17 811	58

Source: ISTAT.

4. Bibliography

Corsi di lingua e cultura italiana per stranieri in Italia. Published by Ministero degli affari esteri.

Repertorio dei corsi di formazione per stranieri offerti dall'Italia. Published by Ministero degli affari esteri.

Guida all'istruzione superiore, Ministero della pubblica istruzione, Roma, 1987. Available from: Istituto Poligrafico dello Stato, Direzione Commerciale, Piazza Verdi 10, 00198 Rome.

Rotary International: **Pronti alla scelta: Facoltà e percorsi alternativi,** 1986. Published by Giunti Marzocco, Florence.

G. Sartoratti, **Una scelta per l'Università, Corsi di laurea e professioni, Scuole dirette a fini speciali**. Edizioni Alborg, Padova, 1986.

C. Boga, **Guida alla scelta delle facoltà e del corso di laurea.** Pirola editore, Milan, 1987.

F. Froio, **Guida completa per la scelta della facoltà**. Mursia editore, 1988.

L. Pusci, **Laurea in ....** Sovera Multimedia editrice, 1988/89.

T. De Mauro, **Guida alla scelta della facoltà universitaria**. Il Mulino editore, Bologna, 1988.

Universitas. Quarterly magazine covering degree courses and university life. F[lli] Palombi editore, Via dei Gracchi 181, Roma.

The abovementioned publications may be obtained from the publishers or from bookshops.

5. Glossary

Accademie di Belle Arti: The academies offer training in the fine arts at 'post-secondary', not university, level. The studies last four years. There are four study specializations: painting, sculpting, interior architecture and stage-set design.

Albo professionale: Register of persons (lawyers, physicians, economic advisers) who practise the same profession to which the registration refers. It entitles persons to practise this profession; for registration it is necessary to pass a State examination.

Assegno di studio: An academic subsidy, also called *presalario*, awarded only to gifted Italian students with good academic records who are lacking in financial means. The subsidies are awarded in a *concorso* (public competition) and only for the acquisition of one *laurea*.

Conservatori di musica: The conservatories are places of training for all branches of music and are therefore subdivided into schools for the various subject specializations (piano, composition, violin, etc.). They offer teaching for beginners and advanced students.

Consiglio di facoltà: The faculty council is a body made up of the teaching staff of the faculty and a student representation. The council's functions include the following: (i) scheduling the various individual courses; (ii) proposing reforms in university teaching methods; (iii) giving opinions on questions the Rector or President present to it; (iv) deciding on and implementing disciplinary measures against students; (v) approving the individual curricula of the students.

Corso di perfezionamento: see *Perfezionamento*.

Corso di specializzazione: see *Specializzazione*.

Corso singolo: Students coming from foreign universities and wishing to take one or more courses at an Italian university may be admitted to these individual courses *(corsi singoli)*, on completion of which they receive a certificate covering their study achievements.

Diploma di maturità: School-leaving certificate awarded upon completing higher secondary studies. All secondary school-leaving certificates with various subject combinations permit entry into any faculty of any university provided they were acquired after a period of secondary education lasting five years. At present the *diplomi magistrali* (pedagogical orientation) and the *diplomi artistici* (art orientation) are being awarded after only four years' upper schooling and only entitle holders to admittance to certain subjects. A supplementary fifth year *(anno integrativo)* and passing the final examination entitle students to enrol in all faculties.

Dottorato di ricerca: A *post lauream* academic degree valid only in the sphere of scientific and scholarly research.

Dottore: An academic title conferred on everyone who has the *laurea*. Thus, there is the *Dottore in lettere, Dottore in ingegneria,* etc., depending on the *corso di laurea* taken.

Esame di laurea: Every student who has passed all the examinations required in the *corso di laurea* is admitted to the *esame di laurea*. This consists of the defence of a written thesis *(tesi)* before an examination commission. Upon successful examination, the student may use the title of doctor.

Esame di profitto: Intermediate examination following various courses as foreseen in the curriculum.

Facoltà: Teaching and research unit of a university.

Immatricolazione: Admission to the first year of the chosen faculty (or the *corso di laurea)* is called matriculation. In order to matriculate the applicant must have the Italian *diploma di maturità* or an equivalent foreign secondary school-leaving certificate, i.e. one entitling the holder to access to a university in the home country.

Immatricolazione con abbreviazione di corso: Registration in an advanced course year for students who have already completed part of a course of study at a university.

Iscrizione: Registration is reserved for those students who have completed the first year at an Italian or foreign university. Registration is possible independently of the number of examinations passed.

Istituti ad ordinamento speciale: The *scuola normale superiore* and the *Scuola superiore di perfezionamento* in Pisa have the responsibility of promoting research as well as teaching in natural sciences and humanities, *inter alia* through postgraduate and advanced studies for students who are simultaneously enrolled at the University of Pisa, and for graduates from Italy (with the *Laurea* degree) and from abroad. Admittance is gained through competition *(concorso)*.

Istituto libero: Private, but State-recognized university.

Istituti o Enti per il diritto allo studio: Regional establishments which provide social services and facilities for students at the individual universities.

Istituti superiori di educazione fisica: These institutes lead to the degree which entitles the holder to teach physical education at Italian schools of every type and at all levels.

Istituto universitario: University establishment which generally has only one faculty.

Laurea: Academic degree awarded after successful completion of all intermediate examinations as provided for in the curriculum as well as of the *Laurea* examination.

Magistero pareggiato: University institution offering courses which nearly all relate to the teaching and social professions.

Numero chiuso: Designation for admissions restrictions at university *(numerus clausus)*. In Italy, the *numerus clausus* is currently only in force for dentistry and orthodontics programmes.

Numero programmato: A restricted number of study places on account of a resolution of the faculty council which bases the decision on the locally prevailing conditions for teaching and research as well as on the opportunities for occupation. This restriction of study places is valid for some *laurea* programmes.

Perfezionamento (scuole di): The institutions of advanced study for students having completed their course *(post-lauream)* are intended to provide profound study of certain subjects and further education or a return to professional life. Admission is subject to limitations. Simultaneous enrolment in two *scuole di perfezionamento* or in a *scuola di perfezionamento* and a *scuola di specializzazione* is not possible, nor can a graduate follow a course at a *scuola di perfezionamento* and a doctoral programme *(dottorato di ricerca)* at the same time. Students enrolled at a *scuola di perfezionamento* must sit annual examinations and a final examination for the diploma degree.

Politecnico: University institution with only two *corsi di laurea*: engineering and architecture. In Italy there are only *politecnici* in Milan and Turin.

Pre-iscrizione: First phase of matriculation (or registration), introduced for foreign students in academic year 1976/77. It is compulsory for all foreign applicants with the exception of the cases listed under 'Application and registration'.

Scuole dirette a fini speciali: The *scuole dirette a fini speciali* are integrated in the university structure and serve to complement the basic principles of higher education. After a two or three year course the student is awarded a diploma for post-secondary studies *(diploma post-secondario)* which entitles the holder to pursue professions for which the *laurea* is not necessary, but which do nevertheless require professional training within the framework of higher education.

Specializzazione (scuole di): These schools award diplomas after completion of the *laurea* which enable the holder to qualify as a specialist in certain professions. They are intended to provide *laurea*-graduates with comprehensive technical capacities in particular professional areas. Admission is subject to limitations. Simultaneous enrolment in two *scuole di specializzazione* or in one *scuola di specializzazione* and one of *perfezionamento* or in a *scuola di specializzazione* and a doctoral course *(dottorato di ricerca)* is not possible. Students enrolled in *scuole di specializzazione* must sit annual examinations and a degree examination for the diploma.

Università: General designation for all higher education institutions in Italy.

6. Diagram of the education system

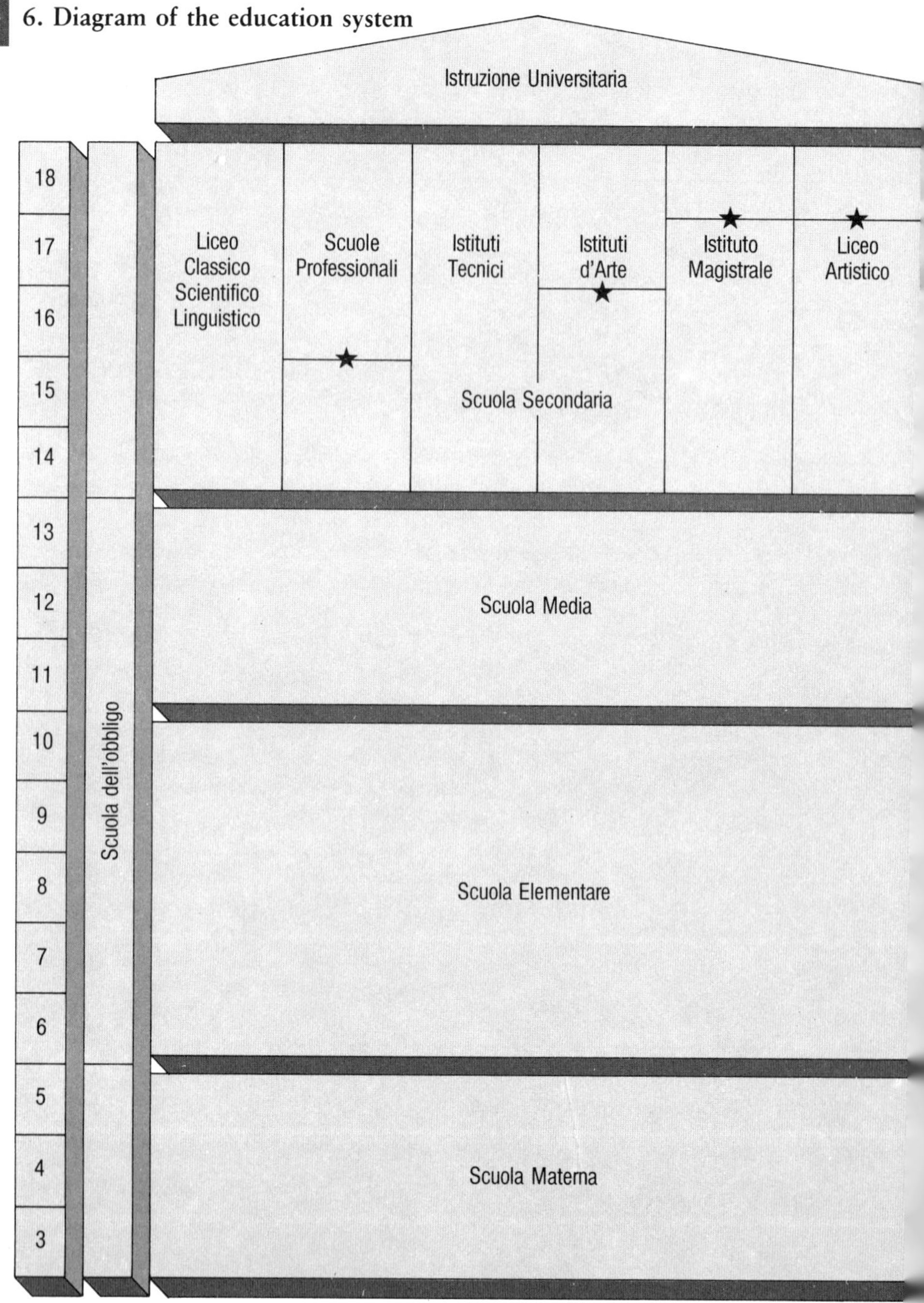
Istruzione Universitaria
18
17
16
15
14
13
12
11
10
9
8
7
6
5
4
3
Scuola dell'obbligo
Liceo Classico Scientifico Linguistico
Scuole Professionali
Istituti Tecnici
Istituti d'Arte
Istituto Magistrale
Liceo Artistico
Scuola Secondaria
Scuola Media
Scuola Elementare
Scuola Materna

Explanations and translations of technical terms on facing page.

Legend

Istituti d'Arte — Colleges of applied art.
Istituti Tecnici — Technical colleges.
Istituto Magistrale — Colleges for educators and primary school teachers.
Istruzione Universitaria — Higher education.
Liceo Artistico — Art-orientated grammar school.
Liceo Classico Scientifico Linguistico — Grammar school (classics, scientific, language orientation).
Scuola dell'obligo — Compulsory schooling.
Scuola Elementare — Primary school.
Scuola Materna — Kindergarten.
Scuola Media — Lower secondary stage.
Scuola Secondaria — Secondary stage.
Scuole Professionali — Vocational schools.
The horizontal dividing lines show that there are intermediate diplomas which do not entitle the holders to higher education access (admissions requirement: five years of secondary schooling).

Luxembourg

L

Organization of higher education

Higher education in Luxembourg is basically confined to:

1. a first-year university course *(cours universitaires)* at the *Centre universitaire de Luxembourg* in the following subject areas: humanities, science, medicine, and pharmacy;
2. postgraduate training at the *Institut universitaire international de Luxembourg;*
3. a three-year course of study at the *Institut supérieur de technologie de Luxembourg*;
4. a two-year course of study in computer science and economics at the *Centre universitaire de Luxembourg.*

Types of higher education institutions

The *Centre universitaire de Luxembourg* offers *cours universitaires* and *cours complémentaires* (see Glossary). The *Institut universitaire international* is under the partial administration of the *Centre universitaire*. The *Institut supérieur de technologie* (IST), which replaced the *Ecole technique*, was established by Grand-Ducal Decree of 21 May 1979.

Student statistics

In 1987/88, a total of 426 students were enrolled at the *Centre universitaire*, 231 of them in the *Département de droit et des sciences économiques*, 79 in the *Département des lettres et des sciences humaines* and 116 in the *Département des sciences*. These 426 students included 91 from abroad.

In 1986, 72 foreign students, most of them from EC countries, were enrolled during the academic periods *(sessions)* at the *Institut universitaire international.*

Most citizens of Luxembourg who wish to continue their education abroad move to France or Belgium. Large numbers also study in the Federal Republic of Germany, in Austria and in Switzerland.

Organization and validation of courses

A Grand-Ducal decree determines the academic structure of the *cours universitaires*, the curricula and the examination procedures. On the basis of this decree, the *cours universitaires* involve the following departments, which are in turn divided into several subject areas:

1. *Département de droit et des sciences économiques;*
2. *Département des lettres et des sciences humaines;*
3. *Département des sciences.*

The *cours universitaires* last one year. Instruction consists of compulsory and optional subjects and is given in the form of lectures and tutorials.

The *Département de droit et des sciences économiques* includes:

1. a sub-department for students who wish to continue their studies at French universities or at universities with a similar course structure;
2. a sub-department for students who wish to continue their studies at Belgian or German universities.

The *Département des lettres et des sciences humaines* includes the following subject areas: philosophy and psychology, classical philology, Romance languages, German, English, history and geography.

The *Département des sciences* includes the following subject areas: medicine (ME), pharmacy (PH), mathematical and physical sciences (MP), chemistry and biology (CB).

During the academic year, which lasts from the first week in October until the end of the following May, the *élèves réguliers* have to write the papers and take the written and oral tests required of them by their professsors. Marks are given at the end of the semester or year on a scale from 0 to 20.

Students who have successfully completed the one-year *cours universitaires* receive the appropriate certificate: the *Certificat d'études juridiques et économiques* from the *Département de droit et des sciences économiques,* the *Certificat d'études littéraires et des sciences humaines* from the *Département des lettres et des sciences humaines* and the *Certificat d'études scientifiques* from the *Département des sciences*.

Students who present one of these three certificates can enrol as a regular student for second-year studies at an Austrian, German, Belgian or French university (for third-year law studies in Belgium). There they can obtain a title or degree which is recognized *(homologation)* or registered *(inscription au registre des titres d'enseignement supérieur)* by the Ministry of National Education and Youth.

The *Institut universitaire international* is divided into three academic departments:

1. the *Centre international d'études juridiques et de droit comparé*;
2. the *Centre international d'études et de recherches européennes*;
3. the *Centre international d'économie politique*.

The initial joint programme of lectures and seminars is followed by specialized, in-depth courses lasting one or more *sessions* of three to four weeks each.

The *Institut supérieur de technologie* is similar to a polytechnic. It is divided into the following subject areas: mechanical engineering, civil engineering, computer science for industrial applications, and electrical engineering. The latter is in turn divided into electronics and electrical engineering for industry.

Studies at this institute last three years (six semesters). The academic year runs from mid-September to the end of June.

Students who successfully complete the course of studies at the *Institut supérieur de technologie* receive the

Diplôme d'ingénieur-technicien. With this certificate they may enrol at certain technical colleges or universities abroad.

Since the 1983/84 academic year, the *Département de droit et des sciences économiques* at the *Centre universitaire* in Luxembourg has been offering two-year courses of study *(cycle court d'études supérieures en gestion)* in the following areas:

— data-processing in industry and administration;
— commerce and banking;
— business management.

In the first year of study there is a joint curriculum for commerce/banking and business management. Specialization in these two areas takes place in the second year of study. In all three subjects, an examination is held at the end of each academic year.

Admission and registration

Initial information

Information can be requested on:

1. studying in Luxembourg and EC countries from the *Centre de psychologie et d'orientation scolaires;*
2. entry and residence in Luxembourg from the *Service de la Police des Etrangers* at the *Ministère de la Justice*;
3. employment opportunities in Luxembourg from the *Administration de l'Emploi.*

(For addresses, see Appendix 1.)

Entry requirements

Holders of a Luxembourg or equivalent foreign secondary school-leaving certificate, regardless of the type of school, can register as *élèves réguliers* or as *élèves libres* (occasional students) for the *cours universitaires* or short courses.

In order to enrol at the *Institut universitaire international*, applicants must have a higher education degree in law, political economy or political science or an equivalent professional qualification. The application for admission must be accompanied by the recommendation of a higher education institution.

The following can enrol in first-year studies at the *Institut supérieur de technologie*:

1. holders of a secondary school-leaving certificate concentrating on technical subjects;
2. holders of an upper-secondary level school-leaving certificate or equivalent diploma.

Limitations and entry examinations

As many foreign students as possible are admitted to the *cours universitaires*, there being no fixed limit. There are no entrance examinations.

The *Institut universitaire international* also admits candidates without holding an entrance examination.

The *Institut supérieur de technologie* admits as many foreign students as possible.

Recognition of foreign certificates and degrees

For certain professional career occupations Luxembourg legislation requires that applicants meet specific admission and educational requirements. The holders of foreign degrees must therefore, in precisely defined instances, have their degrees confirmed by the Luxembourg Recognition Commission *(Commission d'homologation)* prior to taking employment.

The Commission examines degrees submitted to it to see whether they comply with national legislation (especially as regards length of study, admission conditions and courses studied). The following occupations are concerned in particular: secondary school teachers, lawyers, notaries, physicians, dentists, veterinarians, pharmacists.

Access to other academic professions is generally subject to controls by the Recognition Commission *(Commission des titres)* (e.g. degrees in economic and social sciences, political science, architecture and engineering).

In general, academic degrees and certificates are only recognized as such if they involve at least four years of full-time university study.

Application and registration

Applications for admission are not required for the *cours universitaires*, the *Institut universitaire international* or the *Institut supérieur de technologie*.

Applications for enrolment in the *cours universitaires* must be sent to the office of the relevant department by 1 September.

Applications for enrolment in a course of study at the *Institut universitaire international* must be sent to this institute as early as possible (by May at the latest) along with a certified copy of the applicant's degree.

Applications for enrolment in a course of study at the *Institut supérieur de technologie* must reach the director of the institute by 1 September.

Tuition fees

No tuition fees have to be paid for the *cours universitaires* or at the *Institut universitaire international* or *Institut supérieur de technologie.*

Knowledge of the language of instruction, language courses and other courses

French is used in the *cours universitaires.* Foreign students must have a good command of this language. However, the *Centre universitaire* does not demand a language examination or a certificate of proficiency.

At the *Institut universitaire international* German, English and French are used as languages of instruction. Students wishing to study there must have a command of these three languages, although proof of their linguistic competence is not required.

At the *Institut supérieur de technologie* teaching is in German and French. Students wanting to study there must have a perfect command of both languages.

At present there are no special courses at university level in Luxembourg.

Financial assistance and scholarships

Under a law passed on 8 December 1977, the government can grant financial assistance to those wishing to pursue higher education studies. The assistance can take the form of a scholarship, an interest-free loan or a loan with interest.

The following are eligible for this assistance:

1. Luxembourg students;
2. foreign students who have their permanent residence in Luxembourg and have a degree or some other certification of studies completed at a Luxembourg institution or at the *Ecole européenne* in Luxembourg.

The following are considered higher education studies:

1. all university studies of the first and second stages *(cycles)*;
2. semi-academic training (graduate nurse, etc.);
3. training at other higher education institutions (leading, for example, to the *diplôme de gradué*);
4. the *cours universitaires* in Luxembourg;
5. studies at the *Institut supérieur de technologie*.

Applications for the winter semester: Applications for financial assistance must be sent to the *Centre de psychologie et d'orientation scolaires* by 10 July at the latest (for address, see Appendix 1) even if the student has not yet decided on a specific higher education institution.

Applications for the summer semester: students who received financial assistance during the winter semester must reapply by 10 January at the latest.

Details of the application procedure can be found in the brochure *Que faire pour avoir une aide financière de l'État pour études supérieures?* (see bibliography).

The *Institut universitaire international* in Luxembourg awards a certain number of scholarships to students enrolled there. Anyone wanting to apply for a scholarship must submit with his enrolment application the recommendation of a higher education institution or, if he is already employed, of a superior.

L

Entry and residence regulations

Students from EC Member States are subject to the requirements as laid down in Article 11 of the Grand-Ducal Regulations regarding entry formalities for foreigners.

Under this article, foreign students are not required to apply for an alien's identity card *(carte d'identité d'étranger)* if they do not wish to stay in Luxembourg for more than one year and if they at the same time maintain their main place of residence in their respective home country.

However, such students must apply at the Luxembourg Ministry of Justice for a temporary residence permit. This application must include proof of the student's financial means as well as the reasons for the stay in Luxembourg.

A copy of the temporary residence permit will be sent to the local authorities in the community where the student would like to live and where the student's arrival must be announced.

The temporary residence permit may, upon application, be renewed annually.

Social aspects

Social security and health insurance

Foreign students who come from EC countries and who are enrolled in social security and health insurance schemes there may take advantage of the Luxembourg National Worker's Health Insurance Scheme upon presentation of the appropriate form.

Those students who are not insured in their home countries may take out voluntary insurance in Luxembourg. For this they should contact the *Centre d'affiliation et de perception des cotisations commun aux institutions de sécurité.*

Advisory services

The advisory office *Centre de psychologie et d'orientation scolaires* of the Ministry of Education (for address, see Appendix 1) advises foreign students on all questions relating to the everyday life of students in Luxembourg.

Information on employment conditions in the Grand Duchy is available from the *Service d'orientation professionnelle* of the *Administration de l'emploi* (for address, see Appendix 1).

Student employment

Students from EC countries, like Luxembourg students, are dealt with by the *Administration de l'emploi.* It should be pointed out, however, that at present virtually only part-time jobs in hotels are available.

Student organizations

Besides the three most important student associations:

1. *ALUC (Association luxembourgeoise des universitaires catholiques);*
2. *CEL (Cercle des étudiants libéraux);*
3. *UNEL (Union nationale des étudiants luxembourgeois);*

there are some 20 Luxembourg student organizations which cultivate contacts with foreign students and form an umbrella organization: *ACEL (Association des cercles des étudiants luxembourgeois aux universités étrangères).*

Cost of living

The average monthly budget of a student in Luxembourg is difficult to determine. In 1989/90 students living away from home needed at least LFR 20 000 a month.

Accommodation

Students seeking accommodation should either apply to an estate agent or place an advertisement in the newspaper under *demande de location.*

They can also apply to the *Centre universitaire de Luxembourg* for a room in the hall of residence there. In view of the limited number of rooms available (40), foreign students should send in their applications as early as possible, but no later than 1 September. Room rent was LFR 2 500 a month in 1986/87.

Students enrolled in the seminars of the *Institut universitaire international de Luxembourg* are accommodated either in private lodgings or at the *Centre universitaire.* In the latter case, room rent is approximately LFR 3 000 per month. Rooms are available through the secretariat of the Institute.

Services for students

Students enrolled in the *cours universitaires* are entitled to have lunch in the refectory, which is run under the direction of the *Centre de psychologie et d'orientation scolaires* of the Luxembourg Ministry of Education. In the 1989 academic year, the price of lunch was LFR 115.

The *Centre de psychologie et d'orientation scolaires* will provide information on all other services and benefits for students.

L

Appendices

1. Addresses

Luxembourg embassies in EC countries

Belgium
Avenue de Cortenberg 75
B-1040 Bruxelles
☎ 733 99 77

Denmark
The Luxembourg Ambassador in Bonn is responsible for Denmark.

Federal Republic of Germany
Adenauerallee 110
D-5300 Bonn 1
☎ 21 40 08/9

Spain
Calle Claudio Coello 78
E-28006 Madrid
☎ 56 42 474

Greece
The Luxembourg Ambassador in Rome is responsible for Greece.

France
33 avenue Rapp
F-75007 Paris
☎ 45 55 13 37

Ireland
The Luxembourg Ambassador in London is responsible for Ireland.

Italy
3 via Guerrieri (Aventino)
I-Roma
☎ 57 80 456

Netherlands
Nassaulaan
251495 's-Gravenhage
☎ 60 75 16

Portugal
Rua da Janelas Verdes
P-1200 Lisboa
☎ 66 25 44

United Kingdom
27 Wilton Crescent
London SW 1
☎ 235 69 61

Institutions

Centre universitaire
Cycle court
Département de droit et des sciences économiques and Département des lettres et des sciences humaines
162a avenue de la Faïencerie
L-1511 Luxembourg
☎ 216 21

Centre universitaire
Département des sciences
Place Auguste-Laurent
L-1921 Luxembourg
☎ 244 17

Institut supérieur de technologie
Rue Richard Coudenhove-Kalergi
L-1359 Luxembourg
☎ 43 66 61

Institut universitaire international
162a avenue de la Faïencerie
L-1511 Luxembourg
☎ 216 21

Centre de psychologie et d'orientation scolaires du Ministère de l'Éducation nationale et de la jeunesse
29 rue Aldringen
L-1118 Luxembourg
☎ 46 80 25 55, 46 80 25 51

Service de la police des étrangers du Ministère de la Justice
16 boulevard Royal
L-2449 Luxembourg
☎ 47 94-1

Administration de l'Emploi
2 rue Philippe II
L-2340 Luxembourg

Administration communale de la ville de Luxembourg
Hôtel de Ville
Place Guillaume
L-1648 Luxembourg
☎ 479 61

Centre d'affiliation et de perception des cotisations commun aux institutions de sécurité sociale
125 route d'Esch
L-1471 Luxembourg

Caisse nationale de maladie des ouvriers
125 route d'Esch
L-1471 Luxembourg

ALUC (Association luxembourgeoise des universitaires catholiques)
12 avenue Marie-Thérèse
L-2132 Luxembourg

CEL (Cercle des étudiants libéraux)
Boîte postale 1035
L-1010 Luxembourg

UNEL (Union nationale des étudiants luxembourgeois)
Boîte postale 324
L-2013 Luxembourg

2. Bibliography

The following brochures are available free of charge upon request:
From the *Centre universitaire de Luxembourg:*

Structures et programmes, Luxembourg 1988/89; brochure.

From the *Institut universitaire international de Luxembourg:*

Études juridiques et de droit comparé.

Centre international d'études et de recherches européennes;

leaflet.

Centre international d'économie politique.
From the *Institut supérieur de technologie:*

Horaires et programmes; brochure.

From the *Centre de psychologie et d'orientation scolaires:*

Was tun nach dem 6. Schuljahr? 1989 edition; brochure.

Was tun nach der 'Cinquième'? 1989 edition; brochure.

Que faire pour avoir une aide financière de l'État pour études supérieures? 1988 edition; brochure.

Que faire après le lycée?
1989 edition; brochure.

Leaflets on about 60 academic professions; 1988/89 edition.

Guide pratique pour études universitaires in Belgium, France.

Das Studium in Deutschland (BRD), Österreich, Schweiz.

Higher Education in the United Kingdom

Praktische Hinweise.

3. Glossary

Certificat d'études juridiques et économiques: *A certificat d'études supérieures (CES)* awarded by the *Département de droit et des sciences économiques* to students who have successfully completed the one-year *cours universitaires.*

Certificat d'études littéraires et des sciences humaines: *A certificat d'études supérieures (CES)* awarded by the *Département des sciences humaines* to students who have successfully completed the one-year *cours universitaires.*

Certificat d'études scientifiques: *A certificat d'études supérieures (CES)* awarded by the *Département des sciences* to students who have successfully completed the one-year *cours universitaires.*

Cours complémentaires: The *Centre universitaire* offers supplementary training at the *Département de formation juridique* and the *Département de formation pédagogique* as well as practical laboratory training. For admission to the *Département de formation juridique*, the *homologation* of a foreign higher education degree in law is needed. The *Département de formation pédagogique* is responsible for the first year of practical training of secondary school teachers. Required for admission is the *homologation* of a foreign higher education degree entitling the holder to enrol in practical teacher training (degrees in the humanities, sciences, physics, mathematics). A Luxembourg holder of a degree in pharmacy must attend the *cours complémentaires* in the form of practical laboratory training *(stage officinal)* for at least six months.

Diplôme d'ingénieur-technicien: Students who pass the final examination at the *Institut supérieur de technologie* receive the *diplôme d'ingénieur-technicien*. The course of study leading to this diploma lasts three years. Students may continue their studies and take their degrees at certain universities and technical colleges abroad.

Élève libre: Occasional student on the *cours universitaires* who may enrol in one or more courses of his choice. His enrolment requires the approval of a department professor.

Élève régulier: Student on the *cours universitaires* eligible to register for the final examination in his department. He must regularly attend the lectures in his subject area.

Homologation: Titles and degrees awarded to Luxembourg students by foreign universities and other higher education institutions are recognized in Luxembourg by means of official certification.

The system of official certification applies to degrees in the fields of philosophy and philology, physical and mathematical sciences, natural sciences, medicine, dentistry, veterinary medicine and pharmacy. Official certification is required for employment in one of the aforementioned fields.

L

Inscription au registre des titres d'enseignement supérieur: Except for persons who are neither temporarily nor permanently resident in the Grand Duchy of Luxembourg, no one may publicly use an academic title if: (i) he has not acquired the degree under the legal regulations of the country that awarded the degree, and (ii) he does not have his degree entered in the *Commission des titres* of the Ministry of Education, including the name of the university or higher education institution that awarded it and a complete designation of the title acquired.

Academic titles under the Luxembourg Law of 17 June 1963 include, in particular, those of engineer *(ingénieur)*, architect *(architecte)*, licentiate *(licencié)*, etc.

The Netherlands

NL

Organization of higher education

In the Netherlands there is a long tradition of academic freedom and autonomy for the institutions of higher education. These assume responsibility for the content of degree programmes and for research policy. As regards supraregional national policy, the Ministry of Education and Science plays an important role. Although the institutions of higher education are required to implement Ministry policy, they also enjoy a good deal of independence in this area. Academic committees of inquiry under State supervision, however, supervise the quality of the teaching and research. The committees are set up for each study orientation. They compare content and level of the subjects at the various universities. The Ministry of Education and Science has been charged with the supervision of the non-university higher education institutions. With regard to income, the teaching establishments in the Netherlands are largely dependent on the State. They receive an annual budget which is dependent, among other factors, on the number of students registered.

Types of higher education institutions

In the higher education sector in the Netherlands *(hoger onderwijs)* there are two types of higher education institutions: universities *(instelling voor wetenschappelijk onderwijs)* and careers-orientated higher education institutions *(instelling voor hoger beroepsonderwijs)*.

Wetenschappelijk onderwijs (WO) is given at the 13 universities, *hoger beroepsonderwijs* (HBO) at the nearly 100 institutions of higher education in the Netherlands. Both sectors of higher education exist parallel to each other. Students at universities receive training which is orientated towards the independent practice of scientific-academic work. The teaching at the *hogescholen* is of a practical nature and relates directly to future vocational activities.

The length of studies both at universities as well as at the other institutions of higher education amounts to four years for most degree programmes. In practice, the degree programmes at universities usually last longer. From their instigation, the universities and institutions of higher education have represented two different educational forms. In the last few years they have been increasingly regarded as complementary and have been approaching each other. It is, for example, becoming increasingly easy for students to transfer from a course of study at institutions of higher education to the universities and vice versa.

Universities

All universities are involved in research. This research is closely interlinked with the teaching and almost all academic/scientific staff participate in both teaching and research.

Of the 13 Dutch universities, nine

offer a broad range of subjects: the Universities of Leiden, Amsterdam, Groningen, Utrecht, Limburg, Nijmegen, Tilburg, the Erasmus University in Rotterdam, and the Free University in Amsterdam.

Further, there are three universities which mainly offer engineering-orientated degree programmes: the Universities of Delft, Twente and Eindhoven. Finally, there is a university which is specialized in degree programmes in the field of agriculture: the Agricultural University of Wageningen. In addition to these differences in study orientation, there is another division in Dutch university education, three universities having their origins in religious conviction. Thus the Free University in Amsterdam is Protestant-Reformist in origin and the Universities of Nijmegen and Tilburg are Catholic. This difference is of no consequence to the content and level of study. All university training in the Netherlands is on the same level. Apart from these 13 universities, there are another seven theological institutions which are independent of the Ministry of Education and Science.

HBO institutions *(hogescholen)*

The institutions of higher education offering *hoger beroepsonderwijs* prepare students for vocational activities which both require the application of academic/scientific knowledge as well as the capability for practical work. Training through an institution of higher education is mostly orientated towards a specific vocation. During the training, therefore, the emphasis is placed on the practical side.

Institutions of higher education frequently have close relations with trade and industry. In this way they are better able to adjust their study guidelines to relevant career requirements. At present there are more than 90 institutions of higher education. Several years ago there were more than 400. The Dutch Government, however, initiated a merging process in order to improve the efficiency of this educational form. The structure of the institutions of higher education is consequently modified towards that of the universities. The institutions of higher education offer opportunities for study in one or several of the following subjects: engineering, trade and industry, health care, art, education, agricultural science, education/social work, hotels and catering.

The institutions of higher education have great freedom of manoeuvre in the structuring of their study guidelines. The vocational requirements and the needs of the labour market are important criteria in this. Trade and industry therefore strongly influence the policy of these establishments. Furthermore, institutions of higher education generally have strong regional links and frequently maintain close contacts with local industry, for example the Chambers of Trade and Commerce.

Distance University *(Open Universiteit)*

Apart from regular study forms, the distance university *(Open Universiteit)* has been in operation since 1984. The range of studies offered by the distance university comprises university (WO) and higher education (HBO) degree programmes. This new form of

distance study was especially conceived for people who, although they would like to study, are unable to do this full-time, for example, adults who are bound to the home, who are in full- or part-time employment, or who are disabled.

The most important characteristics of the distance university are:

(i) anyone over 18 years of age may register;
(ii) students may compile their own study plan;
(iii) students have free choice in determining when and where they want to study and are not obliged to attend lectures; and
(iv) students may determine their own pace of study.

Studies at the distance university are mainly conducted through writing. Students may obtain information on study conditions, counselling and advice from the 18 study centres that are spread throughout the country.

International studies *(Internationaal Onderwijs – IO)*

In the Netherlands there is also a third type of teaching in the higher education sector: international studies. This form was established in order to offer short-term specialist training courses to citizens of the Third World who hold a degree equivalent to the Bachelor and who already possess some practical experience in the relevant subject area. The courses which last between seven weeks and two years are mainly held in English. There are currently more than 20 Institutes of International Studies offering a total of about 160 various further training programmes for students with an upper secondary school-leaving certificate as well as for academics.

The IO offers degree programmes in many disciplines, including government planning, social sciences, management and building, hydraulic and environmental engineering, electronics, telecommunications, aerospace survey and earth sciences, agricultural sciences, radio and television.

Student statistics

In the 1986/87 academic year, a total of 383 290 students were registered in the higher education sector *(hoger onderwijs)*. Of these, about 2% were foreigners. Of the total number of foreigners (7 777), almost 43% came from EC Member States (see Appendix).

Organization and validation of courses

Universities *(wetenschappelijk onderwijs – WO)*

Dutch academic teaching comprises *doctoraalprogramma's* (diploma programmes) and a number of further postgraduate teaching and research programmes following on to the diploma examination *(post-doctorale programma's)*.

Officially the *doctoraalprogramma's* last four years, concluding with a *doctoraal examen* (diploma thesis). The study programme exerts the student greatly. Because many students do not manage this training in four years, they may take up to six years for their studies.

At the end of the first year, students must take the *propaedeutisch examen*. Anyone not having successfully taken this examination by the end of the second year is not permitted to continue with their studies. The first part of the *doctoraal* studies gives the student a general orientation and introduction into the subject. In the course of the studies, the degree of specialization also increases. With the progress of the studies, the degree of freedom of choice regarding the structuring of the student's individual study plan increases, too. The student concludes the diploma phase with a written paper, which is at least 60 pages long and which represents independent, academic/scientific work.

Those who have concluded their studies may use the title of *doctorandus*, abbreviated *drs.* The titles for engineers *(ir)* and lawyers *(mr)* are equivalent. Graduates may use the internationally better known title of *Master*. For many academics, a diploma degree marks the end of their academic/scientific training; however, there are also opportunities for a continuation of studies. Furthermore, there are graduate studies for academics *(post-doctorale opleiding)* and the opportunity to undertake a doctorate.

Admission to graduate studies *(post-doctorale opleidingen)* following the first academic degree is subject to limitations, since there are too few study places. It must be remembered that the admissions chances vary from subject to subject.

Graduate studies may be placed in the following categories:

1. practical and (for medical professions) clinical experience needed for professional qualification;
2. continuing training in the field of engineering;
3. a series of short continuing training courses, including those aimed at maintaining specialized knowledge in the relevant subject;
4. continuing research programmes, including those in the field of sociology, international law, geology, toxicology and linguistics.

Continuing studies are often a requirement for final professional qualification, for example, in the field of medicine, pharmacy, veterinary medicine and accountancy (two years each), teacher training and dentistry (one year each). The training is primarily practice-orientated. Admission to continuing studies is limited on account of the number of study places. Depending on study orientation, there are, however, various possibilities.

In addition to these continuing training courses for academics, graduates from institutions of higher education may also gain a doctorate, the highest academic title in the Netherlands. The procedure is called *promotie*. The doctorate is primarily a research degree and entitles the holder to use the title of doctor *(dr.)*.

A doctoral candidate is not a student. Frequently, a university employs such a person as a research assistant *(assistent in opleiding* – AIO) or as a researching lecturer *(onderzoeker in opleiding* – OIO). Doctoral candidates may also prepare themselves for their doctorate privately.

Institutions of higher education for vocational training *(hoger beroepsonderwijs* – (HBO)

The degree HBO programmes partially comprise high-level theoretical programmes and partially exercises and practicals *(stages)* external to the higher education institution. The programmes are orientated towards a future profession and so towards the requirements resulting from this. In the final analysis, it is the institution of higher education itself that decides on the content of the study plans. HBO-training leads to the *Getuigschrift van Hoger Beroepsonderwijs* (higher education degree). There are also various possibilities for HBO-graduates wishing to undertake continuing training or a supplementary course of study.

Almost all of the full-time degree programmes last four years. In the first year, general topics which are not necessarily related to the future professional career are covered. This year is concluded with an examination, the *propaedeuse*. Following this, students may specialize in a specific field. Moreover, there is time during the studies to undertake practical exercises *(praktika)* externally to the institution of higher education. The length of this practical depends on the degree programme and varies between several months and one year.

The final section of the training mostly consists of the compilation of a major written paper in the student's subject area. Following completion of four years of HBO-training, the graduate may use the title of Bachelor *(Baccalaureus)*.

Admission and registration

Initial information

Foreign students who would like to study at a university in the Netherlands, may obtain information from:

1. the Deans of Students *(Bureaus Studentendecanen)* or the Foreign Student Services *(Bureaus Buitenland)* at the universities and institutions of higher education *(hogescholen)*;
2. NUFFIC (Netherlands Foundation for International Cooperation), the Dutch organization for international cooperation in the higher education sector in The Hague. NUFFIC has been appointed by the Dutch Minister for Education and Science as the NEIC (National Equivalence Information Centre) within the framework of the Council of Europe *(Raad van Europa)* and as NARIC (National Academic Recognition Information Centre) within that of the EC;
3. the Ministry of Education and Science in Zoetermeer;
4. the Foreign Student Service (FSS) in Amsterdam;

(For addresses, see Appendix 1.)

Foreign students wishing to study at a higher education institution *(hogeschool)* in the Netherlands can obtain information from:

1. the Ministry of Education and Science in Zoetermeer;

2. NUFFIC, the Dutch organization for international cooperation in the higher education sector in The Hague;
3. the Foreign Student Service in Amsterdam;
4. the *Nederlands Centrum Buitenlanders* in Utrecht.
5. the *HBO-Raad* (HBO Council) in The Hague.
   (For addresses, see Appendix 1.)

Entry requirements

The universities and other institutions of higher education may in principle admit students from the Member States of the EC and from other foreign countries. Foreign students should, however, take several factors into consideration.

First of all, there is the language problem: lectures and practicals are held in Dutch.

Moreover, there may be other possible problems, such as adapatation to the structure of the Dutch study regulations, the organization of studies into academic years rather than semesters, the very low number of available scholarships for foreign students, as well as conditions which lie outside the direct responsibility of the institutions of higher education, such as the insufficient availability of accommodation for students.

Admission to university studies is in principle open to applicants who have completed six years of Dutch *(voorbereidend wetenschappelijk onderwijs* – VWO, grammar stream) education. The level of the school-leaving certificate for *voorbereidend wetenschappelijk onderwijs* is relatively high. Foreigners must hold an equivalent certificate in order to be admitted to a university.

Those students may be admitted to studies at the vocational institutions of higher education who hold certificates that are equivalent to the following Dutch secondary school-leaving certificates:

1. *Het voorbereidend wetenschappelijk onderwijs – VWO*
2. *Het hoger algemeen voortgezet onderwijs – HAVO*
3. *Het middelbaar beroepsonderwijs – MBO*

The decision on admission of both Dutch and foreign students lies solely with the higher education institution itself although the general regulations on the assessment of previous education must be taken into consideration. In contrast to the universities, the secondary school-leaving certificates needed for admission do not entitle the holder to any automatic admission to these institutions of higher education. For first-year students with foreign secondary school-leaving certificates, admission to the institutions of higher education is generally more difficult than admission to the universities.

Limitations

There is so much interest in certain subjects at the universities that the number of requests for enrolment is much larger than available capacities. When the situation arises, a selection system valid for the whole country determines which aspiring students will be admitted for the subjects in question.

In the academic year 1988/89 the following subjects came under this *numerus fixus* rule: medicine, dentistry, veterinary medicine, politics and management, general health welfare, social economics, health theory, medical biology, Japanese studies.

Every year, the Minister for Education and Science determines an admission quota for foreigners in medicine, dentistry and veterinary medicine, which is very low. If the number of foreign applicants for admission to one of these three *numerus fixus* subjects surpasses the predetermined quota, the question of admission is decided by drawing lots.

Students who have applied for admission to a subject under the *numerus fixus* rule run a certain risk by coming to the Netherlands early to learn the language, since admissions are not announced until June or later. There is a good chance that foreigners will not be admitted to the *numerus fixus* subjects to which access is difficult.

There are no formal limitations for HBO schools, but in practice very few foreigners are admitted. Most foreigners in this sector of higher education are enrolled at *hogescholen voor technisch onderwijs* and at some art academies.

Recognition of foreign certificates and degrees

Students wishing to study outside of their own countries and desiring information on the comparability of their degrees or school leaving certificates in connection with admission to a specific course of study, should apply (in writing only) to NUFFIC. However, NUFFIC can only give advice and refer the candidate to the competent ministry or higher education institution.

Entry examinations

The universities and *hogescholen* as a rule require no entry examination.

Citizens of EC Member States who have no access to academic education in the country in which they received their secondary education can, in special cases, qualify for admission to WO institutions in the Netherlands by means of an entry examination.

The HBO institutions require no entry examinations. Some art schools do, however, require that applicants be tested in their chosen artistic speciality.

Application and registration

Students who wish to enrol at a Dutch university or *hogeschool* must be authorized to take examinations in their chosen subjects. For this they should apply directly to the university or *hogeschool* in question.

Foreign students should inquire as early as possible about their authorization to take examinations. For this they need to forward a request to the university or *hogeschool* of their choice. The application should include the following documents:

1. authorized copies of school leaving certificates, degrees and transcripts;
2. a complete description of the applicant's past education;
3. personal information (name, birth date and birth place).

Such requests can also be sent directly to the relevant institution for *wetenschappelijk onderwijs*.

For all courses in academic education, first-year students are required to register with the *Centraal Bureau Aanmelding en Plaatsing (CBAP)* in Groningen by means of a standard form. The CBAP is responsible for the distribution of places at the 13 universities. The forms are available every November from the WO institutions, the CBAP and the Ministry of Education and Science. The completed forms must have reached the CBAP before 1 December prior to the academic year in which the student wants to commence his studies.

Upon being authorized to take examinations and receiving a place, the student is sent a registration form from the office of the registrar of the university or *hogeschool* in question. Detailed information is included on registration procedures.

Registration takes place after all administrative formalities have been completed and registration and tuition fees have been paid.

To study at a school for *hoger beroepsonderwijs* the student must apply directly to the school in question.

Students are recommended to submit their applications early, preferably at the beginning of the academic year prior to the year in which they want to begin their studies.

Students who have already begun their studies should register directly with the university or *hogeschool* in question.

Tuition fees

Anyone registering as a student at a university is required to pay HFL 1750 in tuition fees (inclusive of registration fees).

Tuition for students at HBO schools amounts to a maximum of HFL 1 500 per year. These figures apply to the academic year 1988/89.

Knowledge of the language of instruction, language courses and other courses

A good knowledge of the Dutch language is indispensable for studies at universities and schools for *hoger beroepsonderwijs*. Lectures and seminars are given in Dutch and a large part of the prescribed textbooks are in Dutch, so that without a sufficient knowledge of the language the student does not have much chance of studying successfully. There are, however, international courses which form an exception to this rule, the majority of them being held in English, although occasionally also in French and Spanish.

Foreign students who do not have a sufficient knowledge of Dutch and wish to study in the Netherlands, but who have fulfilled all other requirements, are urgently advised to come to the Netherlands approximately six months before the beginning of term at the universities (mid-September) and *hogescholen* (the beginning of August) in order to learn the language. It is also recommended that foreign students continue attending a Dutch language course during their period of study in the Netherlands.

A Dutch language examination is required for admission to studies at the *wetenschappelijk onderwijs* level.

Most universities and colleges offer courses in the Dutch language for foreigners. There are also other institutions offering Dutch summer courses.

The *Haagse Academie voor Internationaal Recht* offers a three-week course in July and again in August on various aspects of international law. The languages used in these courses are English and French.

The European Institute of the University of Amsterdam organizes a two-week course every August on the legal aspects of European integration. The language used is English.

The University of Leiden, the University of Amsterdam and Columbia University of New York jointly offer a one-month English-language course every July on legislation in the United States.

The Ministry of Education and Science organizes a three-week course on the Dutch language and culture in July and August. The course is held in Dutch.

Financial assistance and scholarships

Only seldom can the Dutch universities and other institutions of higher education offer financial assistance to foreign students. Neither, in general, does the Dutch Government grant any educational financial assistance *(studiefinanciering)* to students or their parents who do not have Dutch citizenship.

For students from EC Member States, the following exceptions generally apply:

1. students who have applied for Dutch citizenship, if the Dutch Ministry of Justice has declared that naturalization is to be expected;
2. students who have their place of residence in the Netherlands and who with regard to educational financial assistance have been placed on an equal footing with Dutch citizens through international agreements. These are the children of parents working in the Netherlands who are from another EC Member State;
3. students who have been granted unlimited residence in the Netherlands on the basis of Article 10 of the Law on Aliens. These are:
   (a) students or their parents who have an official permit to practise a profession;
   (b) foreign members of Dutch families;
4. students who are younger than 23 years of age, if their parents have been living continuously in the Netherlands for more than three years and students who have no parents, are married or are older than 18 years of age and have been living in the Netherlands for three years. This exception is only valid in such cases where the residence permit was not issued for professional purposes, and is not limited or restricted to residence with a Dutch person.

There is a limited number of grants available for foreign students, which are awarded by NUFFIC in the context of bilateral cultural agreements between the Netherlands and other States.

These grants have the following common characteristics:

1. they are not restricted to certain subjects;
2. they are only valid for studies in the Netherlands;
3. applicants must hold an academic degree or must already have spent several years studying;
4. the scholarships are generally awarded for a maximum of nine months only.

Applications for the awarding of such grants must as a rule be placed before 1 December of the year previous to the next academic year; they must be placed in the applicants' country of origin at the office responsible for this (normally the Dutch embassy).

NL

Entry and residence regulations

Students who are citizens of an EC Member State are not required to have a temporary residence permit. After arriving in the Netherlands they should request a residence permit from the local police. Requirements for the issuing of such a permit are:

1. possession of a valid identification card or passport;
2. proof of admission as a full-time student to a Dutch institution of higher education;
3. proof of having sufficient financial means (for at least one year) or sources (such as a scholarship or financial assistance from a supranational or international organization);
4. proof of membership in a health insurance scheme.

Social aspects

Social security and health insurance

In the Netherlands students are not automatically insured for medical and other unforeseeable expenses when they register at a higher education institution. Students will have to provide for this themselves.

Proof of having health insurance is a requirement for receiving a residence permit.

Students at universities and colleges can insure themselves with the *Stichting Studentengezondheidszorg* (SSGZ) which gives broad coverage.

There are doctors, psychologists and, occasionally, psychiatrists attached to some Dutch universities who can be consulted free of charge by students registered there.

Students can also insure themselves with the International Student Insurance Service (ISIS) for a maximum period of 18 months. The ISIS policy card provides coverage of medical costs up to a certain limit and provides survivor benefits in case of death.

Advisory services

Universities and *hogescholen* provide advisory services to foreign students through the Foreign Students Service *(Bureau Buitenland)* and Student Affairs Offices *(Bureau Studentenzaken)*.

A number of institutions of higher education have a Dean of Students especially responsible for foreign students.

Student employment
At some universities and *hogescholen* there are student-run student employment offices. The employers pay for the job placement service.

Besides these offices there are commercial job brokers *(uitzendbureaus)* operating all over the country.

In many areas of the Netherlands there are also provincial employment offices under the administration of the Ministry of Social Affairs. These offices offer both job placement service and vocational information.

Students from EC Member States do not need a work permit. However, it is very difficult for foreign students to find a job or part-time work.

The academic load and the scheduling of classes allow little time for gainful employment. Foreign students, in particular, will need all the time at their disposal for their studies. Thus, in the best interest of the students, working and studying at the same time are not advised.

In view of these circumstances, students are urgently recommended not to come to the Netherlands to study if they do not have a financial basis for living here.

Student organizations
There is a great diversity of student organizations in the Netherlands. Besides the traditional student bodies, there are student organizations founded on religion, academic interests, political and philosophical orientation or various other groups based on representing the common interest of their members.

For foreigners there are also different international student clubs.

Cost of living
Experience shows that foreign students living in the Netherlands generally need about HFL 12 000 per year. This is about HFL 1 000 more than is needed by their Dutch counterparts.

These figures are nothing more than a general indication and are subject to revision.

Accommodation
With one exception, the *Technische Universiteit* in Twente, Dutch universities and *hogescholen* have no campuses.

It is difficult to find good accommodation. In large parts of the Netherlands there is a scarcity of suitable rooms at reasonable prices.

Foreign students at universities and *hogescholen* can, just like their Dutch counterparts, register with the Student Housing Services *(Stichtingen voor studentenhuisvesting)* at these institutions. However, long waiting periods should be reckoned with.

The only alternative open to students at the *hogescholen voor beroepsonderwijs* is to find a room in a private household. It is only in the university towns that there is even a limited possibility that foreign students will be assigned accommodation by the Student Housing Services.

The rent for private accommodation varies greatly. Students should reckon with a monthly rent of HFL 250 to 500. Higher rent levels are no exception.

Foreign students are recommended to take steps towards finding suitable housing before coming to the Netherlands.

Services for students

Membership in certain student organizations devoted to representing the interests of their members also entitles students to certain reductions.

There are no special student prices on trains, trams or buses. It is possible, however, to travel cheaply by making use of subscription tickets and route section tickets which generally mean savings for users of public transport.

Foreign students can also profit from low-priced travel offered by student travel agencies.

Facilities for disabled students

Students with physical disabilities and sensory handicaps are not disadvantaged in the Netherlands. Information is available from the Dean of Students at the chosen higher education institution with regard to special facilities for the disabled. It is recommended that applicants point out any disability they may have on submitting their applications. Detailed information and assistance is also available from the *Stichting Handicap en Studie NSS* (Foundation for Handicapped Students).

Appendices

1. Addresses

Dutch embassies in EC countries

Belgium
Wetenschapsstraat 35
B-1040 Brussel
☎ 2 30 30 20

Denmark
Toldbodgade 42
DK-1253 København K
☎ 15 62 93

Federal Republic of Germany
Sträßchensweg 10
D-5300 Bonn 1
☎ 23 80 91

Greece
Leoforos Vassileos Constantinou 5 – 7
GR-Athina
☎ 723 97 01

Spain
Paseo de la Castellana 178
E-28046 Madrid
☎ 45 82 100

France
7 – 9, rue Eblé
F-75007 Paris
☎ 4 306 61 88

Ireland
160 Merrion Road
Dublin 4
☎ 69 34 44

Italy
Via Michele Mercati, 8
I-00197 Roma
☎ 87 31 41

Luxembourg
5, rue C.M. Spoo
L-2546 Luxembourg
☎ 2 75 70

Portugal
Rua do Sacramento à Lapa 4
P-1200 Lisboa
☎ 66 11 63

United Kingdom
38 Hyde Park Gate
London SW7 5DP
☎ 5 84 50 40

Ministries and other institutions

Netherlands Universities Foundation for International Cooperation (NUFFIC)
Postbus 90734
2509 LS 's-Gravenhage
☎ 070 51 05 10

HBO Raad
Postbus 123
2501 CC 's-Gravenhage
☎ 070 62 49 51

Staatsdrukkerij- en uitgeverijbedrijf
Postbus 20014
2500 EA 's-Gravenhage

Foreign Student Service (FSS)
Oranje Nassaulaan 5
1075 AH Amsterdam
☎ 020 71 59 15

Ministerie van Onderwijs en Wetenschappen, Centrale Directie Voorlichting
Postbus 25000
2700 LZ Zoetermeer
☎ 079 53 19 11

Ministerie van Onderwijs en Wetenschappen, Centrale Directie Studiefinanciering
Postbus 30150
9700 LA Groningen
☎ 050 24 91 11

Ministerie van Buitenlandse Zaken, Directoraat-Generaal voor Internationale Samenwerking (DGIS)
Bezuidenhoutseweg 67
Postbus 20061
2500 EB 's-Gravenhage

Centraal Bureau Aanmelding en Plaatsing (CBAP)
Postbus 888
9700 AW Groningen
☎ 050 18 96 66

Nederlands Centrum Buitenlanders (NCB)
Oudenoord 8
Postbus 1 33 13
3513 ER Utrecht
☎ 030 33 45 31

University Assistance Fund (UAF)
Postbus 13001
3507 LA Utrecht
☎ 030 71 12 24

SSZG (Stichting Studentengezondheidszorg)
Postbus 152
2200 AD Noordwijk
☎ 01719 7 09 44

Stichting Handicap en Studie NSS
Willem Barentszstraat 5
3572 PA Utrecht
☎ 030 71 80 21

Foreign students offices *(bureaus buitenland)* of the universities

Universiteit van Amsterdam
Bureau Buitenland
Postbus 19268
1000 GG Amsterdam

Vrije Universiteit te Amsterdam
Bureau Buitenland
Postbus 7161
1007 MC Amsterdam

Katholieke Universiteit Brabant te Tilburg
Bureau Buitenland
Postbus 90153
5000 LE Tilburg

Technische Rijksuniversiteit te Delft
International Office
Postbus 5
2600 AA Delft

Technische Universiteit te Eindhoven
Internationale Betrekkingen
Postbus 513
5600 MB Eindhoven

Technische Universiteit Twente
Bureau Buitenland
Postbus 217
7500 AE Enschede

Rijksuniversiteit Groningen
Bureau Buitenland
Postbus 72
9700 AB Groningen

Rijksuniversiteit te Leiden
Internationaal Contactpunt
Postbus 9500
2300 RA Leiden

Rijksuniversiteit Limburg
Bureau Buitenland
Postbus 616
6200 MD Maastricht

Katholieke Universiteit te Nijmegen
Bureau Buitenland
Postbus 9102
6500 HK Nijmegen

Erasmus Universiteit te Rotterdam
Bureau Buitenlandse Betrekkingen
Postbus 1738
3000 DR Rotterdam

Rijksuniversiteit te Utrecht
Afdeling Internationale Samenwerking
Postbus 80125
3508 TC Utrecht

Landbouwuniversiteit Wageningen
Bureau Buitenland
Stadsbrink 389
6707 AC Wageningen

Nijenrode Universiteit voor Bedrijfskunde
Bureau Buitenland
Straatweg 25
3621 BG Breukelen

NL

2. Survey of courses of study at higher education institutions

Overzicht van studiemogelijkheden aan instellingen voor hoger onderwijs

Degree courses for first-year students at universities

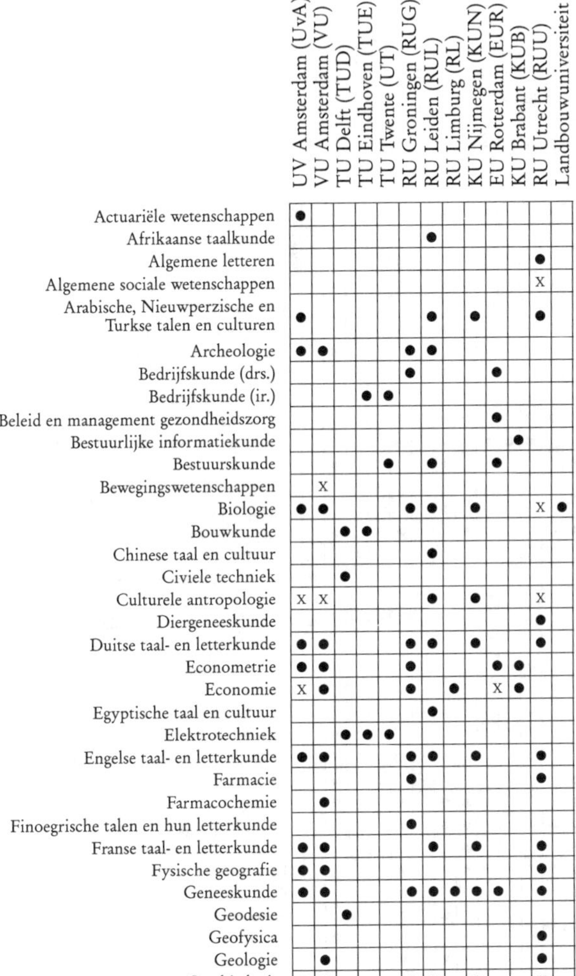

	UV Amsterdam (UvA)	VU Amsterdam (VU)	TU Delft (TUD)	TU Eindhoven (TUE)	TU Twente (UT)	RU Groningen (RUG)	RU Leiden (RUL)	RU Limburg (RL)	KU Nijmegen (KUN)	EU Rotterdam (EUR)	KU Brabant (KUB)	RU Utrecht (RUU)	Landbouwuniversiteit (LU)	
Actuariële wetenschappen	●													Actuarial theory
Afrikaanse taalkunde							●							African languages
Algemene letteren												●		General literature
Algemene sociale wetenschappen												x		Social sciences
Arabische, Nieuwperzische en Turkse talen en culturen	●						●		●			●		Arabian, Modern Persian and Turkish studies
Archeologie	●	●				●	●							Archaeology
Bedrijfskunde (drs.)						●				●				Business administration (drs.)
Bedrijfskunde (ir.)				●	●									Business administration (for engineers)
Beleid en management gezondheidszorg										●				Health care management
Bestuurlijke informatiekunde											●			Computing in administration
Bestuurskunde					●		●			●				Administrative management
Bewegingswetenschappen		x												Theory of motion
Biologie	●	●				●	●		●			x	●	Biology
Bouwkunde			●	●										Building sciences
Chinese taal en cultuur							●							Chinese language and culture
Civiele techniek			●											Civil engineering
Culturele antropologie	x	x					●		●			x		Cultural anthropology
Diergeneeskunde												●		Veterinary medicine
Duitse taal- en letterkunde	●	●				●	●		●			●		German studies
Econometrie	●	●				●				●	●			Econometry
Economie	x	●				●		●		x	●			Economics
Egyptische taal en cultuur							●							Egyptian studies
Elektrotechniek			●	●	●									Electrical engineering
Engelse taal- en letterkunde	●	●				●	●		●			●		English studies
Farmacie						●						●		Pharmacy
Farmacochemie		●												Pharma-chemistry
Finoegrische talen en hun letterkunde						●								Finno-Ugric studies
Franse taal- en letterkunde	●	●					●		●			●		French studies
Fysische geografie	●	●										●		Physical geography
Geneeskunde	●	●				●	●	●	●	●		●		Medicine
Geodesie			●											Surveying
Geofysica												●		Geophysics
Geologie		●										●		Geology
Geschiedenis	x	●				x	x		●			x		History

x = also offered as part-time studies

Degree courses for first-year students at universities

(continued)

	UV Amsterdam (UvA)	VU Amsterdam (VU)	TU Delft (TUD)	TU Eindhoven (TUE)	TU Twente (UT)	RU Groningen (RUG)	RU Leiden (RUL)	RU Limburg (RL)	KU Nijmegen (KUN)	EU Rotterdam (EUR)	KU Brabant (KUB)	RU Utrecht (RUU)	Landbouwuniversiteit (LU)	
Gezondheidswetenschappen RUL							●							Health sciences
Gezondheidswetenschappen RL								●						
Gezondheidswetenschappen KUN									●					
Godgeleerdheid (theologie)	●	●				●	●		●			x		Religion (theology)
Godgeleerdheid (algemene opleiding)		●												Religion (teaching)
Griekse en Latijnse taal en cultuur	●	●				●	●		●					Greek and Latin studies
Indische en Iraanse talen en culturen							●					●		Indian and Iranian studies
Indonesische talen en culturen							●							Indonesian studies
Industrieel ontwerpen			●											Industrial design
Informatica (drs.)	●	●				●	●		●			●		Computer science (drs)
Informatica (ir.)			●	●	●									Computer science (for engineers)
Italiaanse taal- en letterkunde	●						●					●		Italian studies
Japankunde										●				Japanese studies
Japanse taal en cultuur							●							Japanology
Kunstgeschiedenis en archeologie	●	●				●	x		●			●		History of art, archaeology
Landbouwwetenschappen:														Agricultural sciences
landgebruik richtingen —													●	— study area: earth sciences
maatschappijwetensch. richtingen —													●	— study area: sociology
teelt en technologie —													●	— study area: plant and animal breeding, technol
Latijnse taal- en letterkunde	●													Latin language and literature
Luchtvaart- en ruimtevaarttechniek			●											Aeronautical and aerospace engineering
Maatschappijgeschiedenis										x				Social history
Materiaalkunde			●											Materials science
Medische biologie												●		Medical biology
Mijnbouwkunde en petroleumwinning			●											Mining and petroleum production
Muziekwetenschap	●											●		Musicology
Natuurkunde	●	●				●	●		●			●		Physics
Nederlandse taal- en letterkunde	●	●				●	●		●			x		Dutch language and literature
Nieuwgriekse taal- en letterkunde	●					●								Modern Greek studies
Pedagogische wetenschappen	●	●				●	●		●			x		Educational science
Planologie	●								●					Regional planning
Politicologie	x	x					●		●					Political science
Portugese taal- en letterkunde												●		Portuguese studies
Psychologie	x	●				x	x		●		x	x		Psychology
Rechten	x	x				x	x	x	x	x	x	x		Law

x = also offered as part-time studies

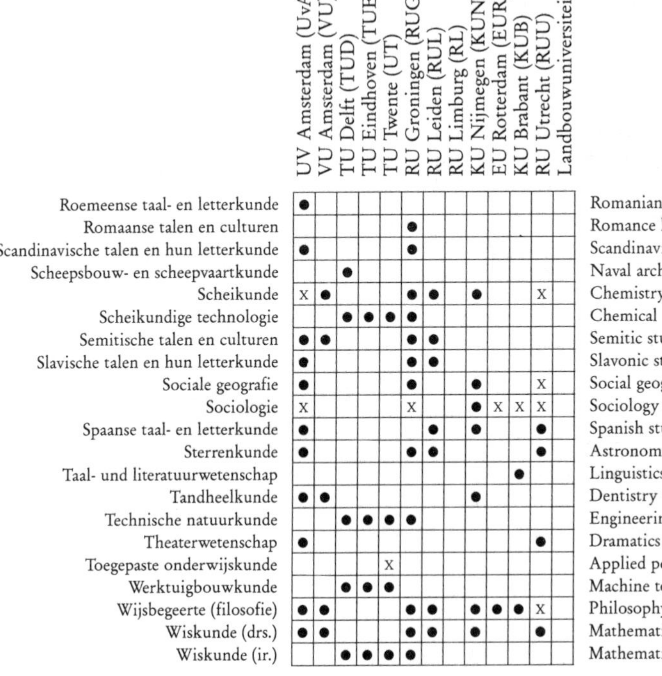

	UV Amsterdam (UvA)	VU Amsterdam (VU)	TU Delft (TUD)	TU Eindhoven (TUE)	TU Twente (UT)	RU Groningen (RUG)	RU Leiden (RUL)	RU Limburg (RL)	KU Nijmegen (KUN)	EU Rotterdam (EUR)	KU Brabant (KUB)	RU Utrecht (RUU)	Landbouwuniversiteit (LU)	
Roemeense taal- en letterkunde	●													Romanian studies
Romaanse talen en culturen						●								Romance languages and literature
Scandinavische talen en hun letterkunde	●					●								Scandinavian studies
Scheepsbouw- en scheepvaartkunde			●											Naval architecture and navigation
Scheikunde	x	●				●	●		●			x		Chemistry
Scheikundige technologie			●	●	●	●								Chemical technology
Semitische talen en culturen	●	●				●	●							Semitic studies
Slavische talen en hun letterkunde	●					●	●							Slavonic studies
Sociale geografie	●					●			●			x		Social geography
Sociologie	x					x			●	x	x	x		Sociology
Spaanse taal- en letterkunde	●						●		●			●		Spanish studies
Sterrenkunde	●					●	●					●		Astronomy
Taal- und literatuurwetenschap											●			Linguistics and literature
Tandheelkunde	●	●							●					Dentistry
Technische natuurkunde			●	●	●	●								Engineering physics
Theaterwetenschap	●											●		Dramatics
Toegepaste onderwijskunde					x									Applied pedagogics
Werktuigbouwkunde			●	●	●									Machine tools engineering
Wijsbegeerte (filosofie)	●	●				●	●		●	●	●	x		Philosophy
Wiskunde (drs.)	●	●				●	●		●			●		Mathematics (drs)
Wiskunde (ir.)			●	●	●	●								Mathematics (for engineers)

x = also offered as part-time studies

The courses of study of the HBO *(hoger beroepsonderwijs)*

There are more than 90 higher education institutions of this type offering practice-oriented studies in many subject areas:

Hoger pedagogisch onderwijs
Training of teachers for the lower and medium levels of schools in general and vocational subjects (16 institutions).

Hoger agrarisch onderwijs
Agricultural studies, under the auspices of the Minister for Agriculture and Fishery (seven institutions).

Hoger gezondheidszorgonderwijs
Training for paramedical professions and in nutrition and health care (25 institutions).

Hoger sociaal-agogisch onderwijs
Studies leading to responsible positions in social work, public welfare and counselling (26 institutions).

Kunstonderwijs
Art studies preparing for various artistic professions, such as dance, drama, music, fine arts, design, fashion (24 institutions).

Hoger technisch onderwijs
The former engineering schools, the schools for laboratory assistants, for shipbuilding and navigation were combined under this heading and concentrated at 27 institutions.

Hoger economisch onderwijs
Besides economics and business administration these schools also offer training in the following subjects: applied home economics, library and documentation science, hotel and catering, journalism (36 institutions).

Detailed information on the various courses of study is provided by:
HBO-Raad
Postbus 123
2501 CC 's-Gravenhage

NL

3. Student statistics

Foreign students in higher education in the Netherlands
(academic year 1986 – 87)

Total number of students	383 290		
Total foreign students	7 777	=	2.03% of total
Total EC members	3 336	=	42.9 % of total foreign students

of which:

Belgium	573
Denmark	48
FR of Germany	1 466
Greece	75
Spain	220
France	139
Ireland	31
Italy	266
Luxembourg	15
Portugal	62
United Kingdom	441
Other European	1 263
Africa	510
Latin America	699
North America	364
Asia	1 238
Oceania	149

NL

4. Bibliography

Vademecum — A concise guide to studying in the Netherlands for foreign students. A short study guide for foreign students, edited by the Foreign Student Service (FSS). The English brochure not only contains general information on courses of study at Dutch universities and other institutions of higher education, but also practical hints. Available free of charge from FSS at the *Ministerie van Onderwijs en Wetenschappen* from NUFFIC, NCB *(Netherlands Centrum Buitenlanders)* and the individual universities and *hogescholen.*

Dutch language courses for foreigners. English, French and Spanish in one volume. Published annually. Free of charge from FSS and NUFFIC.

Studying at a university in Holland — should you? Brochure on study in the Netherlands in the languages English, French, Spanish and German. Describes possibilities and difficulties that foreign students encounter in the Netherlands, 11 pp., free of charge from NUFFIC.

Higher education in the Netherlands. English brochure on higher education in the Netherlands with a survey of courses of study offered by universities and *hogescholen* (HBO). Available from the *Ministerie van Onderwijs en Wetenschappen* and from NUFFIC.

Basic data on international courses offered in the Netherlands. English, with abstracts in French and Spanish. Published yearly. Available free of charge from NUFFIC.

Straks studeren? HAVO edition. Information pamphlet for pupils of secondary modern schools (HAVO), published by the *Landelijke Commissie voor Academische Studievoorlichting,* eight editions per year, HFL 23.75, available from the *Ministerie van Onderwijs en Wetenschappen.*

VWO edition: Information pamphlet for pupils of the academically oriented final classes (VWO), published by the *Landelijke Commissie voor Academische Studievoorlichting,* eight editions per year, HFL 23.75, available from the *Ministerie van Onderwijs en Wetenschappen.*

Het hoger agrarisch onderwijs. Compiled by the department for agricultural instruction *(Directie Landbouwonderwijs)* of the Ministry of Agriculture and Fisheries *(Ministerie van Landbouw en Visserij);* 28 pp., available free of charge from this ministry.

Living in Holland. Brochure giving general information on daily life in the Netherlands with many practical hints that may help foreigners to settle 36 pp., 1988. Can be ordered from NUFFIC (HFL 2.50 plus postage).

Scholarships and fellowships for study and training in the Netherlands. Brochure in English, 11 pp., free of charge from NUFFIC.

Professional upgrading in the Netherlands. Brochure giving a survey of institutions that offer short-term courses in English to foreigners, mainly from third-world countries, who want to upgrade their professional knowledge. 12 pp., free of charge from NUFFIC.

Studie-almanac. Survey of courses of study at universities and *hogescholen.* The almanac, published and updated yearly, provides detailed information and practical hints on higher education in the Netherlands. Publisher: Elsevier. Compiled jointly by VSNU and the HBO-Raad. 480 pp., HFL 24.50

Counterpart. English journal published twice yearly, providing information on the international dimension of teaching and research at the universities of the Netherlands. Published by NUFFIC, available free of charge.

NL

5. Glossary

Doctoraal examen: Examination terminating a course of study at a university and representing a professional qualification. The academic statutes determine and govern the requirements for the *doctoraal examen.* Students in possession of a certificate indicating they passed the *doctoraal examen* with good results can be admitted to an examination for the doctoral degree *(promotie)* after submitting a doctoral thesis.

Extraneus: Registered student at a university who is only entitled to stand for an examination but does not have to pay tuition fees. However, he has to pay examination fees.

Hoger algemeen voortgezet onderwijs (HAVO): Offered at secondary schools with a course duration of five years. The final examination is in six subjects, Dutch language and literature included. It is a form of education preparatory to studies at institutions of *hoger beroepsonderwijs.*

Hoger beroepsonderwijs (HBO): In the case of *hoger beroepsonderwijs* more emphasis is placed on the practical application of the given subject than in the case of *wetenschappelijk onderwijs.* At present there are more than 90 institutions of this kind in the Netherlands. The duration of studies is normally four years. The special form of international instruction *(internationaal onderwijs)* is primarily directed to foreign graduates from developing countries. The duration of such courses is usually not longer than one year, often shorter. Most courses are held in English, some also in French and Spanish, and they are meant to provide additional information to people who already have practical experience in their field of study and work. Detailed information as well as the addresses of all HBO institutions are available from the HBO-Raad (For addresses, see Appendix 1).

Hogeschool: Institution of higher education of the practice-oriented type (*hoger beroepsonderwijs* — HBO).

Numerus fixus: Limitation of the number of students admitted to a specific subject at a university or *hogeschool.*

Propaedeutisch examen: Examination at the end of the first year of study in all subjects at universities or *hogescholen.* The examination is not a professional qualification.

Toehoorder: Student at a university who has surpassed the maximum duration of studies. As a guest student he can continue to attend lectures and he can also take examinations, yet for this purpose he has to pay higher tuition fees than a regular student.

Voorbereidend wetenschappelijk onderwijs (VWO): Form of secondary education preparatory to studying at an academic institution of higher education and having a course duration of six years. The final examination for candidates under 21 years of age includes seven subjects. Candidates reaching their 21st year during the examination year or having surpassed it are examined in six subjects. In every case, Dutch language and literature is an obligatory subject. Candidates taking their examination at an evening school are likewise examined in six subjects only.

Wetenschappelijk onderwijs (WO): The universities are part of the WO. There are 13 universities in the Netherlands.

NL

6. Diagram of the education system

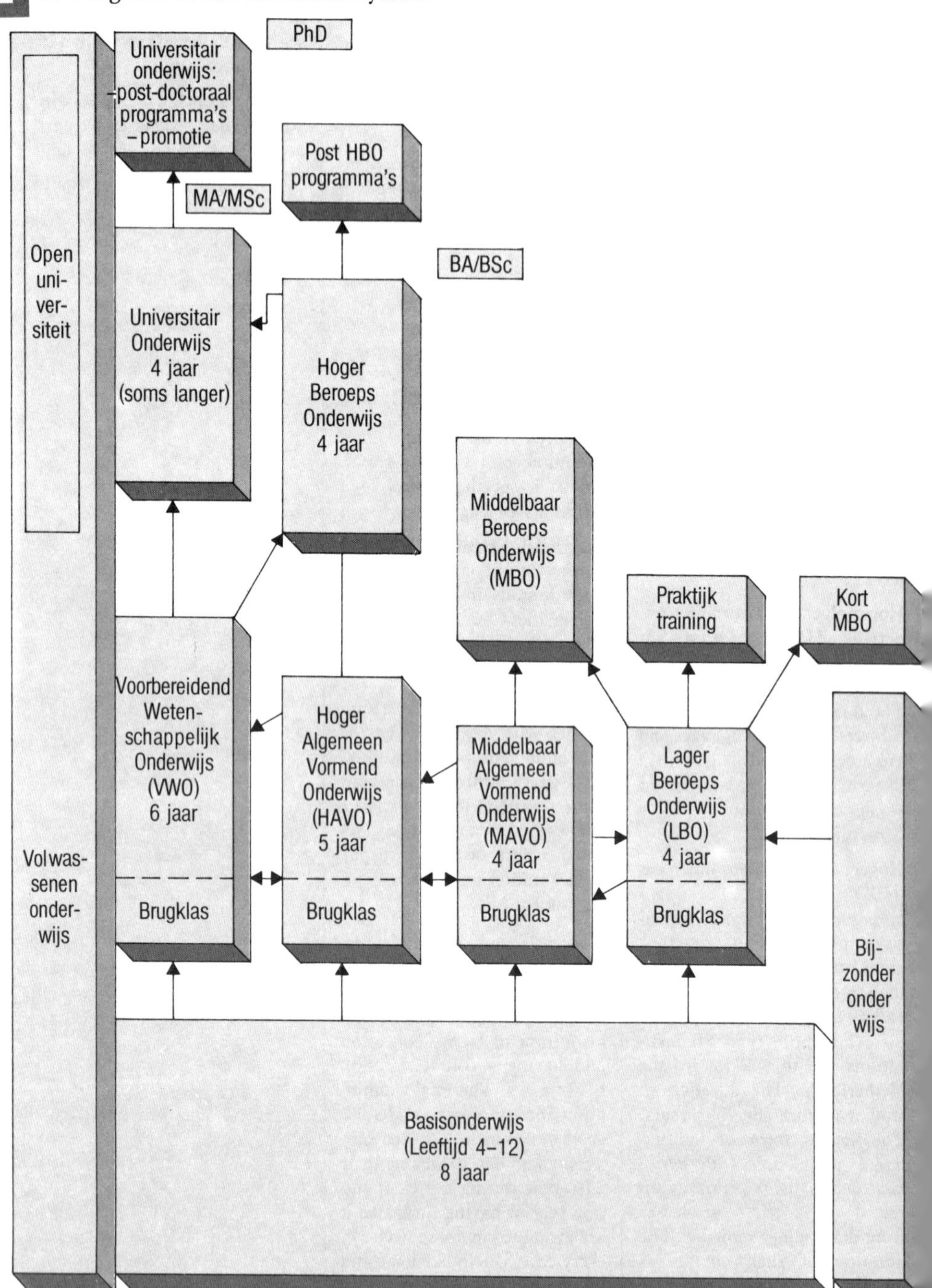
PhD
Universitair onderwijs: -post-doctoraal programma's -promotie
Post HBO programma's
MA/MSc
BA/BSc
Open universiteit
Universitair Onderwijs 4 jaar (soms langer)
Hoger Beroeps Onderwijs 4 jaar
Middelbaar Beroeps Onderwijs (MBO)
Praktijk training
Kort MBO
Voorbereidend Wetenschappelijk Onderwijs (VWO) 6 jaar
Hoger Algemeen Vormend Onderwijs (HAVO) 5 jaar
Middelbaar Algemeen Vormend Onderwijs (MAVO) 4 jaar
Lager Beroeps Onderwijs (LBO) 4 jaar
Volwassenen onderwijs
Brugklas
Brugklas
Brugklas
Brugklas
Bijzonder onderwijs
Basisonderwijs (Leeftijd 4–12) 8 jaar

Explanations and translations of technical terms on facing page.

Legend

Basisonderwijs — Primary education (age 4-12), 8 years.
Bijzonder Onderwijs — Special education.
Brugklas — Transition class.
Hoger Algemeen Vormend Onderwijs (HAVO) — Senior general secondary education, 5 years.
Hoger Beroepsonderwijs (HBO) — HBO* education, 4 years.
Kort MBO — Short senior secondary vocational education.
Lager Beroepsonderwijs (LBO) — Junior secondary vocational education.
Middelbaar Algemeen Vormend Onderwijs (MAVO) — Junior general secondary education.
Middelbaar Beroepsonderwijs (MBO) — Senior secondary vocational education.
Open Universiteit — Open university.
Post HBO programma's — Postgraduate HBO programmes.
Praktijk Training — Apprenticeship training.
Universitair Onderwijs — University education.
Post-doctoraal programma's — post-doctoral programmes.
Promotie — Doctorate.
Volwassenen Onderwijs — Adult education.
Voorbereidend Wetenschappelijk Onderwijs (VWO) — Pre-university education, 6 years.

* *Note:* Dutch government publications in English refer to HBO (hoger beroepsonderwijs) as higher vocational education. The HBO institutes themselves prefer the term higher professional education.

The completion of a university degree is marked by the award of the *doctoraal* certificate, entitling its holder to use the title of *doctorandus*, *ingenieur* or *master*, abbreviated as drs., ir. and mr.
All these titles may be replaced by the Anglo-Saxon title of *Master*, abbreviated as M. after the name and followed — if so desired — by a letter or letters indicating the subject studied.
Graduates of HBO institutions are entitled to use the title *engineer* or *baccalaureus*, abbreviated as ing. or bs. after the person's name. If so desired, the Anglo-Saxon title of *Bachelor*, abbreviated to B. after the name, may be used instead.
Following *postdoctoraal* programmes and a doctorate, students may gain the doctoral degree. The abbreviation of this degree, Dr., may be placed before the holder's name.

Portugal

P

Organization of higher education

In accordance with the general law governing the Portuguese education system (*Lei de bases do sistema educativo*) of October 1986, higher education in Portugal includes both studies at university and at other institutions of higher education (*ensino politécnico*).

University education aims at creating a solid foundation for a student's later profession and at promoting research and innovative and analytical thinking. Education at other non-university institutions of higher education is primarily involved in teaching degree-level subject-specific knowledge which is especially based on the application of research results, and which is thus more closely related to any later occupation.

For a transitional phase during which the general law has not been brought fully into practice, three other institutions of higher education teaching the fine arts and design will also exist — although these are not integrated into the general system of universities and institutions of higher education.

Higher education in Portugal receives public and private support. Consequently, there are both public and private universities and higher education (polytechnic) institutions.

Types of higher education institutions

At present, the following higher education facilities exist in Portugal:

1. universities: 14 public universities; five non-integrated public universities; three private universities (*escolas universitárias*);
2. other non-university institutions of higher education: 14 public institutions (*institutos politécnicos*); three non-integrated institutions (*escolas politécnicas*); 11 private institutions (*escolas politécnicas*);
3. combined universities/institutions of higher education: three private establishments;
4. teaching establishments offering programmes which have neither been integrated into the university system nor into the general higher education system are being offered by three public and three private institutions (*escolas*).

Portuguese universities have the following faculties: arts and humanities, engineering sciences, mathematics and natural sciences, medicine, sport/physical education. The programmes at non-university institutions of higher education (polytechnics) include among others: technology, accountancy and business management, engineering, art and education science. At the as yet non-integrated higher education institutions programmes in the fine arts and design are offered.

Student statistics

For the academic year 1987/88 a total of 119 778 students were registered of which 96 709 were studying at universities and 23 069 at private institutions of higher education. 100 792 of the total number of students were registered at universities, and 18 986 were registered at polytechnics.

In Portugal, 14% of the relevant age group is enrolled in higher education.

In the same academic year 2 333 foreign students were enrolled in Portugal, 1 910 of them at universities. By far the largest group, 1 305 students, came from Portuguese-speaking countries of Africa, and the second largest, 639 students, from South America (mainly Brazil and Venezuela). The number of students from EC countries amounted to 174.

Organization and validation of courses

As a rule, the academic year in Portugal begins in October. Depending on the subject of study, the course can be organized on the basis of years or semesters (two per academic year).

The courses of study at non-university institutions of higher education take an average of three years, at the end of which the students are awarded a *bacharel*. There are also two-year postgraduate programmes leading to a diploma within a specialist field (*diploma de estudos superiores especializados*). Certificates (*certificados*) and diplomas can also be awarded for short study courses.

The degrees *licenciado, mestre* and *doutor* are awarded for university study. Certificates and diplomas can also be awarded for short study courses. The *licenciado* degree is awarded after a course of study lasting from four to six years. The *mestre* degree is awarded after an additional one to two year period of study including the submission and oral examination of an independent academic dissertation (*dissertação*). No special course of study is required for a doctorate, although certain academic criteria must be fulfilled, including the submission and oral examination of a thesis which represents a high-level contribution to current research in its field. Teacher training can take place at universities as well as at other non-university institutions of higher education.

P

Admission and registration

Initial information

Foreign students wishing to study at Portuguese universities and other non-university institutions of higher education should first gather all the relevant information, if possible in their native country, in order to avoid any unnecessary difficulties later. They should consult the Portuguese diplomatic representations in their home countries or write to the following offices: *Ministério da Educação e Cultura* — CIRAD, *Direcção-Geral do Ensino Superior*, or the *Gabinete Coordenador do Ingresso no Ensino Superior* (GCIES) and *Direcção-Geral do Ensino Básico e Secundário*. (See addresses in Appendix 1.)

Entry requirements

Admission to public Portuguese institutions of higher education is dependent upon the number of available student places and is regulated by a national admissions procedure (*concurso nacional*) for both Portuguese and foreign prospective students. The requirements are a 12-year school-leaving certificate and successful participation in a general entry examination (*prova geral de acesso*) regardless of the grade attained. Each institution of higher education may require special entry prerequisites for each degree programme if this is regarded as necessary. The entry examination is intended to assess the prospective student's intellectual level, competence in Portuguese (listening comprehension and capacity for expression) as well as the level of general education. This examination does not reject prospective students, but rather allocates to them a place on a list in order of their achievement. It is to serve as one of the criteria which assign the candidate to the various degree programmes. For admission to the subject areas of physical education and sport, a certain physical aptitude is a precondition, whilst admission to studies in singing and theatre presuppose appropriate talent.

In addition to the admissions procedure for degree programmes at public higher education institutions, there are special programmes for the following groups of persons: (a) applicants who are older than 25 years of age and who have proven their aptitude for higher education studies by passing a special examination; (b) applicants who were already registered for a degree programme at a national higher education institution which is not subject to the control of the Ministry of Education; (c) applicants who have already qualified themselves in middle and higher level courses of the Portuguese education system.

There are also special admissions procedures for special status students, for example, foreign diplomats and their dependants, if they are accredited in Portugal. Further details may be obtained from the GCIES.

Completion of 12 years of schooling is also obligatory for admission to a private institution of higher education. More detailed information regarding the additionally required certificates may be obtained from the higher education institution in question.

Limitations

Restrictions on admission are in force at all Portuguese public and private higher education institutions. The admission of applicants to such institutions is governed by a procedure which takes the results of the applicant's schooling in the 10th, 11th and 12th school years as well as of the general entry examination (*prova geral de acesso*) into consideration. Furthermore, the evaluation of the abovementioned subject examinations which are held at the individual institutions of higher education as well as the order of the examination results may be taken into consideration for an assessment of aptitude.

Each institution of higher education annually reviews the criteria which it applies in order to draw up an order of standing for each of its programmes and in which it will consider the abovementioned criteria.

Recognition of foreign certificates and degrees

Responsibility in questions concerning the recognition of foreign certificates, diplomas and degrees is always a matter for the relevant university or institution of higher education.

Applicants must present all the relevant certificates which confirm successful schooling and must at the same time indicate for which certificate, diploma or degree they require a statement of equivalency (*equivalência*) or of recognition (*reconhecimento*).

Recognition is granted when a statement of equivalency cannot be issued because there is no corresponding course of study in Portugal or because the course of study is not comparable.

A statement of equivalency for a certificate of aptitude for higher education can only be confirmed when the equality of the 10th, 11th and 12th school years and of the study-related subjects of the 12th school year with Portuguese standards can be proven. Applicants must apply for the statement of equivalency at the GCIES branch office (*delegação*) responsible for such matters on the mainland, or respectively at the GCIES offices on Madeira and the Azores.

The statement of equivalency for admission to higher education can be fully or partly issued. If only some of the previous education is recognized as equivalent, then the remaining subjects, with the exception of Portuguese, must be taken and passed by examination. Even if the equivalency of all subjects of the 12th school year has been issued, the applicant must still take an examination in Portuguese language and literature; this is still the case when the 12th school year had specialized in arts and humanities subjects. An examination in Portuguese

P

language and culture is also required for all the other subjects. Equivalency applications must generally be made in April of each year.

Entry examinations

From 1989/90 onwards there will no longer be any entry examinations.

Application and registration

Both Portuguese and foreign students who wish to be admitted to a Portuguese establishment of higher education via the general admissions procedure must normally submit their applications to the GCIES branch offices (*delegação do distritos*) on the mainland or on Madeira and the Azores during July and August. Up to six subjects and establishments in which the applicant would like to enrol may be included on the application form in order of preference. Foreign, as well as Portuguese, students who live abroad must give a Portuguese postal contact address and must name an authorized representative. The GCIES sends the list of the relevant applicants to all institutions of higher education — in accordance with the degree subjects offered by them. The institutions of higher education then determine the order of applicants depending on subject/institution in accordance with the abovementioned criteria.

Tuition fees

Minimal fees are charged for registration and for enrolment to individual subjects. The registration fee (*matrícula*) amounts to ESC 100 (USD 1 = ± ESC 150). The fees for registration, course fees for the *bacharel* or *licenciatura* and all courses lasting, according to the curriculum, one year or one semester amount to ECU 1 200, or respectively ECU 600 at the public higher education institutions. These fee guidelines will change in the course of 1989.

Knowledge of the language of instruction, language courses and other courses

All courses and lectures at Portuguese universities and other non-university institutions of higher education are held in Portuguese. Therefore, a knowledge of Portuguese is required of any student wishing to participate in lectures and classes. As mentioned above, the admissions procedure also presupposes a knowledge of Portuguese, both for the normal examinations as well as for the examinations required for the equivalency procedure. Students whose length of study at another higher education establishment has been recognized and who wish to continue their studies at Portuguese establishments may not be required by all the universities and other institutions of higher education to take a Portuguese language test. However, a lack of Portuguese will make a normal course of study impossible.

In the most important towns in which higher education establishments are to be found, language courses are offered by specialized language schools. In addition to these, some universities and other institutions of higher education organize courses for foreigners on the Portuguese language and culture in the form of summer schools or one-year courses. Details of these courses can be obtained from the *Instituto de Cultura e Língua Portuguesa*.

Financial assistance and scholarships

Students from families with a low income can be exempted from payment of the registration fee and may also apply for a scholarship. If they are not registering at a higher education establishment for the first time, then they will be required to show proof of their schooling and study success. The amount of the scholarship depends on the financial circumstances of the student and of the family.

Foreign students can apply under the same conditions for a scholarship as Portuguese students, if they are stateless or are political refugees or come from countries with which Portugal has a cooperation agreement or if the laws and guidelines of the student's country of origin grant Portuguese citizens the same support under similar conditions.

Entry and residence regulations

Foreign students wishing to enter and stay in Portugal must go to the Portuguese consulate in their country and fill in a form on which they must include the purpose of their stay as well as their address in Portugal.

Students who have been awarded scholarships must present the notice of approval and must also state for how long the scholarship has been granted. Students without a scholarship must provide proof of adequate financial means for the duration of their studies in Portugal. More information can be obtained from the Portuguese consulates and the Central Office for Foreigners (*Direcção-Geral do Serviço de Estrangeiros e Fronteiras*): students should turn to the latter after their arrival in Portugal. (The addresses can be found in Appendix 1.)

Social aspects

Social security and health insurance

Several of the large Portuguese universities have their own medical and social care facilities for their students. In special cases foreign students can also turn to the Health Ministry's medical treatment centres (*serviços de assistência médica e medicamentosa*). On account of bilateral agreements between Portugal and the UK and France, students from these countries can have free medical care in Portugal. Students from other Member States of the European Community are advised to contact the Health Ministry (address in appendix) for more details on access to medical care.

Advisory services

Some higher education establishments have services which will inform and advise students on planning their course of studies and, in some cases, on future employment prospects. In general, however, such an information and advice service has not yet become an integral part of the Portuguese higher education system. The Ministry of Education and Culture is at present compiling generally useful information in this area.

Student employment

It must be pointed out that it is not easy for students to finance their studies through part-time employment. Foreign students are not issued with a work permit so that it is unlikely that they will be able to find employment. Furthermore, the prospects of finding paid part-time work are extremely bad on account of the present employment situation.

Even after Portugal's entry into the European Community, a transitional phase will mean that the opportunities for foreigners from Member States wishing to take up employment will remain restricted.

Student organizations

Most higher education establishments have a student organization which is financed by grants from the university or institution of higher education itself and by the State. These organizations support cultural, political, social and sports activities at the higher education establishments. However, they also supply general information such as on questions of accommodation.

Cost of living

Students' monthly cost of living can only be roughly estimated. This can be expected to be around ESC 55 000 exclusive of study materials. Of this amount some ESC 20 000 can be expected to go towards accommodation, some ESC 25 000 towards food, some ESC 3 000 towards travelling expenses, and ESC 7 000 towards other costs.

Accommodation

Foreign students can apply to the student halls of residence (*residências universitárias*), provided that a bilateral agreement is in force with the students' home country. However, places are very hard to come by on account of the low number of rooms available. Foreign students can also look for private rooms as can Portuguese students who cannot live at home because of the distance. Student societies can offer helpful information here. In Coimbra there are some hostels, so-called *Repúblicas* which the societies administer themselves.

Services for students

Each higher education establishment has social services (*serviços sociais*) which are available to the students. These services maintain refectories and cafeterias and in some places even supermarkets. Should it prove necessary, then one of their administrative functions is to give students legal advice. Students are expected to pay a small fee for this service.

Facilities for disabled students

On account of a special admission procedure, mentally and physically handicapped students have, since April 1985, been granted the possibility of being exempted from attendance at classes and lectures as well as at examinations.

Special regulations governing the application and admissions procedures as well as a special quota (an amendment to the regulations on restricted entry) which only applies to handicapped students are published annually.

In the Ministry of Education and Culture, there is the *Centro de Recursos de Ensino Especial* from which disabled students can obtain their required study materials. The *Centro de Recursos de Ensino Especial* is situated at Av. 24 de Julho, 138, 4º Esq., 1300 Lisboa. It also has a branch office at Rua Bernardo de Albuquerque, 64A, 3000 Coimbra.

Appendices

1. Addresses

Portuguese embassies in European Community Member States

Belgium
115, Rue Defacqz
B-1050 Bruxelles

Denmark
Hovedvagtsgade 6, Mezz.
DK-1103 København

Federal Republic of Germany
Ubier Straße 78
D-5300 Bonn 2

Greece
Odos Loukianou, 19
TT 139
GR-Athina

Spain
Calle del Pinar 1
E-28006 Madrid

France
3, Rue de Noisiel,
F-75116 Paris 16

Ireland
Knocksinna Road
Foxrock
Dublin 18

Italy
Via Gracinta Pezzana, 9
I-00197 Roma

Luxembourg
33 Allée Scheffer
L-2520 Luxembourg

The Netherlands
Bazarstraat, 21
2518 AG 's-Gravenhage

United Kingdom
11 Belgrave Square
London SW1X 8PP

Social services at higher education establishments

Açores
Rua da Mãe de Deus
P-9500 Ponta Delgada

Algarve
Gambelas
P-8000 Faro

Aveiro
Rua Dr. Mário Sacramento, 62
P-3800 Aveiro

Beira Interior
B. Santo António
P-6200 Covilha

Coimbra
Rua Guilherme Moreira, 12
P-3000 Coimbra

Évora
Rua das Alcacarias, 8
P-7000 Évora

Lisboa (Clássica)
Av. da Republica, 84-6º
P-1600 Lisboa

Lisboa (Técnica)
R. Gonçalves Crespo, 20-1º
P-1100 Lisboa

Lisboa (Nova)
Praça do Principe Real, 26-1º
P-1200 Lisboa

Minho
R. do Forno, 30
P-4700 Braga

Porto
Rua da Boa Hora, 18
P-4000 Pórto

Trás-os-Montes e alto Douro
R. Cidade de Espínho, 2
P-5000 Vila Real

Madeira
R. dos Ilhéus, 9-2º
P-9000 Funchal

Note:
In the polytechnic institutions there are committees with responsibility for social services.

Ministries and other authorities

Ministry of Education and Culture
Centro de Informações de Relações Públicas — CIREP
(Information and Public Relations Centre)
Av. 5 de Outubro, 107
P-1051 Lisboa Codex

Direcção-Geral do Ensino Superior
Centro de Informação e Reconhecimento Académico de Diplomas — CIRAD
(Information centre and office for academic recognition of diplomas)
Av. 5 de Outubro, 107 — 9.° andar
P-1051 Lisboa Codex

Gabinete Coordenador do Ingresso ao Ensino Superior — GCIES
(Office for the coordination of student admissions)
Ab. Elias Garcia, 137
P-1000 Lisboa

Aveiro
Rua da Palmeira, 12
P-3800 Aveiro

Beja
Rua Alexandre Herculano, 17-A
P-7800 Beja

Braga
Av. da Liberdade, 12-2º Esq.
P-4700 Braga

Bragança
Rua Dr. Francisco Felgueiras, 18-1º Esq.
P-5300 Bragança

Castelo Branço
Rua Dr. J. A. Mourao, 35
P-6000 Castelo Branco

Coimbra
Rua Feliciano de Castilho, 119-CC
P-3000 Coimbra

Evora
Rua Bernardo de Matos, 12
P-7000 Evora

Faro
Rua S. Luis, 60-3º Esq.
P-8000 Faro

Guarda
Rua Almirante Gago Coutinho, Bloco 4-1º Dto.
P-6300 Guarda

Leiria
Rua Joaquim Ribeiro de Carvalho, Bloco B
Cav. Esq.
P-2400 Leiria

Lisboa
Rua Pinheiro Chagas, 17-r/c
P-1000 Lisboa

Portalegre
Rua Garrett, 5-2º Esq.
P-7300 Portalegre

Porto
Praça Dr. Francisco Sá Carneiro, 251-6alº Esq.
P-4200 Porto

Santarém
Rua Luís de Camões, 16-2º
P-2000 Santarém

Setúbal
Av. Luisa Todi, 33-2º C
P-2900 Setúbal

Viana do Castelo
Largo 9 de Abril, BC 9
P-1900 Viana do Castelo

Vila Real
Rua Marechal Teixeira Rebelo, 151-r/c
P-5000 Vila Real

Viseu
Rua Dr. Francisco Alexandre Lobo, 59-1º
P-3500 Viseu

Direcção-Geral do Ensino Básico e Secundário
(Director-General for Primary and Secondary Education)
Av. 24 de Julho, 138-140
P-1300 Lisboa

Instituto de Cultura e Língua Portuguesa
(Institute for Portuguese Language and Culture)
Praça do Príncipe Real, nº 14-1.º
P-1200 Lisboa

Ministério dos Negócios Estrangeiros
(Ministry of Foreign Affairs)
Largo do Rilvas
P-1300 Lisboa

Ministério da Administração Interna
(Ministry of the Interior)
D. G. do Serviços de Estrangeiros e Fronteiras
(Directorate for foreigners and border questions)
Av. Antonio Augusto de Aguiar, 18
P-1000 Lisboa

Ministério da Saúde
(Ministry of Health)
Serviço de Informaçoes
Av. dos Estados Unidos de América, 75
P-1700 Lisboa

Departamento de Recursos Humanos da Saúde
(Department of Health Care)
Av. Miguel Bombarda, 6-2º
P-1000 Lisboa

Higher education institutions

Public higher education institutions

Universidade Aberta
R. da Escola Politécnica, 141
P-1200 Lisboa

Universidade dos Açores
Rue da Mae de Deus
P-9502 Ponta Delgada Codex

Universidade do Algarve
Quinta da Penha
Estrada da Penha
P-8000 Faro

Universidade de Aveiro
Rua Dr. Mário Sacramento, 62
P-3800 Aveiro

Universidade da Beira Interior
Calçada de S. Martinho
P-6200 Covilha

Universidade de Coimbra
Pátio da Universidade
P-3000 Coimbra

Faculdade de Ciências e Tecnologia
Largo D. Dinis
P-3000 Coimbra

Faculdade de Direito
Pátio da Universidade
P-3000 Coimbra

Faculdade de Economia
Av. Dias da Silva, 145
P-3000 Coimbra

Faculdade de Farmácia
Rua do Norte
P-3000 Coimbra

Faculdade de Letras
Praça da Porta Férrea
P-3000 Coimbra

Faculdade de Medicina
Rua Larga
P-3000 Coimbra

Faculdade de Psicologia e Ciênc. da Educação
Rua do Colégio Novo
P-3000 Coimbra

Universidade de Évora
Rua das Alcacaries, 8
P-7000 Évora

Universidade de Lisboa
Alameda da Universidade
P-1699 Lisboa Codex

Faculdade de Ciências
Edifício C2 — Campo Grande
P-1700 Lisboa

Faculdade de Direito
Alameda da Universidade
P-1699 Lisboa Codex

Faculdade de Farmácia
Av. das Forças Armadas
P-1600 Lisboa

Faculdade de Letras
Alameda da Universidade
P-1600 Lisboa

Faculdade de Medicina
Av. Professor Egas Moniz
P-1600 Lisboa

Faculdade de Psicologia e Ciênc. da Educação
Av. Pinheiro Chagas, 17-1º
P-1000 Lisboa

Universidade da Madeira
P-9000 Funchal

Universidade do Minho
Largo do Paço
P-4719 Braga Codex

Universidade Nova de Lisboa
Praça do Principe Real, 26 r/c
P-1200 Lisboa

Faculdade de Ciências Médicas
Campo dos Mártires da Pátria, 130
P-1198 Lisboa Codex

Faculdade de C. Sociais e Humanas
Av. de Berna, 24
P-1000 Lisboa

Faculdade de C. e Tecnologia
Quinta da Torre
P-2825 Monte da Caparica

Faculdade de Economia
Travessa de Estevão Pinho
P-1100 Lisboa

Universidade do Porto
Rue D. Manuel II
Apartado 211
P-4003 Porto Codex

Curso de Lic. em Ciênc. da Nutrição
Alameda Prof. Hernâni Monteiro
(Hospital de S. João)
P-4200 Porto

Faculdade de Arquitectura
Rua do Golgota, 215
P-4100 Porto

Faculdade de Ciências
Praça Gomes Teixeira
P-4000 Porto

Faculdade de Economia
Rua Dr. Roberto Frias
P-4200 Porto

Faculdade de Engenharia
Rue dos Bragas
P-4099 Porto Codex

Faculdade de Farmácia
Rua da Boavista, 158/68
P-4000 Porto

Faculdade de Letras
Rua do Campo Alegre, 1055
P-4100 Porto

Faculdade de Medicina
Alam. Prof. Hernâni Monteiro
(Hospital de S. João)
P-4200 Porto

Faculdade de Psicol. e Ciênc. da Educação
Rua das Taipas
P-4000 Porto

I. C. Biomédicas de Abel Salazar
Largo da Escola Médica, 2
P-4000 Porto

Inst. Superior de Educação Física
Largo da Escola Médica, 2
P-4000 Porto

Universidade de Trás-os-Montes e Alto Douro
Quinta dos Prados
Folhadela
P-5000 Vila Real

Universidade Técnica de Lisboa
Alameda Santo Ántonio dos Capuchos, nº 1
P-1100 Lisboa

Escola Sup. Medicina Veterinária
Rua Gomes Freire
P-1100 Lisboa

Faculdade de Arquitectura
Largo da Academia Nacional de Belas Artes, 2-2º
P-1200 Lisboa

Instituto Superior de Agronomia
Tapada da Ajuda
P-1300 Lisboa

Inst. Superior de C. Sociais e Políticas
Rua da Junqueira, 86
P-1399 Lisboa Codex

Instituto Superior de Economia
Rua Miguel Lupi, 20
P-1200 Lisboa

Inst. Superior de Educação Física
Estrada da Costa — Cruz Quebrada
P-1499 Lisboa Codex

Inst. Superior Técnico
Av. Rovisco Pais
P-1096 Lisboa Codex

Polytechnic institutions of higher education

Inst. Sup. de Cont. e Administração de Aveiro
R. de Ilhavo — Apartado 58
P-3800 Aveiro

Inst. Politécnico de Beja
Rua de Santo Antonio, 1-A
P-7800 Beja

Escola Sup. Agrária
Praceta Rainha D. Leonor
P-7800 Beja

Escola Superior de Educação
R. de Santo António, 1-A
P-7800 Beja

Inst. Politécnico de Bragança
R. 1º de Dezembro, 8
Apartado 38
P-5300 Bragança

Escola Sup. Agrária
Quinta de Santa Apolónia
Apartado 38
P-5300 Bragança

Escola Sup. de Educação
Bairro da Mãe de Deus
Apartado 38
P-5300 Bragança

Inst. Politécnico de Castelo Branco
R. S. João de Deus, 25-2º
P-6000 Castelo Branco

Escola Sup. Agrária
R. S. João de Deus, 25-2º
P-6000 Castelo Branco

Escola Sup. de Educação
Rua Pedro da Fonseca
P-6000 Castelo Branco

Inst. Politécnico de Coimbra
Rua Pinheiro Chagas, 96-2º
P-3000 Coimbra

Escola Sup. Agrária
Bencanta
P-3000 Coimbra

Escola Sup. de Educação
R. Pinheiro Chagas, 96-2º
P-3000 Coimbra

Inst. Sup. de Cont. e Administração
R. Luís de Camões
Quinta de S. Jerónimo
P-3000 Coimbra

Inst. Sup. de Engenharia
Quinta da Nora
P-300 Coimbra

Inst. Politécnico de Faro
Quinta de Penha — Estrada da Penha
P-8000 Faro

Escola Sup. de Educação
Quinta da Penha
P-8000 Faro

Escola Sup. de Gestão, Hotelaria e Turismo
Quinta da Penha
P-8000 Faro

Escola Sup. de Tecnologia
Quinta de Penha
P-8000 Faro

Inst. Politécnico da Guarda
R. Comandante Salvador Nascimento
P-6300 Guarda

Escola Sup. de Educação
R. Comandante Salvador Nascimento
P-6300 Guarda

Escola Sup. Tecnol. e Gestão
R. Comandante Salvdor Nascimento
P-6300 Guarda

Inst. Politécnico de Leiria
Edificio Maringa
Torre 2, 2º
P-2400 Leiria

Escola Sup. de Educação
Porto Moniz
Apartado 424
P-2400 Leiria

Escola Sup. Tecnol. e Gestão
Edifício Maringa
Torre, 2º
P-2400 Leiria

Escola Sup. de Arte e Design
Edifício Maringa
Torre 2-2º
P-2400 Leiria

Instituto Gregoriano de Lisboa
Av. 5 de Outubro, 258
P-1600 Lisboa

Inst. Politécnico de Lisboa
Campo dos Mártires da Patria, 2-2º
P-1100 Lisboa

Escola Sup. de Dança
Rua dos Caetanos, 29
P-1200 Lisboa

Escola Sup. de Educação
T. Terras de Sant'Ana, 15-A-2º
P-1200 Lisboa

Escola Sup. de Comunicação Social
Campo dos Mártires da Pátria, 2-2º
P-1100 Lisboa

Escola Sup. de Música
Rua dos Caetanos, 29
P-1200 Lisboa

Escola Sup. de Teatro e Cinema
Rua dos Caetanos, 29
P-1200 Lisboa

Inst. Sup. de Contabili. e Administra.
Av. Miguel Bombarda, 20
P-1000 Lisboa

Inst. Sup. de Engenharia
Rua Conselhenro Emídio Navarro
P-1900 Lisboa

Inst. Politécnico de Portalegre
Escola Sup. de Educação
Praça da República
Apartado 125
P-7301 Portalegre Codex

Inst. Politécnico do Porto
R. Dr. Roberto Frias
P-4200 Porto

Escola Sup. de Educação
Rua Dr. Roberto Frias
P-4200 Porto

Escola Sup. de Música
Rua da Maternidade, 13
P-4000 Porto

Inst. Sup. de Contab. e Administra.
Rua de Entreparedes, 48
P-4000 Porto

Inst. Sup. de Engenharia
Rua de S. Tomé
P-4200 Porto

Inst. Politécnico de Santarém
Complexo Andaluz — Apartado 279
P-2002 Santarém Codex

Escola Sup. Agrária
S. Pedro — Apartado 279
P-2002 Santarém Codex

Escola Sup. de Educação
Complexo Andaluz — Apartado 279
P-2002 Santarém Codex

Escola Sup. de Gestão
Complexo Andaluz — Apartado 279
P-2002 Santarém Codex

Esc. Sup. de Tecnol. de Tomar
Av. Dr Cândido Madureira, 13
P-2300 Tomar

Instituto Politécnico de Setúbal
L. dos Defensores da República, 1
P-2900 Setúbal

Escola Sup. de Educação
R. do Vale de Chaves
Lugar da Estefanilha
P-2900 Setúbal

Escola Sup. de Tecnologia
R. do Vale de Chaves
Lugar da Estefanilha
P-2900 Setúbal

Instituto Politécnico de Viana do Castelo
R. Gago Coutinho, 20
P-4901 Viana do Castelo Codex

Escola Sup. Agrária de Ponte de Lima
Praça da República
P-4990 Ponte de Lima

Escola Sup. de Educação
Av. 28 de Setembro — Apartado 51
P-4901 Viana do Castelo Codex

Escola Sup. de Tecnol. e Gestão
R. Gago Coutinho, 20
Apartado 51
P-4901 Viana do Castelo Codex

Instituto Politécnico de Viseu
R. Alexandre Lobo, 55-3º Esq.
P-3500 Viseu

Escola Sup. de Educação
Av. Infante D. Henrique, 76
P-3500 Viseu

Escola Sup. de Tecnologia
R. Alexandre Lobo, 59-2º Dto.
P-3500 Viseu

Escola Sup. de Educação da Madeira
Rua do Castanheiro
P-9000 Funchal

Private higher education institutions

Escola Sup. de Medicina Dentária de Lisboa
Av. Prof. Gama Pinto
P-1600 Lisboa

Escola Sup. de Medicina Dentária do Porto
R. Dr. Roberto Frias
P-4200 Porto

Escola Sup. de C. do Trabalho e Empresa
Av. das Forças Armadas
P-1600 Lisboa

Higher education institutions for the Fine Arts and Design

Escola Sup. de Belas Artes de Lisboa
Largo da Biblioteca Pública
P-1200 Lisboa

Escola Sup. de Belas Artes do Porto
Av. Rodrigues de Freitas, 265
P-4300 Porto

Instituto Sup. de Artes Plásticas da Madeira
Rua da Carreira, 56
P-9000 Funchal

Public higher education institutions which are not subject to the control of the Ministry of Education

Academia da Força Aerea
Granja do Marques
P-2710 Sintra

Academia Militar
Paço da Rainha
P-1100 Lisboa

Escola Náutica Infante D. Henrique
Paço de Arcos
P-2780 Oeiras

Escola Naval
Alfeite
P-2800 Almada

Escola Superior de Polícia
Rua 1º de Maio Nº 3
P-1300 Lisboa

Instituto Militar dos Pupilos do Exército
(Secção do Ensino Superior)
Estrada de Benefica
P-1500 Lisboa

Private institutions of higher education *(Ensino superior particular e cooperativo)*

Universidade Autónoma de Lisboa
Lois de Camões
Rua de Santa Marta, 56
P-1100 Lisboa

Universidade Catõlica Portuguesa
Palma de Cima
P-1600 Lisboa

Fac. Ciéncias Humanas
em Lisboa:
Palma de Cima
P-1600 Lisboa

no Porto:
Rua Diogo Botelho, 1327
P-4100 Porto

no Funchal:
Edifício do Colégio
Largo do Município
P-9000 Funchal

Fac. de Filosofia
em Braga:
Largo da Faculdade
P-4700 Braga

em Lisboa:
Palma de Cima
P-1600 Lisboa

em Viseu:
Largo de Sta. Cristina
P-3500 Viseu

no Funchal:
Edifício do Colégio
Largo do Município
P-9000 Funchal

P

Fac. de Teologia
em Lisboa:
Palma de Cima
P-1600 Lisboa

Instituto Sup. de Teologia
Largo da Faculdade
P-4700 Braga

Escola Sup. de Biotecnologia
Rua Dr. António Bernardino de Almeida
P-4200 Porto

Inst. Univers. de Desenvolv. e Prom. Social
Largo de Santa Cristina
P-3500 Viseu

Universidade Internacional
Estrada de Benefica, 275
P-1500 Lisboa

Universidade Lusíada
Rua da Junqueira, 194
P-1300 Lisboa

Universidade Portucalense
Av. Rodrigues de Freitas, 349
P-4100 Porto

Coop. de Ens. Sup. Artistico (Árvore I)
Passeio das Virtudes, 14
P-4000 Porto

Cocite — Coop. de Tecnicas Avançadas de Gestão e informática
Campo dos Mártires da Pátria, 67-2º Dto.
P-1100 Lisboa

Esc. de Educadores de Infância
Rua do Jardim à Estrela, 16
P-1300 Lisboa

Esc. Sup. de Educação de Fafe
Rua Montenegro
P-4820 Fafe

Esc. Sup. de Educação João de Deus
Av. Alvares Cabral, 69
P-1200 Lisboa

Esc. Sup. de Educação Paula Frassinetti
Av. dos Combatentes da Grande Guerra, 47
P-4200 Porto

Esc. Sup. de Educação Santa Maria
Rua de Guerra Junceiro, 597
P-4100 Porto

Esc. Sup. de Educação Torres Novas
P-2350 Torres Novas

Esc. Sup. de Educação Jean Piaget
em Almada:
Quinta de Areinela (via rápida da Caparica)
P-2800 Almada

em Arcozelo:
Lugar da Igreja
Arcozelo/Vila Nova de Gaia
P-4405 Valadares

Esc. Sup. de Jornalismo
Av. Boavista, 3067
P-4000 Porto

Inst. de Novas Profissões
Av. Duque de Loulé, 47-1º
P-1000 Lisboa

Inst. Sup. de Administração e Gestão
Av. da Boavista, 1043
P-4100 Porto

Inst. Sup. de Assistentes e Interpreti
Rua António Pedro, 24
P-4000 Porto

Inst. Sup. de Ciênc. Educativas
Serra da Amoreira
P-2675 Odivelas

Inst. Sup. de Gestão
Estrada da Ameixoeira, 112/116
P-1700 Lisboa

Inst. Sup. de Línguas e Administração
Rua do Sacramento à Lapa 14/16
P-1200 Lisboa

Inst. Sup. Politécnico Internacional
Estrada de Benefica, 275
P-1500 Lisboa

Inst. Sup. de Matematicas Modernas
Rua das Flores, 59
P-1200 Lisboa

Inst. Sup. Psicologia Aplicada
rua Jardim do Tobaco, 44
P-1100 Lisboa

Inst. Sup. de Serviço Social de Coimbra
Rua Oliveira Matos, 17
P-3000 Coimbra

Inst. Sup. de Serviço Social de Lisboa
Largo do Mitelo, 1
P-1100 Lisboa

Inst. sup. de Serviço Social do Porto
Av. Rodrigues de Freitas, 202
P-4000 Porto

2. Survey of courses of study at higher education institutions

Non-integrated universities and non-integrated *Escolas Universitárias*

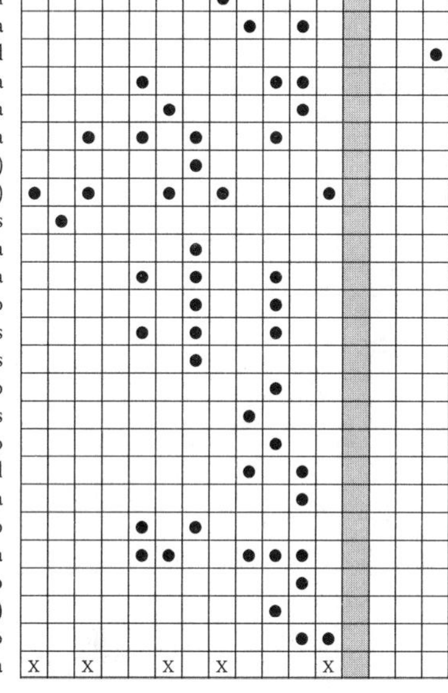

	Açores	Algarve	Aveiro	Beira interior	Coimbra	Évora	Lisboa	Minho	Nova de Lisboa	Porto	Técnica de Lisboa	Trás-os-Montes e Alto Douro	Esc. sup. de medicina dentária de Lisboa	Esc. sup. de medicina dentária do Porto	Inst. sup. de ciências do trabalho e da empresa	
Administração Pública' Regional e Local								●								Public, regional and local administration
Antropologia									●		●					Anthropology
Antropologia Social															●	Social anthropology
Arquitectura					●					●	●					Architecture
Arquitectura Paisagista						●					●					Landscape planning
Biologia			●		●		●			●						Biology
Biologia (Ensino de)							●									Biology (for teaching)
Biologia e Geologia (Ensino de)	●		●			●		●				●				Biology and geology (for teaching)
Biologia Marinha e Pescas		●														Marine biology and fisheries science
Biologia Vegetal Aplicada							●									Applied vegetation biology
Bioquímica					●		●			●						Biochemistry
Ciências da Educação							●			●						Education science
Ciências Farmacêuticas					●		●			●						Pharmacy
Ciências Geofísicas							●									Geophysics
Ciências do Meio Aquático										●						Water management
Ciências Musicais									●							Musicology
Ciências da Nutrição										●						Food sciences
Comunicação Social									●		●					Social/Communications sciences
Dança											●					Dance
Direito					●		●									Law
Economia					●	●			●	●	●					Economics
Educação Exp. e Reabilitação											●					Special pedagogics and rehabilitation
Educação Física (Ens.)										●						Physical education (for teaching)
Educação Física e Desporto											●	●				Physical education and Sport
Educadores de Infância	X		X			X		X				X				Educator training

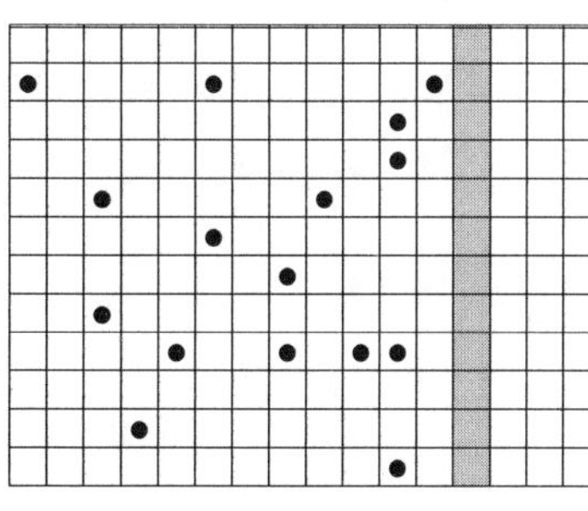

	Açores	Algarve	Aveiro	Beira interior	Coimbra	Évora	Lisboa	Minho	Nova de Lisboa	Porto	Técnica de Lisboa	Trás-os-Montes e Alto Douro	Esc. sup. de medicina dentária de Lisboa	Esc. sup. de medicina dentária do Porto	Inst. sup. de ciências do trabalho e da empresa	**Engineering:**
Engenharia Agrícola	●					●						●				Agricultural engineering
Engenharia Agro-Industrial											●					Agricultural industrial engineering
Engenharia Agronómica											●					Engineering agronomy
Engenharia do Ambiente			●						●							Environmental engineering
Engenharia Biofísica						●										Biophysical engineering
Engenharia Biológica								●								Biological engineering
Engenharia Cerâmica e do Vidro			●													Engineering in ceramics and glass
Engenharia Civil					●			●		●	●					Civil engineering
Engenharia Civil (variante)																Civil engineering (various)
Planeamento e Urbanismo				●												Planning and town planning
Engenharia de Construção Naval											●					Naval construction

● *Licenciatura* programmes
X *Bacharel* programmes (three years)
○ Higher education programmes which are not comparable to an academic degree (two years)

P

Non-integrated universities and non-integrated *Ecolas Universitarias*

	Açores	Algarve	Aveiro	Beira interior	Coimbra	Évora	Lisboa	Minho	Nova de Lisboa	Porto	Técnica de Lisboa	Trás-os-Montes e Alto Douro	Esc. sup. de medicina dentária de Lisboa	Esc. sup. de medicina dentária do Porto	Inst. sup. de ciências do trabalho e da empresa	**Engineering:**
Engenharia de Electromecânica				●												Electrical mechanics
Engenharia Electrónica e Indust.								●								Electronics and industry
Engenharia Electrónica e Telec.			●													Electronics and telecommunications
Engenharia Electrotécnica					●							●				Electrical engineering
Engenharia Electro e Computadores										●	●					Electronics and computers
Engenharia Física					●											Physics
Engenharia Física e Materiais									●							Physics and materials
Engenharia Física Tecnológica											●					Technological physics
Engenharia Florestal											●	●				Forestry economics
Engenharia Geográfica					●		●			●						Geography
Engenharia Geológica			●		●				●							Geology
Engenharia e Gestão Industrial			●													Industrial business management
Engenharia Informática					●				●							Computer science
Engenharia Mecânica					●				●	●	●					Mechanics
Engenharia Metalomecânica								●								Metals mechanics
Engenharia Metalúrgica										●						Metallurgy
Engenharia Metal. e Materiais											●					Metallurgy and materials
Engenharia de Minas					●					●	●					Mining
Engenharia do Papel				●												Paper engineering
Engenharia de Polímeros								●								Polymer engineering
Engenharia de Produção								●								Production engineering
Engenharia de Produção Industrial									●							Industrial production engineering
Engenharia Química					●				●	●	●					Chemical engineering
Engenharia de Sistemas e Informática								●								Sytems analysis and computer science
Engenharia Têxtil				●				●								Textiles industrial engineering
Engenharia Zootécnica	●					●						●				Zoological technology (stock-breeding)
Enologia												○				Viniculture
Ergonomia											●					Labour science
Estatística e Inv. Operacion.							●									Statistics and operations research
Filosofia					●		●		●	●						Philosophy
Filosofia (variante)																Philosophy (various)
História das Ideias									●							History of theory/philosophy
Física			●		●		●			●						Physics
Física (Ens.)				●			●									Physics (for teaching)
Física/Matemática Aplicada										●						Physics/mathematics (applied)
Física Aplicada				●				●								Physics (applied)
Física e Química (Ens.)			●			●	●	●				●				Physics and chemistry
Física Tecnológica							●									Physical technology

● *Licenciatura* programmes
X *Bacharel* programmes (three years)
○ Higher education programmes which are not comparable to an academic degree (two years)

P

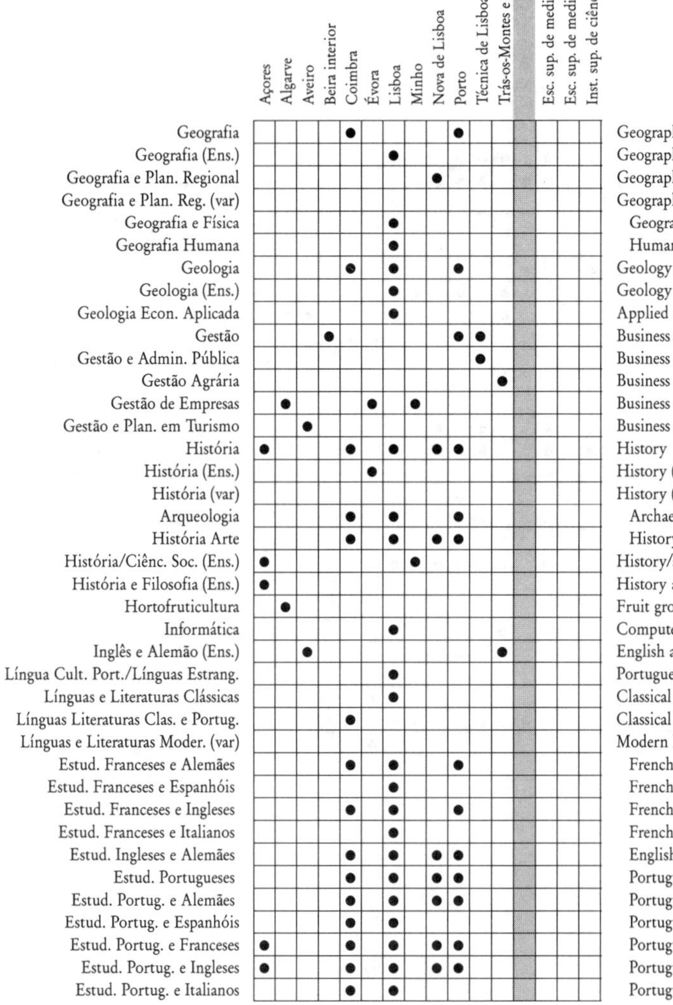

	Açores	Algarve	Aveiro	Beira interior	Coimbra	Évora	Lisboa	Minho	Nova de Lisboa	Porto	Técnica de Lisboa	Trás-os-Montes e Alto Douro	Esc. sup. de medicina dentária de Lisboa	Esc. sup. de medicina dentária do Porto	Inst. sup. de ciência do trabalho e da empresa	
Geografia					●					●						Geography
Geografia (Ens.)							●									Geography (for teaching)
Geografia e Plan. Regional									●							Geography and regional planning
Geografia e Plan. Reg. (var)																Geography and regional planning (various)
Geografia e Física							●									Geography and physics
Geografia Humana							●									Human geography
Geologia					●		●			●						Geology
Geologia (Ens.)							●									Geology (for teaching)
Geologia Econ. Aplicada							●									Applied economic geology
Gestão				●						●	●					Business management
Gestão e Admin. Pública											●					Business management and public administration
Gestão Agrária												●				Business management/agriculture
Gestão de Empresas		●				●		●								Business management/enterprises
Gestão e Plan. em Turismo			●													Business studies/Tourism
História	●				●		●		●	●						History
História (Ens.)						●										History (for teaching)
História (var)																History (various)
Arqueologia					●		●			●						Archaeology
História Arte					●		●		●	●						History of art
História/Ciênc. Soc. (Ens.)	●							●								History/social science (for teaching)
História e Filosofia (Ens.)	●															History and philosophy (for teaching)
Hortofruticultura		●														Fruit growing
Informática							●									Computer science
Inglês e Alemão (Ens.)			●									●				English and German (for teaching)
Língua Cult. Port./Línguas Estrang.							●									Portuguese language and culture/foreign languages
Línguas e Literaturas Clássicas							●									Classical languages and literature
Línguas Literaturas Clas. e Portug.					●											Classical languages and literature/Portuguese
Línguas e Literaturas Moder. (var)																Modern languages and literature (various)
Estud. Franceses e Alemães					●		●			●						French and German
Estud. Franceses e Espanhóis							●									French and Spanish
Estud. Franceses e Ingleses					●		●			●						French and English
Estud. Franceses e Italianos							●									French and Italian
Estud. Ingleses e Alemães					●		●		●	●						English and German
Estud. Portugueses					●		●		●	●						Portuguese
Estud. Portug. e Alemães					●		●		●	●						Portuguese and German
Estud. Portug. e Espanhóis					●		●									Portuguese and Spanish
Estud. Portug. e Franceses	●				●		●		●	●						Portuguese and French
Estud. Portug. e Ingleses	●				●		●		●	●						Portuguese and English
Estud. Portug. e Italianos					●		●									Portuguese and Italian

● *Licenciatura* programmes
X *Bacharel* programmes
○ Higher education programmes which are not comparable to an academic degree (two years)

Non-integrated universities and non-integrated *Ecolas Universitárias*

	Açores	Algarve	Aveiro	Beira interior	Coimbra	Évora	Lisboa	Minho	Nova de Lisboa	Porto	Técnica de Lisboa	Trás-os-Montes e Alto Douro	Esc. sup. de medicina dentária de Lisboa	Esc. sup. de medicina dentária do Porto	Inst. sup. de ciências do trabalho e da empresa	
Linguística							●									Linguistics
Matemática	●		●		●	●	●		●	●						Mathematics
Matemática (Ens.)	●		●	●		●	●	●								Mathematics (for teaching)
Matemática Aplicada										●						Applied mathematics
Matemat. Aplic. e Computação											●					Applied mathematics and accountancy
Matemat. e Ciências da Computação								●								Mathematics and computer science
Matemática/Informática	●			●												Mathematics/computer science
Medicina					●		●		●	●						Medicine
Medicina Dentária					●								●	●		Dentistry
Medicina Veterinária											●	●				Veterinary medicine
Organização e Gestão de Empresas	●														●	Business management (organization)
Plan. Regional e Urbano			●													Regional and town planning
Política Social											●					Social politics
Português e Francês (Ens.)	●		●			●		●				●				Portuguese and French (for teaching)
Português e Inglês (Ens.)	●		●			●		●				●				Portuguese and English (for teaching)
Portug. Latim e Grego (Ens.)			●													Portuguese, Latin and Greek (for teaching)
Probabilidades e Estatística							●									Probability calculus and statistics
Profes. do ens. primário	X		X			X		X				X				Primary school teachering
Psicologia					●		●			●						Psychology
Química			●		●		●	●		●						Chemistry
Química (Ens.)							●									Chemistry (for teaching)
Química Aplicada									●							Applied chemistry
Química Industrial					●											Industrial chemistry
Química Tecnológica							●									Chemical technology
Recursos Faunísticos e Ambiente							●									Protection of fauna and environment
Relações Internacionais								●			●					International relations
Sociologia				●	●	●			●	●					●	Sociology
Sociologia do Trabalho											●					Labour sociology

● *Licenciatura* programmes
X *Bacharel* programmes
○ Higher education programmes which are not comparable to an academic degree (two years)

Studies at polytechnics *(politécnicos)*

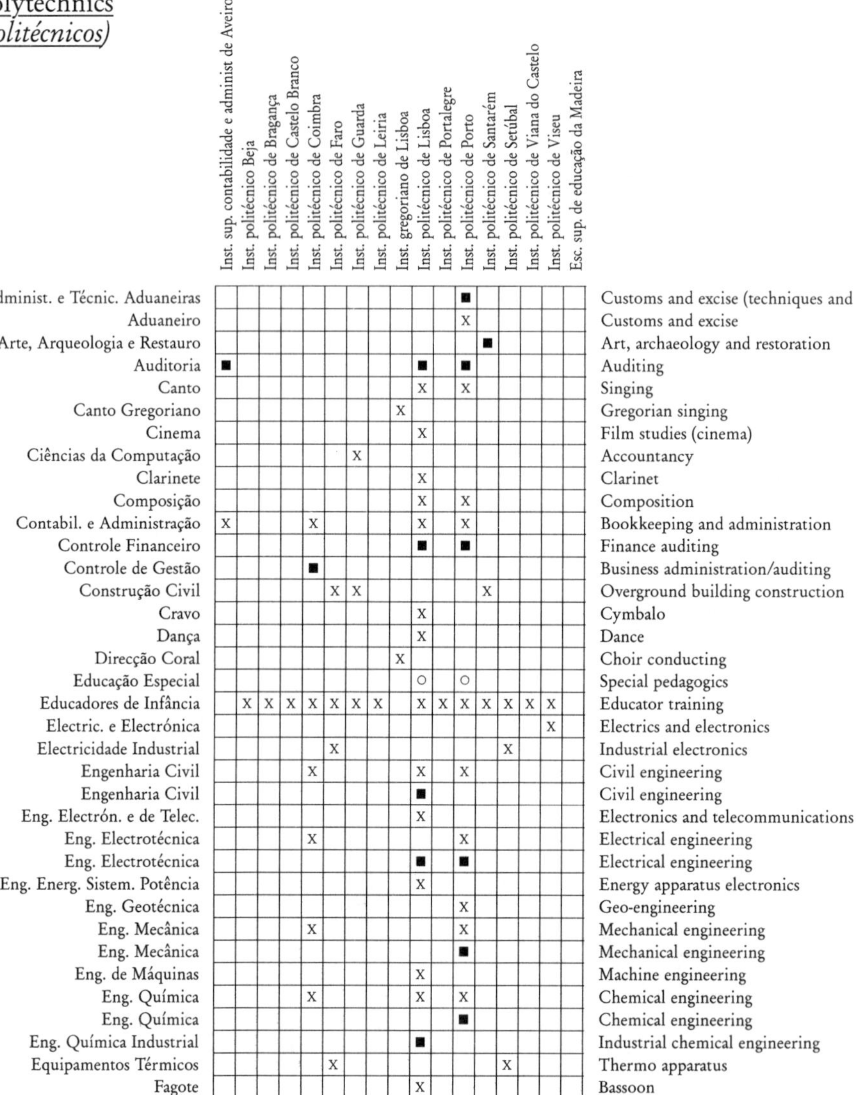

	Inst. sup. contabilidade e administ de Aveiro	Inst. politécnico Beja	Inst. politécnico de Bragança	Inst. politécnico de Castelo Branco	Inst. politécnico de Coimbra	Inst. politécnico de Faro	Inst. politécnico de Guarda	Inst. politécnico de Leiria	Inst. gregoriano de Lisboa	Inst. politécnico de Lisboa	Inst. politécnico de Portalegre	Inst. politécnico de Porto	Inst. politécnico de Santarém	Inst. politécnico de Setúbal	Inst. politécnico de Viana do Castelo	Inst. politécnico de Viseu	Esc. sup. de educação da Madeira	
Administ. e Técnic. Aduaneiras												■						Customs and excise (techniques and administra
Aduaneiro												X						Customs and excise
Arte, Arqueologia e Restauro													■					Art, archaeology and restoration
Auditoria	■									■		■						Auditing
Canto										X		X						Singing
Canto Gregoriano									X									Gregorian singing
Cinema										X								Film studies (cinema)
Ciências da Computação							X											Accountancy
Clarinete										X								Clarinet
Composição										X		X						Composition
Contabil. e Administração	X				X					X		X						Bookkeeping and administration
Controle Financeiro										■		■						Finance auditing
Controle de Gestão					■													Business administration/auditing
Construção Civil						X	X						X					Overground building construction
Cravo										X								Cymbalo
Dança										X								Dance
Direcção Coral									X									Choir conducting
Educação Especial										O		O						Special pedagogics
Educadores de Infância		X	X	X	X	X	X	X		X	X	X	X	X	X	X		Educator training
Electric. e Electrónica																X		Electrics and electronics
Electricidade Industrial						X								X				Industrial electronics
Engenharia Civil					X					X		X						Civil engineering
Engenharia Civil										■								Civil engineering
Eng. Electrón. e de Telec.										X								Electronics and telecommunications
Eng. Electrotécnica					X							X						Electrical engineering
Eng. Electrotécnica										■		■						Electrical engineering
Eng. Energ. Sistem. Potência										X								Energy apparatus electronics
Eng. Geotécnica												X						Geo-engineering
Eng. Mecânica					X							X						Mechanical engineering
Eng. Mecânica												■						Mechanical engineering
Eng. de Máquinas										X								Machine engineering
Eng. Química					X					X		X						Chemical engineering
Eng. Química												■						Chemical engineering
Eng. Química Industrial										■								Industrial chemical engineering
Equipamentos Térmicos						X								X				Thermo apparatus
Fagote										X								Bassoon

X *Bacharel* programmes
O Higher education programmes which are not comparable to an academic degree (two years)
■ Specialist programmes (four semesters)

P

Studies at polytechnicos (*politécnicos*)

	Inst. sup. contabilidade e administ de Aveiro	Inst. politécnico Beja	Inst. politécnico de Bragança	Inst. politécnico de Castelo Branco	Inst. politécnico de Coimbra	Inst. politécnico de Faro	Inst. politécnico de Guarda	Inst. politécnico de Leiria	Inst. gregoriano de Lisboa	Inst. politécnico de Lisboa	Inst. politécnico de Portalegre	Inst. politécnico de Porto	Inst. politécnico de Santarém	Inst. politécnico de Setúbal	Inst. politécnico de Viana do Castelo	Inst. politécnico de Viseu	Esc. sup. de educação da Madeira	
Flauta										X		X						Flute
Gestão						X										X		Business management
Gestão da Empre. Agrícola			X															Agricultural business management
Gestão de Empresas													X					Company business management
Gestão Informática							X											Economic computer science
Informática												X						Computer science
Línguas e Secretariado												X						Languages and the secretariat
Melhoramentos Rurais			X															Land conservation
Manutenção Industrial							X											Industrial maintenance
Oboé										X								Oboe
Órgão									X									Organ
Piano										X		X						Piano
Piano de acompanhamento												X						Piano (accompaniment)
Produção Agrícola		X	X	X	X								X					Agricultural production
Produção Animal		X	X	X	X								X					Animal production
Produção Florestal				X														Forestry production
																		Teaching:
Prof. do Ensino Básico (var)																		Primary school teaching (2nd cycle; varic
Educação Física —				X	X		X	X				X			X	X		— Physical education
Educação Musical —					X		X					X						— Music education
Educação Visual —		X		X	X			X			X	X			X	X		— Visual education
Matemática e Ciências Natureza —			X	X		X		X			X	X			X	X		— Mathematics and the natural sciences
Português e Francês —		X	X	X	X	X		X			X	X			X	X		— Portuguese and French
Português e Inglês —				X		X						X			X	X		— Portuguese and English
Trabalhos Manuais —				X								X			X			— Handicrafts
Prof. do Ensino Primário		X	X	X		X	X			X	X		X	X		X	X	— Primary school
Realiz. Plástic. do Espect.										X								— Stage design
Secretariado de Gestão												■						— Business management/secretariat
Teatro										X								— Theatre
Tecnologia Alimentar						X												— Food technology
Tecnol. Artes Gráficas													X					— Technology (graphic art)
Tecnol. Celulose e do Papel													X					— Technology (cellulose and paper)
Tecnol. Ind. Agroalimentar					X								X					— Technology of industrial-agricultural foo
Violino										X		X						— Violin
Violoncelo										X		X						— Violoncello

X *Bacharel* programmes

O Higher education programmes which are not comparable to an academic degree (two years)

■ Special programmes (four semesters)

Special institutions of higher education

	Autónoma de Lisboa de Luís de Camões	Católica portuguesa	Internacional	Lusíada	Portucalense	
Administ. e Gestão Empresas		●				Business administration and management
Arquitectura				●		Architecture
Ciências Históricas					●	Historical sciences
Ciências Religiosas		●				Religious sciences
Direito	●	●	●	●	●	Law
Economia	●	●		●	●	Economics
Eng. Alimentar		●				Engineering/food
Filosofia		●				Philosphy
Filosofia Humanística		●				Human philosophy
Gestão	●		●	●		Business economics
Gestão e Desenvolvimento Social —		●				— Social development
Gestão de Empresas					●	Enterprise management
História	●			●		History
Humanidades		●				Human sciences
Informática/Matem. Moderna					●	Computer science/modern mathematics
Informática de Gestão					●	Computer science (business economics)
Línguas e Literaturas Modernas (var)						Language and modern literature (various):
Estud. Ingleses e Alemães —	●					— English and German
Estud. Portugueses —	●					— Portuguese
Estud. Portug. e Alemães —	●					— Portuguese and German
Estud. Portug. e Franceses —	●					— Portuguese and French
Estud. Portug. e Ingleses —	●					— Portuguese and English
Matemática					●	Mathematics
Matemáticas Aplicadas	●			●		Applied mathematics
Relações Internacionais				●		International relations
Teologia		●				Theology

● *Licenciatura* programmes

P

Other higher etablishments (Ensino superior particular e cooperativo)

	Cooperativa Ens. Sup. Artístico Árvore I.	Cocíte-coop. Ens. Sup. Técnicas Avançadas de G.I.	Esc. de Educadores de Infância	Esc. Sup. Educação de Fafe	Esc. Sup. Educação de João de Deus	Esc. Sup. Educação Paula Frassinetti	Esc. Sup. Educação Santa Maria	Esc. Sup. Educação de Torres Novas	Esc. Sup. de Jornalismo	Inst. de Novas Profissões	Inst. Sup. de Administração e Gestão	Inst. Sup. de Assistentes e Intérpretes	Inst. Sup. de Ciências Educativas	Inst. Sup. de Gestão	Inst. Sup. de Línguas e Administração	Inst. Sup. Politécnico Internacional	Inst. Sup. de Psicologia Aplicada	Inst. Sup. Serviço Social de Coimbra	Inst. Sup. Serviço Social de Lisboa	Inst. Sup. Serviço Social de Porto	
Animação Cultural	X																				Cultural animation
Arquitectura	●																				Architecture
Assistentes de Administração										X											Administrative assistant
Assistentes de Direcção												X									Executive assistant
Cine-Vídeo	X																				Cinema - video
Comunicação Social									X												Social communication
Desenho	X																				Design
Educadores de Infância			X	X	X	X	X						X								Educator training
Eng. de Informática		●																			Computer science (engineering)
Eng. de Sistemas Dicisionais		●																			Systems analysis (engineering)
Fotografia	X																				Photography
Gestão											X	X		●							Business economics
Gestão Bancária																X					Business economics (banking)
Gestão de Empresas															●						Enterprise management
Gestão Hoteleira																X					Business economics (hotel)
Gestão de Rec. H. P. do Trabalho															●						Personnel management
Gestão Seguradora																X					Business economics (insurance)
Informática de Gestão															●						Business economics (computer science
Línguas e Turismo															X						Languages and tourism
Manualidade Educativa	X																				Arts and crafts education
Org. e Gestão de Empresas										●											Business economics (organization)
Pintura	X																				Painting/art
Prof. do Ens. Básico (1 ciclo)					X			X					X								Primary school teaching/first cycle
Psicologia Aplicada																	●				Applied psychology
Relações Públic. e Publicidade										●											Public relations and advertising
Secretariado															X						Secretariat
Secretariado de Direcção										X											Executive secretariat
Secretariado Internacional																X					International secretariat
Segurança Social																X					Social insurance
Serviço Social																		▲	▲	▲	Social services
Teatro	X																				Theatre
Turismo										X		X									Tourism
Tradutores-Intérpretes												X			X						Translator-interpreter

● *Licenciatura* programmes
X *Bacharel* programmes
▲ Programmes not comparable to an academic degree

Higher education institutions (Colleges of Art and Design)

	Esc. Sup. Belas-Artes de Lisboa	Esc. Sup. Belas-Artes do Porto	Inst. Sup. Artes Plásticas da Madeira	
Artes Plásticas-Escultura	○	○	○	Fine arts – sculpting
Artes Plásticas-Pintura	○	○	○	Fine arts – painting
Design de Comunicação	○			Communications design
Design Comun. (Arte Gráfica)		○		Communications design (graphics)
Design de Equipamento	○			Equipment design
Design/Project. Gráfica			○	Design/graphic projection

O Programmes not comparable to an academic degree (two and three years)

3. Student statistics

Number of foreign students at public higher education institutions, 1985/86

Africa	1 804
America	767
Asia	8
Australia	2
Europe	91
Belgium	2
Bulgaria	1
FR of Germany	16
German Democratic Republic	1
Finland	1
France	27
Greece	2
Italy	6
The Netherlands	1
Switzerland	1
Spain	26
United Kingdom	7
Total	2 672

4. Bibliography

Lei de Bases do Sistema Educativo, Ministério da Educação e Cultura (1987).
General law governing the Portuguese education system (also available in English and French).

Análise Conjuntural — Educação 1985, Ministério da Educação e Cultura, Gabinete de Estudos e Planeamento (Agosto 1986). 191 pp. — ESC 400.00 — Relatório Anual.
Annual report on education system, 191 pp. (August 1986).

Portugal — Equivalência de qualificações estrangeiras de nível superior às qualificações portugueses correspondentes, textos legais, Ministério da Educação e Cultura, Direcção-Geral do Ensino Superior, (Novembro 1986).
Report on the equivalency of Portuguese and foreign studies and degrees, (November 1986, also available in French).

Guia do Ensino Superior, 1989 — Instituições e Cursos, Ministério da Educação, Direcção-Geral do Ensino Superior.
(Guide to higher education institutions and courses).

Guia do Acesso ao Ensino Superior, 1989 — Instituições e Cursos, Ministério da Educação, Direcção-Geral do Ensino Superior.
(Guide to entry procedures to higher education).

Texto Legal do Novo Regime de Acesso ao Ensino Superior — Instituições e Cursos, Ministério da Educação, Direcção-Geral do Ensino Superior.

5. Glossary

Bacharel: degree which is awarded at one of the non-university institutions of higher education after studies lasting two to three years.

Bolsa de estudo: financial support for students whose parents or themselves have insufficient financial means.

Concurso (nacional): computer selection procedure for applicants to higher education which distributes the previously announced number of places for each subject.

Diploma de estudos superiores especializados: diploma which is awarded after two years of study and which entitles the holder to follow a professional or an academic career at one of the polytechnic institutions of higher education *(ensino superior politécnico)* and which corresponds to the *licenciado* degree.

Dissertação: academic research paper which the candidate must present in order to qualify for a *mestre* or *doutor* degree. The academic level must be higher in order for the candidate to be awarded a doctorate.

Doutor: academic degree which is awarded by the universities and which requires a complete course of university study, a *licenciado* degree. Special academic criteria must be fulfilled for the doctorate; it is necessary for the candidate to produce and defend an independent thesis which has been written specifically for the purpose of the doctorate.

Equivalência: a procedure in which an applicant's foreign school and higher education qualifications are adjudged equivalent to corresponding Portuguese qualifications.

Escola superior politécnica: a higher education institution which is placed in the non-university sector.

Faculdade: individual subject areas (faculties), into which a university is divided.

GCIES: Gabinete Coordenador do Ingresso no Ensino Superior: Ministry of Education and Culture department which governs the admissions procedures for the whole of the higher education system: this department has branch offices *(delegações distritais)* on the mainland and on Madeira and the Azores.

Grau: term for a degree after studies at an institution of higher education.

ICALP: Instituto de Cultura e Língua Portuguesa: Ministry of Education and Culture department which is responsible for supporting special courses for foreigners at Portuguese universities.

Inscrição: enrolment for courses after registration.

Instituto politécnico: organizational unit of the non-university sector of Portugal's higher education system within which individual institutes *(escolas)* are classified.

Licenciado: first degree which is awarded at universities after a course of studies lasting four to six years.

Matrícula: formalities connected with initial registration (immatriculation) at an institution of higher education.

Mestre: degree which is awarded after a 1 to 2 year university course of study and which requires a *licenciado* degree. Moreover it is required that the candidate produces and defends an independent dissertation. The *mestre* degree is lower than the *doutor*.

Propinas: fees payable on registration and enrolment for subjects at institutions of higher education. These fees are extremely low at public institutions, although not so at private ones.

Prova geral de acesso: entry examination to establish applicants' competence in Portuguese. Candidates are not rejected but are placed in order of aptitude. The examination counts as one of the criteria used to assign candidates to the various programmes.

Universidade: organizational unit in the university sector of Portugal's higher education system which comprises various schools *(escolas)*, institutes, faculties and/or other departments or units.

P

6. Diagram of the education system

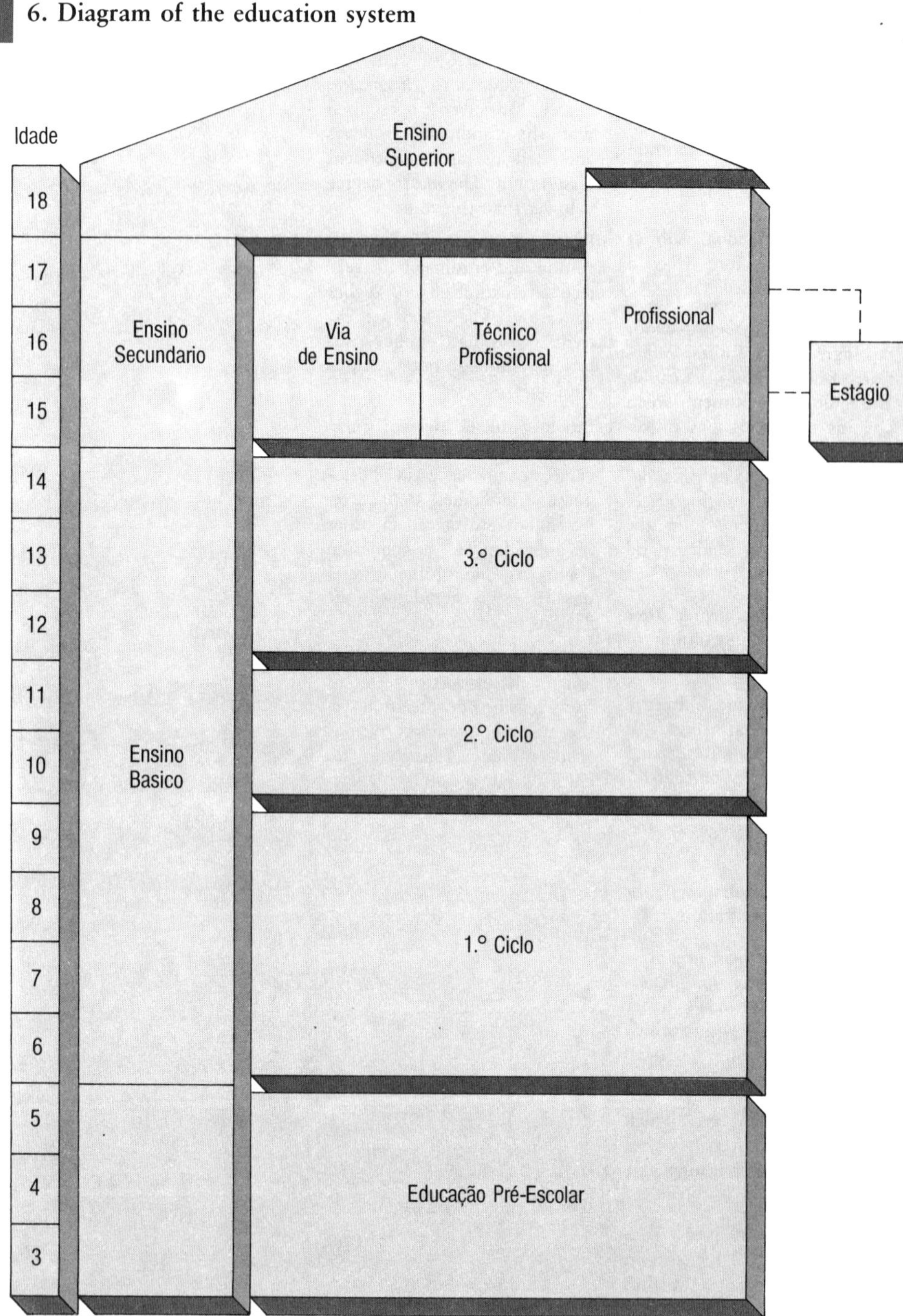
Idade
18
17
16
15
14
13
12
11
10
9
8
7
6
5
4
3
Ensino Superior
Ensino Secundario
Via de Ensino
Técnico Profissional
Profissional
Estágio
3.° Ciclo
2.° Ciclo
Ensino Basico
1.° Ciclo
Educação Pré-Escolar

Explanations and translations of technical terms on facing page.

Legend

Ciclo 1°, 2°, 3°: 1st, 2nd and 3rd cycle.
Educação Pré-escolar: Pre-school education.
Ensino Básico: Primary and secondary schooling.
Ensino Secundário: Vocational level.
Ensino Superior: Higher education.
Ensino Profissional: Career-building courses.
Ensino Técnico Profissional: Technical vocational level.
Estágio: practical.
Idade: Age.
Via de Ensino: Academic level.

United Kingdom

UK

Organization of higher education

Higher education in the United Kingdom is provided mainly by universities and polytechnics, and their Scottish equivalent, Scottish Central Institutions, and colleges and institutes of higher education. It is also provided by a range of other institutions maintained or grant-aided from public funds, such as colleges of further education and colleges of agriculture, art, commerce and technology. Essential differences between the systems in England and Wales, Scotland and Northern Ireland are shown as appropriate.

There are 46 universities in the United Kingdom including the Open University which offers distance learning courses mainly to those resident in the UK, and the University of Buckingham which is independent of direct government aid and is supported by private benefactions and students' fees. There are 30 polytechnics in England and Wales and a number of central institutions and major colleges of technology in Scotland.

Types of higher education institutions

The universities

The universities range from ancient collegiate foundations, such as Oxford and Cambridge in England and St Andrews in Scotland, through the great civic universities of the 19th century such as London and Birmingham, to the smaller campus universities, on suburban sites, such as Exeter, Leicester and Southampton, and the newest, dating from the 1960s, such as Sussex and York or the technological universities such as Aston and Bath. London and Wales are federal universities with constituent but autonomous colleges.

The universities are independent self-governing bodies. Although largely financed through the government, they are not controlled by any government department. They derive their rights and privileges from Royal Charter or from Acts of Parliament and any amendment of their charters or statutes is made by the Crown acting through the Privy Council on the application of the universities themselves. The universities alone decide what degrees they award and the conditions on which they are awarded; they alone decide what students to admit and what staff to appoint.

The polytechnics and central institutions

A distinctive national alternative to the universities is provided in England and Wales by the polytechnics and in Scotland by the central institutions. These are national and regional centres concentrating on higher education for full-time, sandwich and part-time students, with close and direct links with industry, business and the professions.

The polytechnics in England will, from 1 April 1989, be funded through a centralized system similar to that of the universities. The Scottish polytechnics/central institutions and Polytechnic of Wales will continue to be funded by local education authorities.

Degree courses in polytechnics are validated by the Council for National Academic Awards (CNAA), a body required by its charter to maintain standards comparable to the universities.

In addition to degrees, polytechnics run other advanced courses below degree level, especially in business and technical subjects. They offer postgraduate as well as first degrees but are generally more involved with teaching than original research.

Nearly all polytechnics are in the centre of towns and cities — eight of them in or near London.

Colleges and institutes of higher education

The colleges and institutes of higher education constitute a third force in higher education alongside the universities and polytechnics.

Many are the result of amalgamations of teacher training colleges and other colleges, which is why some of them still have a strong teacher training department. In addition to this, the colleges offer advanced courses in a wide range of subjects both at degree level and just below degree level. Like the polytechnics they emphasize the vocational or applied nature of many of their courses. Their degrees are validated by the CNAA.

Further education establishments

There is a wide range of other colleges with a variety of titles — colleges of further education; colleges of art; agricultural colleges; adult education centres; and colleges of education.

The majority of their courses are below degree level but they do also offer many full-time and sandwich advanced courses including first degrees and some postgraduate degrees, and therefore constitute an important part of higher education.

Postgraduate institutions

There are also four other institutions offering mainly specialist postgraduate work: the Manchester Business School and the London Graduate School of Business Studies, Cranfield Institute of Technology, and the Royal College of Art.

Student statistics

In 1986/87 there were 613 000 students on full-time and sandwich advanced courses in the United Kingdom. 57 410 were overseas students, and of these 8 773 were from the European Community. Most EC students in the UK were in social, administrative and business studies, engineering and technology, science, and languages, literature and area studies.

Organization and validation of courses

In most higher education institutions there are three terms each year, usually with only one annual commencement date — in October — for undergraduates. Some institutions may have different arrangements for sandwich and postgraduate students. Teaching methods include lectures and seminars, laboratory classes and other small groups as well as 'tutorials' (where there may be only one or two students in discussion with their teacher).

The University of Buckingham has four terms of 10 weeks each per year.

First degrees

There are several titles for first degrees. In England, Wales and Northern Ireland the best known are BA (Bachelor of Arts) and B.Sc. (Bachelor of Science) which are awarded over a wide range of subjects. Others are more specific and obviously relate to a profession: examples are MB/Ch.B. (Bachelor of Medicine/Bachelor of Surgery), LL B (Bachelor of Laws), and B.Ed. (Bachelor of Education), though some of these, and in particular the B.Ed., may have a relevance wider than the profession to which they are directly related. Degree courses normally require full-time or 'sandwich' attendance at the university, polytechnic or college concerned and usually last three or four years. There are exceptions: e.g. medicine, dentistry and veterinary science take five or six years. In Scotland, the first degree is generally four years for a Master of Arts (MA) degree with honours, and three years for the broad-based ordinary MA which is a particular feature of the Scottish system.

Altogether there is an enormous variety of degree courses. Some are single-subject courses, some are in more than one subject (joint or combined degrees), some are modular and some are 'sandwich' courses. Examinations are not necessarily held annually. At many institutions there are only two major examinations for the Bachelor's degree — one at the end of the first year (Part I) and the 'final' examination at the end of the course.

Postgraduate degrees

Postgraduate degrees are of two kinds: higher degrees by research and higher degrees by instruction. There are also taught classes leading to postgraduate certificates or diplomas offering vocational training or a professional qualification.

Research degrees such as the Ph.D. (Doctor of Philosophy) and certain Master's degrees require the submission of a thesis. A doctorate usually takes three years of study and the thesis is expected to be an original work, which makes a definite contribution to knowledge. Master's degrees by research usually take two years and the thesis would not be expected to reach the same level of originality as that for a doctorate. The degree awarded is usually an MA (Master of Arts), M.Sc. (Master of Science) or M.Phil. (Master of Philosophy). Courses for Master's degrees obtained by instruction usually last one year, nine months of lectures/tutorials, etc. and three months to produce a dissertation. A very wide range of postgraduate courses and research opportunities are available in the UK, so to choose a suitable institution you do need to consult reference sources.

Professional qualifications

One of the distinctive features of the pattern of higher education in the United Kingdom is the part played by professional bodies, which set and maintain standards of working practice in professions such as engineering and accountancy. Some of them set examinations which, combined with working experience, qualify students for increasingly senior levels of membership of the professional association. For example, the Institute of Cost and Management Accountants offers examinations which, together with three years' relevant experience, lead to the title Associate of the ICMA. After a further three years' experience in a senior position an Associate may apply to become a Fellow of the ICMA. In many professions it is necessary to have membership of the appropriate professional body before it is possible to work in that area.

Taking professional examinations can be an alternative to taking a degree. Students taking a degree in a relevant subject first may be exempted from some parts of the examinations. Often these associations set and assess the examinations themselves but do not offer courses to prepare for them. Instead these courses can be taken at polytechnics, central institutions and other colleges.

Teacher training

Most teacher training takes place in faculties or departments of education in universities, polytechnics and institutions of higher education. The two main routes into teaching are a three or four-year B.Ed. course or a one-year postgraduate course leading to the Postgraduate Certificate in Education.

Admission and registration

Initial information

British Council offices in EC countries can give general information and advice to students thinking of studying in the UK. For inquiries about education policy, the Departments of Education for England and Wales, Scotland and Northern Ireland can also be approached.

Entry requirements

Each institution is responsible for drawing up its own regulations about admission, and both the 'general' requirement and the requirements for admission to a particular kind of course may therefore vary in detail from institution to institution. Outside the university sector the CNAA sets minimum entry requirements for courses leading to its awards.

The requirements are expressed mainly in terms of passes in United Kingdom examinations such as those for the General Certificate of Education (GCE) Advanced level or the Scottish Certificate of Education (SCE). Some of these examinations can be taken abroad.

An international or European baccalaureate is acceptable to many institutions, and other qualifications which give entry to universities within the EC will be regarded as the minimum qualification for entry to a British institution of higher education.

To be considered for admission to a first-degree course, students must provide evidence that their education has qualified them to follow a course leading to a degree, and that they speak and understand English well. In addition, there are usually specific 'course requirements' which may vary from one faculty or department to another. 'Course requirements' are intended to ensure that students are adequately prepared or have a sufficient aptitude for the particular subject or subjects they wish to read at degree level.

Mature students without any formal entry qualifications may be considered if they have suitable experience Students should consult *Opportunities in higher education for mature students* and *University entrance: the official guide*.

The qualifications for admission to courses of study leading to professional qualifications other than degrees vary according to the type of course, and students should write directly to the institutions of their choice for details.

A student with the required academic qualifications does not have an automatic right to a place in a British higher education institution. Entry is competitive, and the final decision is up to the institution concerned.

Short-term or 'occasional' students

Some British institutions will not admit students wishing to study for a degree for any period shorter than the usual three or four years of the full course for first degrees in arts or science subjects. However, some will allow overseas students who already have a degree to complete a first degree in arts or science in two years instead of three.

Overseas students often want to attend courses at British institutions of higher education without qualifying for a degree. The institutions vary in their conditions for admitting occasional students during normal term time. Some will not admit them at all, others will only admit, for periods of up to a year, a few recommended students who have a good knowledge of English. The institution will often supply occasional students with certificates of satisfactory attendance.

A number of institutions in Britain are prepared to consider applications from foreign students who are already attending a university in their own country, and who wish to take a one-year or two-year course in Britain, returning to their own country to take their degrees. In all cases the number which can be accepted is small. As regulations vary so much from one institution to another students should write directly to the one in which they are interested, stating their qualifications, the subjects they wish to study and how long they would like to stay.

Postgraduate entry

To be considered for admission to a postgraduate course of instruction or to undertake research in a university or polytechnic, etc., students must have at least a first degree from a university in their own or another country, and must have a very good command of English. But even if students have these qualifications they are not certain to be admitted, as the institutions accept only a limited number of students for postgraduate study and research.

Only those who are strongly recommended by their own universities and show real promise of scholarly ability are likely to be allowed to undertake research. They will normally be expected to carry out independent research under the supervision of the staff of the department in which they are working.

Limitations

Students from EC countries may apply for admission to any course in higher education in the United Kingdom subject to the requirements listed above. It should be noted, however, that in many subjects competition is extremely keen and it is therefore advisable to apply early.

Recognition of foreign certificates and degrees

The National Academic Recognition Information Centre (NARIC), which is operated by the British Council, can give advice on the likely standard which an overseas qualification may be accorded in the UK. This advice is based on information obtained from British educational institutions on the standard they have accorded a particular overseas qualification in the past.

British institutions make their own decisions on the acceptability or recognition they will accord an overseas qualification, and the Centre therefore acts in an advisory role only.

NARIC's publication *International guide to qualifications in education* may be consulted in most British Council offices; it gives information on qualifications obtained in about 140 countries and, where possible, notes have been included on the recognition normally accorded to particular qualifications in the UK.

For advice on the comparability of non-British qualifications with British qualifications the NARIC may be contacted at the British Council, 10 Spring Gardens, London SW1A 2 BN. Copies of certificates with translations into English should be enclosed with enquiries. Enquiries are normally answered within about four weeks.

Entry examinations

An entry examination is not normally required by the institution but individual departments may wish to test a prospective student's knowledge of English. In such cases the department concerned will supply the information.

Application and registration

Students wishing to study as an undergraduate at a university should write first to the Universities Central Council on Admissions (UCCA) for the UCCA handbook *How to apply for admission to a university* and an application form. Applications for admission must be submitted to UCCA which acts as a clearing house and not as a selecting body. It cannot give academic advice; this is available only from the chosen university. The closing date for receipt of forms is mid-October in the year preceding entry for candidates including Oxford and Cambridge in their choice of universities. For other candidates the closing date is mid-December but overseas applicants may continue to submit applications until September the following year.

With the exception of the Open University and the University of Buckingham, all the universities in the United Kingdom participate in the scheme.

Applicants are normally notified in the spring whether they have been accepted or not. Acceptances may be conditional upon certain grades in examinations being attained. UCCA operates a final clearing procedure in August and September to enable candidates hitherto unplaced to have another opportunity, mainly at universities other than those to which their original applications were made. Details of registration dates will be sent by all institutions to applicants who have been accepted.

For the polytechnics and some institutes of higher education, the Polytechnics Central Admission System (PCAS) handles applications for first degree and Diploma of Higher Education courses. It operates in the same way as the UCCA. Application forms and handbooks are available on request from PCAS.

To apply for a B.Ed. course, students should write to the Central Register and Clearing House. For a teacher training course in Northern Ireland, students should write to the Northern Ireland Department of Education. For a Postgraduate Certificate in Education course students should write to the Graduate Teacher Training Registry.

To apply for a CNAA first-degree course in art and design, students should write to the Art and Design Admissions Registry.

For all other courses students should write to each higher education institution which offers courses that interest them, asking for full details and an application form. They will then send all necessary forms and tell the interested student how to proceed. There is no closing date for applications outside the UCCA and PCAS schemes but all entry is competitive so early application is advisable.

Postgraduate courses

Applications for postgraduate courses by instruction or research should be made directly to the institution concerned.

Tuition fees

Tuition and other fees are normally paid on registration which takes place once a year only, in October, except for postgraduate students who can in some institutions register in January or April.

Under current regulations, students who are citizens of European Community countries and who have been 'ordinary residents' in the EC for the three years before the start of their course would normally pay tuition fees at the same level as home students. In 1988/89 fees were about UKL 607 for undergraduates or equivalent and about UKL 1 890 for postgraduates.

Occasional students should obtain information on fees directly from the institution concerned.

Other fees may include an examination fee, CNAA registration fees, and at certain collegiate universities, college fees or dues. All these charges may vary considerably and students should seek information directly from the institution concerned.

EC students may be eligible for reimbursement of their fees if they are taking a first degree course or equivalent in the UK and have not already completed two or more years of higher education. For further information students should contact their local British Council office or the institution where they will be studying.

Knowledge of the language of instruction, language courses and other courses

It is essential to have a good knowledge of the English language before beginning a course of higher education in the United Kingdom. Students must be able to follow lectures in English spoken at a pace to which they may not be accustomed, to produce written work, and to take part in discussions with their teachers and fellow students. If a student has been accepted by a university or college but is in any doubt about his/her ability to meet these requirements, or if an English proficiency test is required by the university or college, he/she should either arrange to take a course in English before leaving the home country or, preferably, come to the United Kingdom well before the higher studies are due to begin in order to take an intensive course in English. Courses in English of this kind are provided at many higher education institutions and range from one week to one year in length. Many institutions can also provide extra English tuition during the course if it is required. In addition recognized private schools of English offer full-time courses, which are listed in the brochure *Learn English in Britain with Arels-Felco 1989.*

In the United Kingdom, except at the University of Buckingham, there are no courses during the summer break. Summer vacation courses are organized by extramural and other departments of some higher education institutions and are open to suitably qualified overseas students and teachers.

The British Council also arranges refresher courses for teachers of English in the summer vacation, and advanced courses at other times of the year on various professional subjects for suitably qualified persons, lasting from a fortnight to 12 weeks. These courses are often organized in conjunction with a university, but they do not count towards any degree in the United Kingdom.

UK

Financial assistance and scholarships

Under current regulations, overseas students who have been 'ordinary residents' in the United Kingdom for three years or more before the start of their course, for purposes other than receiving full-time education, may be regarded as home students. They may be eligible for a local authority award which would cover the cost of tuition fees and maintenance. Citizens of European Community countries who meet a number of conditions, and who enrol on vocational courses in the UK, may also be eligible. Students should write to the local education authority in the area of the UK in which they live, or to the Department of Education and Science.

Details of publications which list scholarships and awards are in the bibliography.

British Council awards to EC nationals are made for postgraduate study only. Application forms are available from the nearest office of the British Council. The latest date for return is usually November of the year preceding the October in which entry is sought.

Information about how to apply for other awards is contained in the books listed in the bibliography.

Entry and residence regulations

Students from EC countries are allowed entry into Britain for a period of six months without formalities of any type. After this they may apply each year to the Home Office for a 12-month extension. Students will need to produce a letter from an educational institution confirming that they are registered as a full-time student and evidence that they can meet the cost of their tuition fees and maintenance. These regulations will not apply to students from Spain and Portugal until 1993. Until then they need to show immigration staff evidence of full-time study and sufficient funds when they first arrive in the UK. They can then apply annually for an extension of their visa like other EC students.

UK

Social aspects

Social security and health insurance

Many institutions require foreign students to pass a medical examination to attend any course. EC students can receive free medical treatment under the National Health Service while they are resident in the United Kingdom. Most institutions have access to or provide a student health service with a full-time doctor.

Advisory services

Many institutions have appointed members of staff as advisers to overseas students. In addition, many have a system of allocating all students to a personal tutor who may help not only with academic matters but also with personal problems. There are also welfare services, psychological counselling services and careers advice is available.

The United Kingdom Council for Overseas Student Affairs (UKCOSA) can provide up-to-date information and advice on rules and regulations affecting the welfare of overseas students in the UK.

Student employment

EC nationals may take up employment during their stay without the approval of the Department of Employment, except in Northern Ireland where special arrangements exist. However, because full-time higher education courses are demanding and intensive, it may not be practicable for students to take paid employment in term time; indeed many institutions do not allow their students to do so.

Until 1993 students from Spain and Portugal will need to obtain permission to work from the Department of Employment.

Student organizations

An active social life has been a traditional feature of higher education in the United Kingdom and typical student societies cover politics, religion, sport, drama and music.

Most higher education institutions have a Students' Union or Students' Representative Council. The President and Executive Committee are members of the student body elected by the students.

Nearly all students' unions are affiliated to the National Union of Students which represents students' interests nationally on such affairs as grants and accommodation.

Cost of living

Costs vary according to the institution or the region. To meet all expenses for a calendar year excluding fees it would be advisable for a single student to have about UKL 5 500 and about UKL 4 800 outside London at 1989 prices. Some will be able to exist on less, some may need more. Some institutions will require a written guarantee that students are able to support themselves. The United Kingdom, like many other countries, experiences steady price rises.

Accommodation

It is advisable when applying for admission to a university for students to indicate on the application form if they wish to apply for a place in a hall of residence.

Most higher education institutions have Accommodation Officers who will help to arrange accommodation. Details of accommodation are sent with the notification from the institution accepting the applicant for study.

Private accommodation can be in the form of lodgings, where students live with a family and some or all meals are provided, or a furnished room where they do their own cooking and cleaning. Students should not expect, particularly in London, to live near their place of study.

Services for students

There is no general concession which allows students automatic reductions on public transport, but there is a scheme run by British Rail which offers reductions on railway fares if a special card is purchased.

The students' unions offer a wide range of facilities such as refectories, common rooms and sports facilities.

Facilities for disabled students

Many institutions of higher education in the UK now provide facilities for students with disabilities, and have designated one member of staff to be 'coordinator for disabled students'. Students' unions also often have someone responsible for promoting the interests of disabled students.

Much will depend, however, on the individual student's handicap and subject of study. Students needing further information should in the first instance seek information from the National Bureau for Handicapped Students, which offers an information and advice service. Their publications include a general leaflet *Applying to higher education: some notes for disabled students, their parents and advisers* (single copies free to disabled students) and leaflets specifically for deaf or blind students. There is no comprehensive list available of facilities at all British institutions of higher education, so for this kind of information students should write directly to the institutions in which they are interested.

UK

Appendices

1. Addresses

Embassies of the United Kingdom in EC countries

Belgium
Britannia House
Rue Joseph II 28
B-1040 Bruxelles
☎ 217 90 00

Denmark
36/38/40 Kastelsvej
DK-2100 København
☎ (01) 26 46 00

Federal Republic of Germany
Friedrich-Ebert-Allee 77
D-5300 Bonn 1
☎ 23 40 61

Greece
Ploutarchou 1
GR-Athina 106 75
☎ 7 23 62 11

Spain
Calle de Fernando el Santo 16
E-28010 Madrid
☎ 419 02 00

France
35, rue du Faubourg St-Honoré
F-75383 Paris
☎ 42 66 91 42

Ireland
31/33 Merrion Road
Dublin 4
☎ 69 52 11

Italy
Via XX Settembre, 80A
I-00187 Roma
☎ 47 55 551

Luxembourg
28 boulevard Royal
L-2018 Luxembourg
☎ 298 64

The Netherlands
Lange Voorhout 10
2514 ED 's-Gravenhage
☎ 64 58 00

Portugal
Rua S. Domingos à Lapa 35-37
P-Lisboa
☎ 66 11 91

British Council offices in EC countries

Belgium and Luxembourg
Britannia House
Rue Joseph II 30
B-1040 Bruxelles
☎ 19 36 00

Denmark
British Embassy
Møntergade 1
DK-1116 København K
☎ 01 11 20 44

Federal Republic of Germany
Hahnenstraße 6
D-5000 Köln 1
☎ 20 64 40

Hardenbergstraße 20
D-1000 Berlin 12
☎ 31 01 76

Rothenbaum-Chaussee 34
D-2000 Hamburg 13
☎ 44 60 57

Brüderstraße 7/111
D-8000 München 22
☎ 22 33 26

Greece
17 Plateia Philikis Etairias
Kolonaki Square
GR-106 73 Athina
☎ 36 33 211

Ethnikis Aminis 9
GR-541 10 Salonica
☎ 23 52 36

Spain
Plaza de Santa Barbara 10
E-28001 Madrid
☎ 419 12 50

Calle Amigó 83
E-08021 Barcelona
☎ 209 13 64

British Institute Bilbao
Residencia Universitaria
Esteban Terradas
Plaza de la Casilla 3
E-48012 Bilbao
☎ 444 58 62

General San Martín 7
E-46004 Valencia
☎ 351 88 18

Instituto de Enseñanza
Edificio Mecenas
Polígono Universitario
Fuente Nueva
E-18003 Granada
☎ 20 19 05

British Institute
Goethe 1
E-07011 Palma de Mallorca
☎ 45 48 55

France
9 rue de Constantine
F-75007 Paris
☎ 45 55 95 95

Italy
Palazzo del Drago
Via delle Quattro Fontane, 20
I-00184 Roma
☎ 475 66 41

Via Manzoni, 38
I-20121 Milano
☎ 78 20 16

Palazzo d'Avalos
Via dei Mille, 48
I-80121 Napoli
☎ 41 48 76

The Netherlands
Keizersgracht 343
1016 EH Amsterdam C
☎ 22 36 44

Portugal
Rua Cecilio de Sousa 65
P-1294 Lisboa Codex
☎ 36 92 08

Casa de Inglaterra
Rua de Tomar 4
P-3000 Coimbra
☎ 39 235 49

Government departments

Department of Education and Science (DES)
Elizabeth House
York Road
London SE1 7PH

Scottish Education Department
New St Andrew's House
St James Centre
Edinburgh EH1 3SY

Department of Education for Northern Ireland
Rathgael House
Balloo Road
Bangor
County Down
N. Ireland BT19 2PR

The Home Office
Lunar House
40 Wellesley Road
Croydon CR9 2BY

Clearing houses for applications

Art and Design Admissions Registry
Penn House
9 Broad Street
Hereford HR4 9AP

Central Register and Clearing House Ltd and
Graduate Teacher Training Registry (both at):
3 Crawford Place
London W1H 2BN

Polytechnics Central Admissions System (PCAS)
PO Box 67
Cheltenham
Glos GL50 3AP

Universities Central Council on Admissions (UCCA)
PO Box 28
Cheltenham
Glos GX50 1 HY

Other organizations

Association of Commonwealth Universities (ACU)
36 Gordon Square
London WC1 OPF

British Council
10 Spring Gardens
London SW1A 2BN

British Tourist Authority
64 St James Street
London SW1A 1NF

Council for National Academic Awards (CNAA)
344-354 Gray's Inn Road
London WC1X 8BP

National Academic Recognition Information Centre (NARIC)
The British Council
10 Spring Gardens
London SW1A 2BN

National Bureau for Handicapped Students
336 Brixton Road
London SW9 7AA

National Union of Students
461 Holloway Road
London N7 6LJ

United Kingdom Council for Overseas Student Affairs
60 Westbourne Grove
London W2 5FG

Universities

University of Aberdeen
Aberdeen AB9 1FX

University of Aston in Birmingham
Gosta Green
Birmingham B4 7ET

University of Bath
Claverton Down
Bath BA2 7AY

Queen's University of Belfast
Belfast BT7 1NN
N. Ireland

University of Birmingham
PO Box 363
Birmingham B15 2TT

University of Bradford
Richmond Road
Bradford
West Yorkshire BD7 1 DP

University of Bristol
Senate House
Bristol BS8 1TH

Brunel University
Uxbridge
Middlesex UB8 3PH

University of Buckingham
Buckingham MK18 1EG

University of Cambridge
The Old Schools
Cambridge CB2 ITN

The City University
Northampton Square
London EC1V 0HB

University of Dundee
Dundee DD1 4HN

University of Durham
Old Shire Hall
Durham DH1 3HP

University of East Anglia
Norwich NR4 7TJ

University of Edinburgh
Old College
South Bridge
Edinburgh EH8 9YL

University of Essex
Wivenhoe Park
Colchester CO4 3SQ

University of Exeter
Exeter EX4 4QJ

University of Glasgow
Glasgow G12 3QQ

UK

Heriot-Watt University
Edinburgh EH1 1HX

University of Hull
Hull HU6 7RX

University of Keele
Keele
Staffordshire ST5 5BG

University of Kent at Canterbury
Canterbury
Kent CT2 7NZ

University of Lancaster
University House
Bailrigg
Lancaster LA1 4YW

University of Leeds
Leeds LS2 9JT

University of Leicester
University Road
Leicester LE1 7RH

University of Liverpool
PO Box 147
Liverpool L69 3BX

University of London
Senate House
Malet Street
London WC1E 7HU

Loughborough University of Technology
Loughborough
Leicestershire LE11 3TU

University of Manchester
Manchester M13 9PL

UMIST (University of Manchester Institute of Science & Technology)
PO Box 88
Sackville Street
Manchester M60 1QD

University of Newcastle upon Tyne
6 Kensington Terrace
Newcastle upon Tyne
NE1 7RU

University of Nottingham
University Park
Nottingham NG7 2RD

University of Oxford
University Offices
Wellington Square
Oxford OX1 2JD

University of Reading
White-knights
Reading
Berkshire RG6 2AH

University of St Andrews
College Gate
St Andrews
Fife KY16 9AJ

University of Salford
Salford M5 4WT

University of Sheffield
Sheffield S10 2TN

University of Southampton
Highfield
Southampton SO9 5NH

University of Stirling
Stirling FK9 4LA

University of Strathclyde
Royal College Building
204 George Street
Glasgow G1 1XW

University of Surrey
Guildford
Surrey GU2 5XH

University of Sussex
Sussex House
Falmer
Brighton BN1 9RH

University of Ulster
Coleraine Co.
Londonderry BT52 1SA
N. Ireland

University of Wales

Constituent colleges

University College of Wales
Aberystwyth
Dyfed SY23 2AX

University College of North Wales
Bangor
Gwynedd LL57 2DG

University of Wales College of Cardiff
PO Box 78
Cardiff CF1 1XL

University College of Swansea
Singleton Park
Swansea SA2 8PP

Saint David's University College
Lampeter
Dyfed SA48 7ED

University of Warwick
Coventry CV4 7AL

University of York
Heslington
York YO1 5DD

Polytechnics

City of Birmingham Polytechnic
Perry Barr
Birmingham B42 2SU

Brighton Polytechnic
Moulsecoomb
Brighton BN2 4AT

Bristol Polytechnic
Coldharbour Lane
Frenchay
Bristol BS16 1QY

Coventry Lanchester Polytechnic
Priory Street
Coventry CV1 5FB

The Hatfield Polytechnic
PO Box 109
College Lane
Hatfield
Herts AL10 9AB

The Polytechnic, Huddersfield
Queensgate
Huddersfield HD1 3DH

Kingston Polytechnic
Penrhyn Road
Kingston upon Thames
Surrey KT1 2EE

Lancashire Polytechnic
Preston PR1 2TQ

Leeds Polytechnic
Calverley Street
Leeds LS1 3HE

Leicester Polytechnic
PO Box 143
Leicester LEI 9BH

Liverpool Polytechnic
Rodney House
70 Mount Pleasant
Liverpool L3 5UX

The Polytechnic of Central London
309 Regent Street
London WIR 8AL

City of London Polytechnic
117 Houndsditch
London EC3A 7BU

The Polytechnic of North London
Holloway Road
London N7 8DB

North East London Polytechnic
Romford Road
London E15 4LZ

Polytechnic of the South Bank, London
Borough Road
London SE1 0AA

Thames Polytechnic, London
Wellington Street
Woolwich
London SE18 6PF

Manchester Polytechnic
All Saints
Manchester M15 6BH

Middlesex Polytechnic
Admissions Office
114 Chase Side
London N14 5PN

Newcastle upon Tyne Polytechnic
Ellison Building
Ellison Place
Newcastle upon Tyne
NE1 8ST

Oxford Polytechnic
Headington
Oxford OX3 0BP

Polytechnic South West
Plymouth PL4 8AA

Portsmouth Polytechnic
Ravelin House
Museum Road
Portsmouth PO1 2QQ

Sheffield City Polytechnic
Pond Street
Sheffield S1 1WB

Staffordshire Polytechnic
College Road
Stoke-on-Trent ST4 2DE

Sunderland Polytechnic
Langham Tower
Ryhope Road
Sunderland SR2 7EE

Teesside Polytechnic
Borough Road
Middlesbrough
Cleveland TS1 3BA

Trent Polytechnic
Burton Street
Nottingham NG1 4BU

The Polytechnic of Wales
Pontypridd
Mid Glamorgan CF37 1DL

The Polytechnic, Wolverhampton
Molineux Street
Wolverhampton WV1 1SB

Scottish central institutions

Duncan of Jordanstone
College of Art
Perth Road
Dundee DD1 4HT

Dundee Institute of Technology
Bell Street
Dundee DD1 1HG

East of Scotland College of Agriculture
West Mains Road
Edinburgh EH9 3JG

Edinburgh College of Art
Lauriston Place
Edinburgh EH3 9DF

Glasgow College of Technology
Cowcaddens Road
Glasgow G4 OBA

Glasgow School of Art
167 Renfrew Street
Glasgow G3 6RQ

The Queen's College, Glasgow
1 Park Drive
Glasgow G3 6LP

Napier Polytechnic of Edinburgh
Colinton Road
Edinburgh EH10 5DT

North of Scotland College of Agriculture
581 King Street
Aberdeen AB9 1UD

Paisley College of Technology
High Street
Paisley PA1 2BE

Queen Margaret College
Clerwood Terrace
Edinburgh EH12 8TS

Rovert Gordon's Institute of Technology
Schoolhill
Aberdeen AB9 1FR

Royal Scottish Academy of Music and Drama
100 Renfrew Street
Glasgow G2 3DB

Scottish College of Textiles
Netherdale
Galashiels TD1 3HF

The West of Scotland
Agricultural College
Auchincruive
Ayr KA6 5HW

Colleges and institutes of higher education

Avery Hill College
Bexley Road
London SE9 2PQ

UK

Bath College of Higher Education
Newton Park
Bath BA2 9BN

Bedford College of Higher Education
Cauldwell Street
Bedford MK42 9AH

Bishop Grosseteste College
Lincoln LN1 3DY

Bolton Institute of Higher Education
Deane Road
Bolton BL3 5AB

Bradford and Ilkley Community College
Great Horton Road
Bradford
West Yorkshire BD7 1AY

Bretton Hall College
West Bretton
Wakefield
West Yorkshire WF4 4LG

Buckinghamshire College of Higher Education
Queen Alexandra Road
High Wycombe HP11 2JZ

Bulmershe College of Higher Education
Woodlands Avenue, Earley
Reading RG6 1HY

Cambridgeshire College of Arts and Technology
Cambridge CB1 1PT

Canterbury Christ Church College
North Holmes Road
Canterbury CT1 1QU

Central School of Speech and Drama
Embassy Theatre
Eton Avenue
London NW3 3HY

Charlotte Mason College of Education
Ambleside
Cumbria LA22 9BB

Chester College
Cheyney Road
Chester CH1 4BJ

Durham New College
Framwellgate Moor
Durham DH1 5ES

The College of Ripon & York St John
Lord Mayor's Walk
York YO3 7EX

The College of St Mark and St John
Derriford Road
Plymouth PL6 8BH

The College of St Paul and St Mary
The Park, Cheltenham
Glos GL50 2RH

Crewe & Alsager College of Higher Education
Crewe Road
Crewe
Cheshire CW1 1DU

Derbyshire College of Higher Education
Kedleston Road
Derby DE3 1GB

Derby Lonsdale College of Higher Education
Kedleston Road
Derby DE3 1GB

Doncaster Metropolitan Institute of Higher Education
Waterdale
Doncaster DN1 3EX

Dorset Institute of Higher Education
Wallisdown Road
Poole BH12 5BB

Ealing College of Higher Education
St Mary's Road
Ealing
London W5 5RF

Edge Hill College of Higher Education
St Helens Road
Ormskirk
Lancashire L39 4QP

Essex Institute of Higher Education
Victoria Road South
Chelmsford CM1 1LL

Gloucestershire College of Arts and Technology
Oxtails Campus
Gloucester

Gwent College of Higher Education
College Crescent
Caerleon
Newport
Gwent NP6 1XJ

Harrow College of Higher Education
Northwick Park
Harrow HA1 3TP

Hertfordshire College of Higher Education
Wall Hall
Aldenham
Watford WD2 8AT

Homerton College Cambridge
Cambridge CB2 2PH

Humberside College of Higher Education
Cottingham Road
Hull HU6 7RT

King Alfred's College
Sparkford Road
Winchester SO22 4NR

La Sainte Union College of Higher Education
The Avenue
Southampton SO9 5HB

Liverpool Institute of Higher Education
PO Box 6
Liverpool L16 9JD

Luton College of Higher Education
Park Square
Luton
Bedfordshire LU1 3JU

Nene College
Moulton Park
Northampton NN2 7AL

UK

Newman College
Genners Lane, Bartley Green
Birmingham B32 3NT

North Cheshire College
Fernhead
Warmington WA2 0DB

The North East Wales Institute of Higher Education
Deeside
Clwyd CH5 4BR

North Riding College
Filey Road
Scarborough YO11 3AZ

Roehampton Institute of Higher Education
Roehampton Lane
London SW15 5PU

Rolle College
Exmouth
Devon EX8 2AT

St Martin's College Lancaster
Lancaster LA1 3JD

St Mary's College
Strawberry Hill
Twickenham
Middlesex TW1 4SX

South Glamorgan Institute of Higher Education
Western Avenue
Llandaff
Cardiff CF5 2YB

Southampton Institute of Higher Education
East Park Terrace
Southampton SO9 4WW

The Suffolk College of Higher and Further Education
Rope Walk
Ipswich IP4 1LT

Thames Valley College
Wellington Street
Slough SL1 1YG

Trinity and All Saints' College
Brownberrie Lane
Horsforth
Leeds LS18 5HD

Trinity College Carmarthen
Carmarthen
Dyfed SA31 3EP

West Glamorgan Institute of Higher Education
Townhill Road
Swansea SA2 0UT

Westhill College
Selly Oak
Birmingham B29 6LL

West London Institute of Higher Education
Gordon House
300 St Margaret's Road
Twickenham TW1 1PT

West Midlands College of Higher Education
Gorway Road
Walsall WS1 3BD

Westminster College
North Hinksey
Oxford OX2 9AT

West Sussex Institute of Higher Education
College Lane
Chichester
West Sussex PO19 4PE

Worcester College of Higher Education
Henwick Grove
Worcester WR2 6AJ

Schools and Colleges of Music (without Polytechnics)

(Scottish Schools of Music and Arts, see under Scottish central institutions)

Bath College of Higher Education
Newton Park
Bath BA2 9BN

Bretton Hall College
West Bretton
Wakefield
Yorks WF4 4LG

Cambridgeshire College of Arts and Technology
Cambridge CB1 1PT

Colchester Institute
Faculty of Music & Art
School of Music
Sheepen Road
Colchester Essex CO3 3LL

Dartington College of Arts
Totnes, Devon TQ9 6EJ

Guildhall School of Music and Drama
Barbican
London EC2Y 8DT

Leeds College of Music
Cookridge Street
Leeds LS2 8BH

London College of Music
47 Great Marlborough Street
London W1V 2AS

Royal Academy of Music
Marylebone Road
London NW1 5HT

Royal College of Music
Prince Consort Road
London SW7 2BS

Royal Northern College of Music
124 Oxford Road
Manchester M13 9RD

Salford College of Technology
Department of Performing Arts/Media Study
Adelphi Building, Peru Street
Salford Manchester M3 6EQ

Trinity College of Music
1 L Mandeville Place
London W1M 6AQ

Welsh College of Music and Drama
Castle Grounds
Cardiff CF1 3ER

Source: British Music Yearbook 1989.

UK

Music, Dancing and Drama Colleges (without Polytechnics

The Arts Educational Schools
14 Bath Road
Chiswick
London W4 1LY

Barbara Speake Stage School
East Acton Lane
East Acton
London W3 7EG

Birmingham School of Music
Paradise Place
Birmingham B3 3HG

Birmingham School of Speech Training and Dramatic Art
45 Church Road
Edgbaston
Birmingham B15 3SW

The Bristol Old Vic Theatre School
2 Downside Road
Clifton
Bristol BS8 2XF

Britten-Pears School for Advanced Musical Studies
High Street
Aldeburgh
Suffolk IP15 6AX

Source: Education Yearbook 1989.

Schools and Academies of Art and Design (without Polytechnics)

Bath Academy of Art
(see under colleges and institutes of higher education)

Buckinghamshire College of Higher Education
Queen Alexandra Road
High Wycombe
Bucks. HP11 2JZ

Canterbury College of Art
(see under Kent Institute of Art and Design)

Derbyshire College of Higher Education
Faculty of Art and Design
Kedleston Road
Derby DE3 1GB

Exeter College of Art and Design
Earl Richards Road North,
Exeter

Falmouth School of Art and Design
Woodlane
Falmouth
Cornwall

Gloucestershire College of Arts and Technology
Oxstalls Lane
Gloucester

Goldsmiths' College (Faculty of Arts)
University of London
Lewisham Way
London SE14 6NW

Gwent College of Higher Education
Faculty of Art and Design
Clarence Place
Newport
Gwent NPT 0UW

Hertfordshire College of Art & Design
Hatfield Road
St Albans
Hertfordshire AL1 3RS

Humberside College of Higher Education
Faculty of Arts: Fine Art, Visual Communication Design, Humanities, Applied Social Studies and Teacher Education
Inglemire Ave
Hull HU6 7LU

Kent Institute of Art and Design
Oakwood Park
Oakwood Road
Maidstone, Kent ME16 8AG

London Institute
388-396 Oxford Street W1
- Camberwell School of Art and Crafts
  Peckham Road
  London SE6 8UF
- Central School of Art and Design
  Southampton Row
  London WC18 4AP

Chelsea School of Art
Manresa Road
Chelsea
London SW3 6LS

London College of Printing
Elephant and Castle
London SE1 6SB

St Martin's School of Art
107 Charing Cross Road
London WC2H 0DU

Loughborough College of Art and Design
Radmoor
Loughborough
Leicester LE11 3BT

Maidstone College of Art and Medway College of Art and Design
(see under Kent Institute of Art and Design)

Norwich School of Art
St Georges Street
Norwich
Norfolk NR3 1BB

Ravensbourne College of Design and Communication
Welden Road
Chislehurst BR7 5SN

South Glamorgan Institute of Higher Education
Faculty of Art and Design
Howard Gardens
Cardiff CF2 1SP

Stourbridge College of Technology and Art
Hagley Road
Stourbridge DY8 1QU

UK

University of Ulster
Faculty of Art and Design
York Street
Belfast BT16 1ED

West Surrey College of Art and Design
Falkner Road
The Hart, Farnham
Surrey GU9 7DS

Wimbledon School of Art
Merton Hall Road
London SW19 3QA

Winchester School of Art
Park Ave
Winchester
Hants. SO23 8DL

Source: Education Yearbook 1989

2. Survey of courses of study at higher education institutions

First-degree courses at universities

	Aberdeen	Aston	Bath	Belfast	Birmingham	Bradford	Bristol	Brunel	Buckingham	Cambridge	City	Cranfield I. T.	Dundee	Durham	East Anglia	Edinburgh	Essex	Exeter	Glasgow	Heriot-Watt	Hull	Keele	Kent at Canterbury	Lancaster
Accountancy/Accounting	○	●	●	○	○	○	○	●	○		●		○	●	○	○	○	○	○	○	○	●	○	○
Acoustics/Acoustical engineering					●					●						●	●							
Actuarial science/Mathematics											○									○			○	
Administration/Administrative science		○		●	●	○		●			●					●			●	●			○	
African languages/studies					○																		●	●
Agricultural economics	○			●						●					●	○		○	○					
Agriculture/Agricultural science(s) [1]	○			○				●				○				○			○					
American/North American studies	●			○	○					●			○		○	●	○	○	○		○	○	○	●
Analytical science	●														●									
Anatomy (human)	○			○	○	●	○			○			●			○			○					
Animal science(s) [1]	○		○	●				●	●	●					○	○	●		[2] ○		●			●
Anthropology/Social anthropology	○			○	●			○		○				○	○	○		●	○		○	○	○	●
Arabic (*see also* Middle/Near Eastern languages/studies)	●			●	●					○				○		○		○	○					●
Archaeology				○	○	○	○			○				○	●	○		○	○					
Architecture			○	○						○			○			○			○	○				
Art/History of art	○						●			○					○	○	○	○	○	○	●		●	○
Astronomy	●			●			●			●				●		●			○			●		
Astrophysics					●									●		○	●		●			●	●	●
Bacteriology (*see also* Microbiology)		●		●	●	●		●		●			●			○	●		●	●			○	
Biochemistry (incl. Biological chemistry)	○	○	○	○	○	●	○	○	○	○	○		○	○	○	○	○	○	○	○	●	○	○	○
Applied/ Technical —								○	●														●	
Medical/Clinical —		●			○	●		●	●				●						●				○	
Biology (*see also* Marine biology)	○	○	○	○	○		○		○	●			○	○	○	●	○	○	●	●	●	○	●	○
Applied —		○	○					○		○				●		●	○		●	●	○		●	
Cell —	○	●		●		●		●		●			●	●	●	●	○	●	○		●	●	○	●
Developmental —	○					●				●			●	●	●	●	○	●	[2] ○		●	●		
Human —	○	○			●			●		●					●	●			●			●		
Biomedical sciences				○		○			●				○											
Biometry										●													●	
Biophysics										●					○							●		
Biotechnology	●		●		●	●		●		●				●			●				●		●	
Botany	○	●		○	○		○	●		○			○	○		○	●	○	○	●	●	●		●
Brewing, Malting, etc.																				○				
Building			○													●				○				
Building economics																●				○				

[1] Incl. Biochemistry, nutrition etc.

[2] Animal development biology.

Source: These tables have been reproduced by courtesy of the Association of Commonwealth Universities from the 'Commonwealth Universities Yearbook 1988', Vol. 1. Editor: T. Craig.

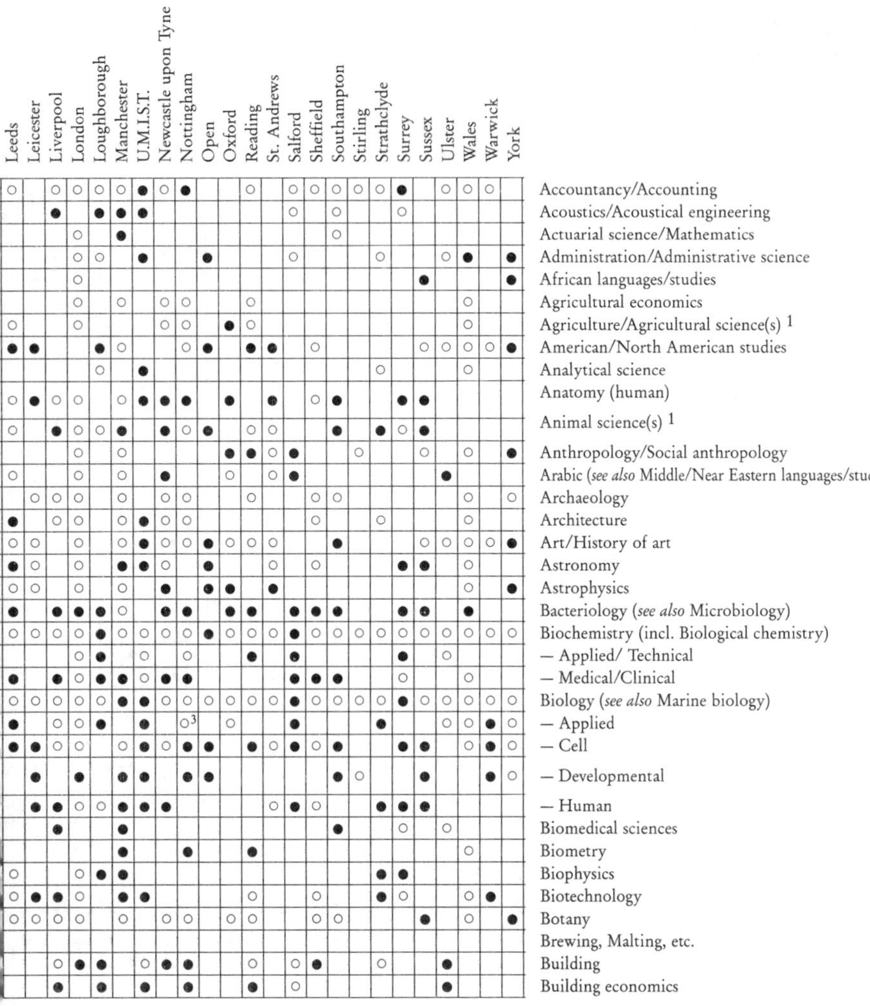

Subject	Leeds	Leicester	Liverpool	London	Loughborough	Manchester	U.M.I.S.T.	Newcastle upon Tyne	Nottingham	Open	Oxford	Reading	St. Andrews	Salford	Sheffield	Southampton	Stirling	Strathclyde	Surrey	Sussex	Ulster	Wales	Warwick	York
Accountancy/Accounting	○		○	○	○	○	●	○	●			○		○	○	○	○	○	●		○	○	○	
Acoustics/Acoustical engineering			●		●	●	●							○		○			○					
Actuarial science/Mathematics				○		●										○								
Administration/Administrative science				○	○		●			●				○				○			○	●		●
African languages/studies				○																●				●
Agricultural economics				○		○		○	○			○										○		
Agriculture/Agricultural science(s) [1]	○			○				○	○		●	○										○		
American/North American studies	●	●			●	○			○	●		●	●		○					○	○	○	○	●
Analytical science					○		●											○				○		
Anatomy (human)	○	●	○	○		○	●	●	●		●		●		○	●			●	●				
Animal science(s) [1]	○		●	○	○	●		●	○	●		○	○			●		●	○	●				
Anthropology/Social anthropology				○		○					●	●	○	●			○			○		○		●
Arabic (*see also* Middle/Near Eastern languages/studies)	○			○		○		●			○		○	●							●			
Archaeology		○	○	○		○		○	○			○			○	○						○		○
Architecture	●		○	○		○	●	○	○						○			○				○		
Art/History of art	○	○		○		○	●	○	○	●	○	○	○			●				○	○	○	○	●
Astronomy	●	○		○		●	●	○		●			○		○				●	●		○		
Astrophysics	○	○		○		○		●		●	●		●									○		●
Bacteriology (*see also* Microbiology)	●		●	●	●	○		●	●		●	●		●	●	●			●	●		●		
Biochemistry (incl. Biological chemistry)	○	○	○	○	●	○	○	○	○	●	○	○	○	●	○	○	○	○	○	○	○	○	○	○
— Applied/ Technical				○	●		○		○			●		●					●		○			
— Medical/Clinical	●		●	○	●	●	○	●	●					●	●	●			○			○		
Biology (*see also* Marine biology)	○	○	○	○	○	●	●	○	○	○	○	○	○	●	○	○	○	○	●	○	○	○	○	○
— Applied	●		○	○	●		●		○[3]		○			●				●			○	○	●	○
— Cell	●	●	○	○		○	●	○	●	●		●	○	●	○	●			●	●		○	●	○
— Developmental		●		●		●	●		●	●						●	○			●			●	○
— Human		●	●	○	○	●	●	●					○	●	○			●	●	●				
Biomedical sciences			●			●										●			○		○			
Biometry						●			●			●										○		
Biophysics	○			○	●	●												●	●					
Biotechnology	○	●	●	○		●	●					○			○			●	○			○	●	
Botany	○	○	○	○		○		○	○		○	○			○	○				●		○		●
Brewing, Malting, etc.																								
Building			○	●	●		○	●	●			○		○	●			○			●			
Building economics			●		●		●		●			●		○							●			

[3] Environmental biology

Note: For full details university/college calendars or prospectuses *must* be consulted.

● = May be studied as part of course leading to first degree

○ = Forms a main part of course leading to first degree

UK

First-degree courses at universities

	Aberdeen	Aston	Bath	Belfast	Birmingham	Bradford	Bristol	Brunel	Buckingham	Cambridge	City	Cranfield I. T.	Dundee	Durham	East Anglia	Edinburgh	Essex	Exeter	Glasgow	Heriot-Watt	Hull	Keele	Kent at Canterbury	Lancaster
Business/Management studies/science		○	○	○	○	○		●	○	●	○	●	●	●	●	○			●	○	○	○	○	○
Celtic studies: Irish	●			○						●						○			○					
Scottish Gaelic (*see also* Scottish studies) —	○															○			○					
Welsh/Welsh studies —	●									●						○			○					
Ceramics —	●							●																
Chemistry —	○	○	○	○	○	○	○	○		○		●	○	○	○	○	○	○	○	○	○	○	○	○
Applied/Industrial —		○			●	●		○									○			●			●	○
Colour —																								
Chinese (*see also* Oriental langs./studies)										○				○		○								
Classical studies/Civilization (Greek and/or Roman)	○			○	○		○							○		○		○	○		○	○	○	
Classics (Greek and/or Latin)	○			○	○		○			○				○		○		○	○		○	○	○	
Commerce		●			○	●										○				●	●			
Computer/Computing science	○	○	○	○	○	○	○	○	○	○	○		○	○	○	○	○	○	○	○	○	○	○	○
Computer systems	●	●			●	○		○	●		○	○	○		○	○	●			●	●	●	○	●
Conflict (incl. Peace, Defence, Strategic) studies						○				●		○				●			●			●	●	●
Dance					●																			
Data processing	●	●				○		●	●		○		●				●			●	○		●	●
Dentistry				○	○		○						○			○			○					
Development studies					●					●					○				●				○	
Drama/Theatre					○		○								○	○	●	○	○		○		○	○
Dutch										○											○			
Ecology	○		●	●	●	●			●					●	○	○	○	●	●		●	●		○
Econometrics (*see also* Economics, Mathematical)	●		○	●	●	●		●	●	●			●	●		●	●	●	○		●	●	○	○
Economic/Economic and social history	○	●		○	○	●	○	●	●	●			●	○	○	○	●	○	○	●	○		○	○
Economics	○	●	○	○	○	○	○	○	○	○	○		○	○	○	○	○	○	○	○	○	○	○	○
Industrial/Technological —		●			●	●																		
Mathematical (*see also* Econometrics) —		●			○	●	○	●	●	●				●				●	○		●	●	○	○
Education [1]	●		○	●[4]			○	○		○				○	○			○	●	●	○		●	○
Electronics	●	○	○		○	○	●	○		●	○	●	○	○	○	○	○	●	○	●	●	○	●	●
Biomedical —																						○	○	
Energy studies/engineering																○			●			●		
Engineering/Engineering science [2]	○	○				●		○		●				○		○		○		○				○
Aeronautical —			○	○			○			○	○								○					

[1] Does not include degrees for which all courses are given in associated institutions.

[2] General or broadly-based engineering courses which do not (or need not) involve specialization in particular branches.

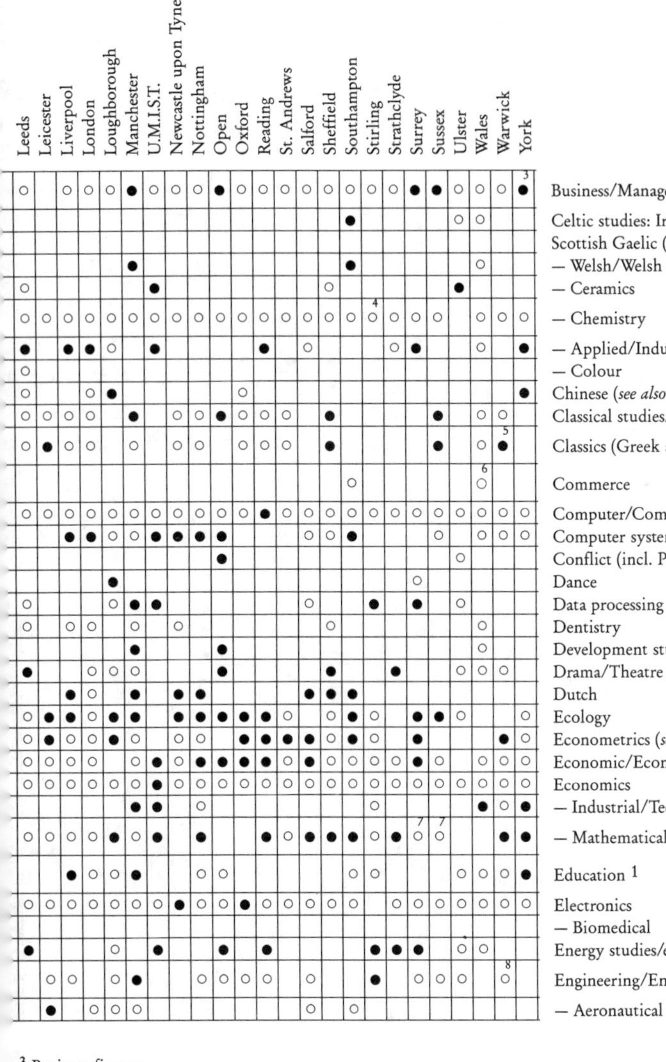

Subject	Leeds	Leicester	Liverpool	London	Loughborough	Manchester	U.M.I.S.T.	Newcastle upon Tyne	Nottingham	Open	Oxford	Reading	St. Andrews	Salford	Sheffield	Southampton	Stirling	Strathclyde	Surrey	Sussex	Ulster	Wales	Warwick	York
Business/Management studies/science	○		○	○	○	●	○	○	○	●	○	○	○	○	○	○	○	○	●	●	○	○	○	●[3]
Celtic studies: Irish																●					○	○		
Scottish Gaelic (*see also* – Scottish Studies)																								
– Welsh/Welsh studies						●										●						○		
– Ceramics	○						●								○						●			
– Chemistry	○	○	○	○	○	○	○	○	○	○	○	○	○	○	○	○	○[4]	○	○	○		○	○	○
– Applied/Industrial	●		●	●	○		●					●		○				○	●			○		●
– Colour	○																							
Chinese (*see also* Oriental langs./studies)	○			○	●						○													●
Classical studies/Civilization (Greek and/or Roman)	○	○	○	○		●		○	○	●	○	○	○		●					●		○	○	
Classics (Greek and/or Latin)	○	●	○	○		○		○	○		○	○	○		●					●		○	●[5]	
Commerce																○						○[6]		
Computer/Computing science	○	○	○	○	○	○	○	○	○	○	○	●	○	○	○	○	○	○	○	○	○	○	○	○
Computer systems			●	●	○	○	●	●	●	●				○	○	●				○		○	○	○
Conflict (incl. Peace, Defence, Strategic) studies										●											○			
Dance					●														○					
Data processing	○				○	●	●							○			●		●		○			
Dentistry	○		○	○		○		○							○							○		
Development studies						●				●												○		
Drama/Theatre	●			○	○	○				●					●			●			○	○	○	
Dutch			●	○		●		●	●					●	●	●								
Ecology	○	●	●	○	●	●		●	●	●	●	●	○		○	●	○		●	●	○			○
Econometrics (*see also* Economics, Mathematical)	○	●	○	○	●	○		○	○		●	●	●	●	○	●	○		●				●	○
Economic/Economic and social history	○	○	○	○		○	●	○	●	●	●	●	○	●	○	○	○	○	●	○		○	○	○
Economics	○	○	○	○	○	○	●	○	○	○	○	○	○	○	○	○	○	○	○	○	○	○	○	○
– Industrial/Technological						●	●		○								○					●	○	●
– Mathematical (*see also* Econometrics)	○	○	○	○	●	○	●		●			●	○	●	●	●	○	●	○[7]	○[7]			●	●
Education [1]			●	○	○	●			○	○						○	○				○	○	○	●
Electronics	○	○	○	○	○	○	○	●	○	○	●	○	○	○	○	○		○	○	○	○	○	○	○
– Biomedical																								
Energy studies/engineering	●				○		●			●		●					●	●	●		○	○		
Engineering/Engineering science [2]		○	○		○	●			○	○	○	○		○			●		○	○	○		○[8]	
– Aeronautical		●		○	○	○								○		○								

[3] Business finance.
[4] Under review
[5] English and Latin literature.
[6] Maritime commerce (Maritime studies).
[7] Economics with mathematics.
[8] Also (Engineering) Design and Appropriate technology.

● = May be studied as part of course leading to first degree

○ = Forms a main part of course leading to first degree

UK

First-degree courses at universities

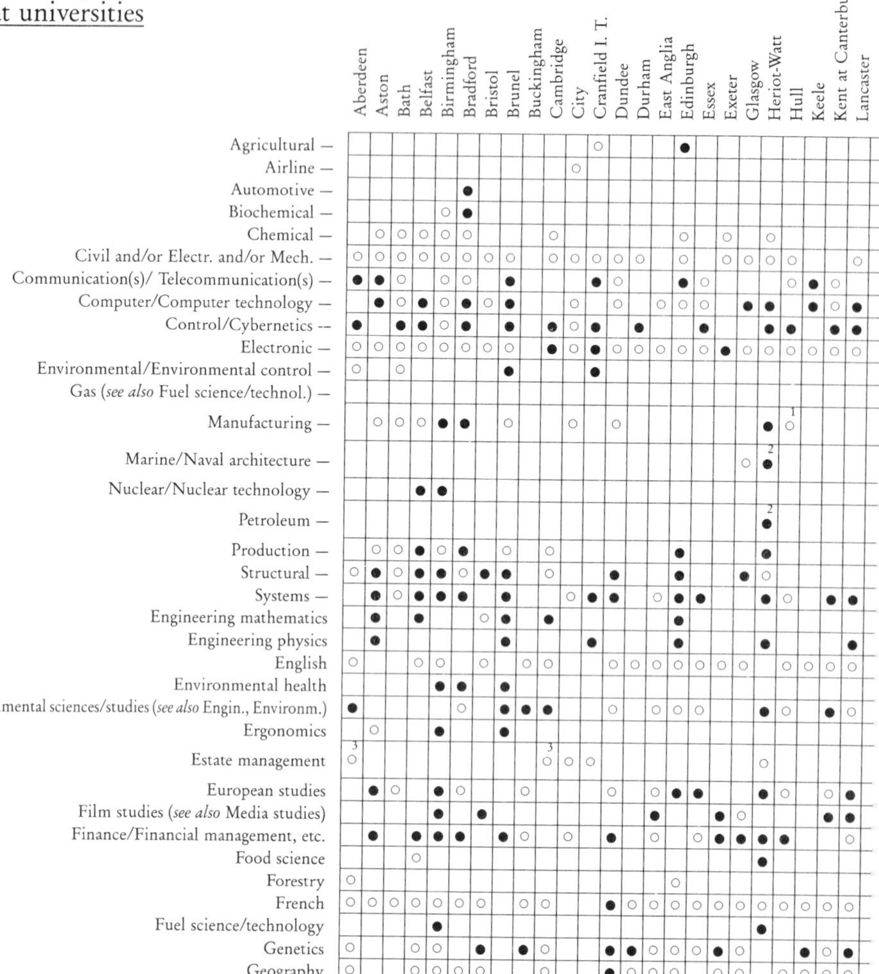

	Aberdeen	Aston	Bath	Belfast	Birmingham	Bradford	Bristol	Brunel	Buckingham	Cambridge	City	Cranfield I. T.	Dundee	Durham	East Anglia	Edinburgh	Essex	Exeter	Glasgow	Heriot-Watt	Hull	Keele	Kent at Canterbury	Lancaster
Agricultural —												○				●								
Airline —											○													
Automotive —						●																		
Biochemical —					○	●																		
Chemical —		○	○	○	○	○				○						○		○		○				
Civil and/or Electr. and/or Mech. —	○	○	○	○	○	○	○	○		○	○	○	○	○		○		○	○	○	○			○
Communication(s)/ Telecommunication(s) —	●	●	○		○	○		●				●	○			●	○				○	●	○	
Computer/Computer technology —		●	○	●	○	●	○	●			○		○		○	○	○		●	●		●	○	●
Control/Cybernetics --	●		●	●	○	●		●		●	○	●		●			●			●	●		●	●
Electronic —	○	○	○	○	○	○	○	○		●	○	●	○	○	○	○	○	●	○	○	○	○	○	○
Environmental/Environmental control —	○		○					●				●												
Gas (*see also* Fuel science/technol.) —																								
Manufacturing —		○	○	○	●	●		○			○		○							●	○[1]			
Marine/Naval architecture —																			○	●[2]				
Nuclear/Nuclear technology —				●	●																			
Petroleum —																				●[2]				
Production —		○	○	●	○	●		○		○						●				●				
Structural —	○	●	○	●	●	○	●	●		○			●			●			●	○				
Systems —		●	○	●	●	●		●			○	●	●		○	●	●			●	○		●	●
Engineering mathematics		●		●			○	●		●						●								
Engineering physics		●						●				●				●				●				●
English	○			○	○		○		○	○			○	○	○	○	○	○	○		○	○	○	○
Environmental health					●	●		●																
Environmental sciences/studies (*see also* Engin., Environm.)	●					○		●	●	●			○		○	○	○			●	○		●	○
Ergonomics		○			●			●																
Estate management	○[3]									○[3]	○	○								○				
European studies		●	○		●	○			○				○		○	●	●			●	○		○	●
Film studies (*see also* Media studies)					●		●								●			●	○				●	●
Finance/Financial management, etc.		●		●	●	●		●	○		○		●		○		○	●	●	●	●			○
Food science				○																●				
Forestry	○															○								
French	○	○	○	○	○	○	○		○	○			●	○	○	○	○	○	○	○	○	○	○	○
Fuel science/technology					●															●				
Genetics	○			○	○		●		●	○			●	●	○	○	○	●	○			●	○	●
Geography	○			○	○	○	○			○			●	○	○	○		○	○		○	○	○	○

1 Engineering design and manufacture.
2 Offshore engineering.
3 Land economy.

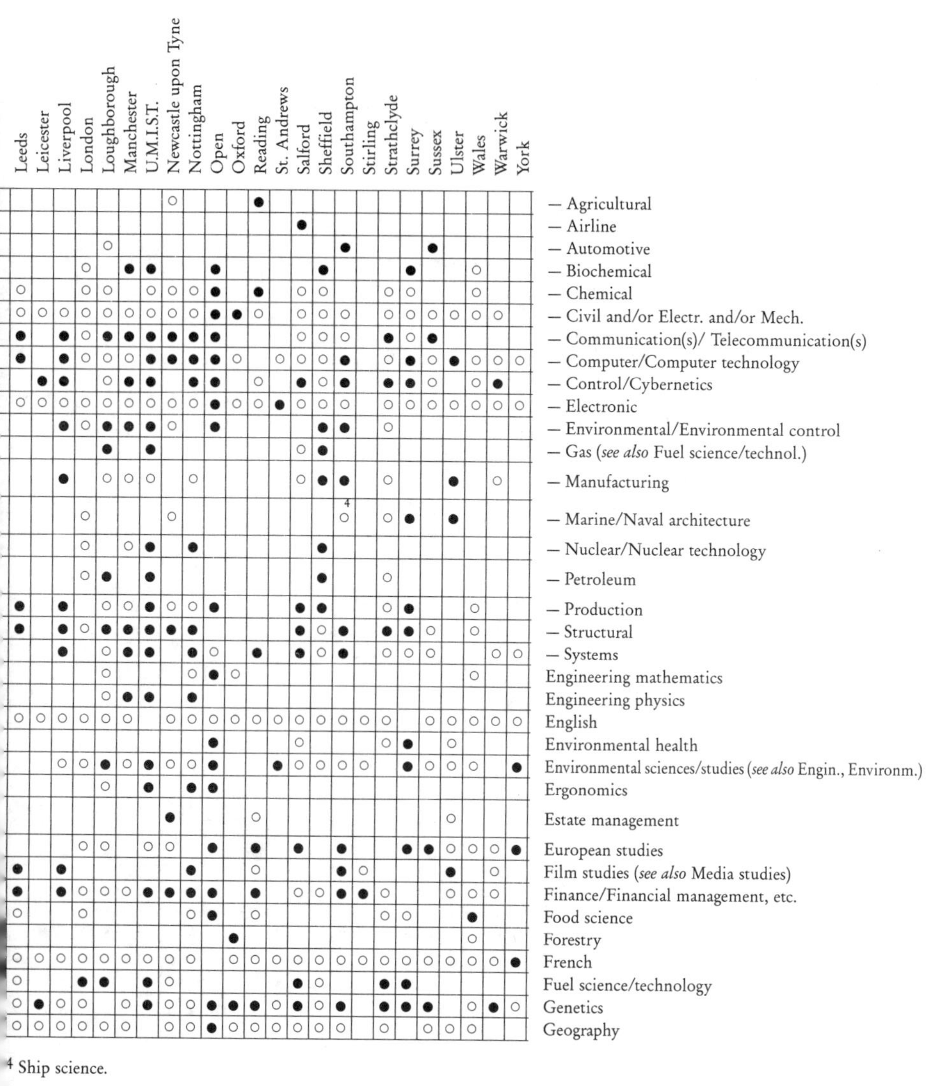

Leeds	Leicester	Liverpool	London	Loughborough	Manchester	U.M.I.S.T.	Newcastle upon Tyne	Nottingham	Open	Oxford	Reading	St. Andrews	Salford	Sheffield	Southampton	Stirling	Strathclyde	Surrey	Sussex	Ulster	Wales	Warwick	York	
							○				●													— Agricultural
													●											— Airline
				○											●				●					— Automotive
			○		●	●			●					●				●			○			— Biochemical
○			○	○		○	○	○	●		●		○	○			○	○			○			— Chemical
○	○	○	○	○	○	○	○	○	●	●	○		○	○	○		○	○	○	○	○	○		— Civil and/or Electr. and/or Mech.
●		●	○	●	●	●	●	●	●				○	○	○		●	○	●					— Communication(s)/ Telecommunication(s)
●		●	○	○	○	●	●	●	●	○		○	○	○	●		○	●	○	●	○	○	○	— Computer/Computer technology
	●	●		○	●	●		●	●		○		●	○	●		●	●	○		○	●		— Control/Cybernetics
○	○	○	○	○	○	○	○	○	●	○	○	●	○	○	○		○	○	○	○	○	○	○	— Electronic
		●	○	●	●	●	○		●					●	●		○							— Environmental/Environmental control
				●		●							○	●										— Gas (*see also* Fuel science/technol.)
		●		○	○	○		○					○	●	●		○			●		○		— Manufacturing
			○				○								○[4]		○	●		●				— Marine/Naval architecture
			○		○	●		●						●										— Nuclear/Nuclear technology
			○	●		●								●			○							— Petroleum
●		●		○	○	●	○	○	●				●	●			○	●			○			— Production
●		●	○	●	●	●	●	●					●	○	●		●	●	○		○			— Structural
		●		○	●	●		●	○		●		●	○	●		○	○	○			○	○	— Systems
				○				○	●	○											○			Engineering mathematics
				○	●	●		●																Engineering physics
○	○	○	○	○	○		○	○	○	○	○	○	○	○	○	○	○		○	○	○	○	○	English
									●				○				○	●		○				Environmental health
		○	○	●	○	●	○	○	●			●	○	○	○	○		●	○	○	○		●	Environmental sciences/studies (*see also* Engin., Environm.)
				○		●		●	●															Ergonomics
							●				○									○				Estate management
			○	○		○	○		●		●		●		●			●	●	○	○	○	●	European studies
●		●						●			○				●	○				●		○		Film studies (*see also* Media studies)
●		●	○	○	○	●	●	●	●		●		○	○	●	●	○			○	○	○		Finance/Financial management, etc.
○			○					○	●		○						○	○			●			Food science
										●											○			Forestry
○	○	○	○	○	○	○	○	○		○	○	○	○	○	○	○	○	○	○	○	○	○	●	French
○			●	●		●	○						●	○			●	●						Fuel science/technology
○	●	○	○		○	●	○	○	●	●	●	○	●	○	●		●	●	●		○	●	○	Genetics
○	○	○	○	○	○		○	○	●	○	○	○	○	○	○		○		○	○	○			Geography

[4] Ship science.

● = May be studied as part of course leading to first degree
○ = Forms a main part of course leading to first degree

First-degree courses at universities

	Aberdeen	Aston	Bath	Belfast	Birmingham	Bradford	Bristol	Brunel	Buckingham	Cambridge	City	Cranfield I. T.	Dundee	Durham	East Anglia	Edinburgh	Essex	Exeter	Glasgow	Heriot-Watt	Hull	Keele	Kent at Canterbury	Lancaster
Geology	○	○		○	○		○			○			●	○	○	○		○	○	●	○	○		●
Applied (incl. Engin./Mining geol.) —	○ [1]	●			●	●								○				○	●	●				
Physical/Geophysics —		●	●	●	●		●			●				○	○	○		○	●		●	●		○
German	○	○	○	○	○	○	○		○	○			●	○	○	○	○	○	○	○	○	○	○	○
Glass technology	●																							
Greek, Modern				○	○					○						○								
Hebrew (*see also* Middle/Near Eastern languages/studies)	○			○	●		●			○				○		○		●	○					●
History	○			○	○	○	○	●	○	○			○	○	○	○	○	○	○		○	○	○	○
History and/or Philosophy of science	●			○		●				○				●		●	●	●	●		●	●	●	○
Home economics																								
Horticulture			○																					
Hotel and catering management																								
Human communication					●	●					○													○
Immunology	●			● [2]	●	●		●		●				●			●		○				●	●
Industrial relations			○	●	●	●		●	●	●				●		●			● [3]	●			○	○
Information science/technology	●	●		○		○		○		○		○		○	○	○				○			●	○
Information studies		●		○				○							○	●								
International relations/studies	○	○			○	●		●		●	●		●	●	●		●		●			○	○	○
Interpreting (languages)						●									○					○				
Italian			●	○	○		○			○				●		○		○	○		○		○	○
Japanese (*see also* Oriental languages/studies)		●							●	○				●		●								
Landscape architecture/studies															●	○				○				
Latin-American studies	○				●		●			●				●		●	○		○					●
Law	○	●		○	○		○	○	○	○			○	○	○	○	○	○	○	●	○	○	○	○
Librarianship																								
Linguistics	●	○	○		●	●				●			●	○	○	○	○	○		●		●	●	○
Marine biology	○			●					○						●			●	●	○				
Maritime studies																								
Marketing		●			●	●			●			●				●				●	●		●	○
Materials science/technology	●	●	○	●	○	●		○		○	●			●			●		●		●			●
Mathematics	○	○	○	○	○	●	○	○	●	○	○	●	○	○	○	○	○	○	○	○	○	○	○	○
Applied/Technological —		○		○	○	○	● [4]	●		●			○		●	●	●	○		●	○	●	○	
Medieval studies					○					●						○		○	○			●	●	○
Media studies (*see also* Film studies)					●			○															● [5]	

1 Petroleum geology.
2 Applied and cellular immunology.
3 Production management.
4 Engineering mathematics.
5 Since 1989.

● = May be studied as part of course leading to first degree
○ = Forms a main part of course leading to first degree

UK

Leeds	Leicester	Liverpool	London	Loughborough	Manchester	U.M.I.S.T.	Newcastle upon Tyne	Nottingham	Open	Oxford	Reading	St. Andrews	Salford	Sheffield	Southampton	Stirling	Strathclyde	Surrey	Sussex	Ulster	Wales	Warwick	York	
○	○	○	○		○	●	○	○	●	○	○	○	●	○	○	●	●	●			○			Geology
●	○		○		●	●	●	●									○	●			○			— Applied (incl. Engin./Mining geol.)
●	○	○	○		●		○	●	●		○	○			○						○			— Physical/Geophysics
○	○	○	○	○	○	○	○	○		○	○	○	○	○	○	○	○	○	○	○	○	○	●	German
														○										Glass technology
			○							○					●				●					Greek, Modern
		○	○		○		●			○		○		●										Hebrew (*see also* Middle/Near Eastern languages/studies)
○	○	○	○		○		○	○	○	○	○	○	○	○	○	○	○		○	○	○	○	○	History
○	●		○		○	●		●	●	●		●			●		●		○				●	History and/or Philosophy of science
																				○	○			Home economics
			○					○			○						○							Horticulture
																	○	○		○	○[6]			Hotel and catering management
		●	●						●											○				Human communication
●	●	●	○		●		●	●			●			●	●		○	●				●		Immunology
○		●	○	●	●	●	●	●	●	●	●		●	●	●	○	○		●		○	●		Industrial relations
				○		●			●	●	○		○	●	○		○	○	○	●		●		Information science/technology
				○													○							Information studies
○	●		○	●	●	●			●	●	○	●			○		●	●	○	●	○	○	●	International relations/studies
●													○							●				Interpreting (languages)
○	○		○		○					○	○		○	●			○		○		○	○		Italian
●			○							○				○						●				Japanese (*see also* Oriental languages/studies)
			●		●		●				○			○										Landscape architecture/studies
●	●[7]	○	○		○		○	●				●		●	○		●					●		Latin-American studies
○	○	○	○	●	○	●	○	○		○	○			○	○	○[8]	○	●	○		○	○		Law
				○													○				○			Librarianship
○		●	○	●	○	○	○	○		●	○		●	○	○	●	●	●	○		○		○	Linguistics
●		○	○	●	●		○	●			●	○		●	●	○	●				○			Marine biology
															●						○			Maritime studies
		●		●		●	○[9]	●					○	●	●	●	○	●			○[9]			Marketing
○	●	○	○	○	○	○		○	●	○	●		●	○	●		●	○	●		○	●		Materials science/technology
○	○	○	○	○	○	○	○	○	○	○	○	○	○	○	○		○	○	○	○	○	○	○	Mathematics
●	●	○	○	○	●	●	●	○	○		○	○	●	○	○		○	●	○	●	○	○	●	— Applied/Technological
●		●	●		○		●	●			○	○		○	●				●		○		●	Medieval studies
		●														○			○	○				Media studies (*see also* Film studies)

[6] Institutional management.
[7] Geography.
[8] Business law.
[9] Agricultural and food marketing.

First-degree courses at universities

	Aberdeen	Aston	Bath	Belfast	Birmingham	Bradford	Bristol	Brunel	Buckingham	Cambridge	City	Cranfield I. T.	Dundee	Durham	East Anglia	Edinburgh	Essex	Exeter	Glasgow	Heriot-Watt	Hull	Keele	Kent at Canterbury	Lancaster
Medicine and surgery	○			○	○		○			○			○			○			○					
Metallurgy/Metallurgical engineering				●	○		●	○		○	●									●				
Meteorology					●									●	●	●								●
Microbiology (*see also* Bacteriology)	○	●	○	○	●	●	○	●		●			○	●	○	○	○		○	○	●	●	○	●
Microprocessors/Microelectronics	●	●		●	●	○		●				●	○	●	●	○	○		●	●	○	●	●	●
Middle/Near Eastern languages/studies (*see also* Arabic, Hebrew)				○	○					○				○		○								
Mining/Mining engineering		●			[1] ○																			
Molecular sciences	●	○					●							[2] ○	●	[2] ○	○		[2] ○		●		○	
Music	○			○	○		○			○	○			○	○	○		○	○		○	○		○
Nursing											●					○			○		○			
Nutrition (human)	○				●				●	●														
Occupational therapy																								
Oceanography															●	●			●	●				●
Operational research	●	●	○	○	●	●	●	●	●	●			●			●	○	○	[3] ○	●	○	●	●	○
Ophthalmic optics/Optometry		○		●		○					○													
Oriental languages/studies (*see also* Chinese, Japanese)		●								○				○		○					○		○	●
Paper science																								
Parasitology	○			●	●	●		●		●									○			●		
Pathology				○	●	●	[4] ○	●		○			○			○			○					
Personnel administration		●				●										●				●		·	●	●
Pest science																								
Pharmacology	○	○	○	●	●	●	○	●		○			○			○			○					
Pharmacy		○	○	○		○																		
Philosophy	○			○	○	○	○		●	○	●		○	○	○	○	○	●	○		○	○	○	○
Physical education [5] (*see also* Sports science/studies)					○																			
Physics/Physical science	○	○	○	○	○		○	○		○			○	○	○	○	○	○	○	○	○	○	○	○
Applied —	○	○	○	○	●			○				●		○			○	○		○	○			○
Chemical —							○									○			○	●		●	○	●
Mathematical —	●			●	○			●		●					○	○			●	○	●		○	●
Theoretical —	○			●	●			●		●				●	●	●	○	○	●	●	●	●	○	○
Physiology (human)	○	●		○	○	●	○	●	●	○			○		●	○			○		●	●		●
Physiotherapy																								
Plant science/Plant biology	○	●	○		○	●	○	●	●	●			●	●	○	●	●					●		●
Politics/Political ccience	○	●	○	○	○	○	○	○	○	○			○	○	○	○	○	○	○	●	○	○	○	○
Polymer science/technology	●			●				○									●		●	●		●		○

1 Minerals engineering.
2 Molecular biology.
3 Production management.
4 Celllular pathology.
5 Does not include courses which form part of B. Ed. curricula.

● = May be studied as part of course leading to first degree
○ = Forms a main part of course leading to first degree

UK

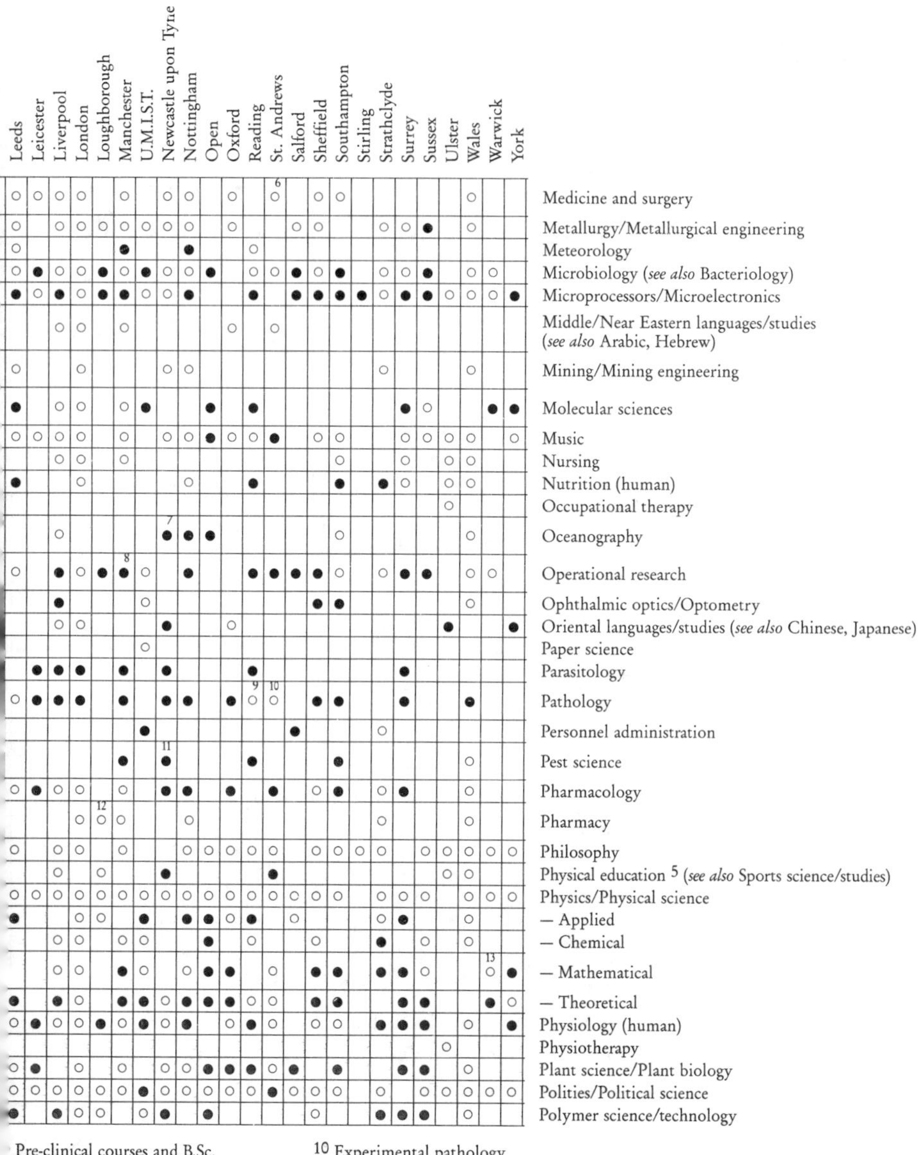

Leeds	Leicester	Liverpool	London	Loughborough	Manchester	U.M.I.S.T.	Newcastle upon Tyne	Nottingham	Open	Oxford	Reading	St. Andrews	Salford	Sheffield	Southampton	Stirling	Strathclyde	Surrey	Sussex	Ulster	Wales	Warwick	York	
○	○	○	○		○		○	○		○		[6] ○		○	○						○			Medicine and surgery
○		○	○	○	○	○	○	○		○			○	○			○	○	●		○			Metallurgy/Metallurgical engineering
○					●			●			○													Meteorology
○	●	○	○	●	○	●	○	○	●		○	○	●	○	●		○	○	●		○	○		Microbiology (*see also* Bacteriology)
●	○	●	○	●	●	○	○	●			●		●	●	●	●	○	●	●	○	○	○	●	Microprocessors/Microelectronics
		○	○		○					○		○												Middle/Near Eastern languages/studies (*see also* Arabic, Hebrew)
○			○				○	○									○				○			Mining/Mining engineering
●		○	○		○	●			●		●							●	○			●	●	Molecular sciences
○	○	○	○		○		○	○	●	○	○	●		○	○			○	○	○	○		○	Music
		○	○		○										○			○		○	○			Nursing
●			○					○			●				●		●	○		○	○			Nutrition (human)
																				○				Occupational therapy
		○					[7] ●	●	●						○						○			Oceanography
○		●	○	●	[8] ●	○		●			●	●	●	●	○		○	●	●		○	○		Operational research
		●				○								●	●						○			Ophthalmic optics/Optometry
		○	○				●			○										●			●	Oriental languages/studies (*see also* Chinese, Japanese)
						○																		Paper science
	●	●	●		●		●				●							●						Parasitology
○	●	●	●		●		●	●		●	[9] ○	[10] ○		●	●			●			●			Pathology
						●							●				○							Personnel administration
					●		[11] ●				●				●						○			Pest science
○	●	○	○		○		●	●		●		●		○	●		○	●			○			Pharmacology
			○	[12] ○	○			○									○				○			Pharmacy
○		○	○		○			○	○	○	○	○		○	○	○	○		○	○	○	○	○	Philosophy
		○		○			●					●								○	○			Physical education [5] (*see also* Sports science/studies)
○	○	○	○	○	○	○	○	○	○	○	○	○	○	○	○		○	○	○		○	○	○	Physics/Physical science
●			○	○		●		●	●	○	●		○				○	●			○			— Applied
		○	○		○	○			●		○			○			●		○		○			— Chemical
		○	○		●	○		○	●	●		○		●	●		●	●	○			[13] ○	●	— Mathematical
●		●	○		●	●	○	●	●	●	○	○		●	●			●	●			●	○	— Theoretical
○	●	○	○	●	○	●	○	●		○	●	○		○	○		●	●	●		○		●	Physiology (human)
																				○				Physiotherapy
○	●		○		○		○	○	●	●	●	○	●		●			●	●		○			Plant science/Plant biology
○	○	○	○	○	○	●	○	○	○	○	○	●	○	○	○		○		○	○	○	○	○	Polities/Political science
●		●	○	○		○	●		●					○			●	●	●		○			Polymer science/technology

Pre-clinical courses and B.Sc. (medical science).
Offshore engineering
Decision theory.
Pathobiology.

10 Experimental pathology.
11 Crop protection.
12 Medical and pharmaceutical chemistry.
13 Mathematics and physics.

UK

First-degree courses at universities

	Aberdeen	Aston	Bath	Belfast	Birmingham	Bradford	Bristol	Brunel	Buckingham	Cambridge	City	Cranfield I. T.	Dundee	Durham	East Anglia	Edinburgh	Essex	Exeter	Glasgow	Heriot-Watt	Hull	Keele	Kent at Canterbury	Lancaster
Portuguese	●			●	●		○			○				●		●	●	●	○		●			
Psychology	○	○	○	○	○	○	○	○		○	○		○	○		○		○	○	●	○	○	○	○
Public administration		●			○	●		●					●	○			○	●	●	●	●		○	●
Refractories technology																								
Religious studies	●				●		○			○					●	○		○			●		●	○
Theology/Biblical studies —	○			○	○		○			○				○		○		○	○		○		○	●
Resource studies/management	●					●		●		○					○	○								●
Russian/Russian studies (*see also* Slavonic/East European)	○		●	○	○	○	○			○				○	●	○	○	○	○	○		○		
Scandinavian languages/studies										○					○	○				●	○			
Scottish studies																○			●					
History —	○												●			○			○					
Literature —	○															●			○					
Slavonic/East European languages/studies (*see also* Russian)				●	●					○				●				●	○		●			
Social administration		●		●	○	●	○	●					●	○		○	●	○	●	●	○		○	○
Sociology/Social studies/science(s)	○	○	○	○	○	○	○	○	●	○	○		●	○	○	○	○	○	○	●	○	○	○	○
Soil science	○			●	●	●				●		●		●	●	○	●			●	●			●
Spanish	○		○	○	○	○	○		●	○				○		○	○	○	○	○	○			
Speech/Speech therapy											○								○					
Sports science/studies (*see also* Physical education)					○														●					
Statistics	○	○	○	○	○	●	○	○	●	●	○		○	●	●	○	○	○	○	○	○	○	○	●
Mathematical —	●	●			○	●		●		●			○	●	●	●	○	○	○	○	○	●	○	○
Surveying, Quantity		●																		○				
Surveying, Topographic science		●		●	●	●				●			●	●		●			○	●				
Textiles																								
Town and country/Regional planning		●		○		●				●			○		●	●			○	○		●		
Toxicology	●		●		●	●		●									●				○			
Transport studies/technology		○				●						●	●						●	●		●		
Typography																								
Urban studies		○			●					●				●	●	●				●	●	●	○	●
Veterinary studies				●			○			○						○			○					
Victorian studies									●															
Virology				●	●	●		●		●			●	●	●		●						●	
Wild-life management										●						○								
Wood science	●																							
Zoology	○			○	○		○	●	●	○			○	○	○	○	●	○	○	●	●	●		●

● = May be studied as part of course leading to first degree

○ = Forms a main part of course leading to first degree

Leeds	Leicester	Liverpool	London	Loughborough	Manchester	U.M.I.S.T.	Newcastle upon Tyne	Nottingham	Open	Oxford	Reading	St. Andrews	Salford	Sheffield	Southampton	Stirling	Strathclyde	Surrey	Sussex	Ulster	Wales	Warwick	York	
○		○	○		○		●	●		○			●	●	○						○			Portuguese
○	○	○	○	○	○	●	○	○	○	○	○	○		○	○	○	○	○	○	○	○	○	○	Psychology
●			●		●				●					●	○		○			○			●	Public administration
														○										Refractories technology
○	●		○		○		○	●	●	●					●	○			●		○			Religious studies
○			○		○		●	○		○		○		○	●						○			— Theology/Biblical studies
●				●												●		●					●	Resource studies/management
○		●	○		○			○		○		○	●	○			○	○	○		○			Russian/Russian studies (*see also* Slavonic/East European)
			○				●						●	●				●			○			Scandinavian languages/studies
																○	●							Scottish studies
												○				○								— History
																○								— Literature
●			○					○						○					○					Slavonic/East European languages/studies (*see also* Russian)
○			○	○	○		○	○	●				●	○	○	○	○	●	○	○	○	○	○	Social administration
○	○	○	○	○	○	●	○	○	○	●	○	●	○	○	○	○	○	○	○	○	○	○	○	Sociology/Social studies/science(s)
●			○		●	●	○	○		●	○			●			●	●	●		○			Soil science
○		○	○		○	●	○	○		○		○	○	○	○	○	○			●	○			Spanish
			○		○		○				○			○						○				Speech/Speech therapy
				○																○				Sports science/studies (*see also* Physical education)
○	●	●	○	●	●	○	○	○	○	●	○	○	●	○	○	●	●	○	○	○	○	○	○	Statistics
●	●	○	○	●	●	●	●	●	●		○[1]	○	●		●		●	●	●	○	○	○[1]	●	— Mathematical
					●	●					○		○					●		○				Surveying, Quantity
				●	●	●	○	●			●				●						○			Surveying, Topographic science
○						○														○	○			Textiles
		●	●	●	○		○	●	●		●			●							○			Town and country/Regional planning
		●	○															●						Toxicology
●				○		●	●	●			●		●		●			●		○	○[2]			Transport studies/technology
											○													Typography
●		●		●	●	●	●		●		●			○	●	○			○					Urban studies
		○	○																					Veterinary studies
	●				●				●												○			Victorian studies
●			●		○		●				●			●				●				○		Virology
							●																	Wild-life management
																					○			Wood science
○	●	○	○		○		○	○	●	○	○	○		○	○				●		○		●	Zoology

1 Mathematics and statistics.
2 International transport (Maritime studies).

UK

Courses of study at polytechnics
Art and design

	Birmingham	Brighton	Bristol	Coventry	Huddersfield	Kingston	Lancashire	Leeds	Leicester	Liverpool	London: City of	London: North
Fine art	●	●	●	●		●	●	●	●	●		
Graphic design	□●	●	●	●		●	●	●	●	●		
3-D design	●	●	●	●		●	□	●	●		●	●
Ceramics	○		○				□		○			
Furniture	○		○			○	□	○	○			
Glass	○											
Industrial design (Engineering)	○				□			○	○			
Industrial design (Marketing)												
Industrial design (Transportation)				○								
Interior design	○	○				○		○	○			○
Jewellery	○						□				○	
Silver/metal												
Silversmithing	○								○		○	
Theatre	○											
Wood/Metal/Ceramics		○					□					
Wood/Metal/Plastics		○	○									
Textiles/Fashion	●	●	●		●	●	●		●	●		
Admin./Business studies		●					○					
Contour fashion									○			
Embroidery	○											
Fashion	○		○			○	○		○	○		
Footwear design									○			
Knitwear design							○		○			
Textile design					□○				○			
Woven & printed textiles	○								○	○		
Multidisciplinary craft/design	□											

● Degree in named areas of study
○ Chief study specialization
□ Higher national diploma in named area of study

Art & design degree course students are generally required to pursue one of four main areas of study, with a further choice of chief study specialization in two of the main areas. Entry requirements for all courses may include a year of preliminary study on a foundation course.

	Manchester	Middlesex	Newcastle upon Tyne	North East London	N. Staffordshire	Plymouth	Portsmouth	Sheffield	Sunderland	Teesside	Trent	Wolverhampton
Fine art	●	●	●	●	●			●	●		●	●
Graphic design	●	●	●		○				□		●	●
3-D design	●	●	●					[●]	●	●	●	●
Ceramics		○			[○]				○			○
Furniture		○									●	
Glass					○				○			○
Industrial design (Engineering)	○		●					○		○		
Industrial design (Marketing)										●		
Industrial design (Transportation)												
Interior design	○	○								○	●	
Jewellery		○						○				
Silver/metal		○						○				
Silversmithing												
Theatre											○	
Wood/Metal/Ceramics	○											
Wood/Metal/Plastics			○									○
Textiles/Fashion	●	●	●	●							●	●
Admin./Business studies				●								
Contour fashion												
Embroidery	○											
Fashion	○	○	○								○	
Footwear design												
Knitwear design											●	
Textile design											○	○
Woven & printed textiles	○	○			○							
Multidisciplinary craft/design			○		●		●		●			

Source: These tables have been reprinted from the leaflet 'The polytechnics, autumn 1988; a guide to full-time and sandwich courses, degree, degree equivalent, HND, DipHE and teaching qualifications'.

UK

Arts, languages and other humanities

	Birmingham	Brighton	Bristol	Coventry	Hatfield	Huddersfield	Kingston	Lancashire	Leeds	Leicester	Liverpool	London: Central	London: City of	London: North	London: South Bank
American studies								◉							
Applied language		●						◉	◉						
Arabic												○			
Art & design								□○			○				
Chinese												○			
Classical civilization														◉	
Combined studies (Arts)					●		●	●		●					
Contemporary studies					●										
Cultural studies											◉				
Dance		○								○					
Drama		○				○				○	◉				
Economic history															
English or Literary studies	●	○	○		◉	○	◉	◉		○	◉	○		◉	
European studies				○	●			○	○		○		○	●	○
Film studies												◉		○	
French or French studies		○	○	○	○	○	◉	◉	●		○	○	◉	◉	○
German or German studies			○	○	○		○	○	●		○	○	○	○	○
History		◉	○	○	◉	○	◉	◉		○	◉	○	○	◉	
History of art & design	●	◉						○		●					
History of ideas					○	○	◉								
Humanities or Modern studies		◉	●	●	◉	●	◉	○		●	○			●	
Italian		○						○				○			
Languages for business	●		□					●	●						
Latin American studies														○	
Linguistics		◉			◉			◉				○			
Music	●	○			○	●	●			○					
Peace and war studies															
Performance or movement studies		◉							●	●					
Philosophy		○			◉	○								●	
Photographic arts		○										●			
Politics or government	●		◉	○		○	◉	◉	○	○	◉	○	◉	○	
Religious studies															
Russian or Russian studies		○									○	○			
Spanish or Spanish studies			○	○	○		○	○	●		○	○		○	○
Theatre studies															

● Degree in named areas of study
○ Chief study specialization
□ Higher national diploma in named area of study

	London: Thames	Manchester	Middlesex	Newcastle upon Tyne	North East London	N. Staffordshire	Oxford	Plymouth	Portsmouth	Sheffield	Sunderland	Teesside	Trent	Wales	Wolverhampton
American studies			○								○				
Applied language							○								
Arabic															
Art & design			○	○		[○]	○							○	○
Chinese															
Classical civilization															
Combined studies (Arts)			●	○							●				
Contemporary studies															
Cultural studies			●		●				●						
Dance			◉												
Drama			◉	○									○	○	
Economic history		○							●						
English or Literary studies	○	◉	◉	○	○	◉	○		○	●	◉	○	○	○	◉
European studies		○		○							○		●		◉
Film studies										○					
French or French studies	○	○	○	○		○	○		◉		○	○	○	□	◉
German or German studies	○	○		○		○	○		◉		○		○	□	◉
History	○	◉	○	○	○	◉	○		●	●	○	○	○	○	◉
History of art & design		◉	◉	●		●	○			●				○	
History of ideas			○									○			
Humanities or Modern studies	●	●	●	●	○	●	○					●	●	●	◉
Italian							●								
Languages for business			○	□			○								
Latin American studies									◉						
Linguistics															
Music			◉	○			○						○		
Peace and war studies											○				
Performance or movement studies			◉	○											
Philosophy	●	○	○		○	○					○	○		○	
Photographic arts		[●]	○			○							●		◉
Politics or government	●	◉	○	○		○	○	◉	●		○	○	○		◉
Religious studies	●													○	
Russian or Russian studies				○					◉						◉
Spanish or Spanish studies	○	○	○	○			●		◉						◉
Theatre studies														○	

UK

Business, social and related professional studies

	Birmingham	Brighton	Bristol	Coventry	Hatfield	Huddersfield	Kingston	Lancashire	Leeds	Leicester	Liverpool	London: Central	London: City of	London: North	London: South Bank
Accountancy or Finance	●	●	●	●	◉	◉	●	●	[●]	◉	[●]	[○]	[◉]	[●]	
Agricultural marketing															
Business information technology			[◉]		◉	●	●	[●]	□				○		
Business studies	[●]	[●]	[●]	[●]	[◉]	[◉]	[◉]	[●]	[●]	[●]	[●]	[●]	[●]	[●]	[●]
Combined studies (Social sciences)					●										
Communication, Media or Visual studies	●	○	○	●							◉	●			
Economics	●	○	◉	◉	◉		◉	◉	◉	●	◉	○	◉	○	○
Education	●	●	●		◉		●	◉	●		●			●	●
European business			○												
Fisheries studies															
Food marketing science															
Health studies														●	
Hotel, catering and institutional management	●	[●]				[●]			[●]					[●]	
Industrial economics				○											
Industrial relations					○								○		
Industrial studies										●					
International business															
International relations/studies				○											
Languages for business	[●]							●	●				○		
Law	●		●	●	◉	●	●	◉	●	◉	●	●	◉	◉	●
Leisure studies									[●]						
Librarianship & information studies	●	●						○	●		●			●	
Manufacturing systems management															
Marketing			□	●	◉	◉				○		○			
Mathematics for business					□										
Nursing			●					●							●
Occupational hygiene															●
Office communication								●							
Operational research					○					○					
Organization studies								◉					◉		

● Degree in named areas of study
○ Chief study specialization
□ Higher national diploma in named area of study

London: Thames	Manchester	Middlesex	Newcastle upon Tyne	North East London	N. Staffordshire	Oxford	Plymouth	Portsmouth	Sheffield	Sunderland	Teesside	Trent	Wales	Wolverhampton	
[○]	[●]	●	[●]	[⊙]	◉	○	[●]	●	[●]	□	[○]	●	[⊙]	◉	Accountancy or Finance
														●	Agricultural marketing
	[●]		□	●		○				○	□				Business information technology
[●]	[●]	●	[⊙]	[●]	[●]	[●]	[●]	[⊙]	[●]	[⊙]	[●]	[●]	[●]	[●]	Business studies
							◉		●						Combined studies (Social sciences)
	●	○	[●]	○		○		●	[●]	[●]		●	●		Communication, Media or Visual studies
◉	◉	◉	◉	●	◉	○	◉	◉		◉		●		◉	Economics
●	●	◉	●			◉			●	◉		●		●	Education
○		●								○		●			European business
							◉								Fisheries studies
									●						Food marketing science
															Health studies
	[●]	[●]				◉		●	[●]			□			Hotel, catering and institutional management
															Industrial economics
		○							○						Industrial relations
									●			●			Industrial studies
●		●					●		●						International business
○			○		◉							○		◉	International relations/studies
○						●				○					Languages for business
	●	◉	●	●	●	○	○		●			●	●	●	Law
					○				●						Leisure studies
	●		●												Librarianship & information studies
				●											Manufacturing systems management
◉	●		□	○			●				[○]		□	◉	Marketing
		●								●					Mathematics for business
				○		●			●						Nursing
															Occupational hygiene
															Office communication
							◉				○				Operational research
															Organization studies

UK

Business, social and related professional studies

	Birmingham	Brighton	Bristol	Coventry	Hatfield	Huddersfield	Kingston	Lancashire	Leeds	Leicester	Liverpool	London: Central	London: City of	London: North	London: South Bank
Physiotherapy				●											
Political economy															
Politics or government	●		●○	○	●○	○	●○	●○	○	○	●○	○	●○	○	
Psychology				○	●○	○		●○			●○	○	●○		
Public or social administration		●□		○	●○	□		●○□	●○	●□		○			
Publishing															
Recreation management									○						
Retailing															
Secretarial studies													○		
Social policy				○	●○				●					●	
Social science/studies	○		●○	●	●		●	●○			○	●○	○	○	●
Society and technology															
Sociology	●	○	●○	○	○	○	●				●○	○	●○	●	
Speech therapy/pathology	●								●	●		●			
Transport and distribution						●									
Travel and tourism														●	
Women's studies												○			

Environmental studies

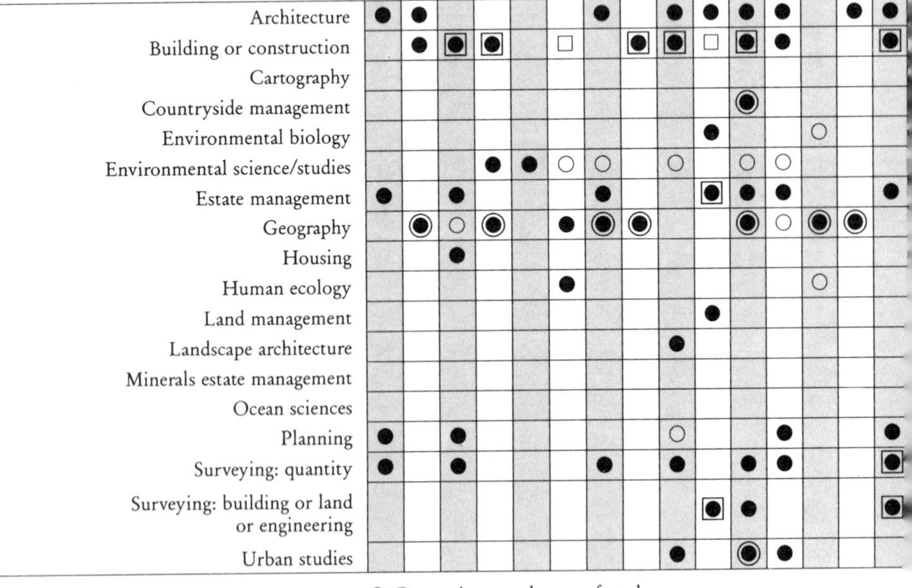

	Birmingham	Brighton	Bristol	Coventry	Hatfield	Huddersfield	Kingston	Lancashire	Leeds	Leicester	Liverpool	London: Central	London: City of	London: North	London: South Bank
Architecture	●	●					●		●	●	●	●		●	●
Building or construction		●	●□	●□		□		●□	●□	□	●□	●			●□
Cartography															
Countryside management											●○				
Environmental biology										●			○		
Environmental science/studies				●	●	○	○		○		○	○			
Estate management	●		●				●			●□	●	●			●
Geography		●○	○	●○		●	●○	●○			●○	○	●○	●○	
Housing			●												
Human ecology						●							○		
Land management										●					
Landscape architecture									●						
Minerals estate management															
Ocean sciences															
Planning	●		●						○			●			●
Surveying: quantity	●		●				●		●		●	●			●□
Surveying: building or land or engineering										●□	●				●□
Urban studies									●		●○	●			

● Degree in named areas of study
○ Chief study specialization
□ Higher national diploma in named area of study

UK

	London: Thames	Manchester	Middlesex	Newcastle upon Tyne	North East London	N. Staffordshire	Oxford	Plymouth	Portsmouth	Sheffield	Sunderland	Teesside	Trent	Wales	Wolverhampton
Physiotherapy					●					●		●			
Political economy	○														
Politics or government	◉	◉	○	○		○	○	◉	●		○	○	○		◉
Psychology		◉	◉	●	◉		○	◉	●		○			○	◉
Public or social administration		●	○	[●]				●	●	[●]		[⊙]	●	[●]	□
Publishing							○								
Recreation management						○				●					
Retailing		●													
Secretarial studies				●											
Social policy			●		○			●							
Social science/studies	○	◉	●	○	◉			○		●	◉	●	●	○	◉
Society and technology			◉		●										
Sociology	●	◉	◉	◉	◉	◉	○	◉	●		○	○		○	◉
Speech therapy/pathology		●													
Transport and distribution				□				◉							
Travel and tourism				●		○	○		○						
Women's studies			○		○										

	London: Thames	Manchester	Middlesex	Newcastle upon Tyne	North East London	N. Staffordshire	Oxford	Plymouth	Portsmouth	Sheffield	Sunderland	Teesside	Trent	Wales	Wolverhampton
Architecture	●	●			●		●	●	●						
Building or construction				[●]			[●]			[●]			[●]	[⊙]	□
Cartography							○								
Countryside management															
Environmental biology							●								
Environmental science/studies	●	◉		●			●	●			●				◉
Estate management	●			[●]	[●]		●		●	[●]			[●]	●	
Geography	○	○	◉	●		◉	○	◉	◉		○		○	○	◉
Housing										[●]					
Human ecology															
Land management									●						
Landscape architecture	●	●													
Minerals estate management										●					
Ocean sciences								◉							
Planning			●				◉								
Surveying: Quantity	●			●					●				[●]	●	
Surveying: building or land or engineering	●				[●]								□	□	
Urban studies									●	●				●	

UK

Engineering

	Birmingham	Brighton	Bristol	Coventry	Hatfield	Huddersfield	Kingston	Lancashire	Leeds	Leicester	Liverpool	London: Central	London: City of	London: North	London: South Bank
Aeronautical/Aerospace engineering			□		□●		□●								
Agricultural engineering															
Building services engineering				●											□●
Chemical engineering															□●
Civil engineering	□	●		●	□●		□●		□		□●	●			□●
Communication engineering	□		○						●		□			□⊙	
Computer-aided engineering						●		□			●	□			
Computer technology	□		○	□●								□			
Control engineering, instrumentation and systems			○	●		□●				○		●			
Electrical engineering	□	◉		□⊙	◉	□●			□		□●	●			□○
Electronic engineering	□●	◉	□○	□⊙	□⊙	□●	□⊙	□●	□●	□●	□●	●		□●	□○
Engineering	◉	●	□	●				□							
Engineering physics															
Engineering product design						□○		□							●
Engineering systems						●									
Engineering with business studies				●		○				●					
Environmental engineering															●
Industrial information technology	●							●							
Information systems	●		●	●		○	●		●						●
Information technology	□	□			□	□●	●	□	□	□●					●
Manufacturing engineering			□	◉	◉		□●		●		◉				
Marine engineering											○				
Mechanical engineering	□	◉	□	□⊙	□⊙	□●	□●	□●	□	□●	□●	□●			□●
Microelectronic engineering															
Microstructural engineering															
Mining engineering															
Naval architecture															
Plant engineering															
Production or industrial engineering	□	□⊙	□	□	◉			□	□	□●	□●				●

● Degree in named areas of study
○ Chief study specialization
□ Higher national diploma in named area of study

	London: Thames	Manchester	Middlesex	Newcastle upon Tyne	North East London	N. Staffordshire	Oxford	Plymouth	Portsmouth	Sheffield	Sunderland	Teesside	Trent	Wales	Wolverhampton
Aeronautical/Aerospace engineering															
Agricultural engineering															[●]
Building services engineering				[●]											●
Chemical engineering					●							[●]		[●]	
Civil engineering	[●]		●		[●]		[●]	[●]	[●]	[●]	●	[●]	[●]	[●]	
Communication engineering	●							[◉]	●		●				
Computer-aided engineering				□	[○]	[●]		●		□		□	●	□	
Computer technology	○	○		○		[●]						[●]			
Control engineering, instrumentation and systems					○	○				●	●	●			
Electrical engineering	[◉]	[◉]	□	[○]	[○]	[◉]	○	[◉]	[●]	□	[●]		[●]	[◉]	
Electronic engineering	[◉]	[◉]	[●]	[○]	[○]	[◉]	○	[◉]	[◉]	[○]	[●]		[●]	[◉]	
Engineering	[●]	(●)		●			[●]		●	[◉]		□			○
Engineering physics										●					
Engineering product design										●					
Engineering systems								●	●						
Engineering with business studies										●					
Environmental engineering				●											
Industrial information technology															
Information systems						●									
Information technology	[○]	●				[●]		●		[●]		□		●	□
Manufacturing engineering				●	○	□		●		(●)	●		●		○
Marine engineering								□							
Mechanical engineering	[◉]	[◉]	[●]	[●]	[●]	[●]	[○]	[●]	[●]	[◉]	[●]	●	[●]	[●]	[●]
Microelectronic engineering			●				○								
Microstructural engineering										●					
Mining engineering													□		
Naval architecture											□				
Plant engineering													●	□	
Production or industrial engineering		○	□	□	[●]		□	□	□	[●]	□		[●]	[●]	□

UK

Materials and Manufacturing technology

	Birmingham	Brighton	Bristol	Coventry	Hatfield	Huddersfield	Kingston	Lancashire	Leeds	Leicester	Liverpool	London: Central	London: City of	London: North	London: South Bank
Ceramic design or technology								□							
Food technology or marketing			□											⊡	⊡
Materials engineering															
Metallurgy															
Polymer or materials				◉	○									□	
Printing															
Textiles or clothing studies						⊡				▣					○

Multidisciplinary courses

	Birmingham	Brighton	Bristol	Coventry	Hatfield	Huddersfield	Kingston	Lancashire	Leeds	Leicester	Liverpool	London: Central	London: City of	London: North	London: South Bank
Combined studies (Arts)		●			●	●	●	●		●	●		○	●	
Combined studies (Sciences)		●		●	●		●	●		●	●	●	○	●	
Combined studies (Social sciences)			●		●		●	●			●	●	○	●	
Modular schemes (multidisciplinary)		△		△				△		△	△	△	△	△	
Dip HE (multidisciplinary)								▼			▼	▼	▼	▼	
Language and science/technology	●		●				●	◉							
Languages and Economics/Geography/Politics							●	◉	○						
Languages and Business studies	▣								●			○	▼		
Business studies and science/technology		●					●		□						

Multidisciplinary modular-degrees (△), Diplomas of higher education (▼) and combined studies courses generally include a range of main subject options (indicated among the symbols ○ and ● shown elsewhere in these charts). For details of the combinations offered, please contact individual polytechnics.

	London: Thames	Manchester	Middlesex	Newcastle upon Tyne	North East London	N. Staffordshire	Oxford	Plymouth	Portsmouth	Sheffield	Sunderland	Teesside	Trent	Wales	Wolverhampton
Ceramic design or technology						[⊙]									
Food technology or marketing		[●]		○						●					
Materials engineering										[●]					
Metallurgy		[○]								[●]					
Polymer or materials	●	[⊙]								[⊙]	[⊙]				◉
Printing		□											□		
Textiles or clothing studies		[●]		○	●							●	□		

	London: Thames	Manchester	Middlesex	Newcastle upon Tyne	North East London	N. Staffordshire	Oxford	Plymouth	Portsmouth	Sheffield	Sunderland	Teesside	Trent	Wales	Wolverhampton
Combined studies (Arts)			●	●		●					●		●	●	●
Combined studies (Sciences)		◉				●		◉	●	●	●		●	●	●
Combined studies (Social sciences)			●			●		◉		●					●
Modular schemes (multidisciplinary)			△	△	△		△	△							△
Dip HE (multidisciplinary)		▼	▼	▼	▼		▼	▼							▼
Language and science/technology						●					●				
Languages and Economics/Geography/Politics			●	●		●				●					
Languages and business studies	○		●								●			□	▼
Business studies and science/technology					●					●	●				

UK

Science and applied sciences

	Birmingham	Brighton	Bristol	Coventry	Hatfield	Huddersfield	Kingston	Lancashire	Leeds	Leicester	Liverpool	London: Central	London: City of	London: North	London: South Bank
Agriculture/Agricultural technology															
Anthropology															
Astronomy					○			◉							
Astrophysics								●							
Behavioural science/studies						●									
Biochemistry				◉	◉	○	○	◉			●	○		○	
Biology/Biological science		○	[⊙]	◉	◉		●	[⊙]		[○]	●	○	◉	◉	[●]
Biomedical science			○		○		○	●			●		○		
Biomolecular science															
Biophysical science							●								
Biotechnology			○		○		●			○		○			●
Chemistry		○	●	◉	[⊙]	[●]	[⊙]	[⊙]		[⊙]	●	○		◉	○
Cognitive science								●							
Combined studies (sciences)		●		●	●		●	●		●	●	●	○	●	
Computer science/studies	[●]	[⊙]	[○]	[●]	[⊙]	[⊙]	●	[⊙]	[●]	[⊙]	[⊙]	[⊙]	[⊙]	◉	[⊙]
Consumer studies															○
Dental technology															
Ecology					○	●							◉		
Electronics	□	○		●	[⊙]			◉		○	□				
Energy studies		○		○											
Engineering physics															
Environmental science/studies				●	●	●	○		○	◉	○	○			
Fisheries science															
Food science			□			○								○	[●]
General science			□									◉		●	
Geography		○	○	◉			●	○			◉	○	◉	○	
Geology					○		◉				○		◉	○	
Home economics									●		●			□	

London: Thames	Manchester	Middlesex	Newcastle upon Tyne	North East London	N. Staffordshire	Oxford	Plymouth	Portsmouth	Sheffield	Sunderland	Teesside	Trent	Wales	Wolverhampton	
							●							●	Agriculture/Agricultural technology
						○									Anthropology
							○								Astronomy
															Astrophysics
			○										●		Behavioural science/studies
○	○			◉									○	◉	Biochemistry
●	[⊙]		●	[⊙]	○	◉	[⊙]	◉	[○]	[⊙]		[⊙]	○	[⊙]	Biology/Biological science
									●						Biomedical science
								●							Biomolecular science
				●											Biophysical science
									●		○				Biotechnology
[●]	[⊙]		●	◉	[⊙]	○	◉	[⊙]	[●]	○	[●]	[⊙]	[⊙]	◉	Chemistry
															Cognitive science
	●				●		●	●		●		●	●	●	Combined studies (sciences)
[⊙]	[○]		[●]	[⊙]	[⊙]	[○]	[⊙]	[●]	[⊙]	[⊙]	[⊙]	[○]	[⊙]	[⊙]	Computer science/studies
			●												Consumer studies
	□														Dental technology
							●								Ecology
			●		●				□						Electronics
													○		Energy studies
									●						Engineering physics
●	○		●	◉		◉	●			●			○	◉	Environmental science/studies
							◉								Fisheries science
	[●]					○			○						Food science
		◉		●										○	General science
○	○	◉	●		●	○	◉	●							Geography
		○		◉	○	◉	◉	◉		◉			○		Geology
	●		●						□						Home economics

Science and applied siences

	Birmingham	Brighton	Bristol	Coventry	Hatfield	Huddersfield	Kingston	Lancashire	Leeds	Leicester	Liverpool	London: Central	London: City of	London: North	London: South Bank
Horticulture	□				●										
Hydrography															
Information systems	●	○		◉			◉		●						
Information technology		□	●		□	[⊙]	●	[●]	[○]	[⊙]		[○]	◉		
Marine biology															
Maritime or nautical studies											[●]				
Mathematics		◉		◉	◉		○	◉		◉	○	○	◉	◉	●
Mathematics for computing							●							●	
Mathematics, statistics and computing		◉	□	□	□		●	[⊙]	□	[○]	●	○	◉	[⊙]	
Medical laboratory science	□		[○]		○					○			○		
Microbiology			○		○							○			
Microelectronics		●					[○]					○			
Neuroscience								●					●		
Nutrition or dietetics						●			●					●	
Operational research				◉	○					○		○			
Pharmacy		●								●	●				
Pharmacology					○										
Photographic science/Graphics technology												●			
Physical science			□	[⊙]	◉		◉					○		○	[○]
Physics		○	●		○		[○]	[⊙]		○	●			○	○
Physiology				○	◉		●	◉				◉	◉		
Polymer or Materials science				●	○									□	
Psychology				○	◉	○		◉			◉	○	◉		
Sports science studies		●									●				
Statistics		○		◉	◉					○	○	○	◉	◉	
Systems analysis/modelling	●	○	●		○	◉	●						○	○	

	London: Thames	Manchester	Middlesex	Newcastle upon Tyne	North East London	N. Staffordshire	Oxford	Plymouth	Portsmouth	Sheffield	Sunderland	Teesside	Trent	Wales	Wolverhampton
Horticulture															
Hydrography								◉							
Information systems						●					●				
Information technology	[●]	●		□		●		●		[●]	●	[⊙]		●	□
Marine biology								●							
Maritime or nautical studies								[⊙]							
Mathematics	[⊙]	○	○	●	◉	○	○	◉	◉	○	◉	◉	○	◉	○
Mathematics for computing										●	●		●	●	
Mathematics, statistics and computing	[⊙]	□	○		◉		●	◉	□	□	●	□		[⊙]	◉
Medical laboratory science		□							●						
Microbiology							○	●							◉
Microelectronics							○			□					
Neuroscience															
Nutrition or dietetics							○								
Operational research						○		◉				●			
Pharmacy									●		●				
Pharmacology									●		●				
Photographic science/Graphics technology		○													
Physical science	[○]	□			◉	[○]	◉							[○]	[○]
Physics		○	○		○	[○]	○	○	●	[○]	◉		○	○	○
Physiology		◉	◉	●	●		●	◉	●		○			○	○
Polymer or Materials science	●	[⊙]				○				[⊙]	[⊙]				◉
Psychology		◉	○	●	◉		○	◉	●		○			○	◉
Sports science studies				●		●							●		
Statistics	○				◉	○		◉	○	●		○			○
Systems analysis/modelling	○					●			○	●		○			○

UK

The polytechnics

Courses and qualifications

First degree courses

Polytechnic degree courses (BA, B.Sc. B.Eng. M.Eng. LL B B.Ed.) lead to the awards of the Council for National Academic Awards (CNAA), a body required by its Charter to maintain standards equivalent to those in the universities. The full-time courses generally last three years; a further year is needed for sandwich courses.

The minimum level of attainment normally required for entry is equivalent to five passes in GCE/GCSE subjects including two at advanced level. Applicants with good BTEC qualifications or AS levels instead of A levels are welcomed. So too are Access course qualifiers and mature applicants who may not hold all or any of the qualifications usually required.

Higher national diplomas

HND courses combine a substantial academic content with an emphasis on one or more major areas of industrial, commercial or design activity. The full-time courses usually involve two years' study; those run on a sandwich basis last up to a year longer. Entry requirements normally include a GCE A level pass (or two AS level passes) or a BTEC National Diploma/Certificate or other equivalent qualification.

These awards can give exemption from parts of the qualifying examinations of professional bodies and, in some cases, advanced standing on first degree courses in related subjects.

Diplomas of higher education

Dip. H.E. courses enable students qualified to enter degree courses to achieve a terminal qualification after two years. Most courses include a number of subjects. Those gaining a Dip. H.E. may be able to proceed to a full degree and/or teaching qualification after one or two years of related study. In some cases the Dip. H.E. may coincide with the first two years of a degree course.

Degree equivalent courses

A number of polytechnic diplomas and the qualifying examinations of some professional bodies have national recognition as degree equivalent qualifications. Initial entry qualifications are generally comparable with those for degree courses. In this handbook such courses are not distinguished from those leading to degrees. Students are advised to ask polytechnics for details.

Teacher training

A substantial proportion of initial (and in-service) teacher training is undertaken in polytechnics.

Other courses and qualifications

Many other full-time and part-time courses are available leading to postgraduate awards, diplomas, certificates and a variety of professional qualifications. It is also possible to study full-time or part-time for taught Master's degrees and higher degrees by research. Polytechnic Academic Registrars or Information Officers will be pleased to provide further information on request.

3. Student statistics

Subjects of study in higher education of students from abroad in the UK, 1985-86

Subject	Universities	Public sector institutions	Total
Education	1 674	140	1 814
Medicine, health and dentistry	3 092	255	3 374
Engineering and technology	8 841	5 255	14 096
Agriculture, forestry and veterinary science	862	26	888
Science	6 242	1 415	7 657
Social, administrative and business studies	10 337	4 012	14 349
Professional and vocational studies	1 472	1 413	2 885
Language, literature and area studies	2 507	159	2 666
Arts, other than languages	1 850	987	2 837
Other subjects	2 573	326	2 899
Total	39 450	13 988	53 438

Source: Statistics of students from abroad in the United Kingdom 1985-86.

Students from the EC in higher education in universities and other public sector institutions, 1986-87

Country	Number of students
Belgium	346
Denmark	154
France	1 246
FR of Germany	2 028
Greece	2 231
Ireland	1 042
Italy	542
Luxembourg	105
The Netherlands	449
Portugal	197
Spain	433
	8 773

Source: Statistics of students from abroad in the United Kingdom 1986-87.

4. Bibliography

General

British qualifications. 19th ed., annual, 720 pp., Kogan Page, 1988, UKL 23.00, pbk UKL 17.50. Covers over 200 different professions and trades, listing what qualifications are available in each field, at all levels, with details of which university, polytechnic or professional body runs relevant courses.

Education Information Service sheets. Available free from British Council offices. They give information on all aspects of living and studying in Britain including information on: courses available in particular subject areas; entry requirements and how to apply; English language tests and training costs; sources of advice and help for students from overseas, etc.

Handbook of degree and advanced courses in colleges and departments of education 1989. Annual, 356 pp., National Association of Teachers in Further and Higher Education/Linneys ESL, 1988, UKL 9.00 (plus UKL 1.00 for overseas post). Directory covering mainly teacher training courses in colleges, universities and polytechnics.

Higher education in the United Kingdom 1989-90: Longman for the Association of Commonwealth Universities, 1988 UKL 13.25. A directory showing the range of higher education courses available at universities, polytechnics and colleges/institutions of higher education.

How to live in Britain 1989. The British Council's guide for overseas students and visitors, annual, 88 pp., Macmillan in association with the British Council, 1989, UKL 1.65. Provides basic information on such topics as immigration, customs, accommodation, prices, medical treatment, public services, and many other aspects of living in Britain.

International guide to qualifications in education. Mansell for the National Academic Recognition Information Centre, The British Council, 1987, UKL 65.00. Provides a summary of education systems and qualifications in over 140 countries, with brief notes on comparability to British qualifications.

Learn English in Britain with Arels-Felco 1989. Annual, 56 pp., Arels-Felco, 1988, free from British Council or British Tourist Authority offices or Arels-Felco, 2 Pontypool Place, Valentine Place, London SE1 8QF. Information on over 300 English language schools in Britain recognized by the British Council.

Statistics of overseas students in the UK, 1985-86. Annual, 48 pp., British Council, 1988, UKL 15.90. A reference guide to the number, countries of origin, subjects of study and location of overseas students in Britain.

Study abroad, 1987-88. 347 pp., Unesco, 1986, UKL 10.25. Gives details of opportunities for further study and training in all parts of the world, and possibilities of financial assistance.

Studying in Britain. British Council, free from the British Council offices. Leaflet describing types of qualifications, application procedures and living in Britain.

Publications mainly or wholly for undergraduate study

A compendium of advanced courses in colleges of further and higher education. Annual, 116 pp., London and South-Eastern Regional Advisory Council for Further Education, 1988, UKL 4.00. Information on all degree, BTEC, HND and other full-time and sandwich courses of equivalent standard offered at polytechnics and other public sector colleges.

Directory of first-degree and diploma of higher education courses 1988-89. Annual, 138 pp., Council for National Academic Awards, 1986, free. A guide to undergraduate and subdegree level courses at polytechnics and colleges leading to CNAA qualifications.

Directory of further education 1988/89. Annual, 944 pp., Hobsons Press for CRAC, 1988, UKL 49.95, Pbk UKL 44.00 A guide to long-term further education courses available at polytechnics and colleges of further and higher education.

Guide for applicants. Annual, 180 pp., Polytechnics Central Admissions System, free with application form.

Guide for young visitors to Britain. The Central Bureau, Seymour Mews, London W1H 9PE, 1989, UKL 2.45. Provides information on travel and accommodation around Britain, opportunities for study, work and leisure activities and sources of assistance.

Guide to the colleges and institutes of higher education 1989. Annual, 143 pp., The Standing Conference of Principals and Directors of Colleges and Institutes of Higher Education, 1988, free. Also a free leaflet 'The colleges and institutes of higher education' from the same address, listing courses available.

Handbook of the Scottish central institutions: courses, entry requirements. Annual, Paisley College of Technology on behalf of the Scottish Central Institutions, free.

How to apply for admission to a university. Annual, 312 pp., Universities Central Council on Admissions, free with application form.

Polytechnic courses handbook 1989/90: full-time and sandwich advanced courses England and Wales. Annual, 500 pp., the Committee of Directors of Polytechnics, 1988, UKL 9.55 (plus postage overseas). A brief description of each of the 30 polytechnics followed by information on courses.

The polytechnics — Autumn 1989: A guide to full-time and sandwich courses. Annual, the Committee of Directors of Polytechnics, free. A leaflet showing which HND, degree, degree equivalent, Diploma of higher education and teaching qualifications at polytechnics.

Scottish Universities Council on Entrance: Scottish universities entrance guide 1989. Annual, 64 pp., supplement 22 pp., UKL 1.50 each. UKL 2.00 for despatch overseas.

University entrance: the official guide, 1989. Annual, The Association of Commonwealth Universities 1988, UKL 9.95 (plus UKL 1.50 postage). Lists 9 000 courses and the subjects and grades needed for entry to them, and gives brief profiles of 82 universities and colleges.

Postgraduate study

British universities' guide to graduate study 1988-89. Annual, 308 pp., The Association of Commonwealth Universities, 1988, UKL 19.50 (UKL 25.00 by air mail). Covers taught courses lasting at least six months.

Directory of postgraduate and post experience courses 1988-89. Annual, Council for National Academic Awards, 1988, free. Lists courses at polytechnics and other public sector colleges, leading to CNAA qualifications.

Graduate studies 1988/89. Annual, 1 008 pp., Hobsons Press for CRAC, 1988, UKL 69.75. A detailed guide to research facilities and courses in the UK.

The grants register 1989-91. Biennial, 852 pp., Macmillan Press, 1988, UKL 65.00. Lists scholarships, fellowships, grants, etc., for students at or above graduate level.

5. Glossary

Bachelor's degree: See 'First degree'.

Campus university: The academic department is the main subdivision with which students identify themselves. The departments are usually grouped together within the same academic complex of buildings.

Central institutions: Higher education institutions in Scotland similar to polytechnics in England and Wales.

Certificate: A document in which success in an examination is formally attested.

College of further education: A college offering post-school education to those aged 16 and above from low-level technical courses and General Certificate of Education courses to BTEC courses. Some also offer degree courses.

College (or Institute) of higher education: A college offering teacher-training courses, undergraduate and postgraduate courses.

College of technology: In general another name for a college of further education.

Collegiate university: The university is subdivided into colleges with which the students identify themselves. All academic departments will usually be represented within each college.

Degree: Academic rank granted by a university or by the Council for National Academic Awards as guarantee of proficiency.

Diploma: Educational certificate attesting the recipient's proficiency.

Federal university: Consists of separate autonomous colleges. The university is the examining body.

First degree: A qualification awarded to an undergraduate after successfully completing a course in higher education at a university or polytechnic or similar institution: BA (Bachelor of Arts), MA (Master of Arts) in Scotland only, B. Ed. (Bachelor of Education), B. Sc. (Bachelor of Science).

GCE (General Certificate of Education): Advanced ('A') level. 'A' levels (normally 2-3) are taken at the age of 18 — two years after GCSE (see below), formerly GCE ordinary ('O') level. The usual minimum entry requirement for British universities is two or three 'A' levels.

GCSE (General Certificate of Secondary Education): Since the summer of 1988 the GCSE has replaced the GCE 'O' level school certificates taken at age 16 (see above).

Graduate: A person who holds an academic degree.

Higher degree: A qualification awarded to a graduate, or a student of equivalent status, after successfully completing an advanced study course either by research or by examination.

Local authority maintenance award: Grant given by local governments to students from the area to attend courses in higher education.

Master's degree: See 'Higher degree'.

Modular courses: Courses in which the course content consists of a number of units of work. Students have a wide, but not unlimited, choice of units which enable them to build up their own course based on interests, abilities and future requirements.

Occasional student: Student who wishes to attend a course of study without qualifying for a degree. The universities vary in their conditions for admitting occasional students.

Open University: The Open University provides tuition by correspondence for students living in Britain and for some students in Belgium (through the British Council). The tuition is supplemented by radio and television broadcasts, residential summer schools, and an extensive counselling and tutorial service operating through a network of local study centres in the United Kingdom.

Polytechnic: An institution of higher learning. Polytechnics offer degree courses and also non-degree courses. The courses are strongly vocational.

Postgraduate: A student who has obtained a first degree and is studying, or researching, for a higher degree or diploma.

Professional qualification: A qualification required before a person can be recognized as competent to practise a profession, e.g. in medicine, law, architecture, accountancy, engineering.

Sandwich course: Degree or diploma course in which periods of academic training at a university or polytechnic alternate with periods of industrial or commercial training. A sandwich course takes a year longer to complete than a full-time degree/diploma course.

Scottish Certificate of Education (SCE): The Scottish equivalent to the GCSE is the standard grade, formally the ordinary grade, and similarly the equivalent to 'A level' is the 'H' grade. The minimum entry requirements for Scottish universities is two 'O' grade passes with three at 'H' grade, or two at 'A' level.

Technical college: Another name for a college of further education.

Tutor: A college teacher who instructs by conference with a small group of students (tutorial); and/or a college teacher who has superivison of an undergraduate.

Undergraduate: A student who is studying for a first degree.

Vocational course: A course which provides the basic academic qualification for a clearly defined career, e. g. medicine, architecture, accountancy, engineering, business studies, teaching.

UK

6. Diagram of the education system

(England and Wales)

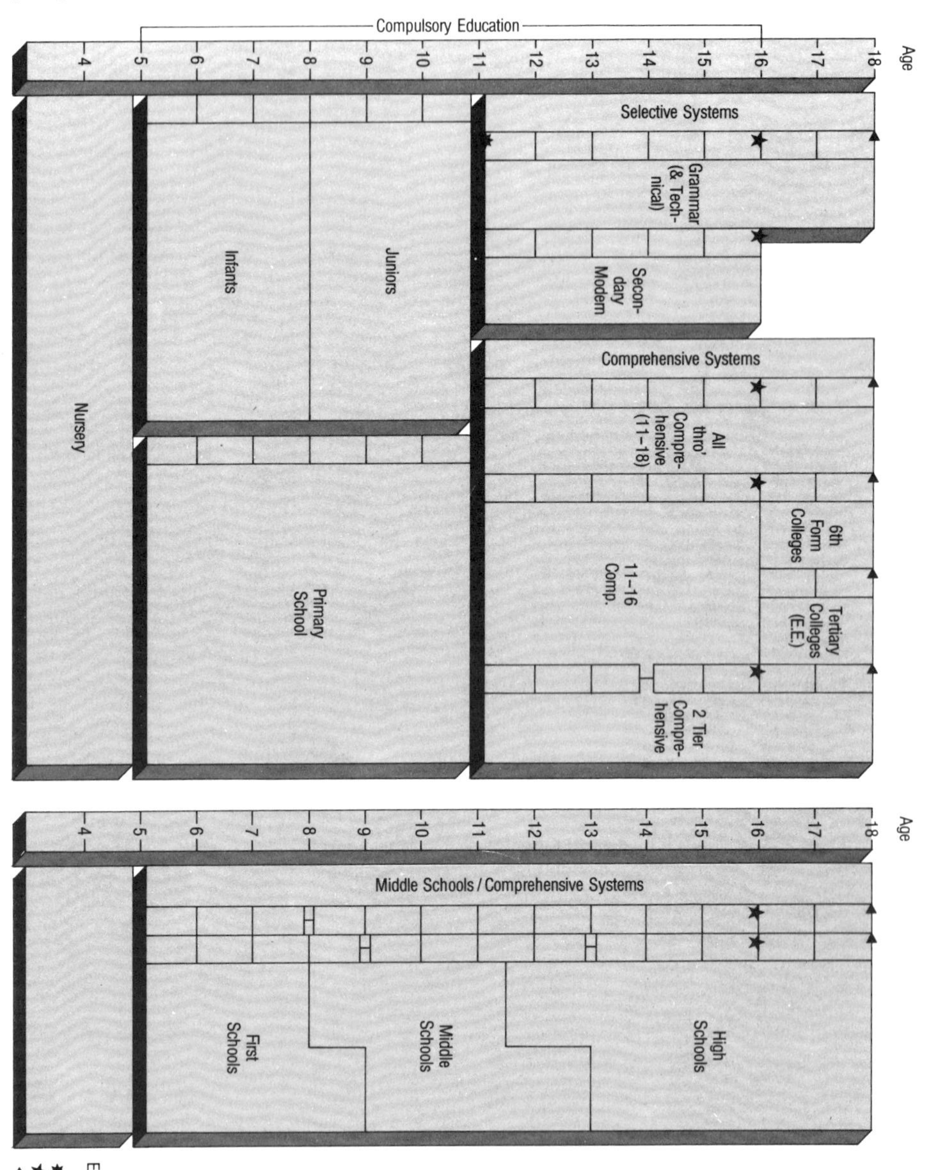
Compulsory Education
Age
4 5 6 7 8 9 10 11 12 13 14 15 16 17 18
Selective Systems
Grammar (& Technical)
Secondary Modern
Nursery
Infants
Juniors
Comprehensive Systems
All thro' Comprehensive (11–18)
11–16 Comp.
6th Form Colleges
Tertiary Colleges (F.E.)
2 Tier Comprehensive
Primary School
Middle Schools / Comprehensive Systems
First Schools
Middle Schools
High Schools
Examinations:
11 +
G.C.S.E.
G.C.E. A-Level

EUR

European University
Institute, Florence

European University Institute, Florence

On 19 April 1972 the Ministers of the six founding States of the European Community signed an agreement on the creation of a European University Institute. Later this agreement was acceded to by Denmark, the United Kingdom and Ireland. The Institute began its academic life in autumn 1976. Greece has been a member of the Institute since 1986, Spain since 1988; Portugal is to accede in the near future.

According to Article 2 of the Agreement it is the 'task of the Institute to contribute to the development of the cultural and scientific heritage of Europe in its unity and variety through activities in the fields of university teaching and research. The studies involve moreover the great revolutionary processes and institutions which characterize Europe in its history and development. They take into account connections with non-European cultures.

This task is fulfilled by teaching and research at university level.

The Institute is also intended to be a place for the meeting and exchange of ideas and experience concerning questions of its fields of study and research'.

The Institute provides research students with an opportunity to attain a doctorate (three-year programme), conferred by the European University Institute in the belowmentioned disciplines or a Master's degree (one-year programme) in comparative, European and international law (LL M).

From the 1989/90 academic year onwards, students will also be offered the opportunity to undertake a one-year course at the economics department to gain a Master's degree.

Organization of the Institute

The Institute is governed by three bodies, these being:

1. the High Council consisting of representatives of the governments of the Member States. It is responsible for the general orientation of the Institute.
2. the Principal, Emile Noël, who directs the Institute;
3. the Academic Council which is generally responsible for questions of teaching and research and, in this capacity, determines the teaching and research programme of the Institute. The Academic Council is composed of the Principal, the Secretary, the Librarian, the professors, representatives of the research fellows and junior research fellows and researchers.

Student statistics

In the last academic year, 230 research students were registered at the European University Institute. Of these, 21 came from countries which are not members of the Institute.

Academic organization

The Institute's specificity lies in the close links maintained between teaching and research, between individual and collective work. The Institute pursues a number of research projects — comparative and interdisciplinary in nature — directed by professors aided by assistants and research fellows. These teams provide a supportive framework for research students coming to the Institute. Work is organized so as to enable research students to produce a doctoral thesis through participation in the research projects.

This organization enables those who come to the Institute to draw the maximum benefit from the Institute's character as a forum for the exchange and discussion of ideas and experience, where high-level researchers from different disciplines, cultures and academic traditions work together on some of the major themes of Europe's past, present and future.

Research students are excellently supported through the favourable ratio of teaching staff to students (27 full-time professors, nine external professors and 10 part-time teaching staff in the 1988/89 academic year). This means that each professor is responsible for the supervision of only a limited number of theses and is thus able to follow the work of the research students very closely.

Secondly, the Institute aims at encouraging the widest possible circulation of ideas within the Institute. The organization of seminars described below is designed to promote exchange of ideas and information on work in progress, and to avoid both the individual isolation of research students and the compartmentalization of the disciplines.

Contacts with the academic world are systematically promoted by bringing large numbers of visiting professors to the Institute. Colloquia held by the Institute provide an opportunity to invite outstanding experts in the social sciences and humanities.

Research students must attend two types of seminar. These are the project seminars for discussing progress on research projects and project-related theses, and the departmental seminars to enable all members of a department to keep informed on the research projects in hand and to exchange views in general. They are weekly, like the project seminars.

Students may also attend project seminars other than those for which they are normally registered.

The teaching and research programme
(as of 1988/89 academic year)

This programme is divided into the four departments of History and Cultural History, Economics, Law, and Political and Social Sciences.

The European Policy Unit is a forum for the critical consideration and discussion of topical political issues within the EC. This is achieved by means of international conferences and workshops and by the assignment of research projects.

The European Cultural Unit concerns itself with European culture and identity issues, taking into account common tradition and national differences. The European Cultural Unit also compares Europe's culture with non-European cultures. The European Policy Unit and the European Cultural Unit work in a similar fashion.

History and Cultural History

Teaching and research in the Department of History and Cultural History are oriented primarily towards:

1. comparative economic, social and cultural history of early contemporary and contemporary Europe;
2. the history of international relations and a comparison of the development of political and social systems in Europe with special attention to European cooperation and integration after the Second World War.

The key research areas within this context are the history of the European Communities, the emergence of industrial society in Western Europe (sixteenth to twentieth centuries), the cultural history of Europe for the same period as well as the largely interdisciplinary field of 'Population, family and society'.

Economics

In the Economics Department, at which it is also possible to gain a British Master's degree (introduced in the last academic year), the research projects are concentrated around the following topic complexes: microeconomic theory and analysis; macroeconomics and economic policy; planned-economy systems and econometry, in all cases with special regard to developments within the EC and OECD.

Law

Research in the Law Department is characterized by three main features; these are (a) Europe-orientated study, which is (b) comparative in approach, and (c) uses contextual methods of research.

After one year of study, students may be awarded a Master's degree in Comparative European and International Law (LL M), which is comparable to the British LL M. Moreover, a doctorate may also be gained after a three-year programme. The requirements for both degrees are theses based on independent research work.

The main research topics in this department are European Community law, its interrelations to European Council law and to European economic law; the law of nations and comparative law; theory of law and interdisciplinary approaches, especially with regard to the various legal traditions within Europe.

Political and Social Science

The teaching and research programme includes political science, sociology, political philosophy and the history of ideas.

Through its work on democratic governmental processes, on European integration, on socio-economic policy and on the history of political ideas, this department forms a link to the research activity of the other departments.

Prospective students who over and above of their political and social science knowledge also have economic knowledge or knowledge in history and social psychology have an especially good chance of being accepted.

The key focuses in the research projects are: social and political theory, especially of the nineteenth and twentieth centuries; social groups and socio-political structures; economic and social policy; European integration and international relations.

Research Group into European Policy

This research group, founded in 1984, is intensively concerned with European questions related to the development of the European Communities. It has an interdisciplinary orientation and has already established the first chair for Community questions (the Jean Monnet Chair) and has Jean Monnet scholarship holders among its members of staff. In the meantime, several specialist groups have been formed for specific question complexes: environmental questions, regional questions, questions of technological development. A database on European cooperation which has been established with the support of the EC Commission facilitates the research work.

Centre for European Cultural Research

The centre was founded in 1987 in order to provide interdisciplinary coordination for research work on cultural questions carried out at the Institute. This research is into contemporary European culture as well as into the cultural past. Research proposals from scientists from outside the Institute may also be accepted. Such scientists are then recommended to apply for a Jean Monnet scholarship. The main activity at the centre involves the organization of conferences and seminars with which the Institute is increasingly establishing itself as a debating forum for questions of European culture.

Admission and registration

The following may apply:

1. research students who wish to write their thesis and gain a doctorate at the Institute within the context of a three-year study period;
2. research students who have started a thesis at their home university and who wish to submit this there after a one- to two-year stay at the Institute. (Appropriately qualified students may be admitted directly to the second year);
3. The Institute accepts jurists and economic scientists who wish to gain a Master's degree within one year under the same conditions.

Within the framework of the EC Erasmus programme (as of 1988), there are cooperation agreements with several universities in force which are primarily intended to make the awarding of joint doctorates possible. Such agreements have been signed with: the University of Parix X-Nanterre, the University of Lille II and the Ecole des hautes études en sciences sociales in Paris; the London School of Economics; the Hochschule Lüneburg.

Entry requirements

The Institute accepts research students who are citizens of an EC Member State with which there is an agreement in force according to which the respective State guarantees to provide a scholarship to higher education graduates from their countries who have been admitted to the Institute. The Institute may also admit students from other countries.

For admission the following minimum requirements generally apply:

(a) students from Belgium who have the *licence/licentiaat (cum laude);*
(b) students from the Federal Republic of Germany who have completed university study and who fulfil the requirements for admission to a doctoral programme;
(c) students from Denmark who have the *kandidateksamen;*
(d) students from France who have the *maîtrise* or a corresponding degree *(cum laude)*;
(e) students from Greece who have the *ptychio;*
(f) students from Italy who have the *laurea cum laude* and if possible a certificate of supplementary studies;
(g) students from the Netherlands who have the *doctoraal examen;*
(h) students from Portugal who have the *licença;*
(i) students from Spain who have the *licencia;*
(j) students from the United Kingdom and the Republic of Ireland who have a good honours degree (at least, upper second);
(k) students from other countries (especially Austria) who have a degree equivalent to the above or proof of the qualifications required for a doctoral programme.

Any additional qualification or research experience or professional experience may constitute an advantage.

Candidates must also have a thorough spoken and written knowledge of at least two official languages of the Institute (Danish, Dutch, English, French, German, Italian, Greek).

The majority of seminars at the Institute are held in English or French.

It should be noted that the Admissions Board will take account not only of the quality of candidates' previous work, but also of the extent to which their proposed research themes fit in with the Institute's ongoing teaching and research programmes.

Admissions procedure

Interested candidates in possession of the required qualifications should ask the Academic Service of the European University Institute for an application form. This form should be filled in and posted by 31 January by registered express mail.

The departments require applicants to enclose a summary of their research topic in one of the main Institute languages with their documents. For the economics department the chosen language should be English.

Applications are first examined by national selection committees, on which Institute professors also sit. Candidates remaining after this preliminary selection are invited to an interview with department members, normally in mid-April. The list of those admitted is decided by the end of April by an Admissions Board appointed by the Academic Council, made up of the Principal, one member of each department and one research student representative.

Admission is given for one year only, advancement to the second and third years following the rules described below.

On 15 June, first-year students must submit to their departments a substantial paper related to their research subject. This may also be a detailed outline or a chapter of their thesis.

Acceptance for a second year is decided by the department upon the basis of this paper. This acceptance constitutes admission to studies leading to the doctorate and implies an extension of grant.

As mentioned above, appropriately qualified research students who have already started their doctoral thesis at their home university may be admitted directly to the second year at the Institute.

Admission to the third year is granted by the Admissions Board on the basis of a certification submitted by the dissertation adviser to the effect that the student's work is progressing satisfactorily.

The doctoral thesis is generally concluded at the end of the third year or within a reasonable period of time thereafter. Third-year research students are provided a scholarship by the Institute.

To defend a thesis, a research student must have spent at least two years at the Institute and played an active part in the seminars relating to his research work. Theses are defended at the Institute before an international examining board appointed by the Academic Council on the proposal of the department concerned. The examining board has from three to five members.

The doctorate is awarded in the following forms:

1. Doctor of the European University Institute in History and Cultural History;
2. Doctor of the European University Institute in Economics;
3. Doctor of the European University Institute in Law;
4. Doctor of the European University Institute in Political and Social Sciences.

Exceptionally, research students may be permitted to defend their thesis at another university.

The Institute is endeavouring to conclude cooperation agreements with a number of universities which may enable doctorates to be conferred jointly by both institutions or only by one of the two (in such cases it is noted that the doctoral studies were partially completed at the other institution of higher education).

Information on the terms of recognition of European University Institute doctorates in the various Member States is obtainable from the Institute's Academic Service.

Tuition fees

No tuition fees are charged.

Linguistic assistance

The Institute offers research students assistance in improving their oral and written knowledge of languages. They are aided as far as possible in writing papers and particularly their theses when these are in a language other than their own.

The language teachers at the Institute — exclusively native speakers — offer German, English, French, Italian and Spanish courses throughout the whole academic year. For new research students, crash courses in English, French and Italian are held in September.

Library

The library is fully computerized, with easily accessible bibliographic and administrative databases. This gives users optimum access to books and documentation needed.

The stock is currently some 300 000 volumes, including microforms. Some 3 000 periodicals are received. Service is extended through inter-library loans.

Computing for quantitative research

The Institute has a high-power PRIME 9955II computer for researchers wishing to do quantitative research. Methodological and technical assistance is also provided.

A considerable range of software and a word-processing system are also available.

The Institute has access to the most important databases of the European Communities, of the International Monetary Fund as well as other international data collections, for example, the Eurobarometer and the ICPSR database at the University of Michigan.

Financial assistance and scholarships

Students admitted to the Institute normally receive grants from their governments. In September 1989 the individual countries granted the following amount of assistance per month:

Belgium:	BFR 26 350
FR of Germany:	DM 1 559
France:	FF 5 000
Greece:	DR 75 000
Ireland:	LIT 800 000
Italy:	LIT 900 000
Luxemburg:	LFR 27 500
The Netherlands:	HFL 1 580
Portugal (through INIC):	ESC 100 000
Spain:	PTA 100 000
United Kingdom:	LIT 1 000 000

Danish research students receive financial support from their government in the form of a salary.

In general German applicants for scholarships must fulfil requirements for DAAD graduate scholarships. Information, including on exceptions, available from: DAAD, Referat 213, Kennedyallee 50, D-5300 Bonn 2.

These government scholarships are normally adjusted annually and are supplemented through extra allowances (family allowances, health and accident insurance, travel expense payments). They are awarded for the first and second academic years. In the third year, the research students are financed through the Institute. In 1988/89 they received a monthly amount of LIT 1.1 million, in addition to the abovementioned allowances.

Austrian research students who are admitted to the Institute also receive a scholarship from their government.

Jean Monnet Research Scholarships:
These scholarships are awarded after a special selection procedure. The closing date for applications is the end of November each year; the scholarships begin on 1 September of the following year. Thirty Jean Monnet scholarships are awarded annually by the Institute itself without participation of the individual State scholarship offices. They are limited to 12 months. Of these scholarships, several are also awarded to researchers coming from non-member States.

Entry and residence regulations

Concerning entry, see the section 'Italy'.

The Italian Ministry of Foreign Affairs issues a special residence permit for the duration of the period of study.

Research students should request information on all other formalities from the Institute.

Social aspects

Belgian, British, German, Irish, Italian and Spanish research students receiving a scholarship from their governments are automatically insured against illness and accidents. Others must conclude an insurance themselves for the first two years of their stay at the Institute. There is an opportunity to join a group insurance. In 1988 the monthly premium amounted to LIT 22 000.

The European University Institute is located at Badia Fiesolana in San Domenico near Florence. The Institute's reception office provides assistance to research students in finding accommodation, i.e. following provisional accommodation during the first month, students may be accommodated either in one of the apartments belonging to the Institute (73 beds) or in an apartment of their choice. Students in the first year or with dependants are given preferential treatment for the Institute's accommodation.

For the children of research students and of the staff there is a day nursery in which small children may be cared for all day and school children in the afternoon.

The Institute operates a self-service canteen at lunchtime in which research students receive reduced rates. There is also a cafeteria, a television and community room, a reading room and a bar.

Sources of information

For any further information concerning its programme or admission requirements, interested students should apply to the academic service of the Institute.

EUR

Appendices

1. Addresses

European University Institute
Academic Service
Badia Fiesolana
5 via dei Roccettini
I-50016 San Domenico di Fiesole (Firenze)
Postbox: Istituto Universitario Europeo CP No 2330
I-50100 Firenze, Ferrovia
☎ (055) 509 21/509 23 38
Telex 571528 IUE
Fax 599 887

National authorities

Belgium
Ministère de l'éducation nationale et de la culture française
Direction de l'enseignement supérieur et de la recherche scientifique
Cité administrative de l'État
Bloc D - 6e étage
B-1010 Bruxelles

Ministerie van Nationale Opvoeding en Nederlandse Cultuur
Bestuur van het Hoger Onderwijs en het Wetenschappelijk Onderzoek
Manhattan Center
Toren 2
Kruisvaartenstraat 2
B-1210 Brussel

Denmark
Rektorkollegiet
Frederiksholmskanal 26
DK-1220 København K

Federal Republic of Germany
Deutscher Akademischer Austauschdienst

(DAAD) Ref. 313
Kennedyallee 50
D-5300 Bonn 2

Greece
National Scholarship Foundation
Lysikratous 14
GR-10668 Athens

Spain
Ministerio Asuntos Exteriores
D.G. de Relaciones Culturales
Dir. de Intercambios y Becas
Calle José Abascal, 41
E-28003 Madrid

France
Ministère des affaires étrangères
Direction générale des relations culturelles
Formation des Français à l'étranger
6, rue Marignan
F-75008 Paris

Ireland
Department of Education
Irish Life Centre
Lower Abbey Street
Dublin 1

Italy
Ministero degli Affari Esteri
Dir. gen. della cooperazione culturale
Ufficio IX
I-Roma

Academic Service of the European University Institute (for address see left-hand column)

Luxembourg
Ministère de l'éducation nationale
Centre de psychologie et d'orientation scolaires
29 rue Aldringen
L-1118 Luxembourg

The Netherlands
Ministerie van Onderwijs en Wetenschappen
Europaweg 4
Postbus 250 000
2700 LZ Zoetermeer

Portugal
Instituto Nacional de Investigacão Científica (INIC)
Av. Elias Garcia 137-6°
P-1093 Lisboa

United Kingdom
Department of Education and Science
HFE3 Branch
Elizabeth House
York Road
London SE1 7HP

2. Bibliography

European University Institute, 1989/90 academic year. Florence, 1989. Leaflet; available free of charge from the European University Institute (English, French).

European University Institute, 1989/90 academic year. Information brochure; 87 pp., available free of charge from EUI or the above addresses (Dutch, English, French, German, Italian and Spanish).

EUR

College of Europe,
Bruges

College of Europe, Bruges

The College of Europe, founded in 1949, is the oldest institution of European studies. It offers university graduates a one-year graduate programme on questions relating to the European process of integration and to the further development of the European Community. Thus it prepares them to tackle the economic, legal, political and social questions, not at the level of a single country but at the level of the European Community, seen as a regional entity open to the rest of the world.

Structure

The College of Europe is governed by an Administrative Council composed of representatives of the 12 States as well as of a number of public and private institutions — e.g. the Commission of the European Communities — that contribute to the budget. This Council is presided over by the Belgian Minister for Education, Mr Daniël Coens.

The Academic Council, which determines the basic orientations of the study and research programme, is composed of professors and elected representatives of the students and former students. Its President is Professor Jerzy Lukaszewski, the Rector of the College of Europe.

Students

The College of Europe merits its name not only because of the orientation of its programme but also because of the highly plurinational composition of its student body. At least 20 different nationalities are represented among the 200 university graduates in law, economics or political science that the College admits each year. These graduates thus have the opportunity to gain experience in plurinational team work and to acquire a solid preparation for a future activity in a European or international field.

Teaching staff

As in most institutions of higher education of its sort, the College of Europe has no permanent professorial staff. Teaching is performed by some 50 lecturers who come from outside at regular intervals. Two-thirds of these lecturers are university professors who provide the College with an indispensable link to the academic world and with the developments in social sciences. The other third is composed of senior officials of the European Community who offer courses close to the economic, legal and political realities of contemporary Europe and refer frequently to the practice of Community organs. The university professors and senior officials who teach at the College of Europe come from at least 10 different nationalities. Thus the students have the possibility to experience different university traditions and methodological approaches.

Programme of studies

The programme of the College of Europe, intentionally limited to one academic year, is condensed and demanding. It prepares students for a life of action and takes its inspiration from Jean Monnet's maxim: 'At a very early age I realized — and this has become the rule for my conduct — that reflection and action are indivisible'. It is constructed in such a way as to, on the one hand, respond to the professional objectives of the students and, on the other hand, to their need for learning and enlarging their intellectual horizons. It consists of:

1. **Specialized studies** in three fields, each of them forming a coherent body of several subjects:
   (a) European administrative studies;
   (b) European economic studies;
   (c) European legal studies.
   Each student chooses one of these three fields according to his or her previous studies.
2. In addition, he or she takes three lecture courses in: **Optional studies.** In this part the student may, according to his or her preference, either opt for courses linked with his or her specialization or for others which place the specialization in a pluridisciplinary context.
3. **Conferences or lectures,** given by prominent personalities in public life pertaining to topical European issues. (A detailed description of the programme may be found in the information brochure of the College, see appendices.)

Teaching methods

In addition to classical lectures, research-orientated seminars, interdisciplinary courses, for example, in human rights, Eastern Europe, defence policy or social policy in the European Community and finally planning exercises are held at the College of Europe from the second semester onwards. It is above all the latter that are especially popular and successful, since these are practice-orientated and so effectively prepare participants for their future professional activity.

Working languages

The two working languages of the College are English and French. Professors choose in which of these two languages they wish to hold their courses and lectures. For examinations, written work and contributions in the working groups, the students may choose one of these two languages. A very good knowledge of the language(s) is therefore an indispensable condition for successful participation at the College of Europe.

Degrees

All students take at least nine examinations. If they pass, they are awarded the Diploma of Advanced European Studies/*Diplôme des hautes études européennes*.

Students who receive this Diploma/*Diplôme* and who have furthermore carried out research work in line with the regulations laid down by the Academic Council and who have written a thesis/*thèse* which was found to be satisfactory by jury receive the Degree of Master of European Studies/ *Diplôme d'études européennes approfondies*.

Library and publications

The library at the College of Europe contains more than 100 000 volumes directly accessible to users. Its collection of books, documents and journals is one of the most voluminous in the world in the field of European integration.

The College of Europe has published more than 50 works covering various aspects of European integration. These works represent, on the one hand, a valuable aid for teaching and, on the other hand, a sum of knowledge and reflection, of great importance for all researchers in European matters.

Admission

Every candidate applying for admission to the College of Europe must have a university degree or its equivalent (for example, a *maîtrise* in the French system or a BA in the Anglo-Saxon system) in economics, law, political science or public administration, and have a good knowledge of English and French.

Applications for admission, and possibly scholarships, should be sent to one of the Selection Committees (see appendices), before the set closing date. Candidates coming from countries where there is no Selection Committee generally apply directly to the College of Europe. Similarly, candidates who wish to study there at their own expense should first contact the Rector's office at the College of Europe prior to 31 March. In some countries, their selection is in each case undertaken by the relevant Selection Committee.

Tuition fees

The total cost for the academic year at the College of Europe is BFR 235 000. This sum includes fees, accommodation, including food (full board and lodging) in a students' hall of residence. Students who wish to live outside the College pay BFR 115 000.

Scholarships

Most of the students at the College of Europe receive scholarships awarded by their governments or by other public or private institutions. Applications for these scholarships must be sent to the national Selection Committee in the student's country (see appendices).

Student residences

Almost all students live and take meals in the College residences. In this way they have an opportunity to rapidly improve their linguistic skills and

EUR

accustom themselves to working in plurinational teams.

Other aspects

For further information on the social and practical aspects of living and studying in Belgium, refer to the section 'Belgium' included in this edition of the *Student Handbook*.

Appendices

1. Addresses

College of Europe

Rectorate of the College of Europe
Dyver 11
B-8000 Brugge

Selection Committees

Belgium
Rectorate of the College of Europe
Dyver 11
B-8000 Brugge

Denmark
Den Danske Europabevægelse
Bremerholm 6
DK-1069 København K

Federal Republic of Germany
Deutscher Rat der Europäischen Bewegung
Bachstraße 32
Postfach 1529
D-5300 Bonn 1

Fritz Thyssen Stiftung
Am Römerturm 3
Postfach 18 03 46
D-5000 Köln 1

Spain
Ministerio de Asuntos Exteriores
Dirección General de Relaciones Culturales
Dirección de Intercambios
Calle José Abascal 41
E-28071 Madrid

Caja de Ahorros y Monte de Piedad de Zaragoza, Aragón y Rioja
Plaza de Paraiso 2
E-50008 Zaragoza

Comunidad Autónoma de la Región de Murcia
Gabinete de la Presidencia
Secretariado para Asuntos relacionados con las Comunidades Europeas
Palacio de San Esteban
E-3005 Murcia

Diputación Regional de Bizkaia
Asuntos relacionados con las Comunidades Economicas Europeas
Gran Via 19-21
E-48001 Bilbao

Diputación Regional de Cantabria
Consejería de la Presidencia
Oficina de Asuntos de la CC.EE.
Calle Casimiro Sainz 4
E-39003 Santander

Gobierno de Canarias
Avenida de Juan XXIII 2
E-Las Palmas de Gran Canaria

Gobierno Vasco
Departamento de Educación, Universidades e Investigación
Avda. Duque de Wellington 2
E-01011 Vitoria-Gasteiz

Junta de Andalucia
Gabinete de la Presidencia
Monsalves 8
E-Sevilla-1

Patronat Català pro Europa
BRUC, 50, 2n
E-08010 Barcelona

Principado de Asturias
Consejería de la Presidencia
Marqués de Pidal 9-2°
E-33004 Oviedo

Real Sociedad Economica Aragonesa de Amigos del País
San Jorge 9
E-50001 Zaragoza

Xunta de Galicia
Consellería de Educacion e Ordenación Universitaria
Edificio Administrativo San Gaetano
E-Santiago de Compostela

France
Ministère des affaires étrangères
Division de la formation des français à l'étranger
6, rue de Marignan
F-75008 Paris

Ireland
Irish Council of the European Movement
32 Nassau Street
Dublin 2

Italy
Ministero degli affari esteri
Direzione generale delle relazioni culturali
Ufficio IX
I-00195 Roma

Luxembourg
Mouvement Européen du Luxembourg
Maison de Cassal
5, rue Large
L-1917 Luxembourg

Malta
Mid-Med Bank Ltd
233, Republic Street
MW-Valletta

The University of Malta
MW-Msida

The Netherlands
Nuffic
Postbus 90734
2509 LS 's-Gravenhage

Portugal
Ministério dos Negócios Estrangeiros
Direcção-Geral das Relaçoes Culturais Externas
Largo do Rilvas
P-1354 Lisboa Codex

Fundação Calouste Gulbenkian
Serviço Internacional
Avenida de Berna 45-A
P-1093 Lisboa Codex

United Kingdom
UK Committee for the College of Europe
UACES Secretariat
King's College
Strand
London WC2R 2LS

Canada
Public Service Commission
300 Avenue Laurier ouest
Ottawa, Ontario K1A OM7
(only for Federal public servants)

Norway
NAVF
Sandakerveien 99
N-0483 Oslo 4

Austria
Bundesministerium für Wissenschaft und Forschung
Minoritenplatz 5
A-1014 Wien

Sweden
Svenska Nationalkommittén för Kulturellt Samarbete i Europa
Sverigehuset
Hamngatan 27
Box 7044
S-10386 Stockholm

or

Svenska Institutet
(same address)

Switzerland
Union européenne
Beaulieustraße 78
Postfach 215
CH-3000 Bern 26

USA
Fulbright grants:
The Institute of International Education
809 United Nations Plaza
New York, NY 10017

2. Bibliography

College of Europe/Collège d'Europe. Bruges, 1989/90. Information brochure, free from College of Europe.

J. Lukaszewski: **Former des Européens pour bâtir l'Europe — L'expérience du Collège d'Europe.** Cadmos (Genève) 1979.

EUR

Erasmus
The European Community
action scheme
for the mobility
of university students

Erasmus

Erasmus — the European Community action scheme for the mobility of university students — was adopted by the Council of the European Communities on 15 June 1987. Deriving its name from Erasmus of Rotterdam, a personalized symbol of European humanism whose teaching and learning were carried out in several different European countries, the Erasmus programme was established with the following main objectives in view:

(i) to increase substantially the number of students undertaking an integrated period of study in another Member State, thereby creating an enhanced supply of graduate manpower with direct experience of the economic and social life of other Member States;

(ii) to promote wide-ranging and intensive cooperation between the higher education institutions in all Member States;

(iii) to promote the mobility of teaching staff, as a means of enhancing the international potential of the universities and improving the quality of training provided with a view to supporting the competitiveness of the Community in the world market;

(iv) to strengthen the interaction between citizens in different Member States with a view to consolidating the concept of a people's Europe.

The programme provides funding for a wide range of cooperative activities:

1. Firstly, Erasmus provides grants to universities, which in this context refers to all types of higher education institutions as defined nationally, for the purpose of designing, developing, operating, maintaining and evaluating programmes for the mobility of students and/or teaching staff. The totality of the programmes thus supported forms what is known as the European University Network. The emphasis is on programmes which enable students to spend a period of up to one year in another Community country for which they receive full academic credit from their home university. Tuition fees are mutually waived. In the case of the staff mobility programmes, preference is given to arrangements whereby the visiting staff members provide integrated teaching input of significant duration (at least one month) into the programmes of the host institution.

In addition, universities may receive support for the joint development of new curricula and for carrying out intensive programmes of short duration involving students and teaching staff from several Community countries. All four types of programmes are collectively known as Inter-university cooperation programmes (ICPs).

2. Secondly — and this is the element of Erasmus which gives the programme both its title and its main focus — Erasmus provides mobility grants to students in the form of top-up grants to help cover the additional costs incurred by students wishing to study for fully recognized periods of three months to one year in another Community country. These costs include such items as language

preparation, cost-of-living differential and, of course, travel. The average target grant Community-wide is around ECU 2 000 for a full year's study, and students of all levels (up to the doctorate) are eligible, though grants are not normally awarded to students in their first year of higher education. Priority is given to students moving to another EC country within the framework of ICPs supported under Erasmus.

Thirdly, the Erasmus programme seeks to promote a number of measures designed to improve the possibilities for students to receive academic recognition or credit for study periods effected and qualifications obtained in other Member States. A network of nationally based information centres on the assessment of foreign educational credentials has been established for this purpose (National academic recognition centres, or Naric). Moreover, from 1989/90 onwards the pilot phase of the European Community course credit transfer system (ECTS), which will span a six-year period, will be started. Within ECTS automatic credit transfer arrangements will be progressively introduced in five subject areas (mechanical engineering, medicine, chemistry, business studies and history) between the total of some 80 institutions which will form the core of the pilot project.

3. Finally, the programme encompasses a number of complementary measures designed to assist in creating a favourable climate for the future development of Erasmus. These include in particular a study-visit scheme to enable university teachers and administrators to visit other Community countries for the purpose of preparing future exchange programmes, to carry out brief teaching assignments or merely to familiarize themselves with aspects of the higher education system in the countries visited. Support is also provided for specific projects of university associations and consortia operating at European level, for the preparation of publications related to university cooperation, and for various information activities.

The Commission of the European Communities is assisted in the implementation of the Erasmus programme by a number of bodies. At the level of overall policy, there is the Erasmus advisory committee, a consultative mechanism chaired by the Commission but consisting of two members from each Member State, one of whom is in all cases a senior academic in order to ensure direct feedback from the academic community. The operational aspects of the programme are handled on the Commission's behalf by the Erasmus Bureau, an external non-profit-making agency, while the student grants scheme within Erasmus is administered on a decentralized basis by nationally designated agencies, coordinated in Brussels and working according to jointly agreed guidelines.

Particularly important with regard to Erasmus is its comprehensive nature: it embraces all 12 Member States of the European Community with a potential student target population of well over six million. It is open to all types of higher education institutions, all academic disciplines and levels of study and provides support for a number of different types of cooperation activity. It is also by far the biggest programme for inter-university co-operation and exchange ever launched at a European level with a budget of ECU 52.5 million in 1989/90.

The response to Erasmus in the academic community has been enormous: already in 1988/89, only the second academic year of operation of the programme, Erasmus is supporting:

(a) 1 091 inter-university cooperation projects, of which 948 involve an integrated exchange of students and 234 an integrated exchange of teaching staff;
(b) 13 000 students;
(c) 2 611 teaching staff members and administrators (within 1 267 'visit' projects) carrying out — singly or in groups — visits to other Member States to prepare exchange programmes, give guest lectures or study aspects of the host countries' higher education systems;
(d) 23 projects launched by associations and consortia of universities;
(e) a number of important publications related to higher education cooperation in Europe, including the Commission's *Student Handbook* but also publications initiated at the grassroots level in the universities.

Erasmus, therefore, is much more than just an exchange programme. It is a flexible and comprehensive instrument for developing greater cooperation and cohesion between the higher education institutions and systems of the 12 Community countries, providing the means whereby despite the diversity which these systems demonstrate and which itself constitutes one of the richest resources of the Community, this diversity will constitute less and less of an obstacle to Community-wide cooperation.

Note: The procedures for applying for financial support under the Erasmus programme are described in the following chapter.

The Erasmus programme: Procedures for application

Under the Erasmus programme financial support for inter-university co-operation and student mobility is provided under four main headings:

(i) financial support to universities;
(ii) mobility grants for students;
(iii) grants for visits for higher education staff;
(iv) grants to associations, university corsortia and publications.

Application procedures are set out extensively in the publication *Guidelines for applicants* which is distributed, with the relevant application forms, to all higher education institutions eligible to participate in the Erasmus programme. Further copies are available from the Erasmus Bureau, an autonomous body of the European Cultural Foundation which assists the Commission of the European Communities in the implementation of the Erasmus programme.

Financial support for universities

Support for universities, which in the context of Erasmus means 'all institutions in the higher education sector recognized by the Member States', is given in the form of grants to Inter-university cooperation programmes (ICP) which can comprise one or more of the following;

(a) Student mobility programmes covering the organizational costs of student mobility between the participating members of an ICP up to a maximum of ECU 25 000 per participating university and year. The grant can typically be used for:
   (i) development and operational costs including costs of planning meetings, supervision of students, evaluation and monitoring;
   (ii) the preparation and translation of essential documentation and teaching materials;
   (iii) costs incurred by the universities in the preparation and orientation of students, especially but not exclusively linguistic preparation;
   (iv) certain information and administration costs.

Grants may not be used to cover normal salaries or capital and infrastructural costs. Any student mobility which results from an accepted programme must involve the full recognition by the home university of the period of study abroad.

(b) Teaching staff mobility. Grants are available to enable ICP staff members to participate in the teaching programme of partner universities. The grant would normally cover:
   (i) the costs of developing and organizing the teacher exchange;
   (ii) grants to teaching staff towards their travel and mobility costs;
   (iii) staff replacement costs up to ECU 2 500 per month in cases where the staff

member is absent for three months or more and the home institution is obliged to employ a temporary replacement.

The minimum period for staff mobility is one month and priority is given to programmes involving reciprocal exchanges.

(c) Joint development of new curricula. Grants, up to a maximum of ECU 20 000 per project, are available to support the direct costs of university staff involved in planning new curricula for partner universities in an ICP. Support includes also the costs of producing, translating and circulating necessary documents but not the full implementation costs.

(d) Intensive programmes. Grants of a maximum of ECU 20 000 per programme are available for short intensive courses involving staff and students from partner institutions. The grants cover the planning costs, the costs of teaching material, and travel and subsistence for participants coming from another Member State.

Applications for Inter-university cooperation programmes are made to the Erasmus Bureau (by the end of October for the following year) on the appropriate form by one coordinating university on behalf of all the partners and it is that coordinating university which is subsequently responsible for the distribution of any grant made to the ICP. All applications must be endorsed by the heads of all the partner universities concerned.

Mobility grants for students

The Erasmus programme is above all a programme of student mobility which allows for mobility grants (maximum per academic year ECU 5 000) to cover the costs of travel, language preparation and higher costs of living in the host university. It is important to remember that Erasmus student grants are only intended to cover the *extra* costs involved in study abroad; all other costs must be met from other sources although students who receive an Erasmus grant remain entitled to any national study grant which they are already receiving and cannot be charged tuition fees by their host university. All students applying for an Erasmus grant must:

(i) be a national of a Member State (or a recognized refugee in a Member State);
(ii) be a registered student on a course in an eligible university intending to study in another Member State for between three and 12 months;
(iii) receive full academic recognition towards the home institution degree or diploma for any study abroad covered by the Erasmus student grant;
(iv) not already be in receipt of a grant from such other Community programmes as Science, Comett or SPES.

Students are normally expected to have completed at least one year of university study before departure and priority is given to students on courses covered by accepted ICPs or to students taking part in the European

Community course credit transfer system (ECTS). These students are nominated by the institutions concerned and should therefore apply through the programme director or departmental ECTS coordinator at their university. ICP programme directors will have already given estimates of student numbers in their ICP applications.

In addition the Erasmus programme also allows for grants to a limited number of 'free movers', i.e. students from eligible institutions who wish to study abroad but who are not covered either by an accepted ICP or by ECTS. 'Free movers' must apply individually to the National Grant Awarding Authority (NGAA) in their Member State by 1 January and must not only satisfy all the conditions of eligibility but also provide evidence from both the home and the host university that they are prepared to accept such conditions as the full recognition of the study abroad period by the home university and the exemption from fees by the host university. In some countries no 'free mover' applications are accepted and in all others the number of such grants is limited. Since 'free movers' by definition lack the support of an ICP or ECTS agreement they must ensure that they have a formal offer of a place at the host institution and that all arrangements for their study-abroad programme are properly completed.

Erasmus student mobility grants are managed on behalf of the Commission by a network of National Grant Awarding Authorities (NGAAs) nominated for this purpose by the Member States. (These are listed in the appendix.) Each year the appropriate budgets for student mobility grants are transferred to the NGAAs who then distribute grants either directly to students or to students via their institutions. The NGAAs are responsible also for ensuring that Erasmus grants are compatible with the national grant programmes in their countries, where such schemes exist.

Grants for visits by higher education staff

The Erasmus programme awards grants of up to ECU 1 500 per person to cover the travel and subsistence costs involved in visits by university teaching or administrative staff to other universities in the Member States of the European Community. Such visits should involve:

(i) preparatory meetings to create, expand or adapt Inter-university cooperation programmes; or
(ii) meetings with colleagues in other universities to improve the quality of teaching and to develop new teaching material; or
(iii) the study of certain aspects of the higher education system, including administrative aspects, in the countries visited; or
(iv) the teaching of a short course at the invitation of the host university; or
(v) the giving of a specialized lecture series at one or more host universities at their invitation.

Applications for visit grants should be made to the Erasmus Bureau on the appropriate application form at least six months before the visits are due to take place.

Grants to associations, university consortia and publications

Erasmus provides limited funding to university associations and consortia and to publications involving specific and innovative projects which make certain aspects of higher education in the European Community more widely known. Support for conferences, seminars, symposia and research is excluded and particular weight is given to initiatives which:

(a) reinforce the European dimension of the association or consortium;
(b) coordinate at Community level the work of national associations;
(c) create new associations at the European level;
(d) increase awareness of study and/ or teaching opportunities in the Member States;
(e) highlight important developments or innovative models for university cooperation in the Community.

There is no specific application form but applicants should submit to the Erasmus Bureau full details of any proposed initiative or publication, including costings and a summary, at least six months before the start of a project.

Detailed information can be obtained from:

Erasmus Bureau
15 rue d'Arlon
B-1040 Bruxelles
Tel. (32 2) 233 01 11
Telefax (32 2) 233 01 50
Telex 635 28

Appendix

Addresses of the National Grant Awarding Authorities (NGAAs) for Erasmus student grants

Belgium (Dutch-speaking)
Vlaams Erasmuscomité
Ministerie van de Vlaamse Gemeenschap
Administratie voor Onderwijs en Permanente Vorming
Bestuur voor Onderwijszaken
Internationale Samenwerking Kunstlaan 43
B-1040 Brussel
☎ (32 2) 513 74 64

Belgium (French-speaking)
Agence Francophone Erasmus
5 rue d'Egmont
B-1050 Bruxelles
☎ (32 2) 512 58 15

Federal Republic of Germany
Erasmus Arbeitsstelle
Deutscher Akademischer Austauschdienst
Postfach 20 08 04
D-5300 Bonn 2
☎ 492 28/88 22 77

Denmark
NGAA (Erasmus)
Direktoratet for Videregående Uddannelser
Undervisningsministeriet
Frederiksholms Kanal 26
DK-1220 København K
☎ (45 1) 92 53 87

Spain
Agencia Nacional Española para becas Erasmus
Secretaria General
Consejo de Universidades
Ciudad Universitaria
E-28071 Madrid
☎ (34 1) 449 74 37

France
CNOUS Erasmus
6-8 rue Jean Calvin
F-75005 Paris
☎ (331) 47 06 61 70

Greece
IKY
Service Erasmus
Lysicratous 14 GR-10558 Athinai
☎ (30 1) 32 54 385

Italy
Direzione Istruzione Universitaria (Erasmus)
Ministero della Pubblica Istruzione
Viale Trastevere 76
I-00153 Roma
☎ (39 6) 58 49 34 12

Ireland
Irish NGAA (Erasmus)
Higher Education Authority
21 Fitzwilliam Square
Dublin 2
☎ (353 1) 61 27 48

Luxembourg
Agence Erasmus
Ministère de l'Éducation nationale
29 rue Aldringen
L-1118 Luxembourg
☎ (352) 46802 5 55

The Netherlands
Nuffic (Erasmus)
Badhuisweg 251
2597 JR 's-Gravenhage
☎ (31 70) 51 05 38

Portugal
Ministério da Educação (Erasmus)
Avenida 5 de Outubro 107-9º
P-1051 Lisboa Codex
☎ (351 1) 76 69 42

United Kingdom
UK Erasmus Student Grants Council
The University
Canterbury CT2 7PD
☎ (44 227) 76 27 12

EUR

ECTS
The European Community course credit transfer system

ECTS: The European Community course credit transfer system

ECTS and the participating institutions

Action 3 of the Erasmus programme provides for the establishment of a European Community course credit transfer system (ECTS) on an experimental and voluntary basis, in order to provide a means by which students undergoing or having completed higher education and training may receive credit for such training carried out at universities in other Member States.

The Commission selected five subject areas (business administration, chemistry, mechanical engineering, medicine, history) to launch the pilot scheme, which will be introduced for a period of six years from the academic year 1989/90. All the higher education institutions in the Community were invited to express their interest in participating in ECTS.

Having received 464 applications from 254 higher education institutions, the Commission selected 81 institutions and three consortia to participate in the ECTS pilot scheme which is based on the principle of 'mutual trust and confidence'.

The 84 institutions have received financial aid from the Commission to facilitate the preparation and the establishment of the system. Their work will be carefully monitored by the Commission and a certain number of Erasmus grants will be awarded to the participating students, provided that they fulfil the usual criteria.

It should be noted that besides the 464 requests for participation in the 'inner circle' of the system, the Commission also received 595 requests for participation in the 'outer circle' from institutions which were not in a position to implement the rules of the 'inner circle' of the system immediately, or because they preferred to introduce the system in subject areas other than the five selected by the Commission.

The institutions which are not selected for 'inner circle' participation may join the 'outer circle' of ECTS and will be kept regularly informed about the work accomplished within the 84 institutions of the 'inner circle'. In this way, the credit transfer system between the universities of all Member States of the Community will have a much greater impact.

The ECTS academic recognition system

The central purpose of ECTS is to provide universities admitting students from another Community country with a quick and objective means of assessing incoming students' previous academic performance. In this way, they may be inserted at appropriate levels into host institution courses, even where there is no specific programme for integrated student exchange with the foreign universities concerned. The scheme is also in-

tended to offer a basis for the academic recognition of intermediate and final qualifications, as well as individual courses, with automatic recognition envisaged in many cases.

A student registered at one of the institutions involved in the ECTS pilot scheme may decide at any time during his/her course to transfer to another ECTS participating institution in another Member State of the EC — provided that he/she sufficiently masters the language spoken in this country. On the basis of the information packages prepared by all participating departments, the student, guided by the ECTS departmental and institutional coordinators, will be able to select those study courses which he/she would like to follow at the ECTS host institution. Following completion of the study period, the ECTS student has three options. First, he/she may return to continue studying at the home institution. The student may also decide to stay at the host institution and take his diploma or degree there. Finally, he/she may proceed to a third ECTS institution in a different EC Member State in order to finish his/her studies there. As long as the student complies with the legal, institutional, departmental and ECTS requirements, he/she will receive a priori automatic recognition for the studies carried out, and not — as is generally the case now — a posteriori and mostly only partial academic recognition.

Through use of these a priori recognition arrangements, which constitute quite a revolutionary concept in Europe, the 'inner circle' of ECTS goes far beyond what is being accomplished in the area of credit transfer in the USA.

Further information

The ECTS system is presented comprehensively in a small brochure obtainable free of charge on request from:

Erasmus Bureau
15 rue d'Arlon
B-1040 Brussels
Tel. (32 2) 233 01 11

EUR

Comett
The European Community
programme on cooperation between universities
and enterprises regarding training
in the field of technology

Comett: The European Community programme on cooperation between universities and enterprises regarding training in the field of technology

The EC Comett programme, which commenced its work on 1 January 1987, after the decision of the Council of Ministers of 24 July 1986, pursues the objective of promoting transborder cooperation between institutions of higher education and industry on the Community level:

(i) by achieving a 'European dimension' in the development and application of new technologies and in the introduction of innovative ideas, the programme aims to strengthen the competitiveness of European industry and to contribute towards the training of a core of highly-qualified experts;

(ii) through the development of training partnerships between institutions of higher education and industry within a European network, through common training programmes and through a constant exchange of experience, the optimal use of all resources in the education sector on the Community level is to be achieved;

(iii) at the local, regional and national levels, Comett is, in constant cooperation with the State authorities responsible, to contribute to a balanced growth of the economy and industry within the Community, including small and medium-sized companies;

(iv) the programme is to promote equal opportunities for men and women in training and continuing training.

For the first programme phase, 1987-89, a budget of ECU 45 million was planned. In fact, ECU 65 million was spent, since the interest of institutions of higher education and of companies in the Member States by far exceeded expectations. In the 'Statistical analysis of Comett projects' of November 1988, the Commission informs readers that during the first three selection rounds a total of 4 249 applications were received from Member States. 1 045 were finally selected for support. A further 300 projects which had commenced in 1987 were extended in 1988. The Comett office estimates that a total of 2 500 companies, 1 000 institutions of higher education, 1 000 other organizations, such as industrial and professional associations, i.e. a total of 4 500 organizations participated in the first programme phase.

The placement of students in practicals which had been estimated at 10 000 places did not initially fulfil expectations: about 4 000 students were exchanged. Now that so-called 'pools' have been formed from which training partners can themselves serve students with training places and scholarships, a strong stimulation of exchange activity is expected for the next programme phase.

Comett II was adopted by the Council of Ministers on 16 December 1988, and was equipped with an ECU 200 million budget. The financial resources for the programme have thus been greatly increased. The second phase begins on 1 January 1990 and will run for five years.

Comett II comprises three programme sections:

Programme Section A: European network of training partnerships between institutions of higher education and industry

For the development and reinforcement of such training partnerships into a European network, both regional and sectoral, as well as transnational cooperation in the field of technological training and continuing training, the Commission may award grants which cover up to 50% of the project costs and which generally end after three years.

Programme Section B: Transnational exchanges of students and personnel

Grants are awarded for the exchange of:

(a) students who are undergoing training from three to 12 months in companies in other Member States;
(b) students who have just completed initial training, are still enrolled at an institution of higher education or who, following graduation and as a transition between their studies and first employment, want to take up a practical for six months to two years in companies of other Member States;
(c) scientists at universities and specialist personnel at companies who are seconded to an institution of higher education or company in another Member State in order to place their knowledge at the disposal of this company or higher education institution and to support the training and practical work there.

The following are considered for exchange: on the part of the institutions of higher education, lecturers, professors and administrators; on the part of industry, employers, training officers, middle management staff, engineers, trade unionists, representatives of the chambers of trade and industry.

40% of the total budget will be placed at the disposal of these exchange measures.

Programme Section C: Joint continuing training projects between institutions of higher education and industry in the field of the new technologies and for multimedia distance training

Three project types may be supported:

(i) crash courses with a 'European dimension' in the technology sector with emphasis given to the latest advanced technologies, but also giving special consideration to the needs of small and medium-sized companies;
(ii) joint development and testing of training projects in the advanced technologies as well as their application, with institutions of higher education and industry from at least two Member States cooperating;
(iii) multilateral agreements on technological continuing training with the objective of introducing distance training systems which make

use of the new training technologies and/or lead to transferable training products.

Additionally, there is a *Programme Section D* which is involved with the development, promotion and evaluation of the Comett programme.

Details on Comett may be obtained from the 'Comett Vademecum' which appears in all Community languages as well as from the Comett office in Brussels:

Comett Technical Assistance Unit
71 Avenue de Cortenbergh
B-1040 Brussels
Tel. (32 2) 733 97 55 57

EUR

Lingua
The European Community programme for the promotion of the teaching and learning of foreign languages within the Community

Lingua: The European Community programme for the promotion of the teaching and learning of foreign languages within the Community

On 22 May 1989, the Council and the Ministers for Education meeting in Brussels adopted Lingua, an action programme for the promotion of training in foreign languages within the Community. Lingua will become operational on 1 January 1990 with, at the very least, a credible five-year budget of ECU 200 million for meeting its broad objectives. Repeatedly in recent years, the Council and Ministers for Education have called for improved foreign language teaching to bring down the communication barriers hindering the free movement of people, goods, services and capital throughout the EC. The prospect of a single European market currently makes this task an especially high priority. The resolution states that all EC citizens should learn two languages other than the mother tongue. Although this aim is still far from achieved, the Ministers and the Commission have at least now moved from appeals to action.

What is Lingua?

EC subsidies and scholarships are planned to promote foreign language teaching at various levels as follows:

(i) Initial vocational training. Whether at school, or in factories and businesses, young people are to have an opportunity to learn two foreign national EC languages. Greater familiarity with the lesser-spoken languages is to be especially encouraged;

(ii) students in higher education, who will be helped to combine their main subject with the study of a foreign language;

(iii) prospective foreign language teachers, who will be encouraged to spend at least three months in the country whose language they wish to teach;

(iv) practising foreign-language teachers who will be able to undertake further training in the language(s) they teach, or gain vocational experience in an appropriate Member State. At least 10% of foreign language teachers and of those responsible for their training are to participate in in-service training projects;

(v) small and medium-sized export-oriented companies which will be helped to train linguistically proficient staff by means of exchange programmes and the development of suitable teaching and learning materials;

(vi) clubs and associations active at European level in the promotion of foreign-language teaching and teaching methods, as well as multilingualism in the mass media.

All measures under Lingua are to be appropriately coordinated with those of the Erasmus, Comett and Youth for Europe programmes, the success of which will depend largely on the extent to which Lingua can deliver the wherewithal for enabling many more young people than previously to move and communicate freely throughout the EC. In this regard, the target sectors are, in the first place, young working people and also the lesser-used languages which are not commonly taught in schools.

EUR

Naric
The European Community
network of national academic
recognition information centres

Naric: The European Community network of national academic recognition information centres

Following the adoption on 15 June 1987 of the European Community action scheme for the mobility of university students (Erasmus), the improvement of academic recognition of diplomas and periods of study between Community countries as a means of stimulating the mobility and free movement of students and university teaching staff is becoming an increasingly important element of Community policy.

In order to improve the present situation in this regard, the Community has agreed to strengthen the exchange of information about academic recognition and equivalence matters, by the establishment of a network of information centres.

To this end, the European Community network of national academic recognition information centres (Naric) was established in 1984. All of the Member States of the European Community have designated national centres, the purpose of which is to assist in promoting the mobility of students, teachers and researchers in the Community by providing authoritative advice and information concerning the academic recognition of diplomas and periods of study undertaken in other Member States. The UK Naric is not empowered to give authoritative advice as the final decision always lies with the UK educational institution or prospective employer. The main users of this facility are higher education institutions, students and their advisers, parents, teachers and prospective employers.

In most cases, the centres designated are also responsible for related work in connection with the implementation of the conventions of the Council of Europe and Unesco regarding academic recognition and equivalence matters.

This edition of the *Student Handbook* contains the names and addresses of each national centre, together with a brief description of their tasks and responsibilities, and the procedures to be followed in each Member State.

The Naric network is coordinated on behalf of the Commission of the European Communities by:

Erasmus Bureau
15 rue d'Arlon
B-1040 Brussels
Tel. (32 2) 233 01 11
Telex 63 528
Telefaxy (32 2)-233 01 50

Belgique

French-speaking

Ministère de l'Éducation nationale
Service des équivalences de l'enseignement supérieur — Direction générale de l'enseignement supérieur et de la recherche scientifique / 1ère direction — CAE
Quartier des Arcades / 6e étage
Rue Royale 204
B-1010 Bruxelles
☎: (32 2) 210 55 11
Person in charge: Ms Chantal Kaufmann

The Centre is an administrative service of the Education Ministry.

It responds to individual requests and prepares decisions to be taken by the Minister.

Decisions

The decision-making power is in the hands of the Education Minister for university degrees and the diplomas defined by the law, as well as for certificates and diplomas delivered by non-university institutions.

The universities decide on recognition matters in the context of certificates and diplomas not defined by the law.

Procedures

The individual student has to submit his requests to the Education Ministry or to the Director of the higher education institution at which he wishes to be enrolled.

The higher education institution will automatically transfer the request to the Ministry if the latter is responsible for the decision.

The decisions of the Ministry are based on the analysis of each individual case and the advice of a consultative body as well as of the responsible service within the Ministry.

België

Dutch-speaking

Ministerie van Onderwijs Bestuur van het Hoger Onderwijs en Wetenschappelijk Onderzoek — Dienst Gelijkwaardigheid
Manhattan Center, toren 2
Kruisvaartenstraat 3
B-1210 Brussel
☎ (32 2) 219 18 80 to 90

The Centre is part of a Directorate of the (Dutch-speaking) Belgian Ministry of Education.

It acts both as an information point and as the deciding authority.

Decisions

The Minister for Education or an official authorized by him takes the decision about recognition and equivalences regarding:

(i) legally determined Belgian university degrees;
(ii) higher education diplomas issued by non-university institutions.

Decisions about university degrees which are legally not determined are taken by the universities themselves.

Procedure

The individual student may put in his request either directly to the Ministry or to the Director of the educational institution where he is (or wishes to be) enrolled. This may be done before, during or after completion of studies abroad.

The higher education institution will automatically transfer the request to the Ministry if the latter is responsible for the decision.

Decisions are based on the well-founded advice of either the responsible ministerial service or of the Inter-university Commission.

Danmark

National academic recognition information centre (Naric)
Undervisningsministeriet — Det internationale kontor
Frederiksholms Kanal 25 D
DK-1220 København K
☎ (45 1) 92 52 01
Telex: 16243 educ dk
Person in charge: Mrs Lis Thomsen

The Centre is part of one of the Divisions of the Education Ministry.

Its task is to provide information to individuals and to institutions about equivalence of foreign qualifications to Danish ones. Information is also available about the recognition of foreign diplomas for professional purposes.

Decisions

Decisions are taken by the individual higher education institution. In cases of clear evidence the Centre may however also give a direct response.

Procedure

For simple information purposes the individual student should address himself to the Centre. Requests for a decision about equivalence and recognition may be sent in either to the Ministry of Education or to the higher education institution. Application forms can be obtained from the Danish Ministry of Education at the above address.

Bundesrepublik Deutschland

Zentralstelle für ausländisches Bildungswesen
im Sekretariat der KMK,
Nassestraße 8
D-5300-Bonn
☎ 49 228/50 10
Telex: 886587 KMK D
Telefax 49 228 50 13 01
Person in charge: Dr Günter Reuhl

The Centre is a special service of the Secretariat of the Standing Conference of Education Ministers of the *Länder* (KMK). It has got a double task:

(i) to act as Information and Documentation Centre in matters of equivalence;
(ii) to assess foreign qualifications in
  (a) individual cases so as to allow for decisions to be taken by higher education institutions, ministries or by other authorities;
  (b) cases of establishing equivalencies of general significance which may lead to resolutions of the Standing Conference of Education Ministers and which may affect the legislation of the individual *Land*.

Decisions

Depending on the type and the level of equivalence or recognition problem, decisions are taken by the individual higher education institution or by the concerned Ministry or authority on the basis of the proposals of the Centre.

Procedure

The enquirer has to submit his request to:

(a) The higher education institution
  (i) for admission to first year courses;
  (ii) for recognition of periods of study abroad (with the exceptions mentioned under (b)).
(b) The local *Länder* examination boards for periods of study abroad in fields like medicine, pharmacy, teacher training.
(c) The Education Ministries resp. Science Ministries
  (i) for recognition of qualifications obtained in the general school and vocational training system (secondary);
  (ii) for recognition of higher education degrees and diplomas (with the exceptions mentioned under (a) and (d).
(d) The Ministries for Health and Social Welfare for recognition of diplomas and degrees in medicine and pharmacy for professional purposes.
(e) The local regional authorities (Chambers of Industry and Commerce, Trade Cooperations, etc.) for recognition of qualifications obtained in initial vocational training.

Ellada

Dikatsa: University centre for the academic recognition of diplomas and periods of study
Leoforos Sygrou, 112
GR-Athinai
☎ (30 1) 922 25 26/922 90 65
Person in charge: Professor Manolis Papathomopoulos

The Centre is a national centre outside the Education Ministry. The 13 members of the administrative council (all university professors nominated by their institution) are appointed by the Ministry of Education. They cover the main fields and branches of study.

It acts both as information point and as decision-taking body on individual cases.

Decisions

Decisions are taken by Dikatsa. These decisions are taken following a consultative process involving about 40 consultative committees, each one of them made up of three university professors. Each committee is responsible for one science subject.

Procedure

A. Foreign university diplomas:
1. Request of application form from Dikatsa.
2. Provide a receipt (Paravolon) from the Bank of Greece (account No 26 031/5).
3. Translated/validated copies of certificates and diplomas to be sent in to Dikatsa.
4. Other certificates and evidence of qualifications to be provided to Dikatsa according to detailed list to be obtained from Dikatsa.
B. Foreign non-university higher education diplomas:
Contact the Institute of Technological Education (ITE)
Leoforos Sygrou, 56
GR-Athinai
C. Foreign primary teacher qualifications:
Contact the Pedagogical Institute
Ermou 15
GR-Athinai

España

Ministerio de Educación y Ciencia
Subdirección General de Cooperación Internacional
Centro de Información sobre Reconocimiento de Títulos y Movilidad de Estudiantes
Paseo del Prado 28, 4ª planta
E-28014 Madrid
☎ (34 1) 230 20 00/230 20 09
Telex: 41306-23801
Person in charge: Sra. Maria Teresa Diez-Iturrioz

The Centre is integrated in the services of the General Subdirectorate of International Cooperation which is part of the General Technical Secretariat of the Ministry of Education.

It is part of the relations with the European Community programme.

Its only function is to give information to Spaniards who wish to go to other Member States to work or to continue their studies and to the citizens of the other Member States who want to do the same in Spain.

The Centre replies to all written requests from other centres of the Naric network or from individuals or institutions wishing to receive information on any particular aspect related to the recognition of a diploma or a period of study, or on any aspect of the exercise of a profession.

Decisions

Decisions relating to diplomas are taken by the Ministry of Education after consultation with the Academic Commission of the Council of Universities.

Procedure

The interested party should address in written form his request for recognition to the Ministry of Education and Science and should be registered at the Ministry's General Registry *(Registro General).*

The request should include personal data concerning the interested party, the nationality, the country of residence, the qualification for which recognition is requested, the university from which the diploma was obtained and the diploma in Spain for which 'homologation' is being requested.

The following documents should accompany the request:
(a) a certificate of nationality;
(b) the original diploma for which 'homologation' is being requested or an original certificate of its expedition;
(c) an academic certificate of the studies undertaken in order to obtain the diploma.

If the diploma to be 'homologated' is at Doctor's level, the following documents should also be included:
(a) record explaining the thesis undertaken;
(b) attested copy of the *Licenciado* degree if it was obtained in a Spanish university, or a credential of its 'homologation' if the title was obtained in a foreign university.

All documents must be official, issued by the competent authorities and authenticated through the diplomatic channels and accompanied by a legal translation into Spanish.

The service competent for the granting of a homologation of the academic diplomas is the Office for Equivalences in the General Subdirectorate for Homologation, Diplomas and Equivalences (Servicio de Convalidaciones, en la

Subdirección General de Homologaciones, Títulos y Convalidaciones).

In the case of diplomas concerning professional medical specialities, the competent body is the State Secretariat of Universities and Research (Secretaría de Estado de Universidades e Investigación).

In the case of partial studies, the competent body is the university in which the interested party intends to continue his studies.

France

Ministère de l'Éducation nationale
Direction des affaires générales, internationales et de la coopération
Bureau d'information, de documentation et de soutien aux établissements — Dagic 8
110, rue de Grenelle
F-75007 Paris
☎ (33 1) 45 39 25 75
Telex: 270 925 EDUNAT F
Telefax (33 1) 45 44 25 75
Person in charge: Mr Jean-Louis Devaux

The Centre is integrated in the services of the French National Ministry of Education. It provides information and advice to universities, higher education establishments, French cultural services abroad and foreign public cultural bodies.

The Centre also replies to any written requests for information from individuals and public or private firms needing to resolve a problem of recognition of diplomas relating to the pursuit of studies or the exercise of a professional activity.

Decisions

Recognition decisions are taken:

(i) by the head of the establishment in which the candidate wishes to register: exemption from studies is granted at the suggestion of a competent committee ruling on each dossier.

(ii) by the Minister for Education for the recognition of diplomas in medicine, pharmacy, odontology.

Procedure

Students should submit their requests to the university or higher education institution where they wish to enrol. The request should be accompanied by the certificate of the diploma in question and a detailed description of the course of study which led to it.

Deadlines must be observed.

The procedure is the same for health studies; the institution channels the candidate's dossier to the competent service of the Ministry of National Education for a decision.

Information and advice services in each university have the task of advising the student as regards enrolment and guidance on the choice of training.

Ireland

Higher Education Authority
21 Fitzwilliam Square
Dublin 2
☎ (353 1) 61 27 48
Person in charge: Mr Brendan O'Dea

The Centre is a national centre operated by the Higher Education Authority which is a statutory body with funding, advisory and developmental functions in relation to third-level education.

It acts as an information point supplying general information to foreign students. Specific queries are passed on to the universities or relevant higher education institutions which deal with queries.

Decisions

Decisions are taken by the higher education institutions.

Procedure

Requests to the higher education institutions should contain precise information about:

(i) the type of qualifications/diplomas held by the enquirer;

(ii) content and length of course leading to qualifications;

(iii) level of qualification (pass/honours);

(iv) type of institution/body which awarded the qualification.

Italia

Cimea
Centro d'informazione sulla mobilità e le equivalenze accademiche
Fondazione Rui
Viale Ventuno Aprile 36
I-00162 Roma
☎ (39 6) 83 21 281 to 283
Telex: 626036 FRUI RM I
Telefax (39 6) 832 28 45
Person in charge: Ing. Alfredo Razzano

The objective of the Cimea is to promote the mobility of students, researchers and teachers by offering information and counselling on academic recognition of diplomas and periods of study undertaken in other Member States of the European Community.

Its services are open to Italian and foreign universities and cultural institutions, to international organizations and to European citizens. Cimea publishes guides and prospectuses and gives answers to written requests made by individuals or organizations on matters relating to:

(i) Italians' academic mobility in EC countries;
(ii) foreigners intending to study or to do research work in Italy.

The Cimea does not have the power to recognize and validate diplomas. Taking into account the autonomy of universities and the institutional competences on the issue, Cimea gives information on the comparability of diplomas and certificates for the purpose of granting recognition and establishing the equivalence of diplomas to promote the free circulation of the citizens of the Community.

The Cimea functions on the basis of an agreement between the Ministry of Public Education and the Rui Foundation.

Decisions

Decisions relating to the academic recognition of foreign diplomas are under the jurisdiction of:

(i) university authorities (academic senate and council of the faculty) for the equivalence of first and second-level university diplomas *(diploma* and *laurea);*
(ii) the Ministry of Public Education after consultation with the National Council of Universities, for the title of 'research doctor' obtained in a foreign university.

Procedure

Those interested, should forward their request to the Italian consulates or embassies of their country of origin. These will be transmitted directly to the university to which admittance is requested or from which academic recognition of the diploma is requested.

Luxembourg

Ministère de l'Éducation nationale et de la Jeunesse
Centre d'information sur la reconnaissance académique de diplômes et des périodes d'études
29 rue Aldringen
L-1118 Luxembourg
☎ (352) 46802 4 70
Telex: 3 311 MENJ LU
Telefax (352) 460927
Person in charge: Mr Ernest Weis

The Centre is a service within the National Ministry of Education.

The Centre cooperates with the 'Commission d'homologation des titres et grades d'enseignement supérieur' and the 'Commission des titres'.

In order to understand the conditions for the academic recognition of diplomas better, it is useful to recall that Luxembourg does not dispose of a proper system of university education conferring final degrees. The country has a 'University Centre' offering courses for the first year of study only.

Luxembourg students returning with a foreign diploma request:

(i) either that their diploma is officially approved ('homologation') — qualifications in the fields of law, medicine, dentistry, pharmacy and veterinary medicine, as well as qualifications leading to a career as an arts or science teacher in secondary education;
(ii) or that their diploma is entered in the register of diplomas of higher education. This register covers all diplomas not governed by the 'homologation' system. There is a commission which is called upon to give an opinion on the protection of foreign certificates and diplomas of higher education.

Decisions

Decisions are taken by the Minister for Education.

Procedure

Individuals should address their request to the Ministry of Education.

Nederland

National Equivalence Information Centre (NEIC)
Netherlands Universities Foundation for International Cooperation (Nuffic)
Badhuisweg, 251
2609 LS 's-Gravenhage
☎ (31 70) 51 05 10
Telex: NL 33565
Telefax (31 70) 51 05 13
Person in charge: Mr Kees Kouwenaar

The Dutch Ministry of Education and Science appointed Nuffic as the NEIC in the framework of the Council of Europe as part of the Naric network of the European Communities.

Nuffic advises ministries, universities and institutions of higher education about questions related to academic recognition and recognition of vocational qualifications delivered by institutions of higher education.

Decisions

The competent Ministries decide on recognition of academic degrees and diplomas. Universities and other higher education institutions decide on the equivalence of periods of study and on examinations.

Procedure

Individual enquirers can submit their request:

(i) to the higher education institution where they want to enrol, for admission to first year courses, for recognition of periods of study and for recognition of diplomas and degrees for the purpose of continuation of studies;

(ii) to the Ministry of Education and Sciences for use of Dutch titles and for the award of teacher qualifications;

(iii) to the Ministry of Social Welfare, Health and Culture for the exercise of (para-)medical professions;

(iv) to the Ministry of Economic Affairs for the creation of an enterprise;

(v) to the local labour exchange for purposes of inscription as an employee.

Portugal

Ministério da Educação e Cultura
Direcção-Geral do Ensino Superior
Centro de Informação sobre Reconhecimento Académico de Diplomas (CIRAD)
Av. 5 de Outubro, 107-9º
P-1051 Lisboa Codex
☎ (351 1 77) 10 82/73 12 91
Telex: 18428 EDUCA P.
Telefax: (351 1) 760984
Person in charge: Mr Manuel Carmelo Rosa

The Portuguese Centre (CIRAD) is part of the Ministry of Education and Culture and has the following tasks:

(i) to act as an information and documentation centre on matters relating to equivalences in higher education in view of the continuation of studies as well as for professional purposes;

(ii) to inform on the administration of academic recognition of diplomas and study periods in view of the continuation of studies or for professional purposes in Portugal and abroad, especially with regard to the Member States of the European Community;

(iii) to prepare studies on the different equivalence systems with regard to higher education and access to higher education;

(iv) to cooperate with higher education institutions towards a uniformization in the application of the legislation on the academic equivalence of studies in and access to higher education;

(v) to ascertain a reciprocal treatment as foreseen by the legislation on the academic recognition of diplomas.

Decisions

Decisions relating to the academic recognition of diplomas are taken by the Scientific Councils of the higher education institutions. Requests are treated on an individual basis, in a case-by-case manner.

Procedure

Requests for recognition of diplomas and study periods have to be submitted to the Scientific Council of a higher education institution in the field of the studies chosen by the applicant.

Access to higher education is to be requested from the Coordinating Cabinet for access in higher education, which is being integrated into the Directorate-General for Higher Education.

United Kingdom

The National Academic Recognition Information Centre (Naric)
The British Council
10 Spring Gardens
London SW1A 2BN
☎ (44 1) 930 84 66
Telex: 8952201 BRITCON G
Telefax (44 1) 839 63 47
Person in charge: Miss Katherine Stewart

The Centre is part of the British Council which promotes cultural, educational and technical cooperation between Britain and other countries.

Using the British Council's worldwide office network it provides an information service on overseas education and provides advice on the comparability in Britain of overseas academic qualifications.

It deals with enquiries from government departments, careers offices, job centres, private employers, universities, polytechnics, colleges, schools and professional bodies as well as students and their parents.

The Centre publishes the *International guide to qualifications in education* and revises it every two to three years.

Decisions

Naric provides information on the recognition likely to be accorded overseas diplomas in the light of specialist advice based on previous decisions taken by interested departments or institutions. The final decision is taken by the institution or employer from which entry, exemption or employment is being sought.

Procedure

Requests for authentication of certificates should be addressed to the consulate of the country of origin. Requests for information about recognition and evaluation should be addressed to Naric. Requests for entry, exemption or employment should be made directly to the institution concerned which has the right to make the final decision.

ERASMUS DIRECTORY OF PROGRAMMES 1989/90

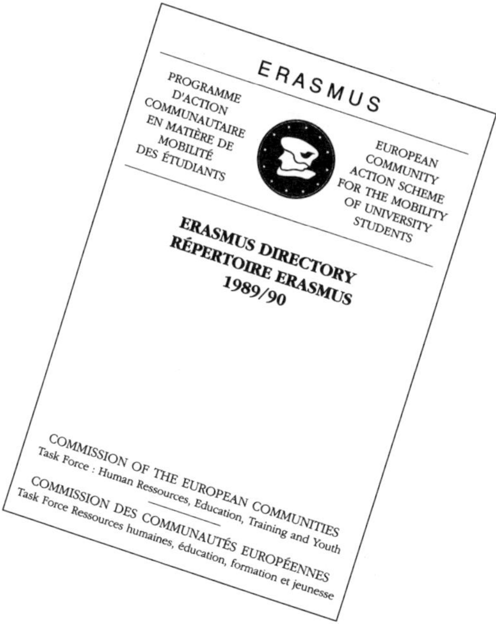
ERASMUS
PROGRAMME D'ACTION COMMUNAUTAIRE EN MATIÈRE DE MOBILITÉ DES ÉTUDIANTS
EUROPEAN COMMUNITY ACTION SCHEME FOR THE MOBILITY OF UNIVERSITY STUDENTS
ERASMUS DIRECTORY
RÉPERTOIRE ERASMUS
1989/90
COMMISSION OF THE EUROPEAN COMMUNITIES
Task Force : Human Ressources, Education, Training and Youth
COMMISSION DES COMMUNAUTÉS EUROPÉENNES
Task Force Ressources humaines, éducation, formation et jeunesse

The *ERASMUS Directory of Programmes 1989/90* gives a comprehensive listing of the 1507 inter-university cooperation programmes (ICPs) funded in 1989/90. It contains:

- a chapter of detailed statistics;
- explanatory notes for potential applicants for all forms of ERASMUS support;
- a complete list of study or teaching visits carried out by teaching and administrative staff;
- a presentation of projects conducted by student and university associations;
- a chapter on the ECTS pilot project;
- three indices enabling programme descriptions to be located rapidly with respect to several search criteria.

The book is an essential tool for those wishing to familiarize themselves with the current development of the European university network, the fields of study covered by ICPs, the types of cooperation financed, the participating institutions and the content of programmes.

The Directory also provides the names of programme coordinators and directors at each participating institution, thereby enabling the reader to make contact easily with possible new partners.

The publication is on sale at the Office for Official Publications of the European Communities, 2 rue Mercier, L-2985 Luxembourg, as well as at the official sales branches of the Office in the Member States.

European Communities — Commission

Higher Education in the European Community — Student Handbook

Sixth edition

Luxembourg: Office for Official Publications of the European Communities
London: Kogan Page
1990 — 516 pp. — 14.8 × 21 cm

ES, DA, DE, GR, EN, FR, IT, NL, PT

ISBN 92-826-0739-9 (Office for Official Publications of the European Communities)

ISBN 0-749-40128-1 (Kogan Page)

Catalogue number: CE-56-89-473-EN-C (Office for Official Publications of the European Communities)

British Library cataloguing in publication data

Student Handbook: Higher Education in the
European Community. — 6th ed.
1. Education, higher — European Economic
Community countries
I. Mohr, Brigitte
II. Commission of the European Communities
378.4 LA628

This sixth edition of the EC Student Handbook which appears in all nine Community languages provides a survey of higher education in the 12 Member States which should be of use to students and their advisers, for lecturers and professors as well as for all those occupied and interested in education and training policies.
In the similarly structured national chapters the text contains a condensed representation of the development of higher education, the types of higher education institutions as well as of degrees, entry requirements, possibilities of obtaining scholarships, and important social questions such as insurance cover, accommodation, cost of living and services for students. This is especially for students who are not yet certain in which Member State they would wish to spend their study period. In this way it is made easy for them to form an idea of what it is like in the respective country and to draw conclusions. The comprehensive appendix following each national contribution contains a list of useful addresses, a tabular survey of the courses on offer at the institutions of higher education (for the first time not only in the original language, but also translated), student statistics, a bibliography, a glossary as well as a diagram of the education system. Information is provided on the European University Institute in Florence and on the College of Europe in Bruges.
The reports on the EC programmes — Erasmus, Comett, the new programme Lingua and ECTS, the experimentally introduced system for credit transfer — show how quickly the opportunities for exchange have increased since the last handbook appeared. The book finishes with a chapter on Naric, the network of national information centres for the recognition of certificates, study achievements and diplomas, which is coordinated and supported by the Commission.

Venta y suscripciones • Salg og abonnement • Verkauf und Abonnement • Πωλήσεις και συνδρομές
Sales and subscriptions • Vente et abonnements • Vendita e abbonamenti
Verkoop en abonnementen • Venda e assinaturas

BELGIQUE / BELGIË

Moniteur belge / Belgisch Staatsblad
Rue de Louvain 42 / Leuvenseweg 42
1000 Bruxelles / 1000 Brussel
Tél. (02) 512 00 26
Fax 511 01 84
CCP / Postrekening 000-2005502-27

Autres distributeurs / Overige verkooppunten

Librairie européenne / Europese Boekhandel
Avenue Albert Jonnart 50 /
Albert Jonnartlaan 50
1200 Bruxelles / 1200 Brussel
Tél. (02) 734 02 81
Fax 735 08 60

Jean De Lannoy
Avenue du Roi 202 /Koningslaan 202
1060 Bruxelles / 1060 Brussel
Tél. (02) 538 51 69
Télex 63220 UNBOOK B

CREDOC
Rue de la Montagne 34 / Bergstraat 34
Bte 11 / Bus 11
1000 Bruxelles / 1000 Brussel

DANMARK

J. H. Schultz Information A/S
EF-Publikationer
Ottiliavej 18
2500 Valby
Tlf. 36 44 22 66
Fax 36 44 01 41
Girokonto 6 00 08 86

BR DEUTSCHLAND

Bundesanzeiger Verlag
Breite Straße
Postfach 10 80 06
5000 Köln 1
Tel. (0221) 20 29-0
Fernschreiber:
ANZEIGER BONN 8 882 595
Fax 20 29 278

GREECE

G.C. Eleftheroudakis SA
International Bookstore
Nikis Street 4
10563 Athens
Tel. (01) 322 63 23
Telex 219410 ELEF
Fax 323 98 21

ESPAÑA

Boletín Oficial del Estado
Trafalgar, 27
28010 Madrid
Tel. (91) 446 60 00

Mundi-Prensa Libros, S.A.
Castelló, 37
28001 Madrid
Tel. (91) 431 33 99 (Libros)
431 32 22 (Suscripciones)
435 36 37 (Dirección)
Télex 49370-MPLI-E
Fax (91) 275 39 98

Sucursal:

Librería Internacional AEDOS
Consejo de Ciento, 391
08009 Barcelona
Tel. (93) 301 86 15
Fax (93) 317 01 41

Generalitat de Catalunya:

Llibreria Rambla dels estudis
Rambla, 118 (Palau Moja)
08002 Barcelona
Tel. (93) 302 68 35
302 64 62

FRANCE

Journal officiel
Service des publications des Communautés européennes
26, rue Desaix
75727 Paris Cedex 15
Tél. (1) 40 58 75 00
Fax (1) 40 58 75 74

IRELAND

Government Publications Sales Office
Sun Alliance House
Molesworth Street
Dublin 2
Tel. 71 03 09

or by post

Government Stationery Office
EEC Section
6th floor
Bishop Street
Dublin 8
Tel. 78 16 66
Fax 78 06 45

ITALIA

Licosa Spa
Via Benedetto Fortini, 120/10
Casella postale 552
50125 Firenze
Tel. (055) 64 54 15
Fax 64 12 57
Telex 570466 LICOSA I
CCP 343 509

Subagenti:

Libreria scientifica Lucio de Biasio - AEIOU
Via Meravigli, 16
20123 Milano
Tel. (02) 80 76 79

Herder Editrice e Libreria
Piazza Montecitorio, 117-120
00186 Roma
Tel. (06) 679 46 28/679 53 04

Libreria giuridica
Via 12 Ottobre, 172/R
16121 Genova
Tel. (010) 59 56 93

GRAND-DUCHÉ DE LUXEMBOURG

Abonnements seulement
Subscriptions only
Nur für Abonnements

Messageries Paul Kraus
11, rue Christophe Plantin
2339 Luxembourg
Tél. 499 88 88
Télex 2515
CCP 49242-63

NEDERLAND

SDU uitgeverij
Christoffel Plantijnstraat 2
Postbus 20014
2500 EA 's-Gravenhage
Tel. (070) 78 98 80 (bestellingen)
Fax (070) 47 63 51

PORTUGAL

Imprensa Nacional
Casa da Moeda, EP
Rua D. Francisco Manuel de Melo, 5
1092 Lisboa Codex
Tel. (01) 69 34 14

Distribuidora de Livros Bertrand, Ld.ª
Grupo Bertrand, SARL
Rua das Terras dos Vales, 4-A
Apartado 37
2700 Amadora Codex
Tel. (01) 493 90 50 - 494 87 88
Telex 15798 BERDIS
Fax 491 02 55

UNITED KINGDOM

HMSO Books (PC 16)
HMSO Publications Centre
51 Nine Elms Lane
London SW8 5DR
Tel. (01) 873 9090
Fax GP3 873 8463

Sub-agent:

Alan Armstrong Ltd
2 Arkwright Road
Reading, Berks RG2 0SQ
Tel. (0734) 75 18 55
Telex 849937 AAALTD G
Fax (0734) 75 51 64

SCHWEIZ / SUISSE / SVIZZERA

OSEC
Stampfenbachstraße 85
8035 Zürich
Tel. (01) 365 51 51
Fax (01) 365 52 21

ÖSTERREICH

Manz'sche Verlags- und Universitätsbuchhandlung
Kohlmarkt 16
1014 Wien
Tel. (0222) 531 61-0
Telex 11 25 00 BOX A
Fax (0222) 531 61-81

TÜRKIYE

Dünya süper veb ofset A.Ş.
Narlibahçe Sokak No. 15
Cağaloğlu
Istanbul
Tel. 512 01 90
Telex 23822 DSVO-TR

UNITED STATES OF AMERICA

UNIPUB
4611-F Assembly Drive
Lanham, MD 20706-4391
Tel. Toll Free (800) 274 4888
Fax (301) 459 0056
Telex 7108260418

CANADA

Renouf Publishing Co., Ltd
61 Sparks Street
Ottawa
Ontario K1P 5R1
Tel. Toll Free 1 (800) 267 41 64
Ottawa Region (613) 238 89 85-6
Telex 053-4936

JAPAN

Kinokuniya Company Ltd
17-7 Shinjuku 3-Chome
Shiniuku-ku
Tokyo 160-91
Tel. (03) 354 01 31

Journal Department
PO Box 55 Chitose
Tokyo 156
Tel. (03) 439 01 24

SVERIGE

BTJ
Box 200
22100 Lund
Tel. (046) 18 00 00
Fax (046) 18 01 25

AUTRES PAYS
OTHER COUNTRIES
ANDERE LÄNDER

Office des publications officielles des Communautés européennes
2, rue Mercier
L-2985 Luxembourg
Tél. 49 92 81
Télex PUBOF LU 1324 b
Fax 48 85 73
CC bancaire BIL 8-109/6003/700

1/90